Frank Sikora • Jazz Harmony

Frank Sikora

Jazz Harmony

Think • Listen • Play
A Practical Approach

 SCHOTT

Mainz · London · Madrid · Paris · New York · Tokyo · Beijing

This book includes additional materials for further study, which are available for download at www.schott-music.com/shop/326750

© 2019 Schott Music GmbH & Co. KG, Mainz, Germany
International copyright secured. No parts of this publication may be reproduced or stored in a retrieval system without the written consent of the publisher.

ED 22091
ISMN 979-0-001-20104-9
ISBN 978-3-7957-4930-9
BSS 56656 · Printed in Germany

Table of Content

Table of Content – PDF-Files

Why yet another Harmony Book?

Ever since I decided to be a Jazz musician, I have been intrigued by the beauty and logic of harmonic systems. It isn't only the intellectual side of things that catches my interest. What fascinates me most of all is the subtle interplay of musical hues and colours, the blending of different textures, the shifting of energy levels, the swell and surge of tension, the way harmonic shapes pulsate – a kaleidoscope of swirling sounds and patterns that has drawn me in from day one. On a less poetic note, I eventually became a dedicated music teacher with a strong desire to share my insights. I started writing this book more than 20 years ago. With hindsight, I have to admit that I've become rather wary (and just a bit weary ☺) of this endeavour. Countless pages of manuscript and just as many postponed publishing dates later, I have come to realise just how questionable, if not preposterous, the attempt can be to capture something that, by its very nature, lives and breathes change and individuality. Improvised music is inherently difficult to put into words. While theory tries to describe a common denominator in music, in other words "the rules", improvisation is more often than not living proof of the fact that it is quite admissible and, ultimately, gratifying to break these rules (and get away with it). In Jazz, theory seeks to define, categorise and verbalise an amazingly colourful and, at the same time, elusive world of sound that defies being approached too systematically.

In light of these reservations, I'd like to begin this introduction with my fundamental creed: *"There is no truth in theory – only in music!"* Music can exist perfectly well without theories and concepts to back it up. Music theory, however, cannot subsist without the real thing. Without the music, theory is no more than inanimate knowledge. Over the years, I have witnessed time and again that those who take to theory too literally are bound to fail miserably as musicians. Formalised thinking stifles music's vitality and diversity all too quickly. This is nothing new. As the German writer Friedrich Hebbel once said: "Bad poets with sharp minds turn out formula instead of character, system instead of passion". How true – and how applicable to music! Those who excel in theory are not necessarily accomplished and persuasive musicians. As the saying goes: "One can know everything but understand nothing".

Let's face it. Who hasn't got a pile of theory books stashed away in some corner? Who doesn't make a dash for the latest publications in the hope of enlightenment? But, let's be honest. Who can state with conviction that this abundance of knowledge has made a substantial difference? Who has ever really struggled through all this material, absorbed it aurally and, most importantly, to whom has it been helpful as a player? Over the many years of working with colleagues and students, I have come to accept that textbooks rarely inspire flexibility, creativity or personality and that piling up knowledge without practical application holds us back rather than helps us move on. Deep down inside, we all know that practising our instruments, working on our repertoire and collaborating with other musicians is so much more important than any piece of writing or academia could ever be. The magic formula is "learn by doing". The well-known bandleader Sun Ra coined a seemingly banal but nevertheless significant phrase: *"The music is you!"* The goal is *your* music. It's *your* job to carve out a niche in music and develop your very personal approach – a book is, at best, a crutch. If we follow this line of thought to its logical conclusion, this book should never have been written (and, to tell the truth, I have often been on the verge of throwing the manuscript in the bin!). So, I guess I'll have to explain why, in spite of my reservations, I have decided to add yet another volume to the steadily growing pile of publications on the subject.

Think, listen, play – theory and practice

There are many well-structured theory books on the market, the majority of which fail to explain how theory translates to practice. On the other hand, there are countless workbooks and play-alongs that are dedicated to the practical side of things but lack the necessary theoretical background. This book attempts to bridge the gap between theory and practice. I don't want to limit myself merely to presenting theoretical facts, nor do I see the study of harmony as a purely intellectual or abstract process. To me, harmony is rather the description of a very real world of sound, which should remain just that – a world that tends to follow certain rules, guidelines and patterns but is nonetheless truly alive and dynamic. Theory in itself is only of limited value (particularly in Jazz). An analytical preoccupation with sound is a lifeless science if it has no bearing on the practical side of music. It is therefore my aim to establish as close a relationship as possible between *theory*, the *ear* and our *instrument*.

Think – An understanding of theory and its vocabulary makes us aware of the enormous reservoir of sounds we have accumulated, internalised and intuitively made use of over the years, and it helps us tap into the multitude of musical memories that lie dormant within us. More importantly, it provides us with the necessary tools to continuously expand our horizons, pointing us towards ideas and concepts not yet within reach. Cultivating our knowledge of theory serves a twofold purpose. Not only does it enhance our ability to describe, explain and categorise the many deeply ingrained songs and recordings that define our musical heritage and personal roots, it is also the key to a whole new world of sound waiting to be discovered and investigated. Music theory is a means of research that will help us move on into the realm of what-ifs and could-bes. It is an exciting playground full of delightful possibilities that should inspire and entice us to explore, experiment, conceive, design, shape, fantasise, invent, create and, above all, have fun.

Listen – Once we are aware of the possibilities and opportunities the study of theory has to offer, we should feel the urge to acquaint ourselves with the sounds that correspond to a particular theoretical concept. Our main objective is a library of mental images, which translates our knowledge of theory into imagined music and establishes a link between the many sounds we've grown up with and the ones we have yet to discover. Just as I assume every Jazz musician to be inherently curious, I would expect the inquisitive ear to be on a perpetual lookout, "on a mission", reassessing what we are already familiar with while scavenging for new and intriguing sounds, probing into the more remote corners of our repertoire and exploring uncharted territory. Ultimately, it's the ear that controls the fingers – the more flexible and versatile the ear, the better we can control the expressive potential of our instruments and the more goal-oriented and successful our daily practice will become.

Play – This book should provide an approach that hopefully will be more practical than what you have been exposed to up until now. Above all, it aims to clear up one fundamental misunderstanding:

The study of harmony = Grammar = Rules

Jazz = Improvisation = Spontaneity

Rules ≠ Spontaneity

Rules do not automatically contradict spontaneity! Theory offers choices. It is up to you to decide which of these choices you want to implement on your instrument. The study of harmony is not meant to channel and control our playing. Neither does it purport to define what is "right" or "wrong", nor should it dictate what to play while improvising. Rather, Jazz harmony attempts to describe what could be called the "lowest common denominator" extracted from the countless improvisations Jazz history has handed down to us. An understanding of harmony shows us that a large part of our daily musical lives is subject to certain rules and conventions. This book will help you understand how these principles work in practice. It would be foolish to ignore them – regardless of whether you apply or deliberately decide to avoid them (one has to know the tradition before it can be thrown overboard). This book aims to show that applying rules will not inhibit your musicality. On the contrary, always consider the possibility that the music you create may sound good just *because of the rules*.

Ultimately, it's not the rules that are the problem; it's what we make of them. Those who slavishly cling to rules readily hand over their responsibilities as musicians to the mechanics of theory. Of course, the music itself will always define, to a certain degree, what is suitable and appropriate. Just as every style has its "dos and don'ts", which you should respect if you want to sound eloquent in a particular idiom, there are many harmonic situations that call for a very specific melodic vocabulary or "grammar", which you have to observe and master if you don't want your solos to sound awkward. But, if you *only* follow the rules, your improvisations will quickly degenerate into sounding like the mindless carrying out of musical duties. The more you allow your world of sound to be determined by concepts and definitions, the more often your knowledge will stand in your way and the less spontaneous your approach to music will become. I call this "paralysis through analysis". Therefore, it is essential to know the rules but not to see them as being set in stone. This book wants you to understand music, but it also expects you to question and expand on this knowledge time and again as a player.

The use of terminology

We are all aware that communication takes place at a non-verbal level in music. Theory attempts to translate sounds into words. And, as theory goes, it tends to be overly exact and meticulous when it comes to choosing appropriate vocabulary. This is most probably the reason why most music courses focus on harmony first, bypassing the more ambiguous topics such as swing feel, phrasing, sound, timing, etc. – things that are generally accepted as being personal and subjective and thus difficult to quantify. Harmony is *the one* subject that seemingly provides us with facts that are readily learnable or teachable. It suggests that there is such a thing as a clear-cut "yes or no", "right or wrong" and "good or bad" in music. As a result, an understanding of harmony and terminology deceives us into believing that we have actually (and quite literally) come to grips with the true nature of music. What a tragic misconception! Words are, at best, an abstract copy of the real thing. The more precise definitions become, the more they limit our flexibility, and the greater the danger of our colourful world of sound turning rigid with the use of formulae.

Unfortunately, the study of harmony has become the territory of many narrow-minded spirits who busy themselves with definitions rather than content or substance, who attempt to label every minute detail of every sound with exact names. Since it is easy to squabble over terminology, theory quickly degenerates into nitpicking or splitting of hairs. If it's all about *how* you describe things and not about *what* you are actually describing, if definitions become more important than their content, then music loses its meaning. Of course, you can't avoid certain musical facts, but arguing about whether a scale is called "HM5" or "Mixoly-dian (♭9/♭13)" or "Spanish-Phrygian" appears to be outrageously foolish. This mindset has no place in my world. A sound is a sound is a sound… – no matter what you call it.

It goes without saying that I have to use specific terminology in this book. But I do not want this terminology to be understood as incontrovertible and indisputable fact. You will find other books on harmony, some of which use a different nomenclature – perhaps not that significantly different, but different enough for the poor souls and afore mentioned nitpick-ers in need of unequivocal terms to run amok. As long as the terminology used in this book is consistent (and it is), I'm perfectly happy. In the end, this book is not about words. My aim is to talk about music without undermining its beauty and transience – knowing that much of what makes good music can never be expressed in writing. So, please, don't get too caught up in definitions and don't let terminology get in the way of your music. This book will be useful as long as you are not searching for precise answers and definite solutions. Read it with a good mixture of naïve detachment and critical distrust. I hope I have put up enough warning signs to help you avoid falling into the trap of taking everything you read as the literal, undeniable truth.

Intellect and instinct

It is said that we experience music with our feet, hearts and minds – in this order! How does music affect the average listener who has virtually no theoretical background, who doesn't have the knowledge, let alone the vocabulary, to understand or describe music on an abstract level? Most people respond to sound in a physical way, perceive music as energy, tension, movement, colour, density… They are touched emotionally, enchanted, enthused, react to moods and atmosphere, to "what comes across". Theoretical considerations play no part in this experience. This is particularly true of Jazz. Like no other style, Jazz has the power to grab us both physically and emotionally – players and audiences alike.

From a musician's point of view, theory gets in the way when it comes to actually making music. Improvisation, as one of the most fundamental elements of Jazz, thrives on the "here and now", the desire to create something magical on the spur of the moment. It relies on intuitive communication with fellow musicians and the willingness to risk venturing into unfamiliar territory without preparation or guarantee of success. This is why some Jazz musicians see theory as something that hampers the spontaneity so essential to improvised music. They see it as an obstruction or interference, even a handicap. And these critics are, at least partly, in the right. In order to perform successfully, it's better not to think about it too much while doing it. Pondering the pros and cons of a line while you're playing doesn't really help the cause.

On the other hand, if intuition seems to be so much more important to making music than cerebral deliberation, why do I propose the sequence "think – listen – play" as the guiding principle of this book? Remembering how I myself got involved in music, and talking to the many colleagues and students I have collaborated with over the years, I am fully aware of the fact that nobody enters the world of music with theory in mind. When you experience music for the first time, as a baby, you listen. Then, as a child, you sing along with your parents or your favourite recordings. Eventually you learn an instrument and it's not until much later (perhaps because you want to go into music professionally) that you really begin to think about music at an abstract level. The natural way of relating to music follows the evolutionary principle of "listen – play – think". So, why would I deliberately subvert the course of nature? What is to be gained by upsetting the natural order of things?

The biggest threat to the purely intuitive musician is *stagnation*. Musicians who only act on instinct rarely manage to venture out of the rut because they are caught up in their habitual likes and dislikes. Because they tend to stick to what feels comfortable they have a hard time grasping and carrying off new ideas. There are musicians who have an uncanny feeling for sound on an intuitive level but whose conscious and analytical ear remains comparatively underdeveloped. These musicians handle familiar situations with extreme confidence but are overwhelmed when something unexpected or unaccustomed comes their way. When running into problems, they are unable to "think" music, to understand what and where the stumbling blocks are, *why* they are stumbling blocks in the first place and how to overcome them.

Once established, routines foster predictability, predictability fosters comfort and comfort fosters routines. In order to break this vicious cycle, we have to make a conscious effort and take ourselves beyond our boundaries time and again. Only if we venture out of our comfort zone will we discover, experience and learn to handle new things. Only if we break our habits will we keep moving and improving. *We only learn what we find out for ourselves.* So, the first step is to evaluate our status quo, our strengths and weaknesses. We have to be aware of where we stand. The second step is deciding where we want to go. This is where theory comes into play. It helps us set goals and shows us how to incorporate them into our practice schedule. The final step is to work on new sounds and practise them until they are firmly anchored in our subconscious and have become part of our intuitive vocabulary. In this way, we encourage a perpetual learning process, integrating the new with the old:

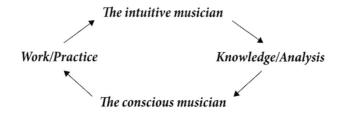

This is how you avoid standstill. Musicians such as Bill Evans and John Coltrane consistently lived this process. They devised theoretical systems, experimented with new concepts and worked them into their compositions and improvisations. Then they would go on stage with new material (in some cases, they even took the risk of recording it). Finally, they listened back to what they had played, continued to work on what appealed to their aesthetic preferences and discarded what didn't.

So, let's accept the fact that improvisation is not just a matter of "feelings". Jazz is no longer a primitive force that erupts from the depths of the soul, unfettered and unexamined. It was certainly possible to go with gut instinct in the early days of Jazz, when melodies and chord progressions were simple enough for musicians to get by on ears alone without prior theoretical knowledge. There were no schools, no textbooks and very few qualified teachers who might have helped along the way. One just listened to colleagues, transcribed records and played concerts. This is no longer sufficient, considering the complexity and variety of the modern Jazz repertoire. You cannot turn history back to its archaic roots. These days, one increasingly has to "think" music. A conscious awareness of sound is vital for focussed and successful practice, though feeling and intuition should always remain our primary goals.

Of course, we would also improve simply by hanging out and playing with other musicians. If we could rehearse and play concerts on a daily basis, we would learn by osmosis. New sounds would gradually seep into our subconscious, merge with our old repertoire and end up at the tips of our fingers sooner or later. For this to happen, though, it would be essential to immerse oneself in a musical environment that constantly provides the ear with new challenges. But, let's be realistic: Who has the chance to rehearse every day, let alone with good (preferably better) musicians? This is why we have to develop the ability to learn without being dependent on external influences. Here, again, theory is the key. If we know how music works, then we know what to practise without having to rely on the help of others.

As musicians, we actually have to integrate two apparently conflicting demands. On the one hand, we have to practise consciously, control what we're doing, develop our perception of sound and diligently transfer all of this onto our instruments. On the other hand, however, we have to act and react intuitively in the heat of the moment while performing. Accordingly, our musical routines should alternate between these two opposing worlds. We need our *intuitive ear* to *make* music. We need our *analytical ear* to *learn* music. The intellect is essential for grasping new concepts. But, as soon as we go on stage, we have to yield to intuition and rely on instincts and reflexes.

In the end, our goal should be to strike a balance between the heart and the mind. There's a quote by an unknown author that says it in a nutshell: *"Think with your heart and feel with your mind"*. Everything we do is partly intuitive and partly rational. The proportions may vary from one person to the next. However, no one is ever entirely analytical, and no one is entirely intuitive. That's why this book takes a holistic approach by addressing both intellect and emotions. I hope this book will help you to both feel and understand music without bringing the two into conflict.

So, let's go back to the initial question – why would I want to add to the plethora of publications? Thanks to the many students and colleagues who urged me on despite my doubts, I have come to believe that my approach is rather unique. Linking theory, ear training and practical application and presenting the three areas of study all-in-one is something no other harmony book does. Balancing the analytical and the intuitive by infusing theory with emotion is also rarely found. In addition, my deep distrust of overly parochial and high-principled theoreticians allows me to view the topic more critically than most theory teachers because, in the end, I will always choose music over theory. I would like to present the study of harmony in a more sensual and playful way than it is commonly done, and it is my intention to encourage methodical thought without losing sight of the spirit and spontaneity of Jazz. Let me know if I have succeeded!

One last piece of advice: Don't feel compelled to work your way through this book chapter by chapter. Instead, start with the sections on ear training ("Listen") and improvisation ("Play") as soon as possible. Feel free to skip around as you please. Your learning curve needn't move sequentially from A to B to C, etc. Sometimes, if you get stuck, it is more effective to move on to something else and return to the initial problem at a later point. More often than not, you will find that your brain has sorted out the issue in the meantime. I'll leave it to you how you want to approach the various topics presented in this book. Enjoy!!!

Think

*"The more ways
you have of thinking about music,
the more things
you have to play in your solos."*

Barry Harris

*"Knowledge is freedom
and ignorance is slavery."*

Miles Davis

First Steps

I'd like to begin with a short anecdote one of my students told me many years ago. In a nutshell, this story illustrates everything I'd like to say in the next 600 or so pages.

During the first session of a master class with saxophonist John Ruocco, John asked the following question: "What does the symbol Fmaj7 mean?" One of the participants wrote on the board:

$$Fmaj7 = F\text{-}A\text{-}C\text{-}E$$

John erased this and replaced it with:

$$Fmaj7 = Sound$$

And that's exactly what I'm all about! Have a look at the following chord progression:

What do you associate with this chord progression? What music do you hear in your mind? Can you conjure up specific sounds simply by looking at the chord symbols? Are they more than just an abstract collection of notes? Do you recognise a particular piece? Does the progression relate to anything you've already played or practised? What seems familiar at this point, what feels obscure? Could you write down the notes of each chord? Can you feel how the tensions add to the underlying four-note structures and how they influence the basic sound of the harmonies? What scale material does each chord imply? Could you notate it? Can you hear melodic phrases, guide tone lines or voicings that go with this chord progression? Are you aware of the formal ups and downs of the changes? Does the progression give you a feeling of development? Do you understand how the chords relate to each other functionally? Could you analyse them? Do you sense the push and pull of the chord progression, the harmonic energy, the feeling of tension and release? Can you sense harmonic phrases, sections, cadences, resolutions, points of rest, a climax…? Are your fingers itching to improvise over this chord progression on your instrument? Can you hear a bass line, a drum groove or possibly even a full band? Anything else…?? Anything at all…???

Every accomplished Jazz musician who sees this progression on paper will not only **understand** it intellectually, but also **hear** it internally. Only if these symbols trigger sounds in our minds and inspire us to pick up our instrument will we be able to **play** convincingly:

Symbol	→	*Sound*	→	*Instrument*
Understand	→	*Hear*	→	*Play*

Over the course of this book, I'd like to show you how to get from symbol to instrument, from understanding to playing. Ultimately, you should be able to not only "think" music, but also to imagine what a symbol sounds like and to make it happen on your instrument.

Tonality

Let there be sound

In all musical cultures, the fundamental structures and principles of sound can be traced back to the laws of physics. *Music is oscillation!* A tone is the result of an elastic body (e.g. a string, bell, plate, column of air, etc.) put into a state of regular – *periodic* – vibration transmitted through air (or any other medium). Our ear interprets the alternating compression and decompression of air molecules (pressure waves) as a specific pitch. Irregular – *aperiodic* – oscillations are perceived as noise. The faster the oscillation or the shorter the oscillating body, the higher the pitch. The following diagram illustrates the characteristics of the most basic waveform – the *sine wave*:

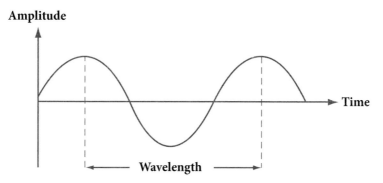

A tone is characterised by the following attributes:

- *pitch* – number of periodic oscillations per second = *frequency*; the frequency is measured in *Hertz* (Hz), named after the physicist Heinrich Hertz (1857-1894);

- *volume* – the amplitude or "peak deviation from zero" of the oscillation, commonly referred to as *sound pressure level* and measured in *decibels* (dB);

- *colour* – the path of the motion within the oscillations, the particular waveform (e.g. sawtooth, square, etc.), the physical properties of the material/matter oscillating as well as the constructive principles of a particular instrument.

Perception of sound by the human ear is limited to the frequency range of about 16 to 20000 Hz. Below 16 Hz, the ear no longer perceives a tone, but rather a pulse (infrasound vibrations). The ability to hear higher frequencies fades with increasing age – down to about 5000 Hz at the age of 60. However, studies have shown that loss of hearing acuity occurs faster and earlier these days. Extreme volumes in discos and the use of headphones dramatically accelerate this loss of sensitivity. Sudden Sensorineural Hearing Loss (SSHL) and tinnitus ("whistling in the ear") have become common diseases of our civilisation. I highly recommend you take utmost care of your hearing and have yourselves examined regularly by a doctor. With the aid of an audiogram you can easily find out what shape your ears are in.

The grand staff

In English-speaking countries and in Northern Europe the first seven letters of the alphabet (A-B-C-D-E-F-G) represent a steadily rising sequence of pitches or notes called *naturals*.

In order to notate pitches, we use a system of five horizontal parallel lines called a *staff* (or stave). The *grand staff* consists of a pair of staves placed at a distance above one another connected by a vertical line on the left. Any staff can be extended upwards and downwards by adding short lines called *ledger lines* above and below either of the staves. The notes (the note heads) are either placed on a line or in the space between two adjacent lines. Two symbols referred to as *clefs* (French: *clef* = key) are placed at the beginning of each staff. A *treble clef* for the upper staff and a *bass clef* for the lower staff establish the position of the notes. The figure below illustrates the distribution of the naturals and how they appear on the grand staff:

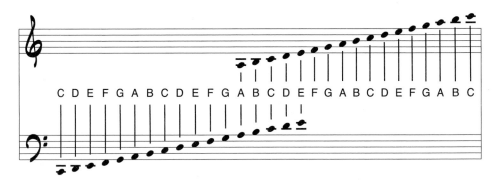

As you can see, the note names on the grand staff repeat periodically. The distance between two notes with the same name is called an *octave* (8 naturals). To avoid the use of too many ledger lines, we often notate single notes or series of notes an octave higher or lower than played, using the abbreviations "8va" (*ottava alta* = an octave above) and "8vb" (*ottava bassa* = an octave below). Double octave transpositions are marked with "15ma" and "15mb" (*quindicesima alta/bassa* = a "fifteenth" above/below; not "16va" or "16vb", a common mistake found in many textbooks and scores).

Note that the distance between the naturals is not always the same. Looking at a keyboard will help you understand this. The white keys are the naturals. You will notice that there are no black keys between the notes B and C or the notes E and F. The distance between the notes of these two pairs is half the distance of the notes in all other pairs (A-B, C-D, D-E and F-G). The note pairs without a black key between them are called *semitones* (also half-tones or half steps) and the others are called *whole-tones* or whole steps. The semitone is the smallest possible distance between two notes in our notation system, although smaller divisions are used in other cultures and contemporary compositions (microtonal music).

The framework of octaves

The octave is the "framework" or "defining" interval (measure of "musical distance") that subdivides our musical universe. Therefore, it merits special attention. Largely as a result of the work of the Benedictine monk Guido d'Arezzo (end of the 10th century), the note C (and no longer A) established itself as the most important reference note of the naturals. Starting with what is called the "Sub-contra C", this is how our system of notation is organised (C is always the lowest note of each octave segment; c′ is also referred to as *middle C*):

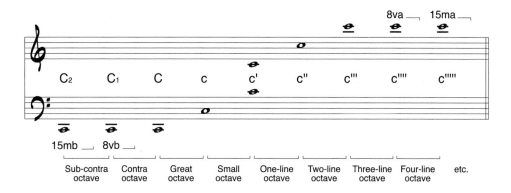

There is quite a bit of confusion concerning the system of labelling octaves. The designation shown above is based on the Helmholtz system of pitch notation, which is used throughout this book. There are, however, several other systems in use. For example, scientific pitch notation starts with C0 (Sub-contra C) and moves on via C1, C2, C3, C4 (middle C) to C8 (c′′′′′ in the Helmholtz system) and beyond.

The above figure illustrates approximately the range within which most of our music is played. Sub-contra C can only be played on a church organ (using the 32-foot Principal = an organ pipe close to 10 metres long), and c′′′′′ can be found in the extreme upper range of a piccolo or violin, for example.

The chromatic scale

The naturals can be raised or lowered by means of *accidentals*, thus creating the notes between the naturals known as *chromatic notes* (the black keys on the keyboard). Naturals are raised by a semitone using the *sharp* sign (♯) and lowered by a semitone using the *flat* sign (♭). All accidentals can be neutralised by the *natural* sign (♮). The name of a chromatic note is derived from either the natural above or below it (e.g. D sharp / D♯ = the note a half step above D, B flat / B♭ = the note a half step below B, etc.). As you can see, the same chromatic note can be reached by either raising the natural below or lowering the natural above by a semitone (e.g. C♯ = D♭, D♯ = E♭, etc.). Notes that are written differently but sound the same are called *enharmonic equivalents*; the principle is referred to as *enharmonic spelling* (enharmonic = in agreement).

By playing all naturals and chromatic notes in a row, we get what is called the *Chromatic scale* (*chroma* = colour) consisting only of semitones constituting the fundamental spectrum of notes in Western music. Here is the Chromatic scale from c′ to c″:

As you can see, even the names of the naturals can be enharmonically changed (E = F♭, F = E♯, B = C♭, C = B♯). A word on notation: On the staff, accidentals appear *before* the note (to its left), but in speech and in text the accidentals come *after* the name of the note (to its right)! For example, we notate "sharp G" but say and write "G sharp". Normally, we use sharps for ascending chromatic lines and flats for descending ones.

Intervals

An *interval* is any pair of notes either played *simultaneously* (at the same time, vertical) or *successively* (one after another, horizontal). In Western music, the system used to measure and label the distance (= gap) between the two notes of an interval is based on the sequence of naturals. The smallest possible interval is called a *unison* – the distance between two exact same pitches (which, of course, is no gap at all). For all other intervals, we use *ordinal numbers* (second, third, fourth, fifth, etc.). Consequently, a second is the distance between two adjacent naturals, a third is the distance between one natural and the next but one, and so on. We measure the distance between two notes by counting the letter names (ABCDEFGABC…) contained within the interval (C to G = C-D-E-F-G = 5 letter names = fifth, F to A = F-G-A = 3 letter names = third, etc.). Always remember that the starting note is included when counting intervals.

In the following table, I have chosen to start on C, but this could have been any note or its enharmonic equivalent:

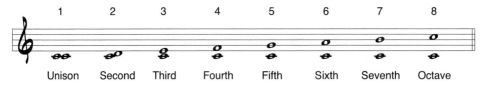

Once we get to the octave, we arrive at a note with the same name as the starting note. The same note sounding one octave apart is referred to as an *octave unison*, whereas the term *perfect unison* is used to describe two notes sounding at the same pitch. Larger intervals (beyond the octave) will therefore be treated as basic intervals plus an octave and are called *compound intervals*. The intervals greater than an octave are called: a ninth (9), a tenth (10), an eleventh (11), a twelfth (12), a thirteenth (13), etc. (in practice, interval names greater than a 13th are rarely used):

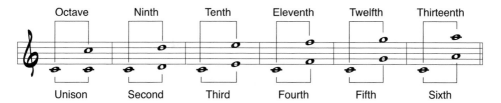

The distance between any two naturals defines the **general name** of an interval. But, remember we talked about the difference between natural semitones (E-F, B-C) and natural whole-tones (C-D, D-E, F-G, G-A). Since both refer to the interval of a second, we need to give each one its own name in order to avoid confusion.

To determine the *specific name* of an interval, the following qualifiers are used: *perfect*, *major* and *minor.* Unisons, octaves, fourths and fifths are perfect intervals (I'll explain later). The others (seconds, thirds, sixths and sevenths) are labelled as either major or minor (e.g. C-D is a major second, E-F is a minor second, C-E is a major third, D-F is a minor third, etc.). Here are all commonly used intervals with their customary numbering and corresponding number of semitones between the two notes of the interval.

Interval name	No. equivalent	No. of semitones
Perfect unison	1	0
Minor second	♭2	1
Major second	2	2
Minor third	♭3	3
Major third	3	4
Perfect fourth	4	5
Perfect fifth	5	7
Minor sixth	♭6	8
Major sixth	6	9
Minor seventh	♭7/7	10
Major seventh	maj7	11
Perfect octave	8	12

The label "maj7", as shown in the table above, is used to make a clear distinction between the major and the minor seventh. "7" is used exclusively for the minor seventh interval as part of a chord, while "♭7" usually designates the interval as part of a scale or melody.

Unusual interval names such as "perfect thirds", "major fourths" or "minor fifths" should be struck from your vocabulary immediately – they are never used in common speech and can result in irreversible brain damage!

The same pair of notes can form two different intervals, depending on which note is at the top and which one is at the bottom. Changing the interval by either raising the lower note or lowering the upper note by an octave is known as **inverting** the interval. Pairs of inverted intervals are known as **complementary intervals**. As a simple means of memorising complementary pairs, just keep in mind that they always add up to 9 (6+3 = 9, 7+2 = 9, etc.).

1/8	♭2/maj7	2/♭7	♭3/6	3/♭6	4/5

In the table on p. 31, we're missing an interval between the fourth and fifth – the **tritone**. This interval divides the octave down the middle, each half consisting of three whole-tones (hence the name). Since there is no such thing as either a major fourth or a minor fifth, we need to extend our vocabulary. The terms **diminished** and **augmented** are used to label intervals in more detail. If we reduce a perfect or minor interval by a semitone (either by lowering the upper note or raising the lower note chromatically), we end up with a diminished interval. Correspondingly, if we enlarge a perfect or major interval chromatically, the result is an augmented interval:

Diminished	←	**Perfect**	→	*Augmented*
Diminished	←	**Minor – Major**	→	*Augmented*

You cannot diminish a major interval or augment a minor interval. Make sure you always refer to intervals as "minor", "major", "perfect", "augmented" or "diminished", rather than just saying seconds, thirds and fourths, etc.

In addition to sharps and flats (♯ and ♭), two more accidentals are in use (though less frequently): "𝄪", the "double sharp", and "♭♭", the "double flat". These raise or lower a natural by *two* semitones. Two examples should clarify the significance of and the necessity for these additional accidentals. Let's start on C♯ and look for the note an augmented fourth (♯4) above it. A perfect fourth above C♯ would be F♯. So, to arrive at the ♯4, we have to raise the F♯ by a semitone. Because the naming of intervals is based on the naturals, we should keep the letter "F" in the name – therefore, the note an augmented fourth above C♯ would have to be called F𝄪 (F double sharp). Conversely, let's try to find a diminished fifth (♭5) above D♭. A perfect fifth above D♭ would be A♭. Flatting the A♭ by a semitone gives us A♭♭ (A double flat).

So, for the sake of consistency, we would occasionally need to use double sharps and flats. Practically speaking (especially in Jazz), however, we avoid this kind of nitpicking. We try to keep things less complicated and easier on the eye. In the two examples above, we would prefer to use the enharmonic equivalent G, not F𝄪 or A♭♭. This may be theoretically wrong, but it simplifies notation. I am generally going to avoid using "𝄪" and "♭♭" in this book, but I would still like you to be aware of the traditionally correct way of constructing intervals.

Here is a list of all commonly used intervals within the octave (brackets indicate enharmonic intervals):

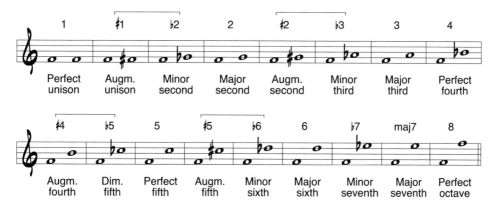

Diminished thirds (♭♭3), fourths (♭4), sixths (♭♭6) and octaves (♭8) as well as augmented thirds (♯3), sixths (♯6), sevenths (♯7) and octaves (♯8) are theoretically possible, but (almost) never used in practice. Logically speaking, the diminished unison (♭1) is a theoretical oddity (Is there anything less than nothing, or is there such a thing as a negative interval?). However, since augmentation or diminution of an interval involves the process of raising or lowering notes, you have to admit a diminished unison (e.g. C-C♭), too, even though it comprises a semitone, just the same as the augmented unison (e.g. C-C♯). At least, that's the way the concept is applied in practice.

Also, be aware of the fact that enharmonic equivalents (e.g. C♯-D♭) are not labelled as perfect unisons, but rather as diminished seconds. If you go to pdf-A ("Tuning Systems"), you will understand that enharmonic equivalents are not identical in pitch – depending on the tuning system, they're merely close. Only with equal-tempered tuning are enharmonic equivalents truly perfect unisons, at least in theory. However, even today, instruments having to control pitch (strings, horns, etc.) will still adjust their intonation (minimally going sharp or flat) with regard to the tonal and harmonic environment of a note. For example, C♯ and D♭ have different functional implications in any key and, accordingly, require differing frequencies.

Assignment

Write down the intervals shown in the above table, starting from all commonly used roots (C, C♯, D♭, D, D♯, E♭, E, F♭, F, F♯, G♭, G, G♯, A♭, A, B♭, B, C♭). You'll realise that you often have to use the accidentals "x" and "♭♭" to construct some of the intervals correctly. In these cases, write down the formally correct version as well as its enharmonically simpler equivalent (for instance, the augmented second of C♯ should be notated as Dx, but you would preferably use an E instead).

The harmonic series

Probably the most important natural sound phenomenon is the *harmonic series* – it is the universal principle in music. What we hear as a single note is actually a combination of various oscillations occurring simultaneously: the "main" note, known as the *fundamental* (the note we hear most clearly, the actual pitch), and a series of subtle, softer, hardly noticeable *partials*, which blend in with the fundamental. These are also known as *harmonic overtones* or just *harmonics*. For the sake of clear terminology – don't mix up harmonics and overtones. The term "harmonic" encompasses all notes in the harmonic series, whereas the term "overtone" refers to all partials excluding the fundamental (e.g. the 1st overtone is the 2nd harmonic).

With the aid of a taut string, we can show how these partials relate to each other mathematically:

1st Harmonic = fundamental	2nd Harmonic (double the frequency of the fundamental)	3rd Harmonic (triple the frequency of the fundamental)	4th Harmonic (quadruple the frequency of the fundamental)

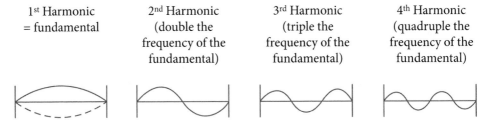

A theoretically endless series of mathematical ratios emerges, each partial a whole number multiple of the fundamental:

$$1 : 2 : 3 : 4 : 5 : 6 : 7 : 8 \text{ etc.}$$

If these mathematical ratios are converted to specific frequencies and corresponding pitches, the following series of notes emerges (based on C):

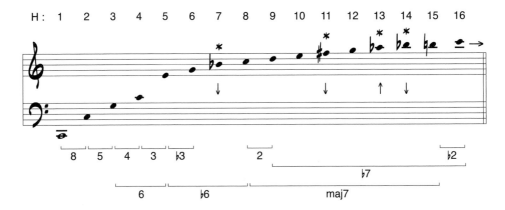

Although this example is based on C, I could have picked any other note as the fundamental. The structure of the corresponding harmonic series would be identical – relatively speaking.

Since our system of musical notation is based on the chromatic subdivision of the octave into 12 equal half steps, some of the notes contained within the harmonic series can only be notated approximately. The notes marked with an asterisk (*) in the diagram are those that deviate, sometimes considerably, from the actual pitch of the harmonic (7:1, 11:1, 13:1, 14:1). The arrows indicate whether the actual pitch is higher or lower than the notated pitch.

The farther away harmonics are from the fundamental (the higher up in the series), the softer they become. The intervallic distance between the overtones also diminishes incrementally. Beyond the 16th partial, the intervals are smaller than a semitone and cannot be depicted using our notation (that's why they will not be discussed any further here). However, they still remain part of the overall sound of every note. The timbre (sound quality) of an instrument depends to a large extent on which harmonics actually resonate and how loud or soft they are. A violin, for example, has a rich and brilliant sound because each note produces many and clearly audible overtones. A clarinet, by comparison, has a subdued, dark or even "hollow" sound, the reason being the almost complete absence of all even-numbered harmonics. So, the fundamental gives us the pitch, the other harmonics characterise the source.

The notes contained in the harmonic series and their corresponding ratios all relate back to the fundamental. The distances between the upper partials of the harmonic series constitute the starting point of our system of intervals. You'll notice that almost all basic intervals within the octave are contained in the harmonic series as a combination of two partials and can, accordingly, also be defined in terms of a frequency ratio:

Perfect unison	1:1 (fundamental)
Perfect octave	1:2
Perfect fifth	2:3
Perfect fourth	3:4
Major third	4:5
Minor third	5:6
Major second	8:9
Minor second	15:16
Major sixth	3:5
Minor sixth	5:8
Major seventh	8:15
Minor seventh	9:16

If the ratios are reversed, they still depict the same interval (1:2 or 2:1 in both cases designate the octave). When calculating frequencies, however, it is of importance whether we use the ratio < 1 (1/2) or > 1 (2/1).

Assignment

You can prove the existence of overtones to yourselves on a piano (not a keyboard):

- With the left hand, very carefully press down the key of any low note (fundamental) without actually playing the note and continue holding down the key (no pedal!).

- With the right hand, now strike each overtone loudly and percussively (immediately releasing the key) while still keeping the fundamental depressed. Take your time and listen closely before you move on to the next harmonic.

You will notice that each harmonic continues to sound even after you release the key. What you are hearing is the sympathetic resonance of the string belonging to the fundamental, which can vibrate freely because its damper is raised. The string is set in motion by the energy of the higher note transferred through the air and through the frame of the piano, activating the frequency of the specific harmonic. If you try the same thing with notes not contained in the harmonic series of the fundamental, these notes will immediately fade away as soon as you let go of the key.

Independent of one-another, people all over the world react to the natural phenomenon of the harmonic series in similar ways, even though they may not be aware of it. All systems governing melody and/or harmony, worldwide, reflect the principles contained in the harmonic series in one way or another.

The root

There are a number of similarities between the music of various peoples and cultures that can be traced back to the harmonic series. The most elementary and perhaps most important aspect of this is that most musical systems in some way relate to a *root, keynote* or *tonal centre*. Even though we may not be aware of it, every one of us has become familiar with tonal music since early childhood and has subconsciously developed an intuitive "feel" for the concept of a root. Cast your mind back to your personal "roots": the nursery rhymes, the Christmas carols, the Folk and Pop songs, hit tunes and jingles you grew up with and which were part of your everyday lives at home, at school, in church and all around you. All these tunes have one thing in common: They relate to a tonal centre.

As soon as a root has been established in our ear, we will subsequently hear all other notes relating to this point of reference as specific intervals. What is commonly known as *tonality* is first and foremost a musical centre of gravity that defines all melodic and harmonic relationships. It is this focal point that determines the forces of attraction and repulsion within a tonal framework or *key*. While the term "tonality" implies the presence of a root as such (e.g. the note F), the word "key" encompasses all notes relating to a tonality (e.g. as part of a Major or Minor scale). I'll talk about keys extensively in one of the following chapters and we will see that the effect of any particular sound depends primarily on its inclination to resolve to the root.

The ability to hear and identify notes relative to the root is called *relative pitch*. Relative pitch relies on a point of reference (e.g. a root). In contrast, there is *perfect pitch* (absolute pitch). This is the ability to recognise pitches without having to refer back to tonal relationships. There are people who have an eidetic (photographic) memory for pitches and their corresponding names. On hearing a sound, they can immediately say "That's an F!" or "These are the notes G-B-D-F♯." At the same time, many people with perfect pitch are unable to determine the intervallic significance of notes or identify tonal relationships. It is not possible to understand tonal implications without a well-developed sense of relative pitch, so perfect pitch is not necessarily an asset at this stage.

Assignment

The basis of good relative pitch is the ability to recognise a root in the first place. Sing melodies you know well: nursery rhymes, Folk tunes, Christmas carols, etc. Start anywhere within your vocal range. Just make sure you can sing a melody comfortably. Take care not to sing sloppily. Follow your mental image of the song and sing in tune as best you can. As soon as you have come to the end of the song, try singing the note that you hear as the strongest point of reference, the note on which your ear "comes to rest". A tip: This will often (but not always) be the final note of the song. Most traditional compositions land on the tonic, thereby reinforcing the tonality and bringing the melody to a close. It is not important to know why you will most probably identify the root seemingly without effort. Since you have grown up with tonal music, you have internalised the presence of a root as an aural reflex. The point of this exercise is to be aware of this automatic response.

There is, however, a problem worth mentioning. In my ear training classes, I often come across students who tend to mistake the fifth (5) for the root (1). This is easy to understand. I have just commented on the importance of the harmonic series and that it has a profound influence on the way we hear. Because the fifth comes right after the fundamental and its octave in the harmonic series, we tend to lock into it very strongly, too. So, when trying to spot the root, always keep in mind that you may be on the wrong track. If you are not completely sure, sing down a perfect fifth to check if the resulting note feels even more like "home".

Now go to the recordings accompanying this book (**tracks 1–38**). Find and sing the root in each example. Try focussing on the bass without being distracted by the piano and drums. The tonal centre is easiest to hear in the bass line. Concentrate on what you believe is the root, sing it along with the recording and check the note on the piano. Then go to the tracklist in the appendix for the correct answers. Repeat this exercise intermittently. Locking into a root and feeling it as a centre of gravity is something you should be able to rely on implicitly.

The circle of fifths

We have already talked about the role of the root as a reference point and the octave as a defining element within our tonal system. Moving up to the next note in the harmonic series, we come across the fifth – the first "foreign" overtone (the 2nd and 4th partials of the harmonic series are simply octave transpositions of the fundamental). It's easy to see why this particular interval is especially important to our perception of sound and why the fifth has become a vital, if not *the*, governing principle of our music. As a matter of fact, it is paramount to most, if not all, other musical cultures worldwide.

One of the central organisational concepts of Western music is the *circle of fifths* (also "cycle of fifths") – a self-contained intervallic system, which incorporates all notes of the Chromatic scale. Starting on C, it moves *up* clockwise in 12 perfect fifths and completes a full circle when reaching B♯, which can enharmonically be respelled as C. Alternately, it can start on C and move *down* counter-clockwise, eventually reaching D♭♭, which can also be seen as an enharmonic equivalent of C. In the most common representation of the circle of fifths (to avoid excessive use of accidentals), the two sequences of fifths C-G-D-A-E-B-F♯ (clockwise) and C-F-B♭-E♭-A♭-D♭-G♭ (counter-clockwise) are joined at both ends by applying the enharmonic equivalent F♯/G♭:

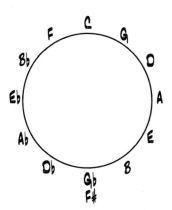
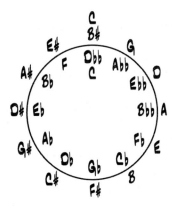

As we'll see later, most of our melodic and harmonic material relates back in some way to the circle of fifths. This may explain why any music that disregards our deeply ingrained awareness of the fifth (e.g. twelve-tone music) is met with rejection or incomprehension by the average listener (and why power chords are so popular ☺).

Chords

Moving up the harmonic series beyond the fifth and its complementary interval, the fourth, we arrive at the major and minor third. The partials 3-4-5, 4-5-6, and 5-6-8 constitute the three inversions of a major triad. It therefore stands to reason that the earliest harmonic structures were triads built in layers of thirds. Maybe this also explains why many of my students find it less difficult to identify major triads than minor sounds, the latter having a more ambiguous quality that is not as easy to grasp for the ear.

Paul Hindemith describes graphically in his *"Unterweisung im Tonsatz"* ("Instruction in Harmony") how a composer, who himself had no aversion to atonality or dissonance, perceives the triad as a natural phenomenon:

"Partials 1 to 6 in the harmonic series (the octave, fifth, fourth, major and minor thirds) and their octave transpositions (double, quadruple and eight times the fundamental) give us the extended triad which, to both the sophisticated and illiterate mind, manifests itself as one of the greatest natural phenomena; as simple and as wonderful as rain, ice and wind. As long as there is music, it will both arise from and resolve back to this most pure and natural of all sounds. The musician is bound to it like the painter to the primary colours, the architect to three dimensions. The triad and its immediate extensions can only be avoided for limited amounts of time in composition if the listener is not to be put into a state of total confusion."

In the next chapter "Chord Symbols", we will take a closer look at triads, four-note chords and their possible extensions.

Whole-tone and semitone

The whole-tone and the semitone appear late in the harmonic series. Their frequency ratios are substantially more complex and therefore not as easily accessible to the ear as a perfect interval. This explains why it took such a long time before the semitone became part of our system of tonality and why it plays such a central role in our harmony. The semitone is the driving force of many chord progressions because its powerful dissonance demands resolution to consonance.

Defining the major or minor second as a specific ratio isn't easy. If you look at the harmonic series, you will realise that, for example, you have two ratios, both of which could work for the major second: 8:9 or 9:10. Go to the chapter "Tuning Systems" (pdf-A) and it will become evident that there are other possibilities for determining the size of a whole step. The minor second is even more challenging. One of the major stumbling blocks in the history of music was to find a way of tuning half steps and, ultimately, arriving at the Chromatic scale as we know it today. 15:16 is one of the most logical ratios because it acts something like an approach to the octave. However, other ratios such as 24:25, 21:22, 16:17 or even 243:256 were used at various points in time. We will take a closer look at seconds when discussing a few of the tuning systems musicians came up with over the past 1500 years (pdf-A).

The tuning note

How are exact pitches determined within the spectrum of frequencies? How do you decide which frequencies correspond to a C, D or E♭, etc.? In early music, the Sub-contra C = 16 Hz was used as a point of reference, probably because this is the lowest frequency the human ear can identify as a note per se. Over the past centuries, *concert pitch a'* has become the accepted standard tuning note. This "concert a" has been subject to great fluctuation over the years. Back in the 17th century, it ranged from 392 Hz in France to 466 Hz in Italy. Later it varied from 422 Hz (Berlin Tuning 1752) to 409 Hz (Paris Tuning 1788) to 435 Hz (International Tuning Conference in Vienna 1885) to the current pitch standard 440 Hz (London 1939).

This shows that the frequencies of all other notes are dependent on the frequency of concert pitch. As concert pitch rises and falls, the entire spectrum of pitches shifts up and down with it. As a result, we are not dealing with an absolute system of pitches, but rather a relative one. For example, two hundred years ago, a c' would have sounded almost a semitone lower.

I'm sure that quite a few of you, who feel insufficiently endowed with talent, will be delighted to hear that you can confuse someone with perfect pitch by setting the tuning note a' to a frequency other than 440. Shifting the point of reference (e.g. by a quarter tone up or down) redefines the entire tonal spectrum and will wreak havoc for anyone who has perfect pitch. This suggests that perfect pitch is not an inherited trait but a "photographic" memory of frequencies acquired intuitively in early childhood to which pitch names are assigned later. In all fairness, I have to add that many people with perfect pitch have the ability to readjust to a "shifted" system and recognise pitches accurately again within a few days.

Before we move on, I'd like to draw your attention to pdf-A once again, a chapter that focusses on the fascinating world of tuning systems. However, here's a word of warning. You may find the topic a bit too technical for your taste. If so, feel free to skip it for the time being (after all, you bought this book to improve your skills as musicians rather than polish up your maths). Return to this chapter whenever your curiosity gets the better of you and you feel ready to delve into a topic that explains how today's music works and why it sounds the way it does.

The effects of the harmonic series

Maybe you're asking yourself why I am going into this much detail in presenting the harmonic series (and the various tuning systems discussed in pdf-A). I believe that every musician's education should include an understanding of how our world of sounds works. One day, when you're sitting in your studio, wondering how to create a good mix, you'll realise just how helpful it is to know the basics of sound production and perception. What do "bass", "middle" and "treble" mean in terms of frequencies? How many Hertz does the lowest note of the double bass have? What is the frequency range of the electric guitar? How do graphic and parametric equalisers work? If you'd like to know more about this, I suggest you start familiarising yourself with basic acoustics, audio engineering and sound design. There are many good books and tutorials available on the market.

The main reason, however, is quite practical. We may have grown up with equal temperament, but we still react to a number of aspects that relate back to the harmonic series and fundamentally define our musical expectations and needs as well as the way we perceive sound. I would briefly like to introduce the perhaps most important characteristic.

Consonance and dissonance

Every interval has a quality that can be explained using the harmonic series. We have seen that the mathematical relationships between the upper partials become more complex as we move away from the fundamental. The farther away from the fundamental we go and the more complex the frequency ratios are, the more *dissonant = rich in tension* an interval becomes (from Latin *dis* = "apart" and *sonus* = "sound"; dissonant = sounding apart). Dissonances trigger feelings of disquiet, conflict and a need for resolution. Vice versa, intervals closer to the fundamental are *consonant = lacking in tension* the intervals become (from Latin *con* = "with" and *sonus* = "sound"; consonant = sounding together). Consonances convey coherence, quiet, stability. In his theory of proportion, Pythagoras stated that the simpler the frequency ratio between notes of intervals, the more consonant the interval. This is surely why the intervals of an octave, fourth and fifth are said to be "perfect" or "pure". The notes of these intervals are closest to the fundamental and their frequency ratios are simple. They therefore produce less tension. On the other hand, it is easy to understand why intensely chromatic music has a rather unsettling effect on some people.

If we arrange all possible intervals found within the octave according to their degree of tension, we end up with the following order (try this out for yourselves on a keyboard!):

The terms "perfect" and "imperfect" are commonly used in music theory when referring to consonances, whereas the attributes "weak/strong", although they quite adequately describe the quality of a dissonant interval, are more colloquial than scientific.

You can see that the principle of complementary intervals is of importance when defining tension levels. Both intervals of a complementary "pair" generate a similar degree of tension (1/8, 4/5, 3/♭6, ♭3/6, 2/♭7, ♭2/maj7).

Augmented and diminished intervals are not mentioned here. They are generally thought of as being dissonant, although the degree of tension strongly depends on the context in which they appear as well as on the melodic or harmonic setting.

The tritone (♯4/♭5) is of special significance. Historically, this interval has generally been taken as dissonant. It was known for a while as the "diabolical interval", "the devil in music" (*diabolus in musica*) because it disrupted the tonal framework of perfect fifths and was seen as a glitch in the divine order of things. Dissonances evoke the desire for resolution. This explains why, also in Jazz, the tritone determines the flow of many chord progressions. These days, however, our musical ear is more receptive to dissonant sounds. As a result, the tension level we sense when hearing a tritone can vary depending on the context. In a simple and basically tonal harmonic environment, the tritone sticks out like a sore thumb and has a strong need to resolve. The Blues, however, is a good example of a type of music where the general tension level is much higher. Here, the tritone blends in as a stable and rather consonant interval (e.g. as part of I7 and IV7). I myself hear the ♯4/♭5 as a weak dissonance, somewhere in the area of a ♭7, when referring to the table above.

The fourth is also an interesting case – here, too, the gods are divided. The fourth, taken on its own, is a perfect (consonant) interval. Then again, it stands out in our tertial harmony (based on layers of thirds) as needing resolution, resulting in a certain amount of tension. This is why layers of fourths seem rather unusual to the ear. Again, our intuitive understanding of sound allows us to hear the perfect fourth as either consonant or dissonant, depending on the context in which it appears.

All this shows that our perception of sound has changed over the centuries. Our tolerance of dissonant intervals has increased. Sounds characterised in the past as extremely dissonant are nowadays heard as mildly dissonant, even as consonant. Even if there are mathematical and physical reasons for varying degrees of intervallic tension, individual habit and our differing socio-cultural environment seem to play just as important a role in how we perceive a sound. Again, go to pdf-A for further information. You will realise that an equal tempered major third at 400 cents is significantly wider than a perfect major third at 386 cents. Both are theoretically considered to be consonant. Our ears, however, have grown up with equal temperament and have learned to appreciate the 400 cents as the "real thing". Conversely, someone who has never heard a perfect major third will hear it as flat, out of tune and mildly dissonant.

Assignment

Find yourself a willing guinea pig, preferably human. Pick a simple tune both of you know really well (e.g. "Jingle Bells" or "Happy Birthday"). And now to the assignment: While one of you sticks to the original key, the other sings the same tune a semitone higher or lower. Concentrate hard on your part. Don't let the other line influence or draw you in. Try putting up with the tension (even if it hurts!). Notice how your intonation wavers and how your voice tries to avoid the dissonances by resolving into the other line, how difficult it is to maintain stable pitch. Now try the same at a distance of a major second, then a minor or major third, then a fourth as well as a fifth. See how it gets easier and how the tension decreases once you switch to a more consonant intervallic relationship.

Conclusion

In summary, it is clear that the harmonic series has had a major influence on the history of music. A closer look reveals that the development of music actually mirrors the structure of the harmonic series, moving along from its simplest and most consonant sounds to the complex and dissonant upper partials. Even the monumental change to equal temperament, an artificial system that has superseded much of what can be called the "true nature of sound", has not succeeded in eradicating the laws of physics. It is a fact that our ears are still influenced by the harmonic series and the tonal organisation implied by it, no matter what kind of music we play or listen to. Even atonality is ultimately nothing but a play on the principles of tonality, principles that invariably pervade our hearing, conditioned by years of exposure to tonal music, whether we like it or not! Composers exploit this fact. If a melody or a harmonic progression coincides with tonal habits and expectations, the listener experiences a sense of smoothness and familiarity. If our expectations are not met, if sounds are used that disrupt or even obliterate the tonal framework, we experience a feeling of tension. It is this interplay of tension and release that accounts for much of what attracts us in music.

Musicians have always had a penchant for stretching tonal boundaries (chromaticism), departing from them (modulation) or disregarding them altogether (atonality). In order to appreciate these concepts, we need to understand the rules governing tonality. Many unusual and exciting sounds are created by breaking the rules, by consciously revoking or temporarily suspending the laws of tonality. This is where the study of harmony comes into play. Harmony describes and explains these laws. You have to understand the norm (the cliché) if you want to appreciate sounds that are special or unusual.

Chord Symbol Notation

Unlike other art forms, music is fleeting and transient. An intense and short-lived experience, it fades fast from our memory, leaving most of us with only a vague and intangible echo. Music notation is an attempt to hold on to these musical moments, permitting us to repeat and savour them again and again.

Musical notation must reflect the music it strives to represent. Notation is not an end in itself. It must always be subordinate to the music, not vice versa. Ideally, differing musical concepts would each have their own distinctive notational system. Conventional musical notation often leaves a lot to be desired when applied to idioms other than Western Classical music. This becomes particularly evident in Jazz where composition and improvisation overlap. Improvisation suggests a high degree of unpredictability – that's what makes it appealing. Composition, in contrast, attempts to control and to determine each sound as accurately as possible. An appropriate system of notation would have to cater to both demands, conveying sufficient important information, while leaving ample room for individual interpretation and chance.

This is why chord symbol notation, which is as informative as it is imprecise, is used to notate chord progressions in Jazz. Although it defines the material for improvisation, it doesn't prescribe how this material is to be used. The emergence of chord symbol notation is arguably one of the most important developments in Jazz, blending improvisation with composition. This "shorthand" conveys a maximum of information with a minimum of means – it is a musical form of stenography, within which lies an inexhaustible abundance of choices for the improviser. A large part of this book is dedicated to the interpretation and application of chord symbols.

Here are the most important chord types, their structural characteristics and the symbols used to represent them:

Triads

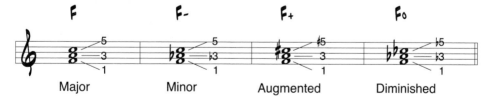

Four-note chords

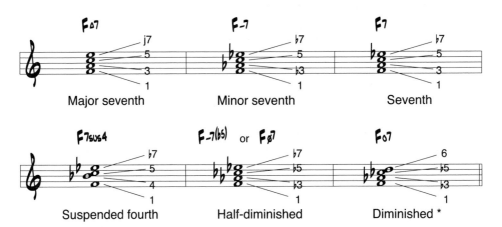

Augmented triads (made up of major thirds only) and diminished four-note chords (made up of minor thirds only) are symmetrical in structure – the layering of thirds can go on and on endlessly without changing the chord. This means that any note within the chord can be treated as the root (e.g. C+ = E+ = Ab+, etc.). Augmented and diminished chords, therefore, can be arranged into groups containing the same notes (watch out for enharmonic spellings!):

$$C_+ \; = \; E_+ \; = \; A\flat_+$$
$$D\flat_+ \; = \; F_+ \; = \; A_+$$
$$D_+ \; = \; G\flat_+ \; = \; B\flat_+$$
$$E\flat_+ \; = \; G_+ \; = \; B_+$$

$$C_{o7} \; = \; E\flat_{o7} \; = \; F\sharp_{o7} \; = \; A_{o7}$$
$$C\sharp_{o7} \; = \; E_{o7} \; = \; G_{o7} \; = \; B\flat_{o7}$$
$$D_{o7} \; = \; F_{o7} \; = \; A\flat_{o7} \; = \; B_{o7}$$

---

* In theory, 4-note diminished chords should be spelled 1-♭3-♭5-♭♭7 following the succession of minor thirds. In Jazz, as already mentioned in the previous chapter, the use of double accidentals ("♭♭" or "x") is not common practice. Accordingly, ♭♭7 is enharmonically spelled as 6.

7sus4 chords are 7th chords with the major third (3) replaced by a perfect fourth (4). In traditional Western music the 4 usually appears as a *suspension* that resolves to the third of the corresponding 7th chord (thus the name *sus4*):

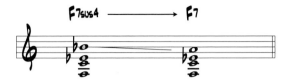

In Jazz, the 7sus4 chord is often used without resolving the suspension. It is treated as a distinct colour in its own right because it has no third and therefore cannot be seen as major or minor.

Here is a summary of the basic chord types and their intervallic structure:

Chord type	Symbol	Intervallic structure
Major	C	1 - 3 - 5
Major seventh	Cmaj7	1 - 3 - 5 - maj7
Minor	C–	1 - ♭3 - 5
Minor seventh	C–7	1 - ♭3 - 5 - ♭7
Diminished	C° / C°7	1 - ♭3 - ♭5 - ♭♭7(6)
Augmented	C+	1 - 3 - ♯5
Seventh	C7	1 - 3 - 5 - ♭7
Suspended fourth	C7(sus4)	1 - 4 - 5 - ♭7
Half-diminished	C–7(♭5) / Cø7	1 - ♭3 - ♭5 - ♭7

Tensions

In Jazz, the chord types I have described so far are rarely used unchanged. By including additional notes, commonly referred to as *tensions*, it is possible to create a variety of colours within one and the same basic chord type. In chord symbol notation, these chord extensions are notated using numbers that represent their intervallic relation to the root. The following table shows the commonly used numbering system for chord tones and tensions added to basic chord symbols:

Distance to root	No. equivalent
Minor second	♭2/♭9
Major second	2/9
Augmented second	♯2/♯9
Minor third	♭3
Major third	3
Perfect fourth	4/11
Augmented fourth	♯4/♯11
Diminished fifth	♭5
Perfect fifth	5
Augmented fifth	♯5
Minor sixth	♭6/♭13
Major sixth	6/13
Minor seventh	7 (not ♭7!)*
Major seventh	maj7 or j7

You can see in the above table that most of the basic intervals are notated up an octave when they appear as tensions (e.g. ♭9 instead of ♭2). Because chords are traditionally constructed by layering thirds from the root up, many of the tensions lie outside the compass of an octave:

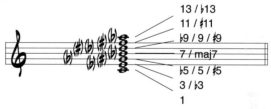

13 / ♭13
11 / ♯11
♭9 / 9 / ♯9
7 / maj7
♭5 / 5 / ♯5
3 / ♭3
1

Let's have a look at the most commonly used extensions (all chords are in root position).

Major chord extensions

---

* The minor seventh is notated as b7 when referring to an isolated interval and as 7 when used as part of a chord symbol.

The label *add9* is used to signify that only the major ninth is added to the triad while the 7th is excluded.

Traditional music theory is based on triads, whereas in Jazz we think mostly in terms of four-note 7th chords. The 7th (maj7 or 7, depending on the chord type) is seen as a fundamental ingredient. This means that a maj7 chord is considered to be a basic sound even though, in traditional harmony, the major seventh interval is seen as a dissonant extension and therefore in need of resolution. In Jazz, however, a maj7 chord is perceived as a stable sound.

Minor chord extensions

The symbols –9 and –11 imply the inclusion of the minor 7th (7); –11 chords may or may not include a major 9th (9). In Jazz, the four-note –7 chord, not the minor triad, is seen as the basic minor colour.

Seventh chord extensions

Here, we differentiate between *diatonic* tensions (9, 13) and *altered* tensions (♭9, ♯9, ♯11, ♭13). Alterations (from the Latin *alterare* = "to change") are chromatic modifications of diatonic tensions or chord tones ("diatonic" meaning "belonging to the scale or key"). ♭9 and ♯9 are a result of lowering or raising the 9 by a half step, the ♭13 relates to the 13, and the ♯11 is derived by either raising the 4 (= 11) or lowering the 5 chromatically:

In the case of X9 or X13, the minor 7th (7) does not have to be notated for the sake of simplification. It is understood as automatically being part of the chord. Sometimes we find the general symbol extension *alt*. This means that the tensions used should only consist of altered notes, without implying any specific alteration.

Of course, tensions can be combined freely. We get particularly interesting sounds when incorporating both diatonic and altered extensions:

Augmented triads

The augmented triad is the only chord in Jazz that has a basic three-note structure (because of its symmetry, extending it by another major third leads us back to the root). Therefore, the 7th (maj7/7) is considered to be a tension and not – as in all other four-note chord types – part of the basic sound. Both possible extensions, +maj7 and +7, are commonly used. The +7 extension is often used in place of a 7(♭13) and is usually interpreted as an altered seventh chord (♯5 = ♭13):

7sus4 chords

These should be treated as seventh chords. In practice, they often have the extensions 9/13 but are rarely used with altered tensions (♭9 is the only alteration found more frequently).

I'll talk about *sus4* chords in more detail in a later chapter (p. 425 ff.).

Half-diminished chords

These rarely contain extensions, probably because the basic chord itself has such a characteristic and unique sound. When tensions do appear, they tend to be 11 or, less commonly, ♭13 or 9.

We will have a closer look at the extensions used with *diminished chords* in a later chapter.

At this point, I'd like you to take a look at the many different ways chords are notated in the textbooks and scores you are likely to come across. The chord symbols used in this book correspond partly to the notation in the original version of the Real Book, the first comprehensive collection of Jazz themes, as well as to the library of symbols found in the notation software *Finale* used throughout this book. Although they conform to internationally accepted norms, there are variants you should be familiar with. These are:

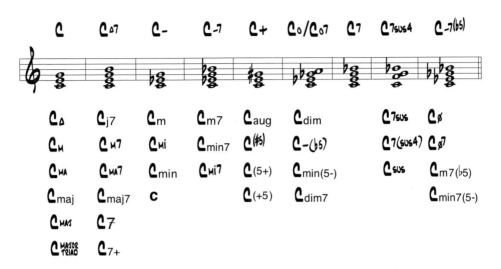

There are also variations in the way extensions are notated. Tensions can be enclosed in brackets or separated from the chord symbol by a slash. With seventh chords, diatonic tensions are usually notated without brackets and altered ones within brackets. As you can see, there is no such thing as a generally accepted or standardised way of notating chord symbols.

In practice, it is particularly unnerving that most lead sheets rarely show more than the basic four-note chords (Gmaj7, G–7, G7, etc.). As a consequence, the chord symbol is of little or no help when it comes to choosing appropriate tensions. We are expected to know or feel which extensions suit each situation best and which ones do not work – quite a problem for the beginner.

Here's a simple rule of thumb: The harmonic context, the key and therefore the function of each chord determine which extensions work best. The relationship of a chord to its tonal centre and key area influences the fact that some tensions fit in smoothly whereas others sound disturbing and out of place. Choosing tensions is a play on expectations. It is possible to define a norm or stereotype, "the way it is expected to sound", for every harmonic situation. Accomplished Jazz musicians are acutely aware of these conventions, not only on a theoretical but also on an aural and intuitive level, regardless of whether they choose to follow them or ignore them. This is not a matter of "right" or "wrong". When it comes to selecting tensions, it is more a question of "inside" or "outside", of consonance or dissonance, of whether a note pleases or rather irritates the ear. It is the musician's choice as to how ordinary or strange a sound should be.

The same applies to the notation of chord symbols. As a result, there is an unwritten rule: If only basic chord symbols are used, you are dealing with the cliché, the expected sound. Only those tensions that are unusual to any particular chord and its function need to be notated. In this way, chord symbol notation is further simplified, much to the disadvantage of the inexperienced player whose knowledge of harmony and repertoire may not yet be up to par. An important question in Jazz harmony is therefore: How do I develop a feel for which tensions to use with which chord in which situation? Most of the following chapters will deal with this question.

Inversions

Chords are built from the root up, resulting in a structure commonly known as *root position*. When placing all notes of a triad or four-note chord as closely together as possible (within the octave), the resulting structure is referred to as *close position*. By changing the vertical spacing and distributing the notes further apart (beyond the octave) we arrive at *open position* voicings (the term "voicing" relates to any particular structure derived from a chord symbol). There are many ways of voicing a chord in close or open position, which we will talk about in detail in the chapter "Voicings" (pdf-E).

Let's go back to chords in close position. If the notes of a triad or four-note chord are rearranged so that the root is *not* the bottom note of the chord, the resulting structure is referred to as an *inversion*. Inversions can be named in two different ways. The first and universally used labelling system is determined by the function of the *bottom* note of the chord (= the bass note) independently of the arrangement of the other notes (close/open position). In symbolic notation, the desired bass note is added to the chord symbol and separated by a slash (e.g. Amaj7/E = Amaj7 with the 5th in the bass; D7/F♯ = D7 with the 3rd in the bass). The second system, one you may not be familiar with because it is predominantly used in German speaking countries, is determined by the *top* note of a chord. As we will see, it is quite often necessary to define chord structures by thinking from the top note down rather than "bottom up". In the chapter "Arranging 101" (pdf-G), we will talk about harmonising a melody for various instrumental settings (piano, guitar, horn sections, vocal groups, etc.). Since the melody is almost invariably considered to be the "lead voice" and consequently the top voice of a chord progression, it also makes sense to focus on the highest note of a chord and construct the desired voicing "top down".

Here are the various inversions and their labels (e.g. C–7 in close position):

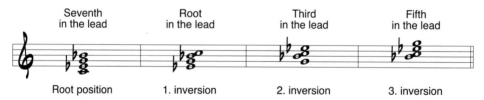

The term "first inversion" always means "♭3 or 3 in the bass" (or 4 with sus4 chords), "second inversion" implies a 5 as the lowest note (or ♭5 as part of a half-diminished or diminished chord) and "third inversion" defines the 7 or maj7 as the bottom note.

Considering the many possibilities of constructing chords through the use of various tensions, inversions and close or open position voicings, the crucial question is: How does a basic chord symbol actually translate into real sounds? The following examples demonstrate only a fraction of the possibilities when interpreting a simple G7:

All these voicings – and many more – represent G7. The examples show that a basic chord symbol tells us absolutely nothing about:

- the available tensions
- the number of notes involved
- the distribution of the notes (chord structure)
- the register of the chord (high, middle or low range)

Again, I'd like to refer you to the chapters "Voicings" (pdf-E) and "Arranging 101" (pdf-G) for further insights into the intricacies and ramifications of chord construction.

Assignment

In the following exercises, write down the chord symbols as notes and, vice versa, mark the chords in the manuscript with appropriate chord symbols. Note that there are exercises in both treble clef and bass clef.

1. Triads in root position:

2. Triads in 1st inversion:

3. Triads in 2nd inversion:

4. Four-note chords in root position:

5. Four-note chords in 1st inversion:

6. Four-note chords in 2nd inversion:

7. Four-note chords in 3rd inversion:

8. Look at the tune "There Will Never Be Another You" on p. 78 and notate the chord progression in the treble clef. Repeat the exercise, each time beginning on a different inversion of E♭maj7. First, write down the complete chord progression using only the inversion you started with (all chords in root position, all chords in 1st inversion, etc.). The result will be a series of chords, which tend to jump around quite a bit. Then, do the exercise again. This time, however, try to move from one chord to the next by changing the notes as little as possible, either by keeping common tones or otherwise moving them up or down in stepwise motion. This principle is called good voice leading and helps the chords to progress more smoothly. You may have to switch to a different inversion for almost every chord to create a good flow.

Modality

"Dizzy's got a very complicated brain, and he comes up with some funny lines that are really a knockout. He's got a whole lot of things that he's figured out for himself – funny oriental-type scales and things. He's always happy to discover new ones, and he uses them in his solos. His mind is always working on those things."

Benny Bailey

The word "modal" comes from the Latin *modus*. Loosely translated, this means the "way" or "manner" in which something is done. In music, it relates to the way in which notes are organised around a tonal centre. Basically, *any* organisational principle can be seen as a form of modality. However, as musicians, we generally associate the word "modal" with scales. Historically, we can easily see why. Music was initially based almost exclusively on melody and rhythm – harmonic relationships evolved from melody at a later stage.

The earliest accounts speak of melodic lines limited to just a few notes. There are, for example, reports of Indian religious chants based originally on only one note (*Sprechgesang* or "speech song") and later consisting of two alternating notes: the higher (*udatta*) and the lower (*anudatta*) – incidentally a fifth apart. Even if there is no melody to speak of in our sense of the word, these are examples of "modality", a "way" or "manner" – admittedly simple – in which tonal material can be organised.

Even within the tradition of European Classical music with its highly sophisticated harmonic language, compositions relied for a very long time on what could, at best, be called linear polyphony (multiple dependent or independent voices or parts). Starting with chorales sung over a drone, a single held bass note (*organum*, 8th/9th century), music evolved into parallel motion of parts (initially in parallel fifths and fourths) and eventually into polyphonic textures made up of independent melodic lines moving in parallel or contrary motion (counterpoint, 13th/14th century). Only as of the 15th century did chords and chord progressions become an integral part of the musical language.

The concept of *scales* or *modes* plays a vital role in Jazz. In this book we are going to concentrate mainly on what is generally known as the *chord-scale approach* – a widely accepted system of harmonic thinking since the 1970s – in which every chord is associated with a particular scale and, vice versa, every scale is related to a chord. Chords convey the vertical aspect in music while scales express the horizontal. Scales translate harmonic structure into melodic movement – both elements of music are inseparable.

So, when I use the word "modality", I mean first and foremost the many types of scales that can be used as a basis for improvisation in Jazz. I'd like to make sure, though, that this is not understood too narrowly. Modality can be used to describe any conceivable combination of notes, be it the Pentatonic scale, our Major scale, the church modes, the Chromatic scale, the twelve-tone principle, Indian *ragas* or just about anything constructed from any number of tones. In essence, the term "mode" generally implies a self-contained system of music in which notes revolve around a tonal centre or tonic. All notes, whether grouped as chords or melodies, establish distinct relationships with the tonic, resulting in the typical and unique colour and character of the mode.

The Pentatonic scale

Probably the oldest system of tonal relationships is the *Pentatonic* (five-note) scale. It is the "proto-scale" to which nearly all scale types used today can be traced back. How is it possible that one and the same scale has managed to establish itself in so many different cultures? Using – as Pythagoras did – only the perfect intervals (octave, fifth, fourth), the Pentatonic scale can be derived in two ways:

- By stacking fifths (and then transposing them back into the octave)

- By linking leaps of fifths and fourths

If we arrange the resulting notes linearly within the octave, we end up with an elementary form of the Pentatonic scale (the intervallic structure of which corresponds to a condensed Major scale):

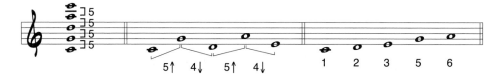

We see that the Pentatonic scale contains only whole tones (8:9) and minor thirds (5:6). Since it avoids dissonances, i.e. intervals with more complex frequency ratios (e.g. ♭2/maj7), it is easy on the ear.

Major and Minor

Most scale types used nowadays are, in contrast to the Pentatonic scale, *heptatonic* (consisting of seven tones). Let's start with the two basic sounds that most probably have influenced your personal musical development from the very beginning and, as a result, are anchored firmly in your subconscious: *Major* and *Natural minor*.

I never really intended to start at square one with this book. There are plenty of theory books you could refer to if you need to catch up on the basics. However, it has become clear to me over the years that many obstacles we stumble upon much later in our musical lives originate with a sketchy knowledge of fundamental theory. Misconceptions that creep into our thinking at the start multiply and spread to other areas later on. That's why I'd like to make a few comments on the construction of scales at this point.

The naturals provide us with the tonal material for both the C Major and A Minor scale:

C Major   A Minor

So far, so good. Here's a question for those of you who already know how to construct scales: How did you get to know Major and Minor scales? How do you remember their structure? Most people learn scales by memorising the sequence of whole steps (1) and half steps (½):

Major: 1 - 1 - ½ - 1 - 1 - 1 - ½
Natural minor: 1 - ½ - 1 - 1 - ½ - 1 - 1

Of course, this principle is simple, easy to understand and applies to **all** Major and Natural minor scales. In the real world, however, we actually find very few melodies that rigidly follow the stepwise motion of a scale. Changes of direction and leaps can obscure the linear structure beyond recognition. Play the following phrase on the piano, sing it and learn it by heart:

Once you've memorised the phrase, listen to it a couple of times in your head and then sing the note you think is the root. Find it on the piano. Chances are, most, if not all of you, will go for a C. Now sing a scale starting on C. Don't think about what you're doing – just let it happen. Rely on your memory of the phrase to guide you through the scale. Play what you have just sung on the piano. It will probably be a C Major scale.

How is it possible that this phrase, despite its many melodic jumps, triggers the unmistakable and automatic response "*Major scale*" in us? Answer: We instinctively zero in on the root (the tonality) and react subconsciously to its intervallic relationship with each other note of the melodic line (the modality). Obviously, it's not necessary to stick to the exact stepwise structure of a scale in order to maintain its distinct character – its particular flavour stands independent of sequence or register of the notes.

In its most basic form, a scale is no more than a technical concept, and a rather artificial one at that. It's easy to wrap your mind around a scale by learning where the half steps occur. The succession of whole steps and half steps, however, tells us absolutely nothing about the most important aspect – sound. Keeping this in mind, think back to the interval series I introduced in the chapter "Tonality" – the one beginning with the octave (as the most consonant interval) and ending with the minor second (as the most dissonant interval). Once a tonal centre is established, every note that follows will have its own unique colour and feeling of tension depending on its relationship with the tonic. And that's what our ears react to.

A scale, then, is a reservoir of notes with individual intervallic qualities. It therefore makes much more sense to describe scales as a series of intervals measured from the root. Here's the numbering applied to the Major and Natural minor scale:

Major: 1 - 2 - 3 - 4 - 5 - 6 - maj7 - 8/1
Natural minor: 1 - 2 - b3 - 4 - 5 - b6 - b7 - 8/1

Even though this is only a slightly different way of seeing things, it has considerable influence on the way we perceive scales and the notes they contain. Using this method makes it much easier to illustrate similarities and differences when comparing any two scales. In the case of Major and Natural minor, we immediately see where they deviate: 3/♭3, 6/♭6, and maj7/♭7. These are the notes that define the specific sound of these two particular scales and help our ear to quickly grasp their individual character.

With this discussion, we have reached a vitally important point. We will realise time and again that the way we think has a considerable influence on the way our ears work, that the terminology we use impacts our perception of music. This is not a bad thing! Terminology should, after all, not only be a means of communication but should also act as reinforcement for the way the ear registers and stores sounds. However, an inappropriate way of memorising theoretical facts or a badly chosen definition can cause problems when trying to connect an abstract concept to the corresponding sound. Instead of blindly accepting and applying terminology, always question whether the terms you use really support the way you hear. Switching from a whole-step-half-step approach to using root-related intervals when learning scales is a good case in point. If you've started out using the former (and 40 years of teaching prove that this holds true for most people) – go for the latter immediately. It will make life so much easier in the long run (and, again, 40 years of cleaning up the mess in my ear training classes proves me right).

To follow up on this idea, here's a final thought before we move on. I like the way the German language picks up the sounds we hear when speaking about major and minor. I believe that most of you would agree that major relates to melodies and harmonies that are bright and vigorous compared to minor with its more subdued and sombre colours. In German there is a strong connection to the Latin origin of major and minor: major = *Dur*, from the Latin *durus* meaning "hard", and minor = *Moll* from the Latin *mollis* meaning "soft". Here, the terminology clearly reflects and quite adequately describes the sounds it represents.

Assignment

It should be clear that the interval series for Major and Natural minor as shown above are standard sequences that can be built on any given root. Write out both scales starting on all possible chromatic roots (C, C♯, D♭, D, D♯, E♭, E, F, F♯, etc.). In order to maintain the correct construction principle (the succession of scale degrees and their intervallic relationships with the root) you will have to alter (raise or lower) certain naturals (ABCDEFG) in every scale other than C Major and A Natural minor (these are the only two Major or Minor scales that are constructed exclusively with notes of the grand staff). I think it is important at this stage that you notate scales using the theoretically correct enharmonic spellings. This means you'll have to use double sharps (x) and double flats (♭♭) in some cases. For example, the maj7 in D♯ Major would be Cx = C double sharp; the ♭6 in G♭ Minor would be E♭♭ = E double flat, and so on. If you use the correct principles to derive the intervals of each scale, you'll notice that in any given Major or Natural minor scale there will only be sharps (♯, x) or flats (♭, ♭♭) and no mixture of the two.

Relative major and minor keys

All musical compositions that are based melodically and harmonically on either a Major or Minor scale are said to be in a particular *key*. To label or signpost the key of a composition and to simplify notation, the required combination of sharps or flats for a particular key are placed at the beginning of each stave (between the clef and the time signature) in order to avoid having to write accidentals again and again every time they are needed. This is known as the *key signature*. The key signature usually applies to the whole piece (there are, however, compositions that work with multiple key signatures). Individual sharps and flats in the key signature can be "cancelled" by placing a *natural sign* (♮) in front of the note to be naturalised. All natural signs apply for the duration of *one* bar only. Additional sharps and flats appearing in the music that are not in the key signature, referred to as *accidentals*, also apply for the duration of one bar unless they are naturalised at some point within that bar.

Go back to p. 57. As you can see, C Major and A Natural minor, although they are fundamentally different sounds, contain the same notes. As a consequence of this similarity, these two keys are said to relate to each other as *relative major* and *relative minor*: A Natural minor is the relative minor of C Major and C Major is the relative major of A Natural minor. Every major key has a relative minor key whose root is a *minor third* below the major. Since both keys contain the same notes, they consequently also have the same key signature. You can see from the table below which keys are related in this way and which key signatures they share:

This, again, shows us the importance of the cycle of fifths. If we arrange all keys in order of increasing number of either sharps or flats starting with C Major / A Minor (no sharps or flats), we see that a pattern emerges – a sequence of fifths forming a circle where F♯ Major / D♯ Minor coincides enharmonically with G♭ Major / E♭ Minor (as shown on p. 38).

Assignment

Draw up the cycle of fifths (C at the top and F♯/G♭ at the bottom) for all major keys. Now, repeat the exercise for all minor keys: A Minor (A–) at the top and D♯/E♭ Minor (D♯–/E♭–) at the bottom. Memorise both cycles by heart.

Neighbouring keys in the cycle of fifths are closely related. This is easily illustrated graphically by falling back on another traditional method of looking at scales. If we "halve" a Major scale by splitting it down the middle, we end up with two identically structured **tetrachords** (*tetra* = "four", hence four-note scale fragment). The structure of this tetrachord is 1-1-½. The lower tetrachord starts on the root and the upper one on the fifth. By adding tetrachords in both directions (maintaining the 1-1-½ structure), we end up with a series of overlapping major keys following the cycle of fifths. In the figure below, we can clearly see how the keys overlap and how neighbouring keys differ by only one note (one sharp or flat):

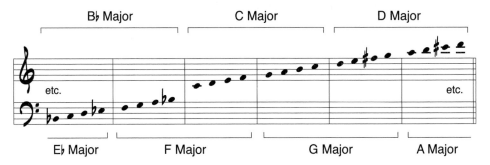

The church modes

In Jazz, in addition to Major and Natural minor scales, we find a whole group of scales that are derived (in name and structure) from the ancient Greek and Byzantine ecclesiastic or *church modes*. Most people, when they initially stumble across the church modes, learn them as "shifts" or permutations of the Major scale. Starting on the various scale degrees of any Major scale and using the same sequence of notes we end up with a variety of different scale types: **Dorian** on the 2nd degree, **Phrygian** on the 3rd degree, **Lydian** on the 4th degree, **Mixolydian** on the 5th degree, **Aeolian** on the 6th degree and **Locrian** on the 7th degree. The Major and Natural minor scales also belong to the church modes and are known as Ionian (1st degree) and Aeolian (6th degree) respectively. Since we can relate all church modes back to the Major scale (Ionian), we speak of the **Ionian system** (e.g. B♭ Major). B♭ Ionian is the "parent scale" and all other church modes can be derived from it:

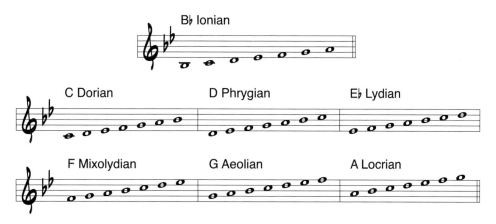

Once you've grasped the concept of how these scales relate to one another, you can easily figure out any one of the church modes. Let's take, for example, G Lydian. Because the Lydian scale is built up from the 4th degree of the Major scale it is based on, G Lydian will have the same notes as D Major/Ionian. All church modes are interrelated in this way: C Mixolydian (F Major) has the same tonal material as A Phrygian, E Dorian and C♯ Locrian; G♭ Lydian (D♭ Major/Ionian) corresponds to B♭ Aeolian, E♭ Dorian or …

WHOA! STOP RIGHT HERE!!!

Let's be honest! Even if you can follow this gobbledygook intellectually – do you really know what these modes *sound* like, and are you able to visualise their specific colours? I doubt it! As neat as this system of derivation may be, it tells us nothing about the actual sound of each individual scale. Because the concept is easy to understand, it tempts us into juggling abstract scale names without our ears having the slightest chance of catching up with this feat of mental gymnastics (the ear, as ever so often, lags behind the intellect!). For this reason, I would strongly recommend you avoid learning and memorising the church modes in this way.

Additionally, the derivation method poses a number of fundamental questions. Firstly, it suggests that the Major scale is the centre of the tonal universe, which is highly questionable, at least from a contemporary point of view. Secondly, it doesn't reveal the fact that each and every one of the church modes is a unique colour in its own right that exists completely independently from any other scale it may be related to theoretically. This is why I'd like to suggest a more effective way of getting to grips with this labyrinth of scales, even though it might mean a little more effort.

I am convinced that new sounds can be understood and mastered by the ear more quickly and thoroughly if they are linked to sounds with which we are already familiar (the known helps us grasp the unknown). Since most of what we are familiar with is based on sounds derived from Major (Ionian) or Natural minor (Aeolian), it makes sense to use these two colours as a point of reference.

If we have a closer look at the intervallic structure of the scales shown above, it is easy to see that they can be divided into two main scale groups – Major and Minor – depending on whether the third is major (3) or minor (♭3). The third determines the basic colour of a scale.

The following table shows the intervallic structure of each of the church modes, highlighting how they correspond to or differ from the Ionian or Aeolian respectively:

Major:	Ionian	1	2	3	4	5	6	maj7
	Lydian	1	2	3	♯4	5	6	maj7
	Mixolydian	1	2	3	4	5	6	♭7
Minor:	Aeolian	1	2	♭3	4	5	♭6	♭7
	Dorian	1	2	♭3	4	5	6	♭7
	Phrygian	1	♭2	♭3	4	5	♭6	♭7
	Locrian	1	♭2	♭3	4	♭5	♭6	♭7

The Locrian scale is included for the sake of completeness. In contrast to the other church modes, this scale has historically never established itself as an independent and self-contained sound (at least I am unaware of any Jazz composition based entirely on the Locrian scale). It is considered to be a "theoretical" mode, the reason being that it has a diminished fifth instead of a perfect fifth and is therefore an unstable sound, which is at odds with the concept of a tonic (here, we see the influence of the harmonic series once again!). There are, however, Folk songs and Rock or Heavy Metal compositions that utilise the dark and disturbing quality of the Locrian mode – for example, "Dust To Dust" by John Kirkpatrick or the first section of "YYZ" by Rush.

The following terms used to delineate the characteristic deviations from Ionian and Aeolian have been coined:

- *Lydian fourth (♯4)*

- *Mixolydian seventh (♭7)*

- *Dorian sixth (6)*

- *Phrygian second (♭2)*

Tunes based on a particular mode usually feature the characteristic note(s) of that mode as an important building block of the melody. A good example is the theme of "Recordame" by Joe Henderson. Here are the first few bars:

The melody moves from A Dorian (bars 1–4) to C Dorian (bars 5–8). In both cases, the Dorian sixth is very prominent, occurring on downbeats. The chord symbols also refer to the use of the major sixth, emphasising the Dorian quality of each four-bar phrase.

More important than the structure, however, is the sound and the atmosphere of each individual mode. What good is it to know how scales are constructed without having a feel for their mood and emotional quality? If we compare the different modes and think of them in terms of their individual colours – taking their intervallic content into account – we can see that a sequence emerges. The spectrum ranges from Lydian, the "brightest" scale (containing only perfect, major and augmented intervals) to Locrian, the "darkest" mode (containing only perfect, minor and diminished intervals). Here is this sequence based on the root G:

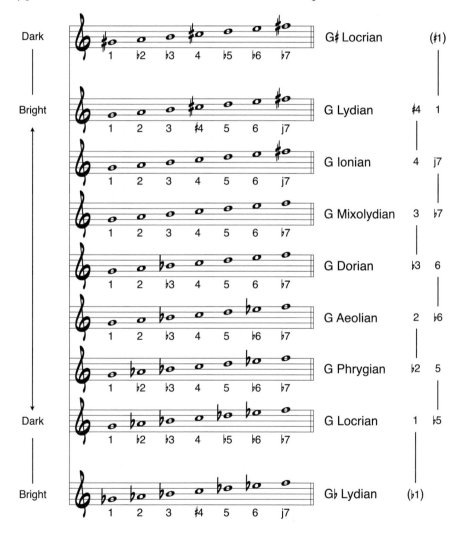

As you can see, each mode differs from the next by only one note. We can continue this sequence chromatically in both directions. By lowering the root of the G Locrian scale by a half step (keeping all other notes) we get G♭ Lydian, the starting point of a new sequence. If we raise the root of G Lydian by a half step, the result is G♯ Locrian. By progressing chromatically from one sequence to the next, we would eventually circle back to G Lydian.

Assignment

Since a major part of this book is about the church modes and their application, it is vitally important not only to understand their construction, but also to get to know their individual colour and unique charm. You will find a number of play-alongs that come with this book. I have tried to choose grooves that match the character of each of the modes and to show the stylistic context within which they are often found. It is no accident that the Dorian example reminds the listener of Miles Davis' composition "So What" and that the Phrygian soundtrack evokes Chick Corea's "La Fiesta". These associations help the ear to classify and remember sounds more easily.

Listen to **tracks 1–9**. It is my great pleasure to introduce you to Hubert Nuss (p), Ingmar Heller (b) and Sebastian Netta (dr). These great musicians will keep us company throughout this book. Find the root of each of the tracks and sing it along with the music. If you have difficulty locating the root, listen closely to the bass. Then turn off the recording and try singing a scale from this root. Sing as slowly as necessary to stay in tune, but don't sing too slowly lest the sound image in your mind should fade away. Keep track of where you are within the scale (e.g. think "now I'm on the 2nd note of the scale, now I'm on the 3rd", etc.). If you get stuck because you are unsure, memorise the scale degree that's giving you trouble. Sing on until you reach the octave, and then return to the root. Repeat this process several times (with and without the recording), speeding it up and slowing it down every once in a while. Don't think too much about what you're singing just yet. At this stage, it's all about intuitively picking up on a sound and holding on to it.

From time to time, make sure you are really singing what you hear. The brain often tricks you into hearing things that are not there, because the ear tends to take the easy way and willingly leans towards anything that is simple to grasp – and that, of course, are the sounds you are most accustomed to. So, be aware of the possibility that your ear may be "bending" an unfamiliar note and moving it closer to what you are more comfortable with. I call this "creating a virtual reality" – even though you may be singing a wrong note you are nonetheless thoroughly convinced that you are in tune with the recording. To avoid this dilemma, sit on each note for a longer period of time asking yourself (while you are singing along with the recording): "Does this note feel right or does it create an unpleasant tension?" Sometimes it may even make sense to sing chromatically up or down to compare the notes next to the scale degree in question. Certain notes will settle in with the recording immediately, while others will set your teeth on edge because they feel so horribly wrong. Once you have done this with every note, put everything back together again to form the scale.

Only when you feel absolutely sure that you're able to sing the scale accurately should you start thinking about the notes in detail!!! Decide first if the sound is major or minor by checking the third (3/♭3). Then go back to the scale degree you weren't quite sure about. In most cases, this will be the characteristic note of the scale – in other words the deviation from Ionian and Aeolian. Finally, sing the complete scale to the recording in slow motion thinking along the way: "This is a ♭2, ♭3, 4, 5, ♭6, ♭7 – I see, this is Phrygian!"

Please don't read on until you have listened to tracks 1–7 and you have established what modes these tracks are in. First write down your answers and then consult the following table. Here's the summary:

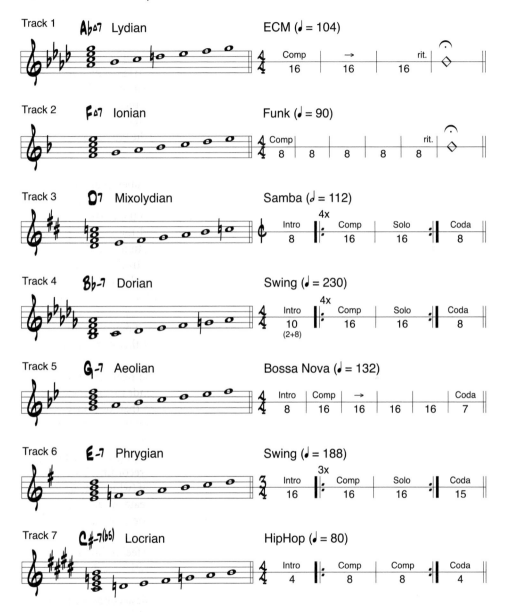

As you've probably noticed, there is a chord symbol attached to each mode. These are the four-note chords you get when you stack up in-scale thirds from the root of each mode. Here, you have a first example of the chord-scale approach mentioned earlier in which every scale is associated with a specific harmonic colour. Of course, these are not the only chords heard in the recordings. The pianist uses the entire scale and plays around with the many other harmonic structures contained within it. All the same, the basic substance of each track relates inherently to its central chord.

Now that you know what mode each track is in, repeat the previous assignment. Concentrate on the major or minor quality of each mode. Sing the interval sequences and make sure you are consciously aware of every note. Stop on the characteristic notes and savour the unique flavour of each mode.

It is essential to establish some sort of emotional rapport with each of the modes. A scale has to become more than simply an abstract collection of notes. Every mode can tell a story, convey a picture and inspire feelings. See if you agree with the following descriptions of the modes while listening to the tracks:

- Lydian: aspiring, floating

- Ionian: stable, earthy

- Mixolydian: searching, urging

- Dorian: pensive, uncertain

- Aeolian: melancholic, sad, romantic

- Phrygian: dark, mysterious

- Locrian: ugly, forceful, vulgar

Do you have the same impression or, at the very least, a similar one? Many of my colleagues and students agree with these characteristics. Of course, other factors such as tempo, groove and style have an influence on the effect of the scale material and how we respond to it. Nonetheless, there is a quality that can be attributed to each mode, regardless of the setting it is used in.

If you recall each sound track, one thing should be perfectly clear. Even if you initially had problems pinpointing the root, in the end there is no question that you eventually do focus on the tonal centre implied by what the musicians play and that there is nothing ambiguous about the root of each recording. This seemingly simple and self-evident fact is important to me because it proves that our ears are capable of perceiving each church mode as an independent, unique colour. Deriving the church modes by referring back to an Ionian "parent mode" works intellectually but denies the ear the opportunity to appreciate their individual sound and colour.

Assignment

There are very few melodies that are entirely in one mode. That's why I have included several examples that will help you become familiar with the modes you may not know so well. Sing the phrases while repeatedly playing the root of each on the piano. This will help you with your intonation and ensure that you don't lose your point of reference. Work slowly and be aware of the intervallic relationships at all times.

C Lydian

G Mixolydian

B♭ Dorian

D Phrygian

These melodic examples require a short explanation concerning the use of key signatures and accidentals when dealing with the church modes. There are three possible systems of notation. The most common method: We use the key signature of the related major key. A phrase in F Phrygian should then have 5 flats (D♭ Major). Unfortunately, this system is highly confusing to the eye and the ear because it relates to Ionian as the "parent mode". Because we associate 5 flats with D♭ Major (Ionian) or B♭ Minor (Aeolian), and not with F Phrygian, the key signature directs our attention to the wrong root:

The simplest and most neutral method: We do without a key signature. The disadvantage is that the notation can become clustered and crowded if many accidentals are required:

The most sensible method – depending on whether we are dealing with a major or minor mode – is to use the conventional key signature for the *parallel* Ionian or Aeolian key (based on the same root). Accidentals or naturals are then used to accommodate the notes "foreign" to the key signature – usually the characteristic note(s) of the mode! Let's take E♭ Lydian as an example. E♭ Lydian is a major mode because it contains a major third (3). We therefore use 3 flats as the key signature, pointing the eye towards E♭ Major and the correct root. Now we add the one accidental necessary to turn it into Lydian. We naturalise the A♭ every time it appears in the music, thus highlighting the ♯4 characteristic of Lydian. This is the method I have used in the above examples and in the rest of this book. The big advantage to the reader is that the key signature refers to the correct tonal centre of the piece of music and the additional accidentals draw our attention to the characteristic note(s) of the particular mode. In the example below, the Phrygian second is visually accentuated by the use of the accidental:

I am aware of the fact that this method of notating modes is not common practice. However, why not start spreading the word and change a notational tradition? There is no reason to stick to something that does not make sense just because it's the way things have always been done.

Melodic and Harmonic minor

Two other scales – *Melodic minor (MM)* and *Harmonic minor (HM)* – are the source of a number of modes which have become more and more accepted in Jazz today as having their own colour, character and application. Listen to **tracks 8 and 9**:

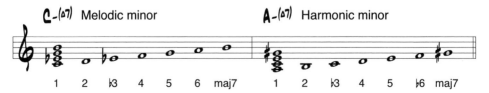

In the same way in which we derive modes from the Major and Natural minor scale, here are the permutations of Melodic minor and Harmonic minor:

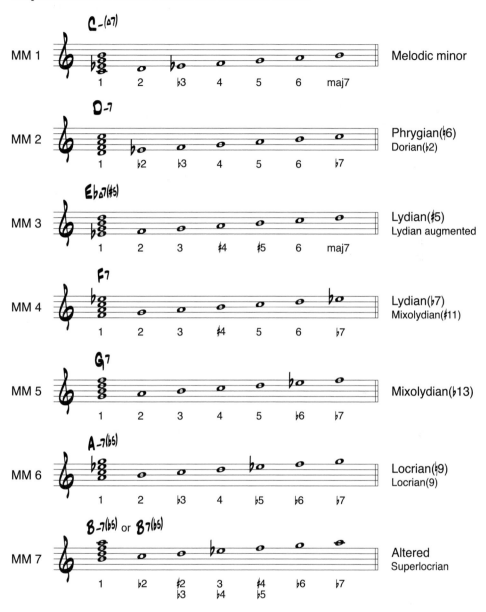

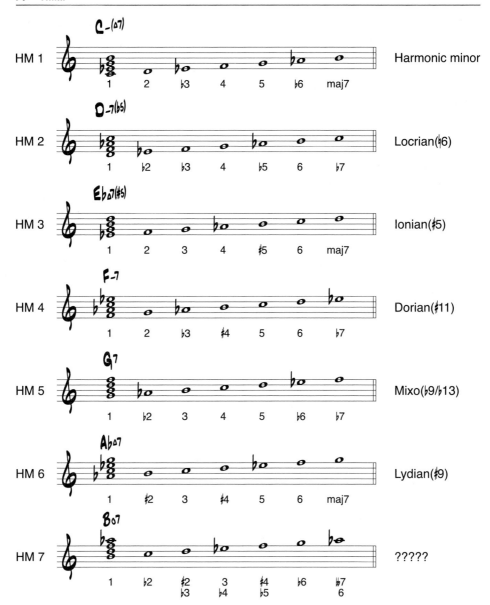

The names of the scales are derived from the church modes with the addition of the characteristic variations of the "parent" scale. While the scales based on the Harmonic minor scale are less commonly found (learn them in any case!), the permutations of the Melodic minor scale are used extensively among contemporary Jazz musicians.

Jazz musicians often use abbreviated names for these scales based on their derivations, for example: MM1, MM2, MM3, or HM1, HM2, etc. For reasons of thoroughness, I have included these names, too. I should warn you again, however, not to see these scales as simple permutations of the original Melodic and Harmonic minors. The concept of starting with

MM and HM as the parent scales and deriving the other modes by shifting the notes from one scale degree to the next was no more than a quick way of showing you how most of these modes came to be. As with the church modes, all these scales can exist as colours in their own right, independent of the Melodic or Harmonic minor parent scales. Labels such as MM2, MM3, etc., though quite often used, are purely technical terms that give you no information as to the sound of a scale. This is why I would prefer your sticking to names that are more closely associated with the characteristic colour of each scale, even if these terms may be a little cumbersome or awkward.

Please note the discrepancy between the scale on the seventh degree of Melodic minor (MM7) and its corresponding chord. The fact is that both a –7($\flat$5) chord and a 7($\flat$5) chord would work with this scale. Initially, the customary method of building chords by stacking thirds leads to a half-diminished chord (e.g. B-D-F-A). For this reason, MM7 is also known as "Superlocrian" in the USA, derived from the Locrian scale by lowering the 4 to the $\flat$4, which is enharmonically the same as 3 (have another look at the table on p. 63). On the other hand, it would be most unusual to include a major third in a minor chord. Because of the major third in the scale, an altered seventh chord with a $\flat$5 (or $\sharp$11) would also be an option. This, however, doesn't conform to our usual layering of thirds (our system of constructing chords implies skipping to every other note in the scale), but it does explain the co-existence of $\flat$3 (= $\sharp$9) and 3. The fact remains that in the "real world" MM7 is used as a scale for seventh chords and is called the *Altered* scale.

When looking at the scales derived from the Harmonic minor scale, we come across one that is hard to name: HM7. It doesn't really fit into our heptatonic system, even if we relate it to the names of the church modes. What do we call a scale that contains both a $\flat$6 and a 6, but neither a $\flat$7 nor a maj7? The difficulty in finding suitable names for some scales suggests that we are talking about colours that are relatively uncommon and, as a result, are difficult for the ear to grasp. Nevertheless, even these are increasingly finding their way into the contemporary Jazz repertoire.

Symmetrical and synthetic scales

Most of the scales we have talked about have evolved naturally over the years. In addition to these, musicians have always looked for alternative scale forms. One of the major breakthroughs in musical research was the discovery of symmetric scales (first used extensively by composers in the early 20th century). Music, by nature, is asymmetric. The laws governing tonal organisation are inherently hierarchic (based on the harmonic series). This means, for example, that in the Major or Minor scale certain notes are more important than others – some notes are chord tones, others are considered to be passing notes, the root carries more weight than a 3rd, a maj7th traditionally has a stronger urge to resolve than a 6th, etc. In addition, the constructional principle of Major and Minor scales – in other words, the sequence of half steps and whole steps – is irregular. As a consequence, it seems logical that musicians should look for symmetry as a counterpart to the naturally evolved melodic and harmonic concepts found in traditional music.

Since most of the well-known and commonly used scales consist of whole steps and half steps, it is understandable that musicians first experimented with various sequences consisting of only minor or major seconds in an attempt to discover new colours. A sequence of nothing but half steps is, of course, a ***Chromatic scale*** (we'll get back to this one a bit later). A sequence consisting exclusively of whole steps leads us to the ***Whole-tone scale*** (WT). Because of its symmetry, this scale is used mostly with augmented triads. They, too, are symmetrical and consist of nothing but major thirds, subdividing the octave into 3 equal parts (two major seconds equal one major third). The four-note extension of an augmented triad leads to a 7th chord when used in conjunction with a Whole-tone scale:

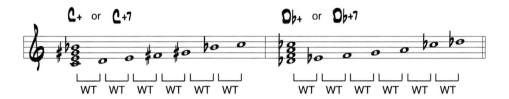

Our chromatic system allows only these two Whole-tone scales (shifting the root by another half step brings you right back to the tonal material of the first scale). In a Whole-tone scale, any note can function as the root. Because of its symmetry, the WT scale tends not to resolve – there is no "weighting" or emphasis on any one of the tones that would convey a definite sense of a tonal centre. However, the ear will quite happily home in on any note emphasised by the bass and relate everything else to this focal point. Every note is equal in terms of its importance. This is why the Whole-tone scale has a very special and unique colouring. Claude Debussy (1862–1918) was the first composer who worked deliberately and extensively with this scale. As a result, many of his compositions have a floating, flowing quality. In Jazz, the Whole-tone scale is less commonly used. It's a very conspicuous colour that does not lend itself easily to creating melodies. Whole-tone phrases tend to stick out considerably when used in a traditional melodic context.

Alternating whole steps and half steps results in two different symmetrical scales: ***Half-tone-whole-tone*** ("½-1", HTWT) and ***Whole-tone-half-tone*** ("1-½", WTHT). Both scales are octatonic (eight-note) and sequentially uniform – their structure repeats itself in minor thirds. Here, too, it is hard to pinpoint a tonal centre. Each scale could imply four different possible roots. Accordingly, there are only three possible "½-1" scales and "1-½" scales:

The French composer Olivier Messiaen (1908–1992) was the first to work consistently with these two types of scales. In Jazz they are very commonly used – however, not specifically as independent sounds, but rather in relation to particular chord types: HTWT with seventh chords and WTHT with diminished chords (see pages 131 and 167). Listen to **track 10**. This example exclusively uses the HTWT scale (the root is C).

These scales all follow the principle of symmetric subdivision of the octave. The octave can be divided into 12 equal parts (Chromatic scale), 6 parts (Whole-tone scale), 4 parts (HTWT or WTHT, which both repeat in minor thirds following a four-note diminished chord), 3 parts (3 major thirds following an augmented triad) and 2 parts (splitting the octave at the tritone). This principle was first systematically presented in the book "Thesaurus of Scales and Melodic Patterns" by Nicolas Slonimsky, a book that was extensively used by John Coltrane in the late 50's and early 60's. Coltrane based a considerable part of his improvisational vocabulary on symmetric patterns, influencing many Jazz musicians on the way. Quite a few of his compositions also made use of symmetric subdivisions of the octave (e.g. "Giant Steps", "Countdown", "Central Park West"). Coltrane was one of the true innovators in Jazz who revolutionised the traditional repertoire and introduced sounds and concepts that play an important role in Jazz to this day.

As we have seen, the Pentatonic scale consists of five tones, the Whole-tone scale has six, the church modes as well as the Melodic and Harmonic minor permutations have seven, WTHT and HTWT each have eight. Of course, it is conceivable to have modes containing even more notes. Olivier Messiaen's *Mode III* is a good example of a nine-note scale. Here it is (the root is C):

Have you noticed the symmetry? Here, too, we come across an equal subdivision of the octave. The scale consists of three identical sections (1-½-½) following a symmetric subdivision into 3 major thirds, which again makes finding its tonality very difficult. Listen to **track 11** – this example, with its ethereal charm and unique colouring, demonstrates distinctly the special character of Mode III. Hubert Nuss' mastery of this unusual sound is remarkable. He told me that it took him several years of hard work to achieve such fluency and to get his ears and fingers accustomed to the scale. This recording is entirely "in scale" (the notes D♭, F and A are consistently missing). In order to provide some structure for the improvisation, we have chosen a simple bass line derived from within the scale, giving us a structural framework to work with. Here's the form:

Intro 8 + 16	8	8	8	8	8	8	8	Coda 12
C	C	B	E	E♭	A♭	G	C	C

You can see that our major/minor system only touches on a very small part of the broad spectrum of sounds that has found its way into the Jazz repertoire. To many of you, some of the modes we have just discussed may sound artificial. Considering traditional listening habits, this is to be expected. However, I do hope that all of you, over time, will learn to appreciate the beauty of track 11. Mode III is a typical example of a constructed and not a historically "grown" scale. It is proof of the fact that musicians are intrinsically curious and continually on the lookout for new ways of doing things. With imagination, an inquisitive mind and the desire to extend ourselves in search of new concepts and structures, any conceivable combination of notes can be used to create a new and valid system of sound. It is only logical that scales such as Mode III should evolve, without which such a striking and shimmering recording could never have come about.

As a final thought, I'd like to offer insights into the world of scale variants by presenting you a small selection of unusual modes. Analyse each sequence of notes (according to its intervallic structure) and try finding a suitable name for each one. By the way, all these scales are used, even if only rarely:

Assignment

Write down all the scales we have discussed starting on every possible chromatic note – without key signatures, using only accidentals.

The Chromatic scale

The Chromatic scale is, in the broadest sense, also a mode. Its symmetric and uniform structure, however, sets it apart from the other more differentiated scale forms. This is precisely what attracted European composers of the early 20th century. They strived to overcome the restrictions and limitations of the music tradition, to break away from tonal conditioning and pave the way for completely new compositional techniques and tonal languages. The Chromatic scale with its neutral character seemed to be a good starting point for this, and the result is what we know today as *serial* or *twelve-tone* music.

The nucleus of a twelve-tone composition is a *series* or *row*, containing the complete Chromatic scale, in which all twelve chromatic notes are considered to be of equal importance. Every series has a unique structure. Initially, only the sequence of pitches was determined by the series, but, eventually, other parameters such as duration, colour, articulation, dynamics, etc. were also "serialised". Compositions were constructed with deliberate attention to every minute detail controlled by the series. Rules were invented to prevent the accidental occurrence of familiar musical relationships. For example, no note was to be repeated until all other notes in the series had appeared, all references to tonality such as triads or cadences had to be avoided, etc.

Let's look at the twelve-tone series from "*Konzert für 9 Instrumente*" (Concerto for 9 Instruments) Opus 24 by Anton Webern (accidentals apply to one note at a time):

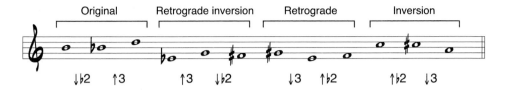

It's easy to see how the intervallic structure of the first three tones determines the structure of the rest of the series. The composer has used Classical variation techniques such as inversion, retrograde, retrograde inversions and transposition (see p. 270 ff.) to construct the full series.

Twelve-tone techniques have occasionally been used in Jazz, too. One of the best-known examples is the composition "Twelve Tone Tune" (TTT) by Bill Evans:

Every line contains the same complete series (with occasional octave transpositions). Here, we find the twelve-tone principle applying only to the melody. The harmony is quite conventional, consisting mainly of –7 and maj7 chords moving down either in fifths or chromatically.

So, the use of twelve-tone rows constitutes a distinct organisational principle. It is a modus operandi, a "way" of organising tonal material. Accordingly, it is possible to see this principle as a form of modality, even though tonality plays a subordinate role if any at all.

World music

If we go one step further and leave behind the well-tempered chromatic division of the octave, we discover a wide variety of tonal systems with modal characteristics in other cultures. While European music is mainly based on the church modes and the major/minor system, very different forms of modality have developed in non-European musical cultures. One of the most prominent examples is the Pentatonic scale, which still plays an important role in Asian music today. Here are several variations of the Pentatonic scale that are, for example, used in Japan or China:

Most of these scales can only be written as approximations in our notation because the tunings used in these cultures are fundamentally different from our equal tempered system (go to pdf-A for further information). For instance, apart from the *Pelog* scale mentioned above, of which there are a number of variations, Gamelan music in Java and Bali uses a tonal system called *Slendro* that subdivides the octave into five roughly equal intervals of about 240 cents. The exact intervals in the tuning named *"Son of Lion"* are (in cents): 245 – 262 – 232 – 236 – 230.

There are other, even more complex, tonal systems. How about a quick detour to India? In contrast to Western music, there is no harmony (meaning chordal structure) in Indian music. For this reason, melody and rhythm have reached a degree of maturity incomparable in complexity and variety to anything we know. The octave is subdivided not into 12 equal parts, but into 22 non-equidistant intervals called **shrutis** (at approximately 22, 70 or 90 cents). It is worth noting that twelve of these *shrutis* correspond exactly to the notes of our Chromatic scale when calculating it according to the frequency ratios derived from the harmonic series (just intonation; see pdf-A). So, if certain *shrutis* are used, we hear a familiar Major scale. However, since the result would not be consistent with the tuning requirements of equal temperament, we would hear some of the notes as slightly sharp or flat. The 22 *shrutis* allow for a far more elaborate subdivision of the octave than our chromatic system. These microtonal steps, in combination with equally essential ornamentations (*gamakas*), such as slides and grace notes, glissandi, accents, subtle resolutions, trills and vibratos, produce what we perceive as the unique colouring of Indian music.

Indian music never modulates (changes key). The tonal centre (*sa*) of a composition persists throughout the whole piece. Even more amazingly (from a Western point of view), it is quite common for any particular traditional Indian musician to use one and the same root for his entire life! The foundation, the tonality or tonal centre, is set by the **tambura** (also *tanpura*). This is a four to six-stringed instrument on which a constant drone is played consisting of the fundamental and the first partials of the harmonic series – usually root and fifth spread out over several octaves (*sa* and *pa*). For every concert, the drone instruments are tuned to a specific fundamental (most commonly C), which is maintained throughout. It is the drone that directs the focus of both the players and the listeners to the intricacies of the melodies with their minute shifts in intonation and at the same time provides a strong foundation for deep emotional expression.

The other musicians play partly composed and partly improvised melodies over this drone, e.g. on the *sitar* (a plucked stringed instrument). The framework for a melody or improvisation is supplied by a **raga**. *Ragas* consist of 5-7 notes and, even though they are not to be mistaken for scales in our sense of the word, they share similarities with our scale system. Every *raga* is based on a **mela** (from *melakarta* meaning "lord of melody") – a system of 72 parent scales in Southern India (Karnatic) – or a **thaat**, a system of 10 parent scales in Northern India (Hindustani), which correspond to some extent to our Major/Minor scales, church modes and their spin-offs. It is said that there are literally thousands of *ragas* derived from these two basic systems.

A *raga* (roughly translated from Sanskrit as "the act of colouring"), however, denotes much more than a simple selection of pitches. Each *raga* has its own set of rules that define ascending (*arohana*) or descending (*avarohana*) phrases, the order in which notes are played, notes of significance (*vadi* and *samvadi*), which *shrutis* to use often or sparingly, which notes to emphasise, how to colour the notes through the use of *gamakas*, etc. One must be able to understand these nuances to fully appreciate the music.

Most importantly, every *raga* evokes a mood – something circumscribed as **rasa**. *Rasa* can be equated with the emotional "essence" transmitted through playing or listening to a *raga*. It is a particular state of mind initiated through the stimulus of a corresponding *raga*. There are *ragas* tied to seasons, rituals, specific times of the day, natural phenomena, particular occasions, etc. For example, *Bhoopaalam*, an early morning *raga*, is usually played from 4-6 am (before sunrise); the *rasa Bhayanaka* (fear) is represented by the *raga Punaaagavaraali*; *Basant* is a spring *raga*, *Dhulia Malhar* is associated with the monsoon, lullabies are often composed in *Neelaambari*, because this is an evening *raga* performed 7-10 pm, and so on.

As you can see, *ragas* are infinitely more complex and subtle in comparison to the simple structure and the rather one-dimensional understanding of scales in Western music. Adding to the complexity of Indian music is the fact that improvisation plays a decisive role. Even within the strict parameters of a *raga*, there is a high degree of freedom of choice. *Ragas* can be played literally for hours on end without ever repeating a single phrase. In addition, there is room for individual interpretation, e.g. different musicians may use different *shrutis* to perform the same *raga,* or a *guru* could be identified by his particular use of *gamakas*. It is this merging of composition and improvisation that may be one of the main reasons why so many Jazz musicians are attracted to Indian music.

Sounds that are unusual to the Western ear have always fascinated Jazz musicians. The desire to search for new colours and combine them with familiar structures is and will remain one of the driving forces in Jazz. I have touched on the world of Indian music to point you towards the many, many sounds out there waiting to be explored. Even though, during the course of this book, we will focus mainly on harmonic relationships rooted in the major/minor system, it should always be clear that we are only dealing with a small fraction of available sounds that are used worldwide or are theoretically conceivable. Keep your ears and eyes open – there's a lot to discover!

The Lead Sheet

"Jazz tunes are great vehicles. They are forms that can be used and reused. The implications are indefinite."

Lee Konitz

Now that you are familiar with chord symbol notation, I'd like to introduce you to our first composition – "There Will Never Be Another You" by Harry Warren:

Do you recognise this chord progression? We were introduced to it in the chapter "First Steps". The chord types in this piece should now be familiar. At least you know which four notes each basic symbol implies.

What you see here is a *lead sheet* – a thematic sketch or "quick score". This slimmed down template contains only the most essential ingredients of a composition: melody, chord progression and formal structure in the simplest possible notation. Sometimes, lead sheets include phrasing and dynamic indications or some sort of loose arrangement.

The lead sheet is meant to be a basis for improvisation. This is why it is kept vague and to some extent imprecise. Again, remember that the notation should always reflect the intention of the music. After all, players should be given the highest degree of liberty to interpret the music as they choose. The more complex, detailed and defined the written music is, the less freedom of choice the player has. This is why only basic chord symbols are used and the rhythmic content of the melody is notated as simply as possible. Nobody would ever give improvising musicians anything more than an outline of a piece, otherwise you would seriously ruin their day. And you would never expect an improviser to follow the music verbatim. Conversely, you can't hand a big band a lead sheet (well, perhaps you could, but it most probably would make for a very interesting musical experience in the negative sense of the word). The larger the ensemble, the more precise the musical information and the notation have to be.

In Jazz, the most common form of improvisation is what we call *"playing the changes"*. If Jazz musicians ask "What are the changes for this tune?", they are referring to the chord progression of the piece. Players then develop their ideas based on this chordal framework, following the harmonic road map as they move along in their solo. One complete harmonic cycle is known as a *chorus*. Improvisations may stretch over several repetitions of the harmonic form. Usually, the soloist will play at least a one-chorus-solo. Listen to **track 41**, "The More I See You", a well-known standard and **track 42**, "Moving Out", an original composition. Both recordings are excellent examples of how improvisations traditionally unfold in mainstream Jazz. We first hear the theme – also referred to as *"the head"* – presented by the full band, and then individual soloists improvise over any number of choruses. The theme reappears at the end, usually cued in by the last soloist by patting his/her hand on top of the head towards the end of the solo to make sure everybody "goes back to the head" the next time the "top of the form" comes around.

A traditional improvisation usually consists of a soloist accompanied by a rhythm section. It would be a mistake, though, to think that only the soloist improvises while the rhythm section slaves away at producing a harmonic and rhythmic "carpet" of sound for the soloist to stand on. Rhythm sections also improvise, even if it is not as apparent to the listener as with soloists. The most important thing in Jazz is the *interplay* within an ensemble – a continual give-and-take where the soloist, to some extent, takes on the role of the leader, but where members of the rhythm section are equally involved in dialogue and providing impetus, interacting with the soloist.

Listen to **tracks 13–19** in one go. Our trio plays "There Will Never Be Another You" in seven different versions. What you're hearing are accompaniments. There is nobody soloing – after all, the various tracks are meant to be play-alongs for *your* improvisations. Notice how different a rhythm section can sound playing one and the same tune. Of course, each instrument fulfils a very specific role within the ensemble. Nevertheless, you should be aware of just how much freedom each player has. Besides, it should now be obvious how little the lead sheet actually tells us about how we are to play a tune and how varied the interpretation of a lead sheet can actually be in practice. Tempo, style, time signature and key are all open to subjective choice. Obviously, there is so much more to the simple guidelines provided by a lead sheet than meets the eye. This is why we will spend a lot of time on how to decipher and interpret lead sheets.

There are a number of lead sheet collections available commercially. The oldest and best known is the "Real Book", *the* Jazz bible – a varied assortment of *standards* (popular tunes mostly derived from musicals or the "Great American Song Book", the backbone of the traditional Jazz repertoire) and compositions by important Jazz musicians, known as *originals* – covering a huge variety of styles. Other recommendations are *"The World's Greatest Fake Book"* (the real book of the 80s with modern tunes in a more professional format), the *"New Real Book"* in three volumes, *"557 Jazz Standards"*, the *"Latin Real Book"* and the *"Real Vocal Book",* just to mention the most common ones. These books cover almost all popular Jazz tunes. Although they sometimes overlap, I can still endorse them all. The "Real Book" and "557 Jazz Standards" contain simple lead sheets, whereas the other collections provide more detailed presentations of the themes (e.g. full arrangements with all horn parts, partly written out rhythm sections, kicks, intros, codas, etc. as played on the original recordings).

You'll quickly realise that you will be in a much better position to make a substantial contribution to your ensembles and at jam sessions if – as all ambitious Jazz musicians should – you can rely on a wide-ranging repertoire of standard tunes you can play anytime without prior rehearsal. This means you have to *learn tunes, learn tunes, learn tunes*! Without an extensive repertoire, no Jazz musician has much of a chance of making it in the business. Buy a good collection of tunes as soon as you can – the best being (as far as I am concerned) the "New Real Book" volumes 1, 2 and 3. They're expensive, but really worth the money!

Almost every lead sheet is based on a specific recording (player/composer and album title are usually mentioned). If you want to work on any particular lead sheet, always try to get hold of the corresponding original recording. If you find other renditions of the piece, please keep in mind that no two Jazz musicians will play the same tune in the same way. On the contrary, they will always try to leave their personal mark on a piece. They will modify the melody by changing the rhythms or using embellishments, add to the harmony and even choose a different time signature or key. In short, they will take liberties with the music. So, the original recording is no more than a starting point. Whoever works creatively with a tune, will want to develop a unique interpretation. This is why there is no such thing as an authoritative version of a lead sheet. Different interpretations of the same tune will produce different lead sheets. It is easy to see how two lead sheets of the same tune based on different recordings can deviate radically from one another and still both be "right". This explains in part the common allegation that many lead sheets contain a number of errors or fail to match the original recordings. In the new Real Books, the tunes supposedly have been checked and authorised by the composers. However, I wouldn't rely on this.

The main reason, however, for the many inconsistencies found in lead sheets is due to a problem that is impossible to resolve. Think about it. Symbols are by their very nature only an approximation of the real thing – which, of course, serves the Jazz cause admirably. In the long run, the main purpose of a lead sheet is not to produce an exact representation of a specific performance or recording, but rather a stylised and generalised likeness of a tune allowing for improvisational freedom. A very complex thing has to be boiled down and packaged into a simple visual representation. Whoever transcribes a recording and extracts a lead sheet has to take a view on what is important and what can be left out. For every melodic phrase, you have to determine which embellishments, rhythmical subtleties, accents, etc. are essential to the basic melody or just supplementary elements added at the whim of the player (have a look at pdf-K, p. 16, and compare the Stan Getz version of "Stella By Starlight" with the stylised lead sheet of the same tune). You have to decide whether to include or leave out extensions on chord symbols, and if you include them, which ones. This sort of decision-making – even with the best of intentions and a clear conscience – is very subjective. As a result, no lead sheet is ever entirely conclusive or unambiguous. Somebody else doing the same job most probably would have come up with a different solution. Therefore, never rely on the ears of others. Check every lead sheet as best you can to see if it corresponds with the recording you are working on. The chapter "Transcription" will help you with this.

How do we handle lead sheets as a player? First, you have to lose your awe of written music. Don't try to be too literal when working with a lead sheet. The "Real Book" – just like any other compendium of tunes – is not a law book, to be followed to the letter. A lead sheet is not set in stone. I would like you to actively question each and every lead sheet and deal with it both responsibly and creatively. Feel free to change it. Give it a new look. Make it your own! Find an interpretation that combines the original with your own ideas – be it by providing a new arrangement, coming up with an interesting reharmonisation, composing additional sections, changing parts of the melody, using a different time signature or switching to another style. Create something that carries your personal handwriting! There are musicians to whom the written note is sacred. Faithfulness to the original is paramount and any deviation would be seen as sacrilege. As a Jazz musician, I take a different stance. You should know and respect the original, but not idolise it. It is your obligation to expand on a lead sheet and free yourself from the constraints of the written note.

It is the concept of using lead sheets that has spurred an evolutionary process in Jazz, which accounts for the many versions found for one and the same piece. Unlike Classical music, Jazz has always made a clear distinction between composing and arranging. This approach has its merits because it makes way for a large variety of choices and solutions. It is generally understood that a Jazz composition initially follows the lead-sheet format and contains no more than the most important aspects of a piece (melody, chord symbols, basic form). In a second step, the composition is arranged for a specific ensemble, which may range from a single instrument to a big band or even a full orchestra. The essentials of the original tune are retained, the final result, however, may sound completely different because parts have been added, the form changed and expanded on, new ideas included, etc. For any lead sheet there can be as many different arrangements as there are arrangers, each version highly personalised and unique. Listen, for example, to "There Will Never Be Another You" played by the Count Basie Big Band (arrangement Buddy Bregman) or Jim McNeely (on "Live at Maybeck Recital Hall"). There you have variety in a nutshell.

As convenient as lead sheets may be, there are, however, pitfalls. Looking at things as an improviser, it is actually one of the greatest drawbacks of the standard Jazz repertoire that it is no more than a collection of lead sheets. Even though having quick and easy access to innumerable compositions is highly user-friendly, the lead sheet has also precipitated a way of thinking and playing that has given rise to a mainstream Jazz scene that has the reputation of being rather bland and monochrome. Lead sheets entice people into playing gigs while keeping rehearsal time to a minimum. More often than not, musicians turn up on stage with the "Real Book" under their arm and, noses buried in their music stands, just barely manage to muddle through a program tacked together at the last minute. In a worst-case scenario, the embarrassing question pops up during the set: "What are we gonna play next?" – highly professional! Adding to this, tunes often unfold according to the ever same old formula: After a short introduction, the theme is presented, followed by endless improvisations, the only variation being the order in which the soloists appear, and a final repetition of the head – end of story.

The results are, at best, tolerable jam sessions. All too often, badly rehearsed bands make it through the themes by the skin of their teeth while hoping for divine inspiration when it comes to soloing (A question on the side: Is it necessary to practise improvisation? Of course not! Improvisation, after all, should materialise like manna from heaven, completely unencumbered by premeditation or the tedious daily grind in the practice room. Yeah, right!!!). The traditional format only works with highly accomplished players who are able to leave audiences with the feeling of having experienced something extraordinary or even magical. Captivating interplay is the key. Sadly, with many bands, the probability is high of having to sit through a non-inspiring and frustrating evening.

I know I'm exaggerating things a bit. Fact is, however, that this recurrent "head-solo-solo-solo-head" format is a source of irritation to Jazz audiences who, in recent years, have become more and more critical and discriminating. Many listeners are voting with their feet and are fleeing in droves from Jazz clubs, where mediocre ensembles reel off predictably insipid concerts. Nowadays, new groups only have a real chance of survival if they present their own fresh sound, exciting arrangements and original compositions, if they say something fascinating with their music and take their audiences seriously.

This does not mean that we should no longer concern ourselves with the standard repertoire. Lead sheets are still by far the most popular means of entering the world of Jazz. And I am in favour of a learning curve that first places emphasis on the tradition before moving on to more contemporary sounds. I do, however, want to make it perfectly clear that lead sheets and the standard repertoire are no more than a first step to a successful career as a Jazz artist.

Diatonic Harmony in Major Keys

If we construct chords on each degree of a scale using only notes from the scale itself, we end up with what is known as a **diatonic** series of chords. The term "diatonic" – from the Greek *diatonos* = progressing / extending / stretching out (through the scale) – traditionally refers to Major and Minor scales and means "using only the seven tones of a scale without chromatic alterations". Given the huge variety of scales used in Jazz, this definition is too limited and I would like to extend it beyond the basic major or minor context. "Diatonic", to me, generally means "in scale" and encompasses every note, interval, melody or chord derived exclusively from *any* particular scale.

In Jazz, we traditionally think in terms of four-note chords, so we'll start with the Major scale and explore the chords that result when diatonic thirds are stacked upon each scale degree (in the key of B♭ Major):

Here's the same series notated with the Roman numerals commonly found in analysis:

$$\text{Imaj7} \quad \text{II–7} \quad \text{III–7} \quad \text{IVmaj7} \quad \text{V7} \quad \text{VI–7} \quad \text{VII–7(♭5)}$$

What we get is a series of general *functions* that applies to each and every Major scale. Every harmonic scale degree has a specific functional significance that is determined by its behaviour in relation to the tonic and the overall key. The tonic acts as a magnet. All other chords react to this force of attraction to differing degrees. As we will see, the function of a chord depends primarily on its level of tension and inclination to resolve.

Imaj7 is always the harmonic point of reference – the most stable chord, referred to as the *tonal centre* or *tonic*. IVmaj7 and V7 are called the **subdominant** and the **dominant** respectively. Imaj7, IVmaj7 and V7 are the primary functions of any major key because they relate to each other by the interval of a fifth (note, once again, the influence of the harmonic series). The dominant is positioned a fifth above and the subdominant a fifth below the tonic – hence "sub"-dominant. We will discuss the other diatonic functions later in the chapter.

F is always the subdominant

For all the years I have been teaching harmony, I have noticed something significant: The greatest difficulty in getting to grips with harmonic relationships seems to be the inability to think equally quickly and effectively in *any* key. Of course, it's not that easy for beginners to find their bearings in keys such as C♯ or G♭ Major. However, to assume therefore that everything must be introduced in the key of C for the sake of simplicity is a tragic misconception

found in almost all theory books. What makes things easier at first just augments the difficulties we encounter when dealing with complex compositions and improvisational concepts at a later point in time.

There is a well-known joke: "What is the subdominant of F? What do you mean? The
subdominant *is* F!!" Like many jokes, there is sadly more than just a grain of truth in this
one. "Many sharps and flats, many enemies!" a popular saying goes. But music doesn't only
happen in the key of C! Composers are not willing to dispense with complex key signatures
for our benefit. No matter how many sharps or flats we are confronted with, we must be able
to approach *all* – and I repeat *ALL* – keys with the same degree of confidence. For this reason, I will present every new topic in a different key. Hopefully, this strategy will help develop your ability to think fast and feel comfortable in all keys by the end of this book.

Assignment

Test your knowledge of all keys from six sharps to six flats and find out if there are any "blind
spots" on your diatonic "map" by filling out the following table (III in Ab Major = C–7; VI in
G Major = E–7; IV in Eb Major = Abmaj7; II in F♯ Major = G♯–7; etc.):

Key	I	II	III	IV	V	VI	VII
Eb Major							
G Major							
Ab Major							
F♯ Major							
Db Major							
B Major							
Gb Major							
E Major							
C Major							
A Major							
F Major							
D Major							
Bb Major							

The diatonic cadence

The simplest way music can progress harmonically is by stepwise movement (up or down)
from one diatonic scale degree to the next. Functional progressions such as II-III-IV-V-I or
IV-III-II-V-I are not unusual. Stepwise root movement over a longer period of time is rare,
though. More commonly, we find what is known as a *cadence* (from Latin *cadere* = to fall).
A cadence is a chord progression that follows the principle of tension and release, moving
from a point of tension to one of resolution. The main objective of any cadence is to "fall"

into a target chord, giving harmonic phrases a distinctive ending. A good analogy is the concept of punctuation with weaker cadences acting as commas, indicating a pause or momentary rest, and stronger cadences corresponding to the full stop, indicating the end of a musical sentence:

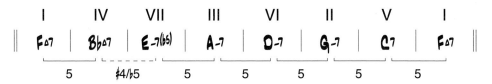

This interplay between tension and resolution is the driving force of any musical progression. Essentially, the musical meaning of a chord is defined by its relation to the tonal environment, its momentum and the amount of tension it creates.

Most chord progressions can be traced back to the ***diatonic cadence*** or ***full cadence***, in which ***all*** diatonic functions of a key are connected in intervals of fifths following the cycle of fifths counter-clockwise (remember the harmonic series and the importance of the fifth). Let's look at the diatonic cadence in F Major:

I	IV	VII	III	VI	II	V	I
F△7	B♭△7	E-7(♭5)	A-7	D-7	G-7	C7	F△7
5	♯4/♭5	5	5	5	5	5	

With the aid of the circle of fifths it is easy to illustrate the root movement of the diatonic cadence:

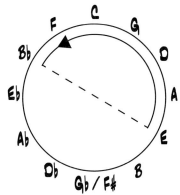

The diatonic cadence increases in harmonic tension as it arches away from the tonal centre and gradually resolves tension as it gravitates back to the tonic. The diatonic cadence is rarely used as a whole. More commonly, shorter segments are extracted. For those of you who already know a thing or two about harmony, it is easy to see why cadences such as V-I, II-V-I, VI-II-V-I or III-VI-II-V-I have become so established in music – these are the progressions that have the strongest urge to resolve back to the tonic chord.

You can see that it is necessary to interrupt the cycle of fifths movement at some point, as there are 12 possible chromatic roots and only 7 diatonic functions. A consistent series of perfect fifths would quickly carry us out of the tonality and into other keys (Fmaj7 - B♭maj7 - E♭maj7 - A♭maj7, etc.). The diminished fifth between IV and VII is necessary to maintain the relationship with F Major. Because E–7(♭5), the diatonic function, and E♭maj7, the expected chord when following the cycle of fifths, differ only in terms of the root and share all other notes, the disruption of the series of perfect fifths is not perceived as dramatic:

Most traditional Jazz compositions rely strongly on progressions based on the cycle of fifths. We will encounter the diatonic cadence (applied as a whole or partially) and its many spin-offs and variations time and again.

Assignment

Complete the following diatonic cadences and learn them off by heart (the given chords are meant to be your points of reference):

I	IV	VII	III	VI	II	V	I
B♭∆7							
	G∆7						
		G–7(♭5)					
			E–7				
				F♯–7			
					E♭–7		
						D7	
							E♭∆7

Voice leading

The more compelling the harmonic flow of a piece, the better the *voice leading*. Good voice leading implies smooth movement of the individual voices (or "parts") from one chord to the next. As a rule, smaller steps between notes lead to more musical coherence than leaps do. Let's look at the diatonic cadence in F Major with the functions written out. The first example seems to move from chord to chord in a haphazard and rather inelegant way. The second, however, follows the *"law of shortest distance"* between notes. In this example, the chords are linked to one another using the closest possible voice leading – either by common tone or by stepwise motion (the interval of a second is the connective tissue of harmony):

Here are the individual voices:

We see that the interval functions 3/7 and 5/1 alternate respectively from one chord to the next, forcing the voices to advance with minimal movement – either stepwise or by common tone (this principle applies regardless of inversion).

The voices containing thirds and sevenths are especially important. They define the quality of each chord and provide – as we will see time and again – *the* characteristic voice leading principle in chord progressions following cycle-of-fifths movement. We will deal with this concept in more detail in the chapters "Guide Tone Lines" and "Voicings".

Assignment

Transpose the individual parts in the above example to the key of Eb Major. Listen to **track 21**. You will hear the complete diatonic cadence in Eb Major. Find the starting notes of the parts on your instrument and sing each voice in turn along with the recording. Repeat each voice several times and try thinking along the following lines as you sing (switch from one perspective to the next each time):

- Now I'm on IV, on VII, on III, etc. (chord function).

- Now I can hear a maj7, –7(b5), –7 chord, etc. (chord type).

- Now I'm singing the 5th, minor 3rd, maj7, etc. of the current chord (function of the note within the chord).

- Now I'm singing the root, the second, the third, etc. of the key (function of the note in relation to E♭ Major = scale degree).

The aim of this exercise is to develop the ability to hear three vitally important things:

- the relation of any note to the current chord and its function (vertical structure);

- the relation of any note to the overall key (horizontal context);

- our expectations in terms of where each note will want to move to within the cadence (voice leading).

Think in terms of actual notes as well as general interval function. The goal, here, is to develop an inner image of sound that will help you recognise musical relationships independent of any particular key.

Basic cadences

If we look at the diatonic cadence, it certainly makes good sense why the dominant chord (V) and the subdominant chord (IV) have assumed such a central role in music: They are both a fifth away from the tonic (I) and therefore directly related to it in the cycle of fifths. The significance of the basic cadences I-V-I, I-IV-I and I-IV-V-I is also easy to see – they generate the strongest feeling of closure (in the key of C – I try to be nice every now and then):

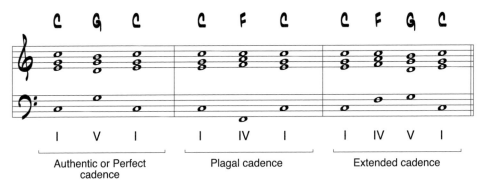

In their most basic form, cadences are limited to triads. Adding the diatonic 7th to the dominant as a fourth voice (V7) increases the chord's tension and thus its need to resolve. The four-note dominant chord contains a *tritone* between the 3 and the ♭7 – a dissonant interval that wants to resolve to a consonance:

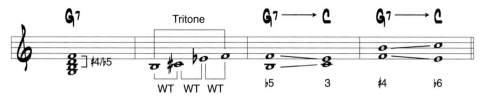

The tritone resolves inwards or outwards chromatically in contrary motion. Depending on the position of 3 and ♭7, the target interval is either a major third or minor sixth (both are consonant intervals).

Leading tones

A note that dictates the need for resolution in a chord or a melody is known as *leading tone*. A leading tone wants to resolve or "lead" to a target note. The semitone – as the smallest possible step – has the most powerful sense of resolution. Traditionally, the term "leading tone" refers to the seventh scale degree of the Major scale (this also applies to Harmonic minor and Melodic minor). The maj7 has the urge to resolve to the octave (= root). Accordingly, many melodies end with the closure maj7-8/1 because this "formula" has the strongest tendency to finalise a melody. I must add, however, that this definition is too restrictive for my taste. For one, limiting the discussion to the basic Major and Minor scales makes it difficult to explain the many other situations in which leading tones play an important role. On the other hand, you will encounter leading tones that resolve by a whole step (though not as strongly as the half step). Generally, any note with a need to resolve should be termed a leading tone.

What is responsible for this urge to move towards a point of resolution? We have already seen that the Pentatonic scale – following the structure of the harmonic series – can be constructed by layering fifths. If we add two more fifths on top and write down the resulting notes within the octave, Lydian emerges (relative to F):

If we stack the notes of a Major scale (Ionian) in intervals of a fifth and compare it to Lydian, we see that Ionian has a slight "flaw" – there is a diminished fifth between the top two notes. Play each stack of fifths at the piano (hold down the sustain pedal so that all notes blend; take your time and immerse yourself in each of the sounds). Whereas the Lydian "layer" has a pure, clear, "floating" or ethereal quality, sounding stable and restful, Ionian contains a sharply dissonant interval. The B♭ in F Ionian has the effect of something foreign in an otherwise homogenous environment characterised by perfect fifths, creating tension that craves resolution. The obvious conclusion is that the 4th degree of Ionian must be a leading tone.

George Russell's well-known work, "The Lydian Chromatic Concept of Tonal Organisation", is based on this hypothesis. His theoretical principle follows the idea that the Lydian scale – when considering the laws of physics – is the most harmonious scale and that, accordingly, the Lydian – and not the Ionian scale – must be the basis of tonal organisation. Despite the fact that the Lydian Chromatic Concept is a brilliant and highly coherent theory, it has never really managed to establish itself (even though it has influenced quite a number of important Jazz musicians such as Miles Davis, Bill Evans and others). Because it stands in radical opposition to how we are accustomed to hearing and thinking music, it remains no more than a fascinating theoretical concept.

Now to the main point: Any diatonic function that contains the 4th degree of a Major scale will have a need to resolve. The 4 will want to resolve down a half step to the 3. This is why we distinguish between unstable *cadence functions* (C) and stable *tonic functions* (T), depending on whether the leading tone is part of the chord or not:

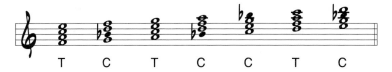

In contrast, the historically evolved leading tone on the 7th degree of the Major scale is harmonically less significant in Jazz. This is easy to see because the Imaj7 chord contains this leading tone but is nonetheless perceived as stable. The characteristic resolution of the 7th degree – the chromatic step to the tonic – plays only a minor role in Jazz harmony. More often, the third of the dominant 7th chord is held over and becomes the major 7th of the tonic chord. Likewise, the reversal of the traditional voice leading pattern (8/1-maj7) can be found in the cadence V7(sus4) - Imaj7 (a typical Jazz progression):

Then again there are many Jazz tunes which make use of the leading tone on the 7th degree in order to strengthen the melodic ending (e.g. "All The Things You Are"):

Because of these incongruities, I like to differentiate between a *harmonic* and a *melodic* leading tone:

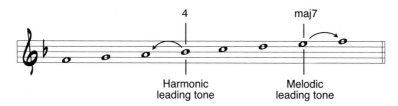

The number of leading tones determines whether a function is perceived as stable or unstable – the higher the number of leading tones, the greater the need for resolution. In order for a chord to have momentum, it has to contain the harmonic leading tone (the melodic leading tone on its own is not enough to destabilise the sound). Functions containing both the harmonic and the melodic leading tone have the greatest need to resolve.

Based on the primary functions I, IV and V, we make a distinction between:

- *tonic functions* (containing none or only the melodic leading tone);

- *subdominant functions* (containing only the harmonic leading tone);

- *dominant functions* (containing both the harmonic and the melodic leading tone).

The following example is in F Major. I have omitted the key signature in order to make the harmonic leading tone more conspicuous:

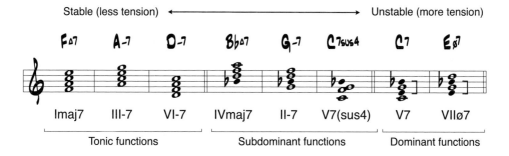

This is why the IV chord and hence the plagal cadence (IV-I) has a weaker cadential pull than the V chord and the authentic cadence (V-I).

V7(sus4) is often considered to be a subdominant function because it contains the harmonic leading tone but not the tritone typical to dominant functions. Nonetheless, it is also perceived as a dominant function because of the strength of its root movement (down a perfect 5th). The sus4 chord's functional ambiguity is increased when voiced as an "upper structure" (a topic which we will discuss in depth at a later stage). In a nutshell: C7(sus4) in the key of F Major can be voiced either as G–7/C = C9(sus4) or B♭maj7/C = C13(sus4). Since G–7 and B♭maj7 are both subdominant functions in the key of F, both variations of the C7(sus4) have a strong subdominant quality. This does not alter the fact that C7(sus4) would still be used as a dominant function (with a lower tension level and a lesser urge to resolve). Sus4 sounds have a special place in Jazz and deserve particular attention. For this reason, we will talk about them at a later point in more detail.

Members of the same functional group are interchangeable because they possess the same level of tension, or, in other words, the same degree of stability. Accordingly, Imaj7 can be substituted with III–7 or VI–7, IVmaj7 with II–7, V7 with VII–7(♭5) and vice versa. Seen from this point of view, the diatonic cadence can be regarded as a combination of two extended cadences (I-IV-V-I) where the primary functions are substituted with secondary functions:

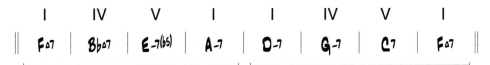

Two other important harmonic principles can be derived from looking at chord progressions in terms of functional groups: *mediant relationships* and *deceptive resolutions*.

Chords whose roots are a third apart (3/♭3) are said to have a mediant relationship (the term "mediant" usually refers to either the third scale degree or the middle note of the tonic triad). Accordingly, III–7 is called the *mediant* (a third above the tonic chord), VI–7 the *submediant* (a third below the tonic chord). Diatonic four-note chords involved in a mediant relationship overlap, sharing 3 common tones in each case. In all functional groups, the secondary functions are related to the primary functions either as a mediant or a submediant:

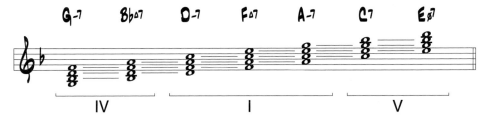

In its most basic form, a deceptive resolution (or deceptive cadence) is the unexpected resolution of V7 to a chord other than the tonic. Usually, V7 resolves to a tonic substitute (most commonly to VI–7), thereby delaying the appearance of Imaj7. I'd like to extend this rather limiting definition. *Any* unexpected resolution of *any* dominant 7th chord – in other words, any surprising harmonic turn – can be labelled a deceptive resolution. We will get to know the deceptive resolution as a vital compositional element.

Stepwise diatonic movement, functional substitutions, mediant relationships and deceptive resolutions are common devices used to upset the compulsive nature of chord progressions following the cycle of fifths and to break the habitual flow of the diatonic cadence, giving the composer the option to jump to an alternative sound before again continuing on the path of the cadence.

The Major/Minor System

Most books on harmony convey the impression that "major is easy and minor is difficult". They treat each colour separately, usually concentrating mainly on major and barely touching on the more complex topic of minor harmony. I have never really felt that it makes much sense to deal with major and minor independently of one another. Even though almost all traditional Jazz compositions are principally either in a major or minor key, they often switch back and forth, leaning for a while towards one colour and then towards the other. In practice, major and minor are inextricably linked to one another. This is why I'd like to talk about the interrelationship between the two as early as possible.

We have already seen that every Major scale (Ionian) has a *relative Minor* scale (Aeolian), which is made up of the same tonal material and shares the same key signature. Its root is a minor third below the major tonic. This is, for example, how C Ionian and A Aeolian form a pair:

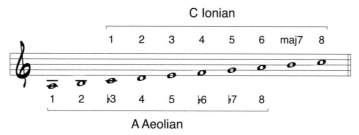

Naturally, both scales contain the same chords, however on different scale degrees. It is important for you to see the correspondence of VI–7 (in the Major scale) and I–7 (in the Minor scale). This is where the two scales latch onto each other. The symbols ♭III, ♭VI and ♭VII are used for the chord functions in minor to make sure that they cannot be confused with the scale degrees III, VI and VII of the Major scale:

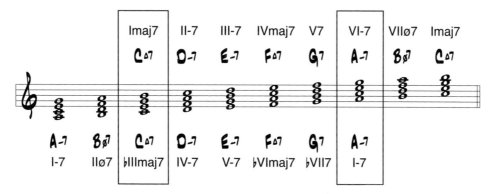

I am fully aware that a traditional theoretician will throw a parabolic fit when confronted with the functional terminology I use for minor keys. In traditional theory, e.g. a third scale degree is labelled as III in both the major and the minor because it is common practice to analyse a chord progression exclusively in either a major or a minor key. This, however, is highly confusing when using a major and minor approach simultaneously. Because I want to blur the boundaries between major and minor, I have to make sure that both are first and foremost separate entities in their own right, which tend to overlap liberally. I make a point of using functional symbols that reflect the appropriate interval relationships when looking at a chord progression either from a major or minor perspective. Accordingly, a function on the third scale degree must be labelled as III in major and ♭III in minor to make it perfectly clear which tonic we are referring to. We will see that it is quite possible (and often necessary) to switch our vantage point from major to its relative minor – and vice versa – at any given point in time (in some cases even every bar).

In Ionian, it is the 4ᵗʰ degree (the harmonic leading tone) that gives the cadence functions II–7, IVmaj7, V7 and VII–7(♭5) their need to resolve. If we see the major/minor system as a unit, then the 6ᵗʰ degree (♭6) of the relative minor key must have the same meaning or function (e.g. E♭ Major / C Minor):

We can conclude from this that the functions II–7(♭5), IV–7, ♭VImaj7 and ♭VII7 must be cadence chords in minor (they all contain the leading tone), while I–7 and ♭IIImaj7 are tonic chords. V–7 is special. Although it has no chromatic leading tone, we still sense it as a (weak) cadence chord. As with the perfect cadence V7 - Imaj7, the root movement of a fifth in V–7 - I–7 automatically creates a feeling of resolution.

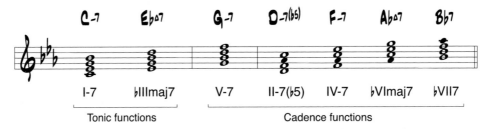

Aeolian is the fundamental colour in minor keys. Accordingly, the primary cadence functions (I, IV, V) are minor chords:

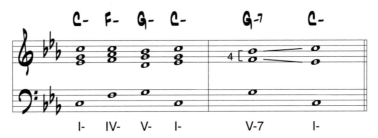

As already mentioned above, the cadence V–7 - I– does not resolve as strongly as V7 - I in major keys because both the chromatic movement of the melodic leading tone (maj7 - 8/1) and the tritone of the seventh chord are missing. In order to create a similarly strong feeling of resolution when moving from the dominant to the tonic in a minor key, the 7th degree of Aeolian must be raised by a semitone. By doing this, we end up with the *Harmonic minor* scale (HM) with its characteristic augmented second between ♭6 and maj7. Now we have the melodic leading tone (maj7 - 8/1) and – as a result – a dominant seventh chord (with a major 3rd!) on the fifth degree of a Minor scale:

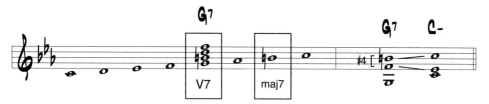

Note that the ♭7 of G7 resolves down to the ♭3 of C–7. Accordingly, the 4th scale degree in minor is also a leading tone. Because it moves by a whole step, it does not resolve as decisively as the 4th scale degree in major.

There is also a diatonic series of chords for Harmonic minor (C HM):

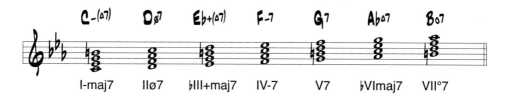

VII°7 can also be interpreted as an "incomplete" dominant – a 7(♭9)-chord without the root – and is often used as a substitute for V7 (we'll look at this sound in detail when we discuss diminished seventh chords). Apart from V7 and VII°7, the functions in this series that deviate from the diatonic chords in Aeolian (specifically I–maj7 and ♭III+maj7) are less commonly used. In summary: *The main purpose of HM is to provide a leading tone and to introduce the major third for the dominant seventh chord (V7).*

The augmented second between ♭6 and maj7 was initially perceived as a flaw within the smooth progression of steps in Harmonic minor. Even J.S. Bach, who was able to conjure up great melodic lines in the worst of situations, sidesteps this problem in his 4th Invention (in D Minor) by displacing the melodic obstacle (the C♯) an octave down, exaggerating it and thereby making it a central motivic element of the theme:

In order to close the "gap" in the HM scale and create smoother melodic phrases, the 6th degree is often raised in addition to the 7th. This gives us the *Melodic minor* scale (MM). This scale differs from the Major scale only in that is has minor third instead of a major third. Traditionally, MM has different ascending and descending forms. The 6th and 7th degrees are raised in the ascending form (6/maj7) – intensifying the effect of the leading tone – and are lowered in descending phrases to support a smooth downward movement (♭7/♭6) resolving to the 5th. The descending form is the same as the Aeolian scale:

This mechanism also applies to Jazz and Pop melodies – as can be seen in the A section of "Autumn Leaves" by Joseph Kosma (in E Minor):

The same principle is even more evident in the composition "Yesterday" by Paul McCartney (in F Major / D Minor):

Depending on the direction of the melody, we often come across differing minor colours within one piece. In Jazz, however, when referring to Melodic minor, we usually have only the ascending form in mind, regardless of whether the music is going up or down, because, to the improvising musician, a scale only defines the available notes and not how they are to be applied.

As the name suggests, the MM scale came into being for melodic reasons. All the same, it has its own diatonic functional series of chords:

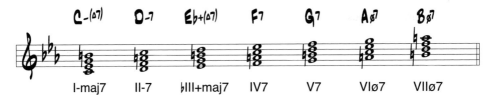

Chord progressions in minor keys often contain a mix of functions derived from Aeolian, HM, MM and/or Dorian. All these scales can function as a parent scale and can subsequently be used as a tonic minor sound:

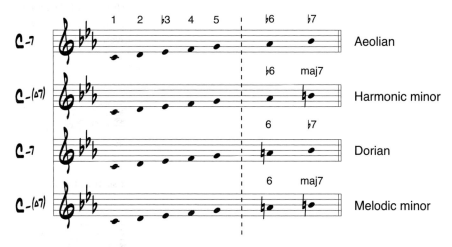

These four scales are identical up to the fifth degree. The variations occur above the 5th and show all possible combinations of sixths and sevenths. Dorian has been included here not only for the sake of completing the table, but also because this scale has established itself as a fully-fledged tonic sound in Jazz. Dorian is – as we will see later – an important source of harmonic functions. Note that C–6 can occur as the basic tonic sound in both Dorian and MM.

This melodic hodgepodge has a direct effect on harmony. The well-known introduction to "Michelle" by the Beatles combines the various minor scale forms in a coherent way (I have changed the original a bit to clarify the principle):

In this example, other chord symbols than the ones given above are conceivable without changing anything in terms of scale allocation: C–maj7 could also be interpreted as G+/B, C–7 as E♭/B♭ and C–6 as Aø7 or F7/A. In the section "Line Clichés" (see p. 245 ff.), we will discuss the use of various minor scale types.

The diatonic cadence in minor

The diatonic or full cadence we talked about in the section on major keys also applies to each corresponding relative minor key, except that the tonic has now shifted. The following diagram shows how the two functional progressions overlap (E♭ Major / C Minor):

				I	IV	VII	III	VI	II	V	I
				E♭ᵒ⁷	**A♭ᵒ⁷**	**Dᵒ⁷**	**G-7**	**C-7**	**F-7**	**B♭7**	**E♭ᵒ⁷**
				|	|	|	|	|			
C-7	**F-7**	**B♭7**	**E♭ᵒ⁷**	**A♭ᵒ⁷**	**Dᵒ⁷**	**G7**	**C-7**				
I	IV	♭VII	♭III	♭VI	II	V	I				

Listen to **track 26** – this is the diatonic cadence in C Minor.

The most obvious difference between the two diatonic cadences is the III in major (G–7) and the V in minor (G7). The latter is changed for cadential reasons. It should be clear that major and minor diatonic cadences, even though they are so closely related, are actually mutually exclusive. As soon as the leading tone appears in a minor key, it automatically triggers the need to move upwards towards the minor tonic (maj7-8/1). In contrast, when V in a major key (V7) appears, the root of the chord and the leading tone draw us just as irresistibly downwards towards the third of the major tonic (4-3 in the major key):

E♭ Major:	III7	VI-7	V7	Imaj7
C Minor:	V7	I-7	♭VII7	♭IIImaj7

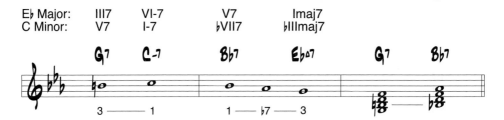

Chord progressions can switch back and forth between major and minor. So, it is quite possible that our ears hear certain progressions alternately as major and minor. Our perception can flip-flop almost instantaneously depending on the appearance of certain notes or sounds. In minor keys, the ♭VII7 announces a move to the relative major key. In major keys a change of III–7 to III7 signals that the progression is about to move to the relative minor. Our ear hears both as dominants (as V7 chords respectively), anticipates a change of tonic and repositions its focus accordingly.

We can see just how closely major and minor keys are interwoven in the first part of J.S. Bach's 4th Invention (BWV 775). The composition clearly begins in D Minor (I-V-I-V-I-V-I) and – after running through a full cycle of the diatonic cadence – ends just as distinctly in F Major:

This example illustrates how the persistent appearance of the leading tone C♯ (implying A7) initially strengthens the feeling of D Minor. As the piece progresses, the A7 chord disappears. Instead, the note C emerges (as part of C7). As a result, the ear gradually loses the feeling of D Minor and leans more and more towards F Major.

Here's a word on notation. It may seem strange to some of you to see a Classical piece of music presented using symbolic notation. It should be clear, though, that every melodic line implies harmony and that it is quite possible to interpret and notate a 2-part invention using chord symbols (analyse the two lines and check out the changes yourself).

The principle of major and minor interdependency is typical for many Jazz tunes. Let's look at the well-known Bossa Nova "Black Orpheus" by Luis Bonfa (the A section):

Fundamentally, this piece is in A Minor. As soon as the leading tone G♯ disappears and the G crops up in the melody, the harmony switches to the relative key of C Major.

There are quite a few Jazz standards that make extensive use of the diatonic cadence. Apart from the notorious "Autumn Leaves" (please analyse!), another good example of this is Paul Desmond's composition "Take Five" (allegedly the best-selling Jazz single ever):

A striking feature of the A section is the rather unusual Aeolian cadence V–7 - I–7 in Eb Minor. Although the leading tone D is missing, we distinctly hear Eb–7 as the tonic because of the numerous cadential repetitions. Additionally, Eb–7 always appears at the (strong) beginning of the bar, while the Bb–7 is positioned at the (weak) end of the bar, acting as a cadence chord and harmonic pick-up.

The B section starts out in Eb Minor (bVI-II-V-I-IV-bVII-bIII). However, as soon as the diatonic cadence has circled to Ab–7 - Db7 and landed on Gbmaj7 for a full bar, thereby giving it more weight than the other chords, our ear zeroes in on Gbmaj7 as a temporary tonic. When Cbmaj7 reappears, the ear now tends to hear the functional progression as IV-VII-III-VI-II-V in Gb Major. Not until the end of the B section at the D.C. (*da capo* = from the beginning) do we encounter the progression Fø7 - Bb7 - Eb–7, with Bb7 re-establishing Eb Minor as the tonal centre. This shows that it is possible to hear different functional interpretations of one and the same chord progression depending on the point of reference. It also demonstrates how willingly the ear switches back and forth between relative minor and major keys. As you can see, it makes no sense to separate two so closely interrelated colours artificially.

The II-V-I Progression

The diatonic cadence rarely appears in full. Usually, we come across shorter segments, the most important being the II-V-I progression. If there is such a thing as *the Jazz cadence* – this is it! There is hardly any other chord progression that has more significance in traditional Jazz. Here are the diatonic functions I, II and V in D Major and D Minor:

The II-V-I progression is the final section of the diatonic cadence:

I	IV	VII	III	VI	II	V	I
D△7	G△7	C#ø7	F#-7	B-7	E-7	A7	D△7
D-7	G-7	C7	F△7	B♭△7	Eø7	A7	D-7

From now on, I will use square brackets to indicate II-V relationships and a curved arrow to show a V-I resolution when analysing chord progressions:

Major: II-7   V7   Imaj7   **Minor:** IIø7   V7   I-7

Miles Davis' "Tune Up" (on the album "Cookin' with the Miles Davis Quintet") is an excellent example of the use of II-V-I progressions in major:

In the first two lines, the maj7 chords are sustained for two bars each and coincide with points of rest in the melody. They certainly stand out more than the other chords. Consequently, we can interpret Dmaj7 and Cmaj7 as tonic functions. The chord progression of "Tune Up" is clearly subdivided into four four-bar sections (following the structure of the melody). Accordingly, lines 3 and 4 have to be seen as part of a harmonic sequence moving down in whole steps. It therefore stands to reason that B♭maj7 in the third line as well as Dmaj7 in the fourth line are also tonic chords (following the harmonic principle set up in the first two lines). This means that the first four-bar section is in D Major, the second in C Major, the third in B♭ Major and the fourth in D Major again. So, "Tune Up" clearly changes key several times. Accordingly, E–7 - A7 - Dmaj7, D–7 - G7 - Cmaj7 and C–7 - F7 - B♭maj7 are II-V-I progressions.

Another frequently played standard is "Blue Bossa" by Kenny Dorham. Here are the changes:

C–7	⁒	F–7	⁒	D–7(♭5)	G7	C–7	⁒
I-7		IV-7		IIø7	V7	I-7	

E♭–7	A♭7	D♭maj7	⁒	D–7(♭5)	G7	C–7	G7
II-7	V7	Imaj7		IIø7	V7	I-7	

"Blue Bossa" is mainly in C Minor with a short excursion into D♭ Major.

In the course of time, the II-V progression established itself as an independent harmonic pattern that often appears without the customary resolution to the tonic (Imaj7 or I–7). This means that a II-V doesn't always behave as expected and isn't automatically tethered to its habitual target chord. It is therefore necessary to introduce a more general definition: *Any –7 or –7(♭5) chord followed by a dominant 7th chord a fifth down can be labelled a II-V pattern.*

Quite often, several II-V patterns are linked to form longer harmonic sequences. II-V's can be connected in a number of ways. Most commonly found are direct or delayed resolutions moving down in fifths:

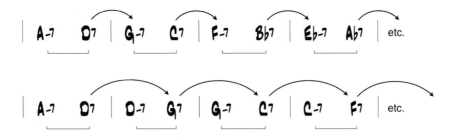

The same, of course, applies to IIø7-V7 chains.

We also find II-V patterns that are shifted either chromatically or by a whole step, e.g. in the A section of Duke Ellington's "Satin Doll":

In contemporary Jazz tunes, the II-V progression can appear as a completely independent harmonic phrase that need not have any connection to a specific tonality or key. You merely have to be able to recognise the pattern as such.

Analogous to the II-V-I progression, it is also possible to extract longer segments from the diatonic cadence (e.g. VI-II-V-I or III-VI-II-V). We will talk about these in a later chapter under the heading of "The Turnaround".

Scales, Chord Tones and Tensions

In most lead sheets, the changes appear as basic four-note chord symbols without tensions. However, accompaniments and improvisations don't thrive on chord tones alone. So how does a pianist, for example, know which extensions to add to the chords provided by the lead sheet? What source of notes does a soloist draw on for his or her melodic ideas? In the previous chapters, we assigned a function to each chord relative to the key. This relationship should be reflected in the improvisational material.

In the old days, improvisers mainly stuck to the chord tones (1-3-5-7) and only rarely ventured into the higher regions of a sound (9-11-13). Chords were approached individually, one at a time, and were interpreted vertically (e.g. by playing arpeggios). This outlook has changed. These days, we think more in terms of chord progressions instead of a series of seemingly unrelated chords. The perspective is more horizontal than vertical, and – as a result – assigning scales to chords appears to be more appropriate.

Let's look at the two different approaches by using a C7 chord (V7) in the key of F Major as an example. We get the tensions for a specific function by stacking diatonic thirds on top of the basic four-note chord until we reach the 13 (the next third would take us back to the root):

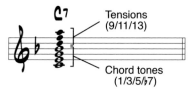

If we re-arrange all chord tones and tensions within the octave, a scale emerges:

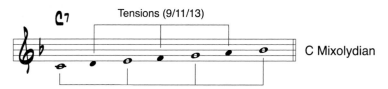

So, principally, chords are nothing but vertical scales and scales are merely horizontal chords – both approaches are inseparably tied to each other. In both cases, the resulting tonal material is made up of *chord tones representing the basic four-note sound* and *tensions that establish the relationship with the key*. In the end, it doesn't really matter which point of view you prefer. As long as you stay within the framework of the tonality and its diatonic ingredients, you will come up with an identical set of notes. But, at the same time, the approach you take does make an enormous difference to the way a solo is structured. This is why I would like to address a topic that is often the subject of heated, rather small-minded and dogmatic discussion between exponents of chord theory on one side and those of scale theory on the other.

A chord-based, vertical concept helps the soloist to stick more closely to the harmony – to *play the changes*, as we say in Jazz. The problem is that our intuitive ear tends to take the path of least resistance and, in doing so, goes for consonant sounds while avoiding dissonances. Consequently, the resulting lines consist predominantly of chord tones (1/3/5/7) and neglect the more colourful extensions that are richer in tension (9/11/13 and their chromatic alterations).

Improvisations that emphasise chord tones (the basic sound of the chord) and use tensions as passing notes sound relatively bland and commonplace, if not boring. Of course, it would be possible to consciously favour upper structures and play triads or four-note arpeggios consisting mainly of tensions. Even though this is heard very often in modern Jazz, our ears will find it more difficult to maintain the relation to the basic chord sound.

In contrast, a scale-based, horizontal approach enhances the melodic contour and the flow of the line. All notes equally support the momentum of a phrase, and almost no distinction is made between chord tones and tensions. However, be aware of the fact that the way we think influences the way we practice, and the way we practice determines the way we play. Those who think predominantly in scales mainly focus on the horizontal aspect and may pay less attention to the vertical structures. Improvisations following a horizontal approach run the risk of losing the connection with the basic harmonic framework and frequently sound like aimless doodling.

As you can see, both approaches are valid, and both have advantages and drawbacks. Since scales and chords are simply different ways of seeing the same thing, it's a question of personal preference as to which point of view suits you more. Personally, I prefer the scale-based approach.

I do not believe that every Jazz musician must re-invent the wheel and unravel the entire history of Jazz from the very beginning. It is completely irrelevant to me whether or not, for instance, Louis Armstrong ever thought in terms of Phrygian, Lydian, etc. (he didn't!). Just because the Jazz greats originally used to think in chords rather than scales, doesn't mean we have to hold on to that forever and ever. We live today, not eighty years ago. Jazz is a highly dynamic art form (thank goodness). Musicians themselves change, and with them the concepts, ideas, sounds, the musical language and the ways of notating music change, too. Therefore, I think it is quite legitimate to use new approaches to simplify or speed up the process of learning Jazz – even if they don't always conform to tradition. Should we respect tradition? *Of course!* – but only as long as we stay open-minded and flexible when confronted with new sounds or different ways of thinking.

To me, scales are the lowest common denominator. They are the bond between melody and harmony and therefore a most elegant means of communication. With scales, we can quickly make ourselves understood within any harmonic context and convey a lot of information with few words. Scales are firmly established in the international language of Jazz today. Why should we do without them just because they didn't belong to the vocabulary of, say, Charlie Parker? Provided we don't forget that scales as such have no or only little expressive power in their own right and that practising scales develops technique and not musicality, there is no danger that they cause us to lose sight of the music itself. Scales are no more than a first step towards creating meaningful solos. As long as we see scales as a way of thinking, as an abstract supply of notes, we won't mistake them for the real thing.

Church modes and diatonic functions

Scales are the reservoirs of sound from which soloists draw their improvisational material. Let's start with chord progressions containing only diatonic functions in major keys. Because all diatonic chords relate back to the same basic scale, the same tonal material can be applied to all functions within the diatonic series (e.g. B♭ Major):

B♭ Ionian ⟶

B♭△7	C-7	D-7	E♭△7	F7	G-7	Aø7
Imaj7	II-7	III-7	IVmaj7	V7	VI-7	VIIø7

When improvising over the chord progression shown below, we could keep things simple and work only with notes from the B♭ Major scale without thinking about each individual chord. Let's try doing just this by playing to **track 20**. Try to be musical, but don't feel compelled to react to every chord. Just go with the flow of your lines:

‖: B♭△7 | F7 | G-7 | D-7 | E♭△7 | B♭△7 | C-7 | F7 |

| B♭△7 | E♭△7 | D-7 | G-7 | C-7 | F7 | B♭△7 | ％ :‖

On the whole, this is quite a useful concept for the inexperienced Jazz musician. It helps overcome inhibitions and generates a reasonably acceptable result. After all, everyone has practised Major scales at some point and has them "at the tips of their fingers".

However, this approach will not be very successful in the long run, mainly because it supports a way of playing that does not respect the individual chord and its specific character. A good solo depends less on the choice of tonal material as such but rather on where particular notes are placed within a melodic line and how they relate vertically to the underlying harmony. The meaning and effect of any note is different from chord to chord – a note that is a chord tone for one function (= low level of harmonic tension) is an extension for the next (= high level of harmonic tension). Indiscriminate use of the same tonal material for every chord will result in everything sounding similar (at least from a melodic perspective). In the end, a melody should reflect the harmonic progression by outlining each individual chord contained within it. Therefore, we have to take a close look at each diatonic function in order to figure out its unique qualities and how it differs from the others.

If we relate the notes of the B♭ Major scale (Ionian) to each of the diatonic functions in B♭ Major and interpret each note of the scale as an independent root, we get a different scale for each chord. What we end up with are derivatives or "shifts" of the Major scale, something we already talked about in the chapter "Modality" when discussing the church modes. In the following diagram, you can see each function and its corresponding scale in the key of B♭ Major, with chord tones and tensions indicated below each scale:

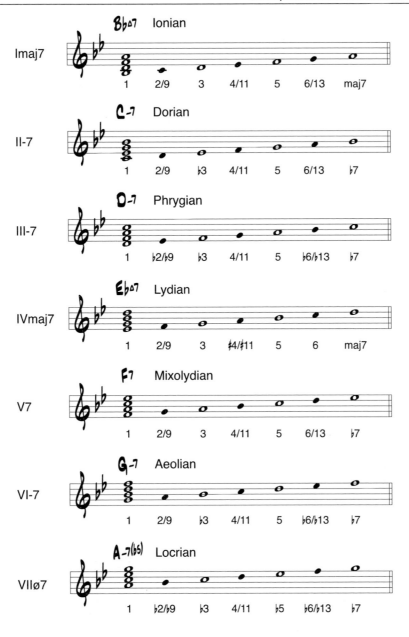

Every one of these scales satisfies both criteria mentioned above by containing:

- chord tones representing the basic four-note sound (1-3-5-7);
- tensions, which establish the relationship with the key (2/9, 4/11, 6/13).

Again, I'd like to post a warning at this point. Although this method of deriving scales is a neat and elegant way of getting the church modes into our heads, please don't make the mistake of confusing cause and effect! It may well be that a II chord implies Dorian, a III chord Phrygian, a IV chord Lydian, a V chord Mixolydian, and so on. But just as a dominant 7th chord can have a life of its own, e.g. as a sus4 chord in "Maiden Voyage" or as a tonic (I7) in the Blues, Mixolydian *itself* can appear as a sound independent of its traditional dominant 7th function. The V7 chord of a major key is Mixolydian, but Mixolydian does not automatically imply V7 exclusively. Mixolydian is Mixolydian is Mixolydian … If you associate each scale only with a single specific function, you'll have problems recognising the same sound in other contexts.

Avoid notes

Dividing scales into chord tones and tensions is primarily a theoretical concept. In practice, not all tensions can really be used as such. Almost every scale contains what we call *avoid notes*. These are notes that present no problems melodically but have to be approached with caution harmonically.

Try this: Play a C7 chord on the piano with your left hand. Now strike the notes D (9), F (11) and A (13) one at a time with the right hand (simultaneously playing the C7). Take your time with each note and ask yourself: "How does this note feel?" You'll probably come up with the following result: The A and the D blend nicely into the overall sound, whereas the F seems to clash with the chord. What we have discovered is an avoid note.

Why does the ear naturally accept certain notes and reject others? In most books on harmony, avoid notes are presented as a simple matter of fact. I would like to explore this topic in more detail and go into the reasons why certain notes don't sound that good. When examining avoid notes there are two aspects to be considered:

- *the function of a chord*;

- *the level of harmonic tension.*

Function

The reason for diatonic cadential functions (II–7, IVmaj7, V7, VIIø7) wanting to resolve is mainly due to the harmonic leading tone (4th degree of the key). Conversely, it should be obvious that the harmonic leading tone, when combined with tonic functions (Imaj7, III–7, VI–7), will have a disturbing and destabilising effect on any member of this functional group. It makes no musical sense to combine a leading tone and the note it wants to resolve to in one and the same sound – something like pushing "stop" and "go" buttons at the same time. Accordingly, 4/11 will be an avoid note when used in conjunction with Imaj7 (Ionian). The same holds true for ♭2/♭9 with III–7 (Phrygian) and ♭6/♭13 with VI–7 (Aeolian):

On the other hand, dominant functions (V7, VIIø7) are highly unstable because they contain two leading tones (constituting the tritone). Both functions want to resolve to the tonic (I). Here, we should take a closer look at the melodic leading tone, the 3 of V7 and the 1 of VIIø7. The melodic leading tone wants to resolve to the root of the key (1), which must therefore be perceived as an avoid note for both dominant functions. Again, it doesn't make sense to incorporate a note that has a tendency to resolve (movement) and the note it wants to resolve to (rest) into one and the same voicing. Accordingly, we should avoid using 4/11 together with V7 (Mixolydian) and ♭2/♭9 with VIIø7 (Locrian) as tensions:

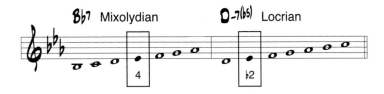

When it comes to the subdominant functions II–7, IVmaj7 and V7(sus4), voice leading plays an important role in terms of avoid notes. Remember the cadences IV-V-I and II-V-I as well as the traditional use of the suspended fourth. In all three cases, we find the same typical mechanism of resolution:

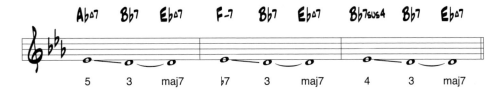

In order not to pre-empt the dominant 7th chord B♭7 in these cadences, the third of V7 (the note D) is treated as an avoid note for the preceding subdominant function:

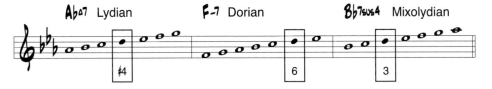

Tension

A more straightforward explanation for avoid notes is that almost all form a minor ninth (♭9) with one of the basic chord tones within the extended chord structure (layering thirds to the 13th). The ♭9 is an extremely dissonant interval that disrupts the consonant framework of diatonic chord progressions:

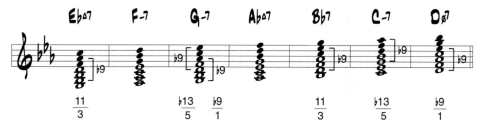

We could formulate a rule saying that any note *a semitone above one of the chord tones* is automatically treated as an avoid note. Play the diatonic chords in the table above on the piano (chord tones with your left and tensions with your right hand). Add the tensions one at a time and see if you can spot the avoid notes just by ear.

The table shows that II–7 (F–7) and IVmaj7 (A♭maj7) don't contain minor ninths. The 13 (in Dorian) and the ♯11 (in Lydian) are therefore treated as avoid notes for functional reasons only (if either II–7 or IVmaj7 appears as part of a cadence preceding V7). In all other cases, neither Dorian nor Lydian contain an avoid note. In modern compositions, where traditional cadences and voice leading play a less important role, both these tensions are quite commonly used.

When screening diatonic functions for avoid notes, we run across another ♭9-situation: ♭6/♭13 with the chord III–7 (G–7 Phrygian). This is referred to as a *conditional avoid note*. The term "conditional" means that whether or not we perceive a note as an avoid note depends on the context. ♭6/♭13 is an avoid note because of the dissonance it creates with the 5th of the chord. If we leave out the 5th (which is possible because the 5th does not essentially define a specific chord quality), the ♭13 can be used as a tension. The resulting chord, however, sounds rather like a tonic with the 3rd in the bass:

Another typical example of a conditional avoid note is the root when used as the final note of a melody. Most traditional Jazz melodies end on 1 or 8 together with the tonic chord, thereby providing the strongest feeling of resolution. The melody note (1 or 8) – being a long note and quite often the top note of a sound – will strongly interact with the underlying harmony (Imaj7). For this reason, we usually find I6 instead of Imaj7 as the final chord because a maj7 would give us a highly dissonant ♭2/♭9-relationship with the root in the melody.

Let's summarise:

Function	Scale	Avoid note	Tensions
Imaj7	Ionian	4	6, 9
II–7	Dorian	(6)	9, 11, (13)
III–7	Phrygian	♭2, (♭6)	11, (♭13)
IVmaj7	Lydian	(♯4)	6, 9, (♯11)
V7	Mixolydian	4	9, 13
V7(sus4)	Mixolydian	3	9, 13
VI–7	Aeolian	♭6	9, 11
VII–7(♭5)	Locrian	♭2	11, ♭13

So, if we look at a scale and subtract the chord tones as well as the avoid note(s), we are left with the tensions that best fit the related function. This means that the function of a chord limits the choice of tensions and defines which extensions are the most appropriate. However, this doesn't imply that other tensions would sound wrong – it's just that they wouldn't give us as strong a connection between the chord and the tonal centre or key of the piece.

The relationships between function and tensions shown in the table above represent the most diatonic and therefore ordinary sounds. Exceptions to the "norm" – i.e. an unusual scale or an unexpected tension – should always occur with due regard to these conventions and not by chance. It is the musician's choice whether he or she wants to act in accordance with a stereotype or not. This has nothing to do with "right" or "wrong". It is more a question of either wanting to opt for the usual, the "inside", or rather search for the unusual, the "outside", as we say in Jazz. However, unconventional sounds create a lot of tension and they can easily feel like mistakes if they pop up haphazardly. That is why we have to know the cliché well if we deliberately want to make "mistakes" by choosing a less commonplace sound. Once we have a grasp of chord-scale relationships, we can decide whether we want to follow the rules or break them, whether we want to go for the expected (no or little tension) or tickle the ear by selecting an unusual option (high tension level).

I should mention again that avoid notes are primarily relevant in a harmonic context where the ear has enough time to settle on a note long enough to be actually aware of the dissonance it creates. In contrast, avoid notes don't pose a problem when occurring as melodic passing notes. We should just be careful not to place them on the strong beats of a bar or to sit on them for too long. Accenting or emphasising avoid notes within a melodic context would give them harmonic significance because the ear registers them as vertically locking into the underlying chord. This doesn't mean that we have to steer clear of avoid notes at all costs. As is often the case, the rule is not followed that dogmatically in practice. It is rather a principle that helps give you a feeling for the way harmony works and provides you with an understanding of why certain notes create more tension than others.

There are many examples of musical situations containing avoid notes that nevertheless seem to work. Take a look at the following passage from the big band arrangement of "Just

Like That" by Peter Herbolzheimer (on the album "More Bebop"). These are bars 28–31 of the theme:

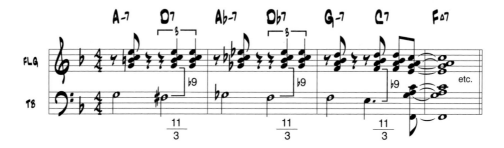

While the trombones – following the fundamental voice leading of a II-V pattern – move nicely from the 7th of the minor chord to the 3rd of the dominant in the second half of each bar, the flugelhorns consistently play the same voicing for both II-7 and V7. As a result, we get ♭9-relationships, which, surprisingly, don't stick out at all (listen to the recording!). The reasons for this are the differences in dynamics and instrumental colours as well as the fact that the flugelhorns play more of a percussive role.

As already stated above, the concept of avoid notes applies primarily to harmonic (vertical) situations. Nonetheless, avoid notes can also be found in a melodic (horizontal) context. Here are two excerpts from "Stella By Starlight" (bars 9/10 and 13/14):

As you can see with both B♭maj7 and Fmaj7, the 4th scale degree (avoid note in Ionian) occurs directly on the downbeat of the bar. Even though the 4th is used as a suspension, which is immediately resolved to the 3rd, it can't really be seen as a passing note. The fact that it appears at such an exposed and accented point in the bar gives it an avoid-note quality. The pianist Bill Evans evades this problem on his album "A Matter of Conviction" by reharmonising both avoid notes using cadence chords that support the idea of the melodic suspension (the voicings differ from the original recording and are simplified for reasons of clarity):

So, when talking about avoid notes, we are referring to sounds that are extremely dissonant and are therefore perceived as unpleasant and disruptive within a traditional context. The more contemporary a composition or style and the more tolerance we have for dissonance, the less significant the idea of avoid notes becomes. Quite to the contrary – in order to free ourselves from conventional listening and playing habits and to create fresh, edgy, unusual sounds, we can deliberately use avoid notes as a source of tension.

Both of the following examples – one of John McLaughlin's favourite guitar chords (1) and a typical brass voicing used by composer Mike Gibbs (2) – illustrate this way of thinking:

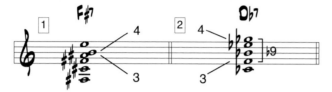

Scales in a minor context

The scale relationships we have just talked about can easily be applied to functions in minor keys by falling back on the major/minor system and equating I–7 (in a minor key) with VI–7 (in the relative major key). The following parallels result (B♭ Major / G Minor):

B♭ Major		Scale		G Minor	
G–7	VI–7	Aeolian		I–7	G–7
A–7(♭5)	VIIø7	Locrian		IIø7	A–7(♭5)
B♭maj7	Imaj7	Ionian		♭IIImaj7	B♭maj7
C–7	II–7	Dorian		IV–7	C–7
D–7	III–7	Phrygian	???	V7	D7
E♭maj7	IVmaj7	Lydian		♭VImaj7	E♭maj7
F7	V7	Mixolydian		♭VII7	F7

The avoid notes we talked about in major keys apply to the corresponding relative minor keys, too.

The dominant in minor

In minor keys, V7 is a special case. The function is not derived from Aeolian but from Harmonic minor. This connection is also reflected in the corresponding scale and the resulting improvisational material (in G Minor):

As shown above, the scale that goes best with D7 is a transposition of G Harmonic minor. In German, *HM5* has established itself as the standard name for this scale – short for: "Harmonic minor starting on the 5th scale degree". Even though this abbreviation makes a lot of sense, it is less frequently found in English speaking countries. Labels such as "Harmonic minor up a perfect 5th" are more commonly used (even though this seems to me a rather cumbersome circumscription). Alternately, the scale is called *Mixolydian(♭9/♭13)* – often shortened to *Mixo(♭9/♭13)* – which also makes sense because this name refers both to the fact that we are dealing with a dominant seventh chord (V7, which is commonly tied to Mixolydian) and that the scale contains the altered tensions ♭9 and ♭13 (with the 9 and the 13 of Mixolydian lowered by a half step respectively). Personally, I prefer HM5, but, for the sake of completeness, I will use both names – HM5 and Mixo(♭9/♭13) – in the course of this book.

HM5 gives us an altered dominant: D7(♭9/♭13). The tension ♭13 (B♭) effectively prepares the ear for the minor quality of the target chord (the B♭ is also the ♭3 of G–7).

The 4th scale degree of HM5 is an avoid note (as in Mixolydian). In addition, the 5th scale degree is considered to be a conditional avoid note because the ♭13 plays such an important role in anticipating the minor quality (♭3) of the target chord. Conversely, when using the 5 – e.g. as part of a 7(♭9)-chord – the ♭13 would become a conditional avoid note. As a rule, we try to avoid the simultaneous use of 5 and ♭13 in same voicing:

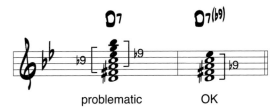

problematic   OK

The tension ♭9, despite its high level of harmonic tension, is *not* heard as an avoid note in a dominant 7th chord. The truth is, I don't really have a satisfactory explanation for this. Maybe it is because the ♭9 causes less of a disturbance within the comparably dissonant context of a dominant 7th chord. A more likely reason, however, would be that we hear the ♭9 as part of a diminished chord on the 7th degree of the Harmonic minor scale. VII°7 is often used as a substitute for the V7(♭9) – omitting the root – and is therefore a sound we are very familiar with.

HM5, with its highly characteristic quality, reminds us of Arabic music or Spanish folklore. This is why it is often known as the Flamenco scale. Its particular anomaly – as in the Harmonic minor scale – is the break in continuity caused by the interval of an augmented second (in this case between ♭2 and 3). In order to close this gap, the raised ninth ♯9 is almost always used in conjunction with the ♭9 in practice. The combinations 9/♭9 or 9/♯9 – in other words a mix of diatonic and altered tensions – do not work. In contrast, combining ♭9 with

♯9 is not a contradiction. Both intervals reinforce the key and have a similar level of dissonance. In many lines they appear next to each other:

So, when I refer to the scale HM5 in the future, it will automatically include the ♯9.

A dominant 7th chord (V7) resolving to a minor tonic (I–7) requires altered tensions –
notably ♭9, ♯9 and ♭13 – to create a close link to the overall minor key. In keeping with this
quality, another scale has established itself as a common alternative to HM5 – the *Altered
dominant scale*, or simply *Altered*. Even though this scale does not generate as close a connection to the key as HM5, it is consistent with the general colour of the function itself. The
Altered scale contains only the most important components of a dominant seventh chord,
the root and the tritone (3/♭7), as well as all possible alterations (♭9, ♯9, ♭5/♯11, ♭13). Altered
doesn't have any avoid notes:

As already stated above, the Altered scale does not create as strong a link to the key as HM5
– the ♯11 is a non-diatonic note that pushes strongly against the tonal environment. On the
other hand, the ♯11 supports the general quality of the function and matches the colour of
the other altered tensions that are diatonic to the key (♭9/♯9/♭13).

Altered and HM5 are mutually exclusive (this means they should not be mixed or used
simultaneously). The ♯11 (♯4/♭5) cannot be combined with either the perfect fourth or the
perfect fifth without causing melodic confusion. Mixing the two scales leads to extended
chromatic movement (♯9-3-4-♯11-5-♭13) that does not lend itself to clear melodic phrases.
So, depending on what the composition indicates, you will have to choose one or the other.

One last word concerning the use of terminology: When I speak of an *altered dominant
chord*, this implies both HM5 (including the ♯9) and the Altered scale as its possible improvisational material. When speaking of *Altered*, I only mean the scale as such.

As you can see, dominant chords use different tensions, depending on whether they resolve to a major or minor tonic chord. Here is what can be termed as the basic stereotype
when dealing with dominant functions:

So – let's summarise. You can attach a scale to any chord. This scale represents the chord type (chord tones 1/3/5/7) and, at the same time, forms a connection with the overall key (tensions 9/11/13). Of course, when improvising over a chord progression, the characteristics of each individual scale will only be clearly audible when the changes move at a fairly slow pace (e.g. in a ballad). The faster the flow of chord changes (e.g. when the chords are moving at half-bar intervals or with up-tempo tunes), the less tangible each scale will be. This is because the scales (or parts of scales) fly by too fast for the ear to register them as distinctive colours. In such cases, the horizontal (melodic) continuity will carry more weight than the vertical aspect of the music (the relationship between melody notes and the chords).

Let's finish this chapter on a critical note. I am very often confronted with the question whether or not it's really necessary to assign a scale to every chord. Everybody knows that, in the end, a good melody is much more than a sequence of scales. Of course, you don't think "scale-scale-scale-Locrian-HM5-Aeolian-Lydian-scale-scale-scale…" while improvising (at least, I hope you don't, because if you do, you're on the wrong track). A good melody is more than the sum of its parts. Although consisting of many phrases, segments, motivic elements and scale fragments, it nonetheless presents itself to the ear as one self-contained whole. A scale, by comparison, is no more than an abstract concept that represents the material used in a melodic situation. Scales can tell you *which* notes to use, but they can't tell you *how* to use them. We will talk about the principles governing the development of good melodies later in this book (from an improvisational as well as a compositional point of view). One thing, though, should be perfectly clear from the start: Practising scales and choosing the right scale for the right chord will *not* help you create good melodies!!! Scales are, at best, a first step.

So, why should we think in terms of chord-scale relationships? Well – it's a neat way of organising music in your head and understanding how melody and harmony relate to each other. Improvisation, after all, revolves around making choices. Using the chord-scale approach helps you limit the multitude of choices and provides you with criteria that will help you practise more effectively. Last, but not least, it makes things easier when trying to analyse and understand the musical vocabulary other soloists use in their improvisations.

Assignment

Have another look at the tables on p. 84 and 86 (you should have filled them out by now). Now, write down the scale that belongs to each of the chord symbols and its respective function. Make sure you always use the appropriate key signature. Name the scales and mark the avoid notes. Write down the intervallic functions as numbers below each note of each scale (e.g. see p. 69).

Secondary Dominants

Jazz tunes very rarely contain diatonic chord functions exclusively. The diatonic framework is usually expanded by an array of sounds creating additional colour without losing the connection to the key. The first new functional group we're going to talk about is *secondary dominants*.

Why should a dominant 7th chord only resolve to a tonic chord (Imaj7 or I–7)? Based on the perfect cadence V-I, with V7 being the *primary dominant*, we can extend the concept by placing a dominant 7th chord in front of *every* diatonic function (II–7, III–7, IVmaj7, etc.). These dominants all resolve down a perfect fifth. In functional notation, the corresponding symbol is "V7 of a specific diatonic target chord" (e.g. V7/III = V7 of III = the dominant resolving to III–7). The following diagram shows all secondary dominant relationships in the key of F Major:

	V7	V7/II	V7/III	V7/IV	V7/V	V7/VI	V7/VII
Secondary dominant	C7	D7	E7	F7	G7	A7	B7
	↓	↓	↓	↓	↓	↓	↓
Diatonic target	Fᴧ7	G–7	A–7	B♭ᴧ7	C7	D–7	E–7(♭5)
	Imaj7	II-7	III-7	IVmaj7	V7	VI-7	VIIø7

V7/VII is a special case. I have not yet come across this function in any Jazz standard. Firstly, it has to do with the instability of the ø7 chord – it just doesn't make a good target chord. Secondly, the B7 chord in this example is the only secondary dominant whose root note is not in key. This doesn't mean that B7 can't be used in the key of F Major. But, as we will see, it works differently.

In practice, secondary dominants can either prepare or replace diatonic functions. This can be seen clearly within the framework of the diatonic cadence:

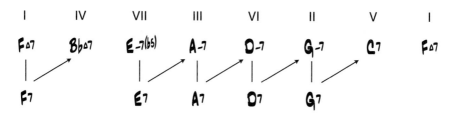

There are two different types of functional symbols we can use to label secondary dominants: a *degree symbol* or a *cadence symbol*. A degree symbol shows the dominant in its diatonic context (e.g. VI7: this sound replaces VI–7). A cadence symbol, by comparison, indicates that the function wants to resolve and points to the expected target chord (e.g. V7/II:

This dominant wants to resolve to II–7). Both systems have their merits because they show the different ways a dominant 7th chord can be perceived within a tonal context. I have already mentioned that your choice of terms or symbols can decidedly influence the way you visualise a sound – a well-chosen symbol can therefore be an important "psychological" aid. This is why you should be familiar with both systems (in F Major):

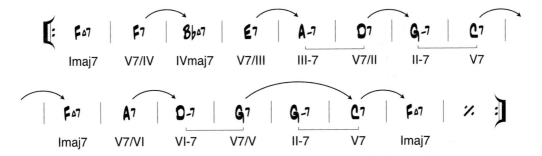

V7/IV	V7/V	V7/VI	V7/I	V7/II	V7/III
F7	G7	A7	C7	D7	E7
I7	II7	III7	V7	VI7	VII7

Let's look at a typical chord progression and its analysis:

F△7	F7	B♭△7	E7	A-7	D7	G-7	C7
Imaj7	V7/IV	IVmaj7	V7/III	III-7	V7/II	II-7	V7

F△7	A7	D-7	G7	G-7	C7	F△7	⁒
Imaj7	V7/VI	VI-7	V7/V	II-7	V7	Imaj7	

Secondary dominants introduce chromatic colouration to the diatonic environment of a major key. I am not talking about squeezing in random chromatic notes here and there as embellishments, but rather about something I prefer to call **functional chromaticism**. What I mean are chromatic "disruptions" appearing at formally important points within a melody or a bass line – especially on strong beats 1 and/or 3 of the bar – giving them harmonic significance.

The following diagram shows the chromatically "filled in" G Major scale:

The chromatic notes create tension relative to the key and therefore have the tendency to resolve to a diatonic target note. The most obvious and, from the ear's point of view, most straightforward association would be to interpret them as leading tones. Chromatic notes are therefore mostly perceived as thirds or sevenths of secondary dominants (of course there are other, though less obvious, ways of explaining them, especially when we take chord tensions into consideration).

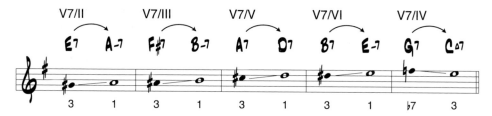

Most improvisations consist of *single note lines* based on the harmonic structure of a composition. When Jazz musicians "play the changes", their melodic lines will "show" the underlying harmony. You can actually "see" the chords just by looking at the tonal material used in the solo and by paying attention to the placement of the notes. If, for example, the chord progression extends beyond the basic diatonic framework (e.g. when the changes include secondary dominants), the melodic lines will inevitably contain chromatic deviations from the key signature. If you can figure out the changes just by looking at a melodic line, you will better understand how Jazz musicians weave their phrases. This is why it is important for you to learn how to "read" a melody harmonically.

I'd like to demonstrate this using an example that may appear to have nothing to do with the world of Jazz – an excerpt from the Sonata for Solo Violin No. 3, 2nd movement (Fugue) by J.S. Bach (BWV 1005). This short passage, in itself, is an awesome work of art. It shows – better than most Jazz improvisations – how effectively a line can reflect harmony (according to contemporary reports, Bach was able to improvise at this astonishing level!).

There is, however, another reason why I want to use this specific example. This book on harmony is meant not only for Jazz musicians. For those of you who have grown up with a Classical music background it is important to realise that many of the melodic phrases you have absorbed over the years as part of your Classical repertoire can also be used in Jazz. Many melodies we find in Baroque music, for example, are quite similar to Bebop lines. By adding a little more chromaticism and using different phrasing and articulation, we could easily transfer the melodies, at least in part, to the Jazz idiom.

Try following the chord progression by playing the roots of the chords on the piano while slowly singing the melody at the same time. You might have to transpose parts of the melody up or down an octave if the lines extend beyond your vocal range. If there is more than one harmonic interpretation indicated for any particular phrase, repeat the passage while concentrating on a different harmonisation each time.

The similarities to Jazz harmony are striking. Although the chord symbol notation may seem unusual to Classical musicians, it shows that Bach's harmony, too, is rooted in cycle-of-fifths movement (turnarounds, II-V-I progressions, secondary and extended dominants). So, traditional Jazz – seen harmonically – can't lay claim to being exceptional, or even revolutionary. Note the median relationships that are interspersed from time to time throughout the piece. This is to avoid the monotony of perpetual root movement in fifths. By substituting chords with median functions, e.g. by replacing a major chord either with a relative minor chord or a secondary dominant a third below or above (C/A–, G/E–, F/A–, C/E7, G/B7, etc.), Bach allows the chord progression to jump to a different place in the cycle of fifths before introducing the next cadential "loop".

This beautiful example shows the extent of harmonic control that can be found in an unaccompanied melodic line. The level of harmonic focus and clarity in each phrase is remarkable. Nothing is superfluous or expendable. Every single note contributes not only to the melodic but also the harmonic flow.

Have a look at the harmonic rhythm (the speed at which the changes move) that can be deduced from the chords outlined by the melody. The chord progression proceeds from one chord per bar to a point where almost every eighth note has an individual harmonic meaning before reverting back to moving at a slower pace. This gradual compression and decompression of the underlying harmony adds to the overall dynamic shape and the driving force of the melodic line.

Assignment

Write up a functional analysis of this Sonata by J.S. Bach. Here are two hints that should help you on the way:

- The chord progression starts in C Major, but modulates to G Major in the fourth line.

- All (!) secondary dominants appear in both keys.

Scales for Secondary Dominants

Although secondary dominants relate to the tonality of a piece of music, they themselves are not diatonic. This means that the corresponding improvisational material must fulfil two criteria: It must reflect the chord and, at the same time, form a connection to the overall key of the piece. Any chosen scale should combine both elements – chord and function. It would be conceivable to use Mixolydian – the most commonly used colour for dominant chords (V7) – with all secondary dominants. In many cases, though, this would only satisfy the chord type and not the key. What we need is a scale for each function that meets both chordal and tonal requirements.

There is a simple way of deriving scales for secondary dominants: Take the chord tones (1/3/5/♭7) and fill in the gaps with notes belonging to the key of the moment. In this way, a scale is completed by adding the tensions which best suit the tonal environment. As a consequence, a scale can be assigned to any secondary dominant dependent on its function (sometimes there are several possibilities). Be sure to remember that at this point we're not yet talking about creating melodies. We are simply defining the basic, unstructured scale material that would result in the closest relationship between the chord and the key. Let's go through the various secondary dominants individually (in the key of F Major):

V7/IV (I7)

We try to remain as diatonic as possible by making only the necessary tonal changes. In this case (V7/IV), the minor 7th – being a chord tone – is inevitably "foreign" to the tonality. All in-between notes, on the other hand, are chosen because they are part of the tonality. The resulting scale for V7/IV is Mixolydian (the 4th degree is an avoid note).

V7/V (II7)

For this function, we also end up with Mixolydian:

V7/VI (III7)

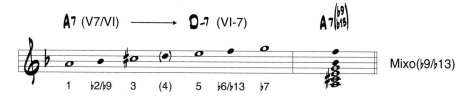

Because of the adjustments we have to make for the sake of tonality, a scale emerges for V7/VI that reminds us of Mixolydian in its basic makeup. But instead of the extensions 9 and 13 commonly associated with Mixolydian, the scale now contains the altered tensions ♭9 and ♭13. In this way, we do justice to both the chord and the tonality.

By comparison, A Mixolydian would be much further removed from F Major and the additional accidentals would clash with the diatonic notes contained in the key:

A7 resolves to D–7 in F Major. If we rewrite the notes of A Mixolydian(♭9/♭13) starting on the note D, the root of the target chord, we get D Harmonic minor. Mixo(♭9/♭13) is nothing other than HM5 – the scale we have already encountered as the most commonly used colour for V7 in a minor key (see p. 113 ff.):

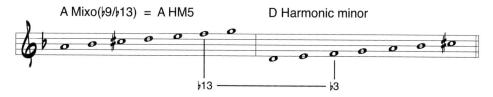

The tension ♭13 (F) is the same note as the ♭3 of D–7. This prepares the listener for the minor sound and establishes a close relationship between the dominant function and its target chord.

As we have already seen in the chapter "Scales, Chord Tones and Tensions" HM5 always includes the ♯9 (♭9 and ♯9 – "the inseparable couple"). In the case of A7, this also makes sense from a tonal point of view: The ♯9 (C) is one of the essential diatonic notes of F Major. In practice, we often go one step further and use Altered as an alternative to HM5. The Altered scale corresponds to the basic colour of the function, characterised by ♭9, ♯9 and ♭13. Logically, the ♯11 fits nicely into the general sound of the dominant (even though the tension is not diatonic to the key):

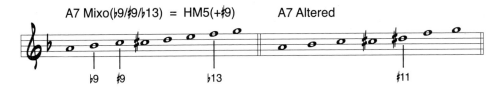

A7 Mixo(♭9/♯9/♭13) = HM5(+♯9)   A7 Altered

Whichever of the two scales you use when improvising is entirely a matter of taste and personal preference (there is no "right" or "wrong").

Let's continue our analysis of secondary dominant functions.

V7/II (VI7)

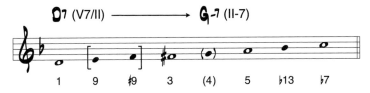

D7 (V7/II) ────────→ G−7 (II−7)

If we stick to the idea of deriving a scale by combining chord tones and key-related tensions, we come up against the problematic combination of 9 and ♯9 already mentioned in one of the previous chapters. Because Jazz musicians usually choose either 9 or ♯9/♭9 (enabling the pianist, for example, to react accordingly) the following scales are commonly used:

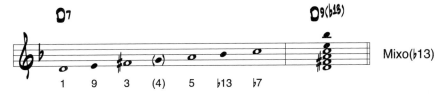

D7   D9(♭13)

                                      Mixo(♭13)

Even if this is the scale that makes most tonal sense, it isn't used very often because of its unusual mixture of tensions (9/♭13). Let's face it – deep down inside, Jazz musicians are actually a rather lazy lot. They look for simplifications and short cuts in order to avoid increasing an already very substantial practice workload. Dominants are therefore usually played either as Mixolydian or HM5/Altered, depending on whether they resolve to a major or minor target chord respectively. Scales containing a mix of altered and non-altered tensions such as Mixo(♭13) are hybrids that mess things up and require additional work. With V7/II, this is what we end up with in practice:

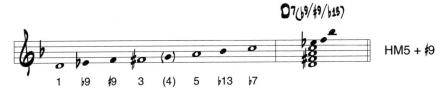

D7(♭9/♯9/♭13)

HM5 + ♯9

Actually, only the ♯9 is anchored in the key. However, because ♭9 and ♯9 are habitually used hand in hand, the ear accepts the ♭9 as a suitable tension, even though it is not diatonic. The use of the Altered scale is once again possible because of the function's inherent altered quality:

Altered

♭9 and ♯11 have no direct relation to the key. Both tensions, however, correspond to the basically altered character of the function defined by ♯9 and ♭13.

V7/III (VII7)

We can derive two scales from this set of notes:

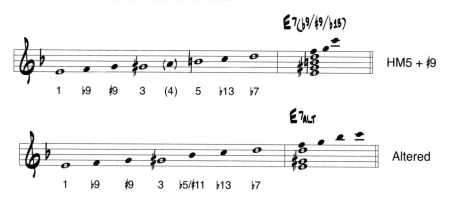

HM5 + ♯9

Altered

With V7/III, you end up with two conflicting scale attributes. Whereas Altered is actually the more "inside" but less conventional sound, HM5 – though the more commonplace scale – is less diatonic because the 5th is "out of key". Of course, both will work.

As you can see, there is more than only one scale that can be used for most secondary dominants. The choice of scales for improvisation depends mainly on the melodic and harmonic context as well as the character of the composition. In case of uncertainty, it's a matter of personal taste.

If we take another look at the derivations we have just discussed, a general rule emerges: Dominants that resolve to major functions (Imaj7, IVmaj7, V7) tend to be Mixolydian, while dominant seventh chords resolving to minor functions (II–7, III–7, VI–7) tend to be HM5/Altered. Here's a summary:

Mixolydian	HM5+♯9 / Altered
V7/I	V7/II
V7/IV	V7/III
V7/V	V7/VI

The 13 prepares us for the major third in the same way as the ♭13 anticipates the minor third of the respective target chord:

This is only the basic theoretical cliché! In practice, you will find a number of exceptions that have become part of every Jazz musician's language.

Altered dominants in major keys

In major keys, the most appropriate scale for V7/I and V7/IV is Mixolydian. However, both functions can also take HM5/Altered. The reason for this is simple. The cadence V7 - Imaj7 follows the principle of "tension-and-release". Since V7 (Mixolydian) and Imaj7 (Ionian) are identical in terms of their diatonic material, the cadential feeling is triggered primarily by the leading tones contained in the dominant, i.e. the tritone (3/♭7). The diatonic tensions of the dominant 7th chord (9 and 13) don't contribute much to the strength of the resolution. Alterations, however, do. They increase the V7's need to resolve because they intensify the feeling of tension by pushing aggressively against both the chord and the key signature. Additionally, they result in chromatic – and thus more compelling – voice leading. Here are the most important resolutions:

When comparing Mixolydian and Altered within the harmonic context of a II-V-I progression in major, you will notice that the Altered dominant moves more energetically into the target chord and stands out more prominently than a Mixolydian dominant because of the non-diatonic tensions (note the additional accidentals):

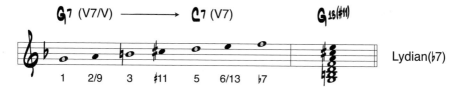

A sound travels around the world

Apart from Mixolydian, another sound has established itself with V7/V (II7) to become the predominant scale associated with this function: *Mixolydian(♯11)* – more commonly labelled as *Lydian(♭7)* or *Lydian Dominant*. Instead of a perfect fourth (4) this scale includes an augmented fourth (♯4/♯11), and therefore no longer contains an avoid note:

Concerning the use of terminology, it is useful to understand how and why specific labels are chosen. The term "Mixolydian(♯11)" relates to the fact that the basic sound is a dominant chord (Mixolydian being the fundamental dominant scale, which is then changed by substituting the ♯4 for the 4th scale degree). The label ♯11 is used instead of ♯4 to imply that we are now dealing with an available tension (the substituted 4 being an avoid note). Lydian(♭7), on the other hand, is derived by assuming that the basic scale is Lydian (usually associated with a major seventh chord), now containing a ♭7 instead of the maj7. I personally prefer the name Mixolydian(♯11) because we are, after all, dealing with a dominant sound, but – for the sake of international consistency – I will use Lydian(♭7) throughout this book.

The function V7/V is a good example of a cliché that has evolved historically rather than being founded on theory. Musical logic and tonal convention dictate Mixolydian as the most suitable scale. In contrast, the choice of ♯11 can neither be justified tonally (the ♯11 being foreign to the key) nor by means of the chord itself. This makes the sound hard to grasp on an intuitive level.

Having taught for well over 30 years, it is interesting to observe that all beginners automatically use Mixolydian for V7/V because it is the most "inside" sound. Proficient Jazz musicians, however, almost invariably use Lydian(♭7) because it is the more exciting colour. As a matter of fact, using Lydian(♭7) over V7/V can be termed a Jazz trademark. Players who use this sound show that they are in touch with the intricacies of the Jazz vocabulary. Lydian(♭7) on V7/V is one of the many "idiomatic musical expressions" you should master if you really want to speak the Jazz language well.

So, how and why has Lydian(♭7) established itself so securely as *the* commonly accepted sound for V7/V? Let's put the question another way. What determines our listening and playing habits most? Of course, it's our roots, our CD collection, our role models and – particularly – our repertoire. Tunes are the universal teachers. Standards (*nomen est omen*) play a central role in this regard, and their influence worldwide has affected the Jazz community's musical awareness. Once a tune is public domain, its melodic and harmonic characteristics likewise become a part of the generally used musical language.

Here are two examples that demonstrate this rather nicely. Question: Who is (arguably) the best-known and most influential Jazz composer of the 20th century? Answer: Duke Ellington. What is his best-known piece? Answer: "Take The A-Train" – at least this is the tune most commonly mentioned (the fact that this composition is actually by Billy Strayhorn, a life-long colleague and companion of Duke Ellington's, makes no difference and is something only Jazz buffs know). Here's another question: Who is the best-known and most often played Latin American composer? Answer: Antonio Carlos Jobim. And what is his best-known piece? Answer: "Desafinado" or "The Girl From Ipanema" (both rank equally high on the list).

Who doesn't know these standards (a rhetorical question)? I have notated the opening bars of both themes in the key of F Major so that you can easily spot the similarities. Sing the melody, play the chord progression on the piano, notice how familiar the sounds actually are and enjoy the ♯11 over V7/V in all its glory:

"The Girl From Ipanema" (see pdf-C) starts out with the same changes: Imaj7 - II7 - II–7. Although the ♯11 does not appear in the melody, we often hear it in the inner voices of the accompaniment as part of the voice leading. Pieces as well known as the ones mentioned above and so obviously "guilty" of using a specific harmonic-melodic "violation of the rules" will inevitably shape our ears and define our expectations and habits. It is clear to me that anything initially "special" will eventually become common practice if it is part of the standard repertoire.

Of course, there is also a theoretical explanation for the use of ♯11 over V7/V. Here is a typical harmonic progression often found in Jazz compositions:

Fᴬ7	A7	D–	G7	G–7	C7	Fᴬ7	℅
Imaj7	V7/VI	VI–	V7/V	II–7	V7	Imaj7	

The D– is deliberately notated as a triad. VI– (in a major key) can be equated with a minor tonic (I–), which is usually played either as Aeolian or Melodic minor (MM). Imagine a soloist who uses MM during an improvisation, misses the change from D– to G7 and, as a consequence, plays the same scale material over both chords. This would result in a ♯11 over the II7:

When listening back to the "mistake", the player says "Wow! That sounds pretty cool, I'll do this more often!" If we are talking about a well-known and often-imitated improviser, the "accidental" phrase could easily proliferate and become a commonly accepted principle. However, I don't think it very likely that II7 and Lydian(♭7) is a sound someone stumbled upon by chance. It is well established that composers such as Ellington or Jobim consciously searched for unusual colours in order to give their music "that something special", something out of the ordinary. This is why I rather favour the more practical explanation based on tunes that have become part of the standard repertoire.

As I mentioned earlier, we often hear this sound in improvisations. Here are the final bars of Phil Woods' solo on "Just The Way You Are" (Billy Joel):

Phil Woods plays the same phrase over II7 and V7 (melodic sequence). In both cases, the ♯11 has a strong tendency to resolve to the 5 (leading tone principle). Notice, however, how the line descends via the 4 and not the ♯11 on the A7 – this shows how the choice of tonal material can be affected by the direction of a line (♯11 upwards to 5, 4 downwards to 3).

I would like to drive home two important points with this rather detailed discussion of a single function. The first is that I want to make sure you are always aware of "why" and "how" a theoretical concept has or might have evolved. I could, of course, take the easy way and say: "These are the rules and here are the corresponding concepts and symbols. Learn everything off by heart, and get on with it." But that is not my approach. I don't simply want to present facts without comment (other harmony books do enough of that!). I would urge you not to take my explanations at face value but to probe deeper on your own and to question or even challenge what you read, even if we're talking about sounds and concepts that are well established in the Jazz community.

My second point is that a theoretical principle and its practical application should not be seen as separate. This book is about the fundamentals of music and the way they relate to the basic vocabulary typical to Jazz. Even if you are an ardent theory hater, you can't refute the fact that countless Jazz musicians have shown with their improvisations that these "rules" actually hold true in real life and produce fabulous results (so ignore them at your own peril). Try to approach every theoretical principle as something alive and breathing and not just as an intellectual puzzle. What good is it to know that you can play Lydian(♭7) over V7/V if you haven't given yourself the opportunity to consciously explore and experience its unique charm?

Let's summarise the various secondary dominants and their scales:

Function	Scale Cliché
V7/I	Mixolydian, HM5/Altered
V7/II	HM5/Altered, Mixo(♭13)
V7/III	HM5/Altered
V7/IV	Mixolydian, HM5/Altered
V7/V	Lydian(♭7), Mixolydian
V7/VI	HM5/Altered

Basically, dominant seventh chords are either Mixolydian / Lydian(♭7) or HM5(+♯9) / Altered. When it comes to functions that allow both options, it's better to pick one or the other so that our band members can react to the lines we are playing.

The following phrase by Bob Berg (from "The Search" on the CD "Short Stories") is a very attractive but rather unusual example of a mixture of these two contrasting scale types. The altered parts of the phrase have been notated enharmonically in order to expose an additional concept hidden behind the scale material. The first altered segment suggests an E major triad, the second a D major triad:

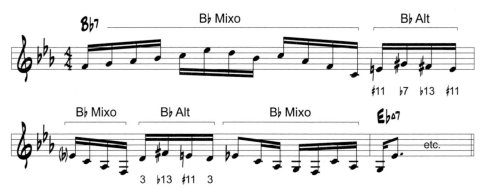

It is quite common to find both scale types used *one after another*, "splitting" the dominant in the process. Usually, a phrase begins with Mixolydian and then switches to Altered to increase the tension and need for resolution just before reaching the target chord:

Split dominants can also be found incorporated in compositions as a set part of the chord progression – for example in the A section of "Wave" (Antonio Carlos Jobim):

The change of scale and the corresponding tensions result in chromatic voice leading, which subtly but effectively moves the listener forward to B–7/E.

Functionally independent dominant scales

We have seen that, for reasons of tonality, all dominant functions are either Mixolydian or HM5/Altered. There are, however, scales that combine Mixolydian and Altered elements and are not clearly linked to either a major or a minor target chord. They are considered to be special colours that can be used with any dominant function. The two most important of these are the *Half-tone-whole-tone* (HTWT) and the *Whole-tone* (WT) scale.

The Half-tone-whole-tone scale

Half-tone-whole-tone is also known as *8-note dominant* because – in contrast with other, mostly heptatonic (7-note) scales – it consists of 8 notes and is used in conjunction with dominant seventh chords. As the name suggests (and as we already know), the HTWT scale is made up of a symmetrical sequence of half and whole steps:

The unusual character of this scale and its resulting chord structures can be traced back to a mixture of altered and diatonic tensions: ♭9, ♯9, ♯11, but 13!

8-note dominant has become one of the most important sounds in modern Jazz. John Coltrane contributed largely to its general acceptance, being the first to use this scale extensively in his improvisations. Here is one of his favourite patterns derived from the HTWT scale, which has often been copied and has established itself as a standard phrase (e.g. it can be heard on the CD "Blue Train" in Trane's solo over the composition "Moment's Notice" at the end of the second saxophone chorus):

Many compositions and improvisations owe their sparkle largely to the HTWT scale. The most striking example of this is the tune "Far Away" by Freddie Hubbard (on "Breaking Point"). The entire theme is based exclusively on two scales – A7 HTWT and D7 HTWT:

Not only the theme but also the improvisations are based on 8-note dominant – at least, the soloists try to be consistent. Hubbard himself is quite relaxed about the scale material and reverts more and more to HM5 along the way – which, of course, is far easier to handle.

"Far Away" is a great tune when trying to come to terms with this unusual scale as a sound in its own right and to habituate the ear. This brings me to an important point. Many Jazz musicians write tunes not only to create wonderful music but also to design vehicles that will help them get accustomed to new sounds. They incorporate concepts they are not yet familiar with and use the resulting compositions as an experimental platform. "Far Away" is a good example of just that (and the title is indicative of this journey into uncharted territory). Written in 1964, it shows how difficult it can be to improvise over material that has not yet become part of the subliminal vocabulary. If you listen to the original recording, you will realise that the solos sound rather choppy, the phrases are unpolished and inelegant and there is no real flow to the lines. It is quite obvious that the whole band is scuffling and holding on for dear life. With the exception of the flute player (James Spaulding), none of the soloists really appears to feel comfortable with HTWT. On a later recording of "Far Away" (on "Stardust", a collaboration with Benny Golson in 1987), the improvisations are much more musical and convincing. Clearly, even the best musicians need time to feel at home with this both exciting and awkward sound. When first introducing HTWT to my students, it usually takes them several months of hard work to fully immerse themselves and become fluent in this scale.

Meanwhile, HTWT has become a staple sound in Jazz. Musicians such as John Scofield and Herbie Hancock are well known for their extensive use of this (no longer) special scale. Today, it is definitely one of the most widely used dominant sounds and is even found in more commercially oriented, Jazz-related styles – as can be heard in Larry Williams' synthesiser solo over "Spain" on "This Time" (Al Jarreau).

Take a look at the first chorus. I have included a functional analysis of the chord progression, indicating the most "inside" corresponding scales. For reasons of simplicity, the analysis is in D Major even though the composition is clearly in B Minor, the relative minor key (we will have a closer look at this analysis at a later point in this book):

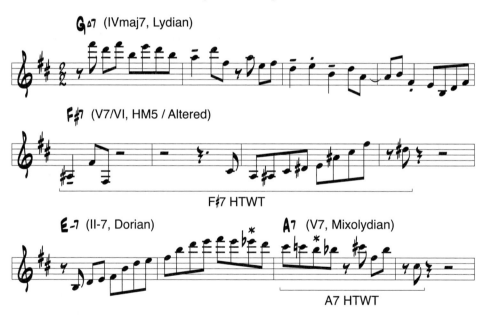

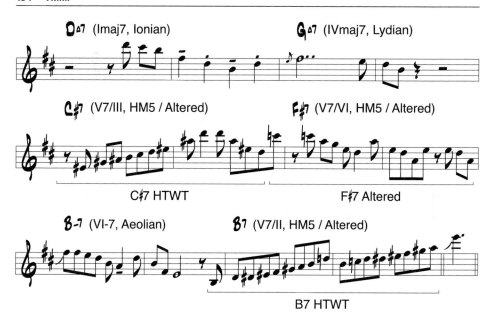

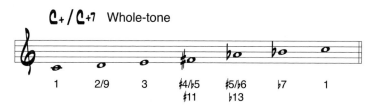

Notice that almost all dominants – regardless of function and scale cliché – are HTWT.

The Whole-tone scale

A slightly less common – also symmetrical – dominant scale, which gets its character from a mixture of diatonic and altered tensions, is the Whole-tone scale. It is hexatonic (6 notes), consists of nothing but whole steps and contains 3 as well as ♭7 (thus its dominant flavour):

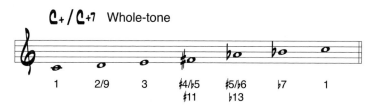

Unlike 8-note dominant, this scale has a rather tiring effect on the listener when used over a longer period of time. Its repetitive whole-tone movement only allows for a limited amount of melodic variation. Additionally, it has little to offer harmonically: Because of its symmetrical structure, only augmented triads, +7 and +7(♭5) chords can be derived from the various scale degrees. Subsequently, Whole-tone is used sparingly, mostly to add colour, in order to avoid the monotony of overuse. Having said this, there are important compositions that employ this scale.

A good example is Wayne Shorter's composition "Juju" on the album by the same name. The introduction (played by McCoy Tyner) and the first ten bars of the theme are melodically and harmonically based on the Whole-tone scale (listen to the improvisations – they are, too!):

This sound can also be found in the realm of Pop music. A well-known example is the intro-duction of "You Are The Sunshine Of My Life" by Stevie Wonder:

In order to avoid confusion when it comes to terminology, there is general agreement on the application of the chord symbol "+7": It is used when the perfect fifth is to be left out, imply-ing the use of the Whole-tone scale. In contrast, the symbol "7(♭13)" indicates that the cor-responding scale includes the ♭6 as well as the 5 (e.g. as in HM5).

As already mentioned above, Half-tone-whole-tone and Whole-tone scales are unique because of their unusual structure and distinctive sound. They can be played over any dom-inant seventh chord – *independently of function*.

In this context, I'd like to make a comment regarding notation. Our traditional notational system is based on the series of naturals (C-D-E-F-G-A-B) organised into seven-note Major or Minor scales and divided into either sharp or flat keys. When music deviates from the key signature chromatically and we need to add accidentals, we try to stick to the sequence of naturals and the consistent use of either sharps or flats in accordance with the key signature. It may even be necessary to use double-sharps (𝄪) or double-flats (♭♭) when trying to achieve correct notation. As a result, notating scales like Half-tone-whole-tone or Whole-tone, which have either more or less than 7 notes, can create something of a problem. Our tradi-tional method of notation doesn't work that well with these scales because, due to their symmetry, they don't fit into the general system of key signatures. The same thing applies to the Altered scale with the ♭9 and ♯9 both being "raised" or "lowered" variations of the same natural. In these cases, it may be quite difficult to stick to the customary practice of consis-tently utilising either sharps or flats. This is why enharmonic equivalents (see p. 29 ff.) are used so much in Jazz. Jazz is richly chromatic and its notation tends and needs to be more flexible. It is not unusual to stumble upon a wild mixture of sharps and flats in one and the same scale or melodic line. Jazz musicians don't go for purism in notation – they go for what is easier to read rather than following whatever may be theoretically correct. Consequently, double sharps and flats are avoided at all cost and even accidentals such as C♭, B♯, E♯ and F♭ appear quite rarely (in these cases the enharmonic equivalents B, C, F and E are used).

Here is an overview of the dominant scales we have talked about:

Scale	Intervals	Avoid notes	Tensions
Mixolydian	1, 2, 3, 4, 5, 6, ♭7	4	9, 13
Lydian(♭7)	1, 2, 3, ♯4, 5, 6, ♭7	none	9, ♯11, 13
HM5+♯9	1, ♭2, ♯2, 3, 4, 5, ♭6, ♭7	4	♭9, ♯9, ♭13
Altered	1, ♭2, ♯2, 3, ♯4/♭5, ♭6, ♭7	none	♭9, ♯9, ♯11, ♭13
Mixolydian(♭13)	1, 2, 3, 4, 5, ♭6, ♭7	4	9, ♭13
Mixolydian(♭9)	1, ♭2, 3, 4, 5, 6, ♭7	4	♭9, 13
HTWT	1, ♭2, ♯2, 3, ♯4, 5, 6, ♭7	none	♭9, ♯9, ♯11, 13
Whole-tone	1, 2, 3, ♯4/♭5, ♭6, ♭7	none	9, ♯11, ♭13

Force of habit

There are two decisive factors when it comes to the choice of what to play in an improvisation. The first of these – *tonality* – has been discussed at length. The ear takes the path of least resistance and chooses the tonal material that deviates the least from the overall key signature. No matter how traditional or modern players want to be, they will inevitably improvise under the influence of or by consciously resisting their tonal reflexes. The second aspect – *habit* – is equally decisive. We must accept that much of what we do is governed by automatic responses.

Like most people, Jazz musicians are creatures of habit who want to get maximum results with minimum effort. It's not really about laziness, but rather about efficiency. Especially when practising scales, the balance between what we put in and what we get out of it is vital. Simply because it isn't possible to work on every single scale in every single key in equal measure, we are forced to make choices. We naturally give priority to the sounds most commonly used in practice. As a result, certain preferences have evolved. Have a look at the following table:

Common	Uncommon	Common
Mixolydian	Mixo(♭13)	HM5+♯9
Lydian(♭7)	Mixo(♭9)	Altered
	Whole-tone	
	Half-tone-whole-tone	

The way the various dominant scales fit into each category reflects our personal musical history and corresponds to our playing and listening habits (this actually holds true for almost anybody who has grown up with Western music). The scales on the left and right are the ones we are generally familiar with. They are the most commonly used dominant sounds. But, even within any one group of scales, there is a hierarchy mirroring our stages of development as musicians. Mixolydian was probably the first dominant mode you came across – of course, without realising it. It is the most "normal" dominant scale in major and is played intuitively because dominant seventh chords appear in almost every tune. We have all been exposed to Mixolydian dominants ever since childhood through a wide variety of music, such as Pop music, Christmas carols, Classical music or Folk songs, etc. Although Lydian(♭7) is similar, it has to be practised with conscious effort to get a grip on the ♯11. You probably have also learned HM5 as the fundamental dominant sound in minor without being consciously aware of it, while Altered is a scale that takes some getting used to (again, the ♯11 is the obstacle to overcome).

The group of scales in the middle are the more unusual sounds. Mixo(♭13), Mixo(♭9), Whole-tone or Half-tone-whole-tone, which all contain a mixture of diatonic and altered tensions, are played far less frequently – in any case, they are not automatically part of our standard vocabulary. These scales may require years of intensive practice before our ears and fingers have "absorbed" them.

This means you can only rely on your instincts when it comes to using Mixolydian or HM5. All other dominant scales require additional work. The stranger a scale is in relation to its tonal environment, the more time you will have to spend on acquiring technical and musical fluency because you can rely neither on intuition nor habit.

Non-altered dominants in minor keys

We have already seen that altered dominants can resolve to major chords. In contrast, a Mixolydian dominant resolving to a minor chord is much less common. This progression seems to create too strong a disruption of the natural flow of the minor cadence. Compare the two following resolutions (in F Minor):

While the tensions ♭9 and ♭13 lead convincingly into the target chord (diatonically and by a half step), the tensions 9 and 13 have a rather unsettling effect on the cadence. Not only do they constitute a weaker resolution (whole step), they also disrupt the tonal framework. Above all, the 13 in the C7 (A) does not sit comfortably with the ♭3 (A♭) of the minor tonic. Any dominant scale containing the 13 will come into conflict with a minor target chord.

In practice, however, we do find examples of this type of resolution. In order to make it acceptable to the ear, it usually appears as a central feature or, at least, as an important part of a composition. This way, the ear learns to tolerate this rather awkward sound. Occurring haphazardly or as an isolated event, it would sound out of place or possibly even wrong. Again, we can't seem to get around our habits.

A good example of this is the opening of the composition "Pools" by Don Grolnick (on "Steps Ahead"):

Not only the conspicuous A in the melody but also the keyboard voicings emphasise the unusual flow of this cadence. More importantly, these 4 bars appear again and again throughout the composition. As part of the solo changes, they also control a major portion of the improvisations (go to p. 325 ff. and take a look at the first chorus of Mike Mainieri's solo).

The composition "Minority" by Gigi Gryce is even more extraordinary and deliberate in this regard:

If we look at this tune from a melodic point of view, it is surprising that the first two lines are entirely in F Major! On the other hand, the chord progression in bars 1–6 clearly relates to F Minor. The D–7(♭5), an inversion of F–6, comes from Melodic minor and G–7(♭5) - C7 - F–7 is, of course, II-V-I.

If we want to draw on the particular colours of a composition when improvising, then we need to acknowledge the connection between the harmony and the melody of the piece. Accordingly, neither D–7(♭5) nor G–7(♭5) can be Locrian – in both cases, there is an uncharacteristic *major second* in the melody. The more appropriate scale for both chords would be *Locrian(♮9)* or simply Locrian(9). Remember that we encountered this scale in the chapter "Modality" as a "shift" (permutation) of Melodic minor. The suffix "9" indicates that the second scale degree (9) can now be used as a tension and is no longer an avoid note (as the ♭2/♭9 is in Locrian):

Accordingly, the C7 must have a scale that relates to the preceding sound, containing both ♭9 (= ♭5 of Gø7) and 13 (melody). The most popular solution is the use of 8-note dominant (HTWT), even if the ♯11 is not part of the melody or contained in the chord (watch out for the key signature):

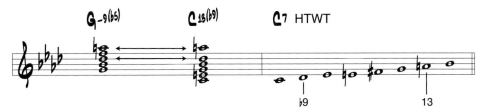

F–7 (bars 1/5) can be interpreted in various ways. It is either Aeolian (relating to the key signature), but it could just as easily be Dorian because of the following D–7(♭5) or Melodic minor if we ignore the 7th in the chord symbol (the latter choice most clearly reflects the melodic line).

As of bar 7, the piece launches into a series of sequential II-V patterns, none of which resolves to its respective Imaj7:

Keeping the melody in mind (which is also sequential in principle), all dominants are Mixolydian, each resolving to a Dorian minor 7th chord. It is not until the very end of the theme that we hear a "normal" minor cadence: C7(♭13) - F–7.

With this last example, I'd like to point out that, time and again, you will need to react to unusual sounds and adapt to musical situations that deviate by varying degrees from traditional chord-scale relationships. *It's the music itself that determines what is right, not theory!* Composers tend to experiment with sounds and inevitably wander off the beaten track. A major aspect of a composer's enjoyment is to lure the listener onto thin ice, to build up expectations only to surprise the ear with an unexpected twist.

Accordingly, every piece of music ends up with its very own sound by either endorsing, changing or ignoring the norm. So, we should always be alert to the possibility of having to depart from theoretical stereotypes and immerse ourselves in something new. To be able to do this, we first have to understand the rules – to break them means to know them! However, if our approach to theory is too dogmatic, we become inflexible and rather helpless when dealing with the unexpected.

Here's a final thought. The musical examples in this chapter are largely exceptions to the rule. There is method in this! I believe that we learn more effectively if we concern ourselves with deviations from the norm. Appreciation for the unusual makes us more aware of the usual (every exception proves the rule). Knowing why something is special will help us better understand how we perceive music. Familiar sounds convey normality, coherency and a sense of wellbeing. They are not likely to spark off an extraordinary response in our ear. On the other hand, unfamiliar sounds and special colours come across as more exciting and surprising. Once we realise why certain sounds have a particular impact and what causes this impression, we can control our music more selectively and effectively.

Tritone Substitution

We already know that the dominant seventh chord's strong tendency to resolve depends on the interaction of 3 and ♭7 – the tritone – within the chord. The tritone splits the octave down the middle. Its only possible inversion is therefore also a tritone. The interval of a tritone is identical to its complementary interval despite enharmonic spelling (♯4 = ♭5). This means that the arrangement of the 3 and the ♭7 within the chord can be reversed without the chord losing its inclination to resolve. As a result, any tritone can imply two different roots:

These two different ways of spelling a tritone result in two dominant seventh chords, either of which can take on the same function in a harmonic context:

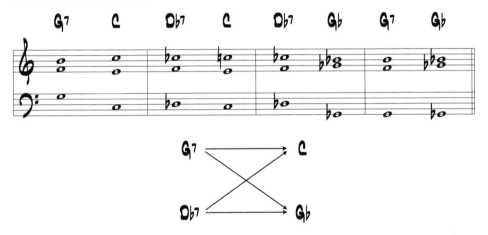

Therefore, every dominant seventh chord has a corresponding *substitute dominant* (SubV). Here are three facts that will help you with the derivation of SubVs:

- The roots of a V7 chord and its corresponding SubV are always a tritone apart.

- A SubV always resolves down a half step.

- V7 chords and their corresponding SubVs are always positioned opposite one another in the cycle of fifths:

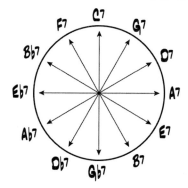

The use of substitute dominants is a first step in breaking the ever-present cycle-of-fifths root movement. If we replace the regular dominant of any II-V-I progression with its substitute dominant, the roots now move chromatically instead of in fifths. II-SubV-I progressions are indicated by dotted brackets (II-SubV) and dashed arrows (SubV-I) in order to tell them apart from a diatonic II-V-I:

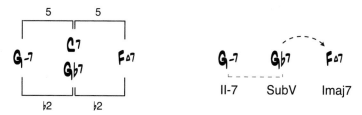

So, any dominant can be replaced with a substitute dominant a tritone away. Accordingly, this principle is called *tritone substitution* and can be applied to both primary and secondary dominants (e.g. in the key of G Major):

	SubV/I	SubV/II	SubV/III	SubV/IV	SubV/V	SubV/VI	
Substitute dominant	A♭7	B♭7	C7	D♭7	E♭7	F7	
	↓	↓	↓	↓	↓	↓	
Diatonic target	G△7	A-7	B-7	C△7	D7	E-7	F#-7(♭5)
	Imaj7	II-7	III-7	IVmaj7	V7	VI-7	VIIø7

The use of SubVs often results in extensive chromatic root movement:

| Imaj7 | SubV/IV | IVmaj7 | SubV/III | III-7 | SubV/II | II-7 | SubV/I |

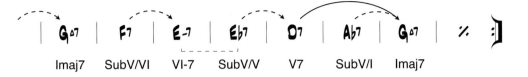

| Imaj7 | SubV/VI | VI-7 | SubV/V | V7 | SubV/I | Imaj7 |

Listen to this example **track 30**, which, however, is in D Major (transpose the above chord progression).

Scales for substitute dominants

Substitute dominants are non-diatonic functions that draw the ear away from the key as a result of their chromatic quality. Accordingly, the material we use for improvisation doesn't have to reflect the key (the diatonic environment) as strongly as is the case with secondary dominants. We could therefore base our improvisations on the chord type alone and – disregarding tonal considerations – go for Mixolydian, the "mother" of all dominant sounds. However, another scale has established itself as the most common choice for all SubV functions: Lydian(♭7). This scale complies with the basic character of the dominant sound and, at the same time, links it to its respective secondary dominant (the ♯4 corresponds to the root of the replaced dominant). Here are the substitute dominant chords in G Major:

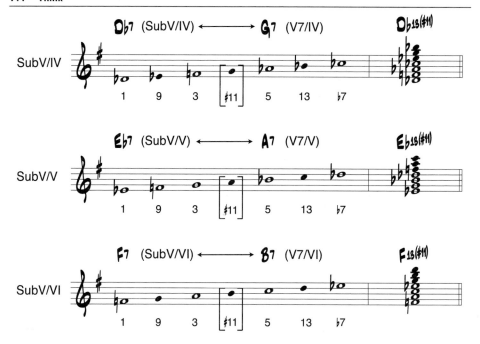

By using Lydian(♭7), an interesting relationship is set up between substitute and secondary dominants. Let's take the dominant seventh pair A♭7/D7 as an example. If we write down A♭ Lydian(♭7) starting on D (using enharmonic equivalents), we end up with D7 Altered as the corresponding scale:

So, a rule emerges:

V7 Altered = SubV Lydian(♭7)

Since we're talking about the same notes, our improvisational material could be drawn from either scale. That said, the ear should be able to tell the difference between the two approaches and acknowledge the distinctive intervallic structure and sound of a chord or melodic phrase, depending on which function (V7 or SubV) they are related to:

Let's remind ourselves that all secondary dominants resolving to a diatonic minor function (V7/II, V7/III, V7/VI) are played as HM5/Altered for reasons of tonality. In light of the correlation between V7 Altered and SubV Lydian(♭7) it surely makes sense that, when choosing scales for the respective tritone substitutes (SubV/II, SubV/III, SubV/VI), Lydian(♭7) is the scale which relates most closely to the tonality.

Conversely, the secondary dominants resolving to major functions (V7/I, V7/IV, V7/V) are played as Mixolydian. It should be equally clear that Lydian(♭7) would *not* establish the closest possible connection with the tonality in conjunction with the corresponding tritone substitutes (SubV/I, SubV/IV, SubV/V). We can see in the diagram on p. 143 ff. that the scale material of precisely these substitute dominants deviates considerably from the diatonic framework (note the many accidentals). Conclusion: For these functions there must be another scale, apart from Lydian(♭7), that is more firmly anchored in the tonality. With this in mind, let's take a look at A♭7 (SubV/I) in G Major:

While Lydian(♭7) has a number of accidentals at odds with the key, A♭7 Altered derives all its notes from G Major apart from the root A♭ (I have deliberately notated the scale enharmonically for the sake of clarity).

The same holds true for D♭7 (SubV/IV) and E♭7 (SubV/V) when using Altered. In both cases, all tensions relate to G Major:

| | 1 | ♭9 | ♯9 | 3 | ♯11 | ♭13 | ♭7 | | 1 | ♭9 | ♯9 | 3 | ♯11 | ♭13 | ♭7 |

Here is an overview of the functions we have discussed and their corresponding scales:

Function	Scale Cliché
SubV/I	Altered, Lydian(♭7)
SubV/II	Lydian(♭7)
SubV/III	Lydian(♭7)
SubV/IV	Altered, Lydian(♭7)
SubV/V	Altered, Lydian(♭7)
SubV/VI	Lydian(♭7)

Extended Dominants

If we connect either secondary dominants or substitute dominants in cycle-of-fifths root movement, we end up with what is called ***extended dominants***. The following two chord progressions in C Major are extreme examples. In practice, we usually come across shorter "chains" of no more than three or four dominants.

Secondary dominants:

Substitute dominants:

The root movement can be nicely illustrated with the cycle of fifths:

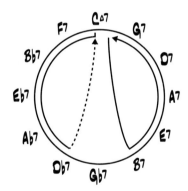

A combination of secondary and substitute dominants is also quite common:

| A⁷ | D⁷ | G⁷ | Cᐃ⁷ || ⟶ | A⁷ E♭⁷ | D⁷ A♭⁷ | G⁷ D♭⁷ | Cᐃ⁷ ||

We can create another variation of extended dominants by placing the corresponding II–7 chord in front of each dominant (V7). In this way, we obtain an interlinked series of II-V patterns that obscures the otherwise obtrusive cycle-of-fifths root movement and cushions the transition between the dominants:

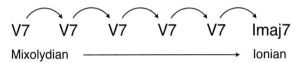

Let's have a look at the possible material for improvisation. How do we handle a chain of dominants? It is quite possible to treat every seventh chord as an isolated sound, consequently assigning the most common scale – Mixolydian – to each dominant:

V7   V7   V7   V7   V7   Imaj7

Mixolydian ⟶ Ionian

In practice, this only holds true for progressions where the changes move at a slower pace, introducing a new chord every two bars or more. A good example of this is "Sweet Georgia Brown" by Pinkard/Bernie:

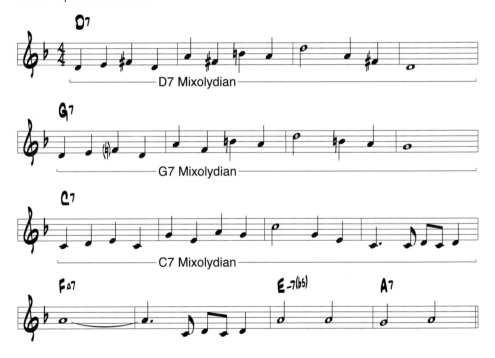

Here, the sound of each individual chord plays a more significant role than the tonal centre (F Major). Because the ear spends a considerable amount of time with each chord, it tends to zero in on each dominant as a sound in its own right rather than making the connection to the overall tonality.

If the harmonic rhythm is faster (changes occurring in one-bar intervals or even every half bar), the tonal association has a far greater impact on the ear. Now the extended dominants are perceived as a succession of secondary or substitute dominants linked to a key area. This, of course, influences the choice of scale material for improvisation (in G Major):

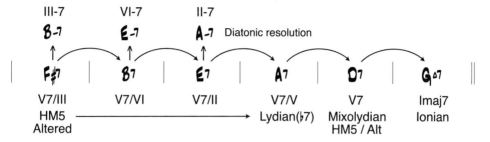

To show that this bit of theory actually holds true in practice, let's look at a piece that could hardly be more commercial and, in consequence, more in keeping with a "public standard": "Mr. Sandman" by Ballard & Morris. This world-renowned evergreen illustrates the "norm" more conclusively than most Jazz tunes:

Almost every bar contains a ♭13 or a 13 as the primary melodic element, suggesting the corresponding scale (HM5 or Mixolydian) as well as establishing a connection between the dominant and the major or minor character (3/♭3) of the anticipated diatonic target chord. The fact that none of the dominants resolves quite as expected, instead moving on to another dominant chord, is of little importance. The ear is influenced by what has happened up until this moment and will automatically treat a dominant as part of the overall key if the preceding chord progression has provided a clear sense of the tonality. The unexpected resolution will create a moment of surprise, brought about by the appearance of another dominant, which in turn implies a new diatonic resolution, and so on, and so on … Besides, the tonality is clearly outlined by the melody: With the exception of the last bar, the entire melody is in G Major.

Based on the same principle, we can illustrate the extended dominant chain derived from substitute dominants:

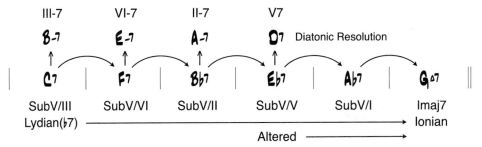

Dominant seventh chords are therefore dealt with according to their functional characteristics, *no matter whether they resolve as expected or not!*

As already stated above, extended dominants sometimes consist of a mixture of secondary and substitute dominants. A typical example of this is the A section of "There Is No Greater Love" (Isham/Jones):

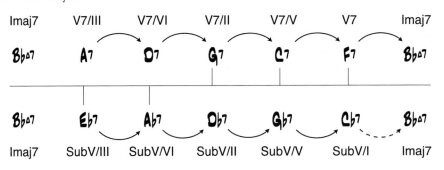

Here's the analysis:

The melody verifies what we spoke about earlier in terms of scale relationships. Eb7 and Ab7 are Lydian(b7), C7 could be either Mixolydian or Lydian(b7) and F7 is Mixolydian (the melody doesn't contradict this choice of scales). Only the G7 (V7/II) is probably Mixo(b13) rather than HM5 – notice the A = 9 in the fourth bar. The b13 = Eb, though not contained in the melody, is nonetheless part of the sound, anticipating C–7 as the diatonic target chord.

The fact that C7 appears instead is irrelevant when choosing the scale for G7. The chromatic passing notes don't need to be taken into account in the analysis.

Chord progressions can contain both tonally based extended dominants as well as functionally independent ones. Probably the most appropriate example of this is the composition "Jordu" by Duke Jordan:

In the A section, the minor tonic alternates with its relative major at each point of resolution. The preceding dominant seventh chords clearly relate to the overall tonality. However, there's a catch. So far, we have only spoken about dominant functions in major keys. Remember, however, that the major and minor systems interrelate harmonically. Even if the basic key of "Jordu" is clearly C Minor, the ear will readily switch to E♭ Major as the related tonal centre (see p. 98 ff. for more on this). Accordingly, the functional and scale analysis could look like this when thinking in E♭ Major:

D7	G7	C-6	F7	B♭7	E♭△7		A♭7
V7/III	V7/VI	VI-6	V7/V	V7	Imaj7		SubV/III
Alt / HM5	HM5 / Alt	MM / Dor	Lyd(♭7)	Mixo	Ionian		Lyd(♭7)

A word on the improvisational material for C-6: The tonic scale in minor keys is invariably either Aeolian or Melodic minor. The major 6th in the chord symbol and the tenor saxophone line (2nd voice) leading up to it clearly point to Melodic minor. But, if we take into account the B♭ (♭7) in the theme (bars 2 and 6), we could also consider Dorian, which contains both 6 and ♭7. Of course, these things hardly matter while soloing because the changes and the corresponding scales are handled less restrictively and therefore the colouring of the C minor chord is entirely at the player's discretion.

In contrast to the A section, it is hard to decide what the key of the B section is. Although the chord progression starts with G7 (V7 in C Minor), it quickly moves away from the starting key, advancing through the cycle of fifths with half-bar extended dominants. As the changes progress, it becomes increasingly difficult to hold on to C Minor or E♭ Major. The melody amplifies this gradual loss of tonal orientation, since it consists only of chord tones, which are embellished by chromatic approaches. Accordingly, it would make no sense to stick to a choice of scales based on tonal considerations. Even D♭6 and C♭6, the chords to which both extended dominant chains resolve, can hardly be seen as tonal points of reference. How are we supposed to interpret extended dominants functionally if the key has not been clearly established or the melody gives us no distinct indication of the tonality? Since we cannot assign functions to the dominant chords, they are best interpreted as Mixolydian.

In conclusion, we can say that if a tonal reference point has been established, then we choose scales for the dominant seventh chords that reflect the key. If no clear tonality is apparent, or if the dominants in a progression move at a slow pace, our ear perceives them as independent colours and we choose Mixolydian.

The Chromatic Dominant System

When adding up all secondary and substitute dominants within any specific key, we end up with a set of 12 dominant seventh chords – one on each note of the Chromatic scale. This means that *every* single dominant seventh chord has a function in *every* key. The following table shows all possible dominant functions and how we would expect them to resolve in the key of D Major:

Function		Dominant	Diatonic target (in D Major)	
I7	V7/IV	D7	Gmaj7	IVmaj7
♭II7	SubV/I	E♭7	Dmaj7	Imaj7
II7	V7/V	E7	A7	V7
♭III7	SubV/II	F7	E–7	II–7
III7	V7/VI	F♯7	B–7	VI–7
IV7	SubV/III	G7	F♯–7	III–7
♭V7	SubV/IV	A♭7	Gmaj7	IVmaj7
V7	V7/I	A7	Dmaj7	Imaj7
♭VI7	SubV/V	B♭7	A7	V7
VI7	V7/II	B7	E–7	II–7
♭VII7	SubV/VI	C7	B–7	VI–7
VII7	V7/III	C♯7	F♯–7	III–7

Try to imagine how each one of these resolutions sounds. First of all, play the tonic (Dmaj7) on the piano and sing the corresponding Major scale up and down a few times in order to establish the tonal centre firmly in your ear. Then play one of the dominant seventh chords followed by its diatonic target chord. Repeat this procedure a number of times, while singing the melodic lines suggested in the following table. I have only included two of the most important ones in each case (there are, of course, many more). The lines contain the essential chord tones, also referred to as **guide tones**, which voice-lead each chord progression as smoothly as possible:

Sing these examples with and without accompaniment and try to imagine the changes. It should be possible, over time, to develop an inner sense for harmonic movement even though you are only singing single notes. Experienced musicians can actually hear more than is being played. They can hear a B♭ and visualise it as part of an E♭maj7 or as the first note of "There Will Never Be Another You". One isolated note can spark the inner image of a chord, a melody, a harmonic sequence or even a complete piece of music. In the same way, we are able to use individual voices as a starting point when visualising a chord progression. This means we can, in fact, hear other parts in our mind in addition to the lines we are singing or playing: the bass line, the vertical chord structures, tensions, etc. – in other words, a "cloud of sound" triggered only by a sequence of single notes.

Once a key has been established, the ear automatically anticipates the most likely resolution of any dominant seventh chord. Our listening habits prevail, even if the dominant seventh chord does *not* resolve the way we expect it to. In contrast to traditional chord progressions, where dominants almost invariably resolve as predicted, we find a much less restricted way of dealing with dominant seventh chords in modern compositions. Basically, *all* secondary or substitute dominants can be *randomly* approached and resolved. *But this doesn't change their function or sound in relation to the key!* The functional significance of a dominant is not bypassed simply because it appears or is resolved unexpectedly. It is the composer's choice either to satisfy the "norm" or to toy with the expectations of the listener by using unexpected harmonic turns (e.g. deceptive resolutions) in order to introduce an element of surprise or to create tension. This play on expectations is a common compositional device that does not change the fundamental quality of a dominant.

However, there are dominant seventh chords that have freed themselves from their original functions and their inclination to resolve. Specifically, I7, IV7 and ♭VII7 often appear as independent colours (notice the use of degree symbols rather than cadence symbols, suggesting that these sounds have little or no inclination to resolve). We will get to know these functions later in the chapters "Modal Interchange" and "Blues".

Assignment

Analyse the following dominant chords in relation to their respective keys. Determine their function and write down the scale that most strongly relates to the key. Name the scales and parenthesise avoid notes if they occur:

Analyse the following chord progression. Determine functions and scales:

1.

‖: Ab△7 | ∕. | Db7 | ∕. | Ab△7 | ∕. | C−7 | F7 |

| Bb−7 | ∕. | Gb7 | ∕. | Bb−7 | Eb7 | C7 B7 | E7 A7 :‖

2.

| Eb−7 | Ab7 | D7 | Db△7 | C−7 | Cb7 | Bb7 | A7 | Ab△7 | ∕. ‖

Secondary and Substitute II-Vs

As we've seen, any diatonic function can be approached by means of a dominant seventh chord (V7 or SubV). In a second step, any dominant can be preceded by a corresponding –7 or –7(♭5) chord. This "extends" the secondary or substitute dominant, forming a II-V pattern, thereby creating a second functional "layer", which can expand the diatonic framework dramatically without actually leaving it altogether.

Secondary II-V progressions

Let's start with secondary II-V patterns (in B♭ Major):

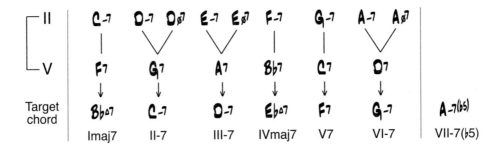

As with secondary dominants, VIIø7 can be disregarded as a diatonic target chord. In accordance with their respective diatonic resolutions, the various II-V progressions are labelled as II-V/II, II-V/III, II-V/IV, etc.

Diatonic minor functions (II–7, III–7, VI–7) are often approached by the minor cadence IIø7 - V7 rather than by II–7 - V7, the latter being more appropriate for target chords with a major quality (in the key of B♭ Major):

II-V / II **D**–7(♭5) **G**7 **C**–7 (II-7)

II-V / III **E**–7(♭5) **A**7 **D**–7 (III-7)

II-V / VI **A**–7(♭5) **D**7 **G**–7 (VI-7)

The minor cadences II-V/III and II-V/VI are more frequently used because of their tonal coherence: E–7(♭5) (♯IVø7) and A–7(♭5) (VIIø7) relate more closely to the key of B♭ Major than E–7 and A–7. Inversely, with II-V/II the D–7 (III–7) is the more suitable choice from a diatonic point of view, whereas Dø7 (IIIø7) works against the tonality:

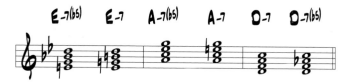

Let's take a look at an eight-bar phrase in which all secondary II-V patterns are linked to form a typical chord progression:

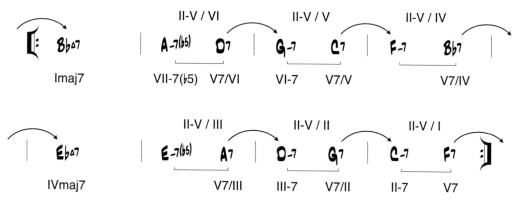

The non-diatonic II–7 and II–7(♭5) chords in this analysis have not been given functional labels. It is sufficient to see them as part of the II-V pattern. On the other hand, it would be possible (and useful to the ear) to, for example, label Eø7 as ♯IV–7(♭5) or F–7 as V–7, thus specifying the scale degrees on which the sounds occurs.

At this point, I'd like to emphasise the importance of thinking about tonal relationships in more comprehensive terms. The above analysis may seem to be pedantic, but it shows that even complex chord progressions can be seen within a broader tonal context. You could, on the other hand, interpret every II-V pattern as an isolated harmonic phrase with its own tonal centre. The analysis would then look like this:

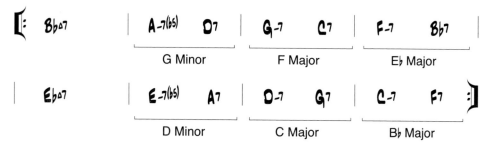

This is, of course, nonsense! A new key in almost every bar? Those who follow this line of thinking will improvise in the same way. The result would be no more than melodic patch-work instead of an integral flowing line. In addition, we would end up playing Dorian on each and every one of the II–7 chords. Sadly, there are teachers who endorse this approach. However, even if this may seem to be a welcome simplification for beginners, it does no justice to the minor 7th functions that are diatonic to the key (notably III–7 and VI–7):

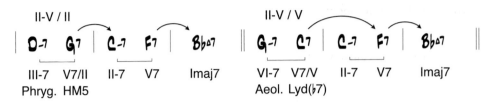

II-V / II					II-V / V				
III-7	V7/II	II-7	V7	Imaj7	VI-7	V7/V	II-7	V7	Imaj7
Phryg.	HM5				Aeol.	Lyd(♭7)			

A good example is the A section of "One Note Samba" (Antonio Carlos Jobim). Because of the unmistakeable tonality (B♭ Major) outlined by the melody, consisting only of the fifth (F) and the root (B♭) of the key, the D–7 must be played as the IIIrd degree (Phrygian), despite the fact that the chord progression starts on this sound and it is not yet apparent that the whole piece is in B♭ Major. The purpose and diatonic relevance of the D–7 becomes obvious as soon as the phrase is repeated and resolved to B♭maj7 in bar 8:

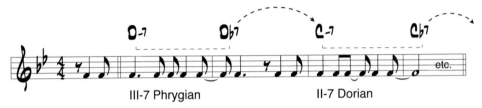

This doesn't mean, though, that you can't play Dorian over a III–7 chord as part of II-V/II. A good example of this is "Satin Doll" (Duke Ellington). Here, Dorian presents itself as the more suitable option for III–7 because of the obvious sequential nature of the melody (shift of the entire two-bar phrase up a whole step). The ensuing dominant should be Mixolydian in both cases – seen as a continuation of the preceding Dorian minor chord. As a consequence, E–7 (Dorian) and A7 (Mixolydian) support the melodic principle (sequence) but work against the key to a certain extent (in C Major):

So, to sum things up, here are the preferred scale choices for secondary II-V progressions:

- Non-diatonic II–7 chords are **Dorian**.
- IIø7 chords are **Locrian**.
- Diatonic II–7 chords are played according to their function in the overall key.

We don't have to concern ourselves with the dominant seventh chords. Their tonal material complies with the scales we have already established for secondary dominants.

An interesting thing about secondary II-V progressions is that they can influence the subsequent diatonic resolution and its tonal material. Let's take the II-V/IV in B♭ Major as an example. In this case, the tonal material of the II-V progression is extended into the following target chord (IVmaj7) and turns what would normally be a Lydian function into an Ionian sound:

We could therefore establish the following rule: If approached directly by Imaj7 (or any other diatonic function), IVmaj7 continues to be Lydian. On the other hand, if IVmaj7 is preceded by a cadence (V7/IV or II-V/IV), the function is more likely to be Ionian.

The important thing is that, for every secondary II-V progression, you should know of at least one composition that shows the use of this particular sound. This will help your ear to integrate it as part of your musical language. Here are a few examples. Bear in mind that, in some cases, the II-chord of the II-V pattern can be either –7 or –7(♭5):

II-V/II

- The II-chord usually corresponds to **III–7** because it is the diatonic option (can be heard in nearly every closing turnaround).

- Less often heard with **III–7(♭5)**: e.g. in "Desafinado" or "Black Orpheus" (analyse the latter composition in the relative major key).

II-V/III

- Often appears with **♯IV–7(♭5)** because it is the more diatonic sound: e.g. in "Stella By Starlight" and "The Days Of Wine And Roses".

- Very rarely heard with **#IV–7** because it clashes with the key: e.g. in "Misty" (B section) and "Summer Samba" (without its expected resolution)

II-V/IV

- A very common sound (to be found in almost every piece in this book!): e.g. in "Stella By Starlight" and "There Will Never Be Another You".

II-V/V

- Usually interpreted as **VI–7 - II7**, this is a progression found in every other standard: e.g. "There Will Never Be Another You".

II-V/VI

- Very common with **VII–7(♭5)**: e.g. "A Child Is Born", "There Will Never Be Another You", "Parker Blues", etc.

- Rarely used with **VII–7.**

Assignment

I didn't mention a composition for VII–7 (as part of II-V/VI). Your assignment is to find an example yourself. In addition, look for at least one more composition for each of the other secondary II-V patterns.

Secondary Sub(II-V) progressions

Substitute dominants can also be "extended" to form II-V patterns (in C Major):

	SubII	A♭–7	B♭–7	C–7	D♭–7	E♭–7	F–7	
		↓	↓	↓	↓	↓	↓	
	SubV	D♭7	E♭7	F7	G♭7	A♭7	B♭7	
		↓	↓	↓	↓	↓	↓	
Target chord		C△7	D–7	E–7	F△7	G7	A–7	B–7(♭5)
		Imaj7	II-7	III-7	IVmaj7	V7	VI-7	VII-7(♭5)

With Sub(II-V) progressions, it is no longer necessary to make a distinction between the major or minor quality of the target chord. Sub(II-V) patterns are sometimes so far removed from the tonality that the choice of how we treat them depends solely on the general sound of a II-V. Here is an example of the typical use of Sub(II-V)s in the key of C Major:

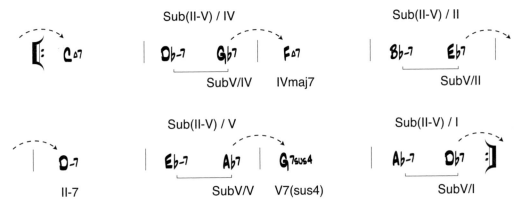

Sub(II-V) progressions sound quite unusual. Although they rarely appear in traditional compositions, they play an important role in modern improvisation – as we'll see later.

A few words on the improvisational material for Sub(II-V) patterns: Because they often deviate strongly from the diatonic framework, we can practically ignore tonal considerations when choosing what to play. The II–7 chords are therefore usually played as *Dorian* – following the scale principle of II-V patterns. When it comes to the dominant seventh chords, we could work along the lines of the substitute dominants we have already talked about: They are either Lydian(♭7) or Altered. But! – since a II-V progression is heard as a unit, the II–7 has an immediate and profound effect on the subsequent dominant. Accordingly, V7 would rather be Mixolydian (e.g. A♭–7 - D♭7 in C Major):

As a rule, the scales we derived for substitute dominants – Lydian(♭7) and/or Altered – apply only if the SubV appears on its own and is not part of a Sub(II-V) progression.

Considering all possible permutations of secondary II-V and Sub(II-V) patterns, we can see that we now have four II-V options at our disposal:

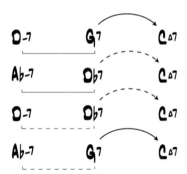

The cadential effect is basically the same for all four possibilities. The differences lie only in the movement of the root (resolving down a fifth or chromatically) and the extent in which the pattern deviates from the tonality. As shown above, I will use solid arrows for dominant seventh chords resolving down a perfect fifth, solid brackets for II-V patterns, dashed arrows for dominant seventh chords resolving down a half step and dashed brackets for II-SubV patterns over the course of this book when analysing chord progressions.

Assignment

To finish off this chapter, here's a bit of a brainteaser: Translate the following diagram into a real chord progression. The C7 and the functions are given as points of reference. Be sure to begin by determining the tonality first:

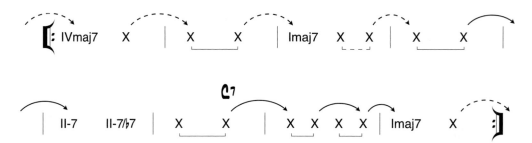

Diminished Seventh Chords

Every four-note diminished seventh chord consists of two interlinked tritones:

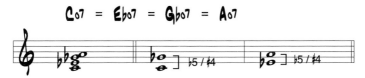

The two notes of a tritone can be interpreted as either 3/♭7 or ♭7/3 of a dominant seventh chord. This allows us to relate any tritone to two different roots. The two resulting dominants are a V7 and its corresponding SubV. Taking both tritones, we can translate any four-note diminished seventh chord into four different dominants (please note that enharmonic spelling is inevitable when dealing with diminished chords):

If one tritone of a diminished chord is seen as 3 and ♭7 of a dominant, the other tritone automatically gives us 5 and ♭9 of the same dominant chord. This means that every diminished seventh chord can be interpreted as a 7(♭9) chord with four different roots (again watch out for enharmonics):

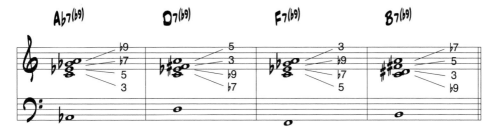

This means that the root of any diminished seventh chord always functions either as the 3, 5, ♭7 or ♭9/♭2 of a dominant seventh chord. As a result, any diminished seventh chord can replace 4 different dominant chords and resolve in 4 different directions.

Confused? Let's see if we can clear up the mess. Before looking at the table further down, consider the following facts:

- Because of their symmetrical structure (they are made up of minor thirds exclusively), there are only three groups of diminished chords. Have a look at p. 44 for a reminder. All chords within each group contain the same notes (e.g. C°7 = D#°7 = F#°7 = A°7). By shifting the notes of a four-note diminished chord up a half step or a whole step, you get the other two groups. Shifting all notes up a minor third results in the same material and just gives you an inversion of the original chord.

- Within each group, any diminished chord can replace any one of the corresponding dominants. So, C°7 can replace Ab7, B7, D7 and F7 (the same holds true for D#°7, F#°7 or A°7, the other three members of the same group). Again, enharmonic spelling is a must.

- Because any diminished chord can replace 4 different dominants, it can consequently resolve to any one of 4 possible target roots. For example, C°7 (replacing Ab7, B7, D7 or F7) can theoretically resolve to Db, E, G and Bb (as can D#°7, F#°7 or A°7, the other members of the group). In practice, however, the root of a diminished chord is most commonly interpreted as the 3rd of the corresponding dominant. The diminished chord then resolves **up a half step** to the target chord (e.g. C°7 replaces Ab7 and re-solves to Db).

This being said, here's the table. Only the roots of the target chords are given because diminished chords can resolve to any chord type:

C°7	Ab7 → Db	C#°7	A7 → D	D°7	Bb7 → Eb
D#°7	B7 → E	E°7	C7 → F	F°7	Db7 → Gb
F#°7	D7 → G	G°7	Eb7 → Ab	G#°7	E7 → A
A°7	F7 → Bb	A#°7	F#7 → B	B°7	G7 → C

Assignment

Let's see if you've grasped the concept. Here are 24 resolutions. Please mark them either true (✓) or false (x). Translate each diminished chord into the 4 corresponding dominants and check if one of these dominants and the given target chord form a V-I relationship. If you have to, refer back to the table, but I'd prefer you work out the answers in your head before taking a peek in the solutions folder.

F°7 → A–7	Db°7 → Fmaj7	A°7 → D7	B°7 → Ebmaj7
G°7 → E7	Eb°7 → D–7	G#°7 → Cmaj7	E°7 → G–7
C°7 → Bb7	D°7 → Amaj7	Bb°7 → G–7	F#°7 → C#7
B°7 → Fmaj7	A°7 → C7	C#°7 → Amaj7	F°7 → Eb–7
E°7 → A–7	Ab°7 → Gbmaj7	D#°7 → E–7	G°7 → Db7
Gb°7 → Bb7	A#°7 → G–7	D°7 → F#maj7	C°7 → G7

Many resolutions that involve diminished chords create bass lines that are rather awkward (e.g. G°7 → Bmaj7: Though possible, the root movement is rarely found in practice). It is therefore no coincidence that in the table on p. 164 the root of each diminished chord is the 3rd of the dominant chord it is paired up with. As already mentioned above, this reflects the fundamental concept governing most diminished chord functions. In a nutshell, a diminished chord corresponds to a 1st inversion 7(♭9) chord (= 3rd in the bass), which – following the leading tone principle – chromatically resolves up to the root of the target chord. Here's an example:

$$C\sharp°7 = A7(\flat 9)/C\sharp \quad \rightarrow \quad Dmaj7, D{-}7, D7$$

Diminished chord functions

Diminished chords usually appear as connecting elements between neighbouring diatonic functions. They replace secondary dominants and allow for chromatically **ascending** bass lines as opposed to the descending bass lines characteristic of secondary and substitute dominants.

Let's take a look at the most important functions (in F Major):

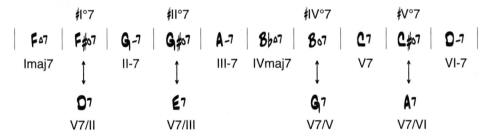

Here's the summary:

♯I°7	replaces	V7/II
♯II°7	replaces	V7/III
♯IV°7	replaces	V7/V
♯V°7	replaces	V7/VI

In practice, we find two additional resolutions for ♯II°7 and ♯IV°7 that employ the same chromatic voice leading in the bass:

G-7	G♯°7	F△7/A		B♭△7	B°7	F△7/C
II-7	♯II°7	Imaj7/3		IVmaj7	♯IV°7	Imaj7/5

A good example of the functions ♯I°7 and ♯II°7 is "Once I Loved" by Antonio Carlos Jobim:

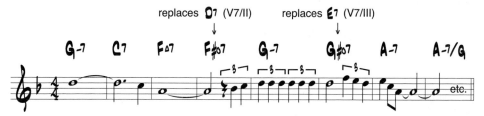

We rarely find ♯IV°7 and ♯V°7 in Jazz standards, but they are almost seminal to Gospel and Blues. The following common chord progressions show the traditional use of these two functions with the triad-based harmony typical to these styles:

Listen to **tracks 31** and **32**. All diminished seventh functions we have talked about so far are on these tracks.

One of the few situations in which we find ♯IV°7 in Jazz is in bars 25–29 of Frank Churchill's "Someday My Prince Will Come":

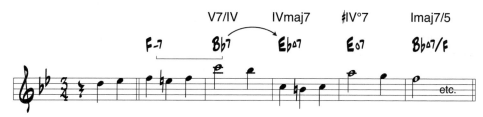

In the first few bars of "I Remember Clifford" by Benny Golson, we encounter the ascending chromatic movement from IVmaj7 via ♯IV°7 to V7 and ♯V°7 to VI–7:

The diminished functions discussed up to this point introduce what I like to call *functional chromaticism* to the diatonic environment by linking diatonic functions chromatically. There are, however, two diminished functions that are less conspicuous because, unlike ♯I°7, ♯II°7, ♯IV°7 and ♯V°7, their roots occur on diatonic degrees: III°7 (replaces V7/IV) and VII°7 (replaces V7/I). This doesn't alter the fact that they, too, appear as chromatically ascending functions: III°7 → IVmaj7 and VII°7 → Imaj7. There is no real need to go into more detail concerning these two sounds because they occur all the time – not necessarily as part of the changes but as passing chords created by the bass playing the leading tone when approaching the root of the target chord. Here's an example (in F Major): Fmaj7 - F7 - F7(♭9)/A - B♭maj7 can be heard as Fmaj7 - F7 - A°7 - B♭maj7 because of the bass line.

Scales for diminished chord functions

Since we are dealing with symmetrical structures when it comes to diminished seventh chords, we should also look for symmetry in the improvisational material. This is achieved by uniformly filling in the gaps between the notes of the chords either with half steps or whole steps. What we end up with are two symmetrical scale forms: Whole-tone-half-tone (WTHT) and Half-tone-whole-tone (HTWT):

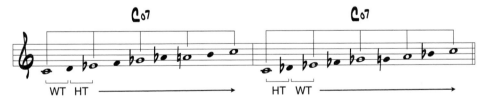

While HTWT has become one of the most important sounds used with dominant chords (see the discussion on the 8-note dominant scale on pages 131 ff.), it is the WTHT scale that has established itself as the best working option for diminished seventh chords (I'll explain why in just a second). For this reason, WTHT is also referred to as the *Symmetric diminished* scale, clearly linking it to diminished chord functions.

It is easy to understand why WTHT is the more appropriate scale for diminished chords than HTWT. Since the non-chord tones in WTHT create 2/9 intervals with the chord tones, they can all be used as tensions. In HTWT, on the other hand, all passing notes form ♭2/♭9 relationships with the chord tones. This means that they are extremely dissonant (too dissonant within the rather traditional sound of a diminished chord) and have to be treated as avoid notes (remember: Every note a half step above a chord tone is an avoid note):

As stated above, all non-chord tones of WTHT are available tensions. Let's have a look at the way they are applied. Of course, we could simply add tensions to the basic four-note structure, consequently creating 5-note, 6-note, 7-note or even 8-note voicings. Duke Ellington, for example, was known for a voicing technique commonly referred to as "combination diminished". Because WTHT is a symmetric scale, the tensions also add up to a diminished four-note chord, as shown in the table above. By combining two diminished chords – e.g. F°7 (the basic chord) in the trombones and E°7 (the tensions, voiced as an inversion of G°7) in the trumpets – Ellington created brass voicings with a beautiful buzz, each tension paired up with a chord tone by a maj7 interval. Play it on the piano and find out for yourself.

How do we add tensions to diminished chords while retaining the four-note structure of the harmony? This is usually achieved by substituting a chord tone with an adjacent tension, usually the one a whole step above. Here are a few examples (don't forget enharmonic equivalents):

Of course, any voice (or more than one chord tone) can be replaced with tensions:

Apart from the WTHT scale, which is a functionally independent scale for *any* diminished seventh chord, there is an alternative for most diminished functions that relates more closely to the tonal environment. In this case, notes taken from the key signature are used in addition to the chord tones to fill in the gaps. Let's look at the function ♯I°7 (F♯°7) in F Major as an example:

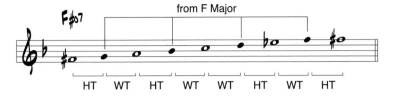

The in-between notes taken from F Major outline a G–7 chord and anticipate the expected resolution of F♯°7. The resultant scale is obviously no longer symmetrical, but it does relate more closely to the tonal centre and – more importantly – to the dominant that was replaced by the diminished seventh chord. In this example, the F♯°7 chord takes the place of D7 (V7/II). If we rewrite the same scale material starting on the note D, the relationship becomes apparent:

The result is HM5(+♯9), the most common sound for V7/II (see secondary dominants). Using WTHT for F♯°7 also works, but it would create much more tension. Be aware of the following correlation when looking at F♯°7 and D7 in the key of F Major:

D7 HTWT (8-note dominant) = F♯°7 WTHT (Symmetric diminished)

So, as a general rule, if a diminished chord is WTHT, the corresponding dominant is HTWT. Considering the fact that HTWT (8-note dominant) is a special colour for all dominant functions, the same must hold true for any diminished chord played WTHT (Symmetric diminished). We've already talked about the difficulties in coming to grips with 8-note dominant from a player's point of view. The more comfortable you are with 8-note dominant, the easier it will be to handle WTHT, and vice versa.

The same considerations apply to all other diminished seventh functions resolving to minor chords. In addition to ♯I°7 (replacing V7/II and resolving to II–7), we also have ♯II°7 (replacing V7/III and resolving to III–7) and ♯V°7 (replacing V7/VI and resolving to VI–7). In these three cases, we can assign the notes of HM5(+♯9) – as the standard scale for the secondary dominants mentioned above – to their corresponding diminished functions. The fact that we are relating the same notes to two different roots is irrelevant when considering the resulting sound. Both functions – the secondary dominant and its diminished replacement – ultimately resolve to the same target chord and can therefore be associated with the same scale material.

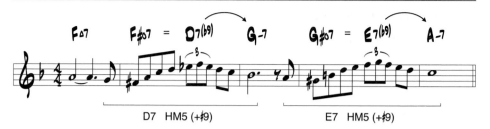

$\sharp$IV°7 (replacing V7/V and resolving to V7) is the exception. Because V7/V is most often played as Mixolydian or Lydian($\flat$7), HM5(+$\sharp$9) would be rather out of place. This is why we usually use WTHT for $\sharp$IV°7.

In conclusion, there are two options:

- We could use WTHT regardless of function and apply it to any diminished chord. Please remember, however, that this creates the same deviations from the tonality as would be the case when using HTWT with dominant functions.

- We could pick the tonal option and go for HM5(+$\sharp$9) of the substituted secondary dominant. As explained above, this works well with $\sharp$I°7, $\sharp$II°7 and $\sharp$V°7 because the corresponding dominants tend to be played as HM5/Altered. The same goes for III°7 (replaces V7/IV) and VII°7 (replaces V7). Even though the corresponding dominants are normally Mixolydian (the most "inside" sound), it is also quite common to use HM5/Altered. Again, the exception is $\sharp$IV°7 because V7/V can only be played as Mixolydian or Lydian($\flat$7) – HM5 would be highly unusual.

Either approach will work equally well. However, WTHT would be the option that creates more tension and is more difficult to handle.

Descending diminished chord functions

To round off this chapter, I would like to go into a couple of special cases where the relationship between the diminished chord and a corresponding dominant is not that obvious.

$\flat$III°7

In contrast to the other diminished functions we have talked about, this one resolves *downwards* (this is also suggested by the functional notation). $\flat$III°7 resolves to II–7. The B section of "Someday My Prince Will Come" (bars 9–16) shows this harmonic relationship nicely:

♭III°7 can be interpreted in the following two ways:

- As a deceptive resolution of ♯II°7 (= ♭III°7);

- As an inversion of ♯IV°7 (same chord tones) whose resolution to V7 is delayed by the insertion of II–7.

Personally, I find the second option more convincing. Have a look at the following two progressions (in F Major):

Since C7(sus4) can also be written as G–7/C (see p. 425 ff.), it actually makes sense to interpret ♭III°7 as an inversion of ♯IV°7 with the bass line moving in a different direction. B°7 (♯IV°7) resolving up to C7 and A♭°7 (♭III°7) resolving down to G–7 (II–7) are two interpretations of the same chord progression (A–7 is a tonic substitute for Fmaj7). So, when it comes to descending diminished functions, we're not just simply dealing with a case of chromatically inserted passing chords but rather with sounds that still maintain a clear relationship with dominant seventh chords, though in a less obvious way than ascending diminished functions.

♭VI°7

This function also resolves chromatically by downward bass movement. The target resolution can be any chord on the fifth degree of the key – for instance V7, Imaj7/5 or V–7 (as part of a II-V/IV progression). The latter (♭VI°7 resolving to V–7) is most common. An example of this is the beginning of "Wave" by Antonio Carlos Jobim:

We can analyse ♭VI°7 either as a deceptive resolution of ♯V°7 (= ♭VI°7) or – more likely – as a reinterpretation of V7(♭9). We can use the same approach as we did for ♭III°7: In "Wave" the B♭°7 sounds like a substitute for A7(♭9) resolving to D7(sus4) = A–7/D, which is reinterpreted as a II-V/IV progression (A–7 - D7 - Gmaj7).

The interesting thing about ♭III°7 and ♭VI°7 is the fact that they are the only descending diminished chord functions, the reason being that both are part of a set cadential progression, which only occurs in conjunction with two diatonic target chords – Imaj7 and IVmaj7 (in D Major):

F♯–7	F°7	E–7	A7	Dmaj7		B–7	B♭°7	A–7	D7	Gmaj7
III–7	♭III°7	II–7	V7	Imaj7		VI–7	♭VI°7	V–7	V7/IV	IVmaj7

As you can see, both chord progressions are identical with regard to root movement and chord types.

Diminished chord functions without root movement

In addition to diminished chords resolving chromatically, there are functions that resolve without any root movement, the most prominent example being I°7. This is how it occurs in Richard Rodgers' "Spring Is Here":

The chord symbol A♭°, chosen deliberately instead of A♭°7, indicates that the chord tone F is replaced by the tension G in the melody.

The theme of "Donna Lee" by Charlie Parker serves as a good example of how this harmonic principle also applies melodically (bar 28):

How do we account for this functional relationship? As with ♭III°7 and ♭VI°7 we have to take a small mental leap and interpret I°7 as an inversion of ♯II°7 whose expected resolution to the tonic function III–7 is replaced by Imaj7.

In the meantime, this progression has established itself so strongly in the repertoire of most Jazz musicians that I°7 is often inserted as a spontaneously played preparation for Imaj7, even if it doesn't appear in the original changes. Here are two examples (the first two bars of "Misty" and "On A Clear Day"):

In both cases, the appearance of the tonic chord is delayed by insertion of the diminished function I°7. In a broader sense, this can be interpreted as a suspension of Imaj7.

Because ♭III°7, ♭VI°7 and I°7 are less obviously tied to dominant functions, they are almost exclusively played as WTHT.

Modal Harmony

"The music has gotten thick, guys give me tunes and they're full of chords. I can't play them ... I think a movement in Jazz is beginning away from the conventional string of chords, and a return to emphasis on melodic rather than harmonic variation. There will be fewer chords but infinite possibilities as to what to do with them."

Miles Davis, 1958

During the 1950s, Jazz underwent a period of dramatic change. At the same time as Bebop was evolving into its more aggressive form, *Hard Bop*, something else was being born as its antithesis – *Cool Jazz*. Soloists such as Miles Davis and arrangers like Gil Evans belonged to the first proponents of this new ideal, deliberately separating themselves from the extrovert mainstream of the time. While Hard Bop was characterised by the open display of virtuosity, extreme tempi and high-strung, frantic phrases, Cool Jazz was the epitome of understatement and restrained, controlled intensity – ascetic, intellectual, even seemingly cold.

From a historical point of view, the central work heralding the appearance of this new development was undoubtedly the album "Birth of the Cool", masterminded and recorded by Miles Davis in 1949/50. For the first time, spontaneous improvised music was deliberately structured and channelled through composition. Improvisation, arrangement and composition flowed seamlessly into one-another with the soloist's function being a subordinate part of the overall concept of the piece, bowing to the whims of the composer. Groundbreaking ensembles such as the *Modern Jazz Quartet*, the *Gerry Mulligan Quartet* and even larger ensembles such as the *Gil Evans Orchestra* evolved out of this initial project, characterised by the subtle play on colours and delicately crafted sonic landscapes.

In Cool Jazz, we come across for the first time what is known as *modal composition*. The emergence of this approach can be described as a reaction to the increasingly complex chord progressions heard in Bebop and Hard Bop. Two famous pieces highlight this stylistic transition: "Giant Steps" by John Coltrane (on the album by the same name) and "So What" by Miles Davis (on "Kind of Blue"). Recorded almost simultaneously ("So What" on 22 April 1959, "Giant Steps" on 15 August 1959), they clearly embody two highly antithetical approaches to composition and improvisation.

"Giant Steps", with its fast tempo, rapid chord changes and sudden modulations, is *the* typical example of a composition in which improvisation is increasingly dominated by the chord progression and where the melody is in danger of merely being a subordinate accessory to the harmony. The tune is deceptively simple – consisting of nothing but V-I and II-V-I relationships. The frequent modulations, however, make this chord progression incredibly difficult to improvise on (you can hear the pianist Tommy Flanagan hanging on for dear life on the original recording). Even today, there are but few Jazz musicians who are capable of soloing competently on this piece, of "playing the changes" and at the same time creating melodically convincing lines, without being hampered or inhibited by the convoluted harmony. The danger of being caught up in an artistic dead-end street is all too present when dealing with tunes that force the soloist to fall back on mechanistic, rote-learned fingerings and set patterns. Here's the lead sheet for this both challenging and highly innovative piece:

In contrast, "So What" was the first and probably best-known representative of a group of compositions taking a radically different route, which dispensed almost entirely with chord progressions in the conventional sense and, instead, attempted to give the individual sound more room to unfold. Despite its simplicity, "So What" was downright revolutionary. It helped lead Jazz away from harmonically overloaded and cluttered compositions and a vertical, chord-based way of thinking that slavishly focussed on the changes. The new concept favoured a more horizontal approach with an emphasis on melodic shape, indulgence in sound and modality (thus the term "modal"). As a result, improvisations were more transparent and – following the axiom "less means more" – gave higher priority to timbral shading and motivic development, reinforcing the expressive and creative potential of the musicians.

Let's have a look at the structure of "So What". The form is AABA (32 bars) subdivided into four eight-bar sections. Here's the A section:

The tonality (root) is D. The mode (scale) used is Dorian. The A section is exclusively in D Dorian. The B section is an upward chromatic shift of the A section to E♭ Dorian (you can see that the pick-up notes leading into the B section in the second ending already suggest E♭).

D Dorian	D Dorian	E♭ Dorian	D Dorian
8	8	8	8

Here are the first 16 bars of Miles Davis' solo:

How simple, straightforward and unpretentious, but how impressive and convincing! This improvisation breathes in a completely different way from the solo on "Giant Steps" (see

p. 568). While the eighth-note lines aggressively carve their way through the harmony in "Giant Steps", the solo on "So What" thrives on an initial motivic idea that is calmly and cautiously developed, soaring higher and higher from phrase to phrase and returning to the starting point in a compellingly shaped melodic arc. Where Coltrane hardly allows the listener (or himself) to catch one's breath, Miles Davis plays with a relaxed feel, allowing rests, pauses and space to take on musical importance.

Staple tunes such as "So What" initiated what is generally associated with the term "modality". It becomes evident just how widespread this perception is – even to this day – when I ask my students how they relate to the concept of modal Jazz. Here are some of the catchwords and phrases they invariably come up with:

- church modes;

- 50s and 60s Cool Jazz;

- no chord progressions or functional harmony;

- improvisation on one scale;

- open sounds, quartal harmony (voicings in fourths).

Based on "So What", these observations, of course, are quite accurate. Dorian is a church mode. "Kind of Blue" is seen as one of the key recordings of the Cool Jazz era. There are no chord progressions in the traditional sense of the word ("soundscapes" would provide a better description). The improvisations are based on one scale type and the harmonic material is predominantly structured in layers of fourths rather than thirds.

And yet, these initial compositional attempts are worlds apart from what has happened modally since then. "So What" must be seen as the starting point of a significantly wider-reaching evolutionary process. I'd like to try and trace this development in the course of this chapter.

Modal soundscapes – the "new simplicity"

Initially – as is so often the case – things were taken a bit too far. Recordings appeared, featuring players improvising over the same basic modal colour for hours on end. Compositions often consisted of no more than a bass ostinato (repeated bass pattern) to which a simple theme was played. On the other hand, this reduction to an elementary modal approach now seems to have been essential in order to purge Jazz of its over-cooked harmonies.

Have another listen to **tracks 1–11**. They will give you some insight into how beautiful modal soundscapes can be. Enjoy the sense of calm and coherence they radiate compared to pieces where the harmony is busier. Of course, you're not really hearing anything new. Most of these are familiar sounds, albeit approached from a different angle. For instance, take the Phrygian scale (track 6), which is actually something you've known about and used for some time. Now, however, we're no longer talking about a traditional functional context, where Phrygian is linked to the third degree in a major key (III–7). Here, we're experiencing the Phrygian mode as a colour in its own right.

Avoid notes

At this point, we have to review the concept of "avoid notes". It should be evident that the concept of avoid notes, as we have already learned, is restricted to a specific context. Up until now, we have assigned a scale to a chord depending on its function within a key. In this context, certain notes are considered to be disruptive for tonal reasons. Now we are looking at the same scale freed of its functional constraints. As a result, what used to be an avoid note within the functional environment assumes a vital role and becomes the exact opposite – the very sound that characterises the scale! Again, let's take Phrygian as an example: While the ♭2/♭9 is an avoid note when used in conjunction with III–7, it is precisely *the* note that most distinctly distinguishes Phrygian from most other minor modes. So, if we need to express the unique colour of a mode, we have to incorporate *all* notes of the scale, which includes what has been previously defined as avoid notes.

The same is true for modal voicings. They have to include the avoid notes if they are to convey the essential flavour of the mode. Here are a few examples of voicings that represent the characteristics of each of the church modes (accidentals apply only to each chord – the lowest note is always the root):

Following up on our discussion of the church modes on p. 63 and their colour gradation, ranging from Lydian (bright) to Locrian (dark), let's look at a series of chords that shows the progressive darkening as we move through the modes. Each chord contains the characteristic note of the corresponding scale and resolves to the next chord with smooth voice leading:

Modal vamps

The next significant step in the historical development of modal Jazz was to combine various modalities. It was popular to improvise over **vamps** (a harmonic "loop" repeated many times). In the modal context, this was less about a specific chord progression than working with a series of "episodes", each in a particular mode. Here's an example of an eight-bar modal vamp:

The root stays the same while the modal colour changes. Notice how the mood of the vamp evolves from bright (Lydian) to dark (Locrian). We will see that this kind of play on colour is an important concept used in composition.

Of course, it is possible to change not only modalities but also tonalities. A good example of this is "Flamenco Sketches" (also on the album "Kind of Blue") – a ballad without a theme (!) consisting of a series of improvisations over mostly four-bar modal sections:

The accompaniment is based on the given chord symbols, but additional diatonic colours are used from each scale to create movement. Over the Cmaj7 (Ionian), for example, the piano randomly switches to D–7, Ab7(sus4) is alternately played as Ab7, etc. Whereas the structure is maintained throughout the first two solos (4-4-4-8-4), it gradually disintegrates during the ensuing improvisations. The form is expanded; four-bar sections are repeated spontaneously. In one case – at the end of John Coltrane's solo – we can even hear G–7 played as a five-bar phrase.

In this piece, it is only in parts possible to identify functional relationships between the various colours. Whereas Cmaj7, Ab7(sus4) and Bbmaj7 are unrelated, we could indeed talk about a functional progression when analysing Bbmaj7, D7(b9/b13) and G–7: Imaj7 - V7/VI - VI–7. It is worth noting that during John Coltrane's and Miles Davis' solos all sounds are 4 bars long – with the exception of D7, which is always 8 bars! Dominant seventh chords, of course, want to resolve, and the ear expects D7 to cadence to G–7, which it does. It is therefore a clever compositional device to "stretch" the D7. This counterbalances its cadential effect and stabilises it, so that it can be heard as a sound in its own right and not as V7. As a result, it no longer interacts that strongly with the preceding and ensuing harmony.

On "Flamenco Scetches", we can hear that Cannonball Adderley is still having some difficulty adjusting to this new concept. He, of all people – the powerhouse of the alto saxophone, the master of fast runs – seems to have had quite a hard time playing "in scale" exclusively and limiting himself to the available diatonic material. Time and again, in his phrases, we hear the chromatic passing notes and approaches so typical to Bebop and Hard Bop. Though he manages to capture the lyrical quality of the recording in his improvisation, he obviously doesn't feel all that comfortable with the idiom and is in search of appropriate lines. In addition, the players are not entirely in agreement on the D7. Miles plays Phrygian (the major third of the sound only appears in the piano) while Coltrane clearly uses HM5(+♯9).

Functional modal harmony

This book was initially published in 2003. Since then it has been discussed in many forums by amateurs and professionals alike – something I find both flattering and amusing. Amusing, because some of these discussions are downright nasty and dogmatic – especially when it comes to dealing with the concept of *functional modal harmony*. I frequently come across the notion that modal Jazz (or the concept of "modality" in general) has nothing to do with actual chord progressions. There seems to be a general misconception that modality and functional harmony contradict each other and are mutually exclusive systems, which have to be dealt with separately. Mixing up the two is something that quite obviously displeases hardcore aficionados of this rather old-fashioned point of view. To be blunt – I thoroughly disagree, and music proves me right.

I firmly believe that terms and definitions are closely linked to their historical origin and that they only have importance and validity for a limited period of time. Church modes emerged around 600 AD – at a time where harmony did not yet exist. Functional harmony did not evolve until the 15th century and was subsequently almost exclusively tied to our major/minor system. Today, 1400 years later, church modes are again used in Jazz. But times have changed. So, let's get a few things straightened out and dismiss a fundamental misunderstanding!

Most theory books make a clear distinction between functional (chord-based) and modal (scale-based) compositions and concepts. What they seem to ignore, however, is that these are simply two different ways of looking at the same thing. After all, a mode defines the tonal material and not its organisation or the way it is applied. It is therefore beside the point whether we are talking about a melody or a chord progression – if either relates to any specific mode, they are both modal.

In the end, it all depends on how narrowly we define the term "modal". In my world of modality, there are indeed chord progressions, functions and cadences. Don't forget that a tune like "Silent Night" relates to the Major scale, not only because of the melody but also because of the harmony – and the Major scale is just as much a mode as any other. We have always lived with modality as a basis for the sounds we know. "Modal Harmony" is nothing special, but rather a natural part of our musical heritage. We all grew up with progressions in major (Ionian) and minor (Aeolian, HM, MM) keys. The actual problem is that we're simply not used to thinking in terms of "modality" when it comes to talking about major and minor.

Conversely, it is logical and valid to interpret church modes not just melodically but also harmonically. Why should Phrygian be treated differently from Ionian? Why should we think of harmonic functions and scale degrees within our Ionian/Aeolian system and discard this approach when dealing with other modes? To me, the labels "functional" and "modal" are not mutually exclusive. Quite the opposite – they are inseparable. In music today, most situations can and must be argued both from a functional and modal perspective.

Earlier on in this book, I made the assertion that "if we construct chords on the various degrees of *any* scale using only the notes belonging to this scale, we end up with a diatonic series of chords". From this, it should be clear that *every* mode provides us not only with a horizontal, melodic, aspect, but also with a vertical, harmonic, one. Accordingly, every mode has its own and unique functional harmony. Major and minor keys (modes) only cover a tiny part of the myriads of colours theoretically possible.

That said, let's have a look at the church modes, their diatonic functions and characteristic chord progressions. I have chosen the root C for all modes so that the similarities and differences are easy to see:

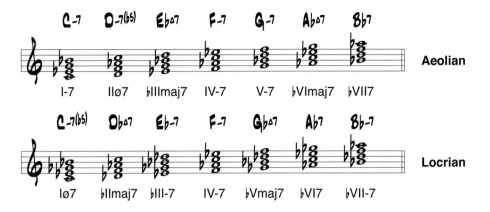

Of course, Locrian is only included for the sake of completing the table. This scale has never really established itself as an independent sound and a harmonic system of reference. The ø7 chord is far too unstable to act as an effective tonic.

Assignment

Write out the table of functions as shown above, starting on all possible roots. This is admittedly a lot of work, but it will help you become more flexible in your thinking.

Naturally, other scale forms can be investigated in the same way. Although I have had to limit this book to the church modes (the most commonly used sounds) for reasons of space, please remember that *each and every* scale has its own harmony. Let's take one of the more unusual modes and look at the chord structures it contains – HTWT (watch out for enharmonic notation):

Apart from the expected three-note or four-note diminished chords (a °7 chord can be found on every degree of the HTWT scale), we can extract a number of triads and four-note chords that are also diatonic ingredients of this scale. Here's the decisive point: Because the HTWT scale is symmetrical, with its structure repeating in minor thirds, all chord types derived from the root C must necessarily reappear based on the roots E♭, F♯ and A.

Of course, we cannot really speak of true functional harmony because of this scale's symmetry – a distinctive root is missing, which is needed in order to define functional

(= hierarchical) relationships. Nevertheless, there are a number of composers both in the Classical and Jazz worlds that have made good harmonic use of the HTWT scale (e.g. Olivier Messiaen, Charles Mingus, Duke Ellington, etc.). Listen to **track 10**, which is exclusively in HTWT. If you listen closely, you can hear two variations on how the scale is applied. On the one hand, you will hear HTWT used horizontally as a dominant scale (whenever the band turns on the heat). On the other hand, there are sections where the band seems to drift and the sounds have a more floating quality. Here, you hear harmonies taken from the scale, which, to some extent, relate to one-another functionally (even though, at times, this may be difficult for the less experienced ear to discern).

Modal cadences

Each mode has its own unique harmonic momentum; each contains tonic sounds, cadence chords and typical cadential phrases. We must, however, free ourselves from the notion that the usual major and minor cadences (V-I, IV-I, II-V-I, etc.) also apply to other modes. Each mode is subject to its own laws. Here are a few thoughts on the matter:

- Tonic sounds are functions that have a comparatively low energy level (little or no need to resolve). In addition to the tonic (I), this applies, of course, primarily to sounds on the IIIrd and/or VIth degrees. They form mediant relationships with the tonic and share many common tones.

- In contrast, functions on the IInd or VIIth degrees are almost always cadence chords because they have no notes in common with the tonic and therefore have a strong need to resolve. Stepwise movement is typical to modal cadences.

- The characteristic note of each mode is always involved in one of the half steps within the scale. Because the half step has the strongest tendency to resolve, it stands to reason that chords containing the characteristic note are cadential functions.

- Furthermore, we will experience all chords that generate the familiar major and minor cadence root movement (V-I and IV-I) as cadence functions.

- The –7(♭5) chord plays a rather special role in most cases. It is rarely used in a modal context because it contains a tritone (1/♭5), which would possibly confuse and even mislead the listener into hearing a different tonal centre.

- Seventh chords should also be treated with care. They, too, contain the tritone (although not quite as exposed as in the ø7 chord). In many cases, these functions are used in triadic form, avoiding the tritone between 3 and ♭7.

With these points in mind, let's have a look at the church modes and their typical cadences. The following functional progressions are presented in the form of four-note chords. But, please don't forget – especially within the context of modality – that triads are often used.

Dorian

I–7	II–7	♭IIImaj7	IV7	V–7	VIø7	♭VIImaj7
T	C	T	C	C	–	C

IV7 is a cadential function because we are so used to hearing IV-I as a fundamental cadence. The same applies to V–7. Although the function does not contain the mode's characteristic note, it does create a cadential feeling because of the root movement of a fifth. To sum things up, here are the typical cadences in Dorian (F Dorian):

I-7	II-7	I-7		I-7	IV7	I-7		I-7	V-7	I-7		I-7	♭VIIj7	I-7

‖ F-7 G-7 F-7 ‖ F-7 B♭7 F-7 ‖ F-7 C-7 F-7 ‖ F-7 E♭△7 F-7 ‖

Phrygian

I–7	♭IImaj7	♭III7	IV–7	Vø7	♭VImaj7	♭VII–7
T	C	(T)	C	(C)	C	C

♭III only sounds like a tonic function when used as a triad (a seventh chord would be too unstable). In addition, ♭III7 – when used in conjunction with ♭VImaj7 or IV–7 – would inevitably lead the ear to interpret this incorrectly as a V7 - Imaj7 cadence or the deceptive resolution V7 - VI–7 in Ionian. ♭VImaj7, even though it is related to the tonic as a mediant, is obviously a cadence function because the root of the chord (♭6 in the key) has a strong tendency to resolve to 5. Here are the common cadences in F Phrygian:

I-7	♭IIj7	I-7		I-7	IV-7	I-7		I-7	♭VIj7	I-7		I-7	♭VII-7	I-7

‖ F-7 G♭△7 F-7 ‖ F-7 B♭-7 F-7 ‖ F-7 D♭△7 F-7 ‖ F-7 E♭-7 F-7 ‖

   An interesting thing about Phrygian is the possibility of using V–7(♭5) as a cadence chord (V-I). It is very similar to an altered dominant (Locrian and Altered differ in only one note) and therefore conveys a strong feeling of resolution. The pianist McCoy Tyner, for instance, often uses this principle when playing over V7.

Lydian

Imaj7	II7	III–7	♯IVø7	Vmaj7	VI–7	VII–7
T	(C)	T	–	–	T	C

II is a good cadential function when used as a triad. II7, on the other hand, needs to be treated with caution because this sound – especially when used in combination with Vmaj7 (V-I in Ionian) and III–7 (deceptive resolution) – would immediately suggest Ionian cadences and divert the ear to the wrong tonic. V or Vmaj7 is problematic because this function corresponds to the Ionian tonic. Try as you might, it is almost impossible to interpret the chord progression Fmaj7 - Cmaj7 - Fmaj7 as I-V-I in F Lydian. The ear immediately switches to IV-I in C Ionian as the much more familiar sound. Find out for yourselves – as soon as you play Fmaj7 and Cmaj7 alternately, the ear will promptly turn to Cmaj7 as the tonic, despite your determined attempts to hear Fmaj7 as Imaj7. Lydian is probably the one mode that is hard to establish cadentially. On the one hand, it simply contains too few cadence functions that convincingly resolve to the tonic. On the other hand, the ear is quick to hear Imaj7 in Lydian as IVmaj7 in Ionian. This leaves us with just a few effective cadences in Lydian (F Lydian):

Imaj7	II	Imaj7	Imaj7	VII-7	Imaj7
F△7	G	F△7	F△7	E-7	F△7

Using the root of the tonic as a pedal tone, over which various Lydian functions are shifted back and forth, is also quite common: e.g. F/F, G/F and C/F (F in the bass and the triads F, G and C alternating above).

Mixolydian

I7	II–7	IIIø7	IVmaj7	V–7	VI–7	♭VIImaj7
T	C	–	–	C	T	C

I7 is a tonic sound we'll encounter again once we talk about the Blues. Since all of us are familiar with the Blues, it's easy for us to accept I7 as a tonic (this is why the tritone between 3 and ♭7 is no problem). The triad (I) is naturally more stable – the disadvantage, of course, being the fact that it is not possible to identify the sound as a Mixolydian tonic. We could also use I7(sus4) to avoid the tritone. IV (as well as IVmaj7) is a hazardous sound when used in conjunction with I7. In this case, the ear automatically switches to the parallel Ionian context (F7 - B♭maj7 will not be heard as I-IV but rather as V-I in the key of B♭). V– (as well as V–7) is a cadence chord because it satisfies our V-I needs, even if the leading tone and its expected resolution are missing. Here are the cadential formulas typical to Mixolydian:

I7	II-7	I7	I7	V-7	I7	I7	♭VIIj7	I7
F7	G-7	F7	F7	C-7	F7	F7	E♭△7	F7

Aeolian

Even though we have already discussed the Natural minor scale, we need to talk about it here, at least for the sake of completeness. It stands to reason that the strongly established relationship between Aeolian and its relative major cannot be ignored. Despite this, it is possible to suppress our tendency to switch to the relative Ionian and to concentrate only on the primary Aeolian colour. We have already talked about the distribution of tonic and cadential functions on p. 94 (please have another look!):

I–7	IIø7	♭IIImaj7	VI–7	V–7	♭VImaj7	♭VII7
T	C	T	C	C	C	C

Modality and aural perception

It should be our objective not only to perceive modes as unique melodic colours, but also as independent harmonic frameworks. The danger, here, is that the ear – following the path of least resistance – has a strong tendency to switch to the relative Ionian or Aeolian key. Essentially, we hear and locate tonal centres according to our listening habits and musical backgrounds. For most of us, these are based on the traditional major/minor system (e.g. we would be more likely to hear a chord progression in B♭ Ionian than in C Dorian, and our ear would be inclined to gravitate towards A♭ Major when we hear C Phrygian).

Let's compare, for example, the tonic and cadential functions in C Dorian and B♭ Ionian. Both modes incorporate the same notes and therefore contain the same diatonic chords.

	Tonic functions	*Cadential functions*
C Dorian	C–7, E♭maj7	B♭maj7, D–7, G–7, F7
B♭ Ionian	B♭maj7, D–7, G–7	C–7, E♭maj7, F7, Aø7

The functional significance of all maj7 and –7 chords is inverted depending on the tonal centre: Tonic functions in C Dorian are cadence chords in B♭ Ionian and vice versa (F7 and Aø7 – as already explained earlier – are exceptions). This means that one and the same chord can have a different functional connotation within the same diatonic environment depending on our choice of tonal centre. For you to be able to recognise this change in functional quality, you will have to break out of the rut of your traditional listening habits.

If you want your ear to be capable of exploring new territory, you first have to examine the way you think. The more one-sided your thinking is, the more difficult it will be to identify a new sound or concept when it crosses your path. For example, if you only think in terms of Aeolian and Ionian categories, you'll have difficulties recognising Dorian or Phrygian chord progressions. But, as soon as you're able to say: "Somehow this piece sounds minor, but there's something slightly strange going on – maybe it's Dorian", you've all but won the battle. The more options you have while assessing a situation, the easier it will be for your ear to cope with new sounds and concepts. A simple example will prove the point. Go to **track 33**. I'll give you one clue to work with: The root of the first sound is a C. Now listen to the recording and try to figure out the chord progression. Don't read on. See if you can come up with an answer first.

OK, let's continue. While listening, you could have been thinking along the following lines: "I hear a two-bar pattern, which is repeated many times. I hear two different chords, one bar each. The root of the first chord is a C. The root of the second chord is down a perfect fifth. The first chord sounds minor, the second is a dominant chord. Conclusion: I'm hearing C–7 and F7."

Now comes the important part. I'd be willing to bet that most of you – as any Jazz musician – will immediately identify this harmonic phrase as a II-V pattern (expecting Bbmaj7 = Imaj7 as the target chord). But, wait a minute! Let's use those grey cells, ignore the recording for a moment and ask ourselves: Are there other ways of analysing C–7 - F7? Well, here are three basic interpretations (and – believe me – there are many more):

C–7	F7	
II	V	in Bb Ionian
I	IV	in C Dorian
V	I	in F Mixolydian

All three possibilities should make sense when referring back to the various church modes and their diatonic functions. And – even more importantly – all three options should cross your mind while you're listening.

Now, let's go back to the recording. Which one of the possibilities mentioned above describes best what you are hearing? Finding a viable solution has a lot to do with making assumptions and evaluating probabilities. Consider the following facts: Bbmaj7 never appears; C–7 is played in the first bar of the two-bar pattern, whereas F7 occurs in the second bar (the first bar carries more weight in a two-bar pattern). What do we deduce from this information? Since the harmonic pattern never resolves to Bbmaj7 and F7 appears in the weak bar of the pattern, everything points to C–7 as the most plausible tonic chord. The functional progression would therefore not be *II-V* (in Bb Ionian) but rather *I-IV* (in C Dorian):

To make sure that you're on the right track, alternately sing the roots Bb, C and F to the recording. Hold each note for some time to give your ear the opportunity to immerse itself in the music and evaluate how the sung note corresponds to the accompaniment. You'll probably find it relatively hard to hold on to the note Bb as the tonic (it actually creates quite a lot of tension). The note C produces a far more secure feeling of "locking into the sound", clearly supported by the bass line and reinforced by the fact that C–7 appears in the first bar of the two-bar pattern. F, on the other hand, does not create as strong a feeling of "being at home". This confirms what we already suspected: C–7 is I–7 and F7 is IV7 (sounding something like a Blues subdominant).

Simple as this little example may be, it shows two things. For one, you are quite capable of switching to modalities other than Ionian or Aeolian. Once a tonal centre has been clearly established, your ear will readily accept chord progressions based on other modes. The main thing, though, is the fact that you will not hear certain relationships if you don't know they exist. Knowledge helps the ear. The more you know, the more you hear. Recognising a chord progression as being based on a Dorian tonic implies that you know what Dorian is and which diatonic functions pertain to this mode. Without this knowledge, you won't even start looking in the right direction. So, learn your modes and you will enter into a multi-faceted world of sound.

Many pieces use the Dorian I–7 - IV7 pattern. Typical examples are "Oye Como Va" by Carlos Santana (Dorian is his "trademark" scale) or "Chameleon" by Herbie Hancock, which consists of little more than the following bass vamp (bass riff):

Without being consciously aware of it, most of us know compositions that are written exclusively in one or another of the church modes discussed above. A nice example is "Scarborough Fair" by Simon and Garfunkel:

Both the melody and the chord progression are entirely in E Dorian:

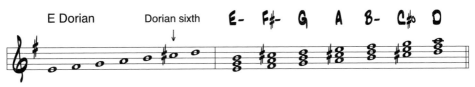

The diatonic chords have been written in triadic form because these are the sounds that are more commonly used in Folk and Pop music.

Assignment

Try to find more pieces that have been set in modes other than Ionian or Aeolian (melodically and/or harmonically).

What we have discussed in this chapter is only a first step – and a small one at that – towards an understanding that will open doors to music worldwide – be it compositions by Eric Satie or Bela Bartok, Folklore from Iceland, music by Chick Corea, Gregorian chants or Indian *ragas*. It would go way beyond the scope of this book to delve into all these wonderful sounds. In the following chapters, we will mainly stick to modal concepts and their application in Jazz and popular music in general. But I do hope you take me up on the offer to investigate and explore the many exciting musical venues around the world.

Modal Interchange

Originating in the United States, a highly elegant terminological system has established itself in the musical community. This concept provides us with a powerful analytical tool that helps describe and categorise almost all types of music and their harmonic and melodic mechanisms independent of stylistic considerations. This system incorporates two sets of principles: *tonality* and *modality* on the one hand and *diatonicism* and *chromaticism* on the other. While the first two terms define the material, the other two specify the way the material is used. This chapter explores how these concepts relate to one another, how they interact and what their impact is on Jazz composition and improvisation.

Let's look at definitions first and straighten out our terminology to make sure that we're talking about the same thing:

- *Tonality*: the tonal centre, the root or point of reference

- *Modality*: the choice of notes and the way the material is organised and structured

- *Diatonicism*: remaining exclusively within the boundaries of any specific modality and its melodic or harmonic ingredients

- *Chromaticism*: the departure from the diatonic framework through the use of material or principles foreign to the modality (in this context, the term "chromaticism" is used in a more general sense as a synonym for "deviation" or "discrepancy")

Here is the A section of "I Mean You" (Thelonious Monk, Coleman Hawkins) illustrating how these four elemental principles co-exist and interact:

The tonality is F, the modality is the Major scale (actually major Pentatonic), and the melody is strictly diatonic with the exception of bars 3 and 4, which deviate from F Major chromatically.

Let's start with the principles of tonality and modality. Considering the definitions above, music can be categorised as follows:

- *unitonal / unimodal* – in one tonality and mode

- *polytonal / unimodal* – in more than one tonality but in only one mode

- *unitonal / polymodal* – in one tonality but in more than one mode

- *polytonal / polymodal* – in more than one tonality and mode

For the sake of clarity: D Phrygian and D Lydian have the *same tonality* but *different modalities* (unitonal/polymodal), A Dorian and Bb Dorian have *different tonalities* but the *same modality* (polytonal/unimodal).

Be aware of the fact that the concepts described above can occur *sequentially* or *simultaneously*. For example, polytonality/unimodality may imply the use of the same mode and two *consecutive* tonalities (e.g. moving from F Ionian to A Ionian as in "Polka Dots And Moonbeams"). Many modulating standards fall into this category. The use of *concurrent* tonalities (bitonality) is quite common, too (e.g. as in Igor Stravinsky's "Petrushka", where the first clarinet plays a melody outlining a C major chord, accompanied by the second clarinet playing a variation of the same melody in F# Major). The same applies to unitonality/polymodality. Tunes can work with various modes based on the same tonic consecutively (e.g. as in "I'll Remember April", which switches from G Ionian to G Dorian in the first 8 bars) or simultaneously (e.g. as in Bela Bartok's "Seven Sketches, No. 2" for piano, where the left hand plays in C Phrygian and the right hand in C Lydian).

Let's have a closer look at each of these categories.

Unitonal/Unimodal

All compositions that are exclusively in *one tonality* and *one modality* fit into this category. This applies to most children's songs, nursery rhymes as well as to almost all Folk songs (worldwide). Their melodies and harmony (if there is any harmony at all) relate to a single root and to the same scale material throughout. All sounds used are diatonic and taken from one mode. Modality is quite clearly not a Jazz invention or a term pertaining only to Jazz, but rather a way of structuring sound that has been with us for centuries in all musical cultures around the world. What was celebrated as a revolution in Jazz (the focus on modality) is, in fact, nothing more than a return to our musical origins.

We should realise, though, that this group of compositions also includes most *non-modulating* Jazz standards. This is where the qualifiers "diatonicism" and "chromaticism" come into play. Whereas Folk music, nursery rhymes and Christmas carols are almost always purely diatonic, the concept of chromaticism plays an increasingly important role in Jazz themes. The more complex a piece is, the more chromatic passing notes and embellishments we are likely to come across in the melody and the more chromatic deviations we find from the diatonic harmony (secondary and substitute dominants, secondary II-V progressions, altered tensions, etc.). This doesn't change the fact that these compositions are based on *one* specific root (unitonal) and *one* specific modality (unimodal). Here's an example: "There Will Never Be Another You" is in Eb Major (tonality: Eb, modality: Ionian). The melody contains just one little chromatic exception to the scale of Eb Ionian (the A in bar 13), and the harmony is essentially diatonic: All chords appearing at important points in the form belong to Eb Major (the secondary dominants and II-Vs introduce chromatic material but are clearly linked to diatonic target chords).

Polytonal/Polymodal

This group consists of compositions in *any number of tonalities and modalities*. Many contemporary Jazz compositions fall into this category. Here, the harmony often meanders from one tonality to the next or moves in a way that makes it difficult to pinpoint specific tonalities in the first place. The same goes for the modalities – today it is perfectly normal to mix different modes and their diatonic functions. Without going into detail, I'd like to mention tunes such as "Dolphin Dance" (H. Hancock) or "Invitation" (B. Kaper) as good examples of this kind of thinking. Alas, we won't have the time and space in this book to discuss these compositions (I'll save them for Volume 2).

There are, of course, less complex tunes that fall into this category. A simple example of this is "Flamenco Sketches" (see p. 179), since each modal section relates to a different root and a different mode. Another typical example would be "Blue Bossa" (see p. 102). This piece is predominantly in C Minor and modulates for a short time to D♭ Major. We therefore have two tonalities (C and D♭ = polytonal) as well as differing modalities (Aeolian and Ionian = polymodal).

Polytonal/Unimodal

Compositions such as "So What" or "Impressions" (John Coltrane) belong to this group. "Impressions" is very similar to "So What": identical tonalities (D/E♭), same modality (Dorian) and form (32 bars, AABA), just at a much faster tempo. The A section of "Maiden Voyage" (p. 422 ff.) is also polytonal/unimodal: D7(sus4) and F7(sus4) are four-bar Mixolydian phrases based on two different roots. "Maiden Voyage" shows that a harmonic concept need not be sustained throughout the whole composition (the B section is actually polytonal/polymodal – check it out!). I mention this, because changing the harmonic principle is a compositional technique often used as a means of creating contrast (an example for this kind of thinking can be found when comparing the A and B section of "On Green Dolphin Street").

In the previous chapter, I pointed out the historical significance of the composition "So What". But what was really that radically different? In the end, it was only the amount of time spent in one mode that separated it from earlier compositions. So, as a challenging thought, consider the fact that a tune like "Giant Steps" falls into the same category as "So What". It revolves around the three tonal centres B, G and E♭ (polytonal) and it moves through chord progressions (V-I or II-V-I) that are all diatonic to the Ionian mode (unimodal). In contrast to "So What", the tonal centres change so rapidly that our ear has a hard time keeping track. This doesn't alter the fact that "Giant Steps" can indeed be seen from a modal point of view.

Unitonal/Polymodal

Here, the tonality stays the same and only the modality changes. In its simplest form, this can be achieved by placing different harmonies over a *pedal point* (also "pedal tone", "organ point" or simply "pedal") – a sustained note, typically found in the bass. The term comes from organ music where the bass lines and low notes are played on a set of foot pedals. Although pedal points usually appear in the bass, we sometimes find them in the top voice with chords moving underneath (inverted pedal point) or in the middle register as part of the inner voices (internal pedal point). Sometimes, the bass plays a pedal point in conjunction with a rhythmic pattern and/or alternating with the upper octave as a form of ornamentation.

As stated above, a pedal point is a sustained bass note acting as the foundation for a longer harmonic passage. To create a polymodal environment, the harmonic structures above the pedal tone are chosen in such a way that the resulting progressions generate changing scale relationships. Theoretically, any note can be used as a pedal point. In practice, however, we predominantly find *tonic pedals* and *dominant pedals* – the bass note being either the root or the fifth of the key.

A good example of a tonic pedal is the A section of "On Green Dolphin Street" (by Bronislaw Kaper). The changes consist of a series of major triads moving over an E♭ pedal:

G♭/E♭ is another way of notating E♭–7 (G♭ = 3, B♭ = 5, D♭ = ♭7). This gives us a choice of several minor scales for improvisation: Aeolian, Dorian and Phrygian. Keeping the tonal centre E♭maj7 (Imaj7) in mind, E♭ Dorian would be the best choice because it deviates least from the key signature of E♭ Ionian. Let's look at the tonal material of F/E♭. Relative to the E♭ pedal, the notes of the F triad have the following intervallic functions: F = 2, A = ♯4, C = 6. Considering the scale of the previous chord (E♭ Dorian) with its D♭ (♭7), Lydian(♭7) would establish the closest relationship with the key. The same procedure would work for F♭/E♭. The notes of the F♭ triad have the following functions: F♭ = ♭2, A♭ = 4, C♭ = ♭6. Here, we could use either Phrygian or Locrian. Because of the preceding sounds (all include the B♭ = 5), the best choice would be Phrygian (Locrian has a ♭5 and no 5).

What is the principle behind this kind of a progression? At first glance, it's simply a series of chromatically descending major triads. Beneath the surface, however, we find a fascinating interplay of colours. Remember how we put the church modes in an order, ranging from Lydian, the brightest, to Locrian, the darkest? There are many compositions that put this bright/dark gradation to good use. In "On Green Dolphin Street", we hear light and shade alternating, brought about by an oscillation of bright and dark colours. The result is a sort of undulating modal landscape consisting of musical hills and valleys:

E♭ Ionian		E♭ Dorian		E♭ Lydian(♭7)	E♭ Phrygian	E♭ Ionian
E♭△7	٪	G♭/E♭	٪	F/E♭	F♭/E♭	E♭△7
Bright		Dark		Bright	Dark	Bright

An even more impressive example of this is the composition "Naima" by John Coltrane – in my opinion one of the most beautiful ballads ever written. If we analyse the A section of "Naima" in the same way as we did with "On Green Dolphin Street", the following choice of scales emerges:

What we have here is essentially a dominant pedal in the key of A♭ Major with various major 7th chords moving above the E♭, resolving to an A♭maj7 in the fourth bar. Play the sounds on the piano (E♭ in the left and the maj7 chords in the right hand) and try singing the scales. Take your time and concentrate on every note, and see if you can confirm the scale relationships.

Here, we find a first step towards a combination of modal and functional aspects. In essence, the A section of "Naima" is actually nothing more than a stretched out V-I progression. But, if we look and listen closely, we'll notice a sophisticated play on colours. The three-bar dominant becomes increasingly obscure and dark. It starts with Mixolydian (the brightest colour), moves on to Dorian and Locrian (which, of course, are not dominant scales) and ends with Altered. In the United States, the last scale is often known – for good reason – as **Superlocrian** because we get an Altered scale by chromatically lowering the 4th degree of Locrian (4 → ♭4 = 3), thereby extending the sequence one step beyond the church modes (see p. 63). Accordingly, Altered could be seen as being one level "darker" than Locrian:

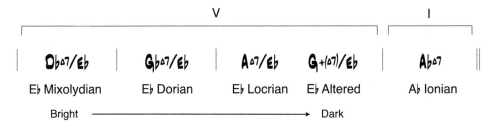

Assignment

Here is the B section of "Naima". The chord progression is based on a B♭ pedal point (this, by the way, demonstrates the use of pedal tones other than tonic and dominant). Analyse the sounds using the same method as above and try to determine the corresponding scales:

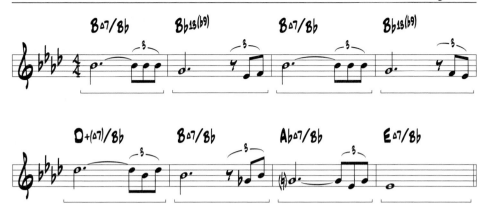

Despite the indisputable modal nature of this piece, we discover a functional concept when linking the formal aspects of the piece to its harmonic essence. The main sounds in the A section (Eb7 and Abmaj7) and the B section (Bb7) form a harmonic progression that is distinctly functional: Bb7 - Eb7 - Abmaj7 is nothing but a simple variation of a II-V-I cadence, drawn out beyond recognition. Compositionally speaking, this is a highly original and creative way of using and redesigning a traditional harmonic pattern. With its unusual distribution of functions (an eight-bar II, an inflated V and a tiny, one-bar tonic), its exciting modal colours and the lovely melody, this piece is nothing but a stroke of genius.

Functional polymodality – modal interchange

The use of differing modal colours over a pedal point is the simplest example of unitonal/polymodal harmony. If we go one step further and apply this principle to diatonic functions derived from the many different scales available to us, we finally arrive at the actual subject matter of this chapter – *modal interchange* (MI for short). Here is the basic principle: The functions of *different modalities* are combined within the *same tonality*. If, for example, a composition is in F Major (Ionian), the chord progression could also contain sounds derived from F Dorian, F Phrygian, F Lydian, etc. In this way, traditional diatonic harmony can be enriched with a multitude of refreshing colours without departing from the tonal centre by switching to another key (modulation). So, to put it in different words, modal interchange describes the process of *parallel modes trading functions*. Just to make sure that there is no misunderstanding: *Parallel* modes have the same root whereas *relative* modes have the same key signature.

Here's an example of how MI-functions work. We have already looked at bIImaj7 as one of the most important cadence chords in Phrygian. Listen to the chord progression on **track 34**:

	F Phrygian		F Ionian	F Phrygian
‖: F-7	Gbᐃ7 :‖:	Fᐃ7	Gbᐃ7 :‖
I-7	bIImaj7	Imaj7	bIImaj7

Initially, the ♭IImaj7 chord (G♭maj7) is introduced in its customary Phrygian context resolving to F–7. After a few repetitions, you can hear the same function alternating with Fmaj7 (Imaj7) instead. Now, the *Phrygian cadence chord* is combined with an *Ionian tonic*. Despite the different tonic colour, we can still clearly recognise the typical Phrygian cadential movement. So, G♭maj7 is a good example of an MI-function in F Major (or, seen conversely, Fmaj7 would be a modal interchange function in F Phrygian).

Having talked about chord progressions in major keys almost exclusively so far, I'd like to restrict myself to discussing the most commonly used MI-functions in a major context for the time being. It should be clear, however, that modal interchange is a principle that can be applied to any modality – *all* modes relating to the same root can trade functions with one another.

In the following table, you will find the most important MI-functions used in major keys. They can be derived by referring to the table of church modes on p. 181 ff. and picking out the functions that are non-diatonic in major:

Function	*Mode of Origin*
♭IImaj7	Phrygian / Locrian
♭IIImaj7	Dorian / Aeolian
♭Vmaj7	Locrian
♭VImaj7	Phrygian / Aeolian
♭VIImaj7	Dorian / Mixolydian
I–7	Dorian / Phrygian / Aeolian
IV–7	Phrygian / Aeolian / Locrian
V–7	Dorian / Mixolydian / Aeolian
VII–7	Lydian
II–7(♭5)	Aeolian
♯IV–7(♭5)	Lydian
I7	Mixolydian / Blues
IV7	Dorian / Blues / MM
♭VII7	Aeolian

Dominant seventh chords are generally not perceived as MI-functions. Ultimately, any dominant would be interpreted either as a secondary or substitute dominant. The ear will always hear them first and foremost in conjunction with their expected resolutions. However, as already mentioned on p. 154 and seen in the table above, there are three seventh chords that are sometimes used independent of their dominant functions and live lives of their own.

Many MI-functions have more than one possible mode from which they could originate. This is of considerable importance to the derivation of improvisational material, as we'll see in a moment. Again, I want to remind you that we arrived at the sequence of scales – ranging from Lydian to Locrian – by simply changing one note when moving from one mode to the next. We will take Ionian as the point of reference for the following discussion because it is the central colour of the chord progressions we are going to talk about. The following table shows that a scale – tonality remaining unchanged – deviates more strongly from Ionian the further away it is positioned:

Scale	Deviations	
Lydian	♯4	
Ionian	4	maj7
Mixolydian	3	♭7
Dorian	♭3	6
Aeolian	2	♭6
Phrygian	♭2	5
Locrian		♭5

Now to the decisive point: If an MI-function can be derived from several different modes, we select the mode of origin that is ***closest*** to Ionian and contains the least dissimilarities, thus establishing the strongest possible link between the key and the MI-function. This prevents the ear from perceiving these sounds as strange and softens their potential dissonance.

Let's have a look at the various MI-functions one by one (in C Major – yes, I'm trying to be nice):

♭IImaj7

This function can be derived from Phrygian as well as Locrian. Phrygian takes preference because it deviates less from Ionian than Locrian. If we notate C Phrygian from the root D♭, we get *Lydian* as the appropriate scale for ♭IImaj:

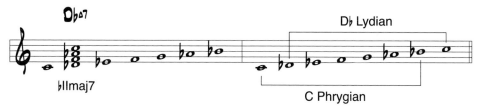

In the A section of "Lucky Southern" by Keith Jarrett, ♭IImaj7 is prominently placed at the climax of the eight-bar phrase. Within the diatonic context of D Major, E♭maj7 appears in its expected role as an MI cadence chord resolving to Dmaj7 (watch the repeat!). The A (= ♯11) in the melody confirms the choice of Lydian as the corresponding scale:

♭IImaj7 is a popular closing chord – especially with melodies ending on the tonic root (1/8). If the last note of a melody lands on 1 or 8, we have to harmonise it with I6 or I(add9) and not Imaj7 to avoid the collision of 1/8 in the melody and maj7 in the chord (remember the discussion on conditional avoid notes). As a result, the final sound of a tune often feels a little colourless and boring. In contrast, ♭IImaj7 gives the close a nice shimmer. Additionally, it is formally more exciting to leave the ending open by avoiding the expected final resolution to the tonic.

Please note that ♭IImaj7 resembles what is referred to as the *Neapolitan sixth chord* (N6) in Classical music. The Neapolitan chord is a major triad built on the ♭II scale degree of any key (major or minor). Traditionally, the triad appears in its first inversion (3rd in the bass) – hence the "sixth" (the root of the chord is a 6th above the bass). The N6 usually precedes V, intensifying the harmonic resolution to I (in A Minor):

♭IIImaj7

This function can be derived from both Aeolian and Dorian. Because Dorian is the better choice (closer to Ionian), we end up with Lydian as the scale for ♭IIImaj7:

In the B section of "Night And Day" by Cole Porter, we repeatedly come across ♭IIImaj7 (alternating with Imaj7):

♭Vmaj7

This MI-function comes from Locrian (the only option). Its tonal material for improvisation therefore has to be *Lydian*:

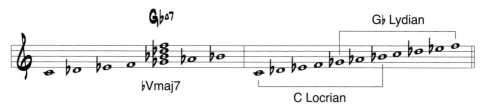

♭Vmaj7 is hardly ever used, probably because, as I've mentioned before, Locrian is not one of the "naturally grown" modes. It has not established itself as an independent tonic colour. Subsequently, it has only limited significance as a source of "borrowed" functions. As a result, Locrian functions are hard for the ear to grasp. In addition, of all MI-functions, ♭Vmaj7 is the one that differs most from the diatonic surroundings in terms of the key signature (Locrian – Ionian) and tends to clash considerably with the basic Ionian texture. As far as I know, there are no traditional compositions in which ♭Vmaj7 appears in direct relation to Imaj7 (if someone can bring me a standard with this functional progression, I'll take you out to dinner and give away a substantial amount of my accrued royalties from this book!).

   ♭Vmaj7 does, nevertheless, sometimes appear embedded within the harmonic flow of things – for example in "Israel" by John Carisi (bars 7–11 as heard on the original recording, not as notated in the Real Book version!):

Thinking in terms of harmonic sequences will help clarify the issue: The progressions Cmaj7 - D–7 - E♭maj7 and E♭maj7 - F–7 - G♭maj7 are identical when looking at both root movement and chord types. Here, G♭maj7 evolves naturally out of the preceding passage and leads effectively to the G7 chord. The C (= ♯11) in the melody supports the choice of Lydian for ♭Vmaj7.

This discussion shows us why some of the theoretically possible MI-functions have not made it into the standard repertoire. Their impact on a traditional harmonic context is simply too strange.

♭VImaj7

This function is derived from either Phrygian or Aeolian. Because Aeolian is closer to Ionian than Phrygian, ♭VImaj7 takes *Lydian* for improvisation purposes:

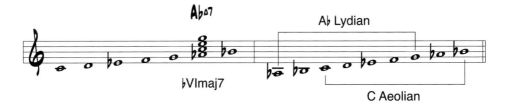

♭VImaj7 is normally used as a chromatic link between the diatonic V^th and VIth degrees or their substitutes/variants – like, for instance, in "A Child Is Born" by Thad Jones (bars 25–28):

Sometimes, we find ♭VImaj7 in connection with two other MI-functions – ♭IImaj7 and ♭III-maj7. Here are the last two bars of the standard "Lady Bird" by Charlie Parker:

The interesting thing about this progression, which consists only of major seventh chords, is its similarity to a dominant turnaround (extended SubVs) with its cycle-of-fifths root movement and a chromatic resolution back to the tonic (Imaj7).

It's not that uncommon to find ♭VImaj7 prepared by the corresponding dominant or even a II-V progression. Again, "Lady Bird" (bars 5–10) is a typical example of this:

We should ask ourselves, though, whether the ear actually hears A♭maj7 as a modal interchange function or rather as a short modulation (change of key) to A♭ Major with A♭maj7 as the tonic.

In this case, the Lydian scale for improvisation over ♭VImaj7 is not necessarily the best choice. Both B♭–7 and E♭7 contain the note D♭ and strongly imply a resolution to an Ionian target chord (D♭ = 4, used as a melodic passing note over the A♭maj7, is more plausible than D = ♯11). This can also create the impression of a modulation. In any case, always be aware of the possibility that the tonal material of a function is influenced and changed by the preceding sounds.

♭VIImaj7

This function comes either from Dorian or Mixolydian. The latter takes preference (closest to Ionian), and the best scale for improvisation would be *Lydian*:

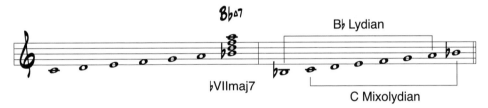

A typical application of this function can be found in McCoy Tyner's composition "Three Flowers" (in E♭ Major):

I–7

I–7 is used as a direct alternative to Imaj7. It can be derived from Dorian, Phrygian or Aeolian. Dorian is the most suitable choice (closest to Ionian) and therefore the best scale for improvisation. In the composition "I'll Remember April" by Gene de Paul, Imaj7 and I–7 appear alongside one another on equal terms:

In this example, both I–7 and I–6 are related to Dorian. Generally speaking, we could go one step further and take any of the minor tonic forms – borrowed from HM/MM (I–maj7), Phrygian or Aeolian – as a modal interchange function.

IV–7

This is probably the most popular of all MI-functions. If there were such a thing as *the* "tear-jerker-chord", IV– would be the prime candidate. Its bittersweet and melancholic quality has contributed to many a love or heartbreak song. Listen to "In My Life" (Beatles) or "Wake Me Up When September Ends" (Green Day) and you'll hear what I mean.

  IV–7 can be derived from Phrygian, Aeolian or Locrian. Aeolian is the best choice because it differs the least from Ionian. IV–7 must therefore be played as Dorian:

IV–7 is used mostly in combination with or as a substitute for the diatonic IVth degree. In most cases, it resolves directly back to Imaj7. However, it can also appear as a passing chord that is inserted between IVmaj7 and III–7 (or Imaj7/3). The ending of "Lucky Southern" (Keith Jarrett) is a typical example (bars 24–28):

Notice the Dorian 6th in the melody over the G–7 chord.

In many cases, IV–7 is expanded into a II-V progression by adding the corresponding dominant seventh chord. The beginning of "Just Friends" (John Klenner) demonstrates the use of this progression (the piece is in G Major, so it starts with the subdominant!):

So, how do we interpret F7? We either choose Mixolydian (a logical continuation of C Dorian) or analyse it as the function SubV/VI (expected sound = E–7) with a deceptive resolution to Gmaj7. In the latter case, the most suitable scale for improvisation would more likely be Lydian(♭7). The #11 (B) complies with the major third of Gmaj7. Both options are found in practice. F7 corresponds to the modal interchange function ♭VII7 listed in the table on p. 196. We will talk about this function later in the chapter.

In "Joy Spring" by Clifford Brown (F Major), the II-V progression B♭–7 - E♭7 appears in the fourth bar. The first and therefore most conspicuous melody note is an A♭ (♭7 of B♭–7). As part of the voice leading A♭-G, the A♭ influences the scale material of E♭7. This is why we would rather choose Mixolydian for improvisation:

However, in "Lady Bird" (in C Major), the melody clearly shows the #11 (E) and therefore determines that we should use Lydian(♭7) on the B♭7:

With IV–, we would create an even stronger link to the main modality (Ionian) if we choose Melodic minor and IV–maj7 or IV–6 as the corresponding chord symbol. The major seventh of IV–maj7 points to the major third (3) of the tonic, establishing a closer connection to the tonal centre than IV–7 Dorian:

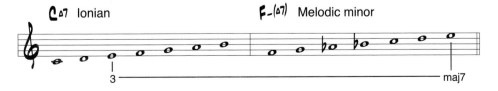

In "God Bless The Child" by Arthur Herzog and Billie Holiday (bars 4–7), this link is very clear, both melodically and harmonically. The G (major third in E♭ Major) is the central melody note that holds together the entire phrase:

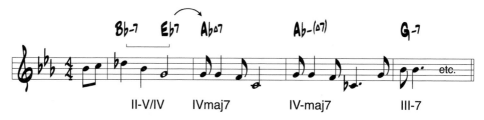

Expanding IV–maj7 (Melodic minor) into a II-V pattern will result in Lydian(♭7) for the dominant chord. In this way, both sounds incorporate the same notes (e.g. B♭–maj7 - E♭7 in F Major):

Bars 4–9 of "The Days Of Wine And Roses" (in F Major) support this idea:

Lastly, "A Child Is Born" by Thad Jones is an example of IV– that allows for Dorian as well as Melodic minor. Here's the A section:

E♭–6 is IV–6. The pedal point B♭ does not affect the function. Since IV–6 is contained in both Dorian and MM, the soloist can switch from one scale to the other as desired while improvising. However, take a close look at the tune: The melody plays a very important role in the analysis. The ever-present D influences not only the entire A section but also the scale material of E♭–6. Considering this, Melodic minor and not Dorian would be the better choice (D = maj7). On the other hand, the tune is not set in stone when it comes to playing a solo – there is much more freedom in the choice of material during an improvisation.

V–7

We have already dealt with this function as part of a II-V/IV in the chapter on secondary II-V progressions (e.g. Cmaj7 - G–7 - C7 - Fmaj7). However, V–7 also appears as an independent colour and can be derived from Dorian, Mixolydian or Aeolian. Mixolydian gets the vote, as it is closest to Ionian. So, for V–7, the most appropriate scale is Dorian:

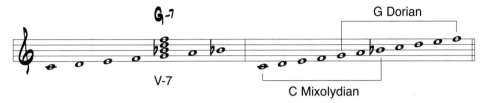

At the beginning of "Dolphin Dance" by Herbie Hancock, we find V–7 alternating with Imaj7:

II–7(♭5)

This function is derived from Aeolian (the only option) and takes the Locrian scale:

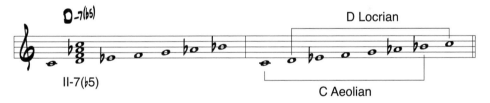

II–7(♭5) gives us the opportunity to prepare a major tonic (Imaj7) with a minor cadence (II-V). A typical example of this is the composition "I Love You" by Cole Porter:

In this context, V7 is usually HM5 or Altered (as a continuation of IIø7 Locrian). The melody of "I Love You" is evidence of yet another possibility (take note of the A in the melody over C7) – I'll come back to this later.

In the same way in which II–7 and IVmaj7 constitute a functional pair in major (sub-dominant functions), IIø7 and IV–6 belong together in a minor context (both chords contain the same notes). It is easy to see and hear this connection in "All Of You" by Cole Porter:

If a minor II-V progression can be used in a major key, then the opposite – resolving a major II-V progression to a minor tonic (I–7) – must work too. A good, though quite rare example showing both MI options can be found in the B section of Stevie Wonder's "You Are The Sunshine Of My Life":

The chord progression modulates from C Major to A Major and back. Starting in the key of C Major, Bø7 - E7 prepares A–7 (VI–7) as the expected target chord. Amaj7 pops up instead. Once the new major tonic has been established and confirmed with the help of B–7 - E7 (II-V in A Major), A– suddenly reappears (I–/VI–) and turns the progression back to C Major. In order to soften the effect of the change from Amaj7 to A–, the melody moves from C♯ (= 9 of B–7, which can still be seen as part of A Major) to C (= ♭13 of E7), which sets up the A– and creates a smoother transition.

For II–7(♭5), there is an alternative scale we have already come across in a different context: Locrian(9), derived from the Melodic minor scale (MM6). The 9 in Locrian(9) indicates that we are now dealing with an available tension for IIø7 and not with an avoid note, as would be the case with ♭2/♭9 in Locrian. Locrian(9) establishes a closer relationship with a major key than Locrian because the 9 corresponds to the major third of Imaj7:

Since we perceive every II-V progression as a harmonic unit, any changes we make to the II chord will automatically influence the V chord. If we allow the characteristic notes of Locrian(9) – ♭5 and 9 – to carry on as part of the ensuing seventh chord, they become ♭9 and 13 respectively. Remember that this specific combination of altered and non-altered (diatonic) tensions can only be found in two of the more common dominant scales: Half-tone-whole-tone or Mixo(♭9). I prefer HTWT as the more exciting scale for V7 when extending Locrian(9) into its corresponding dominant:

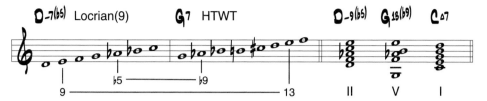

The following scale pairs are those most commonly used in practice:

II-7(♭5)		V7
Locrian	→	HM5/Altered
Locrian(9)	→	HTWT

The second scale combination is surely the more contemporary sound. Nonetheless, it can sometimes be found in traditional standards. Have another look at the beginning of "I Love You" (p. 205). On the C7 chord, the melody contains both D♭ (♭9) and A (13), implying HTWT. Even though G–7(♭5) is not clearly Locrian(9) in this case, it is safe to assume that whatever applies to C7 will also be relevant to the preceding II chord. While improvising, it is possible to ignore the tune and rely on the more commonly used scales (Locrian and HM5/Altered).

♯IV–7(♭5)

This function comes from Lydian (the only option) and therefore goes with the Locrian scale for improvisation:

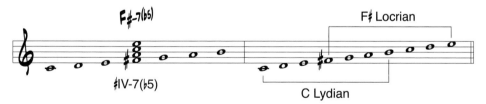

We have already encountered this function as part of a secondary II-V progression: II-V/III (e.g. Cmaj7 - F♯ø7 - B7 - E–7 etc. in the key of C Major). Used as an independent sound, this function is normally found as a chromatic link between the IVth and Vth degrees, e.g. as a substitute for ♯IV°7 (similar colour) or ♯IV7. Typical progressions include IVmaj7 - ♯IVø7 - V7 (ascending) or V7 - ♯IVø7 - IVmaj7 (descending). Instead of V7, we often hear V7(sus4) or Imaj7/5.

♯IVø7 is often used as the starting chord of a longer progression that resolves towards the tonic with a chromatically descending bass line. "Night And Day" is a good example of this (from bar 9):

An interesting variation of this chord progression is often used e.g. in Bossa Nova tunes – not as part of the actual composition but rather as an extension of the final cadence (as a *coda*). Here, ♯IVø7 appears as a substitute for Imaj7 (deceptive resolution: e.g. II–7 - V7 - ♯IVø7) and serves as the kick-off for a long harmonic phrase, which eventually resolves to the tonic. This reinforcement at the end of a tune is particularly effective when the melody lands on the root of the key (1 or 8) and is sustained in the upper voice as a melodic bracket with the chords moving underneath (inverted pedal):

Apart from Locrian – the best choice tonally – we often find Locrian(9) used as an alternative for improvisation (see IIø7). The reason for this is simple. The ear obviously links ♯IVø7 to two other functions, hearing it either as a part of V7/V or as an inversion of VI–6. If we consider the standard scales for these functions – Lydian(♭7) for V7/V and Melodic minor for VI–6 – it is quite obvious that they are identical to Locrian(9) for ♯IVø7. Even the "special" notes that give each scale its characteristic flavour match (in C Major):

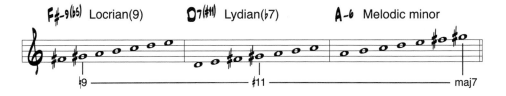

♯IV–7(♭5) is one of the most important sounds when it comes to generating interest because it gives a composer the option of using a non-diatonic root in combination with chord tones that are diatonic to the key. Compare Fmaj7 (IVmaj7) and F♯ø7 (♯IVø7) in the key of C Major – with the exception of the root, both chords contain the same notes. There are quite a few tunes that employ this similarity as a means of creating surprise – e.g. by setting up IVmaj7 with a II-V/IV and then resolving to ♯IV–7(♭5) instead (deceptive resolution), positioning the sound at an important point in the form (at the beginning of a section or at the climax) or using it as the starting point of a modulation. You will come across this special sound in a multitude of Jazz standards (e.g. "Stella By Starlight", "The Days Of Wine And Roses" or "When Sunny Gets Blue", to name a few).

Non-dominant seventh chords

Apart from I7 (from Mixolydian) and IV7 (from Dorian), both of which we will deal with in detail in the next chapter as the essential colours of the Blues, the most important of these non-dominant functions is ♭VII7 (derived from Aeolian):

Even though ♭VII7 is actually the same chord as SubV/VI, the function works in a different way. For one, it usually does not resolve to VI–7. As already mentioned above, ♭VII7 is often used as an extension of IV–7 but can also appear as an independent sound without the preceding IV– chord. This is why it is preferably labelled using the degree symbol (♭VII7) rather than the cadence symbol (SubV/VI).

The interesting thing about ♭VII7 – in contrast to SubV/VI – is that it is normally played as Mixolydian and not Lydian(♭7). Therefore, ♭VII7 can also appear as a 7(sus4) chord. Whereas the ♯11 in Lydian(♭7) establishes a strong link to the major third (3) of the key, the 4 in Mixolydian – e.g. as part of a 7(sus4) chord – has the opposite effect: It implies the minor third (♭3) of the parallel minor key. Accordingly, ♭VII7(sus4) acts as a true MI-function and not as a substitute dominant:

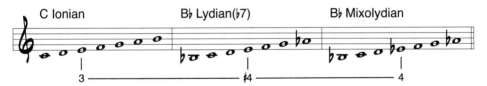

A good example of ♭VII7 (Mixolydian) can be found in the B section of "Mornin'" on p. 413.

As I mentioned before, ♭VII7 is often preceded by IV–7 or IV–maj7. The resulting II-V pattern would be expected to resolve down to VI–7, the ♭VII7 being SubV/VI, with IV–7 expanding it to a Sub(II-V)/VI. However, more often than not, the progression cadences back to Imaj7 instead – e.g. Cmaj7 - Fmaj7 - F–7 - B♭7 - Cmaj7. Even though this would be labelled a deceptive resolution, implying a special case, it is by far the most commonly found alternative. It is so firmly established as one of the basic cadence patterns that it has a name of its own and is frequently referred to as the ***backdoor cadence*** because it circles back to the tonic and resolves from below rather than above.

Here is a summary of the MI-functions used in major keys:

Function	Scale	Mode of Origin
♭IImaj7	Lydian	Phrygian
♭IIImaj7	Lydian	Dorian
♭Vmaj7	Lydian	Locrian
♭VImaj7	Lydian	Aeolian
♭VIImaj7	Lydian	Mixolydian
I–7 / I–6	Dorian	Dorian
IV–7 / IV–6	Dorian	Aeolian
IV–6 / IV–maj7	Melodic minor	–
V–7	Dorian	Mixolydian
II–7(♭5)	Locrian / Locrian(9)	Aeolian
♯IV–7(♭5)	Locrian / Locrian(9)	Lydian
I7	Mixolydian / Blues	Mixolydian / Blues
IV7	Mixolydian / Blues	Dorian / Blues
♭VII7	Mixolydian	Aeolian

Note that all maj7 chords are Lydian and all –7 chords are Dorian. This is no coincidence. Because MI-functions should be heard as part of an already established tonality and not as new tonal centres or tonic sounds, it is vital that they have a distinct and different identity from the two sounds which have the strongest tendency to assert a feeling of tonality: Imaj7 (Ionian) and I–7 (Aeolian). Using Lydian or Dorian instead helps the ear avoid latching onto the MI-functions too strongly.

It is important to realise that you will only start hearing these sounds as MI-functions if you are truly familiar with all modes as a source of functional and cadential relationships. Only once you've internalised a mode harmonically will MI-functions really start making sense to the ear.

Many harmony books refer to certain MI-functions as belonging to the *subdominant minor* group, based on the fact that IV–7 is one of the most, if not *the* most, important MI-function used in major keys. The significant note of IV–7 is the ♭3, which corresponds to the ♭6 of the key (e.g. in C this would be the A♭ of F–7). All MI-functions containing the ♭6 of the key are considered to be a member of this group. This holds true for the following sounds: ♭IImaj7, II–7(♭5), IV–7, ♭VImaj7 and ♭VII7 (in C Major this implies D♭maj7, Dø7, F–7, A♭maj7 and B♭7). For some people these functions represent everything there is to modal interchange. This seems to be a rather narrow view because there are, of course, many other MI-functions, as can be seen in the table above. And again – please always remember this – the functions we've discussed represent only a small fraction of the multitude of sounds that can be generated by applying the concept of modal interchange.

An excellent example of the use of MI-functions is the composition "Beatrice" by Sam Rivers:

The melody relates almost exclusively to F Major (with minor deviations in bars 6 and 15). In essence, the melody revolves, for the most part, around the F major triad. We therefore hear a well-established tonal centre F and Ionian as the primary mode. Let's have a look at the functional analysis (MI-functions are in frames). The mode of origin is indicated above each chord:

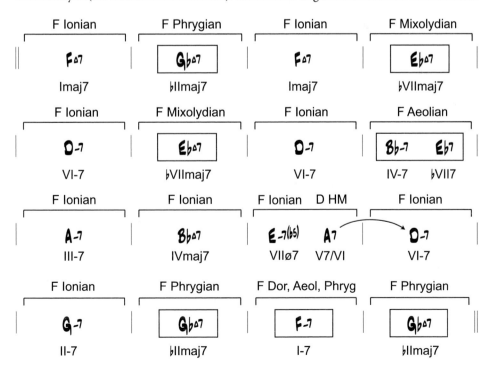

With the exception of A7 (bar 11), all chords can be attributed to a mode based on the root F as diatonic functions. F–7 (bar 15) can be interpreted and played in a number of ways:

- F Dorian forms the closest relationship with the main mode of F Ionian (smallest difference in number of accidentals).

- F Aeolian is what most of us are used to hearing for a minor tonic (I–7).

- F Phrygian is the most effective link between the preceding and ensuing G♭maj7 chords (♭IImaj7 in Phrygian).

All three options are equally justifiable from a sound point of view. Since the melody doesn't provide any clues (it consists only of notes pertaining to all three scales), the choice of scale is a matter of personal taste. I would probably play Phrygian because, to me, harmonic flow and the resulting melodic coherence is the most important thing. But, find out for yourself which option is the most satisfactory.

There are three possible approaches to dealing with improvisational material when it comes to progressions like these. Either we get our bearings from the root of each chord (1), the various F modalities (2), or from the Major scales implied by each of the chords (3):

	F△7	G♭△7	F△7	E♭△7	D-7	etc.
1)	F Ionian	G♭ Lydian	F Ionian	E♭ Lydian	D Aeolian	
2)	F Ionian	F Phrygian	F Ionian	F Mixolydian	F Ionian	
3)	F Ionian	D♭ Ionian	F Ionian	B♭ Ionian	F Ionian	

All three approaches result in the same thing (the scale material is identical in all cases). In the end, it depends on which approach you find easiest to use. By the way, I have only included the third option for the sake of completeness. As I have mentioned before, thinking only in terms of Ionian is a mnemonic that has its drawbacks because it misleads the ear.

Modal interchange in minor keys

So far, we have only discussed chord progressions based on major keys, where most MI-functions are derived from parallel minor modes. It stands to reason that the opposite exists too: minor chord progressions containing MI-functions derived from parallel major modes. The simplest choice of function would be to replace a minor tonic (I–7) with a major tonic chord (Imaj7). This can be found, for example, in "Alone Together" (Arthur Schwartz), which is almost exclusively in D Minor, but resolves to Dmaj7 instead at the end of the A section. Other good examples of this are "Daahoud" by Clifford Brown or "Israel" by John Carisi. A Jazz standard that seesaws between major and minor is "Here's That Rainy Day" by Jimmy van Heusen. While the A and B sections are predominantly in F Minor, the entire C section is in F Major.

A popular harmonic device found in European Classical music was the *Picardy third* (from French: *tierce de Picardie*), e.g. extensively used by J.S. Bach. The term refers to a composition, section or harmonic phrase in a minor key ending on a major tonic instead of the expected minor tonic. Again, the A section of "Here's That Rainy Day" is a good example. It starts out in F Minor and ends on an Fmaj7 chord.

I could now start from scratch and go through all MI-functions used in minor keys. But, please remember that any mode with its diatonic attributes can act as the primary colour of a composition and that any other parallel mode can supply MI-functions. The fact is that, up until now, we have only touched on a small number of the many progressions that relate in some way to the concept of modal interchange. It should be clear that not even another 100 pages would be enough to run through every conceivable functional relationship. It would be a futile and merely academic endeavour of little practical value to attempt cataloguing the many imaginable combinations of all existing modes and their diatonic functions.

I'd like to close this chapter with a sweet and simple example that shows in a nutshell the coexistence of modal and functional concepts. Here's the composition "Little Sunflower" by Freddie Hubbard:

This piece, a mixture of modal soundscapes and functional relationships, combines a Dorian and an Ionian tonic with a Phrygian cadence chord. D Dorian is the primary mode: D–7 = I–7. E♭maj7 (♭IImaj7 taken from D Phrygian) and Dmaj7 (Imaj7 in Ionian or Lydian) are therefore MI-functions.

With the concept of modal interchange, we have taken an important first step on the road towards discovering an abundance of (as yet) unknown sounds. I am convinced that the study and understanding of harmony should not only encompass the analysis of music that already exists as part of our familiar vocabulary but should also stimulate an ongoing exploration of new harmonic concepts. So, do your research – with curiosity, openness, imagination and the enjoyment of designing, conceiving, analysing, structuring, shaping and experimenting with the many sounds yet to be invented …

Assignments

1. Go to **track 35** and see if you can figure out the function of each sound simply by listening to the recording.

2. Analyse the composition "Elm" by Richie Beirach (in the New Real Book). This is a prime example of a piece using modal interchange!

The Blues

The Blues is probably America's most influential contribution to 20th century music world-wide and one of the most important elements of Jazz. There are literally countless books, biographies and studies on the origins, artists, lyrics, emotional implications as well as the political, ethnic and sociological aspects of the Blues. Despite this enormous wealth of available material on the subject, it is unlikely that it can fully capture and convey the spirit, the lifestyle and the diversity of moods – the proverbial "blues feeling" – inherent to the Blues.

The Blues is traditional Folk music – or rather "down-to-earth music for down-to-earth people". It should not be seen as an academic or highbrow art form that we could learn by theorising, philosophising or by reading books. This chapter on the Blues makes no pretense at an attempt to replace what we should do in terms of playing, listening and *experiencing* the Blues, making it part of our personal language through everyday involvement. In this context, we'll have to restrict ourselves to describing the melodic, harmonic and formal aspects of the Blues as it appears in both traditional and more contemporary forms.

The vitality of the Blues is the result of a merging of opposites. The sound of the Blues evolved by bringing together the music of West African people displaced by slavery and the musical tradition of European settlers in North America. The aboriginal music of Africa had no harmony as such. At best, it can be described as a linear, parallel movement of various voices in ritualistic chants or antiphony (call-and-response singing) based on simple Pentatonic scales. Its emphasis was on rhythm (polyrhythm) and expression through dance. In contrast, European music had developed a highly sophisticated harmonic and melodic language over the centuries (at the expense of rhythm as well as physical involvement!). How do these differences influence the sound of the Blues?

Blues melody

Let's start with the one element that most clearly distinguishes the Blues from other styles: melody. Blues melodies originate from field hollers, work songs and call-and-response shouts of the North American plantation workers. The sacred counterpart of the secular Blues is Gospel music, which is deeply rooted in Negro Spirituals – religious songs often based on Biblical themes that conveyed messages of faith, hope and freedom.

The distinctive colouring of the Blues is a result of conflicting elements. The African slaves, forced to live subserviently in a foreign culture, confronted with unfamiliar music, felt compelled to adapt their mostly minor pentatonic melodies to songs predominantly based on the Major scale. Let us compare these two sounds (based on the root F):

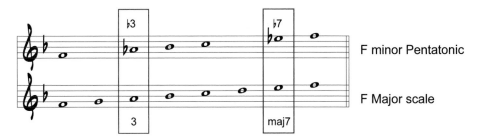

F minor Pentatonic

F Major scale

The differences lie in the third and the seventh. It is easy to imagine how early slaves, in a rather self-conscious effort to reconcile their own melodic traditions with the music of their subjugators, might have wavered back and forth between the colours ♭3/♭7 (minor Pentatonic) and 3/maj7 (Major scale), even singing notes somewhere in between or using glissandi to get from one interval to the other. These "hybrid" notes are commonly referred to as *blue notes*, blurring the dividing line between major and minor (have a good listen to some old recordings of blues singers!). Traditionally, blue notes are considered to be "tonal glitches" – notes that cannot be pinpointed in terms of pitch and reflect a much more liberal approach to intonation. Blue notes are often also referred to as "bent notes" – microtonal shadings that are virtually impossible to write down in conventional notation.

Even though the explanation given above is the generally accepted view on the evolution of blue notes, I would like to take a slightly different stand. To me, a blue note is not one but *two* notes that occur simultaneously or in immediate succession. Think about it – if blue notes were micro-tonally positioned between ♭3 and 3 or ♭7 and maj7, then piano players could not play the Blues (which, of course, is nonsense). The piano is an instrument with fixed pitch that cannot adjust intonation in the same way a horn or string player can. So – to me – a blue note is not a microtone, but the co-existence of two conflicting notes. It's the dissonance created by ♭3/3 or ♭7/maj7 sounding together that creates the typical Blues feel. We will get back to this when talking about Blues harmony.

During the 1940s, a third blue note appeared: the *flatted fifth* (♭5/♯4). Through increased use of SubV functions, tritone substitutions, Altered and Lydian(♭7) scales, chromatic approaches in walking bass lines and the resulting exposure of the tritone, the flatted fifth became one of the most prominent elements of the Bebop language and, subsequently, part of the Blues. In Blues, the ♯4/♭5 is used predominantly as a chromatic link – a kind of "slide" tone between the fourth (4) and the fifth (5) or as a grace note.

The traditional Blues scale is therefore an extended version of the minor Pentatonic scale (in F):

Blue Notes

1   ♭3   4   ♯4/♭5   5   ♭7   1

Here are some typical Blues patterns in F. Practise these at about 80 beats per minute (BPM) until you have fully absorbed them (singing and playing). The blue notes are particularly conspicuous at slower tempos:

Note that the patterns mostly consist of descending lines. This is an inherent attribute of the Blues scale and consistent with the very nature of the Blues. The blue notes (♭3, ♭5, ♭7) tend to exert a downward pull and give melodies a melancholy quality – a wistful or even mournful inflection that is often considered quintessential to the "Blues feel".

Blues form

The lyrics of old Blues songs generally follow a three-part format:

1st phrase: statement / question
2nd phrase: repetition / reinforcement
3rd phrase: conclusion / answer

Here's what the famous Blues singer John Lee Hooker sings in the last verse of his "Wandering Blues":

„*Since you've been gone baby, I haven't been a bit of good,*
  Since you've been gone baby, I haven't been a bit of good,
'Cause I never get the loving, that I really should."

The form implied by these lyrics is similar to that of Classical tripartite music (compositions following a three-part or ternary form based on the principle of "theme – repetition/variation – contrast") and was probably influenced by European tradition. Nevertheless, consistency in form was not yet found in early Country Blues (Folk or Rural Blues) songs. Old Blues recordings show that the duration of the verse was often varied freely depending on the flow of the lyrics. Initially self-accompanied, Blues singers would spend as much time with a phrase as was needed, before moving on to the next. Only with the migration of black musicians into the major cities did Urban Blues (or City Blues) appear. Blues singers were now often accompanied by other instrumentalists and a more structured approach became necessary. As a result, the standardised 12-bar form divided into three four-bar phrases – the AAB Blues form – was born:

The same form established itself in instrumental Blues. A good example of this is "The Blues Walk" by Clifford Brown (in B♭):

Another Blues category is referred to as **_Riff Blues_** ("riff" = repeated phrase). Riff Blues also follow the customary 12-bar form, but all three four-bar sections are identical. Here are two well-known examples:

"Bag's Groove" (Milt Jackson)

"Sonnymoon For Two" (Sonny Rollins)

As the Blues evolved, the standard four-bar subdivision gradually eroded and the 12-bar structure was rather heard as one long melodic phrase (e.g. "Au Privave" by Charlie Parker and "Isotope" by Joe Henderson).

Blues harmony

Blues Harmony emerged from early American Church music. In particular, the ever-present "Amen", set to a plagal cadence (see p. 88) at the end of most hymns, served as the source of the two most important functions used in the Blues – I and IV (in F):

At first, Blues compositions revolved almost exclusively around these two sounds (the earliest recordings show that sometimes only the tonic was used). It is also conceivable that the guitar – the most popular instrument in the accompaniment of Blues – played a decisive role. The tuning of the guitar E-A-D-G-B-E naturally emphasises the interval of a fourth. Listen to John Lee Hooker, for example, accompanying himself in his "I'm Wandering" (The Blues Collection 1: Boogie Man, track 17, wrongly labelled "Wandering Blues"). It is easy to hear that he plays the bottom two open strings E and A with a steady rhythmic drone, occasionally interspersed with little riffs and fills. As a result, his accompaniment sounds as if it consists only of the functions I and IV (V does not occur at all).

The Vth degree did not appear until much later in the development of the Blues. Once established, the harmonic structure of the Blues can be said to correspond to an elongated version of the extended cadence I-IV-V-I. Here is the 12-bar functional sequence of a traditional Blues:

While Blues harmony is based on simple *major* functions, the melodies – as we've seen earlier – are primarily based on the *minor* Pentatonic scale. Both layers affect one another and, in this way, generate the peculiar tension distinctive of the Blues. The first and most obvious result of this blending of opposite colours becomes apparent when we expand the basic triads I, IV and V into four-note chords by adding notes from the Blues scale (in F):

F Blues scale

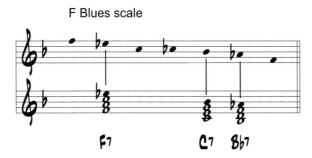

As you can see, not only the dominant (C7) but also the tonic (F7) and the subdominant (Bb7) are seventh chords. The unusual thing: I7 and IV7, in contrast to traditional interpretation, are *NOT dominant functions!* I7 is perceived as a *stable* seventh chord without need for resolution.

The following chorus in "Sack Of Woe" by trumpeter Nat Adderley nicely illustrates the mingling of minor melody with major harmony:

This solo exclusively uses the basic Blues scale and helps clear up a widespread misconception. Up until now, we have always assigned one or more scales to every chord dependent on its function. This leads us to the general assumption that the tonal material changes from one chord to the next. *This is not the case with the Blues!* The tonic Blues scale applies to *every* chord in a chord progression irrespective of its function and chord type, regardless of any clashes and tensions. Here are the intervallic relationships between the Blues scale and the functions I7, IV7 and V7:

F7	1	♯9	4	♯11	5	♭7	1
B♭7	5	♭7	1	♭9	9	4	5
C7	4	♭13	♭7	maj7	1	♯9	4

Play each chord on the piano and sing the Blues scale r-e-a-l-l-y slowly, so that you can savour the effect of each and every note. You'll notice, for example, that the 4 (usually an avoid note in 7th chords) plays a vital melodic role. ♯4/♭5 of the tonic also creates considerable dissonance with IV7 as a ♭9 and V7 as a maj7 (!), even if it only appears as a chromatic passing tone. It wouldn't be the Blues without these wonderful "dirty" notes.

We can also derive the typical extensions of the basic harmony from the table above. Notice that V7 uses altered tensions (♯9/♭13). The most interesting thing, though, is the use of ♯9 for I7. This, too, is a trademark of the Blues: major third and minor third (♯9 = ♭3), both used as part of the tonic chord. By the way, this clash (3 against ♯9 on I7 and V7) is what I hear as blue notes. In Blues, the ♯9 does not appear together with ♭9 or ♭13, as it is customary for altered dominant seventh chords within the context of standard Jazz progressions. After all, I7 in Blues is not a dominant chord in the usual sense (it does not have a dominant function). The tensions ♭9 and ♭13 appear exclusively in dominant functions and are not part of the tonic Blues scale. ♯11/♭5 – being one of the blue notes – is, of course, also an important tension for I7.

One thing before we move on: We haven't yet talked about the matter of notation. Which key signature do we use when dealing with melodies that are predominantly based on minor-pentatonic material and harmony that focusses primarily on major key functions? The quick answer to this difficult question: The chord progression wins! Even if the melody sticks closely to the basic Blues scale, the key signature will still be based on the changes. It is common practice to notate a Blues in major and to add the necessary accidentals to the melody.

Blues scale versus Mixolydian

Over the years, Blues melodies gradually departed from the basic Blues scale. In the late 1940s, I7, IV7 and V7 were increasingly interpreted as independent dominant seventh chords and thus often played as Mixolydian. This was a direct consequence of the rising awareness of church modes associated with Bebop. It was also customary to use chromatic passing notes, approaches and embellishments in improvisation (see p. 250 ff. and the Blues chorus on p. 257).

It is interesting that most soloists strictly separate the two approaches, clearly using either the basic Blues scale or Mixolydian (with chromatic embellishments) and not mixing the two. However, it is quite common to switch repeatedly from one "philosophy" to the other and back during a solo. This only works, though, if either approach is applied exclusively for a certain amount of time. While the Blues scale can be played over any chord without a second thought (horizontal approach), using Mixolydian (vertical approach) implies that the scale material changes from chord to chord. Due to the different character of the two playing concepts, it is virtually impossible to merge both "philosophies" and still come up with convincing lines. Have a look at the Blues chorus on p. 228 and compare it to Nat Adderley's solo shown above. The two examples couldn't be more contradictory in nature, but they both – each in their own way – express the Blues.

All the same, there are phrases typical to the Blues that combine the two concepts. If you mix the notes of F, B♭ and C Mixolydian on the one hand with the F Blues scale on the other, this is what you would get:

| 1 | 2 | ♯2/♭3 | 3 | 4 | ♯4/♭5 | 5 | 6 | ♭7 | maj7 | 1 |

The result is known as the "extended Blues scale". Notice that only ♭2 and ♭6 are missing. These two intervals are never heard in traditional Blues phrases. They do, however, appear under certain conditions (we'll get back to these two notes in just a second). Of course, the extended Blues scale is not used in its entirety (working with so much chromaticism would sound strange). Have a look at a few typical phrases derived from this material:

The tensions used commonly these days with I7, IV7 and V7 are derived from the extended Blues scale as well:

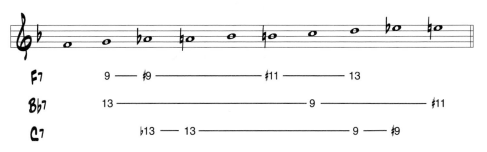

Despite the variety of available tensions, improvisers tend to fall back on the following conventions:

- On I7, 9 and ♯9 are never used together. The combinations ♯9/13, ♯9/♯11 and ♯11/13, on the other hand, work really well with a Blues tonic. If we want the sound to be less grating, we could also turn to 9/13 as the more conventional extensions derived from Mixolydian.

- With IV7, any combination of 9, ♯11 and 13 will work well.

- With V7, the most common combinations are ♯9/♭13 or 9/13 (the more consonant sound). Again, ♯9 and 9 are never mixed. The same holds true for ♭13 and 13. However, ♭9 and ♯11 are often used as additional tensions. Within an F Blues, we are talking about C7 and the notes D♭ and F♯/G♭. These relate to F as ♭6 and ♭2 – the two notes that were missing from the extended Blues scale. With V7, however, they can be used, since both reinforce the quality of an altered dominant seventh chord.

With this approach – and because of the extensive chromaticism of the extended Blues scale – certain "rules" have to be observed, the most important being the treatment of IV7 in bar 5. Because it is quite common to play the major third (3) of the key on I7, it is important to switch to ♭3 on IV7 (= ♭7 of IV7). So, don't sit on 3 when playing over IV7!

It is interesting that I7 can have two different functions. Although harmonically stable as a Blues tonic, I7 can also be interpreted and played as a secondary dominant (V7/IV) in the fourth bar to prepare IV7 more convincingly:

I7 Blues			V7/IV HM5/Alt	IV7 Blues
‖ F7	⁄.	⁄.	F7	B♭7 ‖

This interpretation can be found in many improvisations. Whereas basic Blues phrases are usually played over the first three bars (I7), we often hear HM5 or Altered lines in the fourth bar (played as V7/IV), driving the seventh chord forward towards IV7 and intensifying the cadential effect.

Extended Blues

The original 12-bar Blues progression has been increasingly changed and diversified by introducing passing chords and small harmonic detours. On the following pages, you will find a number of harmonically modified Blues forms. Have a good look at the various progressions in terms of functions and scale relationships (I have provided a rough analysis using arrows and brackets). Let's start with the basic Blues as a point of reference:

Here are three frequently used variations:

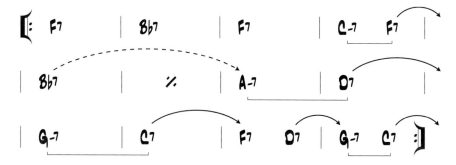

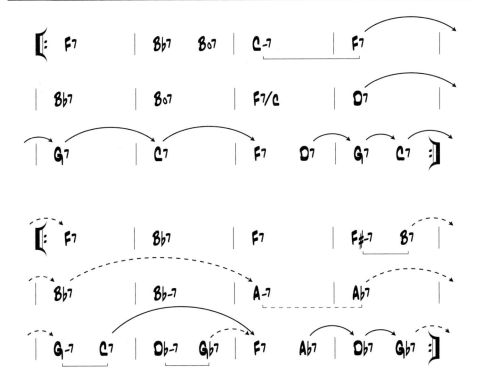

It is still possible to recognise the backbone of the basic Blues in the previous examples: I7 in bars 1 and 11, IV7 in bar 5, cadence chord(s) at the end (bars 11/12) before returning to the beginning of the form. However, the original changes have been added to by insertion of secondary and substitute dominants, secondary II-V progressions as well as diminished passing chords. These sounds are derived from the parallel major key. What we have here is actually a type of modal interchange. In our examples, the main functions come from F Blues and the harmonic variations from F Major, using diatonic and related functions.

The three chord progressions shown above contain the most important and common harmonic variations found in a traditional Jazz Blues. In practice, they are combined freely, sometimes even changing from one chorus to the next. This means that, when playing a Blues, you have to *be prepared* – you need astute ears because you never know which version is going to happen. Every Jazz musician has his or her personal preferences and habits. You may even run into a scenario where you've got the soloist, the pianist and the bass player each drawing on a different set of changes. In the end, playing the Blues is, as always in Jazz, a matter of communication and finding common ground.

After having played, listened to and analysed literally thousands of Blues solos, it is clearly evident to me that there are three equally popular strategies on how to improvise over an extended Blues:

- Play the Blues scale (regardless of the consequences).

- Play the changes using the chord-scale relationships discussed in the chapters on secondary, substitute and extended dominants, secondary II-Vs, diminished chords, etc.

- Play a combination of the first two approaches (something that is actually done quite often). The principle is simple: Begin each chorus with the basic Blues scale and typical archaic Blues phrases over I7 and IV7 (bars 1–6). Halfway into the chorus, switch to the chord-scale approach and concentrate on each individual change (bars 7–12). So, again, you're not mixing the two "philosophies", you're using *one or the other*.

Parker Blues

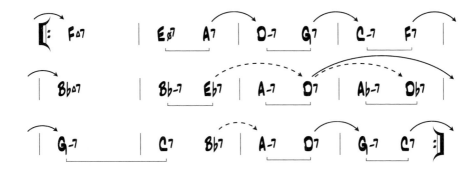

This popular Blues progression, attributed to the great saxophonist Charlie Parker, is unusual in that it contains the functions Imaj7 and IVmaj7 instead of I7 and IV7. It, too, shows the increasing influence of major key harmony and may, incidentally, be one of the reasons why Blues compositions tend to be notated with major key signatures.

The form begins with a long series of II-Vs following the cycle of fifths, leading into a sequence of chromatically descending II-Vs in bars 6–10 and ending in a two-bar turnaround (in bar 11, A–7 substitutes Fmaj7). The best-known example of this type of harmonic progression is the composition "Blues For Alice" by Parker himself. There are many pieces by other musicians that have the same chord progression with simply a new theme written over it (for example "Freight Train" by Tommy Flanagan).

Improvisations over the changes of a Parker Blues rarely work with the basic Blues scale. At best, you can hear little bits and pieces popping up every now and then. Mostly, though, solos relate to the scale material discussed for diatonic functions, secondary dominants, SubVs, secondary II-Vs and Sub(II-V)s.

Minor Blues

Strictly speaking, a minor Blues is a contradiction in terms. If we agree on the fact that the typical "flavour" of the Blues stems from the clash of minor melody and major harmony, changing the harmony to minor would obliterate everything that makes the Blues special.

Let's look at a minor Blues using the same 12-bar form and distribution of functions as found in the major Blues:

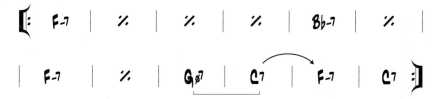

So, what makes this chord progression, which could easily be mistaken for any other minor tune (e.g. "Blue Bossa"; note the title – the allusion to the Blues is no coincidence, as we will see), a typical Blues? Since the blue notes ♭3/3 and ♭7/maj7 are no longer relevant in a minor Blues, it is only the third blue note – the flatted fifth (♭5/♯4) – that can produce the typical Blues feel. Without the ♭5, no minor Blues would really sound like the Blues. It is worth mentioning that the minor Blues did not evolve until well into the 1940s. Without having done much research myself, I think it is highly likely that it was the emergence of Bebop and the ♭5 as one of its most important intervals that made the minor Blues possible in the first place.

Melodically, a minor Blues is characterised by the ♭5, which is used indiscriminately throughout a solo (disregarding the changes). But, how do you show the minor Blues when it comes to harmony? The 12-bar form is an important feature, but it's not enough to clearly authenticate the sound of the Blues. However, there is one chord that has established itself as the central harmonic function in the minor Blues: ♭VI7. In a C minor Blues, we're talking about A♭7 (SubV/V, when thinking in terms of minor functions), which appears in bar 9 of the 12-bar form – the one place where you can really be sure that you are dealing with a minor Blues. In preparation of G7 (V7), A♭7 contains the G♭ (♭7), which corresponds to the flatted fifth (♭5) in the key of C Minor and substantiates the characteristic Blues feel harmonically.

A typical example that shows the use of ♭5 melodically and harmonically is "Mr. P.C." by John Coltrane on "Giant Steps" (dedicated to Paul Chambers):

Other good examples would be "Equinox" by John Coltrane or "Footprints" by Wayne Shorter (the latter has a Dorian tonic!).

A word on the side: I mentioned the tune "Blue Bossa" a few paragraphs ago and pointed out the word "Blue" in the title. Look at the changes (p. 102). The piece is basically in C Minor with a short detour to D♭ Major. The first 8 bars follow the same functional progression as a minor Blues (the slightly different chord distribution doesn't change the likeness). The interesting part of the tune is the modulation to D♭ Major. D♭maj7 is set up with E♭–7 - A♭7. The important note of the II-V in bars 9 and 10 is the G♭ (♭3 of E♭–7 and ♭7 of A♭7) – the flatted fifth in the key of C Minor, positioned exactly where it would appear in a traditional minor Blues (in bar 9!). It is the composer's choice that A♭7 (♭VI7 in C Minor) does not resolve to G7 (V7) but moves on to D♭maj7 (as the new tonic) instead. Note that we are now dealing with a 16-bar form and not the traditional 12-bar Blues because the changes need time to return to C–7 in a relaxed way after modulating to D♭ Major. Compositionally, "Blue Bossa" is a very clever example of how the traditional minor Blues stereotype can be transformed into an original and unique standard. The title, of course, is the give-away and shows that this transformation was intentional and that the composer was fully aware of the similarities.

Because of the variety of minor scales, there are more diatonic colours to choose from than in major keys. Apart from Aeolian, it is possible to draw on HM, MM, Dorian (as, for example, in "Footprints" by Wayne Shorter) or even Phrygian as functional sources. Theoretically, there should be many different minor Blues progressions out on the market. However, extended variations such as the following are relatively rare compared to the diversity of major Blues progressions (in F Minor):

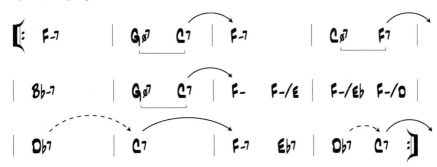

As with a major Blues, it is possible to use either the minor Pentatonic or the Blues scale over the entire chord progression. This would be a bit tiring in the long run because the characteristic flavour of the Blues, which results from the clash of major harmony and minor melody, is missing. For this reason, most soloists tend to switch from the basic Blues colour to actually playing the changes with due regard to every individual chord.

Contemporary trends

The Blues form has developed over the years and moved further and further away from its humble origins. It is obvious that this has had a profound effect on improvisation. Naturally, the characteristic colour of the Blues scale continues to play a central role. It is possible to use the Blues scale to great effect, creating gorgeous colours and "crunches" by combining "earthy" melodies with complex harmonies within the context of extended Blues progressions. As time has passed, the melodic concepts have changed. Much of the scale material used in Jazz standards has found its way into the Blues.

Here are six choruses by Sonny Stitt on the alto saxophone over an F Blues. It's not a spectacular solo, but it clearly shows how far improvisations had already advanced in the early 1950s when compared to the basic Blues scale approach. I'm not going to tell you which recording the solo is on. I don't want you to listen. Try to "read" the lines. See if you can extract the changes simply by analysing the phrases. You're sure to make some interesting discoveries. To give you a few pointers – you'll find a very vertical, chord oriented approach, use of Half-tone-whole-tone, chromatic sequences, approach patterns and passing notes, etc. Sonny Stitt even outlines Fmaj7 during the first three bars of almost every chorus (note the E in the lines), only switching to F7 in bar 4 (note the E♭) – something that may relate to the harmonic ideas introduced by the Parker Blues:

The metamorphosis of Blues melodies also affected the harmonic concepts. The strictly formalised harmony of the Blues became a palette for composers who enjoyed modifying and manipulating the traditional Blues changes. One of the most beautiful examples is "Goodbye Pork Pie Hat" by Charles Mingus. This both passionate and grief-stricken obituary of the tenor sax player Lester Young (he used to wear a classic felt "pork pie" hat) shows in the most enthralling way how the complexity of modern harmony can lend surprising angles to the archaic Blues form without impairing its integrity:

The fact that we're still talking about the Blues, despite the complex harmony, can be seen in the 12-bar form, the tonic sound F7 (I7) and the melody consisting almost exclusively of F Blues (F minor Pentatonic; for reasons of clarity and contrary to common practice I have used the key signature Ab Major / F Minor). How can we explain the intricate changes? Three principles govern the harmony of this Blues:

- reharmonisation – substitution and extension of the basic Blues changes;
- modal interchange;
- Half-tone-whole-tone as a source of melodic and harmonic material.

Let's have a look at the first two bars. I'd like to demonstrate how the principle of chord substitution turns the basic Blues functions into a highly original chord progression. The process of reharmonisation could well have looked like this:

	Bar 1	Bar 2	Bar 3	Bar 4	
Original harmony	F7	Bb7	C7	F7	Basic functions of the Blues (I7, IV7, V7) in condensed form
1st step	F7	G-7	C7	F7	IV7 replaced by II-7 (both are subdominant functions)
2nd step	F7	G7	C7	F7	II-7 replaced by V7/V
3rd step	F7	Db7	Gb7	F7	Replacement of G7 and C7 by their tritone substitutes
4th step	F7	Db7	Gb△7	B7	Replacement of Gb7 by Gbmaj7 (bIImaj7) and F7 by B7 (tritone substitution)

As the piece proceeds, modal interchange continues to play a vital role. Even though the tonic F7 suggests a Blues in F Major, we can find many chords relating to F Minor. Bars 3+4 are a kind of turnaround in F Minor (see p. 237). Bb-7 in bar 5 is IV-7 in F Minor. G-7 in bar 6 can be interpreted as II-7 in F Major or as IV-7 in D Minor (the relative minor key). So, in bars 5 and 6, where IV is usually found in the Blues, we encounter a play on modal interchange subdominant functions.

G-7 - C7 would normally cadence back to F7 (the tonic being the expected function in bar 7 of the Blues form). D7 appears instead – a delightful harmonic "side-step" that is easy to explain. Remember that Half-tone-whole-tone has a melodic as well as a harmonic symmetry (repeating in b3-intervals). Subsequently, F7 HTWT must automatically also contain Ab7, B7 and D7 (see p. 182). The D7 is clearly a HTWT substitute for F7. That Charles Mingus was actually thinking HTWT shows in the melody: The notes Ab (b5/#11), B (13) and F (#9) clearly indicate HTWT as the scale of origin (no other dominant scale contains this combination of tensions). The G7 in the same bar supports this line of argument: Both E (13) and Bb (b3/#9) in the melody point to HTWT.

Bars 7–9 follow a long, chromatically descending sequence of dominants: D7 - G7/Db7 - Gbmaj7 (implying C7) - B7 - Bb7, with Gbmaj7 replacing C7 for melodic reasons and as an allusion to bar 2. In bar 10, C7 is the cadence chord back to F7. Eb7 is interpolated as a HTWT-substitute for C7 to keep the chord progression moving at half-bar intervals. Bars 11 and 12 correspond to bars 1 and 2. What a tune!!!

Because of the tricky reharmonisations, "Goodbye Pork Pie Hat" is a difficult piece to solo on. I have heard highly accomplished Jazz musicians fail while working their way through the convoluted changes and trying to capture the mood of the piece at the same time. Of course, you could attempt to catch every chord, but, as illustrated by the melody, the basic Blues scale is probably the most effective choice for a convincing improvisation. Here you have an exceptional example of a brilliantly sophisticated harmonic scheme that allows or even calls for a basic and simple soloing approach.

Long-metre Blues

Jazz musicians have consistently attempted to break away not only from the melodic and harmonic constraints but also from the "tyranny" of the 12-bar framework, resulting in a number of compositions that fall into the category known as *long-metre Blues*. This usually means the elongation (mostly doubling) of the basic form. I'd like to introduce you to a few long-metre variants of the Blues types we've spoken about.

Let's start with "The Healer" by Wilton Gaynair. This composition is a basic Blues with a 24-bar form and an unusual harmonic twist at the end:

Take note of the atypical melody. The phrases consist mainly of diatonic arpeggios, and the elementary Blues scale is nowhere to be heard (perhaps with the exception of bars 10/11 because of the E♭). All chords are Mixolydian, whereas E♭7 (SubV/II) and D♭7 (SubV/I) could also be Lydian(♭7) for tonal reasons.

Other long-metre Blues following the basic Blues format are "The Sidewinder" by Lee Morgan (a straight-8ths funky Blues in E♭), "Footprints" by Wayne Shorter, a 3/4 Blues in C Dorian in which the usual A♭7 - G7 (♭VI7 - V7) cadence at the end is substituted with D7 -

Db7 (tritone substitution) or "Foreign Correspondent" by the Yellowjackets (with its unusual HTWT-melody).

A further good example is "Bluesette" by Toots Thielemans – a 24-bar composition derived from a Parker Blues in 3/4 time:

While the opening passage closely follows the Parker Blues format all the way up to Ebmaj7, the progression then modulates to Db Major and Cb Major via a series of II-V-I patterns. While Dbmaj7 is clearly Imaj7, Cbmaj7 can be analysed either as Imaj7 Ionian or bIImaj7 Lydian in Bb Major. If we take the latter analysis, the transition from Cbmaj7 to Cø7 would be particularly smooth because Cb Lydian and C Locrian both consist of the same notes apart from the root (check this out!). With Cø7 - F7 (modal interchange II-V) we are back in the original key. "Bluesette" is one of the best known and most often played Jazz standards there is – and proof that it pays to compose. According to Toots Thielemans himself, these 24 bars have guaranteed him a life-long basic income from royalties (and not a bad one, either!).

A long-metre Blues usually consists of an exact augmentation of the number of bars from 12 to 24, doubling each function. The basic 12-bar form, however, can also be expanded in other ways. Typical examples of this are "Sticks" by Cannonball Adderley (a 14-bar Blues) and "Soul Station" by Hank Mobley (on the album by the same name), a 16-bar extended Blues with an unusual functional progression (listen and analyse!).

The 24-bar long-metre Blues itself can also be expanded. A good example of this is the title "Snakes" by Bob Berg (on the album "The Search") – a high-energy minor Blues that starts out as a 24-bar long-metre Blues, extending into a 32-bar form by means of a harmonic loop (bVI7 - V7) and a modal-interchange ending (bVImaj7 - bIImaj7). The tune has quite a special melody – very angular with many twists and turns (as the title suggests). For lack of space, I will just give you the changes:

Fast Latin

```
‖: C-7 | ∕ | ∕ | ∕ | ∕ | ∕ | C7 | ∕ | F-7 | ∕ | ∕ | ∕ | C-7 | ∕ | ∕ | ∕ |
| Ab7 | ∕ | G7 | ∕ | Ab7 | ∕ | G7 | ∕ | Ab7 | ∕ | G7 | ∕ | Abo7 | ∕ | Dbo7 | ∕ :‖
```

Two more examples of the extended Blues form in a major or minor key are the 26-bar (!) theme "Yearnin'" and the 16-bar Blues "Stolen Moments", both by Oliver Nelson and to be found in the chapter "Arranging 101" (pdf-G).

Finally, I'd like to mention the use of the 12-bar Blues as the A section of an AABA song form:

With its eight-bar bridge, the form usually encompasses 44 bars. Good examples of this are "Locomotion" by John Coltrane and "Unit Seven" by Sam Jones. The composition "Moving Out" on **track 42** also follows this format.

Blues has come a long way. It always was and still is an omnipresent sound in Jazz – no matter how advanced or complex the harmony may be. The Blues is an integral part of Jazz, if not its origin. Blues is the spice that gives every sound its pungent taste and earthy smell. If you don't know what to say, play the Blues! If you get lost while improvising, play the Blues!! If you want to sound hip, play the Blues!!!

The Turnaround

We have seen that the patterns V-I and II-V-I are derived from the diatonic cadence, and we have discussed how they can be applied as preparatory sounds for diatonic target chords – as secondary or substitute dominants and as secondary II-V or Sub(II-V) progressions. Back-tracking one step further in the diatonic cadence provides us with the functional progression VI-II-V-I, commonly referred to as the *turnaround* or *turn-back* (in F Major):

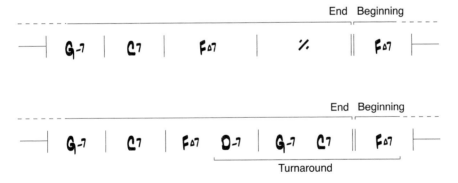

The initial use of the turnaround was based on a practical necessity. During improvisation, the chord progression of a composition is usually repeated several times. Since the first and last chords in a chorus are often identical (the tune ending and beginning on I), the chord progression tends to stagnate when moving from one chorus to the next. In such a case, a short cadential loop is inserted before the repeat in order to avert harmonic standstill, to signpost the end of the form and to drive the piece on towards the beginning of the following chorus by circling back to I (hence the name):

Over the years, the turnaround has become established as an independent harmonic formula. It is the foundation of many chord progressions – mostly as a four-bar or two-bar cycle, depending on whether the chord changes occur once every bar or in half-bar intervals. The starting point of the turnaround can vary without changing its functional sequence. More frequently than VI-II-V-I, you will find the shifted versions I-VI-II-V or II-V-I-VI. The fourth permutation (V-I-VI-II), however, is almost non-existent, the reason being its awkward distribution of tonic and cadence functions (we'll talk about this topic in the chapter "Harmonic Rhythm").

Turnarounds in major keys

A turnaround can be varied without changing its cadential structure by using substitutions. The basic scale degrees I-VI-II-V-I are each replaced by related functions. Here are the most important substitutions (in F Major):

I	VI	II	V
F△7	D-7	G-7	C7
A-7	D7	G-7(b5)	Gb7
A-7(b5)	Ab7	G7	Gb△7
A7	Ab△7	Db7	G#△7
Eb7	F#△7	Db△7	
F7	Ab△7		

The following selection of turnarounds shows the most common combinations of these functional replacements. Take note that this is by no means an exhaustive list. There are many more variants that can be derived from the above substitution table:

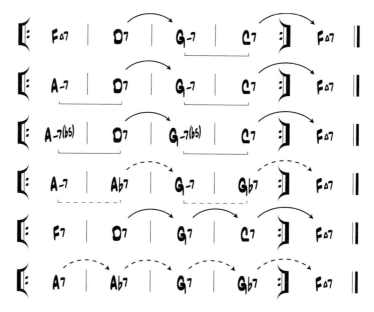

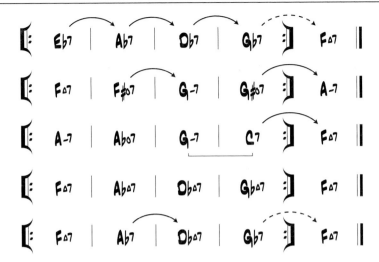

Turnarounds in minor keys

Although the turnaround plays a less prominent role in minor keys, there are, in analogy to I-VI-II-V-I in major, a number of harmonic loops that have a similar effect. In a minor context, the fundamental progression is, of course, I-♭VI-II-V-I (based on the scale degrees of Aeolian). However, many further options are available if we consider the fact that we can also draw on the diatonic functions of Melodic minor and Harmonic minor as well as Dorian or Phrygian. The tonic minor chord (I–7) in the turnarounds shown below could be substituted with I–6 or I–maj7 (from MM/HM):

We often find turnarounds based on a mixture of the various minor scales. This is how we could analyse the second turnaround:

F-7	D-7(b5)	G-7(b5)	C7
I-7	VIø7	IIø7	V7
Aeolian	MM	Aeolian	HM

Listen to **track 29** – a recording of the preceding turnaround (however, in G Minor: G–7 - Eø7 - Aø7 - D7). Note the change of colour halfway into the track. What you are hearing is a change of scale on the two half-diminished chords (VIø7 and IIø7). Instead of Locrian, the more traditional and tonal choice, the pianist now uses Locrian(9), which, in both cases, clashes strongly with the overall feel of G Minor (Aeolian). On the dominant (V7), he switches to HTWT, which is a logical follow-up of the preceding Aø7 played Locrian(9).

And yet again, the turnaround

The turnaround has become a central element of the Jazz vocabulary. As an essential ingredient of hundreds if not thousands of Jazz and Pop tunes, it is second nature to any Jazz musician and therefore firmly anchored in our musical consciousness. As a result, we are likely to interpret just about any two-bar or four-bar harmonic loop as a turnaround – regardless of whether it relates to the functional sequences shown above or not. As long as the loop follows a logical harmonic progression and resolves to a target chord every two bars (half-bar changes) or four bars (changes occurring once per bar), we are bound to hear it as a turnaround.

Listen to **track 12**. This recording begins with the basic diatonic turnaround in F Major and then moves through the most commonly found variants as listed on p. 236 ff. (each progression is played twice). After having reached the last turnaround, the musicians open up and slip into an extended improvisation. Even though they continue to follow the general concept of a four-bar turnaround, they gradually depart from traditional functional progressions on the way. The tonal boundaries become increasingly blurred, extended and chromatically distorted. The chords start to sound more and more dissonant, ambiguous and harder to define in terms of functions, basic chord symbols or specific voicings. Ultimately, the only remaining distinctive feature is the repetitive nature of the four-bar cycle and its inherent feeling of tension and release. Even though we end up with a seemingly haphazard series of sounds at times, we still retain the sense of a turnaround. After a while, the improvisation returns to the tonal centre of F Major and the musicians pass through the various turnarounds in reverse order until they again reach the starting point – the diatonic I-VI-II-V-I progression. Note, however, that the improvisations have a different quality on the way back. They are less diatonic (in scale) and have more of a chromatic flavour – as if the short detour into harmonic no-man's-land has left its mark and made the musicians more daring.

With this example, I'd like to illustrate how traditional harmony can gradually break away from its basic functional stereotypes and eventually be transformed into something new and fascinating. What you have just listened to is a history of Jazz harmony condensed into 8 minutes – from the most traditional beginnings all the way to the chromatic, dissonant and almost atonal world of contemporary Jazz. We have to know the old formulas, understand their origins and appreciate their habitual application in order to follow (and create!) new trends in harmony. Many exciting sounds found in music today can be traced back to elementary principles – even though some of these innovations may be hard to explain or impossible to notate using common musical language or traditional functional symbols. Most have developed through incremental stages over a considerable period of time to what is considered today to be state of the art. Even those musicians, who can be seen as the true musical avant-garde, have all served long apprenticeships and paid their dues by first following the path of their many predecessors. Change doesn't happen overnight. It is the result of creative thinking, hard work and respect for tradition, spurred on by a need for transformation and an acumen for new sounds.

You will find a summary of all the chord functions we have discussed up to this point in the file pdf-B – "Overview of Functions".

Guide Tone Lines

Flowing harmony depends on good voice leading. *Guide tone lines* – a series of single notes threading their way through a chord progression – play a vital role in connecting harmonies. They give a progression of vertical structures (chords) horizontal motion (melody) by joining the scale material (chord tones and tensions) of the individual chords in the closest possible way, mostly by common tones or stepwise melodic movement.

We have already seen an example of good voice leading when discussing the diatonic cadence (p. 87). Remember in particular the minimal movement of thirds and sevenths. 3/♭3 and maj7/♭7 are the essential guide tones – the connective tissue – of any sequence of chords and provide the characteristic voice leading in a traditional context. All cycle-of-fifths progressions contain two primary guide tone lines. One starts on the third, the other on the seventh. Here is a typical example:

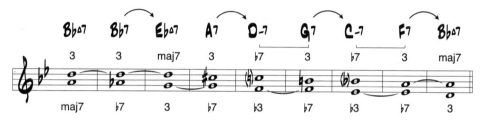

Extended dominants work in the same way. Have a look at the following example:

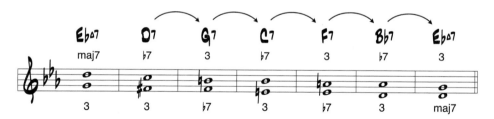

Every seventh chord resolves chromatically, with 3 and ♭7 (the tritone) alternating positions from one chord to the next, resulting in two chromatic lines.

Chromatic voice leading of the tritone also applies to progressions containing both secondary and substitute dominants (watch out for enharmonic equivalents):

With the aid of this voice leading principle, even non-pianists can manage simple accompaniments at the keyboard. Here's how to do it: The left hand plays the roots and the right hand takes care of the thirds and sevenths. By way of illustration, let's have a look at the chord progression of "Tune Up" (lead sheet on p. 101 ff.):

There are numerous melodies that are nothing but variations or embellishments of guide tone lines based on thirds and sevenths. A good example is the theme from "All The Things You Are" (A section):

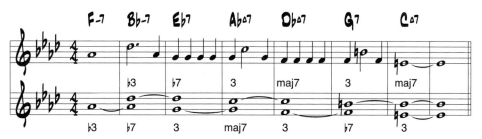

One of the most beautiful examples of a theme based almost entirely on guide tone lines is the composition "Line For Lyons" by Gerry Mulligan (on the album "Gerry Mulligan – Paul Desmond Quartet", Verve MGV-8246). The remarkable thing about Gerry Mulligan's quartets was that they dispensed with the piano and relied solely on bass and drums for the rhythm section. It's not as if the harmony were missing. It's easy to make out the chord progression at any given point. While the bass provides the foundation, the alto sax and the baritone sax play melodies that are embellishments of the thirds and sevenths of each chord. To the ear, this three-part counterpoint comes across as a harmonic unit even though there are hardly any vertical structures to be heard.

The following transcription shows the two horn parts as well as a condensed version that depicts the underlying guide tone lines. Watch out for the baritone sax; it is first written in bass clef (as it sounds) while the corresponding guide tone line is notated in treble clef:

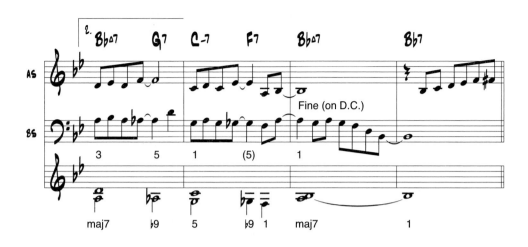

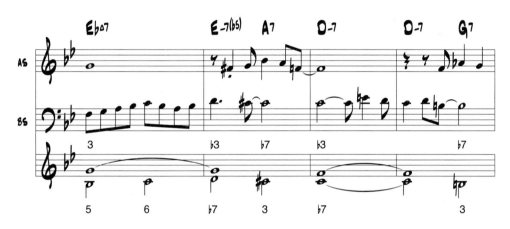

Find the recording, sing/play the two guide tone lines (first one, then the other), compare each line with the actual horn parts and check out the analysis. You'll realise that you can't just focus on the most conspicuous notes (e.g. the long notes). In some cases, the guide tones are camouflaged by the active melody and merely pop up as eighth notes at the points of resolution from one chord to the next. Note the guide tone line accompaniment of the baritone sax behind the alto sax solo.

There are many recordings of "Line For Lyons". The most impressive, in my humble opinion, is a live recording by Chet Baker (tp) and Stan Getz (ts) on "The Stockholm Concerts" (1983). The rhythm section sits out and leaves the stage to two masters interacting at the peak of their creative potential. The relaxed way they trade off phrases and make their ideas mesh is proof of the fact that there is no need for a harmony instrument or a bass if you rely on guide tone lines as the connecting principle.

Please don't get the impression that guide tone lines consist only of thirds and sevenths. *Any* note (chord tone or tension) can be used to voice-lead a chord progression, and *any* line that produces forward melodic motion and a strong sense of direction will act as a guide tone line. The A section of "Darn That Dream" (Jimmy van Heusen) is an impressive example:

Analyse each individual guide tone (*) and its relationship with the corresponding chord and you will discover a colourful mixture of intervallic functions. Note that the theme has an additional guide-tone-line-like ingredient. The melody begins on a d′ and lands on a d″ at the climax in bar 4. In bar 5, we again hear the d″ before descending back to the starting note. The octave d′-d″ bracketing the melody adds to its structural integrity:

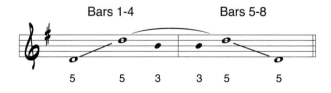

There are melodies that are made up of a combination of several guide tone lines. Let's have a look at "Take The A Train" (Billy Strayhorn):

The B section sounds highly coherent, not only because of the clear four-bar motivic repetition but also because of the many guide tone lines that tie into both the preceding and ensuing A sections (the form is AABA):

"Take The A Train" demonstrates that guide tone lines can be exclusively descending or ascending, move in a wave-like fashion or consist of repeated notes.

The line cliché

A widely used variant of the guide tone line is the *line cliché* – a voice leading principle found mostly in a minor context. A line cliché adds movement to a static harmonic situation and usually appears as a *descending* or *ascending* connecting element between the 5 and the 8/1 of a chord – either as part of the bass line or as an active inner voice. Infrequently, a line cliché serves as the basic substance of a melodic phrase. Line clichés usually progress stepwise. They can be chromatic (e.g. 1-maj7-♭7-6-♭6-5), diatonic (e.g. 1-♭7-♭6-5) or a combination of both.

A good example for the progression "1-maj7-♭7-6 (-♭6-5)" is the piece "In A Sentimental Mood" by Duke Ellington (A section). Here, the line cliché can be found in one of the middle voices (neither bass nor melody are involved):

There are pieces, however, in which the line cliché is in the bass, for instance in the ballad "My Funny Valentine" by Richard Rodgers:

We hear the line cliché as a melodic element in the composition "On Green Dolphin Street" by Bronislaw Kaper:

The same line cliché is commonly used within the context of II-V progressions, with the line connecting both chords:

The composition "Israel" by John Carisi – a relatively complex minor Blues, first heard on the legendary album "Birth of the Cool" by Miles Davis – is based on the cliché variant 5-#5-6-♭7 (-maj7-1). Here's the tune:

And here is the line cliché from within the progression:

As mentioned above, we also find combinations of ascending *and* descending line clichés (e.g. 5-♯5-6-♭6-5). Everybody knows the notorious James Bond motive that shows the use of this cliché in a minor key. One of the rare examples in major is the introduction to "Lucky Southern" by Keith Jarrett:

Line clichés don't actually have any functional significance. They are simply a means to harmonic variety, bringing motion and impetus to otherwise stationary chords.

Guide tone lines and improvisation

Time and again, we will see that guide tone lines play a decisive role in improvisation. Many solos emanate an extraordinary feeling of confidence and fluidity precisely because important and conspicuous notes in individual phrases as well as longer passages follow consistent voice leading. This provides strong forward impulse to the melodic flow. A good example of this is the famous solo by Phil Woods on "Just The Way You Are" (by Billy Joel):

The lowest notes in each bar (marked with an asterisk) add up to a long line, giving this solo remarkable coherence despite differing motives and phrases in the upper parts of the lines.

Guide tone lines are therefore the connecting element between melody and harmony. They turn a series of vertical harmonic components (chords) into flowing linear motion (melody) by linking chord tones and/or tensions horizontally as closely as possible. I will often refer back to this topic in the following chapters.

Assignment

Devise various guide tone lines for the following progression. Make sure each guide tone line fulfils <u>one</u> of the listed criteria:

    a) Use mainly thirds and sevenths.

    b) Use mainly tensions.

    c) Use as many common tones as possible.

    d) Keep the GTLs moving in only one direction (exclusively descending or ascending).

    e) Stick mainly to whole notes (only *one* note per bar or chord).

    f) Use mixed note values (several notes per bar or chord).

Eb△7   D-7(b5) G7(b9) C-7   Bb-9   Eb13(b9)

Ab△9 Db7(#11) Eb△7   C-11   F13(#11)   F-9   Bb7   Eb△7

Chromaticism

It seems that it always was and always will be the desire of Jazz musicians to explore tonality, continually expanding on it, gradually suspending it and eventually abandoning it entirely, as is the case in Free Jazz. Chromaticism plays an essential role in this process. It is the deviation from diatonicism that disturbs our perception of tonality and initially irritates the ear. However, it is important to realise that chromaticism and diatonicism do not contradict one another. Quite the opposite: It is the interplay of these two elements that creates the intensity and sense of vitality so typical of many Jazz lines. Over the years, characteristic chromatic formulae and patterns have evolved. First appearing in the early 40s and playing a prominent role in Bebop, they have become an indispensable part of the Jazz language and are used in improvisations to this day.

Fundamentally, we distinguish between *functional* and *ornamental* chromaticism. We have already talked about functional chromaticism in some detail in the chapter on secondary dominants. We will deal mainly with ornamental chromatisicm in this chapter. As the name suggests, ornamental chromaticism has no functional meaning. It serves to colour (Greek: *chroma* = colour) and embellish an otherwise strictly diatonic environment. As a consequence, chromatic notes occur for the most part on offbeat eighth notes, while in-scale notes appear mainly on the beat. In this way, the tonal quality – scale character and corresponding harmony – of the melodic material is retained and continues to be recognisable, despite extensive chromatic ornamentation. Here is an example:

Although this phrase has the entire Chromatic scale worked into it, C Mixolydian can still clearly be heard throughout as the skeleton of the line. Notes foreign to the scale are either *passing notes* (bar 1), part of an *embellishment* or *approach pattern* (bar 2) or a *chromatic sequence* (bar 3).

Passing notes

Chromaticism is often used as a melodic link or connecting element between two scale tones. Lines containing chromatic passing notes have a more flowing, even floating quality, although they are harmonically diffuse and harder to grasp than a purely diatonic melody. Chromatic passing notes are used …

… to stretch or prolong phrases or to delay resolutions:

… to fill out phrases:

… to achieve better phrase placement with respect to the form and to improve the timing of a line in such a way that it resolves more convincingly:

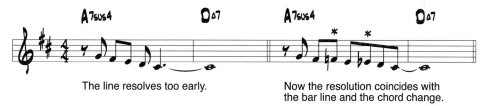

The line resolves too early.   Now the resolution coincides with
                                                the bar line and the chord change.

… to give phrases more drive and direction:

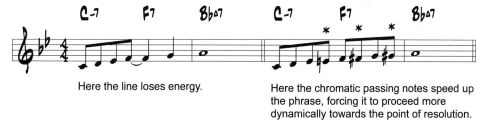

Here the line loses energy.   Here the chromatic passing notes speed up
                                        the phrase, forcing it to proceed more
                                        dynamically towards the point of resolution.

… to accelerate the phrase by increasing its rhythmical activity:

Although the last chromatic passing note (A♭) occurs on the beat, it is the next note (G) that closes the phrase (anticipation of the next bar).

Embellishments / approach patterns

Embellishments are melodic devices that are used to prepare and zero in on target notes in an assertive way. This happens with the help of ***approach patterns***, which converge on important points within a phrase either ***in scale*** (diatonically) or ***out of scale*** (chromatically):

Here are the approach variants for the notes of a Cmaj7 chord. Sing and play the following lines:

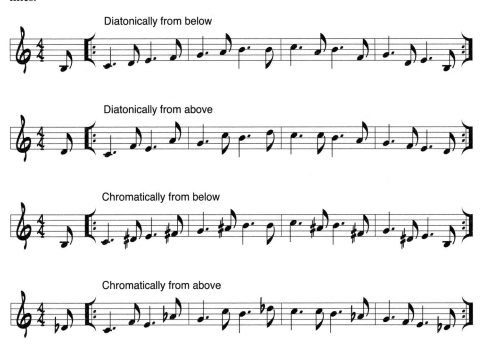

Transfer these exercises to other chord types, for example C–7 or C7. Any note can be the target of an approach note. The following example shows chromatic approaches from below (partly diatonic and partly out-of-scale; approach notes have been notated with an "x" note head):

Approach notes foreign to the scale can sometimes occur **on** the beat without causing a disturbance if there is a motivic idea governing the structure of the line. In the following example, the chromatic approach notes don't feel wrong because the melodic sequence (diatonic arpeggios in G Mixolydian) makes the line sound logical:

With an approach pattern or embellishment, a target note is approached from above and below by more than one approach note, encircling it in the process (Cmaj7):

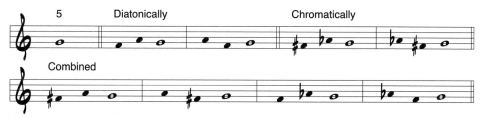

All these patterns are theoretically possible. Practically speaking, however, we most commonly find approach patterns resolving diatonically from above and chromatically from below (following the leading tone principle as found in the third (3) of a dominant chord resolving up chromatically to the root of its target chord). A few examples should illustrate this:

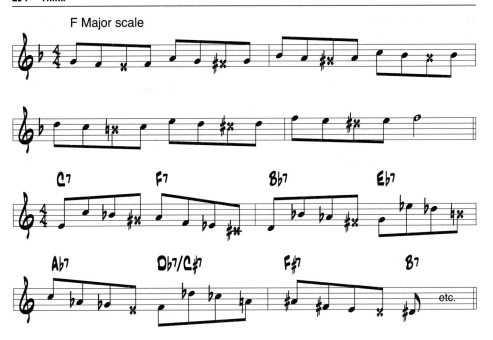

The target note can also be prepared from above or below by means of two chromatic steps – known as a *double chromatic approach*. In this way, we can construct longer chains of embellishments:

The following line is an extreme example of a chromatic line based on the turnaround:

This line can be interpreted in the following way (approach notes = black note heads; target notes = white note heads):

A line often played by the guitarist Wes Montgomery shows how approach patterns can be combined with guide tone lines:

By grouping the notes a little differently, we end up with even longer approach patterns ("x" note heads are approach notes):

The longer the embellishment, the harder it is to maintain the line's tonal orientation, especially if the chromatic notes, as in the above example, occur on a strong beat (e.g. C♯ over D7!). We therefore have to learn to listen ahead and to visualise the target note *before* we get to it if we want an approach pattern to resolve convincingly.

The following example should help develop the ability to anticipate a target note, its position in the line and, accordingly, the necessary design of the approach pattern. The target notes (marked with an asterisk) create a simple guide tone line, making the melodic focal points even more conspicuous:

As you can see: As long as a line locks into the harmony from time to time, it is not important how it meanders from one target note to the next. Homing in and landing is what counts – and nothing else!! It doesn't matter at all that we are no longer thinking in terms of scales over F7 and G7. Because a chromatic embellishment provides such a strong feeling of resolution when landing on its respective target note, it is irrelevant what material was used to reach it. Any line will work, as long as it resolves "on the button" – irrespective of whether the notes are "right" or "wrong" in relation to the key or the scale of the moment.

It is important to realise how essential accurate "phrase timing" is. Start an approach pattern too late or too early and the line will not feel "right" because the placement of the target note will feel "wrong" – even if it is just an eighth note off. Jazz musicians who are truly familiar with the intricacies of the idiom can hear immediately if someone has genuinely mastered chromatic vocabulary or is just "faking it".

Another example, also by Wes Montgomery, shows how effectively a line can be conceived, and how well thought-out an approach pattern can be:

In this example, it is not possible to remove a single note without destroying the phrase. Every note contributes to the flow of the line. All of Wes Montgomery's improvisations have this powerful forward drive.

To conclude, I'd like to use a Blues chorus to summarise the principles discussed above:

Assignment

Sing and play this chorus at about 120 BPM until you can do it by heart. Now sing and play it in slow motion. Only then will you be in a position to really appreciate every twist and turn contained in each phrase. Analyse the material in terms of scale relationships as well as functional chromaticism, chromatic passing notes and approach patterns.

Chromatic sequence

In more contemporary improvisations, we find not only single notes but also parts of a line or even entire phrases shifted chromatically against the tonality. The most commonly used technique is referred to as *pattern displacement* or *sidestepping*, whereby a series of notes is shifted and used sequentially without regard to key, scale or changes. Let's take a little two-note motive as an example:

Here's an example of how this pattern could be used in a real improvisation:

The displacement of patterns involving intervals of a perfect fourth is particularly popular. Phrases incorporating extended use of fourths sound unusual enough as they contrast melodies that reflect the structure of traditional harmony based on layers of thirds. Shifting quartal structures chromatically compounds the effect. A good, albeit extreme, example of the thematic use of fourths is the composition "Freedom Jazz Dance" by Eddie Harris. The harmonic framework for the entire theme is Bb7 Mixolydian. The leaps in fourths are marked with brackets:

Of course, it is also possible to displace longer phrases. Here are two examples:

Both lines are good examples of another displacement technique: the use of *substitute changes*. This term refers to a soloist superimposing a reharmonisation known only to him/her over the original chord progression. While the other musicians keep playing the original changes, the soloist moves, at least part of the way, on a different harmonic plane.

I would like to introduce this concept – first used consistently by Charlie Parker – by referring to two solo excerpts from the piece "Tune Up". The first improvisation is by Wes Montgomery (on the album "Movin' Along", 1st version, 2nd chorus):

Have a close look at the chromatic inserts Eb–7 - Ab7 and Db–7 - Gb7 (bars 4 and 8). Both II-Vs are played only by the soloist and act as a kind of chromatic "suspension", which is resolved in bar 5 and 9 respectively. In bar 4, the chromatic effect is only faintly noticeable because the motive dominating the first half of the chorus advances so elegantly through the transitional area. In bar 8, the line moves more freely and stands out from the diatonic framework more distinctly. In the second half of the chorus, the two chromatic approach patterns (AP) and the inserted Bb7 are worth noting.

Whereas the amount of chromatic modification in the above example is relatively small, the following excerpt by Miles Davis (a composite of two choruses from the album "Cookin' with the Miles Davis Quintet") is the epitome of chromaticism:

Chromatic thinking within a traditional environment doesn't get much more extreme than this. Combining Dmaj7 with A♭ Major and Cmaj7 with G♭ Major means mixing key signatures that are as far apart from one another as possible, resulting in maximum tension. Similarly, in the second half of the chorus, the original chord progression is hardly recognisable. The numerous chromatic sequences, passing notes and embellishments all but completely conceal the underlying changes and the corresponding chord-scale relationships.

Inside – outside

Pattern displacement and ***substitute changes*** are indispensable techniques for an approach to improvisation that has become a natural part of any contemporary Jazz soloist's repertoire: the ***inside-outside*** concept. Its appeal lies in the back-and-forth between diatonic (inside) and non-diatonic (outside) passages, the tension derived from the clash of familiar and unfamiliar sounds.

The principle is easy to explain but quite difficult to implement, at least from a psychological point of view, because the soloist has to learn to play "against the grain". Basically, we're elevating the concept of a chromatic passing note or an approach pattern, both of which work at the level of the beat or the single bar, to the level of an entire phrase or even section as a means of deliberately surprising the listener. In essence, we will hear a line that begins diatonically, leaves the tonality for a short time (tension), before returning to its tonal origins (release). The effect is quite startling. At first we are lulled by the soloist's playing the changes, adhering to traditional chord-scale relationships and fulfilling tonal expectations. As soon as the soloist starts playing outside (which usually happens quite suddenly), our immediate reaction is "What's going on? This feels all wrong!" But, because the line is presented with conviction, we quickly realise that the unusual choice of material is clearly intentional. For the avid Jazz listener, the perception switches to "Wow! This sounds hip!", though I'll concede that, to some, an outside phrase may still sound strange or even unpleasant. As the line slips back smoothly into the tonality our response will be "Oh, we're back home!" Outside phrases are usually short excursions (a few bars at the most) – otherwise the concept loses its impact. In the chapter "Licks and Tricks", I will discuss strategies and propose exercises that will help you become familiar (and, hopefully, comfortable) with inside-outside playing.

John Coltrane was one of the first to push this concept with determination. The album "A Love Supreme" (1964) – one of his central works – demonstrates extensively how the principles of tonality and modality can be gradually modified and transformed. I'd like to show you a typical passage from the first part, "Acknowledgement". While a complete transcription would be beyond the scope of this chapter, the basic idea is easily explained. The starting point is the following phrase:

From this phrase, Coltrane extracts a short motivic idea, which he then develops freely over a harmonic ostinato in F Minor (*ostinato* = a musical idea that is persistently repeated, derived from the Italian for "stubborn"; compare English: obstinate). The following illustration shows the condensed solo structure:

The improvisation follows this motivic master plan. The phrases progress through the cycle of fifths, moving further and further away from F Minor at first and then gradually arching back to the original key. It's easy to see how the number of accidentals in the music increases and diminishes, illustrating the extent of the deviation from the primary key. Of course, this is a very mechanical representation of this inspired improvisation. Coltrane uses the motivic idea in a far more liberal way, skipping back and forth, slipping in and out, playing with different levels of dissonance by moving further away from F Minor or returning to the diatonic environment intermittently.

Lines that sound tonally "wrong" but feel structurally "right" have a unique and sometimes strange quality within a diatonic context, which takes some getting used to. For those of you who are looking for non-tonal sounds for your repertoire, I can recommend the "Thesaurus of Scales and Melodic Patterns" by Nicolas Slonimsky, briefly introduced in the chapter "Modality". It is a mathematically conceived collection of interval exercises – a mind-boggling and challenging compendium of melodic shapes, which extends far beyond the world of traditional scales. The book will not tell you how to apply the material, nor does it supply information beyond the actual notes, so you will have to figure out a lot for yourself. However, it is a wonderful tool for every advanced improviser that will definitely expand your musical vocabulary, no matter what instrument or style you play. I, personally, love to work with this book as a source of inspiration (as a player as well as a composer) by randomly choosing any one of the intervallic shapes and using it as a starting point for a melody. As already mentioned, John Coltrane made extensive use of this book over a number of years and based quite a few of his compositions and improvisations on the ideas presented in this unique compilation of melodic patterns.

Unfortunately, as a result of the inside-outside concept, many people tend to believe that anything goes in Jazz. In principle, this may be true. Of course, it is almost impossible to define a universally accepted "right" or "wrong", Jazz being an idiom that is open to so many outside influences, while relying on a highly personalised language and an individual approach. Any departure from the diatonic framework, e.g. breaking tonal rules, adds spice to the sounds we use. It is, however, a huge mistake to believe that we can simply play just about anything, anytime. Quite to the contrary, playing outside requires an enormous amount of tonal understanding and control. The saxophonist Ramon Ricker rightly said:

"You can't play hip outside if you can't play hip inside!"

It is the combination of "inside" and "outside" that creates the special effect of this improvisational technique. Without the "inside" there cannot be an "outside" – one spawns the other. For the concept to work effectively, certain tonal cornerstones have to be respected and observed for the "outside" to sound meaningful and not "wrong". John Coltrane sums this up beautifully:

"No matter what you play, always play the cadence!"

If we resolve our phrases with determination at the right places in the form, in other words, if we "play the cadence", then it is basically unimportant how we reach the final note of a melodic line. Any phrase, be it diatonic or chromatic, inside or outside, will work, if it comes to rest at a harmonic focal point and is played with conviction. No matter how strange the tonal material may be – the ear will accept it as long as the line "homes in" and "lands". In the end, it is simply a question of our personal aesthetics, tolerance and stylistic taste as to how much chromaticism or strangeness a composition or improvisation can take. In the chapter "Licks and Tricks", we will take a closer look at the practical implications of the inside-outside approach.

Form

Any composition thrives on the presence of two aspects: *structure* and *aesthetics*. These refer respectively to what we could call "external form" (design) and "internal form" (the effect a piece has on the listener beyond the written music). *Structure* encompasses everything that relates to the logic and organisation of the music: the design of the melody and the harmony, the rhythmical and metrical framework, the subdivision of the complete work into smaller formal sections, etc. – in other words: the components we can *quantify* as well as the rules that govern their behaviour. *Aesthetics*, on the other hand, refers to the mood a piece conveys, to a feeling of coherence, balance, continuity, sensuality, passion, etc. and circumscribes the *qualitative,* less tangible spirit and soul of a composition. The fact that the term "aesthetic" no longer denotes "the beautiful" in the classical sense of art is self-evident – these days, dissonances, noise and even repulsive sounds quite commonly determine the character and impact of music.

Aesthetic appreciation has a lot to do with an eye both "for detail as well as the whole" and an intuitive understanding of the interdependency of many, often seemingly contradictory factors, which can only be taught or learned to a limited extent. The ability to consciously perceive music as consisting of more than the sum of its parts, to hear a sort-of "grand total" and to put this understanding into effect in our own music, is a skill we acquire and develop gradually over time. One day, it's just "there", and we don't consciously realise how this insight came about.

I therefore hope that the material covered in this chapter (and the chapters to follow) will enhance your awareness of the essential structural aspects and aesthetic qualities of good music, even though some of these ingredients are hard to put into words. I would like to shed some light on the understanding of what makes music feel "right" and not just talk about abstract musical concepts and formal rules.

Song forms

Music thrives on contrast. As we'll see later on in this book, the interplay of tension and release constitutes the driving force of harmonic and melodic activity. When considering Western musical forms, we come across the same three compositional building blocks contending for influence time and again:

- Repetition
- Variation
- Contrast

Repetition helps the listener, who is quite capable of grasping structural components and formal relationships intuitively, to follow and remember thematic elements. Variation changes what the listener knows, creates something new without losing touch with the familiar and prevents stagnation of the musical flow. Contrast introduces something different – it is the break with the initial thematic idea, fulfilling the need for change.

These three factors are inseparable. Only in conjunction with one another do they create a dynamic musical contour – each element complements the others. Too much of the same leads to monotony, too much contrast leads to chaos. Most Jazz compositions therefore look to strike a balance between these extremes – they attempt to radiate inner coherence without being too repetitive and they contain moments of surprise without losing thematic integrity.

As a result, particular formal structures that strive to maintain equilibrium between thematic continuity and contrasting passages have evolved over time and become established in our thinking. In traditional Jazz, many tunes follow a 32-bar configuration divided into four eight-bar sections – the most common of these forms being labelled *AABA* (e.g. "Nardis" by Miles Davis – see pages 360 ff.):

8 bars	8 bars	8 bars	8 bars
A	**A**	**B**	**A**
Statement (Theme)	Repetition (Variation)	Contrast (Bridge)	Recapitulation (Ending)

The B section is known as the **bridge** (it bridges the A sections). This provides the necessary contrast in an otherwise rather uniform setting.

Compositions that take the AABA format are, of course, not always 32 bars long. There are pieces that follow a 64-bar form (16-16-16-16) such as "Cherokee" (Ray Noble), "Nica's Dream" (Horace Silver) or "Love For Sale" (Cole Porter). A variation on AABA form is *ABA* – as, for example, in pieces like "One Note Samba" by Antonio Carlos Jobim (16-8-16), "Infant Eyes" by Wayne Shorter (9-9-9!) or "Stablemates" by Benny Golson (14-8-14!). Also, "Little Sunflower" by Freddie Hubbard (see p. 213) belongs to this category with its AABBAA form (8-8-8-8-8-8; sometimes the last A section is omitted because many musicians have the feeling that it upsets the balance of the composition).

Many Jazz standards are based on this or a similar form. One of the most important formats besides AABA is *ABAC* (e.g. "The More I See You" – see p. 315 ff.):

8 bars	8 bars	8 bars	8 bars
A	**B**	**A**	**C**
Statement (Theme 1)	Contrast (Theme 2)	Repetition (Theme 1)	Ending (Theme 2)

In ABAC format, the B and C sections are often similar and – as a result of their position in the form – differ only in the ending: Whereas the B section flows nicely into the repeat of the A section, the C section usually contains the overall climax of the melody and brings the piece to a close.

A close relative of ABAC is *AA'*, sometimes labelled as *AB* (not quite correctly because the letter B suggests a completely new idea, which is usually not the case – quite often, more than half of A is repeated in B). Assuming we have 32 bars, we hear two uninterrupted 16-bar sections that have no clearly discernable subdivisions and can't be broken down any further (e.g. "The Days Of Wine And Roses" – see p. 281 ff.):

The labels A and A' are used because of the different endings of the 16-bar sections, which are otherwise identical.

A less frequently used form is *ABCA* (e.g. "Stella By Starlight" – see p. 399 ff.):

Pieces that comply with this form are more complex than the average Jazz standard. They are harder to follow for the listener because the piece moves through three differing formal sections before returning to the original idea.

Two-part (AA') or four-part (AABA, ABAC, ABCA) subdivisions of a piece are not the only commonly used tune formats. Three-part subdivisions are also quite popular – as in the Blues:

Almost the entire traditional Jazz repertoire can be boiled down to one of the basic forms mentioned above and a small number of spin-offs – not really much to choose from, considering a style of music that places so much importance on individuality and variety. Why is there such a limited range of formal concepts?

One reason is down to the historical roots of many Jazz standards. Most of them originate from the "Great American Songbook". Although there is a specific collection of tunes that goes by this name, what it actually refers to is the American song heritage going back as far as the 19th century. Apart from the Blues, these songs, mostly evergreens, themes taken from well-known musicals or film melodies, are the basis of the Jazz repertoire – hence the term *song forms*. With their fairly simple structure – most pieces consist of four-bar or eight-bar phrases in 4/4 or 3/4 time – they have fashioned every Jazz musician's perception of form for decades.

The second and probably more likely reason should be obvious to every Jazz player – improvisation is a matter of feeling and intuition. The more we need to think while soloing, the more difficult it becomes to play in a spontaneous and relaxed state of mind. It seems logical that simple, easy-to-grasp forms would establish themselves as the prevailing standard in the Jazz world. Soloists have to battle on many fronts simultaneously and have more than enough on their plate, coping with changes, timing, interplay, etc. Why make the job even more challenging than it already is by adding yet another layer of complexity?

By contrast, many modern Jazz compositions are of more intricate and asymmetrical formal design. Here, we can no longer rely solely on feeling and reflexes. This may explain why, since the 1960s, fewer and fewer pieces have established themselves as Jazz standards. Sophisticated formal structures are a challenge for the intuitive soloist because they require more conscious effort while playing. The more complex the formal makeup of a tune, the more difficult it is to achieve a natural flow of ideas. In extreme cases, it is only the person who has written the piece who can improvise on it confidently.

This doesn't change the fact that even the more recent compositions are often based on traditional song forms to a certain extent. It almost always comes down to the old game of taking long-established formulae and adapting or varying them. A good example is the piece "Yes Or No" by Wayne Shorter. If you want to check out the entire composition, have a look in your Real Book. Here's the form of the tune:

14 bars	14 bars	16 bars	14 bars
A	**A**	**B**	**A**

For our purposes, I'd like to concentrate on the rather unusual A section. As you can see, the A section has 14 bars and is asymmetrical, while the bridge – in contrast – is quite conventional in its formal approach. This shows nicely how traditional concepts can be reversed without changing the original principle. Normally, the A sections are "home base" and the B section provides contrast by introducing different material. Here, it is the symmetrical B section (!) that contrasts the asymmetrical A sections.

The A section itself follows an irregular AABA format (form within form):

The succession of four-bar motives ("A sections") is interrupted by a two-bar "bridge", which accelerates both the melody and the harmony, providing contrast as well as the climax of the

14-bar phrase. In the last four-bar phrase (the third "A section"), the whole thing comes to rest. Note the sustained D in the melody, which winds down the energy in comparison to the E in the first two "A sections".

It is precisely the formal limitations of the traditional Jazz repertoire that have inspired musicians to strive for more stimulating compositional variety. This is why there are a number of examples of extended and/or asymmetrical song forms. Most of these are a play on the basic forms we have talked about earlier, with variations on the length of the individual sections. Here are a few examples of standards demonstrating unusual formal proportions:

AABA

"All The Things You Are" (8-8-8-12) by Jerome Kern
"Gregory Is Here" (16-16-8-16) by Horace Silver
"I Remember You" (8-8-8-12) by Victor Schertzinger
"Moonlight In Vermont" (6-6-8-8) by Karl Suessdorf
"Naima" (4-4-8-4) by John Coltrane
"Pannonica" (8-8-8-9) by Thelonious Monk
"Speak No Evil" (14-14-8-14) by Wayne Shorter
"Wave" (12-12-8-12) by Antonio Carlos Jobim

ABAC

"A Foggy Day" (8-8-8-10) by George Gershwin
"Airegin" (8-12-8-8) by Sonny Rollins
"Desafinado" (16-16-16-20) by Antonio Carlos Jobim
"Moment's Notice" (8-8-8-14) by John Coltrane

It is not uncommon to find yourself struggling with the form, rather than the changes. So, when learning pieces, concentrate firstly on the structure. This will help you understand the chord progression better. In most lead sheets, the end of each formal section is marked with a double bar line.

Assignment

Browse through your own repertoire and determine the formal structure of your favourite compositions. A better understanding of the formal design of a piece will help you a lot with your improvisations.

Now that we have dealt with the structural framework typical of a wide range of Jazz standards, I'd like to introduce you to a number of factors that influence the structural integrity, the dynamic contour as well as the psychological impact of both melodies and chord progressions, and which, in many cases, determine the personality and beauty of a composition or improvisation. You will find that much of what touches you as a listener is owed to a feeling of "rightness", which is first and foremost a result of the dynamic flow and captivating design of the music.

The Motive

Music is forward motion! This is why the horizontal aspect of a piece (the movement itself) has a stronger impact on the listener's perception than the vertical aspect (any particular moment in time). Accordingly, we're generally more aware of melody than harmony, a melodic phrase is more meaningful than a single note, and harmonic development (voice leading and the principle of tension and resolution) tends to have more significance than any isolated chord. This implies that looking closely at melodies often reveals more information about the structure of a composition than harmonic analysis. Although this book is primarily devoted to the study of harmony, it is essential for us all to come to grips with the basics of melodic design.

It is hard to imagine an effective melody that consists of a random series of notes. In language, stringing together a haphazard assortment of letters would result in nonsense. So, just as speech relies on words, phrases and sentences, melodies are made up of smaller groupings of notes, longer segments and sections that create a meaningful whole.

The smallest independent component of a melody is the **motive** – a short rhythmic and/or melodic idea that is usually presented at the beginning of a piece and is developed gradually as the composition unfolds. Initially, "motif" (from French: *motif*) was the only accepted spelling, making a distinction between "motif" (recurring pattern) and "motive" (reason, incentive). Today, however, the spelling "motive/s" is omnipresent in music, and I'll use it throughout this book.

As Arnold Schönberg puts it in his "Fundamentals of Musical Composition", the purpose of a motive is to provide "unity, relationship, coherence, logic, comprehensibility and fluency to a musical fabric." The motive remains recognisable within the composition as a self-sufficient thematic building block because of its intervallic and rhythmical structure. Motives are not limited in length or duration. As long as we get the feeling that we are talking about a self-contained melodic idea, it makes no difference whether a motive consists of two notes or a phrase spanning several bars. We'll see later how a catchy and effectively developed motive can determine the character and structure of an entire composition.

With motivic thinking, we try to create maximum melodic effect with a minimum of tonal material. It is amazing how many possibilities there are to be found in just a single initial motivic idea. Let's take the following phrase:

I'll now show you how this little motivic idea can be established, varied and developed by the use of specific tools.

Repetition

Almost all melodies evolve along the lines of the principle "repetition – variation – contrast". It may seem self-evident, but any idea must be repeated first before it is recognised as a motive. I place so much emphasis on this seemingly obvious fact because Jazz musicians have a tendency to avoid repetition (probably for fear of being perceived as lacking in creativity and imagination). It cannot be stated often enough: If you want to establish any musical idea as a motive you have to repeat, repeat, repeat…

Of course, blatant repetition is not the key to an exciting and inspiring improvisation. While repetition generates motivic identity and clarity, it also can produce monotony. For this reason, the concept of developing and gradually transforming the original idea, creating increasingly intense and dramatic lines in the process, is more important than simply rehashing the same phrase over and over again. Accordingly, the principles of variation are quintessential to any convincing solo.

I may add that the concept of extreme repetition also has its merits when seen as a means of creating music with a trance-inducing and hypnotic quality. Furthermore, there have always been artistic movements endorsing simplicity and the use of limited material. *Minimalism* – a genre of music originating in the 1960s and developed by composers such as Steve Reich, Philip Glass or Terry Riley – is known for its repetitive structures, elementary patterns and subtle transitions. Psychedelic, Experimental and Art Rock groups and artists such as The Velvet Underground, Brian Eno, King Crimson or Tangerine Dream explored minimal music techniques. New Age and Techno are also heavily influenced by Minimalism. With few exceptions, however, Jazz has never really picked up on this style as a source of inspiration.

Inversion, retrograde and retrograde inversion

Let's start with a set of variation techniques that are tools of the trade for every Classical composer regardless of style (e.g. they are quintessential to Baroque music and 20th century serial compositions alike). The general concept: Melodic phrases are modified by mirroring their intervallic structure. The mirroring of a phrase along the horizontal axis is known as *inversion*. This means that the direction of every interval is turned "upside down" (inverted). An inversion can be *exact* (sometimes also called "real") or *diatonic* (also "scalar" or "tonal"), depending on whether the phrase is mirrored exactly (this may imply the phrase leaving the key of the moment) or is adjusted to fit the tonal environment and the chord progression:

Reversing the order of the tonal material by reading a phrase backwards is known as *retrograde* (mirroring on the vertical axis). This usually affects the notes or sequence of intervals, but not the rhythms:

We refer to *retrograde inversion* when both techniques are applied to a phrase simultaneously (backwards and upside down). Here, too, we distinguish between exact and diatonic modification:

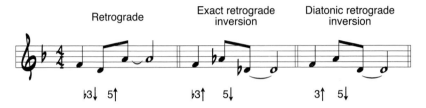

These traditional variation techniques are relatively mechanical in nature and mathematical in design. I have included them for the sake of completeness and because they are of central importance in many stylistic periods of Western European music, even if they have not really been established in the world of Jazz and are – if at all – rarely used as strictly as in Classical music as compositional devices. No Jazz musician will think in terms of inversion or retrograde while improvising, even though, while fiddling around intuitively with the notes of a motive, a soloist may well come up with variations that correspond to the techniques discussed. Nonetheless, you should be aware of these techniques, since they have had a profound influence on composition over the past 500 years.

Rhythmic variation

Two musical terms come to mind, here: *augmentation* and *diminution*. Originally, these techniques meant the exact doubling or halving of each and every note value. For our purposes, we'll stick to a more general definition by saying that any rhythmical expansion or contraction of a motive can be labelled as an augmentation or diminution respectively:

Syncopation and *rhythmic displacement* (sometimes the term "metric displacement" is used) also change the way a motive sounds by shifting its points of accent:

Tonal variation

Changing the notes while retaining the rhythms is one of the most effective ways of altering the motivic shape:

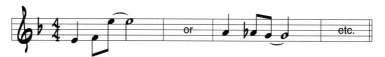

It is not only my personal perception that motivic recognition seems to be more the result of the rhythmic structure than the tonal material of a phrase. It is the rhythmic quality of a motive that has the greater impact on interplay (the way the band responds to your ideas when improvising). It is the one aspect that fellow musicians catch on to most rapidly.

Transposition and sequence

Transposition means the repetition of a motive at a different pitch. A transposition can be *exact* (real) or *diatonic* (tonal), depending on whether the structure of the motive remains identical or is adjusted to fit the key or scale of the moment:

A *sequence* is the consecutive restatement (repetition) of a motive or phrase at different pitch levels – a series of transpositions that usually displays a particular concept. Most sequences uniformly move in one direction (ascending or descending). They also tend to follow a systematic intervallic principle. Most often, sequential patterns are transposed stepwise (however, any type of intervallic displacement is possible). We differentiate between *diatonic* and *modulating* sequences. Here are a couple of examples:

Diatonic sequence descending stepwise:

Diatonic sequence ascending in thirds:

Modulating sequence (using exact transpositions):

Embellishment

A motive can be *ornamented*, *expanded* or *extended* (diatonically or chromatically) by either inserting or adding notes without changing its fundamental design:

Ornamentation may also involve the use of trills or turns.

Fragmentation and subtraction

Fragmentation is the process of isolating and then using and developing a segment of a motive. *Subtraction* is the process of simplifying a motive and "boiling it down" to its elementary ingredients (intervals, rhythmical structure, etc.):

| Fragment | Development of the fragment | Subtraction |

It should be obvious that both variation techniques work especially well with longer phrases. The shorter the motive, the harder it is to isolate a fragment or further simplify a motivic idea.

Reharmonisation

This is one of the prime variation techniques used in Jazz. Colouring a single melody note or a phrase in different ways is particularly effective when trying to achieve different levels of tension or attempting to change the mood of the music subtly. The harmony of a motive can be modified by…

…inserting additional chords:

…partly or wholly replacing the original chord progression:

The more complex a motive, the harder it is to find adequate reharmonisations because **all** melody notes have to fit the new chord or chord progression. Our motive is quite short and, accordingly, provides us with a multitude of harmonic possibilities. In the example above, note the different sound "qualities" depending on the intervallic relationship between the melody note(s) and the corresponding chord(s). While the original harmonisation is fairly simple with the melody consisting of nothing but chord tones, the suggested reharmonisations are far more colourful because the melody notes are now predominately tensions: 13 over C7(sus4), ♯11 over B7 and ♭13 over A7. Good reharmonisation requires awareness and control of the amount of tension created. We will talk about this in depth in the chapter "Harmonisation & Reharmonisation" (pdf-F).

Variation of phrasing and articulation

Unfortunately, phrasing and articulation are variation techniques that Jazz musicians tend to neglect. Classical composers seem to be far more attentive to the different ways notes or phrases can be shaped. It is possible to achieve a surprisingly wide variety of effects by specifying indications in terms of articulation (staccato, legato, tenuto, portato, accents, etc.), phrasing (swing or straight eighths, anticipations, grace notes, glissandi, drops, slides, slurs, ghost notes, etc.) as well as dynamics (see p. 511 ff. for more on this):

In practice, we come across the techniques discussed above both individually or in combination with one or more of the others. It should be clear that any motive allows for an almost inexhaustible number of ways in which it can be varied.

Let's have a look at a remarkable example of extensive and consistent motivic development – the composition "Just Like That" by Peter Herbolzheimer (on the album "More Bebop"). The main motive should be an old friend by now:

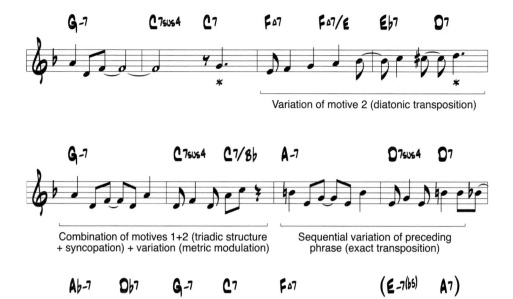

Variation of motive 2 (diatonic transposition)

Combination of motives 1+2 (triadic structure
+ syncopation) + variation (metric modulation)

Sequential variation of preceding
phrase (exact transposition)

Continuation of sequence (1-bar acceleration,
chromatic displacement) and ending

My comments should be self-explanatory. What I think is worth mentioning, though, is the little dotted quarter note – marked with an asterisk (*) – appearing repeatedly on 3+. It is important to realise that even a single note – if connected to a rhythmic concept and consistently built into the theme – can develop a motivic life of its own.

Basically, any structural feature – be it melodic, rhythmic, harmonic or formal – will acquire motivic significance as soon as it appears more than once. Take a look, for instance, at bars 7–9. You will see several inversions creating a descending bass line moving in contrary motion to the melody, which at this point happens to be motive 2 (the contrasting idea). Every time motive 2 appears (in bars 11–13 as well as bars 23 and 24), we come across the same harmonic concept (use of inversions and descending bass line). This is, of course, no coincidence – it's a trademark of this piece and most definitely a motivic idea.

Motive and improvisation

Motivic thinking plays a vital role in improvisation. There are Jazz musicians who can develop long passages based on a single motive or musical cell. When this is done with conviction, the impact on the listener is overwhelming. When hearing this kind of soloing, you sense nothing but unequivocal control, confidence and determination. You feel without a doubt that this is exactly how this solo was supposed to unfold. Even though there would have been innumerable other, equally convincing alternatives, the final result radiates such logic and integrity that there is no mistaking: "This is the way it was meant to be, everything fits, not a single note is out of place".

We encounter this type of clarity in the lines of all great players – a decisive and focussed motivic approach that accounts for their solos' tremendous energy. One of the masters, whose improvisations display this breathtaking quality, is the pianist Bill Evans. Let's have a look at the first 8 bars of his solo on the composition "Time Remembered" (on the album "Since We Met"):

The way Bill Evans develops the opening motive is exquisite. Listen to how he coaxes it up towards the climax of the phrase in bar 4, gradually changing its melodic and rhythmical design and compressing it towards the end of the passage, where it finally cascades back to its starting point. Bill Evans definitely was a true master of improvisation. The way he gave his ideas sufficient time and space to unfold, turning a single, tiny little phrase into something magnificent is magical and the sign of pure genius.

In later chapters in this book, we will repeatedly come back to talking about the motivic aspect of improvisation and its significance. Let's try to bring some of this magic into our own playing.

Harmonic and Melodic Rhythm

A musical composition is like a book in which letters, words, sentences, paragraphs and chapters are linked to form the whole. Music – harmonically and melodically – is constructed along very similar lines. This implies that single notes or isolated chords say little or nothing on their own. Only as part of the greater picture can they have any real meaning. Up until now, we have concerned ourselves mainly with the smaller units of musical structure. This chapter will serve as an introduction to the formal grammar of longer phrases and facilitate the understanding of the compositions presented later on in this book.

Harmonic rhythm

A chord progression is more than just a shapeless succession of non-related harmonies. It is rather to be seen as a rich unfolding landscape of tension and resolution. An analogy should illustrate what I mean. We know that rhythm is founded on a regular pulsating series of beats, which is divided into bars by emphasising certain beats. The resulting time signature (2/4, 3/4, 4/4, etc.) is based on a recurring sequence of *strong* (stressed) and *weak* (unstressed) beats. The little lines in the following figure illustrate the degree of stress of each beat:

As a result of the different relative stress or weight levels given to each of the beats, a periodic cycle of rhythmic tension and release occurs in any sequence of bars. The main stress always falls on the first beat of the bar – on count *one*. The ensuing, comparatively weak(er), beats generate an increase in tension (rather like breathing in), which is released abruptly on the first beat of the next bar (rather like breathing out):

At this point, we should briefly talk about the most common rhythmic weight pattern in Jazz – placing the emphasis on beats two and four rather than on one and three in a 4/4 bar. By shifting the attention away from the strong beats 1+3 inherent to Western European music, the weaker counts 2+4 take on more significance. By upgrading the weak beats and counterbalancing the traditional weight pattern, we get a more even and uniform pulse that disguises the bar line, giving rhythmical phrases a more floating quality and improvisers more freedom in the placement of their ideas. This doesn't alter the fact that all of us – Jazz musicians or Classical musicians, amateur or professional alike – still tend to feel beats one and three as "heavier". It's part of our musical heritage, our roots – whether we like it or not. Just how firmly the traditional positioning of strong beats is ingrained in our subconscious can be experienced time and again, with concert audiences mercilessly and inexorably clapping along on 1+3, even if the drummer is clearly emphasising 2+4 on the hi-hat or snare.

Chord progressions also follow this rhythmic principle of tension and release. Since the chord changes in most standards occur regularly (at half-bar, one-bar, two-bar or, more rarely, four-bar intervals), it is possible to speak of a harmonic pulse. This pulse is not perceived as a uniform flow of harmonies but rather as a sequence of periodic ups and downs, subdividing the chord progression into groups of bars and sections (usually indicated by the use of double bar lines). These sections of 4, 8, more rarely 12 or 16 bars can be referred to as *multi-measure* or *multi-bar phrases*, *periods* or *units*. In mainstream Jazz, the eight-bar period is the most widespread.

For a Jazz player it is important to develop an intuitive awareness of the duration of multi-measure phrases. It is imperative we eventually arrive at a point where it is no longer necessary to consciously count bars. In contemporary Jazz, it is quite common to temporarily manipulate and obscure the formal structure by making use of polyrhythmic superimpositions and metric displacements without actually abandoning the form. For this reason, a feel for multi-measure units must be firmly anchored in our subconscious if we want to handle complex rhythmical situations without getting lost (this is particularly important for eight-bar and 16-bar periods). In contemporary compositions, where odd-bar phrases and asymmetrical structures are quite common, it is the deviation from our deep-rooted reflexes that helps us grasp unusual formal events.

In multi-measure units, it is the succession of alternating strong (S) and weak (W) harmonies that determines the flow of the section. Chord progressions tend to oscillate in waves, regularly moving from a lower to a higher level of tension and back again – rather like breathing in (weak = tension) and breathing out (strong = release).

Chord changes every half bar:

$$ \text{S} \quad \text{W} \mid \text{S} \quad \text{W} \mid \text{S} \quad \text{W} \mid \text{S} \quad \text{W} $$

Chord changes every bar:

Chord changes every two bars:

The *frequency* of the chord changes in conjunction with the periodic rise and fall of *tension levels* within a chord progression is known as *harmonic rhythm*.

As we go from "weak" to "strong", we move from harmonic tension to resolution:

- *Weak* = cadence chords and unstable functions (motion/tension)

- *Strong* = target chords and stable functions (rest/release)

Here is a typical example:

It is easy to see why this turnaround has managed to establish itself as one of the most popular and commonly used harmonic phrases – it corresponds to the weight pattern of a 4/4-bar translated into a four-bar unit. Fmaj7 and G–7 are target sounds occurring in the "stronger" bars 1 and 3. Both chords are prepared by dominants (cadential functions), which appear in the weaker bars 2 and 4. Fmaj7, the tonic sound, is particularly strong and therefore acts as a "one" in the harmonic phrase, whereas G–7, a secondary diatonic degree (a subdominant function), is not quite as stable as Fmaj7 but still strong because it is preceded by D7.

Let's look at a seemingly insignificant variation of the same turnaround (actually the most basic version of I-VI-II-V):

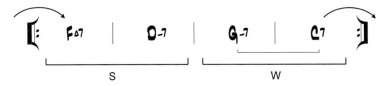

As you can see, bar 2 no longer contains a dominant chord. Now, the first two bars are strong (Imaj7 and VI–7 both being tonic functions) and bars three and four are weak (both II–7 and V7 being cadence chords wanting to resolve).

Two conclusions can be derived from the comparison of the two turnarounds shown above. For one, it is not always practical to look at a chord progression one chord at a time. Chords of similar functions (either "strong" or "weak") can occur in groups, not necessarily coinciding with the harmonic frequency: Even though our second turnaround has a harmonic frequency of one chord per bar, the strong-weak distribution follows a two-bar pattern. Secondly, a chord can have a different meaning depending on its relationship with the immediately preceding or subsequent harmonies. It is the environment of a chord that determines whether it should be considered strong or weak. In our examples, G–7 is perceived as strong when preceded by D7. Following D–7 (a tonic function), however, G–7 is weak in comparison because it is a diatonic cadence chord in the key of F Major.

These principles are often varied in order to create special effects. For example, we can modify the harmonic rhythm of a phrase by speeding up or slowing down the frequency of the chord changes:

Acceleration (increase in tension):

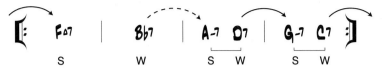

Deceleration (decrease in tension):

Another common means of creating contrast is the deliberate reversal of the usual placement of strong and weak chords within a multi-measure phrase. In the following example, the cadence chords appear in strong bars and the corresponding target chords occur in weak bars, giving the chord progression a completely different feel:

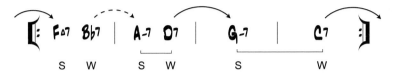

The Jazz standard "The Days Of Wine And Roses" (Henry Mancini) illustrates how the harmonic rhythm of a chord progression can contribute decisively to the dynamic contour of a composition:

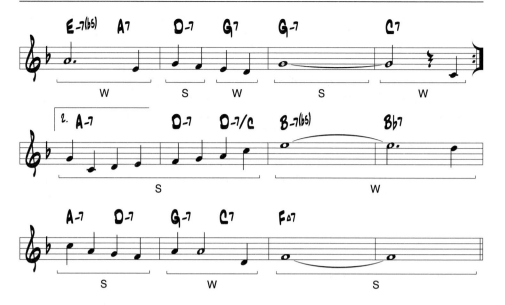

Be aware of the fact that, for now, we are primarily discussing harmonic material. We will return to this piece for a more detailed melodic analysis at a later point. Furthermore, when dealing with formal aspects, it is important to understand that we are not talking about cut and dried facts but rather general tendencies. It is therefore necessary that you learn to distinguish between more or less important features of a composition. Not every note or chord has the same significance or is equally relevant to the overall development of the piece. So, don't try to be too nitpicky and hyper-analytical. There is no need to understand every twist or turn of a composition. As long as you grasp the gist of things, I'm perfectly happy.

The first 8 bars of "The Days Of Wine And Roses" follow a two-bar harmonic pulse. Don't get distracted by the Eb7 in bar 2. Two bars of D7 and G–7 clearly indicate that the chord progression moves at two-bar intervals. The two Eb7 chords in bars 2 and 8 do not affect this basic pulse: The first Eb7 is only a passing chord resolving to D7, and the second is no more than an extension of Bb–maj7 (II-V pattern). The melodic movement underpins the harmonic pulse (sing the theme keeping the two-bar pulse in mind and pay attention to the motivic phrases). If you listen very carefully, you can hear an eight-bar turnaround (Fmaj7 - D7 - G–7 - C7) in which C7 chord is replaced by another cadential formula (the backdoor cadence Bb–maj7 - Eb7 = IV–maj7 - bVII7). In bar 9, the A–7 appears as a tonic replacement for Fmaj7 (strong). At the same time, it serves as the logical resolution of the preceding Bb–maj7 (chromatic shift: IV-III).

Bars 9 to 12 raise the level of energy. The harmonic frequency is speeded up (single-bar pulse). We hear a four-bar turnaround (III-VI-II-V), which still follows the two-bar S/W-distribution of bars 1–8: A–7 and D–7 (both tonic chords) are strong, G–7 and C7 (both cadence chords) are weak. The melodic activity increases, too. In bars 13/14, the rate of the chord progression accelerates even more (half-bar changes). And here Mancini comes up with something really neat: As an additional boost of energy, he also reverses the harmonic rhythm. Eø7 - A7 are both weak. Eø7 can be seen as an upper structure of C9, thereby extending the harmonic tension of bars 11+12 into bar 13 and establishing the high point of the first half of the tune with a harmonic exclamation mark before resolving to D–7 in bar 14. With D–7 (S) and G7 (W) we return to the initial S/W-distribution. Following the subtle transition from G7 (non-diatonic = weak) to G–7 (diatonic = strong), the chord progression eases back into a more relaxed one-bar pulse in bars 15/16 (G–7 - C7), setting up the second half of the composition, which we will get to in a short moment.

As you can see, the harmonic rhythm is of vital importance to the construction of this composition. In conjunction with the melody, the harmony is a calculated part of the design, a significant component governing the ebb and flow as well as the highs and lows of "The Days Of Wine And Roses", creating a convincing dynamic arch from beginning to end.

Let's have a look at a simple example to substantiate the significance of harmonic rhythm. The following comparison shows just how firmly the traditional distribution of "strong" and "weak" is anchored in our subconscious – a fact that can be used to alter the meaning of a chord progression decisively:

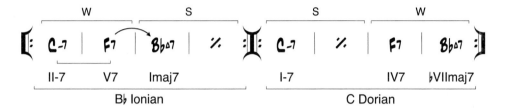

Alternately play both chord progressions on the piano. Keep a steady tempo and make sure you repeat each harmonic phrase a number of times (the second one in particular). Listen closely and compare! The first version in B♭ Ionian follows the course of an ordinary II-V-I progression. B♭maj7 is clearly the tonic (strong). In the second version, the feeling of emphasis shifts (especially if we repeat it often enough). Gradually, C–7 establishes itself as the tonic, and the ear loses its connection with B♭ as the primary root. We start hearing C as the new tonality and Dorian as the modality. The B♭maj7 no longer occurs in a strong bar, but in a weak one, and consequently turns into a cadence chord in need of resolution (♭VIImaj in Dorian)! So, bear in mind that changing the allocation of chords can give a chord progression a completely different feel.

The commonly found alternation of strong and weak chords plays a vital part in functional perception. Haphazardly changing the expected position of cadence and target chords will result in awkward harmonic phrases. This explains an issue I raised in the chapter "The Turnaround" (on p. 235), where we talked about the permutations of I-VI-II-V. I mentioned the fact that one of these variants – specifically V-I-VI-II – cannot be found anywhere in the standard repertoire. Now, it should be apparent why. V-I-VI-II translates into W-S-S-W, which is completely at odds with traditional S/W weight patterns and their habitual distribution of functions. No matter whether we look at it from a one-bar or a two-bar perspective, it just doesn't feel right.

Being aware and in control of the harmonic rhythm is of decisive importance to every composer and improviser. In addition, an understanding of how the positioning of chords affects the impact of a composition or an improvisation provides us with a fundamental tool for harmonic analysis. Let's have a look at the harmonic rhythm of "There Will Never Be Another You". Here's the lead sheet and the analysis:

The chord progression starts out with a two-bar tonic (S). In bars 3 and 4, don't make the mistake of looking at every chord individually. Although the changes seem to speed up (one chord per bar), both Dø7 and G7 are cadence chords (II-V/VI) and therefore have the same functional meaning (W). This automatically sets up a pattern, with "strong" and "weak" functions alternating every two bars (two-bar pulse). The pattern is repeated in bars 4–8: C–7 is strong, whereas Bb–7 and Eb7 (II-V/IV) are both weak. In bar 9, the harmonic rhythm accelerates (one-bar pulse): Abmaj7 (S), Db7 (W) and Ebmaj7 (S) clearly indicate a general increase in energy. Now comes the interesting part. As a tonic substitute, C–7 is strong, too, whereas F7 is weak by comparison. Obviously, the chord progression deviates from the previous alignment of "strong" and "weak" by reversing the harmonic rhythm. This reversal marks the high point of the first 16 bars (F7). The ensuing F–7 is strong, since it is diatonic and therefore has less energy than F7 (non-diatonic). With B♭7 (W) the chord progression returns to the usual S/W-distribution, easing back into the low energy level of E♭maj7 in bar 17.

For the most part, the second half of the tune is self-explanatory. Worthwhile mentioning, however, is the last line. The tune reaches its climax in bars 28/29. E♭maj7, though strong, is merely a brief respite within an otherwise highly intense environment. In bars 29–31, it would be possible to analyse each chord individually. On the other hand, it also makes sense to interpret the harmony summarily as an extended cadential phrase (W) heading back to E♭maj7 (S).

When improvising, your solo should reflect this analysis. During the first 4 bars, try to keep your cool. Don't start out with a flurry of notes. Take it easy on the E♭maj7 (S), play relaxed (long notes, lower range of the instrument, simple rhythms, etc.). Add a bit of activity in bars 3 + 4 (W). Repeat this scenario in bars 5–8, though, at a higher energy level. Ease off a bit on the C–7 (S) and pick up speed again in bars 7 + 8 (W). In bar 9, you have to resolve the preceding cadence (A♭maj7 is strong). However, in order to account for the acceleration of the harmonic pulse, you should now play more energetically, especially on the D♭7 in bar 10 (W). Once you hit E♭maj7 in bar 11 (S), make sure that you don't come down too far. In the grand scheme of things, this E♭maj7 has quite a different meaning than the one at the beginning of the tune. Even though both are strong, the E♭maj7 in bar 11 is only a moment of repose before heading for the climax of the first 16 bars. So, you have to let up just a bit on the E♭maj7 before starting to push again towards the end of the bar. Try to keep the momentum on the C–7. Build up towards the F7 where you should outline the high point of the first section, e.g. by playing more actively (busy lines, animated rhythms) while using the higher range on your instrument. On reaching the F–7, you will have to come down again. The B♭7, though more active than the preceding F–7, should be no more than a short burst of energy before settling back into E♭maj7 in bar 17. We'll talk about the second half of the tune in more detail in a later chapter.

Assignment

1. Draw up a graph that reflects the sequence of events as described above. Start with a baseline subdivided into 17 bars and add a wavy line above it that follows the ups and downs of the harmony with a clear high point in bars 13 + 14.

2. Improvise to the play-along **track 13**, following your diagram. Overdo things at first by playing "stop (S) and go (W)" to get a feel for the peaks and valleys of the chord progression. At a later point, you should try to go for smoother transitions from S to W and back again by playing phrases that cross the bar line.

3. Try to figure out how you would have to shape the second half of each chorus to bring it to a convincing close. The following discussion of "melodic rhythm" will help you along the way.

Melodic rhythm

Melodies derive their vitality from highs and lows, lively passages and restful moments, just as chord progressions do. This is what we mean by *melodic rhythm*. In nearly every Jazz standard, the melodic and harmonic rhythms occur synchronously. A change from "strong" to "weak" in the harmonic rhythm is usually accompanied by an increase in melodic activity and intensity: strong = release/rest, weak = tension/motion. Here are a number of factors (arranged as opposite pairs) that influence the energy levels of a melodic line:

Strong	*Weak*
inactive passages	active lines
on the beat	syncopations
downbeats	pick-ups
long notes / rests	smaller note values
steady rhythms	erratic rhythmic patterns
low(er) notes	high(er) notes
descending lines	ascending lines
smaller intervals	larger intervals
stepwise movement	leaps (angular lines)
chord tones	tensions
target notes	leading tones
diatonic notes	chromatic notes
in scale	out of scale
inside	outside
melodic clichés	something unexpected

As you can see, these melodic factors can be subdivided into four basic groups:

- rhythmic quality of a phrase;
- direction / range of a line;
- tonal function of the material;
- psychological considerations.

Please do not assume that my list of criteria differentiating between "strong" and "weak" is in any way exhaustive. For example, when soloing, don't forget that dynamics, phrasing and articulation also come into play as a means for adding impact and emphasis to the shape of a melody. At this point, however, I would like to focus on the actual melodic material.

Most melodic phrases alternate back and forth between these differing aspects – in conjunction with the harmonic S/W-distribution. A good, but rather mechanical, example of conventional melodic development (also reflected in the harmonic rhythm) is the A section of "Autumn Leaves":

"Autumn Leaves" is a straightforward example of a melody oscillating between movement and rest. In many cases, however, it is not that easy to determine whether a phrase (or part of a phrase) is strong or weak. Quite often, features from both sides of the spectrum appear simultaneously, cancelling each other out. When analysing a melody, the important thing is to detect which side outweighs the other. There is always an imbalance in one or the other direction – no matter how slight or subtle it may be. A good example of this is the A section of "There Is No Greater Love":

Whereas the theme clearly follows the traditional S/W-rhythm as of bar 3, the beginning is somewhat less clear. Is bar 1 strong or weak? The preparatory pick-up leading into the down-beat suggests bar 1 to be strong. In addition, we are used to hearing the beginning of a melody as strong. However, the melodic activity and the higher register seem to indicate that it is weak. The answer lies in the comparison of bars 1 and 2. Even though they appear to be identical (both bars follow the same melodic contour), there are small differences:

- the functions of the notes on counts one (bar 1: B♭ = root; bar 2: F = fifth of the key; this produces a feeling of I-V = stable moving to unstable);

- the direction of movement into the first beat of each bar (descending into bar 1 = re-lease of tension, ascending into bar 2 = build-up of tension);

- exclusively diatonic material in bar one, as opposed to chromatic material in bar 2.

Even though we are only arguing about details, the balance in bar 1, on the whole, tips in favour of "strong".

Let's go back to "The Days Of Wine And Roses". Although the melody is not as predict-able as that of "Autumn Leaves", we clearly see how it mirrors the harmonic rhythm we discussed earlier on in this chapter. Even though we sense a single-bar S/W-rhythm in the first 9 bars (pick-up – long note – pick-up – long note, etc.), we can also make out a two-bar melodic rhythm that alternates between "strong" and "weak", supporting the harmonic pro-gression. Observe the motivic development: Bars 1 + 2 revolve around the long note A (no melodic movement = strong) and swing up to the comparatively higher note C (= more energy = weak) in bars 3 + 4. In bars 5 + 6, the melody dips down again (less energy =

strong) and we hear a diatonic motive with D as the lowest, most conspicuous note. In bars 7 + 8, the motive is repeated, but now it contains the important chromatic note Db (non-diatonic = weak).

In bar 9 the melodic activity increases. Nevertheless, this bar is clearly strong from a melodic point of view – mainly because of the low note C, which is the resolution of the guide tone line D-Db-C in bars 5–9. While the chord progression continues to follow the two-bar harmonic rhythm (A–7 - D–7 = strong, G–7 - C7 = weak), the melody picks up speed and switches to a one-bar melodic rhythm (bar 9 = strong, bar 10 = weak, bar 11 = strong, bar 12 = weak, and so on). D–7 in bar 10 (a tonic function = strong) counterbalances the active melody, which arches up to the melodic high point of the first half of the piece in bar 11. Here, things are not entirely clear. Melodically speaking, the note C feels strong (long note preceded by an active and ascending line). Harmonically speaking, however, it is weak – a powerful tension (11 of G–7) and a high note, supported by the cadence chords G–7 - C7 (both weak). We have already discussed the reversal of the harmonic rhythm in bars 13 + 14: Eø7 - A7 are both weak. The A in the melody (tension 11 = weak) adds to the harmonic excitement. Although the melody is quite lively in bar 14, this serves to set up the feeling of "strong" in bar 15, where the long melody note G (phrase ending on 1 of G–7) as well as the harmonic rhythm, which switches from half-bar to single-bar chord changes, clearly indicate a release in tension.

The melodic analysis of "The Days Of Wine And Roses" shows two things. For one, we are always talking about subliminal tendencies, not hard-core facts, when dealing with the principles of harmonic and melodic rhythm. This means that many things are open to interpretation and second-guessing. The other thing we should realise is that minor details can be of major importance to the whole, and a single note can have great impact on the overall feel of a line.

Assignment

Find a play-along of "The Days Of Wine And Roses" (e.g. Aebersold, Volume 40, 'Round Midnight) and play a solo that follows the suggested melodic contour. Focus on the formal ups and downs rather than the actual notes. Try pacing yourself by controlling the activity of your lines. You will find that your solos will start making sense from a formal point of view, even if you hit the occasional wrong note.

We have seen that the harmonic rhythm can be reversed (weak-strong instead of strong-weak). Where this is the case, the feeling of melodic movement usually changes along with the harmony – as it does in the B section of "There Is No Greater Love" (Isham Jones):

Note how both the harmony and melody return to the original strong-weak rhythm before reaching the beginning of the next formal section. In bar 6, G–7 is, of course, strong because we have already heard the same phrase twice, forming our expectations. However, unlike in bars 2 + 4, the melody does not pause on a long note. It flows energetically onward, coming to rest in bar 7. G–7 - C7 is therefore the crossover point, at which the chord progression and the melody simultaneously switch from W-S back to S-W.

As we've already said, the harmonic and melodic rhythms usually move concurrently and reinforce one another. Naturally, exceptions prove the rule. But even when it comes to these exceptions, the basic rules are not simply broken randomly. A divergence of harmonic and melodic rhythms only works if it happens systematically and follows a certain structural concept so that the ear can adjust to the unusual formal development. In the first 8 bars of "There Will Never Be Another You", the melody and changes are not in agreement – the melodic activity coincides with static harmony and vice versa. This is clearly intentional and indicates compositional design because the switch happens at regular intervals (every two bars):

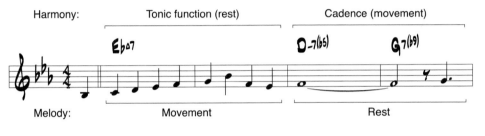

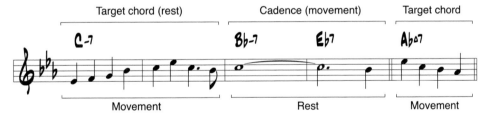

Even at the level of the single bar, many melodies reveal formal structure – strong beats coincide with little or no movement, weaker beats with increased melodic activity. If we halve a bar, the first half is strong and the second is comparatively weak:

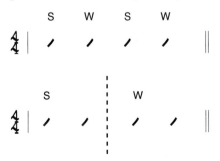

This explains the effect of the pick-up. Since there is no release without prior tension, the pick-up produces forward motion, driving towards a target note on the downbeat of the following bar. This is why many phrases do not begin on the first beat of the bar (strong) but rather on a weaker beat (e.g. on count four of the previous bar). This makes the melodic lines sound livelier. Most Jazz musicians hate lines that highlight the first beat of the bar and, consequently, draw attention to the bar line. The saxophonist Jerry Bergonzi once said: "Never start on one, never end on one". I find this to be a bit dictatorial, but it definitely proves the point.

A good example of a melody that not only demonstrates the link between harmonic and melodic rhythm in the multi-bar period, but also shows the typical distribution of tension and release within each individual bar, is the A section of "Misty" by Erroll Garner:

Of course, this analysis breaks down the melody to the level of the bar. If you look at the melodic rhythm in a more general way, it clearly coincides with the harmonic rhythm, switching from strong to weak and back every bar.

Both on a small and large scale

As already noted, the principles I have talked about in this chapter are not hard facts but rather tendencies. To make things even more complicated – these principles operate on different formal levels concurrently. The S/W-distribution is not only discernible at the level of the single bar or the multi-measure phrase but also on a larger scale. If we investigate the flow of energy within a 32-bar ABAC form, it quickly becomes apparent that the eight-bar units as well as the 16-bar sections of the composition also relate to one another in terms of tension and release. If we go one step further, we could even perceive two consecutive choruses of a solo to be "strong" and then "weak" respectively:

Bar 1	Bar 2	Bar 3	Bar 4
S	W	S	W

4-bar unit 1	4-bar unit 2	4-bar unit 3	4-bar unit 4
S	W	S	W

A section (8 bars)	B section (8 bars)	A section (8 bars)	C section (8 bars)
S	W	S	W

First half of theme (16 Bars)	Second half of theme (16 bars)
S	W

First chorus (32 bars)	Second chorus (32 bars)
S	W

Alternating strong and weak phases occur on all levels *simultaneously*. So, in order to explain or analyse any particular melodic or harmonic event correctly, we can't just zero in on the immediate bar in question. We have to be conscious of all other formal layers at the same time because they interact and influence each other and can actually weaken or strengthen the effect of a specific melodic phrase or chord.

I'd like to take yet another look at "The Days Of Wine And Roses". Up until now, we have only discussed the first half of the composition. How does the build-up and release of tension develop in the second half? Bars 17–24 are identical to bars 1–8. So let's move on to bars 25–29. Based on what we have seen in the first half of the tune (bars 9 + 10), both A–7 and D–7 are strong, even though the melody is quite active (try to recall the reasoning behind this). In bars 27 + 28, we finally reach the climax of the composition. We will discuss the concept of "high points" in more detail in a later chapter, but I briefly want to mention a few factors governing climaxes.

Of course, the melody is the most significant element to consider, E being the highest note of the melody and the melodic leading tone in F Major (both aspects suggesting "weak"). This, however, is not the only aspect. Take note of the bass line that progresses from D–7 via D–7/C to Bø7. It accelerates the chord progression (implying a half-bar harmonic pulse) and moves in contrary motion to the melody, thereby adding to the excitement immediately prior to the climax. The choice of target chord supports the melodic high point brilliantly: B–7(b5) is not only a very unstable type of chord, but also the only function with a non-diatonic root in the course of the tune (discounting Eb7, which is merely a passing chord). The melody note E is a strong tension (11) and enhances the effect of the chord. The ensuing Bb7 prolongs the feeling of excitement (E = #11 in the melody), after which both melody and chord progression cadence back to Fmaj7 (S) via A–7 - D–7 (S) and G–7 - C7 (W).

And now for the most important issue: In bar 27, not only are we talking about the highest melody note E and B–7(♭5) at the level of the bar. We are also dealing with the second half of a four-bar period (weak), the C section (weak within the ABAC format) as well as the second half of the tune (weak compared to the first half). This means that all formal layers highlight the climax by pointing in the same direction, supporting each other and amplifying the feeling of "weak":

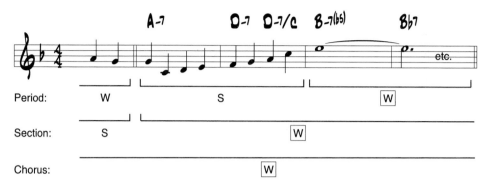

Some of you may argue that the melody comes to rest on the Bø7 (suggesting "strong"), even though this is the climax of the theme. The climax, on the other hand, is the point of maximum tension and excitement, which should be heard as "weak" by the listener! This apparent contradiction is clarified when we realise that, even though we have landed on a point of emphasis on the level of the bar (downbeat), the high point has been positioned at the "weakest" possible and therefore most dramatic spot of the entire composition. If we consider the superordinate layers of the formal structure, the long note is no more than a short moment of rest, a suspension in time, a "freeze" within an otherwise highly energetic environment (the eye of the hurricane), which actually accentuates the sense of drama.

Even if the relationship between melodic and harmonic rhythm is not always immediately evident, it is necessary to regard this as one of the most important principles governing the construction of a composition or the flow of a solo. It is amazing how strongly most people react to this formal phenomenon. Having taught Jazz Composition classes for many years, I have discussed and analysed thousands of tunes taken from the standard Jazz repertoire as well as originals written by the students themselves. These discussions have proven, time and again, that whenever the melodic rhythm fails to coincide with the harmonic rhythm, the listener experiences a feeling of unease and disorientation. On the other hand, compositions tend to sound logical and convincing when both elements are in agreement.

Of course, the same applies to improvisation. When analysing solos that convey a strong feeling of coherence, it is usually the formal control exercised by the soloist that proves to be the crucial factor. You will eventually realise that an understanding of the harmonic and melodic rhythm of a piece will help you pace your own improvisations better. Being able to control the activity and intensity of your lines by following the ups and downs of the chord progression will make your solos so much more expressive and meaningful. You will find a number of exercises in the chapter "Playing the Form".

Assignment

I would like to show you that you are quite capable not only of analysing a melody or chord progression from a theoretical perspective but also of following the emotional contour of a recording aurally and translating it into the concepts we talked about in this chapter.

Prepare a 32-bar grid on a piece of manuscript paper with four bars per line. Listen to track 41, "The More I See You". Listen closely to the theme as well as Hank Mobley's two solo-choruses a number of times and determine:

- the harmonic frequency or pulse (the location of the chords);

- the strong-weak distribution of the changes and the melody.

First, ask yourself: "Where do I actually hear a new chord?" Tick each one on your grid. Then figure out the strong-weak pattern (marking each chord or bar either as S or W). It would make good sense to concentrate only on one of the two factors each time you listen to the recording (otherwise you'll overtax the ear). Don't worry about chord types, harmonic patterns or specific functions. If you recognise something familiar, fine. But, please, don't base your analysis on abstract knowledge. Theoretical assumptions are not what we are looking for. Just concentrate on the energy levels and the way a chord and the corresponding melody feels. Rely on your intuition. Don't try to be overly precise in your evaluations – remember that we are talking about tendencies only. Some things may be ambiguous, so it's OK not to be 100% sure. One last thing: Practise switching from one formal layer to another. Focus your attention on the single bar as well as the 4-bar, 8-bar and 16-bar sections and the way they relate to each other. You will find the answers to this assignment in the chapter "Form and Improvisation" on p. 317.

Melodic Contour and Climax

Every composition consists of a number of sections, delineated not only by short motives but also by longer melodic and harmonic phrases, which evolve in a clearly designed way. These phrases are – besides motivic continuity and harmonic rhythm – the first and foremost reason why we perceive any piece as formally structured and subdivided into smaller entities.

In most popular styles, melodic design is what primarily outlines each section and, in turn, an entire composition consisting of several sections. When we look at the subdivisions of a typical 32-bar standard (AABA, ABAC, ABCA), we often come across the following layout:

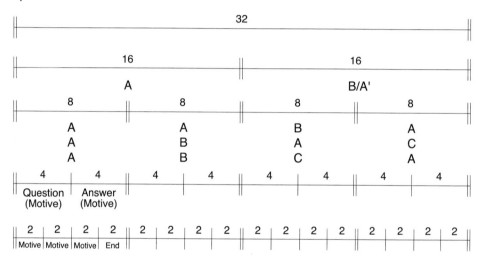

As this diagram suggests, music unfolds on various formal levels simultaneously. The motive is the smallest unit. The melodic phrase is the next level, superordinate to the motive. Let's have a look at the criteria that influence the development of longer melodic phrases. We have seen earlier that the majority of multi-measure units in traditional Jazz consist of 4 or 8 bars. This means that groups of 4 and multiples of 4 predominate. Most commonly, we find eight-bar phrases subdivided in one of two different ways (S = strong, W = weak):

- as a self-contained line determined by a two-bar motivic pulse that comes to a close at the end of the melodic phrase, e.g. like in the piece "A Child Is Born" by Thad Jones:

- as a line divided into two four-bar motivic segments that follow the principle of question (antecedent phrase) and answer (consequent phrase), e.g. like in "Here's That Rainy Day" by Jimmy van Heusen:

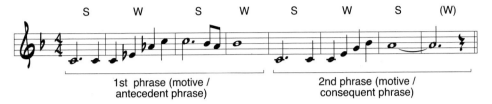

1st phrase (motive / antecedent phrase)

2nd phrase (motive / consequent phrase)

Notice that both versions conform to a clear motivic concept, which is brought to a close at the end of the formal section. For a melodic phrase to be perceived as a unit, as an integral musical idea, it has to come to rest temporarily in order to give the ear the feeling of completion. Let's focus our attention on the shape and especially the ending of a phrase.

Phrase shape and phrase ending

At this point, it would be interesting to compare linguistic syntax and melodic structure, intimating the close relationship between spoken language and music. The language of every culture, country, population or age group is unique. Many attributes characteristic of the indigenous melodic vocabulary of Folk and Art music can be traced back to speech patterns. The rise and fall of a spoken sentence (intonation), the way in which syllables are emphasised, the punctuation – all of this can be found in melodies as well and is an inextricable part of our musical heritage. In the Western European cultural context, too, there are particular linguistic mechanisms that have a bearing on melodic design. Here are three simple examples of how sentences are pitched:

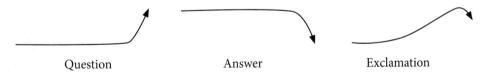

Question   Answer   Exclamation

Similar patterns of inflection are at play in music. The direction of a melodic line has a profound influence on its dynamic quality and the effect it has on the listener. Ascending lines build up tension (question = breathing in), whereas descending lines diminish the energy level (answer = breathing out). It's easy to spot this principle in the theme of the Jazz standard "Here's That Rainy Day" (ABAC form):

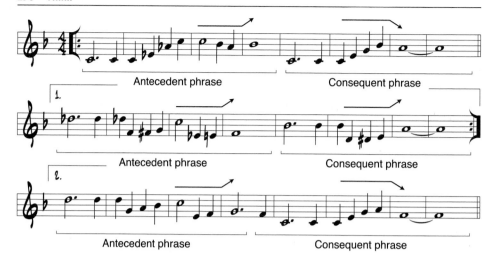

Antecedent phrase   Consequent phrase

1.

Antecedent phrase   Consequent phrase

2.

Antecedent phrase   Consequent phrase

Follow the contour of the melody. Whereas each antecedent phrase with its initial statement (exclamation) and rising ending remains "open" (question), the consequent phrase closes with falling motion (answer). However, there is one exception to the rule: The B section finishes with an ascending phrase, too, so as to prevent the piece from coming to an end at this point. It is also interesting that, in each formal eight-bar section, the antecedent ends on "weak" (bar 4) and the consequent ends on "strong" (bar 7). Remember that odd-numbered bars are usually strong and even-numbered bars are weak. This gives the ending of the melodic phrase additional weight and intensifies the feeling of closure.

Apart from the direction the melody takes, the last note of a phrase and its tonal significance plays a vital role. In the A section, the antecedent comes to rest on B♭ (4 in F Major = unstable leading tone with a need to resolve), whereas the consequent lands on A (3 = stable target note). In this way, tonal considerations contribute to the contour of the melodic phrase by adding to the feeling of resolution and decline in tension at the end.

Have a look at the lead sheet (it's not in the book). The piece modulates briefly to A♭ Major at the beginning of the B section. This change in key itself produces tension in the antecedent, which is then resolved at the end of the B section when the piece returns to the initial key of F Major in the consequent. The last note in each motivic phrase underpins this process. While we end up on D♭maj7 (IVmaj7) and an F in the antecedent (6 in A♭ Major = a weaker tonal function, which wants to resolve to 5), the consequent ends as it does in the A section: on the 3 (stable chord tone).

The C section, which brings the composition to a close, further reinforces the overall concept. Only now, after the G (2 = unstable) in the antecedent, the decisive concluding twist appears, with the melody nose-diving into the root, the most stable and tension-free point of the entire theme.

The melodic axis

The coherence of a phrase is most strongly determined by melodic points of emphasis and how they relate to one another. Melodic contour can almost always be narrowed down to a few distinctive and important notes, which represent the essence of the melody, the *melodic axis*. Have another look at the chapter "Guide Tone Lines". The compositions we talked about there are good examples of themes that can be whittled down to just a handful of melodic focal points.

The concept of reducing a composition to its essentials and thereby revealing its basic architecture is attributed to Heinrich Schenker (1868–1935), an Austrian music theorist. Schenker perceived every composition as a multi-layered structure governed by the hierarchy of tonal relationships, each layer being an elaboration of an underlying simpler layer. He devised a system of *subtractive analysis* by which he would strip a composition of all superfluous frills and break it down into its essential components, ultimately arriving at the structural core in its most condensed, purified and undiluted shape, referred to as *Ursatz* – the formal nucleus. His aim was to penetrate the surface, the *foreground*, and understand the complexities and intricacies of a composition by seeing them in relation to a simplified model, the primary level or *background*.

Without going into the rather complex details of Schenkerian analysis, let's apply this principle of reduction to the melody of "Here's That Rainy Day" (p. 296). The backbone of each section of the theme is immediately apparent if we zero in on the melodic essentials:

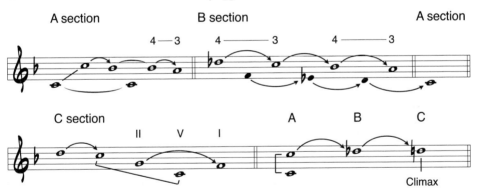

The A section begins with a strong rise in tension (octave leap), which then gradually dissipates (5-4-3). In the B section, the highest notes constitute a stepwise descending line (4-3 in Ab Major and 4-3 in F Major), accompanied by a secondary, subtler guide tone line, which consists of the lowest notes in the phrase and leads back into the second A section. The C section starts out a little like the B section, skips the voice leading Bb-A (4-3), which we have heard a number of times already, and ends the composition with a melodic II-V-I pattern. Note how the octave leap (C-C) in the A section re-appears in reverse direction, acting as a frame or bracket for the whole melody.

Assignment

Let's practise this approach to melodic analysis and apply it to one of the most famous themes ever composed. If there were a prize for the "perfect" phrase, the A section of "Over The Rainbow" by Harold Arlen would be a serious contender (first sung in the film "The Wizard of Oz" by Judy Garland). Why is it that this relatively tricky melody (large range, big leaps) is so easy to sing and has actually found its way into the basic repertoire of children's songs? How is it possible that this piece has enjoyed so much airplay over the past 70 years, not only in its original version but also in countless interpretations and covers by renowned musicians such as Eric Clapton, Jeff Beck or DJ Marusha (as a techno arrangement!)? The answer lies in the "rightness" of the melody, manifest in a quality that appeals to musicians and audiences alike, above and beyond any stylistic preferences. This is great music, pure and simple, and it's all about developing an eye (and ear!) for this sort of quality. Here it is (and be sure to dig deep!):

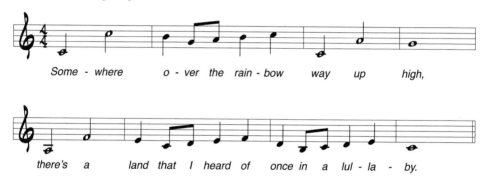

You'll find the analysis in the solutions folder.

Melodic phrases in comparison

Having said all this, how do individual melodic phrases interrelate, how do they connect to become a coherent whole? Bearing in mind the build-up and release of tension within a theme, it seems to make sense that the transitions between formal sections should play a decisive role. The following diagram shows the typical phrase structure of a 32-bar AABA format:

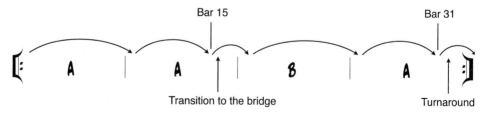

All three A sections, although fundamentally the same, pursue different objectives. Each A section needs a slightly different ending dependent on where it appears in the piece. A1 should lead back to A2 without interrupting the flow towards the end of the phrase. Consequently, A1 will either keep moving melodically and harmonically or, if it does come to rest in the last two bars, land on a weak note (with a need to resolve), to prevent too strong a feeling of closure and a loss of energy. In contrast, the second A section brings the melodic phrase to a close with a clear ending within the section (usually in bar 15) in order to make room for new thematic material in the B section. The last bar of A2 often contains a preparatory melodic and/or harmonic transition leading into B. The bridge builds up a high level of energy, culminating in the climax of the composition, and then arches back into the last A section, gradually calming down the composition. The 3rd A section, finally, concludes the piece with a decisive close in the second-to-last bar. A3 and A2 are often identical or at least similar (discounting the transition to B in A2 or a possible turnaround in A3 leading back to A1 when the form repeats).

The composition "Misty" by Erroll Garner is a perfect example of a typical AABA format:

Although the first A section comes to rest in bar 7, it ends with an ascending line (question) and lands on the melody note G (3 in E♭ Major), which doesn't really leave the listener with a definite feeling of closure. The active harmony underpins this by cadencing into the next section with a turnaround (half-bar harmonic rhythm). The second A section also comes to rest in bar 7. This time, however, the melody resolves to the root E♭ with downward movement (answer). Together with the tonic chord, this generates a clear-cut ending (the A♭7 ensures that the energy level doesn't drop to a total standstill). In bar 8 (A2), a long melodic pick-up sweeps into the bridge with a flourish. The B section also has a self-contained melodic contour, which is subdivided into two four-bar motivic phrases (antecedent and consequent) with a climax in the second half. Note how the melody lands on the Bb (5 in Eb Major = dominant feeling) and nicely ties over into the pick-up of A3, setting up the last A section with the help of the chord progression (two-bar turnaround). A2 and A3 are identical, excluding the Ab7 and the pick-up into the B section. In the absence of this melodic transition, there is a strong sense of finality.

In comparison, the phrase structure of an ABAC song format is relatively simple:

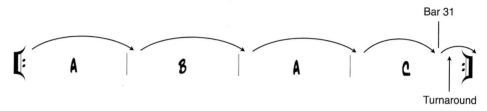

Try to figure out the way phrases develop in other song forms (e.g. ABA, AAB, ABCA, etc.) and look for compositions that demonstrate each of those forms.

The climax

Every composition follows a dynamic curve that usually begins at a lower energy level, gradually progresses to a maximum, then winds down again and finally tapers off to a distinct ending. A good piece of music is like a well-told story. It doesn't get to the punchline too quickly. There should be a basic theme, various sub-plots, which accelerate or delay the progress of the narrative, various conflicts and convolutions, false leads, points of deception, unexpected twists, trumped-up conclusions and renewed complications, before reaching a powerful climax and the final resolution of the drama. Here's a graphical representation of this scenario:

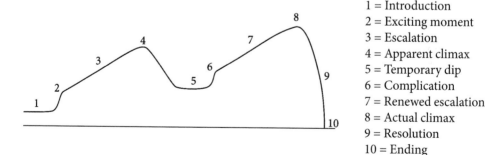

1 = Introduction
2 = Exciting moment
3 = Escalation
4 = Apparent climax
5 = Temporary dip
6 = Complication
7 = Renewed escalation
8 = Actual climax
9 = Resolution
10 = Ending

A typical Jazz composition follows the same or at least a similar design. It usually has an easily recognisable climax, which is reached by way of a wave-shaped trajectory. The piece advances through a number of secondary climaxes, taking care not to upstage the main climax in terms of energy or significance. It is almost a law of nature that the actual high point of a piece should occur relatively late. The climax is what the composition is all about. It is its point of culmination, its central message. If it is reached too soon or is badly prepared, the composition will lose its sense of direction and meander around aimlessly. This is why the main climax is almost always found in the final third or quarter of a composition (remember, exceptions prove the rule!). Good improvisations exhibit the same kind of structural attributes.

The diagram shown above can serve as a template for quite a number of Jazz standards. Here is, for example, the melody of "Someday My Prince Will Come" by Frank Churchill, which follows the same strategy of tension and release:

The basic structure of this 32-bar tune is an ABAC format that matches the following dynamic curve (the similarity to the previous diagram is self-evident):

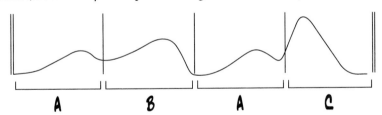

Whereas the climax of an ABAC scheme is usually found at the beginning of the C section, the melodic contour of an AABA form reaches its climax a little earlier – in the course of the B section (usually towards the end):

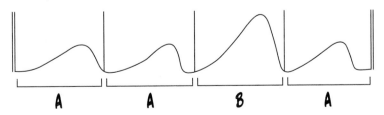

Every composition, therefore, has its own energy curve with secondary climaxes in every section and a point at which the energy reaches its overall peak. "A Child Is Born" by Thad Jones is a particularly typical example of this:

The following tension diagram shows the course of the melody:

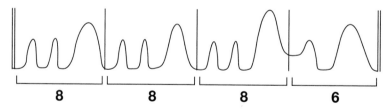

Every two-bar phrase – linked to the strong-weak distribution of the chord progression – alternates back and forth between rest (relaxation) and motion (increase in tension). Each individual section follows a dynamic curve that comes to rest after having reached the climactic point in the second to last bar. The main climax of the whole composition appears almost exactly three quarters into the piece (bar 23). As you can see, the ebb and flow of the energy is controlled at all formal levels. Even though "A Child Is Born" may be an "ideal case" and therefore a rather stylised example, most pieces more or less follow the same principle.

Let's have a closer look at the primary climax of a composition. What does it take to create the overall high point? Which elements contribute to the feeling of maximum tension? The most common and obvious feature is that the climax usually coincides with the highest note in the melody (this generalisation holds true for more than 90% of all Jazz standards and Pop tunes). Additionally, it is almost always made noticeable by a conspicuous compositional feature or an unusual sound, a sort-of musical exclamation mark – a surprising intervallic leap, a melodic tension, an interesting rhythmical feature, a dissonant chord or voicing, an unexpected function, a speeding up of the harmonic and/or melodic rhythm just before reaching the climax, etc.

The primary climax of "A Child Is Born" (bar 23) bears out what we have just talked about. It is the highest note of the theme as well as a tension (F = 9 of E♭maj7). Even more interesting, albeit more subtle, is the harmony at this point. Throughout the composition, the MI-function E♭–6 has been established as the prevailing colour. Now, at the climax, the more unusual function in this context, the diatonic IVth degree in B♭ Major (E♭maj7), appears for the first and only time. This moment of surprise is amplified by the deceptive resolution occurring just before the climax (D7 shifts to E♭maj7 instead of resolving to G–7).

Let's recapitulate: The primary climax should not appear too early, and the secondary climaxes should not exceed the main one. With this in mind, let's go back to the composition "Just Like That" (on p. 275 ff.). I love using this tune as a prime example of a composition gone astray. It's not that I would want to be critical of as great a composer and arranger as Peter Herbolzheimer, but I do want to point out that even highly accomplished musicians don't always turn out masterpieces. From a motivic point of view, the melody is admirably crafted. Considering its overall structure, however, having gotten off to a great start, the piece then loses momentum towards the end. Don't get me wrong – on the whole, we are still talking about a good composition (and the original recording is a really nice big band arrangement, too). It's just that the first half promises more than the second half actually delivers. I have played this piece to many people and inevitably the majority, students and colleagues alike, sense that something doesn't feel quite right. Think back to the dynamic curve of the average ABAC tune and compare the secondary climax in the B section with the main climax in the C section. Here's the melodic diagram:

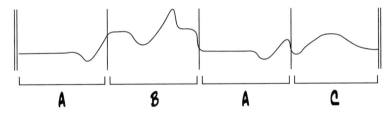

Simply by looking at the diagram, it is easy understand why "Just Like That" would leave the listener with a vague feeling of disappointment. Let's consider the B section and the first climax. A number of factors catch the eye (and ear): the modulation to E Major, the increase in melodic activity, the way the phrases soar higher and higher in contrary motion to the descending bass line, culminating in the D♯ in bar 13 – all of this is well designed and contributes to a successfully staged high point. In addition, D♯ is the leading tone (maj7) in the key of E Major as well as a tension (11) in relation to the accompanying A♯–7(♭5), which is a conspicuous and special chord function in E Major (♯IVø7). In a nutshell, this is what a good climax is all about – great preparation, powerful exclamation mark, perfectly positioned before the theme tapers off again and resolves into the second A section. The problem: This climax is all too powerful for a first half – and it's hard to top. After all, we still have the second half of the piece coming up, and that's where the primary climax should be. By comparison, however, the second half of the composition is out of balance and a bit of a letdown. As if the tune has used up its ammunition, it doesn't live up to the expectations set up by the B section.

The second A section is merely a repeat of the first 8 bars with a slightly different ending. So, let's have a look at the C section, which should provide the primary climax and bring the piece to a satisfactory close. And that's where the tune runs into problems. Now, it is no longer possible to use a modulation to create excitement. There just wouldn't be enough time to get back to the initial key (D Minor / F Major) in a relaxed way and to end the piece within the form without rushing. Neither is it possible to outdo the high D♯ from the first half. Why not? We need to know that "Just Like That" was designed as a tenor sax feature. The D♯/E♭ is the highest note available on most tenor saxophones (see pdf-G for instrumental ranges). Of course, Peter Herbolzheimer could have solved this problem by transposing the whole composition down a whole step to C Minor / E♭ Major and, as a result, opening up the high range of the tenor sax for a top note that would exceed the climax in the B section. But then again, composers are reluctant to switch once they have settled on a starting key. It's hard to relinquish an initial concept because, even in equal temperament, every key has a certain quality linked to the instrumentation and the musical ideas. Changing key implies changing the mood and the intensity of the piece considerably.

For lack of better options, Herbolzheimer was forced to turn to other strategies. His choice (whether consciously or not) was the use of rhythmic displacement and chromatic sequencing (A–7 - D7, A♭–7 - D♭7, G–7 - C7) to create the necessary tension in the C section. However, it is more of an artificial and mechanical kind of tension rather than an increase of energy flowing naturally from the composition and by no means as strong a climax as the overpowering high point in the B section. Herbolzheimer himself was quite aware of this problem, including his own inability to find a more than adequate solution for the dilemma. He admitted that he was not altogether happy with the tune, and his choice of title reflects "just that" – that it is no more than a little ditty on the side without greater merit. I do find it worthwhile noting that the discussion of "Just Like That", although it may seem rather academic to some of you, clearly proves that the listener intuitively picks up on structural inconsistencies of a piece. We're not just talking about technicalities. The architectural make-up of a composition is something we react to at a gut level, amateurs or professionals alike. A musician, however, should be aware of and capable of controlling these parameters.

Assignment

Examine your own repertoire in terms of form and melodic contour.

The master plan

Let's remember our dear old friend Mr. Schenker and his concept of simplification. Composers are generally in control of not only the melodic, harmonic and rhythmical details, but also of the formal structure, the overall shape, of their compositions. No matter whether they consciously follow a premeditated concept or whether they link various passages intuitively, it is always possible to find what I like to call the *master plan* of a composition – the most basic governing principle, corresponding to the primary level, the *Ursatz*, in Schenkerian analysis.

Have another look at the melodic synopsis of "Here's That Rainy Day" shown on p. 297. We have reduced each eight-bar phrase to just a few important notes, which form the melodic axis of a section. However, if we dig down even deeper, we will discover yet another level of structural integrity. Just as each section is held together by a basic principle (e.g. a guide tone line), the formal sections themselves are linked in a similar way. Go to the last part of the diagram. There you will find the master plan of "Here's That Rainy Day". The highest notes of each section add up to a separate line (C-Db-D), which leads compellingly to the climax in bar 25. It doesn't matter that these melodic cornerstones are far apart. The ear still picks them up subliminally as the connecting element that weaves its way from section to section and propels the dynamic progress of the entire composition.

As evidence that such construction principles pertain to any style, have another look at the C Major Sonata by Bach on p. 120. So far, we have only analysed the way the melody effectively reflects the harmony and commented on the remarkable clarity of the phrases. The most amazing thing about this line, however, is its formal structure. Although not initially noticeable, you will find a large-scale mirroring of motivic segments. The first half of the passage – the "original" – is presented in retrograde in the second half. The mirror axis (or pivot) is located at the end of bar 12. Keeping in mind that the line modulates from C Major to G Major, here are the corresponding cross-connecting bars:

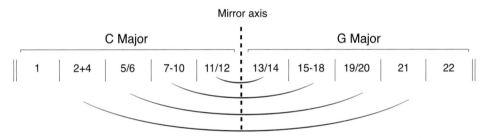

The motivic two-bar or four-bar parcels are repeated in reverse order in the new key as of bar 13. The mirroring is not that evident at the beginning and at the end of the passage because it is part of a longer composition and is linked to the preceding and ensuing sections in a musical way. Nevertheless, bar 21 corresponds to the second half of bars 2 + 4, and bar 22 mirrors bar 1 – at least in principle.

These few bars demonstrate the incredible compositional genius of Johann Sebastian Bach. The thing I find most remarkable, however, is the fact that the highly complex form and its mirror symmetry are not immediately apparent to the ear. Neither is the master plan obtrusive nor does the music feel mechanical. Bach achieves this by cleverly concealing the axis of symmetry. Relentlessly spurred along by an extended guide tone line (marked with asterisks), the ear is tricked into following the powerful surge of the melodic line to the asymmetrically placed climax in bar 15. In addition, because music moves forward in time, it is highly unlikely that you can actually hear the reversal of the motivic groups (you'd need a pretty good memory and perceptive ear to make the connection). This is the kind of master plan, which is revealed rather through analysis than through listening to the music.

None of this is built into these compositions coincidentally! Of course, it is quite possible that Jimmy van Heusen or J.S. Bach developed an intuitive and finely honed sense of proportions and structure during the course of their lives. However, you can't get something from nothing – this level of control doesn't just happen. At some point or other, these great composers practised and developed the instinctive ability to simultaneously control every melodic and harmonic detail as well as the composition as a whole. It is likely that they eventually reached a level of craftsmanship that no longer called for conscious effort. Be that as it may, composing (or improvising) "in the zone" and arriving at great results calls for a highly sharpened and immediately accessible set of tools and skills.

One last thing, when looking at the previous examples: It is worth noting that, despite the details of construction and form, the music is not lost. This, to me, is the decisive point: Neither Bach nor van Heusen give the impression that they want to show us how clever they are, or that they would abandon musical criteria and their emotional impact on the listener in favour of a compositional principle. For them, a system is never an end in itself.

The two master plans we have just discussed should give you a basic idea of what to look for when analysing a composition. Every composition has a master plan of some kind and every master plan is unique. Sometimes it is quite simple and blatantly obvious (as in "Here's That Rainy Day"). More often than not, however, it can only be detected and deciphered by scrupulously looking for connections beyond the obvious structural features (as in Bach's sonata). Finding the master plan of a composition is of paramount importance because it will tell you *why* a composition unfolds the way it does. It is what makes a composition special, what separates it from others and gives it its distinctive quality. And this understanding will help you when practising the piece on your instrument.

"Saving All My Love For You"

To sum up the previous chapters, I would like to recapitulate all the formal elements we have discussed using just one example. In contrast to the many Jazz tunes I have quoted so far, I have chosen a Pop ballad which I'm sure you are all familiar with: "Saving All My Love For You" (by Michael Masser and Gerry Goffin). Whitney Houston's Grammy-Award-winning cover version, recorded in 1985, became a No.1 hit in the USA, the UK and Ireland. I know, I know – this is a kitschy nightmare for the Jazz aficionado. But I do want to appeal to the not-quite-converted-to-Jazz people, and, at the same time, show the hardcore Jazz crowd that these formal factors apply irrespective of genre.

I have chosen 6/8 as the time signature for the following lead sheet to make it easier on the eye (12/8 is also an option). It would have been more correct to notate the piece in slow 4/4 (it's a ballad, after all), but we would be up against a melody teeming with triplets:

D.S. al Coda

I would ask you to listen to the tune first (without consulting the lead sheet). Immerse yourself in the music without analysing it from a melodic, harmonic or rhythmic point of view. Focus on the form exclusively. Feel free to jot down whatever you deem important on a sheet of paper. Once you're done, you should have gathered a fair amount of information on the following topics:

- the general form of the complete recording;
- the length (number of bars) and structure of each individual section;
- the motivic material;
- the harmonic and melodic rhythm;
- the climax;
- the master plan.

Don't move on before you have listened to the recording several times (it would make sense to concentrate on a different aspect each time).

Form

Let's begin with the general layout of the recording. It starts out with an eight-bar introduction (a four-bar turnaround, which is repeated). The song then follows an AABA format, which is extended by adding a last, slightly different A section (A') and a long fade-out (I have not included the intro, A' or the fade-out on the lead sheet for reasons of space). Notice the differing lengths of the various A sections: A1 = 22 bars, A2 = 20 bars and A3 = 26 bars. Despite this irregular formal structure, we don't get the feeling that the composition sounds awkward. Quite the opposite – we will see that the asymmetry is a natural result of the melodic and harmonic development within each of the individual formal sections. I would even go so far as to say that *because* the composition follows a particular strategy the A sections *have to be* different (more on this later). The B section, as opposed to the A section, is 16 bars long and thus corresponds to traditional formal expectations. As we have already discussed, this is a frequently used compositional device to bring about contrast: Whereas each A section contains an odd number of bars, the B section displays a more conventional structure (remember the composition "Yes Or No" by Wayne Shorter; see p. 267). Here's the formal outline of "Saving All My Love For You":

8	22	20	16	26	?	
Intro	**A**	**A**	**B**	**A**	**A'**	Fade-out

Harmonic and melodic rhythm, motives, melodic contour

In this piece, as in many others, it doesn't make much sense to talk about harmony and melody separately. Both aspects influence each other profoundly.

A section

Just to make things perfectly clear: The A section pursues a single objective, namely to prepare for and highlight the *hook line* – also known as the "hook". The hook is the most important lyric line of a Pop song, its selling point. It must therefore have a memorable melodic and/or rhythmic quality. It is usually found in the chorus and often serves as the title of the song. The term comes from marketing-speak, literally meaning to "hook" or "grab" the attention of the listener (they want to sell records, don't they?). Without a hook, a song has little commercial potential. The hook line "… so I'm saving all my love for you" appears in bars 17 + 18. Everything that happens before this is part and parcel of a steady increase in tension, driving us towards the hook and the climax of the A section.

The first A section starts out quietly with two four-bar phrases, each based on a turnaround in A Major and a continuation of what we already heard in the introduction. Although the harmonic pulse is one chord per bar, we still sense two-bar groupings. This is partly due to the harmonic rhythm of the diatonic turnaround, which follows a traditional two-bar strong-weak weight pattern: Amaj7 - F♯–7 (tonic sounds = strong) and B–7 -

E7(sus4) (cadence functions = weak). The melody supports the harmony with its motivic flow. Each four-bar phrase is made up of two transposed two-bar motives (antecedent and consequent). Whereas each antecedent has an ascending close, which is extended over the bar line and ends on F♯ (6 in A Major = weak tonal intervallic function), the consequent closes on the downbeat and the root of the key.

As of bar 9, the tempo increases. The harmonic pulse is still one chord per bar. The strong-weak distribution, however, speeds up, with the chord progression oscillating between F♯–7 (strong) and B/F♯ (weak) every bar. B/F♯ is the first sound to depart from the key of A Major (= more tension). The F♯ pedal in the bass and the two-bar repeat in the harmony also add to the surge of energy. The motivic phrases reflect the acceleration of the harmony. A second, single-bar motive now appears, see-sawing between C♯ (3 = strong) and B (2 = weak). Bars 9–11 create a feeling of suspenseful expectation and act as a sort-of springboard for things to come.

In bar 13, the moment we have all been waiting for arrives. The bass line suddenly accelerates, descending diatonically, while the melody branches off energetically in the opposite direction. But, don't get too excited, we haven't quite reached the peak yet. The harmonic rhythm is still one chord per bar (strong-weak) despite the bass line suggesting a half-bar pulse (both Amaj7/G♯ and F♯–7/E must be seen as inversions). We'll come back to bars 13–16 when we talk about the master plan. For now, it suffices to point out that bars 15 +16 demonstrate a remarkable bit of compositional control. This is a palpable moment of restraint, a built-in breather that gives us a chance to come up for air before the grand finale and signals: "Watch out, something important is about to happen!" It's an exclamation mark that announces the upcoming hook line.

In bar 17 the chord progression and the melody finally reach the climax. With a burst of speed, the hook line confirms what was subliminally introduced in bars 13/14 by the bass line – now, at last, the changes follow a half-bar pulse. An additional element of suspense is generated by the deceptive resolution at the beginning of bar 17 – C♯7 resolves to Dmaj7 and not, as expected, to F♯–7.

The motivic development of the A section underpins the acceleration we have already discovered in the harmony. Two-bar motives in bars 1–8 and one-bar motives in bars 9–12 give way to a third, half-bar motive in the hook line as the melody finally reaches its high point and then comes to a close:

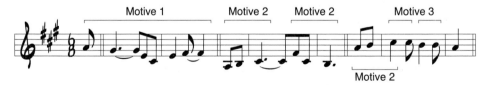

This shows, once again, that the melodic development is closely related to the way the harmony progresses. All formal levels act in concert with the intention of driving the A section towards its climax. Here's the summary (the melodic rhythm is displayed above the chord progression and the harmonic rhythm below):

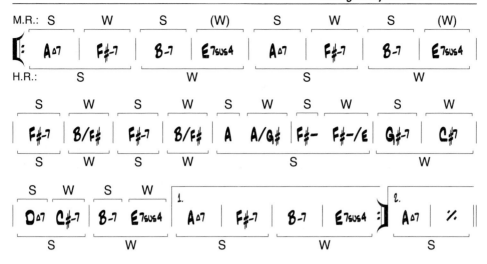

Let's have a look at the transitions from A1 to A2 and A2 to B. Before moving on into the next formal section, the energy of the climax must be diminished to a point where it corresponds to the energy level of the next section and makes the transition feel logical. To a certain extent, this already happens with the melody and chord progression descending stepwise into the final note of the hook. However, when moving from A1 to A2, the energy level has to be brought down even further (an immediate transition into the second A section would neither have been harmonically sensible nor melodically possible). A1 comes to a close with the same four-bar turnaround we already heard in the introduction. The ear remembers and automatically expects another A section. At the same time, the harmony loses momentum by switching back to the one-bar pulse with its two-bar strong-weak distribution. So, we need the four-bar interlude to prepare for the much lower energy level and the slower harmonic rhythm at the beginning of the second A section.

Unlike A1, A2, ends on two bars of Amaj7 and not the turnaround. Since the piece is moving towards the B section and an overall increase in energy, a four-bar transition would have been too much. The tonic is a definite point of closure and signals the end of the first major part of the song. However, the tension should not drop to rock bottom. Two bars of Amaj7 are just sufficient to create the necessary respite. At the same time, the shortened moment of rest ensures that the energy level is not completely lost (listen to how the drummer fills the gap and sets up the B section). Now it should be clear why the A sections have varying lengths without producing an unsettling feeling. The acceleration of the harmony and the different endings result in an asymmetrical formal structure that feels perfectly natural.

B section

The analysis of the 16-bar B section is child's play compared to the A section. It is subdivided into four four-bar harmonic phrases. Each phrase consists of a II-V-I. G♯–7 | C♯7 | F♯–7 | is VII–7 - III7 - VI–7 (II-V/VI in A Major). The G♯–7 creates a first pinprick of suspense because it is not entirely "in key" (G♯ø7 would be the diatonic VIIth degree). B–7 | E7 | Amaj7 | is, of course, II–7 - V7 - Imaj7 in A Major. The two-bar harmonic rhythm is deliberately inverted (weak-strong), which – as we already know – is a very commonly used compositional tool for creating contrast. Since the target sounds are 2 bars each, the II-V progressions are perceived as two-bar units. The melody supports the harmonic rhythm (active phrases on the II-Vs, little or no activity on the target chords).

From bar 9, the chord progression modulates, reinforcing the increase in the tension of the B section. D♯–7 | G♯7 | C♯maj7 is II-V-I in C♯ Major. D♯–7 serves as a link between the two keys. It can be seen as ♯IV–7 in A Major, which again adds to the tension level (the more diatonic version would be D♯ø7 = ♯IVø7), and as II–7 in C♯ Major. It is therefore a dual-function chord. F♯–7 | B7 | E7(sus4) is the transitional area where the piece returns to the initial key of A Major. Again, we have to see this II-V-I as a dual-function chord progression: F♯–7 - B7 is IV–7 and ♭VII7 in C♯ Major and, at the same time, VI–7 and II7 in A Major. E7sus4 serves both as the target chord for F♯–7 - B7 as well as the cadence chord back to Amaj7. Accordingly, it is both strong (resolution of F♯–7 - B7) and weak (dominant of Amaj7). In this way, an effective link is established between the B section and the third A section, with the piece returning to the initial strong-weak distribution of the chord progression:

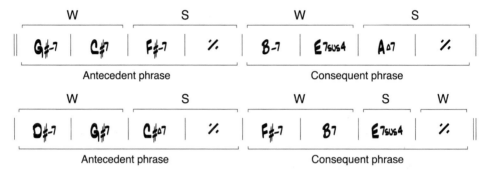

As you can see, the B section can be divided into two eight-bar subsections, each consisting of a four-bar antecedent and a four-bar consequent. This can be best understood by focussing on the phrase endings. In the antecedent phrases, the melody continues into bar 4, which doesn't give us a clear feeling of closure (question), whereas the consequent phrases end on the downbeat of bar 3, signifying a strong sense of finality (answer).

The master plan

Finally, let's look at the overall shape, the "master plan" of the composition, made visible by reducing the individual formal sections to their essential notes and applying the principles of Schenkerian analysis presented in the previous chapter. Here is the condensed theme (compare this with the lead sheet):

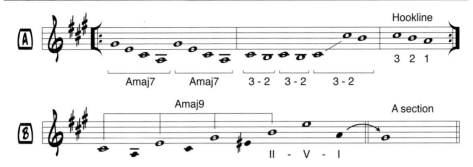

A section

In the opening passage, the melodic focal points constitute a descending Amaj7 arpeggio. In this way, the initial key of A Major is firmly established by the melody. From bar 9, we hear the notes C♯ and B alternating. This sets up a strong need for resolution to the root – an expectation that is not (yet) satisfied. Instead, the tension intensifies further. Remember the harmonic-melodic rhythm? At this point, we feel an increase in the energy level triggered by the aggressive surge of the melody and the acceleration of the bass line descending in contrary motion. Now the function of bar 13 should be clear. The melody is readying itself for the high point of the A section. The motivic phrase (C♯-B) is moved up an octave to a higher and more energetic register where it is repeated and expanded. In bar 15 the theme almost comes to a standstill on the note B – as if the melody were catching its breath before plunging into the closing phrase (the hook). The craving for resolution becomes almost unbearable. At last, with the climax of the A section, the melody satisfies our needs by resolving to the eagerly anticipated root. The final note (A) gradually fades out while the chord progression quiets down again accompanied by the turnaround we already heard in the intro. The melodic development of this section shows how cleverly the composer exploits our expectations in order to create a sense of drama and achieve the desired effect of spotlighting the hook line.

B section

The primary melodic substance of the entire B section is an ascending Amaj9 arpeggio (or rather C♯-7, which is almost the same thing) – a reversal of the melodic focal points we came across at the beginning of the A section: a descending Amaj7. As with any well-written tune, the B section doesn't just introduce new material for the sake of contrast. It feeds on elements that have already been presented and uses them in a different way. This adds to the coherence of the overall melody. Notice how the melodic cornerstones forge a close link between the opening key of A Major and the new key of C♯ Major. This cushions and elegantly camouflages the otherwise dramatic modulation in bar 9 (the E♯ in bar 11 is the very first and only important note not diatonic to the initial key). The melody continues on its ascent, increases in tension and eventually reaches the top note E in bar 15, which is hammered firmly into the ear by the driving rhythm in bars 13 and 14. This is where the tune reaches its primary climax, placed exactly where we would expect it in an AABA form: towards the end of the B section. The transition to the following A section is equally effective and cleverly constructed.

Again, take a look at the melodic focal points. They correspond to the roots of a II-V-I progression in A Major. We actually hear a melodic cadence that leads us back seamlessly to the third A section. The note A at the end of the B section (the pick-up) – a seemingly negligible eighth note – is not that insignificant after all.

The climax

We still have one problem to solve. Let's remember: The main objective of any memorable Pop song is to successfully choreograph the hook line. In most cases, the hook line is the central phrase of the chorus. Unfortunately, "Saving All My Love …" doesn't have a chorus. The hook line is the final phrase of every A section (the verse). Moreover, the melodic climax of the tune is prominently located at the end of the B section. This, again, means that one of the main features of any successful Pop song – the synchronicity of the hook line (text) and the climax of the melody (music) – is missing. The composer was fully aware of this apparent contradiction. So, how does he make it work? As a first step, he compensates for this incongruity by repeating the hook line at the end of the third A section (the hook appears three times). The repeats extend A3 to 26 bars. This draws our attention back to the central statement of the piece. Note that the last repeat does not end on the root (the A) but on the same note as the climax in the B section (a high E). This, however, is not enough. To reinforce the message of the song even more, the composer does something rather clever. He slips in a four-bar solo (played by Tom Scott) and adds a last, shortened A section. The solo acts as cross-fade. It serves as the end of A3 as well as the first 4 bars of A' and ensures that the energy level stays right up there. This last A section is far more intense than the previous A sections. Whitney Houston gives it all she has, the bass is pounding away, the saxophone is wailing, the strings are rejoicing, and when the song finally fades out with several repeats of the hook line and the last statement "for you …" the focus is back where it should be. There can no longer be doubt in anybody's mind – this is what the tune is all about.

Great choreography! And quite a lot of information! Not bad for a stupid old Pop song, is it? You'll have to admit – you probably didn't expect this seemingly shallow tearjerker to be this complex. Hidden beneath the glitzy surface, we discover a fascinating array of psychologically fascinating considerations and stratagems that belie the tune's sleek appearance. Here you have the fine art of songwriting. Being able to package musically demanding material in a way that appeals to the ear of the mainstream listener is something that requires an enormous amount of compositional acumen and sensitivity. Don't make the mistake of underestimating Pop songs as a matter of principle. They can often show us how to say complicated things in the simplest of ways.

Form and Improvisation

You might be asking yourselves why I'm going into so much detail about formal principles in a book on harmony. The reason is – as always – *practical*. I am absolutely convinced that a well-developed sense of form (after good timing) is the single most important quality of any Jazz musician – and experience has proven me right time and again. Have you ever wondered why some improvisations come across as aimless doodling while others radiate breathtaking excitement and determination? The answer is simple. Only when soloists succeed in transforming their ideas into intelligible musical words and sentences, will they tell a coherent and expressive story comprehensible to the listener. The way in which a solo evolves is far more important than the tonal material itself. Playing the correct notes won't get you anywhere if they don't translate into meaningful phrases. Formal control is paramount. It's not so much about *what* you play, it's more about *when* and *how* you deliver your lines.

Everything we have discussed and said about composition so far is equally valid to improvisation. The play on energy levels, the rise and fall of tension, the structure of the phrases, the architecture and storyline of a convincing solo – all of this is subject to the same principles. Basically, a good improvisation is nothing more than a successful spontaneous composition. That, however, is a tall order! It takes years of practice and experience to reach the high level of coherence to be found in the improvisations of the Jazz greats.

So – where to begin? The easiest way to achieve a meaningful result as a soloist is to follow the build-up and release of tension in the theme and empathise with the harmonic and melodic ups and downs of a composition. I'd like to illustrate this correlation by using "The More I See You" (Harry Warren) and Hank Mobley's tenor sax solo (on the album "Roll Call") as an example. Listen to the original recording on **track 41** and then take a look at the lead sheet below. It's a simplified version of the theme as played by Hank Mobley (notated an octave higher than the actual sound for reasons of readability):

If you haven't completed the assignment on p. 293 (at the end of the chapter "Harmonic and Melodic Rhythm"), don't read on. I would prefer you to give the exercise a try before we delve into the formal details of the tune.

Let's start with the basic formal structure. This 32-bar composition is divided into eight-bar sections following ABAC format. Next, let's have a look at the harmonic and melodic rhythm. The chord progression begins with a two-bar pulse. Both bars of Aᵇmaj7 are, of course, strong. Bᵇ–7 and Eᵇ7 are therefore not heard as separate sounds but rather as a two-bar unit (weak) cadencing back to Aᵇmaj7. The melody clearly reinforces the harmonic rhythm by beginning in the lower range in bars 1 + 2 (strong) and moving to a higher pitch level in bars 3 + 4 (weak). It is also possible to hear a one-to-a-bar melodic rhythm because of the pick-ups (weak) preceding the long notes in bars 1 + 3 (strong). Then again, because of the two-bar phrases and the way they relate to one another, the first motive has less energy (strong) than the second (weak). In addition, the main melody notes and their tonal significance play an important role. The first bar begins with an Aᵇ (the root), thereby signalling the tonic melodically (strong). In bar 3, in contrast, we hear an Eᵇ on the first beat (the fifth), which produces a strong dominant effect (weak). Even if the harmonic and melodic rhythms are not 100% synchronous in the A section, they are still closely interlocked.

In comparison to the A section, the B section should provide contrast and a higher level of tension. Both the harmony and the melody contribute admirably to the expected increase in energy. The piece departs from the key of Aᵇ Major and modulates to E Major. This modulation, introduced by the dominant B7, creates a considerable amount of unrest, which is briefly resolved when we arrive at the new tonic Emaj7. Most importantly, the harmonic rhythm is reversed: Bars 9 + 10 (B7) are weak and bar 11 (Emaj7) is strong. Again, the melody supports the harmonic rhythm. The enharmonic switch from E♭ (bar 8) to D♯ (bar 9 = leading tone in E Major) in the melody sustains the energy level into the B section, augmented by an increase in melodic activity and a further rise in pitch in bar 10.

Having reached Emaj7, both the melody and the chord progression speed up (one-bar harmonic and melodic rhythm). Within the framework of the first 16 bars, this acceleration comes across as a brief burst of activity, marking a first climax and powering the piece into the second half. The tune modulates back to the initial key of A♭ Major (bar 13). Harmony and melody return to the traditional strong-weak distribution. In the A section, B♭-7 - E♭7 was perceived as a unit because the harmonic rhythm suggests a two-bar pulse. Now, the same two chords have a different connotation. Since the chord progression follows a one-bar pulse, B♭-7 is strong and E♭7 is weak.

The second A section is basically a repeat of the first 8 bars. However, take note of the transition to the C section. Here, the energy level increases significantly in comparison to the first A section. Even though the chord progression once again consists of a two-bar II-V progression (E♭-7 - A♭7), it is, in contrast to B♭-7 - E♭7, no longer diatonic (= more tension). The melody accentuates this rise in tension. While the first A section ends on an E♭, the melody jumps to the note F at the end of the second A section. Despite the lapse of time, our ear registers the difference in pitch and perceives the higher note as a melodic exclamation mark that prepares us for important things to come.

At the beginning of the C section we reach the highest note of the theme – the primary climax of the composition. Unlike the B section, the chord progression doesn't modulate (we are too close to the end of the piece for a modulation to work effectively) and the harmonic rhythm is no longer reversed (here, too, there wouldn't be enough time to return to the initial strong-weak pattern in a relaxed way). Instead, the melodic and harmonic activity contributes to the high level of tension. The chord changes as well as the motivic phrases are now one-per-bar. This intensification clearly signals that the end of the piece is approaching. In bars 5 + 6 of the C section, the harmony and melody accelerate one last time (half-bar movement) in order to bring everything to a final close. Needless to say, the II-V in the last bar is not part of the composition, but the link to the next chorus during solos.

Let's summarise what we've analysed so far:

S		W		S		W	
A♭△7	⁒	B♭-7	E♭7	A♭△7	⁒	B♭-7	E♭7
W		S	W	S	W	S	W

W		S	W	S		W	
B7	⁒	E△7	E♭7	F-7	B♭7	B♭-7	E♭7
S			W		S		W

S	W	S	W	S		W	
A♭△7	⁒	B♭-7	E♭7	A♭△7	⁒	E♭-7	A♭7
S	W	S	W	S		W	

D♭△7	D♭-6	A♭△7	D♭-7 G♭7	A♭△7 F-7	B♭-7 E♭7	A♭△7	(B♭-7 E♭7)

A graphic representation of "The More I See You" would correspond to the melodic and harmonic contour of an ABAC format as shown on p. 301.

How does this formal structure affect Hank Mobley's improvisation? Here's the solo (two choruses, notated "as is"):

Since this chapter is about form, I'll leave it to you to investigate the tonal material and do an analysis of this solo. You'll find that Hank Mobley plays with incredible control, no matter how fast or slow his lines are. You will not discover a single wrong note throughout. His lines are flawless and the coherence of his phrases is amazing. I have marked a few guide tone lines with asterisks (*) so that you can see how compellingly the solo is held together by stepwise movement of important notes and confidently positioned resolutions. Even if he never was front rank in terms of media coverage, Hank Mobley must be considered to be, without exaggeration, one of the greatest tenor sax players of the 20th century.

Let's start with the opening of the solo. I have deliberately included the last few bars of the theme (as played by Hank Mobley) because the transition to the improvisation is proof of remarkable formal ingenuity. Compare the lead sheet with the transcription. Instead of concluding the melody on the A♭, Mobley leaves the ending suspended in mid-air – a clever twist that serves two purposes. On the one hand, it prevents the energy level from dropping to zero. After all, this is where the recording launches into the solo section and should take off rather than convey a feeling of closure. On the other hand, it gives Mobley the opportunity to use the momentum of the theme as a springboard for his solo. He does play the A♭ – however, not as the final note of the melody but as the first note of his solo pick-up. The slightly delayed resolution links the end of the theme and the beginning of the solo beautifully. I hope you share my enthusiasm for this seemingly insignificant detail. But it is precisely the little things that impress me most, simply because they best demonstrate the amazing level of intuitive control that distinguishes the great soloist.

The long solo pick-up arches into the first A section, which almost entirely mimics the theme on a formal level. The motivic phrases are two bars each, they alternate between rest and motion every bar, and the relationship of the main melody notes to one another – i.e. their energy level and tonal significance – mirrors the strong-weak distribution of the melody. Hank Mobley not only duplicates the ups and downs of the motives but also their rhythmical structure. Note that most phrases in the A section of the theme don't end on "one", but tend to disguise the bar line by spilling a little into the next bar. We see this particular detail in Mobley's lines, too (in both A sections!).

The energy level increases in the first two bars of the B section (weak). Hank Mobley plays more actively and employs the higher register of the instrument (= more energy). Notice how confidently he resolves the leading tone D♯ in bar 9 (weak) to the E in bar 11 (strong) after whipping through a string of eighth notes. Again, here's proof of Mobley's awe-inspiring melodic foresight. From bar 12 (weak), the solo plunges into a long phrase, which peaks at the first intermediate climax in bar 14 and then comes to rest again in bar 15.

In the second A section, the improvisation returns to the sparse phrasing we heard at the beginning of the solo. Here we hear the connection with the theme even more strongly than in the first A section (particularly from a rhythmical point of view). In bar 23 (E♭–7) the solo lands on the same melody note as the theme (F). Notice the short guide tone line working its way up from F via G♭ (bar 24) to the A♭ in bar 1 of the C section.

The C section is a miniature masterpiece in itself. The formal control Hank Mobley displays in the final 8 bars of the first chorus is absolutely startling. Let's remind ourselves – the primary climax of the theme was in bar 1 of the C section. This was necessary from a compositional point of view so that there would be enough time to gradually diminish the energy level and bring the melody to a convincing close within the constraints of the 32-bar structure. An improvisation over only one chorus would probably have copied this formal approach. Because Hank Mobley plays more than one chorus, his plan of attack has to be different.

Hank Mobley's first chorus reaches its climax in the C section, as would be expected. However, it makes no sense to fire off all your bullets in one burst here – after all, there's a second chorus coming up, which should outshine the first. Having said this, there are several things to consider. For one, the C section must be more energetic than the B section so that the chorus as a whole has a convincing contour and feels right. Then again, the C section should bring the first chorus to some kind of a close. However, taking into account that there's a second chorus, the solo should not be allowed to run out of steam. Additionally, there is a third aspect to bear in mind: Although the C section should end the first chorus, it should also help advance the solo smoothly into the next chorus.

Hank Mobley successfully manages to pull all this off. By simply looking at the transcription, it is easy to see that the C section is more energetic than the B section. With the A♭ in bar 1 of the C section, the solo lands on the same climactic note as in the theme (the ear of both the player and the listener remembers this sort of thing subconsciously). After a short pause (the calm before the storm), Mobley dives into a long line of eighth notes that keeps up the flow but doesn't surpass the climax (this gives him enough space to add to the tension level at a later stage during the second chorus by using the full upper range of the instrument). Notice how the little motivic fragments in bars 29 + 30 paraphrase the half-bar harmonic rhythm of the theme.

To avoid any doubt whatsoever that we are indeed heading for a second chorus, Mobley repeats what he already did at the junction of the theme and the beginning of the solo. In bar 6 of the C section, he stops on the G (leading tone in A♭ Major) without playing the resolution, avoiding the obvious conclusion of the chorus and retaining the tension. Instead, he plays an awesome pick-up phrase (again, starting on the A♭!) as an introduction to the second chorus. For the first time, we hear a flurry of sixteenth notes (= even more energy). It is fascinating with just how much dead-certainty he hits the A♭ on the downbeat of the first bar of the following A section despite the breakneck tempo of the line. As if he were to point out that "this is exactly the note I wanted to land on", he relishes the point of resolution for a short moment, only to carry on, following the momentum of the phrase and extending it into the second chorus. What a transition!

I fully realise that what I have been saying up until now might sound awfully abstract (it is in the very nature of an analysis to sound bookish because it involves taking something apart that only works and comes across as a whole). It should also be obvious that no Jazz musician ever thinks along these lines when improvising. There is simply not enough time. However, I'd like to give you an idea of why some improvisations move us while others leave us cold, even if every note is in place. I encourage you to look beyond the surface of a solo and develop and eye (and ear!) for what is good in an improvisation (if you can put it into words, you can practise it). I hope – despite my somewhat dry and technical language – that I can heighten your perception and appreciation of the beauty and elegance Hank Mobley's solo emanates. There is no denying that he was one of those gifted musicians whose ability to do just the right thing at the right time deserves the admiration of any astute listener (the formal correlation between the theme and his solo is certainly no coincidence). But, even though Hank Mobley's control of all musical parameters is evident in every note he plays, he is not infallible.

Considering the build-up and release of tension, let's have a quick look at how a solo consisting of two choruses could (or should?) evolve. Two basic versions are conceivable:

- The soloist plays a full second chorus, tapering off at the end of the C section and finishing up in the first few bars of the following A section (the disadvantage for the next soloist is that he or she will have to wait until the previous soloist is done). In this version, the design of the second chorus would be similar to the first, only at a higher energy level. The whole solo would follow a continuous, wave-shaped contour, with the final climax occurring in the last C section:

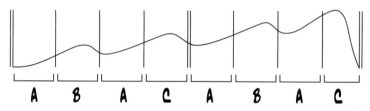

- The solo is completed within the 32-bar form of the second chorus. In this version, the structure of the second chorus would differ from the first. The improvisation should reach its maximum towards the end of the B section and gradually die down over the last 16 bars. In contrast to the first chorus, the final C section would have less energy than the preceding B section because the solo has to be brought down to a fairly low level well before reaching the end of the form:

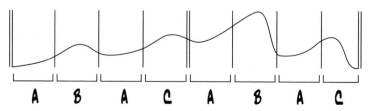

You might argue that there are other possible ways of structuring a solo – and, of course, you'd be right. However, the two versions shown above are the most commonly used strategies, backed up by countless improvisations.

Assignment

Before we move on, I would like you to go back to the recording – **track 41** – and listen to Hank Mobley's solo (several times, if necessary). Ask yourself: "How do both choruses relate to one another? How does the second chorus feel when compared to the first?" Don't think about the actual notes. Just go for the ups and downs of the lines and the energy level of each section.

Now, let's have a look at the second chorus. The first A section gets off to a flying start, following up on the powerful transition. We still hear two-bar phrases, but they are rhythmically more active and use almost the entire range of the tenor sax. Even the strong-weak distribution is harder to distinguish because the busy phrases obscure the bar lines (= more unrest). This was to be expected after the spectacular pick-up leading into the second chorus. So far, so good.

Now we get to the decisive moment of the whole improvisation. How often has it happened to you that you wanted to play something and the fingers just couldn't do it? All of us are familiar with the situation where we have a general notion of where we want our solo to go, but we don't quite have the technical ability to carry it off. I guess that Hank Mobley found himself in just this situation at the beginning of the B section.

If you listen very carefully, you will hear a tiny, hardly noticeable trip-up at the beginning of the B section (in the transition from bar 1 to 2). I've marked the spot in the transcription. This glitch can clearly be attributed to the saxophone – and, mind you, Hank Mobley was known to never make mistakes. I believe he wanted to follow up on what he had set up in the preceding A section – to go hell for leather and play a mind-boggling B section. He most probably had a particular phrase in mind. But, the very moment he started to play, he must have realised that he was never going to make it. So he immediately backed off. I'll take my assumptions one step further. I believe that Hank Mobley could already sense disaster looming ahead. Good soloists can hear their next idea well in advance. Again, if you listen closely to the phrase preceding the B section, you can hear that Mobley's timing is slightly off (his phrasing usually is impeccable) – as if he could already feel impending doom. It could be that being in the studio held him back (he may well have risked it live on stage). The courage to take risks is one thing, but ruining a recording is another. A lesser soloist might have gone for it, with the likelihood of sounding like a dog's dinner. Hank Mobley, however, played it safe. In the split second he became aware of the hole he had dug for himself, he aborted the attempt. After a brief pause for reflection, he started picking up the pieces and carried on playing. Now that he no longer could play what he had had in mind, he was forced to accept the fact that the result would not sound as convincing and coherent as the initial idea most probably would have. Every sudden change of plan affects the overall picture.

As I have said, this is no more than conjecture. I don't mean to suggest that I can read minds, but it is a fact that the B section is lacking in power. I have played this solo to many students and colleagues. Almost all agree with me (without any coercion!) that the second chorus sounds less compelling than the first. Although the improvisation is perfect in terms of the notes played (don't forget to analyse the chord-scale relationships), it still leaves us with a vague feeling of disappointment. Even though the closing passage (the final C section) is structured beautifully, the musical "coitus interruptus" at a decisive point of the solo clouds the overall impression, as if a promise was given and not kept. I would like to emphasise that I do not intend to judge whether Hank Mobley should or should not have taken the risk. I just feel the need to show with this example how a small moment can affect the impact of an entire improvisation and be of enormous importance to its overall success. This, again, emphasises the need for us all to develop an eye for detail as well as for the whole.

I'll just briefly go into the rest of this improvisation. After the rather unsuccessful B section, another A section follows, which brings down the energy level even further. It is apparent that Hank Mobley is still taking no chances and tries to get his ideas back on track. Only in the C section does he come to an authoritative end and conclude the solo with a powerful, albeit late, climax (active rhythm, high register, etc.). The last four bars gradually wind down the tension (notice the descending guide tone line resolving into the last note).

Let's summarise this solo in a diagram:

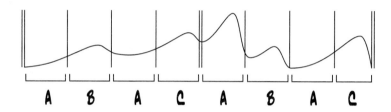

Conclusion: If Hank Mobley had not started the second chorus on such a high energy level, he would have been able to step up the pace in the B section and top the preceding A section. Irrespective of which of the two solo strategies suggested earlier in this chapter he may have chosen in the end, every section would have logically followed the formal master plan of the tune to result in the perfect improvisation. Unfortunately, he couldn't deliver the goods at a crucial moment. A successful strategy also depends on the ability to assess your own resources and limitations and to stay within the scope of feasibility while you're playing. So, don't use up your ammunition too soon. If you peak too early, where do you go from there? Don't get carried away! And don't get me wrong – Hank Mobley, in my opinion (and not only mine), is still one of the greats and merits utmost respect. This solo was chosen for its instructional value, and by no means is it meant to denigrate a man of his standing. But, as we all know, learning from our mistakes is what life's all about.

With this example, I wanted to show you how important it is to be in tune with the structure of the theme while improvising. It is not enough to simply hit the right notes. How they are played and where they occur is just as important – and the composition will provide the necessary clues. This obviously does not mean that we have to be slaves to a composition to the last detail. But it will help our soloing considerably if we approach an improvisation with a certain amount of respect for and an understanding of the formal anatomy of a tune. In addition, the example demonstrates how difficult it is, even for top soloists, to do the right thing at any moment and keep the overall musical result in perspective at the same time. A feeling for proportion in small and large terms, paying attention to detail while keeping an eye on the whole, is an admirable quality – especially if we keep in mind that these are processes that have to take place on a subliminal level for a solo to come across as spontaneous rather than contrived.

Here is a second example of a great solo, which proves that it is indeed possible to control every detail of an improvisation from beginning to end without ever losing touch with the overall dynamic flow. This is Mike Mainieri's solo over "Pools" (by Don Grolnik on the album "Steps Ahead"). For reasons of space it isn't possible to talk about the whole improvisation, so I'll introduce you to the first of four choruses. I do believe, though, that this excerpt suffices to show how masterfully Mike Mainieri develops his lines:

When the album hit the market, many of my colleagues raved about this improvisation in particular (some could actually sing or play it note for note). I, too, was really impressed by the recording. However, after having transcribed the four choruses, I have to admit I was a bit stumped. At first glance, I was unable to find anything that would justify my enthusiasm. Neither the actual notes played nor the rhythmical structure of the lines seemed unusual or overly exciting. But I still *knew* there was something very special about this solo.

It is entirely possible that my memory has romanticised this improvisation over the years. Today, my first reaction would probably be more along the lines of: "Yeah, he knows what he's doing. Good solo." We learn as we get older, see things a little more soberly and are not that easily overwhelmed. The magic of hearing the recording back then has been replaced by something more tangible – respect for a musician who has obviously done some serious shedding, now that I understand how and why the solo works (as is often the case, the magic tends to fade when we get to know things better). This, however, doesn't alter the initial impression I had of this improvisation.

Let's start with the harmony:

As you can see, the changes consist of nothing more than a couple of simple V-I progressions in G Minor and F Minor. The 32-bar formal structure is made up of two 16-bar sections, each of which is subdivided into four four-bar phrases. Nothing unusual here! Worth mentioning, though, is the asymmetrical harmonic rhythm of each four-bar phrase: 3 bars of "strong" and one of "weak". An analysis of the tonal material sheds no light on the matter – the minor chords (G–7 and F–7) are Dorian, the seventh chords (D7 and C7) are Altered or HTWT. So, where is the appeal in this solo? You can probably guess that, in the end, it was the formal integrity of the solo that fascinated everybody. I must admit, however, that it took me quite some time to get to the bottom of this. We tend to focus too much on the harmony and the chord-scale relationships – a predilection and habit that isn't easy to shake.

Let's have a look at the solo from a formal point of view. It starts with an extended pick-up (D7) targeting the downbeat of the first bar. After this, nothing much happens (G–7). In bar 4 (D7), the line accelerates, only for it to calm down again almost immediately. In bar 7, the solo almost comes to a standstill in the lowest register of the vibraphone before again picking up speed on the D7. As of bar 9, the melodic activity intensifies. We are now well into the first half of the chorus, which in itself demands dynamic development. In bars 15 + 16, the improvisation reaches its highest point so far and sets up the second half of the chorus with a sweeping pick-up. The same principle is continued over the next 16 bars, however at a higher energy level. After all, the chorus as a whole also calls for a general increase in tension, with the second half displaying more energy than the first. Let's summarise: While the phrases over G–7 and F–7 (strong) are comparatively laid back in terms of movement and dynamics, we hear an aggressive shift in register, more rhythmical activity and sudden leaps on D7 and C7 (weak).

You'll find that the same structure is continued throughout the following three choruses, gradually increasing in energy. The solo follows a wave-shaped contour, which is driven primarily by the rhythm and the register of the lines. Whereas we hear eighth notes as the smallest note value almost exclusively in the first chorus, eighth-note triplets crop up during the second chorus and longer passages of 16th notes and even 32nd notes appear in the choruses three and four. At the same time, the lines progressively move up into the higher register of the instrument. The main climax is reached at the beginning of the fourth chorus. After that, the solo gradually dies down and ends in the second half of the last chorus with sparse and wispy lines, a lot of sustain pedal and short motivic fragments. When you listen to the recording, notice how the rhythm section interacts with the soloist and supports him (especially in the last chorus). Here is a graphic representation of the solo:

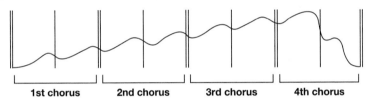

1st chorus   2nd chorus   3rd chorus   4th chorus

It is remarkable how Mike Mainieri creates a beautiful and powerfully persuasive melodic arch over the full 4 choruses while simultaneously maintaining impeccable control on all other formal levels. Every four-bar phrase, every 16 bar section and each individual chorus is a work of art in itself. Even in the heat of the moment, with lines flying all over the place, he never loses his bearings. It is amazing how he manages to exploit the entire range of the vibraphone (F1 to f‴) without ever exceeding the boundaries of the instrument. I'm sure you all know what it feels like wanting to develop an idea, only to discover that you've "run out of instrument". Mike Mainieri stretches the musical and instrumental limits to the max without ever crossing the line to disaster.

Great improvisations are often a matter of luck. Even the very best soloists have days when they don't manage to pull off the big one. Of course, it is easier to control the formal aspects of a piece such as "Pools" with its rather simple chord progression. Whatever the case may be – it should be your goal to be able to express musical thoughts with similar determination and clarity. The analysis of Hank Mobley's and Mike Mainieri's solos proves that there are indeed generally valid criteria – beyond all questions of style – that define good soloists.

In this and the previous chapter, we focussed on the larger picture. I hope I have succeeded in drawing your attention away from minute occurrences at the bar-to-bar level and back to fundamental principles and phenomena concerned with energy, the general ebb and flow of a solo and its psychological effect on the listener, aspects which appeal to the senses rather than the intellect. Of course, this book should help you develop an analytical approach to music. However, getting too obsessed with details can result in losing sight of the wood for the trees. Breaking down musical structures into their constituent parts should therefore be no more than a first, deliberate step. Far more important is the process of putting everything back together again in such a way that it has emotional impact, that the ingredients add up to an experience, which touches the listener because it is more than just the sum of its parts.

Assignment

Find the recording of "The Opener" by Bill Evans (on the album "I Will Say Goodbye"). This was one of the first solos I happened upon that really blew me away. It was only much later that I realised that I was intuitively reacting to the solo's perfect design and not so much the actual notes or chord-scale relationships. Apart from Bill Evans' incredible phrasing and timing, this is as close to a perfect solo as you will ever come. What caught my ear was the fact that this improvisation made sense on each and every zoom level. Whatever Bill Evans plays, it is impeccably positioned in relation to its immediate environment as well as the solo as a whole. Every note, every bar, every four-bar phrase, every 8-bar or 16-bar section and each chorus is wonderfully executed and underscores its location in the grand scheme of things. I'm not going to give you the transcription because I don't want you to look at the music. Just listen closely and follow the theme as well as the two ensuing piano choruses.

First, listen to the theme and determine its basic formal structure (song form, harmonic and melodic rhythm, climax, etc.). Even though it is played out of time (rubato), it shouldn't be too difficult to extract the pertinent information. Prepare a time line on a piece of paper and subdivide it into 4-bar sections. Then, listen to the complete solo several times, try to focus on a different magnification level each time and see if you can draw a graph that mirrors the energy curve of each four-bar phrase as well as each of the larger sections in relation to one another (something like the diagrams on p. 322). Start off with the general shape and the way the two choruses relate to each other before you start breaking down the improvisation into shorter sections. Enjoy the solo and soak it up.

Let's wrap up this chapter with a brain teaser. There is one wrong note in this solo. Try to find it. It's easy to miss because Bill Evans camouflages it by doing what every great soloist does: He turns his mistake into a motivic idea, which he immediately incorporates into the next few phrases, transforming the mistake into a logical continuation of the line. How do I know this was a slip-up? Well, it's the only note in the entire solo that doesn't fit the chord progression, and you can hear Bill Evans shying away from it immediately.

Analysis

What is the point of analysis? Why would a musician want to tear a composition apart and investigate its structural elements? Wouldn't it be so much more fun just to play without prior mental gymnastics? Well – that approach will work with a handful of simple tunes but not with the major part of the standard repertoire, never mind more contemporary compositions. So, here are a few important reasons and objectives to consider:

- *Conceptual insight* – You will develop the "eye for detail and the whole" I mentioned earlier once you have grasped how the music unfolds formally, how the composition evolves with the use of repetition, variation and contrast, how it is subdivided into sections, phrases, motives, etc. and how these relate to each other. You will understand why certain things happen at a specific point in the tune (modulations, secondary and primary climaxes, etc.) and how the harmonic and melodic rhythm influences the flow of energy. You'll acquire know-how that you can put to use when writing your own music.

- *Practice efficiency* – You will be able to practise in a more goal-oriented way once you are familiar with the special features of a piece, the easy and difficult passages, what you already know, what is new, etc. You will learn to focus on what is important without getting caught up in insignificant detail or wasting time on things you are familiar with and can already do.

- *Chord-scale relationships* – Analysis will help you understand how the changes work functionally, how to choose the appropriate scales and determine the available tensions for each individual chord.

- *Improvisation* – You will be able to improvise more confidently once you have an overview of the structure of a composition.

- *Comparison with other compositions* – It will be easier to distinguish which aspects are exclusively typical of a particular composition, which features coincide with other pieces and in which respect a tune differs from others.

- *Memorising tunes* – You will be able to memorise pieces more quickly and effectively once you have a feel for the important landmarks of the piece. It is easier to picture a tune in your mind if you can visualise the chord progression and the way it evolves structurally – an image that will become more elaborate as time goes by.

- *Comparison of various soloists* – Analysis will help you appreciate how different soloists deal with the same piece, how they implement its basic substance and structure, how they personalise and change it (e.g. reharmonisation). This will help you understand the soloist's approach.

- *Transcription* – Your transcriptions will be more accurate because you will be able to analyse and evaluate a recording of the tune better.

- *Learning to ask the right questions* – Analysis is not just about stating obvious facts. Understanding how a tune or an improvisation works has a lot to do with figuring out *what* the concepts behind the music are, *how* a composer or improviser applies them and *why* something happens at a specific point in the composition.

Before we get down to business, I'd like to issue two friendly warnings (or maybe not so friendly!):

Every analysis must be corroborated by the ear!
The more complicated and "brainy" an analysis is, the more unlikely it tends to be.

The discussion of "Saving All My Love For You" most probably gave you first insight into what an analysis is all about – and, I'm sure you realise by now that there's a lot more to it than just talking about chord functions and chord-scale relationships. Considering the many different aspects an analysis should cover, it makes sense to approach the job systematically. The following example – the first A section of the well-known ballad "Misty" by Erroll Garner – will illustrate the individual steps in the process. I know we have already talked about this tune several times in other chapters. However, the road to success is paved with repetition. So bear with me:

Form

Always, always, always begin with the form. It makes good sense to start with the big picture and work your way down to the details. First, figure out the general structure of a piece (overall form and number of bars, subdivision into sections and multi-measure units, the harmonic and melodic rhythm, the motivic structure of the melody, placement of the climax, etc.). This will give you an initial rough overview. It is advisable not to take this seemingly simple first step lightly, even if many of the structural components appear to be obvious. Any good improvisation follows the contour of a composition. Your solos will sound more articulate if you understand the formal design of the theme.

Our example consists of one coherent eight-bar phrase starting out with a one-bar harmonic pulse. Ebmaj7 and Abmaj7 are strong. Both Bb-7 - Eb7 and Ab-7 - Db7 should be seen as one-bar units (weak). In the second half of the section, the harmonic rhythm speeds up (two-bar turnaround with a half-bar pulse). Note that the one-bar strong-weak distribution continues: E♭maj7 - C–7 (S) and F–7 - B♭7 (W). Only in the last two bars do we hear a true half-bar harmonic rhythm: G–7 (S), C7 (W), F–7 (S), B♭7 (W). Initially, the melody develops in two-bar motives, then changes to half-bar motives in bars 5 + 6 and comes to a standstill in the last two bars (end of the phrase) while the harmony continues its half-bar movement and drives the first A section on to its resolution at the beginning of the next section. The general contour of the melody is interesting, too, in that the climax of the eight-bar phrase occurs unusually early (in bar 2). The melody then gradually arches back following the guide tone line C-B♭-A♭-G (top notes of the phrases).

Key

Now we determine the key. Obviously, the key signature is the first thing you should go for. But, watch out! Especially when dealing with modal compositions, the key signature is sometimes not correct or misleading (go back to p. 67 ff. where I have already pointed out this problem). If you're not sure, have a look at the first and, more importantly, the last chord of the piece (excluding a cadence or turnaround that may be indicated in the lead sheet at the end as a turn-back to the beginning of the tune). But again, be careful! Not all tunes start with the tonic (e.g. the standard "Just Friends" begins on IVmaj7). Of course, the melody is also a good indicator.

Don't forget that tunes may modulate, i.e. switch to another tonality, without changing the overall key signature. We will look into modulations and how they affect analysis in one of the next chapters. For now, we will restrict ourselves to standards that have *one* tonal centre. In our example, the key signature of 3 flats and E♭maj7 as the first chord clearly indicate the key of E♭ Major.

Chord functions

Again, start with the simple things and gradually proceed to the more obscure or complex parts of the chord progression. As a first step, we look for diatonic functions:

‖: E♭△7		B♭–7 E♭7	A♭△7	A♭–7 D♭7
Imaj7			IVmaj7	

E♭△7 C–7	F–7 B♭7	G–7 C7	F–7 E7 :‖
Imaj7 VI-7	II-7 V7	III-7	II-7

Next, we bracket II-V patterns (a solid bracket for II-Vs and a dashed bracket for II-SubVs):

E♭△7		B♭-7	E♭7		A♭△7		A♭-7	D♭7
Imaj7					IVmaj7			

E♭△7	C-7		F-7	B♭7		G-7	C7		F-7	E7
Imaj7	VI-7		II-7	V7		III-7			II-7	

Then we label the various dominant seventh chords and mark their resolutions – only if they resolve as expected – with arrows (a solid arrow for resolutions down a perfect fifth and a dashed arrow for chromatic resolutions):

E♭△7		B♭-7	E♭7		A♭△7		A♭-7	D♭7
Imaj7			V7/IV		IVmaj7			♭VII7

E♭△7	C-7		F-7	B♭7		G-7	C7		F-7	E7
Imaj7	VI-7		II-7	V7		III-7	V7/II		II-7	SubV/I

Finally, we analyse the remaining chords (diminished chords, modal interchange, etc.):

E♭△7		B♭-7	E♭7		A♭△7		A♭-7	D♭7
Imaj7		II-V/IV			IVmaj7		Sub(II-V)/VI	
		or					or	
		V-7	V7/IV				IV-7	♭VII7

E♭△7	C-7		F-7	B♭7		G-7	C7		F-7	E7
Imaj7	VI-7		II-7	V7		II-V/II			II-7	SubV/I
						or				
						III-7	V7/II			

If you're still uncertain about any chord – skip it for now or hazard a guess.

Chord-scale relationships

Now it should be easy to find suitable scale material for each chord. Where there are alternate scale choices, make your selection according to the harmonic-melodic relationships. *Always consider the melody and the way it relates to the underlying chord progression!* First, go for the important notes (long, on-the-beat or accented notes). Analyse their intervallic function. If you see chromatic notes (out of key), try to decide whether they relate in some way to the attached chord or should rather be seen as a chromatic embellishment (passing note or part of an approach pattern). If you come across a melodic section (several bars) containing accidentals, always consider the possibility of a modulation. Should all of this still not give you a clear result, the decision becomes a question of personal taste.

Back to our example! With the exception of the Db in bar 2, which must clearly be analysed as b3 of Bb–7, the melody is entirely in key. This means that our basic scale analysis will be mostly diatonic in the key of Eb Major. *With every chord, always go for the scale cliché first!* Of course, there may be (and usually are) more scale options beyond the restrictions of the key and the melody – e.g. if you want to increase the amount of tension, you would deliberately choose a scale that deviates from the cliché. However, it is important to understand which scale is closest to the key and would consequently create the most "inside" feel. So, here's the scale analysis:

$E\flat^{\vartriangle 7}$	$B\flat^{-7}$ $E\flat^7$	$A\flat^{\vartriangle 7}$	$A\flat^{-7}$ $D\flat^7$
Ionian	Dorian Mixolyd.	Ionian (Lydian)	Dorian Mixolyd. Lydian(b7)

$E\flat^{\vartriangle 7}$ C^{-7}	F^{-7} $B\flat^7$	G^{-7} C^7	F^{-7} E^7
Ionian Aeolian	Dorian Mixolyd.	Phrygian HM5 Altered	Dorian Altered

With Abmaj7 (IVmaj7), you have two options. If you take the preceding II-V progression into account, you'll realise that both the melody and the chords (Bb–7 - Eb7) contain the note Db. So, if you are looking for continuity of sound, then Ab Ionian would be the logical and more appropriate choice because it also contains the Db (4). On the other hand, if we base our decision on the key and the function, then Lydian would make more sense. However, the D (♯4) would really stick out because of the preceding II-V and would not be that easy to handle when improvising. Db7 could be either Mixolydian (as a follow-up of Ab Dorian) or Lydian(b7), which sets up a closer connection with the key. C7 is HM5 because there is a G (5) in the melody (for this reason, Altered would only be an option if we discount the melody). The E7 has to be Altered because the G (♯9) in the melody dictates the general character of the sound.

As you can see, we should never treat a chord as an isolated event but rather as part of its tonal environment (key and melody) as well as relative to the immediately preceding and following sounds (harmonic context). It should also be obvious that the scale choices we have discussed relate only to the theme. In an improvisation, these chord-scale relationships would still apply in principle. However, since the melody is no longer an issue, the soloist is free to choose as he or she pleases. An analysis should never be the be-all and end-all of your approach to playing the piece – there are many ways of interpreting a chord progression. In the section "Play" (starting on p. 537), we will see how far we can remove ourselves from the restrictions of the basic scale material without actually abandoning it altogether.

Assignment

Have a look at the lead sheet of "There Will Never Be Another You" on p. 78. Examine the piece, its formal structure (the overall form and its subdivisions, melodic and harmonic rhythm, motives, melodic contour, climax, etc.) as well as harmonic functions and chord-scale relationships. The analyses in the following chapters will help you with this. Write everything down. We will come back to this piece in the chapter "Improvisation".

Analysis in minor keys

In the chapter "The Major/Minor System", we dealt only with the basic diatonic functions in Aeolian, Harmonic minor and Melodic minor. As a result, most of us have little more than a rudimentary knowledge of what is going on in minor keys, and this falls very short of what we need to analyse complex pieces in minor. Besides, I don't want to make the same mistake as so many books on Jazz harmony, which stubbornly insist on avoiding the topic (as if there are no pieces in minor keys that consist of anything more than elementary functions).

On the other hand, it stands to reason that it would be an extravagantly laborious and time-consuming undertaking to work through the entire list of functional relationships in minor keys to the same extent as in major keys (secondary and substitute dominants, secondary II-Vs, diminished chords, modal interchange functions, etc.). This smacks of theory for theory's sake. It would just add to an already dense jungle of functions and bring about a plethora of new symbols. The big question is: Do we really need them? There are good reasons why I don't want to open this can of worms. Just think of the many functions we talked about in major keys (there are more than 50). Just think of doing the same in minor (based on Aeolian, HM and MM). Just think of the fact that every church mode (or any other of the commonly used scales) can stand on its own and would deserve the same treatment. Just think of the zillions of modal interchange functions and relationships that would have to be accounted for. I hope, you agree with my assessment that we don't want to go down that road. Even though I love to get deeply involved in theory, there's a limit.

Much of what is taught at music schools all over the world is based on theoretical systems that date back to the 18th century and focus mainly on diatonic harmony. While music evolved and has become increasingly complex and chromatic, these systems have resisted change and have lagged behind. Sadly, they provide only a limited view on tonal harmony. The old systems fall short of providing effective tools for analysing music as it is composed, played and perceived today. I believe it is time for a change of paradigm. I want to shake up the tired old ways of looking at harmony in minor keys. I know some of you may not agree with my line of thinking. Well, so be it.

I'd like to start out with a simple example to give you an idea of the problem and to propose a practical solution. Let's have a look at B♭-7 in the key of D Minor. Can you imagine what it sounds like? The logical functional description would be ♭VI–7. Does that help in any way? We didn't come across this function when discussing minor keys. It's neither diatonic in Aeolian nor in any other of the minor scales containing a ♭6 scale degree (check!) with the exception of Harmonic minor, which, as we know, only serves the purpose of providing a minor key with the function V7. Now, play the two chords D–7 and B♭–7 on the piano. Make sure you establish D–7 as your tonic. Switch back and forth between these two chords while always keeping the tonal centre D in mind. Does the B♭–7 feel strange? Most probably not! As a matter of fact, I'm sure it will sound rather commonplace to you. Here's the decisive question. Why should an unfamiliar function feel so ordinary?

The answer is quite simple. If we switch to F Major, the relative major key of D Minor, we immediately see that B♭–7 is IV–7, one of the most frequently used modal interchange functions and therefore a good old friend. This implies that, when analysing B♭–7 in D Minor, we are introducing a new symbol (♭VI–7) for something we already know as IV–7 in F Major. Two different symbols for one and the same sound within the same diatonic environment – does that make sense? As far as I am concerned, no! This example shows that, when analysing chord progressions in minor keys, we would have to learn a whole new set of functional symbols without actually adding to the vocabulary of sounds we have already become accustomed to and filed away.

This is why I would prefer to advocate a more pragmatic and practical approach, which is simple and effective, though not all that well founded in terms of music theory: We can analyse minor compositions – at least partly – in the relative major key. Since the major/minor system links two basic colours, which often interrelate and are hard to isolate anyhow, this trick would seem legitimate. So, if we see I–7 (in minor) as VI–7 (in major) or, vice versa, Imaj7 (in major) as ♭IIImaj7 (in minor), then we can easily trace back a minor chord progression to the many functions we have already discussed in detail in major keys.

At first glance, this approach seems to belittle minor keys as mere appendages to major keys – something I try to avoid. In truth, I see minor and major as "partners in crime". They both share the same key signature. To me, they are so closely related that a separation simply doesn't make sense. After all, we are only looking at the same chord progression from a different angle. Besides, the ear tends to flip-flop readily. Even if a tune is clearly in minor, the ear will switch to the relative major key at the slightest opportunity. Last, but not least, one of the main reasons for analysing a chord progression is to define the appropriate chord-scale relationships. Since any minor key and its relative major share the same pool of notes, the resulting scale clichés will also be the same, irrespective of whether we analyse a chord in minor or its relative major.

As shown above, it's not sensible to have two different symbols – e.g. ♭VI–7 in minor and IV–7 in major – representing the same sound. The opposite – one and the same functional symbol representing two completely different sounds – is even more of a problem. Let's take the changes of Chick Corea's composition "Spain" as an example. Listen to Al Jarreau's version on the album "This Time". Stop the introduction just before reaching the theme and sing the note you think is the root. Check this note on the piano – it should be a B. If you sing a scale from this note, you will most probably end up with a minor scale (Aeolian, HM or MM). The tune is clearly in B Minor.

Now analyse the changes. Proceed systematically by first pinpointing the functions that are diatonic in B Minor. Your analysis of the chord functions and their corresponding scales should look something like this:

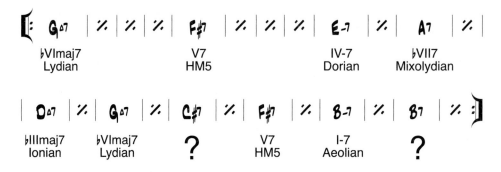

Whereas most of the chords can be interpreted as diatonic sounds in B Minor (derived from Aeolian or HM), C♯7 and B7 pose a problem. We could, of course, label them as secondary dominants in B Minor based on their expected resolutions. Accordingly, C♯7 would be seen as V7/V (target chord F♯7 = V7) and B7 as V7/IV (target chord is E−7 = IV−7). However, there's a catch: These are functional symbols we have already used when analysing secondary dominants in major keys. The problem: We have learned to associate these functions with a corresponding scale cliché. Let's take C♯7 as an example. The symbol V7/V triggers Mixolydian or Lydian(♭7). This, however, would put us on the wrong track because this is the scale cliché pertaining to this function in *B Major*. Remember the principle of scale derivation: chord tones plus key-related tensions. If we go for the most diatonic solution in *B Minor*, C♯7 would be Altered (D = ♭9, E = ♯9, G = ♯11, A = ♭13). This means we get two contradicting scales for one and the same function (V7/V) depending on whether it appears in a major or its parallel minor key. I'm sure you agree that it makes very little sense to use the same Roman numeral symbol for two entirely different sounding situations – chaos would by inevitable.

In order to avoid this mix-up, I again suggest we take a mental leap into the relative major key and interpret C♯7 as V7/III and B7 as V7/II in D Major instead. The advantage is that we automatically associate the correct scale clichés: C♯7 Altered and B7 HM5(+♯9). The following diagram illustrates that we can think in D Major and still arrive at a satisfactory result in B Minor:

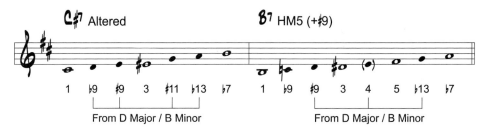

Since D Ionian and B Aeolian contain the same notes, it simply doesn't matter which of the two we choose as our point of reference – both lead to the same scale results. One of the main objectives of any analysis is to derive the material for improvisation. To me, it is irrelevant how we get there, as long as we arrive at a satisfactory solution. As I said before, I believe in the practical side of things. I therefore find it perfectly admissible to use the switch to the relative major key as an elegant shortcut, even though this approach may be deplorable from a theory-buff's point of view. But, is it really worth opening Pandora's box of minor functions just for the sake of being overly exact theoretically?

Besides, it may well be that your ear wants to hear parts of the chord progression in the relative major key anyhow. I have already mentioned that the ear tends to take the path of least resistance and will automatically fall for the easiest interpretation. The allocation of functions is based on our listening habits. It would, of course, be theoretically correct to analyse the passage | E–7 | A7 | Dmaj7 | Gmaj7 | as | IV–7 | ♭VII7 | ♭IIImaj7 | ♭VImaj7 | in B Minor. However, it is much more likely that the ear switches to D Major and hears the familiar functions II-V-I-IV instead.

The C♯7 may still be a functional question mark. As a logical continuation of the cycle-of-fifths root movement and as part of the diatonic cadence, it can be heard either as VII7 (V7/III) in D Major or as II7 (V7/V) in B Minor (I can actually make my ears flip-flop and hear either one). Only with the F♯7 and its resolution to B–7 does the ear definitely return to B Minor. We could analyse B7 as V7/IV (I7) in B Minor (we expect E–7 = IV–7) because we have just heard the tonic (B–7), and, secondly, we know this progression from the minor Blues (in bar 4 we often hear an altered dominant leading to the subdominant). However, I would not hesitate to analyse B7 as V7/II in D Major. In the end, it makes no difference – the functional analysis serves primarily to determine the scale material (see p. 133 ff.).

One last thought on "Spain". At the beginning of this chapter, I mentioned the ability to ask the right questions as one of the important goals of any analysis. Well, here's a question you should be asking: Why is it that we don't seem to have a problem with B7 resolving to Gmaj7 instead of E–7 on the repeat? Why does the unusual bass line not bother the ear? Why does something that looks strange sound run-of-the-mill? Again, this is easier to explain in D Major: E–7 (II–7) and Gmaj7 (IVmaj7) are both subdominant functions and contain almost the same notes. Obviously, the ear accepts Gmaj7 as a substitute for E–7.

Let's summarise: *All scale clichés we have so far determined for functions in major keys also hold true for their relative minor keys.* This means we don't have to be familiar with more than the basic diatonic sounds in minor. All non-diatonic sounds can be analysed in the relative major key, and I don't care if I have theory teachers from all over the world furiously banging at my front door. Besides, the many musicians I have interviewed on the subject of functional perception in major and minor confirm my view on this matter.

Of course, if a tune is in minor, it's in minor and there's no way around it. Even if we switch to the relative major temporarily for the sake of analysis, it is still important to keep the actual tonal centre and the basic minor functions in mind and ear. Only if the chord progression gets too obscure should we go for a change of perspective for clarification.

As a last example, let's have a look at another Chick Corea tune: "Crystal Silence". Here's the A section:

A Minor:	I–7	V–7	♭VImaj7
C Major:	VI–7	III–7	IVmaj7
	Aeolian	Phrygian	Lydian

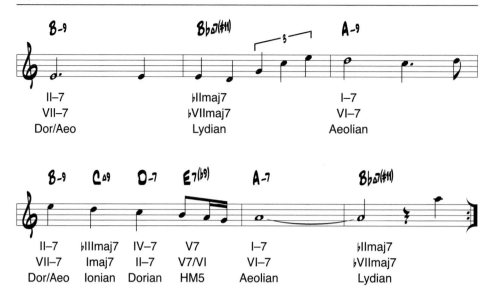

This chord progression can (and should) be analysed in A Minor exclusively, even though it contains several non-diatonic sounds. A–7 is I–7 (Aeolian), E–7 is V–7 (Phrygian) and Fmaj7 is ♭VImaj7 (Lydian). As indicated in the lead sheet, we could also think in C Major (A–7 = VI–7, E–7 = III–7, Fmaj7 = IVmaj7, thus confirming the scale analysis). However, once we move on, it should become apparent that it makes more sense to stay in A Minor. Interpreting B–7 as VII–7 and B♭maj7 as ♭VIImaj7 in C Major would be a rather artificial way of looking at things. Analysing B–7 as II–7 and B♭maj7 as ♭IImaj7 is much closer to what the ear perceives. A–7, as the tonic, is far too strong to be ignored. Of course, both B–7 and B♭maj7 are clearly non-diatonic in A Aeolian. We can interpret them as modal interchange functions. Since, in practice, B–7 usually includes 9 (C♯) as a tension, it is played either as Aeolian (taken from A Mixolydian) or Dorian (from A Ionian). I personally prefer the former choice because of the G in the melody in bars 3 + 5. B♭maj7 (♭IImaj7 from A Phrygian) is played Lydian, which is confirmed by the melody. The last 3 bars are clearly in A Minor, too. I hope you agree that there is no need to switch to C Major.

Assignment

Listen to the original recording of "Isn't She Lovely" by Stevie Wonder (1976, on the album "Songs in the Key of Life"). The key signature has four sharps. Decide whether you'd rather hear it in E Major or C♯ Minor. Transcribe and analyse the chord progression (functions and scale relationships).

"All Of Me"

Let's have a look at a tune that has made it around the world. Written by Seymour Simons (music) and Gerald Marks (lyrics) in 1931 and first recorded by Vaudeville star Belle Baker, "All Of Me" is one of the most (over)played tunes of the traditional Jazz repertoire. I can already see some of you rolling your eyes, thinking: "Why on Earth does he have to pick such a trite piece as his first example of an analysis?" To be quite honest – I'm not that partial to "All Of Me" myself. It's not that I don't like it. It just feels a bit old-fashioned and outdated. The melody is clichéd, the chord progression is highly predictable and the corny lyrics don't really help either. So, why would I choose it?

First of all – almost everybody knows it. I'm sure you can conjure up some kind of mental image of the tune without having to refer to a recording. And that's a good thing because it supports my stipulation that every analysis should be linked to and backed up by a sound in your mind. The better you know a tune, the easier it will be to make that connection.

Secondly, never underestimate something that comes across as plain or unpretentious. "All Of Me" is such a simple tune at first sight (and listening to it doesn't really change that first impression). However, as soon as you start digging, you'll discover that there is more to it than meets the eye. Even a seemingly straightforward standard can be remarkably intricate beneath the surface and reveal surprising qualities. Many renditions of this tune by contemporary Jazz greats prove that, despite (or perhaps because of) its simplicity, "All Of Me" can inspire more than just a run-of-the-mill performance.

Last, but not least, "All Of Me" is a great tune to lead you through the various stages of an analysis. It will show how deeply you can delve into a piece and that there is more to an analysis than just figuring out the chord-scale relationships. It is a wonderful example of how the various aspects of a composition interact. And, hopefully, by the end of this chapter, you will have to concede that "All Of Me" is actually a compositional stroke of genius.

Here's the lead sheet taken from the old Real Book (the original recording is in key of B♭ Major):

Before you read on – try to come up with your own analysis first! And make sure you really dig deep!!

Form

OK, let's get down to the analysis! As suggested in the previous chapter, we'll start with the form. The basic structure of "All Of Me" is simple: The piece follows a 32-bar AB format with two 16-bar sections – at least that's what's indicated in the lead sheet. However, since bars 1–8 and bars 17–24 are identical, shouldn't we rather speak of an AA' (16/16) or an ABAC (8/8/8/8) format? How can we tell the difference? The question must be: "Are bars 9–16 a continuation of the first 8 bars or do they introduce something new and contrasting?" Sing the first 16 bars of the melody. If you can feel two distinct eight-bar sections, the form is AB (8/8). If not, it's safe to say that the first half of the tune should rather be seen as a unit, and that speaks in favour of a 16-bar A section. So, what do you think? If you are not sure, you'll find the right answer just by looking at the lead sheet and the melody in particular (the rhythmic structure of the motivic phrases). Since the tune is notated 4 bars to the line, it is easy to see that the first 4 lines look almost the same when comparing the first bar of each line vertically, then the second bar (observe the quarter note triplets), and so on. You'll find slight differences towards the end of each line depending on its function in the overall scheme of things. For example, you will sense a slight interruption of the flow at the end of the first 8 bars, but that pause feels more like taking a breath than a true separation of the first and second eight-bar section. Obviously, the first 16 bars must be perceived as a unit. If you are not entirely convinced yet, I'll provide more proof as we move along.

Bars 17–24 are the same as bars 1–8. We'll call this section A', since the melody doesn't continue as in the first half of the tune and we're talking about 8 and not 16 bars. Again, just by looking at the lead sheet, you can see that the last 8 bars of the tune are completely different. This is the contrasting element, the B section. So, we have our first surprise. For a 32-bar tune, the subdivision of the form is rather unusual: AA'B (16/8/8). There is no other (!) standard I know of (and I know many!) that follows this format.

Melody

Remember that melodic analysis is an important step towards understanding how a tune works. So, let's have a look at the motivic makeup of the melody. Again, the melodic structure seems straightforward at first glance and, again, there's more to it than meets the eye. The first 8 bars clearly consist of two-bar segments (motive – motive – motive – end of phrase). The second 8 bars, however, are just as clearly divided into antecedent and consequent, each 4 bars long (sing the melody and you will feel how the length of the motivic phrases changes). Because of the different phrase subdivision, we could interpret the first 16 bars as two separate eight-bar sections. But, hold on, there's more! If you look closely, you will notice that bars 5–8 (motive – end of phrase) anticipate the four-bar motivic structure of bars 9–16 (antecedent and consequent). What initially points to two separate eight-bar sections is in actual fact proof of their connection. What we hear is a "formal cross-fade" from a two-bar to a four-bar motivic structure – further evidence supporting a 16-bar A section without a conclusive formal break. The last eight bars once again follow a two-bar motivic pulse (motive – motive – motive – end of phrase):

Motive	Mot.	Mot.	End	Antecedent	Consequent	Mot.	Mot.	Mot.	End
2	2	2	2	4	4	2	2	2	2

Let's continue. Remember our dear friend Mr. Schenker and his method of subtractive analysis by which he would condense a melody to its structural core. Apart from the obvious motivic patterns, an overall concept emerges if you carefully filter out the melodic focal points (phrase beginnings, long notes, high/low notes, etc.) and relate them to one another. Here's the "master plan" for the A section:

Bars 1 - 9

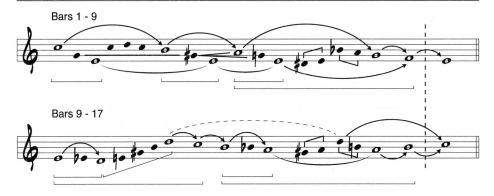

Bars 9 - 17

If you analyse the main guide tone line, you will make an interesting discovery: The condensed melody of the A section (bars 1–16) is nothing but an embellished C Major scale descending over more than an octave. The note E in the first 6 bars acts as kind of melodic pedal point and provides additional cohesion. The descending line (C-B-A-G) and the E both converge on the final target note F in bar 7. Note that the F is a leading tone and therefore not a stable note in the key of C Major. It wants to resolve to the E, and that's exactly what happens in bar 9. It's a bit like posing a question that has to be answered in the following bars. This, too, is an element that confirms our initial assumption that the first 16 bars should be perceived as a unit.

Now we come to an interesting point. Consider the psychology of the primary descending guide tone line C-B-A-G-F-E-D (bars 1–10). Which note would we expect to hear next? Of course, a C, since that's the next logical step! But this would bring the melody to a crashing end! Landing on the root of the overall key is something that reduces the energy level to zero. Although this commonly occurs at the very end of a piece (as the final resolution), it's not something that should happen when you're not even halfway into the tune. So, how does the composer solve this dilemma? An ingenious solution is the sudden surge in bar 10 that carries the melody up to the D and repeats it an octave higher. This takes the line to a more energetic register (the E7 arpeggio just fills the gap and creates movement). Now that the tune can't fizzle out, the energy level is no longer an issue, and the D can resolve to the expected C without the line losing momentum. Note that the high D serves a further, even more important purpose. It not only ensures the continuation of the line but also marks the climax of the first 16 bars. So, the octave leap is a very cleverly designed melodic device that kills two birds with one stone.

This leaves us with one final question: "How did the composer come up with the last 8 bars of the tune?" When looking at the melodic contour, we can see that bars 1–24 are obviously related. The closing passage, however, appears to be taken from a different piece. So, how does the B section tie in with the rest of the composition? Here again, we'll realise how important it is to look at the bigger picture. What this piece has been lacking until now is a contrasting element and a definite high point. Accordingly, the last eight bars should meet the following criteria: create contrast, state the primary climax and bring the piece to a close. As you can see, the B section consists of two-bar motivic phrases. At first sight, there is seemingly no connection to the melodic material presented in the first 24 bars. But, let me assure you, we have heard bars 25 + 26 before. Where? If you like brainteasers, then don't read on until you have at least tried to figure it out for yourself.

OK, here's the solution. Go to bar 11. Can you see the link? Compositionally, this is something that is done very often. You pick an important feature of one section and use it as the basic component for another part of the tune. Seymour Simons utilises the high point of the A section (the notes D-C) as a spin-off and expands on this little idea to create the B section. Clever, isn't it? The listener's ear subconsciously makes the connection and accepts the closing passage as a logical extension of bar 11:

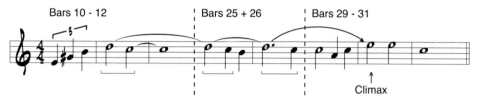

Since the final motivic idea (derived from bar 11) needs a bit of time and space because it first has to be stated and then developed, the main climax of the tune doesn't appear until bar 30 – unusually late for the average standard. The overall high point (the E) is actually part of the closing turn just before the melody resolves to the root at the end of the piece. Note that the E surpasses the high point of the first 16 bars (D in bar 11). Again, this is something the ear registers subliminally.

"All Of Me" a trite tune? I don't think so. I hope you are at least a bit surprised at the many interesting aspects the piece has so far divulged (and we haven't even started talking about the harmony yet). Our Schenkerian analysis shows that there is not a single superfluous note in the melody. You couldn't take anything out without ruining the tune. Every note contributes in some way to the overall flow. Even the chromatic passing notes are a vital part of the motivic structure. It should now be apparent why "All Of Me" is so popular – not only among sing-along Dixieland audiences all over the world but also among the many Jazz musicians who enjoy using it as a session tune. Only a formally well-constructed composition that says complex things in an effortless and understandable way could ever hit the mark as this has. Whether you like the tune or not, "All Of Me" is a great piece of music, plain and simple!

Harmony

Let's look at the changes and the chord-scale relationships. We are in the key of C Major. The chord progression starts and ends on C6 (the turnaround in the last two bars is not part of the composition). The first two bars are therefore I6 (Ionian). E7 is V7/VI. It makes no difference that A7 (VI7) appears instead of the expected diatonic target chord A–7 (VI–7). The most likely scales for E7 are HM5 or Altered. Since the first melody note in bar 3 is a B (the 5 of E7), HM5 is the more appropriate choice (Altered does not contain a perfect fifth). During an improvisation, however, we could consider using Altered because we don't have to worry about the constraints of the melody. On the other hand, we should take into account that "All Of Me" is a very traditional tune (remember, it was written in 1931 and the melody consists mostly of arpeggios and chord tones). Altered – as a rather aggressive and contemporary sound – would therefore not really be "in style". In bar 5, the E7 resolves to A7 (extended dominants). A7 is V7/II and sets up the following D–7 (II–7). The best choice of scale for A7 is also HM5 since the melody contains the notes E (= 5, so Altered is not an option) and B♭ (♭2/♭9). We can ignore the D♯, which is simply an auxiliary chromatic embellishment. The D–7 is, of course, II–7 Dorian.

In bar 9, E7 (V7/VI) appears once again. The corresponding scale is HM5 (check the melody). E7 resolves to A–7 (VI–7 Aeolian) as expected. A–7 and the ensuing D7 (V7/V) form a II-V progression (II-V/V). The D7 could be either Mixolydian or Lydian(♭7). The melody doesn't indicate which scale would work best – so, you're the boss. The notes E♭ (bar 9) and B♭ (bar 13) are chromatic passing notes that don't need to be taken into account when considering the chord-scale relationships (they are, however, important in order to preserve the rhythmic structure of the motives and to ensure motivic continuity). D7 resolves – delayed by D–7 (II–7 Dorian) – to G7 (V7 Mixolydian).

The shift back to E7 in bar 9 is entirely unexpected (G7 would have been the logical follow-up). There is no connection to the preceding D–7. To understand why this doesn't sound strange, we have to look at the harmonic rhythm. Of course, we could have examined this aspect when considering the form (and, as I've said, you should always look into this topic at an early stage of your analysis). However, I wanted to save it for the following discussion. The strong-weak distribution of the first 8 bars is easy: C6 (S) - E7 (W) - A–7 (W) - D–7 (S). Now, have a closer look at bars 5–8. The usual harmonic rhythm of a four-bar phrase is reversed (A7 = weak, D–7 = strong). This reversal is continued over the next 8 bars (supported admirably by the melody): E7 (weak) resolves to A–7 (strong), the D7 (non-diatonic = weak) is followed by D–7 (diatonic = strong). This, by the way, is yet another piece of evidence in support of a 16-bar A section. During the last two bars of the A section (D–7 - G7), the harmonic rhythm switches back to its initial alignment to ensure a logical preparation of C6 in bar 17 (strong). So, it is the quality of the chords that justifies the unusual harmonic progression in bars 8 and 9 (D–7 - E7). Here again, we run across a compositional feature that shows the clever design of the piece and the level of control exercised by the composer. Here's the summary:

C6	⁒	E7	⁒	A7	⁒	D–7	⁒	E7	⁒	A–7	⁒	D7	⁒	D–7	G7 ‖
S		W		W		S		W		S		W		S	W

D–7 - G7 leads back to C6 (II-V-I) and the repeat of the first 8 bars. So, let's jump to bar 25. F6 is IV6 (Lydian). Note the B = ♯4/♯11 – the Lydian fourth – in the melody! F–6 is IV–6 (modal interchange) and takes Dorian or Melodic minor as a scale (the characteristic major 6th appears in the melody). Cmaj7 (Imaj7 Ionian) and E–7 (III–7 Phrygian) should not pose a problem (Cmaj7 is sometimes omitted in the lead sheet). The A7 (V7/II) is an old friend, too. We should, however, realise that HM5, which we have used consistently for A7 so far, does not reflect what is going on in the melody. The note B (2/9) implies two alternatives: Mixo(♭13) or Whole-tone (both of these scales contain the B and the F = ♭13 diatonic to the key). D–7 - G7 - C6 is II-V-I (the E = 6/13 in the melody on G7 suggests Mixolydian). The harmonic rhythm of the B section follows the usual strong-weak distribution: | F6 (S) | F–6 (W) | Cmaj7/E–7 (S) | A7 (W) | D–7 (S) | G7 (W) | C6 (S).

The C6 chord used at the beginning and the end of the tune is deliberately chosen as a substitute for Cmaj7 to prevent the ♭2-clash between a major seventh in the chord and the root/octave in the melody:

Let's summarise our harmonic analysis:

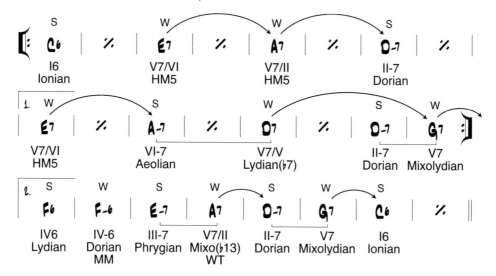

Improvisation

Find a play-along for "All Of Me" (e.g. Aebersold, Volume 95) and give it a try. It's a great tune to work with, since the two-bar changes are not that complicated and you can spend time with each chord. See if you can follow the harmonic rhythm and create lines that are as coherent and conclusive as the original melody. A simple melody, transparent form, cohesive harmony – all these attributes are hallmarks of a well-designed Jazz standard. We should not ignore these things. We should incorporate them into our improvisation (simplicity certainly benefits a solo more than artificial complexity). Start working with chord tones at first and connect them as smoothly as possible. The ear training exercise on p. 465 ff. will help you with this approach.

The following improvisation by the trombonist Trummy Young over the second half (A'/B) of "All Of Me" on the album "Ambassador Satch" (1956) by Louis Armstrong consists almost entirely of chord tones and arpeggios. It is a wonderful example of "playing the changes" (watch the bass clef!):

Note the variation on the changes in bars 25–27: F6 - F–6 - Cmaj7 is replaced by F7 - F♯°7 -
C/G (IV7 - ♯IV°7 - I/5). This gives the solo a bluesy touch.

Then again, such a straightforward chord progression – used independently of the theme
– could offer an opportunity to musicians who like to experiment and create suspense by
combining familiar sounds (e.g. simple changes) with contemporary concepts (e.g. rhythmically or formally exciting ideas). An amazing example of this way of thinking is the composition "Line Up" by the pianist Lennie Tristano (on the album "Lennie Tristano", 1955). This
unusual recording has no actual theme; it is – as Tristano stated himself – a conceptual improvisation, a largely through-composed solo based on the changes of "All Of Me". "Line Up"
is in A♭ Major. I have transposed the transcription to C Major to make it easier to compare
with our lead sheet. Take the trouble to play this solo note for note, phrase by phrase, and
analyse it. Here are the first three choruses (again, watch the bass clef!):

I'd like to quote Ted Gioia, pianist, critic and music historian. His review of this recording sums things up better than I could ever have done: "When this track was first released, it attracted enormous attention … but not for the music. Tristano had "tampered" with the tapes by recording the piano part over a separate rhythm track, manipulating the music in the process. Tristano never provided details and got testy when questioned about his method. But it appears that he brought the bass and drums down to half speed, and recorded the piano on top of this slower version, then accelerated the playback rate of the combined performance. A certain ethereal and detached quality permeates the finished product. The piano sound possesses a strange, unnatural crispness, and the question was raised whether Tristano was trying to "trick" people into thinking that he could play faster than was actually the case. The controversy would be less pronounced today, when studio splicing, dicing and "fixing" are a high-tech art. But the sad result of this brouhaha was that it distracted attention from Tristano's brilliant performance. "Line Up" is one of the great linear improvisations in the modern Jazz heritage. Students could profitably study this solo, learning from its crystalline structure, unlocking the artistry of its phrasing, the rhythmic relationship of melody to the ground beat, and the harmonic implications of Tristano's lines. The chord changes are borrowed from "All Of Me", but instead of the romantic sensibility of that standard, Tristano offers a diamond-hard coolness purged of all emotional excesses. This is as pure and abstract as music can get. At any speed, "Line Up" is a masterpiece."

The explanations I have included in the solo transcription should help you understand this extremely complex improvisation (passages conforming to the expected chord-scale clichés have not been commented on). Here are a few more thoughts on Tristano's performance. From a present-day perspective, we will not discover anything momentous when analysing the solo material and the chord-scale relationships. For that time (1955), however, the approach was highly unusual. The many chromatic passing notes, approach patterns (AP) and displacements, the use of Pentatonic scale material, the occasional reharmonisation or superimposition of substitute changes – all of this sounds quite daring within such a traditional context. Moreover, all dominants tend to be Mixolydian (including V7/II and V7/VI), which adds to the ambiguous feeling of tonality.

The most remarkable aspect, however, is Tristano's persistent toying with the form and his treatment of phrasing. Starting the solo in bar 9 (!), compressing or expanding the duration of a chord, anticipating or delaying resolutions, displacing phrases away from traditional rhythmical focal points by beginning a line on beats two or four or even on offbeat 8th notes, playing over the bar lines, controlling the dynamics and the phrasing with attention to each individual note (e.g. ghost notes), shifting accents within the line away from the usual four-note groupings – all these strategies demonstrate the conscious effort to go against familiar ways of playing, to break away from the habitual harmonic and melodic vocabulary and venturing into new territory,

Here's one last fact: "Line Up" was recorded 6 months *before* Trummy Young's solo. This shows how different two practically concurrent interpretations of the same composition can be. It also illustrates a fundamental paradigmatic shift – from a distinctly vertical (chord-based) soloing concept to an increasingly horizontal (scale-based) and chromatic way of improvising. Whether extreme modifications such as the ones presented in Tristano's solo make a positive contribution to the composition or whether they cause the piece to miss its mark stylistically is open to discussion. Lennie Tristano sidesteps this problem cleverly by completely abandoning the theme, making way for the aesthetics of his own melodic language. To me, every tune is a playground, a vehicle that serves the intentions of the player. Even if every well-known theme automatically triggers certain expectations among listeners, I believe it is the obligation of the Jazz musician to find a personal approach to interpreting a tune.

Lennie Tristano was certainly one of the great pioneers of modern Jazz. He was one of the most significant pianists and teachers of the 1950s (e.g. as head of his own "school" in Chicago), a master who, despite the unobtrusive way in which he worked, inspired a whole generation of Jazz musicians.

"'Round Midnight"

One of the best-known and most beautiful Jazz ballads ever written, this masterpiece proves that Thelonious Monk was not only one of the Jazz greats as an improviser, a pianist with a unique and unorthodox style, but also a composer capable of highly sensitive, atmospheric and poetic pieces full of dissonant harmonies, angular melodies and unexpected quirks. Time and time again, I come across Jazz musicians who approach "'Round Midnight" with utmost respect – not only because the piece is by Monk, but also because it takes quite some getting into. I often hear that the harmony is complicated, elusive and hard to figure out. Of course, the key signature (6 flats) is no cakewalk and adds to the confusion. Every Jazz musician has, at one time or another, poked around at this piece in an attempt to shed some light on its seemingly enigmatic content. As a result, countless versions have been recorded. Allegedly, "'Round Midnight" is the most-recorded Jazz standard ever (in *allmusic.com*, an online music guide, it appears on over 1000 albums). It serves as the title and the main tune of an acclaimed movie starring Dexter Gordon (soundtrack by Herbie Hancock), and one critic has even labelled it the "National Anthem of Jazz" (according to *jazzstandards.com*). One of the most authoritative recordings can be found on Miles Davis' album "'Round About Midnight" (1956).

In truth, it doesn't matter which version we choose to look at. What is important is that you know at least one. Once you have acquired an initial understanding of this piece, it should be comparatively easy to make sense of the many other versions. The following lead sheet is taken from the old Real Book:

D.C. al Fine (A2, no repeat)

Form and melody

As already mentioned in the previous chapters: Always begin an analysis by clarifying the form of a piece. "'Round Midnight" follows the typical AABA format of the average 32-bar Jazz standard. A1 leads back into the second A section, whereas A2 closes within the eight-bar phrase to provide space for the B section. The tune climaxes towards the end of the eight-bar B section, only to return to A3 (same as A2) and the conclusion of the piece. Nothing special here, so let's move on to the melody and the harmony.

Unlike "All Of Me" with its highly predictable if not tediously repetitive thematic design, "'Round Midnight" has an almost conversational, even rambling, quality. As if somebody were talking to no one in particular, the tune seemingly meanders from one phrase to the next with a relaxed and almost soporific feel (the lugubrious mumblings of an inebriated customer in a smoky bar). Nonetheless, the melody follows a very coherent motivic concept. We can see that the A section progresses in two-bar phrases. The 16th-note sweeps occurring on the second beat of bars 1, 3 and 5 are clear indication of a "motive - motive - motive - ending" subdivision. The melody soars higher and higher, reaches a climax in bar 5 and then ebbs away towards the end of the section. Note that A1 ends on a Bb (5 in the key of Eb Minor = open ending), linking it to the first note of A2, while the second A section ends on the root (closure).

And now Monk does something very clever. Instead of creating contrast by introducing entirely new melodic and harmonic material, he uses the concluding phrase of the first A section as a motivic link and starting point of the B section. Bars 7 + 8 of A1 reappear in the first four bars of B with only minor melodic and harmonic alterations: Cb7 is substituted with the II-V pattern Cø7 - F7, which is almost the same thing, since Cb7 and F7 are tritone substitutes. The second half of the B section may seem different at a first glance. But, even though the harmonic and melodic rhythm speeds up and the motives are now half-bar phrases, bars 5–8 are no more than a spin-off derived from bars 1 + 2 – a simplification of the initial two-bar phrase (note the stepwise sequential quality of the motives). This melodic and harmonic connection guarantees a strong sense of continuity and unity. Notice how the B section ends on a Bb (as A1), setting up the first note of A3.

The climax also deserves a closer look. Don't make the mistake of automatically going for the highest note. In "'Round Midnight", this won't get you far. Even though the two highest notes of the tune (Gb-F) occur in the A section, they appear in the middle of bar 5 and are therefore not as prominently positioned as the Eb on the downbeat of bar 7 in the B section.

To ensure that the E♭ is perceived as the primary high point of the composition, the motivic frequency and the harmonic rhythm accelerate in the 2 bars prior to the climax. In addition, Monk harmonises the E♭ with E♭7 – a special sound (a Blues tonic) that creates tension in an E♭ Minor environment, thus enhancing the melodic high point admirably.

Let's have a quick look at the harmonic and melodic rhythm of "'Round Midnight". In ballads, the harmony generally tends to be richer and more elaborate. Due to the slower tempo, there is more space for intricate chord progressions. As a result, it usually makes little sense to look at each chord individually. You often have to think in terms of harmonic patterns where two or more chords have the same or similar meaning and must therefore be regarded as a unit. The actual harmonic rhythm may therefore be obscured to a certain extent by the harmonic activity. Here, we're dealing with tendencies rather than hardcore facts.

In the A section, things start out in the usual fashion. Bar 1 is strong (Cø7 is nothing more than an inversion of E♭–6). Both Fø7 and B♭7 have a similar cadential quality – so bar 2 is weak. This sets up a clear strong-weak pattern. Accordingly, bar 3 is strong (A♭7 can be interpreted as an extension of E♭–7). Bar 4 is clearly weak (4 chords to the bar, II-Vs that deviate from the tonality, chromatic notes in the melody). A♭–7 (bar 5) feels like a point of resolution and must therefore be strong. The D♭7, however, should be seen as weak, not only because it's a dominant but also because of the ensuing E♭–7, which is clearly strong. Obviously, the harmonic rhythm accelerates in the second half of the A section. The end of the A section is not that obvious. A♭7 (bar 6) could be either strong (same as bar 3) or weak (dominant chord). Personally, I would go for the former, since C♭7 in bar 7 is clearly weak (a cadence chord that wants to resolve to B♭7). B♭7 (bar 8) is ambiguous because it serves two functions. For one, it is the resolution of C♭7, which would make it strong. At the same time, it is V7 in the key of E♭ Minor and therefore weak. As you can see, one and the same chord may have different implications. Here's the summary (we'll talk about the B section at a later point in this chapter):

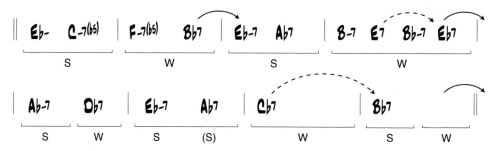

Harmony

Whenever I discuss "'Round Midnight" with my students, here's my first question: "What effect does this piece have on you? Does it sound strange, straight-ahead, coherent, awkward, illogical, surprising, etc.?" Most of the answers are down the line of: "Even if I don't really understand what's going on and how the chords work, the piece sounds very familiar and logical." And something that sounds matter-of-fact must be easy to explain (an unusual chord progression would not feel familiar)! So, clearly, our mind categorises this piece as "complicated", but our ears say: "Everything's cool!" And, as is often the case, the ear is on the right track. The problem is that we simply have less understanding of harmonic relationships in minor keys (the tune is clearly in E♭ Minor according to the key signature as well as the melody and the first/last chord of the tune). Before we start with the analysis, we should therefore clarify the basic functions in E♭ Minor. It makes sense not only to look at Aeolian as the most important tonic minor scale, but also at HM and MM (the enclosed chord symbols represent the important sounds found in "'Round Midnight"):

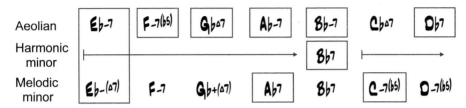

As already explained earlier on in this book, Harmonic minor's sole purpose in life is to supply minor keys with a V7 dominant chord. Therefore, we don't have to worry about the other diatonic functions contained in HM.

A section

Let's tackle the chord progression. The first two bars are clearly a turnaround. The functional progression I-VI-II-V doesn't allow for any other interpretation. It shows, however, how liberally you can combine the functions of the various minor modes. E♭– (I–) is deliberately notated as an undefined triad – neither sixths nor sevenths are included. This chord could be anything that sounds like a minor tonic: Aeolian, HM, MM (theoretically even Dorian or Phrygian). The available four-note extensions of the E♭ minor triad are therefore E♭–6, E♭–7 or E♭–maj7. Since Cø7 is clearly from MM (VIø7), we could either go for E♭–6 or E♭–maj7. In this way, the first bar can be played using just one scale. Accordingly, Cø7 would be Locrian(9), which contains the same notes as E♭ Melodic minor. Fø7 (IIø7 from Aeolian or HM) and B♭7 (V7 from HM) constitute a II-V progression. Fø7 is Locrian, followed by B♭7 played HM5 or Altered (a matter of taste, since the melody does not indicate which of the two is more appropriate). An attractive variation would be the use of Locrian(9) for both Cø7 and Fø7 and, as the logical follow-up, HTWT for B♭7. That would give the first 2 bars a nice buzz (the second half of **track 29** will give you an idea of what this sounds like).

Bar 3 should not be a problem: E♭–7 is I–7 (from Aeolian) and A♭7 is IV7 (from MM). At first glance, E♭–7 - A♭7 could also be seen as a II-V pattern. However, since we are in the key of E♭ Minor, I-IV is the more likely analysis. This naturally affects the choice of scales. E♭–7 is clearly Aeolian (as a tonic minor chord) and A♭7 is Lydian(♭7), the "shifted" version of E♭ Melodic minor (the origin of the function IV7):

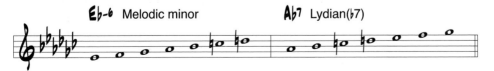

If we reconsider the II-V analysis for E♭–7 - A♭7, the choice of Dorian and Mixolydian would be an option, too. This would allow us to play the whole bar using the same material (besides, the idea of a Dorian minor tonic should not be all that foreign to us). Here is the analysis so far (the functions and their origin):

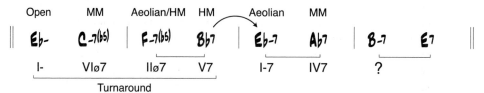

Open	MM	Aeolian/HM	HM		Aeolian	MM		
E♭-	C-7(♭5)	F-7(♭5)	B♭7		E♭-7	A♭7	B-7	E7
I-	VIø7	IIø7	V7		I-7	IV7	?	

Turnaround

Now comes the moment of truth. How on Earth do you explain B–7 and E7 in the key of E♭ Minor? At first guess, it could simply be an out-of-key II-V resolving chromatically to B♭–7 - E♭7. And that's the way it's usually analysed (as a chromatic harmonic sequence). Both chords could also be seen as Sub(II-V)/I in E♭ Minor with a deceptive resolution to B♭–7 (instead of E♭–7). Out-of-key II-V, chromatic sequence, Sub(II-V), deceptive resolution? All of this would indicate a highly unusual sound. However, all my students agree that, when listening to the recording, the actual sound suggests something quite familiar and doesn't feel out-of-context at all. And if something sounds familiar, the explanation should be simple, too.

Remember! Whenever we are dealing with tunes in minor keys and we run up against chord progressions that are hard to explain, we should always consider the option of switching to the relative major key for clarification. So, let's try to solve the problem by shifting the perspective to G♭ Major. And, lo and behold, all of a sudden everything falls into place. The chord progression B♭–7 - E♭7 - A♭–7 - D♭7 (bars 4 and 5) now makes perfect sense. What we see (and hear!) is a simple turnaround in the key of G♭ Major: III–7 - VI7 - II–7 - V7. The final confirmation for this analysis is the E♭–7 in bar 6. Whereas the E♭–7 in bar 3 is clearly heard as a minor tonic (I–7), the E♭–7 in bar 6 is rather heard as VI–7 (Aeolian), the relative minor of G♭ Major. My students corroborate this time and again. Obviously, the ear has shifted to G♭ as the new tonal centre and now interprets D♭7 - E♭–7 as a deceptive resolution (V7 - VI–7) in G♭ Major.

If we continue to think in G♭ Major, A♭7 is V7/V (or II7), C♭7 is SubV/III (or IV7) and B♭7 is V7/VI (or III7). With B♭7, the chord progression returns to E♭ Minor at the end of the A section. While D♭7 clearly pointed to G♭ as the tonic, B♭7 and the leading tone D pushes the chord progression back to E♭–, the initial tonal centre. Be aware, however, that we are not really talking about a modulation when switching from E♭ Minor to G♭ Major and back. Modulation implies a change of key signature, and that's not what's happening here. It therefore makes no sense to separate the two colours artificially (by referring to a modulation), since both key areas are interrelated and share the same basic functional environment (with the exception of B♭–7 = III–7 in G♭ Major and B♭7 = V7 in E♭ Minor).

Now that we know how to interpret the changes functionally, it is easy to determine the corresponding scales. Again, remember that it makes no difference which perspective we use – E♭ Minor or G♭ Major. Because of the joint key signature, the diatonic material on which we base our conclusions is the same and, consequently, the choice of scales would be the same, too. Here we go: B♭–7 is Phrygian, E♭7 is HM5, A♭–7 is Dorian, D♭7 is Mixolydian, E♭–7 is Aeolian, A♭7 is Lydian(♭7), C♭7 is Lydian(♭7), too, and B♭7 is HM5.

A word on the Cb7, which is obviously used as a replacement for Cbmaj7 (the diatonic Aeolian function). A strong bluesy undercurrent pervades the tune, contributing to its poignant "after hour" mood. Remember that the function bVI7 is paramount to the Blues feeling in minor. Cb7, apart from being a SubV of Bb7, is also bVI7 in Eb Minor – *the* most important function of a minor Blues (many soloists like to play Eb Blues over the last two bars of the A1 section). Just to show how closely related Eb Minor and Gb Major are: Cb7 is also IV7 in Gb – next to I7 *the* most important function of a major Blues.

Did we miss anything? Ah, yes! We still haven't solved our little brainteaser: B–7 - E7. Whenever we are working on tunes with key signatures that flaunt a gaggle of flats or sharps, enharmonic spelling becomes a major issue. Sadly, lead sheets are not very consistent when it comes to accurate notation (you should always make a point of checking alternate spellings if you chance upon something strange). If we notate B–7 - E7 enharmonically as Cb–7 - Fb7 and analyse both chords in Gb Major, we end up with the functional progression IV–7 - bVII7. So, the riddle is solved. And it is also easy to understand why the listener doesn't get the impression of anything unusual. Cb–7 (IV–7) and Fb7 (bVII7) are the most frequently used modal interchange functions. They will always sound commonplace and familiar in the context of Eb Minor or Gb Major, irrespective of whether Eb–7 or Gbmaj7 is perceived as the tonic (here, the backdoor cadence doesn't resolve to the expected tonic Gbmaj7, but rather to III–7, a tonic substitute). Because of the II-V sequence, the choice of scales would be Dorian for Cb–7 and Mixolydian for Fb7.

Here's the functional summary of the first A section as of bar 4 (based on our analysis in Gb Major):

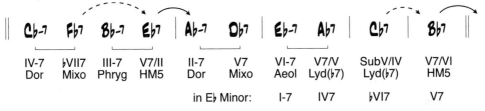

Cb–7	Fb7	Bb–7	Eb7	Ab–7	Db7	Eb–7	Ab7	Cb7	Bb7
IV–7	bVII7	III–7	V7/II	II–7	V7	VI–7	V7/V	SubV/IV	V7/VI
Dor	Mixo	Phryg	HM5	Dor	Mixo	Aeol	Lyd(b7)	Lyd(b7)	HM5
				in Eb Minor:		I–7	IV7	bVI7	V7

The first 6 bars of the second and third A section (A2/A3) are usually played the same as A1. It is worth mentioning, however, that A2 and A3 often end on Ebmaj7 (!) instead of Eb–6 (indicated in the lead sheet). In this case, a D is sometimes played in the melody (the Eb doesn't go so well with the maj7 chord). Monk himself played this version, keeping the Eb in the melody in spite of the Ebmaj7 in the left hand (he obviously liked the resulting dissonance).

Assignment

Write down the scales mentioned above and see if you agree. Don't forget to use the key signature and to add accidentals as needed.

B section

Let's turn our attention to the B section. Our ear has switched back to Eb Minor in the meantime. Cø7 (VIø7 Locrian) and F7 constitute a II-V-pattern resolving to Bb7 (V7 HM5). At this point, I would like to remind you of one of the problems we may run into when analysing chord progressions in minor. Remember my saying that it's not a good idea to have one and the same symbol denoting two different functional situations? F7 is V7/V in E♭ Minor and that's what you can call it because that's what it is. However, don't fall into the trap of assuming that V7/V in minor works the same as V7/V in major. In major, V7/V would take Mixolydian or Lydian(♭7). In minor, however, Altered is the more diatonic choice. As you can see, the same symbol (V7/V) stands for two entirely different situations – and that's exactly the kind of mix-up we should try to avoid. For the sake of scale analysis, it would be better to switch to the relative major key. V7/V in E♭ Minor corresponds to V7/III (or VII7) in G♭ Major, and that implies Altered. If this approach seems too confusing, or if you want to avoid the discussion altogether – go for the key signature. The key signature will tell you which tensions go best with the F7 chord: G♭ (♭9), A♭ (= G♯ = ♯9), C♭ (♭5/♯11) and D♭ (♭13) are all part of E♭ Minor. Therefore, the most logical choice of scale is Altered.

Let's move on. Of course, we could analyse A♭–7 - D♭7 - G♭maj7 as a II-V-I in G♭ Major. However, our ears are tuned to E♭ Minor at this stage. It therefore makes more sense to stick to the basic minor functions: IV–7 - ♭VII7 - ♭IIImaj7. Besides, the changes whiz by too fast (quarter-bar rhythm) and return too quickly to E♭ Minor for the ear to be able to settle on G♭ Major. Again, when defining the chord-scale relationships, it makes no difference whether we think in E♭ Minor or G♭ Major: A♭–7 is Dorian, D♭7 Mixolydian and G♭maj7 Ionian.

We have already discussed C♭7 and B♭7 at the end of both A sections. Now for the closing passage: E♭7 appears at the climax of the B section and could, of course, be Mixolydian. However, we already talked about the Blues inflection of "'Round Midnight". Therefore, it is not that far-fetched to analyse E♭7 as a Blues tonic. Because the Blues scale is almost identical to the minor Pentatonic scale, their tonics are interchangeable. What comes next is a sequence of seventh chords, all of which we have already analysed earlier: D♭7 (♭VII7), C♭7 (♭VI7) and B♭7 (V7). There are soloists who use the E♭ Blues scale for the full two last bars of the B section. We could, of course, interpret each dominant chord individually, as shown in the following summary of the B section:

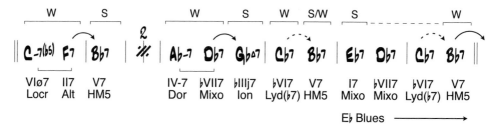

I have added the strong-weak distribution of the chord progression in the above diagram. In the B section, both the harmonic and melodic rhythms are reversed (a means of creating contrast). Bar 1 (Cø7 - F7) is weak, bar 2 (B♭7) is strong. You might argue that B♭7, as a dominant, can't be strong. Of course, it can! The II-V preparation (weak) and the active melody provide for a strong feeling of resolution when reaching the B♭7, which sits around for a full bar and can therefore only be seen as a target chord (strong). With A♭–7 - D♭7 (weak), G♭maj7 (strong), C♭7 (weak) and B♭7 (strong), the harmonic rhythm accelerates, driving the piece towards its climax. B♭7 is both strong and weak, since it is also the V7 of E♭7. Remember the A section – there, too, B♭7 was a dual-function chord. The last two bars are not that clear. Essentially, we're dealing with a minor turnaround that gradually progresses from "strong" (Eb7) to "weak" (Bb7).

All in all, "'Round Midnight" is not quite as mysterious as it is often thought or made out to be. This doesn't mean that there is nothing more to discover about the piece. As already mentioned at the beginning of this chapter – there are many different versions of "'Round Midnight". Inserting additional passing chords or substituting parts of the original changes is common practice. Here are three examples:

- In the A section, Thelonious Monk himself liked to play Ab–7 - Db7 instead of Bb7 in the second half of bar 2, and then Cø7 (an upper structure of Ab7) for all of bar 3, resulting in a chromatically descending bass line to B–7 in bar 4.

- Personally, I like using the following chord progression for the last 2 bars of A2 and A3 (quarter-note pulse): | Cø7 Cb7 Fø7/Bb Bb7 | Ebmaj7 |.

- At the end of the B section, the chord progression Eb7 - Db7 - Cb7 - Bb7 is often added to by inserting the corresponding II–7 chords and expanding the dominants into a series of II-V patterns (quarter-note pulse): Bb–7 - Eb7 - Ab–7 - Db7 - Gb–7 - Cb7 - F–7 - Bb7. The nice thing about this reharmonisation is the fact that the melody no longer relates to each dominant chord as the root (a rather plain sound). Instead, the main melody notes now start out as the tension 11 of each –7 chord and – in conjunction with the acceleration of the chord progression – thereby greatly enhance the climax of the piece (check it out!).

Your job is to listen to other interpretations of "'Round Midnight" and compare the changes. And now it's up to you to develop your own version.

"Nardis"

This piece, written in 1958, is attributed to Miles Davis, although he never recorded it himself! It is more closely associated with Bill Evans who recorded it a number of times. One of the most beautiful versions can be heard on his album "Explorations" (1961). Controversy still surrounds this tune, particularly regarding the origin of its harmonic structure, which clearly shows Evans' influence. Davis and Evans collaborated extensively and "Nardis" is only one of several compositions where the question as to who takes the credit is yet to be settled. Here is the lead sheet:

The tune is based on the old faithful 32-bar AABA format (I'll leave it to you to work out the harmonic rhythm of the chord progression). Melody and harmony, however, are special. With its dark and somewhat oriental flavour, "Nardis" is an unusual and pioneering piece for its time.

One sharp in the key signature implies E Minor (Aeolian). On the other hand, the chord progression leans strongly towards E Phrygian – especially because of the opening turn E–7 - Fmaj7 (I–7 - bIImaj7). Assuming this to be true, let's take a refresher and look once again at the diatonic functions in E Phrygian:

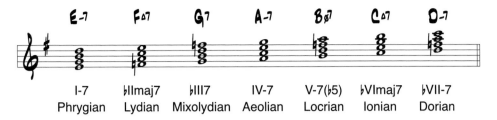

E-7	Fᴧ7	G7	A-7	Bᴓ7	Cᴧ7	D-7
I-7	♭IImaj7	♭III7	IV-7	V-7(♭5)	♭VImaj7	♭VII-7
Phrygian	Lydian	Mixolydian	Aeolian	Locrian	Ionian	Dorian

As you can see, the A section can be analysed almost completely in E Phrygian:

E-7	Fᴧ7	B7	Cᴧ7	A-7	Fᴧ7	Eᴧ7	E-
I-	♭IImaj7	V7	♭VImaj7	IV-7	♭IImaj7	Imaj7	I-
Phrygian	Lydian	HM5	Ionian	Aeolian	Lydian	Ionian	Phrygian

B7 and Emaj7 extend the diatonic Phrygian limits, deviating from the modality, but not the tonality (E). We can therefore interpret them as MI-functions: B7 from E Harmonic minor and Emaj7 from E Ionian. The B section is also easy to analyse:

A-7	Fᴧ7	𝄇 2	D-7	G7	Cᴧ7	Fᴧ7
IV-7	♭IImaj7		♭VII-7	♭III7	♭VImaj7	♭IImaj7
Aeolian	Lydian		Dorian	Mixolyd	Ionian	Lydian

But, is "Nardis" really a Phrygian piece? There is another, rather quaint, clue that would point us in just that direction. Many of the pieces written in the early days of Modal Jazz were composed in one mode exclusively. And as much as I'd like you to view all church modes as unique and independent tonic sounds, I am perfectly aware of the fact that we all first learned them as displacements of the Major scale. In addition, most of us have the unfortunate habit of thinking in C. Now picture a trumpeter like Miles Davis, who used the piano as a composer, but was by no means a pianist. I can just see him fiddling around with the white keys and coming up with modal tunes such as "So What" in D Dorian or "Nardis" in E Phrygian. It is astonishing to think that one of the most important movements in the history of Jazz may have originated in the dabblings of an amateur piano player.

And that's all there is to this analysis. Easy, isn't it? Sadly, as logical as it might sound, it is nothing but hypothetical drivel. This is a typical example of a purely theoretical analysis that is *not* backed up aurally. If you listen to the original recording, you will hear a secondary line (an inner part) in bars 3 and 4 of the A section that upsets the apple cart big-time:

Follow my train of thought! Even though the line is entirely chromatic at first (bar 3), it still has a scale connotation in relation to B7 because of the notes on the strong beats, i.e. G♯ (13) on beat 1 and G (♭13) on beat 3. This suggests that B7 is a "split" dominant – the first half of the bar is Mixolydian and the second half is HM5. More importantly, the next bar (Cmaj7) clearly implies C Lydian with the F♯ = ♯4/♯11 on beat 1 and the E on beat 3. This automatically influences A–7 in bar 5, which, accordingly, is no longer Aeolian but rather Dorian (C Lydian = A Dorian with the F♯ carrying on into A–7 as the 6/13, the characteristic note in Dorian). As a result, the entire system of functional derivation shifts. Because the note F♯ is so prominent, it also influences the tonic E–7. Therefore, E–7 must be Aeolian (F♯ = 2/9 rules out Phrygian). The key signature with one sharp is obviously correct.

Let's have a look at the first A section of Bill Evans' solo:

This excerpt shows clearly that Bill Evans did actually hear E Aeolian and not E Phrygian as the central sound. The conspicuous F♯ leaves no room for doubt. However, I would like to show you this improvisation for another, more important reason: It is interesting that the characteristic chords Fmaj7 and Emaj7 do not appear at all, at least not in this A section (neither in the left nor right hand). Bill Evans reduces the changes to the elementary functions in E Minor (have another look at the accompaniment). This example shows that a solo doesn't have to reflect every tiny detail of the harmonic structure. The freedom to reharmonise, replace, extend or, as in this case, to simplify the original changes arbitrarily is common practice while improvising.

In a more subtle way, Bill Evans nevertheless follows a modal-interchange approach by alternately (and rather randomly) using different scales for B7: Mixolydian(♭13) in bar 3, HM5/Altered in bar 6 and HTWT in bar 8. Incidentally, his play on rhythms is lovely. The shifted quarter-note triplets conceal the bar lines and give the whole phrase a floating quality.

Let's get back to the chord progression of "Nardis". Even though the functional analysis in E Aeolian remains the same as in E Phrygian, the chord-scale relationships do not:

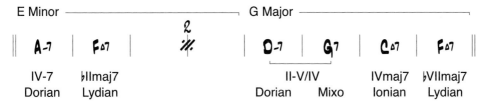

Now that the perspective has changed, Fmaj7 (♭IImaj7 from Phrygian), B7 (V7 from HM) and Emaj7 (Imaj7 from Ionian) are MI-functions.

The B section, too, looks quite different (it makes sense to partially base the analysis on G Major rather than on E Minor):

E Minor			G Major			
A-7	F△7	2 ./.	D-7	G7	C△7	F△7
IV-7	♭IImaj7		II-V/IV		IVmaj7	♭VIImaj7
Dorian	Lydian		Dorian Mixo		Ionian	Lydian

Cmaj7 would actually be Lydian in E Aeolian. If, however, we consider the chord progression leading up to Cmaj7 and the note F prominently contained in every one of the preceding chords (Fmaj7 - D-7 - G7), then C Ionian would be the better choice. Nonetheless, Cmaj7 is quite obviously a IVᵗʰ degree (when thinking in G Major) and proof of the fact that the piece is in E Aeolian and not E Phrygian. Early modal compositions moved predominantly in one scale and followed a horizontal approach. Accordingly, improvisations were usually very diatonic and had a laid-back, almost ethereal quality. Bill Evans' solo, in part, speaks a different language. Here, the lines switch from a modal to a functional, chord-based approach. Whereas the phrases seem expansive, airy and rhythmically open in the A section and at the beginning of the B section, the improvisational concept changes with D–7 - G7 - Cmaj7. Suddenly, we hear everything we would expect of a typical Bebop line: chromatic approach patterns, altered dominants, eighth-note movement, intense beat-related phrasing, etc. In other words, the solo changes its philosophy to a predominantly vertical feel, which speaks in favour of E Aeolian and a functional rather than a modal concept.

The analysis of "Nardis" is intended to show that seemingly insignificant details (e.g. an inconspicuous inner voice) can strongly influence how we hear and, as a result, interpret an entire composition. Don't merely scratch the surface of your lead sheets, but rather dig deep into the inner layers of the recording.

Finally, I would like to point out the unusual colouring of the theme in the A section. If we reduce the melody to its central (characteristic) notes, we end up with a rather strange scale (notated downwards in order to accentuate the connection to the melody):

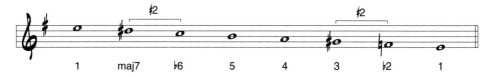

This is known as the **Double Harmonic major** scale – referring to the two augmented seconds, which remind us of the characteristic interval in Harmonic minor (thus "double harmonic"), and the major third (thus "major"). Melodies based on this scale have a distinct oriental flavour. That is why it is sometimes referred to as the Arabic scale or the "Gypsy Major" scale. Though not commonly used in Western music, since it doesn't fit traditional chord progressions, it does appear in some of Claude Debussy's compositions (e.g. "La Soirée Dans Grenade") in an attempt to evoke a Spanish Flamenco mood. It is also identical to the South Indian *Melakarta* "Mayamalavagowla" and the North Indian *Thaat* "Bhairav".

In practice, as the improvisation by Bill Evans goes to show, Jazz musicians usually follow a relatively orthodox strategy when playing over "Nardis" in accordance with the functional analysis above and the corresponding chord-scale relationships. As a rather refreshing way of improvising over this tune, it would be worth considering a modal approach by using Double Harmonic major throughout the A section *irrespective of the changes* and switching to a chord-scale approach in the B section as a means of contrast. Try it. Find a play-along (e.g. Aebersold Volume 50, "The Magic of Miles") and see if you can make the scale work.

A good example of how to use this scale (though not on "Nardis") is Kenny Garrett's solo on "Sing A Song Of Song" from the album "Songbook" (1997). Of course, he is not entirely consistent. You can hear him slipping in and out of the scale, mixing it with lines based on the changes of the tune. However, it is the strange colour of Double Harmonic major that pervades the solo and gives it its unique flavour.

For the sake of tying up loose ends, I'm sure you'll agree that if there is a Double Harmonic major scale, logically speaking, there must also be a **Double Harmonic minor** scale. Well – here it is:

In Europe, this scale is also known as the "Gypsy Minor" scale. It contains two augmented seconds as well as a minor third and can be seen as a permutation of Double Harmonic major starting on the 4th scale degree. I have mentioned these two rather unusual scales to remind you that Jazz musicians have always searched for musical inspiration in cultures other than their own. Especially when experimenting with modal concepts, compositions using scale forms indigenous to countries outside the Western hemisphere are not at all uncommon.

Rhythm Changes

It is quite popular in Jazz to "borrow" the changes from frequently played standards or popular songs (in part or as a whole), to compose a new melody, give it a different title and – hey, presto! – we have a new piece. It's a convenient way to generate a large number of seemingly different and original tunes with a minimum of effort! Since melodies and melodic phrases have a high recall value, it goes without saying that they are protected by copyright. The same goes for recordings and lyrics. On the other hand, it is almost impossible to protect chord progressions – they don't fall under copyright restrictions. Personally, I do indeed have qualms about the fact that you can simply expropriate any set of changes, add a new melody and call it an original. Of course, there are chord progressions that can be seen as "public domain" (e.g. the 12-bar Blues), and I am fully aware that many standards contain more or less the same harmonic clichés. However, I would find it highly questionable to steal (that's what I call it) the highly distinctive changes of "Giant Steps" and use them as if they were my own (as was done by Arun Luthra with "Third Event" or by John McLaughlin with "Do You Hear The Voices You Left Behind?").

Be that as it may, many popular tunes share the same or almost the same set of changes. To name just a few well-known pieces that were derived from others – here's a short list: "Prince Albert" and "Dixie's Dilemma" from "All The Things You Are", "Half Nelson" from "Lady Bird", "Ornithology" from "How High The Moon", "Donna Lee" from "Back Home Again In Indiana", "Fried Bananas" from "It Could Happen To You", "Scrapple From The Apple" from "Honeysuckle Rose", "Background Music" from "All Of Me" and "Hot House" from "What Is This Thing Called Love".

Apart from the matter of copyright, there is a second good reason why these tune spin-offs, also referred to as **contrafacts**, are so popular. Once we feel comfortable improvising on a tune because we've worked the changes over and over again, it is nice to use the same chord progression with other tunes, too. Seen another way, always having to learn and internalise a completely new chord progression for every new composition would be quite a challenge. So, it is very enticing to be able to create a multitude of new melodies without having to worry about the harmony. After all, it is the melody that gives a composition its distinctive character. For the average listener the changes are no more than an obscure cloud of sound, which comes alive only in conjunction with the melody or a solo.

A particularly important example of a collection of tunes using one and the same set of chords is referred to as **Rhythm Changes**. Every theme belonging to this group of compositions is based on the chord progression of the world-famous Broadway hit "I Got Rhythm" by George Gershwin. Every Jazz musician should know how to improvise on Rhythm Changes. They are – apart from the Blues – the most popular thing played at jam sessions. Compositions such as "Oleo" (Sonny Rollins) or "Moose The Mooche" (Charlie Parker) should therefore become an integral part of your repertoire. The good thing: You'll only have to learn the melodies.

Here's the original chord progression and its functional analysis in B♭ Major. The general form is AABA (32 bars divided into four eight-bar sections):

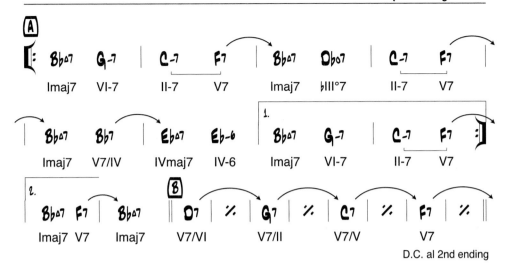

The scale choices for the A section shouldn't be too hard to figure out – try it for yourself. With the exception of Db°7, we have already talked about all other functions in the chapter "All Of Me". You'll find the basic scale clichés confirmed by many improvisations.

The A section consists of two-bar cadential loops that can be reduced to the following formula:

Turnaround	Turnaround	I → IV/IV-	Turnaround
2	2	2	2

There are numerous variations that have evolved from this basic formula without significantly changing the original chord progression. Here is a typical example (analyse the chord-scale relationships):

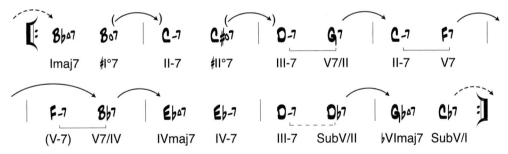

It is typical for many soloists to play with a marked Blues feel over Rhythm Changes. Playing the Blues makes a lot of sense when thinking in terms of turnarounds consisting primarily of seventh chords:

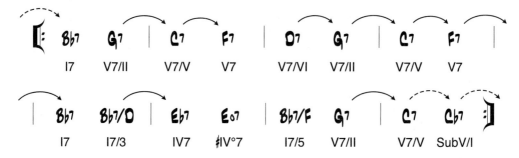

Basically, this version of the A section looks like an abbreviated (eight-bar) Blues format with chords added in the first 4 bars and a slightly unusual functional distribution (IV7 in bar 6 and not 5). Because Rhythm Changes are mostly played at a hell-for-leather tempo, it is not at all easy to elaborate on every harmonic detail and come up with good lines at the same time. The Blues gives us the opportunity to use one and the same colour throughout without risking a major catastrophe because of the fast-moving changes.

Let's have a look at the B section. It is worth noting that many Rhythm Changes compositions have no specific melody for the B section. It is often improvised by any one of the players (it may even provide space for a drum solo). There are two different ways of looking at the chord progression and the corresponding chord-scale relationships. On the one hand, it can be seen as a sequence of Mixolydian dominants independent of tonality (the two-bar harmonic rhythm reduces the tonal influence considerably). On the other hand, there are many improvisations firmly anchored in the tonality. Accordingly, the choice of scale material is more diatonic:

Of course, the more unusual dominant colours (HTWT, WT, etc.) or even phrases deliberately played "outside" – e.g. lines that are chromatically shifted against the changes – are not that uncommon.

The B section, too, is often expanded on through interpolation of additional chords. Here's an example (in Bb Major) where every dominant chord (V) is preceded by its –7 chord (II), creating a sequence of interlocking II-V patterns:

Now for the important thing: All possibilities mentioned above (and more) are combined freely during an improvisation. This implies that there is no "standardised" one-and-only chord progression for Rhythm Changes. The appeal lies in the spontaneous linking of various versions (three cheers for a good ear and quick reaction time!). To make things worse: Soloist and rhythm section may play different versions simultaneously. Despite the clash of changes, there is no real problem because each individual part sounds coherent in itself and the fundamental formal structure (two-bar turnarounds, IV in bar 6, etc.) is the same for both the soloist and the accompanists.

I would like to quote a number of well-known Jazz musicians to demonstrate what I have been talking about from a practical perspective. Let's start with the first one-and-a-half choruses of Miles Davis' solo on "Oleo" (on the album "Bags' Groove"). Before you read on, try to figure out Miles Davis' concept. In other words, analyse the lines and deduce the changes they imply:

The first two A sections demonstrate a soloing concept that could hardly be simpler! The melodic analysis shows that Miles Davis is obviously improvising over the most basic of turnarounds: B♭maj7 - G–7 - C–7 - F7. The phrases consist almost entirely of chord tones and the notes on the strong beats clearly imply diatonic changes. He even ignores the harmonic sidestep into the subdominant in bar 6 and simply continues soloing over the basic turnaround. This works for the simple reason that the piano drops out for both A sections and the bass lines are very basic, too (so Miles Davis is free to do whatever he feels like doing).

What is quite unusual, though, is what happens in the bridge. Have another look at the first two bars. How does the line relate to D7 (the chord you would expect at the beginning of the B section)? How do you explain the D♭ in bar 1? Things fall into place once we realise that Miles Davis plays a two-bar phrase in bars 1 + 2, repeats it with a slight variation in bars 3 + 4 and then shifts it down chromatically in bars 5 + 6. So, we're hearing a motivic sequence. While the tonal material makes very little sense over D7 in terms of chord-scale relationships, the line morphs into G7 Altered (watch out for enharmonic spelling) and then eases back into the diatonic environment of B♭ Major on the C7. So, the passage progresses from *outside* (D7) via an aggressive but familiar colour (Altered on G7) back to *inside* (Mixolydian on C7) before ending the phrase. What incredible control – Miles Davis must have anticipated exactly how the line would unfold well before playing the first note of the B section. This is what good soloing is all about: Come up with a clear idea, hear where it wants to go and how it should develop well ahead of time, have the necessary technique to pull it off and bring the phrase to a satisfying close.

The piano enters with the B section. So – let's have a look at the piano voicings (I've simplified the rhythms):

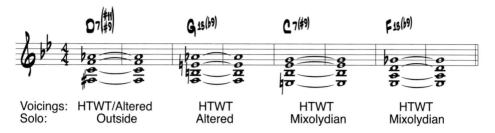

Voicings:	HTWT/Altered	HTWT	HTWT	HTWT
Solo:	Outside	Altered	Mixolydian	Mixolydian

The voicings are very aggressive, create a lot of tension (as would be expected of a contrasting B section) and follow a clear concept. Voicings 1 + 2 have the same top note, while the bottom three voices are voice-led down a half step. Voicings 2–4 are structurally identical and are simply shifted down chromatically ("constant structure").

Now, here's the interesting thing. What makes this passage fascinating is the fact that improvisation and accompaniment don't match. If you compare the scales that can be attributed to either the solo or the voicings, you'll realise that the tensions are not compatible (e.g. on G7 the melodic phrase hits a high Eb = b13 while the voicing contains an E = 13). Surprisingly, this works (and quite admirably so). Listen to the recording. I'm sure – even though you now know there is an inconsistency, you still won't have the feeling that something is "wrong". Since both the solo and the accompaniment are highly consistent (each in their own way) and work with the same structural strategy (chromatically descending sequence), they can coexist without causing major problems.

After the aggressive B section, the piano drops out again. The improvisation returns to its relaxed and easy-going approach. Now we don't even hear the turnaround anymore. In the 3rd A section, the phrases circle around a Bb major triad most of the time (only in bar 6 does the Eb triad appear). The second chorus begins as an unadulterated Blues. Both A sections are almost exclusively in the Bb Blues scale. It is not until four bars before the next bridge that the solo returns to the chord progression.

Let's summarise! In order to pull off nursery-rhyme-like lines or Blues in the A section and a sophisticated inside-outside concept in the B section one has to be endowed with coolness, self-assurance and, apart from the necessary musical and technical skills, a healthy dose of cheek. Miles Davis has all of this and more. The solo also shows that you don't have to observe each and every chord as long as you give everybody the feeling that you know what you're doing. Live and learn!

The next two A sections are good examples of "playing the changes". The first line is by Sonny Rollins (also on the Miles Davis album "Bags' Groove", 1st tenor chorus, 2nd A section). The phrase clearly outlines the chord progression:

The second example is by John Coltrane (recorded in 1956 on "Relaxin' With The Miles Davis Quintet"; 4th tenor chorus, 1st A section):

As you can see, it is possible, despite the fast tempo and the half-bar changes, to take every chord into account and come up with a coherent, logical line.

Let's have a look at three examples of improvisations on the B section. The first is by Wynton Kelly (on Miles Davis' "Live at the Blackhawk, San Francisco", 1961) and can be heard in the theme (the bridge in "Oleo" doesn't have a set melody and is usually improvised):

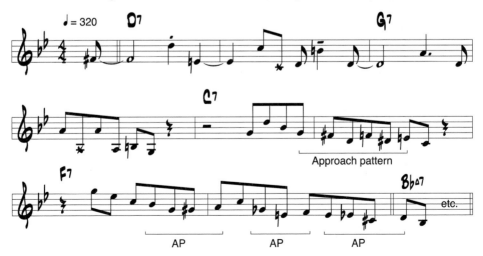

If we ignore the approach patterns and the chromatic notes contained within, all seventh chords are clearly Mixolydian (analyse!).

The following example is by trumpeter Louis Smith ("Oleo" on his album "Just Friends", 1978). It is worth mentioning that he starts out by playing the first part of the recording without the rhythm section (*a cappella*), carrying the responsibility for the formal, harmonic and rhythmic flow of the solo *all by himself* (at this crazy tempo!). Here's the bridge of the 1st chorus:

Despite the many chromatic passing notes (*) and approach patterns (AP), we can clearly identify the chord-scale relationships. D7 (V7/VI) is still strongly linked to Bb Major. The Eb (b9) and the Bb (b13) both point to HM5 as the corresponding scale. G7, C7 and F7, on the other hand, are obviously Mixolydian, the colour of the individual dominant prevailing over all tonal considerations.

A beautiful B section by Miles Davis appears in the recording of "Oleo" mentioned above (on "Live at the Blackhawk", 3rd chorus). This passage shows that a simple idea effectively performed is all you need for a good solo:

The basic idea is merely a chromatically ascending guide tone line (9 - b7 - #11 - 9). What makes the line come alive is its rhythmical quality and the compelling way Miles Davis phrases each note.

I could go on and on and on. I'll leave it up to you to check out the zillions of Rhythm Changes recordings available out there. Always keep the Boy Scouts motto in mind: *Be prepared*!!! You better be, if someone should count in "Oleo" at BPM = 280 during your next jam session. I don't want to see you slinking off the stage just because you're afraid you won't cut it! So – do your homework, transcribe and practise, practise, practise…

Finally, here is a list with a small selection of well-known Rhythm Changes compositions. Once you have learned three or four themes by heart (the changes are more or less the same), you will be well equipped for your next session:

Anthropology	Oleo	Cottontail
Boppin' A Riff	Red Cross	Dexterity
Celerity	Rhythm-A-Ning	The Theme
Crazeology	Salt Peanuts	One Bass Hit
Moose The Mooche	The Serpent's Tooth	Tuxedo Junction
Move	Steeplechase	Lester Leaps In

Assignment

I claim there has never been a single Jazz musician who hasn't written at least one Rhythm Changes composition during the course of his or her career. Now it is your turn to add another unique, incomparable theme to this collection and bequeath another masterpiece to the world of Jazz. On your marks, get set, go!

Modulation

So far, we have restricted ourselves to tunes in one key only. Now I'd like to talk about compositions that pass through any number of keys. A piece that changes key is said to *modulate*. Modulation is an essential compositional device that creates variety and emotional impact. The psychological incentive of any modulation is to raise the level of tension, to create suspense, trigger an emotional response in the listener and, ultimately, to stop the audience from getting bored. Its effect depends on whether the piece modulates to a closely related or a more remote key. The greater the difference between the key signatures, the more dramatic the modulation will sound. The more notes the two keys share, the less obtrusive it will be (e.g. Bb Major and F Major are very closely related, Bb Major and E Major are only remotely connected).

Traditional Jazz standards are usually in one primary key represented by the key signature. In most cases, they start out in this primary key, briefly modulate and return to the initial key at the end. Modulations are not necessarily accompanied by a change of key signature. The primary key signature is generally maintained throughout the piece. However, if a new tonal centre persists for a longer period of time (e.g. a full section), the composer may temporarily change the key signature. Pieces may move through several keys before settling on a new tonal centre or returning to the home key. The time spent in any one of the keys can also vary considerably.

Contemporary Jazz compositions, in contrast, are often written without a key signature, either because they don't have a clear sense of tonality in the first place or because they float through several tonalities without settling on one particular tonal centre conclusively. As a consequence, a key signature would not be in character with the composition.

In the analyses we have undertaken so far, I have tried to call attention to the high level of harmonic integrity of many compositions. In Jazz, we have come to accept a large number of functions as key-related. Even though many of them create a lot of tension because they are highly chromatic in terms of the diatonic substructure, they are still linked to the fundamental tonal environment by means of cadential relationships or other connecting principles. That is why chord progressions may deviate dramatically without actually losing their tonal affinity. For example, secondary Sub(II-V)s or some of the modal interchange functions may sound quite distant, but they still are considered to be part of the key because they relate to or resolve back to a diatonic function. The ear hears a strong digression from the key but accepts the strangeness because the chord progression quickly returns to the basic tonality.

This is where Jazz harmony differs considerably from Classical music. In Classical music theory, the tonal environment is defined in a far more restrictive way. In traditional analysis, key affiliation is almost exclusively limited to the basic diatonic functions. For instance, the switch from a major key to its relative minor (or vice versa) is already regarded as a modulation – something I don't agree with, since both key areas share the same key signature. Even minor deviations from the diatonic material are perceived as a breach of tonality and, potentially, a change of key. A simple example should suffice to demonstrate the extent of this way of thinking. In a magazine for the Classical guitarist that intermittently presented Jazz topics, I once came across a harmonic analysis of the standard "Misty". According to this analysis, believe it or not, "Misty" modulates 12 times! Every non-diatonic II-V is interpreted as a new key area. What nonsense! After all, the melody is almost entirely in E♭ Major.

In Jazz, not every harmonic departure from the diatonic framework is a departure from the key. The functional environment within one tonality is much broader and varied and thus harder to pin down. It just isn't possible to contain it within the boundaries of late 18th century harmonic and analytical conventions. But, even in Jazz, there are limits! And that's where we have to start talking about modulations.

I like to divide the concept of modulation into four basic categories:

- *Direct* modulations

- *Pivot* modulations

- *Transitional* modulations

- *Implied* modulations

These four types of modulation cover most of what we will come across in the traditional Jazz repertoire. I might add, again, that the more contemporary Jazz compositions often follow other harmonic and structural principles. On the one hand, the tonalities are not always clearly defined and chord progressions elude a distinct key signature. On the other hand, many compositions that belong to the more modern Jazz repertoire have a tendency to "drift" through various key areas without actually settling on a definite tonic. In these cases, it is virtually impossible to provide an unequivocal functional analysis. Functional analysis implies a hierarchy of harmonic relationships based on the existence of a tonal centre. Without this point of reference, chord progressions are ambiguous and functionally ambivalent.

There's a whole other world of harmonic relationships to be explored beyond the scope of functional harmony. Polytonality, polymodality, pantonality and intervallic or mathematical concepts provide melodic and harmonic strategies that often defy functional interpretation. For the sake of this book, we will stick to examples that have a clear sense of tonality.

Direct modulations

This refers to a sudden change of tonality – a direct and unprepared shift from the primary key to a new key area. Direct modulations often appear at important structural points of a composition, e.g. at the beginning of a new section as a means of creating contrast. Usually, one section ends on the tonic of the initial key and the next section begins with the tonic of the new key:

In Pop music, it is quite common to use direct modulations towards the end of the recording to create additional excitement by moving the whole piece up a half step (or, less often, a whole step).

Sometimes, the original tonal centre is directly followed by a secondary diatonic function of the new key (II–7, III–7, etc.), e.g. when setting up the new tonic with a cadence:

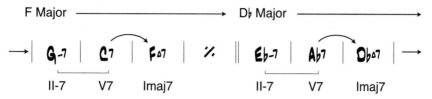

| II-7 | V7 | Imaj7 | | II-7 | V7 | Imaj7 |

The opposite also happens, where a new tonal centre follows a secondary diatonic function of the original key:

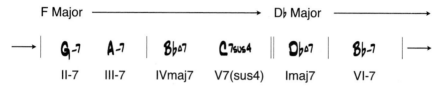

| II-7 | III-7 | IVmaj7 | V7(sus4) | Imaj7 | VI-7 |

Direct modulations tend to happen rather abruptly. The advantage of this is that it is easy to determine the exact point of modulation. On the other hand, this type of modulation often comes across as being a bit clumsy and inelegant. For this reason, a lot of importance is placed on the smoothest possible transition from one key to the next. The easiest way to achieve this is to aim for good voice leading in the chord progression or to use common tones in the melody. The latter principle, in particular, is an established compositional tool for cushioning glaring breaks with the tonality. In the following example, the note C (5 in F Major and the maj7 in Db Major) serves as the link:

This too, is an essential concept you should work on when improvising on progressions containing direct modulations. Finding the notes that tie together both keys will give your phrases more coherence and better flow across the point of key change. This is particularly important when you're up against a quick succession of key changes, also referred to as *chain* or *sequential modulations*, where the ear only has little time to settle on a new tonal centre and establish it as a stable point of reference. Let's have a look at the B section of "Have You Met Miss Jones" (Richard Rodgers) as an example:

This chord progression leaves the primary key F Major, quickly passes through the keys of Bb Major, Gb Major, D Major and back to Gb Major (watch the accidentals), only to return to the original key with the beginning of the final A section. Bbmaj7 can still be seen as IVmaj7 in F Major, but it is rather played as Ionian than Lydian because of the preceding dominant F7. All other maj7 chords are tonal centres in their own right (Imaj7 Ionian), which are set up by their respective II-V patterns. Here, we have a quick succession of direct modulations. Both the melody and the harmony progress sequentially, with the two-bar patterns descending in major thirds. The problem lies, then, less in whether we can recognise the points of modulation (that's straightforward), but rather in the rapid switch from one tonality to the next. This is especially noticeable when improvising. It is not easy to create flowing melodic lines when trying to connect a string of relatively unrelated keys (Bb Major: 2 flats, Gb Major: 6 flats, D Major: 2 sharps). Having hardly arrived at a new tonic, the ear already has to prepare for the next modulation. Note the transition from Dmaj7 to Ab–7 in bars 5 and 6. This is a nice example of the melody linking one key area to the next by means of a common tone. In bar 5, you see a D major triad in the melody, which is continued into the next bar, completing a Dmaj7 arpeggio (Db = C#). The ear accepts the key change despite the brutal modulation because C#/Db (maj7 in D Major and 5 in Gb Major) is diatonic in both keys.

Pivot modulations

This is probably the most frequently used type of modulation. It works by way of a single chord or a short chord progression common to both the original and the new key. The overlap of functions is the point at which the tune "pivots" between the two tonal centres. In analysis, the common chord or chord progression is labelled with its function(s) in both the initial and the target key, since the pivot point or pivot area can be heard either way. Pivot modulations are more flowing and subtler than the comparatively abrupt direct modulation. Here are a couple of examples:

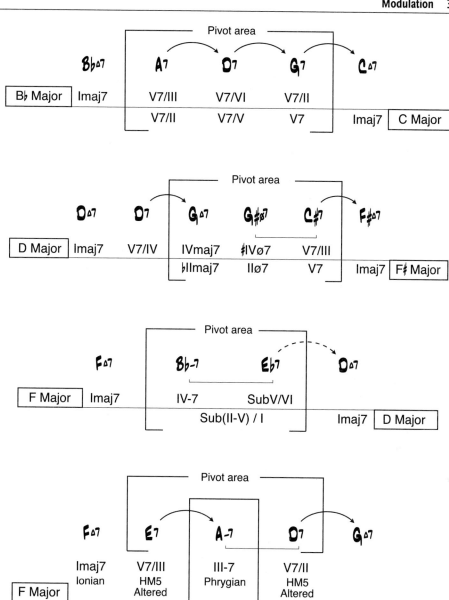

By nature, seventh chords are particularly well suited to being pivot chords, since every chromatically available dominant relates to any key either as a secondary or a substitute dominant. Functional reinterpretation of dominants is a simple means of changing key. Consequently, II-V patterns and extended dominants make good pivotal progressions, too.

The last example nicely shows the actual problem of many pivot modulations. Sometimes it is possible to assign different scale material to the chords in the pivot area depending on their functional interpretation. This could be the case, for instance, if neither the melody nor the chord symbol clearly implies a choice of scale. How does this affect improvisation? The decision is based on whether we are looking for a gradual or a more sudden key change. If we change to the new scale material early on in the modulation (even if the chords could still be interpreted in the initial key), the appearance of the new key will feel less surprising. The ear registers the departure from the expected scale sound. It senses that something unusual is happening and can adjust gently to the change of key:

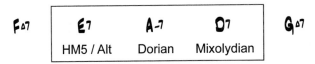

If, however, we stay in the original key for as long as possible, the new tonic will come as a surprise and will rather be heard as an unexpected shift of tonality (almost like a direct modulation) because, initially, nothing in the modulation points to the new tonal centre:

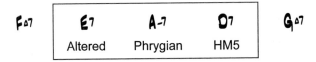

When you practise, try both approaches in your improvisations and discover for yourselves which of the two alternatives sounds more plausible and more musical to your ear.

Transitional modulations

Up until now, we have talked about switching from one key to the next in a clearly defined way, where modulations occurred either immediately (direct) or over a relatively short period of time (pivot point or pivot area). Transitional modulations, by contrast, take a more gradual approach. The piece moves through a longer phase of transition – hence the name – where the initial key is gradually lost and there is no clear indication of what the new key will be. The transitional area is heard as a loose progression of sounds without a distinct feeling of tonality. It usually follows a logical connecting principle (e.g. sequential II-Vs or extended dominants) and gradually erases the old key before finally establishing a new tonal centre. The ear perceives the transitional section as a sort-of harmonic and melodic no-man's-land. Consequently, it can neither be analysed in the original nor the new key.

I won't give you an example of a transitional modulation at this point. The analysis of "Falling Grace" later in this chapter should clarify the problems you are likely to encounter when dealing with ambiguous chord progressions.

Implied modulations

This is not really a modulation in the true sense of the word. The chord progression tempo-rarily departs from the original key and gives the impression of a modulation without car-rying it through by distinctly establishing a new tonal centre. It does, however, set up the expectation of a key change to come and implies a new tonic (hence the name). Usually, the melody stays rooted in the initial key (no accidentals) while the changes deviate strongly.

As an example, here is the B section of the Jazz ballad "Misty" by Erroll Garner (in E♭ Major):

In bars 5 and 6 of the B section, we arrive at the formally most important point of the tune, the climax. Here we come across the chord progression A–9 - D13, which we could analyse as II-V/III. However, in the key of E♭ Major, II-V/III is commonly played as A∅7 - D7. A∅7 would be Locrian and D7 Altered. Consequently, A–7 (Dorian) and D7 (Mixolydian) are clearly out-of-key. That is why I have deliberately included the tensions you'll usually find in the accompaniment. They accentuate the break with E♭ Major. While the chord progression indicates a modulation to G Major, the melody is still diatonic in E♭ Major. Instead of con-firming the new tonic Gmaj7, the tune resolves to G–7(♭5) and quickly cadences back to E♭maj7 at the beginning of the last A section. So, A–7 - D7 is hardly more than a brush of colour foreign to the tonality and simply a pseudo-modulation that emphasises the high point of the composition.

One last thing: The F7 in bar 6 (taken from the lead sheet in the old Real Book) is often omitted and the D7 is played a full bar. However, it is usually played as a split dominant (half a bar of Mixolydian and half a bar of Altered) to accommodate the melody. The switch to D7 Altered cushions the return to E♭ Major. Moving from D7 Mixolydian to G–7(♭5) Locrian would be a rather brutal transition (a difference of 5 accidentals). Here, this kind of thinking makes sense, since individual sounds are far more noticeable within the context of a ballad than at a higher tempo.

Modulation and analysis

When analysing a tune we believe to contain a modulation, there are two essential questions to consider:

- Does the tune truly modulate?
- At what point does a modulating tune lose its connection with the starting key?

Let's tackle the first problem. What is a true modulation? As stated at the beginning of this chapter, a modulation can be defined as a change of key. Even though this sounds simple enough, things are not always cut and dried. Does this always imply a switch to a different tonal centre? Must the key signature change too? Or both?

There are a number of clues that will help you identify modulations. As a rule of thumb, you're most probably dealing with a modulation if one or more of the following points apply. It's a true modulation if …

- … both the chord progression *and* the melody depart from the initial key. As long as a theme remains faithful to the key signature, we should try to analyse the chord progression within the primary key. As soon as we see accidentals in the melody that stick around for a certain period of time (several bars) and occur on the stronger beats of the bar (so we're not talking about chromatic embellishments or passing notes), it is safe to assume that a modulation has occurred.

- … we come across predominantly non-diatonic chords when analysing a chord progression and have to resort to functional symbols that are highly improbable or simply make no sense in the primary key (e.g. Vmaj7, ♭II–7, etc.).

- … the feeling of key change persists for a certain amount of time (several bars or even a complete section). If, however, we hear a strange chord and the tune very quickly returns to the primary key (we're only talking about a bar or two) we should instead consider modal interchange.

- … non-diatonic maj7 or –7 chords occur at strategically important places in a composition – for instance, at the beginning or the end of a formal section or at focal points of the harmonic rhythm. Maj7 and –7 chords, in particular, are most likely to produce a tonic feeling, especially if they are preceded by a cadence (e.g. V7 or II-V) and are confirmed by additional diatonic material in the new key.

The first bullet point above is probably the most important. The stronger a melody relates to a particular Major or Minor scale, the more clearly we are able to sense a specific tonality, no matter how complex or strange the changes may be. I am often amazed at the fact that extreme reharmonisations of predominantly diatonic melodies do not baffle the ear as much as one might imagine. Even chord progressions that clearly leave the tonal framework are not necessarily heard as modulations as long as the melody stays in the original key. So, for a true modulation, the melody has to switch keys – more so than the harmony.

As I said at the beginning of this chapter, the impact of a modulation depends – amongst other things – on the difference between the key signatures of the primary and the new key.

Let's have a look at a few scenarios starting in the primary key of C Major (no sharps or flats):

C Major → E Major (→ 4♯):

This is definitely a modulation, since we have a clear change of tonal centre and distinctly differing key signatures. Emaj7 is a target chord that is neither diatonic in C Major nor interpretable as a modal interchange function.

C Major → E Minor (→ 1♯):

This is tricky business. Not only is the target chord diatonic in the initial key (III–7), the key signature is not significantly different either. For this to be heard as an unequivocal modulation, there has to be a clear cadential preparation (e.g. F♯ø7 - B7) with the leading tone (D♯) being prominently featured either in the melody and/or the chord progression. Likewise, the note F♯ should be introduced to emphasise the break with C Major and to indicate the switch to the key signature of one sharp. In addition, the tune will have to spend some time in E Minor for the ear to accept E–7 as a new tonic and not hear it as III–7 in the original key.

C Major → G Major (→ 1♯):

At first sight, this is almost the same situation as the one before (same change of key signature), since G Major is simply the relative major of E Minor. The big difference, however, is the fact that Gmaj7 is not diatonic in C Major and there is no modal interchange function Vmaj7. In this case, the ear will readily make the switch to G Major. This, of course, is not a dramatic change of key, since C Major and G Major only differ in one note (F/F♯).

C Major → A♭ Major (→ 4♭):

At a glance, this should be a straightforward modulation, since we have a clear change of both tonality and key signature. If, however, A♭maj7 is **not** prepared by a cadence (V7 or II-V) and the tune quickly returns to the primary key, chances are high it will rather be heard as a modal interchange function in C Major (♭VImaj7). Again, the factor of time is important. If A♭maj7 just pops up for a bar or so, it is most probably an MI-function. If, on the other hand, the A♭maj7 appears at an important formal point of the tune and sticks around for some time, supported by other diatonic functions in A♭ Major, it is more likely to be perceived as a new tonic.

C Major → A Minor (0♯/♭ → 0♯/♭):

Even though this is a change of tonality, we don't have a change of key signature. To me, this is not a true modulation. Switching from a major key to its relative minor (or vice versa) is no more than a change of perspective within the same diatonic environment (and, as we know, the ear readily tends to flip-flop between the two anyhow). If, however, the change of tonic persists for a longer period of time (e.g. a full section), reinforced by a recurring leading tone (G♯), the ear may also accept this as a modulation.

C Major → C Minor (→ 3♭) or vice versa:

This is a change of key signature but not of tonality, since the root remains unchanged. It is therefore more likely to be a case of modal interchange. If, however, the change of colour persists for more than just a few bars (preferably a full section) and is backed up by other functions taken from C Minor, the ear will perceive it as a new diatonic environment and, consequently, as a modulation.

When reviewing the scenarios above, we can draw several conclusions (let's summarise in the starting key of C Major with a modulation to another major or minor key):

- Genuine modulations require a change of key signature *and* of tonal centre (e.g. C Major → E Major or C Major → F♯ Minor). If it's either/or (e.g. C Major → C Minor or C Major → A Minor), the tune will have to remain in the new key for a certain amount of time for the ear to have a chance of re-orientating itself and to adjust to the new tonal centre and its diatonic environment.

- If the root of a target *major* key is *diatonic* in the primary key (C Major to either D, E, G, A or B Major), we're clearly dealing with a modulation since we are changing both the tonal centre and the key signature. Since the resulting maj7 chords are all non-diatonic in C Major, our ear will invariably hear them as unexpected colours and, consequently, as new tonics (exception: Fmaj7 will not be heard as a new tonic because IVmaj7 is the more likely interpretation).

- If the root of a target *major* key is *non-diatonic* (C Major to either D♭, E♭, G♭, A♭ or B♭ Major), it is quite possible that we're dealing with a modal interchange function. If, however, the new tonic is set up by a cadence and confirmed by additional diatonic material in the new key, we're likely to hear a modulation. In these cases, the tune has to spend a certain amount of time in the new key for the ear to adjust.

If we look closely, a general pattern emerges. Let's visualise the cycle of fifths. We'll stick to C Major as our primary key:

- If the tune modulates *clockwise* (to the major keys G, D, A, E or B), the ear should have no problem in picking up the target chord as a new tonic. Note that the roots of these target keys are all diatonic to the primary key. This actually helps the ear in accepting the target chord as Imaj7, since we are expecting different chord types for the diatonic roots.

- If the tune modulates *counter-clockwise* (to the major keys F, B♭, E♭, A♭ or D♭), the new tonic may act as an MI-function (or in the case of F as a diatonic function). Here, time and context play an essential role. It is vitally important for the melody and the chord progression to introduce the new key clearly, and the new key will have to be reinforced by additional diatonic material.

Of course, the diagram shown below can be adjusted to any primary key other than C Major or A Minor simply by rotating it accordingly:

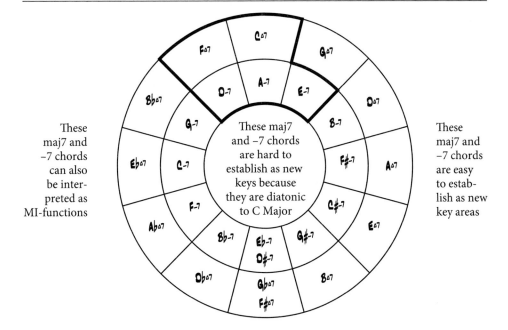

These maj7 and −7 chords can also be interpreted as MI-functions

These maj7 and −7 chords are hard to establish as new keys because they are diatonic to C Major

These maj7 and −7 chords are easy to establish as new key areas

When starting out in C Major, G♭/F♯ Major is the most remote key. It is located at the opposite end of the cycle of fifths and it provides the most dramatic change of key signature. G♭maj7, though also a modal interchange function in C Major (♭Vmaj7), is so far removed from C Ionian that you will more likely hear it as a new tonic.

The diagram also works when looking at modulations from major to minor keys (and vice versa). Note that the diatonic functions II−7, III−7 and VI−7 are difficult to establish as new tonics in their own right. We feel perfectly comfortable with the concept of setting up a diatonic function (e.g. D−7 = II−7 in the key of C Major) with a preceding secondary or substitute dominant (A7/E♭7) and treating it as a temporary tonic, something that is also referred to as *tonicisation* in Classical theory. However, for this to be a modulation, the tune (melody and harmony) would have to spend ample time in D Minor and switch from D Dorian to D Aeolian/HM as the primary mode (introducing the leading tone C♯ and the note B♭) to emphasise the change of key and to give the ear a chance to adjust. Whereas tonicisation is simply a brief detour within the primary key, modulation is a more extended excursion into a different diatonic environment.

The same goes for the modal interchange functions I−7, IV−7 and V−7 (counter-clockwise modulations). For these keys, cadential preparation of the new tonic and a certain amount of time for the ear to settle in are paramount if they are to be heard as a true change of key. All other minor keys (arrived at by clockwise modulations) are easy to establish and identify, since they are neither diatonic to the primary key nor can they be interpreted as a modal interchange chord.

Before we move on, here's a word of warning and advice. In this chapter, I have liberally used the term "change of key" when referring to a modulation. This, however, is not quite correct and potentially misleading. Historically speaking, the key-concept is invariably tied to either Ionian (Major) or Aeolian (Minor), and the key signatures reinforce this correlation. Modulations are traditionally seen as a change of key from or to an Ionian or Aeolian tonic. However, things have evolved. A tonic no longer need be Ionian or Aeolian. Any mode can serve as a tonic sound. And with a different tonic scale comes a whole new set of diatonic relationships and functions. So, one of the first problems to deal with is the definition of a "key". If we're not aware of the existence of tonic scales other than Ionian or Aeolian, many contemporary harmonic relationships and subsequently certain modulations will elude us.

This problem is compounded by the fact that key signatures, too, are linked to Ionian and Aeolian. We have already talked about this dilemma in the chapter "Modality" (p. 67 ff.). Here's an example. Which key signature should we expect for F Phrygian? Do we use 5 flats with the danger of the eye and ear being deflected towards Db Major or Bb Minor? Or no key signature at all, resulting in rather messy notation cluttered with accidentals? Or 4 flats, with a Gb added as an accidental? As much as I prefer the third option, since it points us immediately towards F Minor and highlights the characteristic note in Phrygian (b2), the usual practice is to go for 5 flats – and that is highly misleading. Since there is no consensus as to the use of key signatures with modes other than Ionian and Aeolian, you will always have to be on the lookout for a tonic irrespective of the key signature.

As pointed out at the beginning of this section, the second fundamental problem is being able to locate the point of modulation. There is no hard and fast rule for this. However, here are a few thoughts that will help. As I have already emphasised in the chapter "Analysis", any analysis *must* be corroborated by what the ear hears. Otherwise, practically speaking, analysis is simply not worth the effort! After all, analysis should support us in establishing a mental image of a piece and help us along when improvising. First and foremost, we can and should rely on our ear intuitively. Since we have grown up with tonal music we will always be aware of and react to a tonal centre – without necessarily knowing why. Even the inexperienced ear is capable of picking up sounds that are not consistent with the diatonic environment. We should assume that we have reached a point of key change or an area of transition …

- … if we are confronted with an unusual sound or a situation in which we feel insecure about our perception of tonality and this feeling of insecurity persists.

- … if we have difficulties locking into a root with certainty.

- … if chords no longer seem to make functional sense or melody notes and chord extensions no longer correspond to the tonal cliché in relation to the primary key.

With experience, your ear will learn not only to pinpoint sounds foreign to the primary key, but also be able to hear both backwards and forwards at the same time. It will react to where the music came from (ante-modulation) and anticipate where it wants to go (post-modulation). And you will hear the point or area of transition not as an unsettling moment of uncertainty but rather as an exciting twist of sound before the ear locks into the new tonality.

Even if the ear is a good indicator, you should not rely on it blindly without reflecting on what you heard. Since the ear always takes the path of least resistance, it is easily misled by anything out of the ordinary. That's why we should also turn to analysis for verification. If we can still come up with a sensible functional explanation, it's more likely that our ear is just reacting to something that jars our sense of tonality (non-diatonic functions, unusual tensions, etc.). Only if the analysis gets increasingly convoluted and results in absurd theoretical explanations and constructions, should you start looking for a new tonal centre. This is healthier than stubbornly holding on to the initial key.

"Falling Grace"

While things are usually quite straightforward with direct and pivot modulations, transitional and implied modulations can pose quite a problem. Using "Falling Grace" (Steve Swallow) as an example, I would like to demonstrate that we sometimes have to dig deep when it comes to the analysis of modulating compositions. As with a large jigsaw puzzle, the linking of small bits of information eventually leads to the complete picture. Here's the lead sheet:

Seen on its own, the A♭maj7 could be a tonic (especially since it is sustained for two full bars). However, we should take note of the D = ♯11 in bar 2. It would imply that A♭maj7 is Lydian, whereas Imaj7 is usually Ionian. A possible interpretation could be IVmaj7 – the most elementary interpretation of a Lydian function. Assuming this to be true, the changes could be analysed as follows (inversions do not change the basic functional analysis):

‖ A♭△7	∕	D7/F♯	G-7	F-7 B♭7	E♭△7/G D7/F♯	G-7/F ‖ ⟶
IVmaj7		V7/III	III-7	II-7 V7	Imaj7 V7/III	III-7

Well, that was easy. However, things are not what they seem to be. This analysis would be fine if it weren't for the melody and – though small and seemingly insignificant – the note A in bar 7. The G–7 is therefore not Phrygian (♭2 = A♭) and, consequently, not III–7. Sing the first 7 bars and you'll see what I mean: The melody will give you a strong feeling of B♭ Major in the first 6 bars with a switch to G Minor in bar 7. This has to be taken into account when assigning functions. Even though the melody points to G Minor in the end, the following functional analysis is in B♭ Major (remember that it always makes sense to partially analyse minor chord progressions in the relative major key):

‖ A♭△7	∕	D7/F♯	G-7	F-7 B♭7	E♭△7/G D7/F♯	G-7/F ‖ ⟶
♭VIImaj7 (!)		V7/VI	VI-7	II-V/IV	IVmaj7 V7/VI	VI-7

The tonal centre G–7 (I–7 in G Minor or VI–7 in B♭ Major) is approached chromatically by A♭maj7 from above and D7/F♯ from below. Clearly, "Falling Grace" begins on a modal interchange function! However, it is highly unlikely that we would hear the above analysis in the first chorus. Firstly, the note A, a crucial note in terms of tonal orientation, only appears in bar 7. Secondly, it is impossible to recognise the MI-function ♭VIImaj7 as such without first having established the corresponding tonality.

It is only then possible to understand the functional progression once the chorus is repeated. So, let's quickly look at the second half of the tune. The last 10 bars of the composition should not pose a problem. C♯°7 (♯II°7), B♭maj7/D (Imaj7/3), E♭maj7 (IVmaj7), E∅7 (♯IV∅7), A7 (V7/III), D–7 (III–7), D♭7 (SubV/II), C–7 (II–7), F7 (V7), B♭maj7 (Imaj7) and E♭maj7 (IVmaj7) can all be analysed in B♭ Major. The melody also gives us a clear impression of B♭ Major. Now that the tonal centre is firmly anchored in the ear, the beginning of the repeat can also be heard in B♭ Major and, subsequently, the A♭maj7 as ♭VIImaj7.

Even though the primary key does not become apparent until the second half of the tune and the chord progression does not start out with a clear sense of tonality, the primary key of "Falling Grace" is clearly B♭ Major. That is why I have notated the piece with two flats. The lead sheet in the Real Book sidesteps the problem of having to define a primary key by dispensing with a key signature altogether, which doesn't do justice to the tune. So, make sure you don't take every lead sheet as the ultimate truth, especially when dealing with modulations and the appropriate choice of key signature.

We now get to the purpose of this example. In bar 9 the chord progression leaves the original key of B♭ Major or G Minor. Fmaj7 would be Vmaj7 in B♭ Major, which makes no sense functionally. So, what is it? The first thing that comes to mind is a pivot modulation with G–7 and C/E either analysed as VI–7 - II7 in B♭ Major or as II–7 - V7 in F Major. Consequently, Fmaj7 must be a new tonic (Imaj7). But, beware! As of bar 9, something interesting happens in the melody: We encounter an increasing number of accidentals. First, E♭ is replaced by E, then B♭ becomes B, and finally an F♯ is added in bar 11. The melody implies a change of key signature from 2 flats to 1 sharp and that again implies a modulation to G Major or E Minor (1 sharp). This is confirmed by the chord progression in bars 10–14: F♯ø7 - B7 - E–7 and A–7 - D7 - Gmaj7 are the corresponding II-V-I progressions.

With this in mind, Fmaj7 can hardly be interpreted as a new tonic. What initially looks like a simple pivot modulation to F Major is actually something quite different. The answer to the riddle is again to be found in the melody and its formal structure. Let's look at the melody in the first two bars of "Falling Grace". The opening motive – a long note followed by a descending quarter-note triplet – reappears in bars 8 and 9 with minor modifications (slightly shifted and contracted), but still clearly recognisable:

Assuming that composers approach their work systematically, we could expect the melodic similarities to be paralleled harmonically. Lo and behold – Fmaj7 and E–7 are related to one another in the same way as A♭maj7 and G–7 in the opening passage. The similarities become even more apparent if we hypothetically place an Aø7 before the D7 and turn it into a II-V progression: Quite evidently, A♭maj7 - Aø7 corresponds to Fmaj7 - F♯ø7. The Fmaj7 chord is therefore ♭VIImaj7 (Lydian) in G Major, the concluding tonal target chord of the A section. C/E is therefore not a genuine dominant but nothing more than a logical link between G–7/F and Fmaj7. Because Fmaj7 is Lydian, C/E could conceivably be Ionian (!) apart from Mixolydian – the B♭ (♭7) in Mixolydian would correspond to the preceding G–7/F while the B (maj7) prepares the ♯11 of Fmaj7.

Even if this analysis (a transitional modulation from B♭ Major / G Minor to G Major / E Minor) makes theoretical sense, your ear will only be able to follow it if you know the piece inside out. On the one hand, nothing in the transitional section points to the new tonal centre G Major. On the other hand, without a clearly established tonality, it is impossible to interpret any chord as a modal interchange function. Nevertheless, now it should be easy to define the chord-scale relationships for bars 7–14:

G–7/F	C/E	F∆7	F♯–7(♭5)	B7	E–7	A–7 D7	G∆7
Aeolian	Mixo/Ion	Lydian	Locrian	HM5	Aeolian	Dor Mixo	Ionian

Apart from this transitional modulation, "Falling Grace" contains a pivot modulation that leads us back to the original key in bar 15 via C–7 (IV–7 in G Major or II–7 in B♭ Major).

Whew! I hope you've managed to follow all this! Transitional modulations are sometimes only decipherable by painstaking detective work. The ear, too, needs time to grasp the rather convoluted harmony of "Falling Grace" – not least because of the excessive use of inversions. Of course, inversions make no difference to the functional interpretation. However, they lend the chord progression a certain diffuse, floating quality, which further obscures the harmonic relationships. For this reason, I would like to mention once again, how important it is to keep the melody in mind when struggling with harmonic analysis. The melody can often provide more clues about the harmonic relationships in a composition than the harmony itself.

This example also shows the importance of screening the whole piece before launching into a detailed analysis. It's easy to be led astray if you work your way through the tune bar by bar. Sometimes, the last section of a tune will give you more pertinent information than the beginning.

However, I'd like to emphasise that the above explanations and guidelines do not comprise a patent remedy for every composition. All pieces that modulate follow their own laws, which need to be recognised and evaluated individually. And – last, but not least – we have to accept that there is rarely just one way of hearing a modulation and that not everybody deals with modulations in the same way. Deciding on how long to stay in the original key, when to make the switch to the new key and choosing the appropriate scale material for the area of transition is a matter of personal preference and at times a challenge even for the seasoned ear. A lot depends on personal listening experience and understanding of repertoire. The more tunes you have analysed, the easier it will be to spot a modulation as such, to appreciate its mechanics and to find a way to make it work for you as a player.

Modulation and repertoire

As usual, it is important to find tunes that back up our theoretical knowledge. Beyond the compositions presented in the following chapters, you should therefore know (know = know how to play) a fair number of pieces pertaining to every one of the modulation categories presented above. Independent of what types of modulation the pieces contain, I suggest that you also make sure your repertoire includes at least one composition for each chromatically possible target key (I → ♭II, I → II, I → ♭III, etc.). This is the best way to develop a mental image that will help you get through modulations when improvising. Here are a few randomly chosen examples (major tonic → major tonic):

I → ♭II   "Joy Spring", "Body And Soul"

I → II   "I Can't Get Started", "Lazybird"

I → ♭III   "Here's That Rainy Day", "On Green Dolphin Street", "I'll Remember April"

I → III   "Polka Dots And Moonbeams", "Desafinado", "The Song Is You", "Prelude To A Kiss", "I Love You"

I → IV   This is not really heard as a modulation since the target sound (IVmaj7) is diatonic; an exception, for example, is "Good Bait", which works as a modulation because the complete A section (both the melody and the harmony) is simply shifted up a perfect fourth and the transposition comes across as an abrupt change of tonality (direct modulation).

I → ♭V   "Pensativa" (because of the radical change in the key signature, this is an unusual modulation)

I → V   "Could It Be You", "Seven Steps To Heaven" – This modulation is hard to hear because the change of key signature is only minimal. It was, however, one of the most common modulations in Classical music for a long time (this makes sense if you consider the tuning problems before the arrival of equal temperament; the closer two keys are in the cycle of fifths, the more compatible they become in terms of tuning requirements).

I → ♭VI   "Confirmation", "Darn That Dream"

I → VI   "You Are The Sunshine Of My Life", "When Sunny Gets Blue", "Almost Like Being In Love"

I → ♭VII   "Tune Up", "Afternoon In Paris", "Once I Loved" (a very common modulation)

I → VII   "Airegin", almost always found as a modulation back to the original key (not I → VII, but rather ♭II → I): e.g. "One Note Samba", "Bluesette"

Analyse all the above compositions. They are good examples, since they belong to the standard repertoire of any Jazz musician. You will notice that the modulations almost always take place in the bridge. From a compositional point of view, in elementary song forms (AABA, ABAC, etc.), the B section is usually the element of contrast and, consequently, should be distinct from the A section. Modulation is an effective way to achieve contrast.

If we examine the standard repertoire, we find that modulations to the IIIrd degree (III or ♭III) and to the VIth degree (VI or ♭VI) are especially common. The reason for this is that it is easy to prepare the new key or to modulate back to the original key by using customary cycle of fifths root movement. Modulations to keys a whole step down (I → ♭VII) are also common for the same reason (prepared by II-V). Analyse the following chord progressions and make sure you know where the initial key ends and where the new one begins (look for pivot chords or pivot areas and apply dual-function analysis):

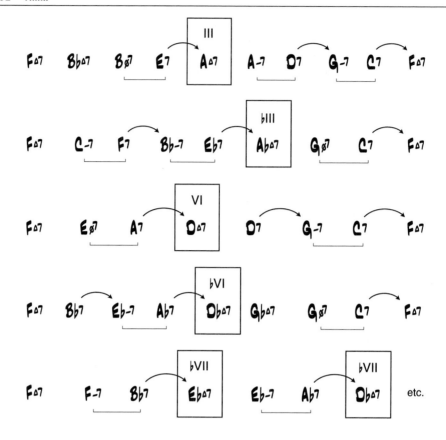

For the sake of completeness, you should take pains to scan all other combinations of modulations systematically (major → minor, minor → major, minor → minor) and look for examples in your repertoire. For reasons of space, I am not going to work through all possibilities mentioned above. It's not that hard to do if you remember that you can re-interpret a minor tonic (I–7) as a VIth degree (VI–7) of the corresponding relative major. For example, modulating from E♭ Major to E Minor corresponds to a modulation from E♭ Major to G Major because both E Minor and G Major share the same key signature and the same diatonic material.

As I have already said at the beginning of this chapter, make sure you don't mistake the switch from a major key to its relative minor key or vice versa for a modulation (e.g. from E♭ Major to C Minor). A true modulation, to me, implies a change of key signature. Relative major and minor keys, however, are so closely interrelated that it makes no sense to separate the two colours artificially. Even if the ear switches back and forth between the two tonic chords as the point of reference (e.g. E♭maj7 and C–7), we're only looking at different perspectives of the same thing.

Look for modulating compositions in your own repertoire and use the guidelines presented in the following chapters. However, even if you are under the impression that my reasoning is sound and my analysis is presented with authority, things are not always indisputable. Many chord progressions are open to more than one interpretation, mainly because it is not always possible to determine the exact point of modulation. Even though the ear is usually a reliable guide, it could still mislead you because there is often more than one way of hearing the same modulation. So, bear in mind that you will not always find clear solutions when it comes to analysing modulations. In the end, it is more important that you decide on a logical and aurally convincing interpretation of the chord progression. After all, the objective is to play the piece with confidence.

Assignment

1. To round up our discussion on modulation, your first assignment is to analyse "Peace" by Horace Silver. Write down the functions above the chords. Mark the II-V progressions with brackets and dominant resolutions with arrows. Mark the modulations (the pivot point or area of transition between the two keys, dual functions, etc.):

2. Write down the corresponding scale choices (with avoid notes in brackets). Don't look at the answers in the solutions folder until you've completed the assignment. If there is more than one scale possibility, then choose the one that is most diatonic to the key of the moment (closest to the tonality). If you come up against a dual-function chord, decide whether you would want to interpret it in terms of the initial or rather the new key (a question of personal choice and preference). Make sure to watch the overall key signature! Since this is a fairly short tune, which doesn't stay in any one of the keys for a long time, the indicated key signature (2 flats) applies to all parts of the piece. In some cases, you will have to add quite a number of naturals, sharps or flats to notate the scales correctly.

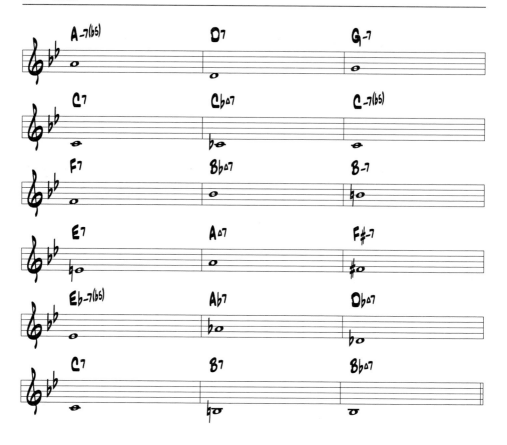

In the following chapters, make sure you always try to come up with your own analysis first before you read my commentaries and explanations!

"All The Things You Are"

The composition "All The Things You Are" by Jerome Kern has become one of **the** most important Jazz standards there is (on *jazzstandards.com* it ranks No. 2 just behind "Body And Soul"). This piece is often associated with a certain amount of bravura – it is usually played very fast and, due to its many modulations, poses a serious challenge to any soloist. It's definitely high up on the list of favourite jam session tunes and has been used (or rather abused) for many a "cutting contest" amongst those Jazz musicians who relish going up on stage to show off how skillfully they can whip through the tune (something I rather disparagingly refer to as "pissing contests" amongst boys). Here's the lead sheet:

Form and melody

As with the previous analyses – always check out the form first! You should notice that bars 9–16 are a repetition of the first 8 bars at a different pitch level. Bars 17–24 are different (contrast). As of bar 25, the tune returns to the melodic and harmonic material we already heard at the beginning of the piece. The last section, however, is extended to 12 bars (instead of the usual 8!). In conclusion, "All the Things You Are" follows a simple AABA' format (8/8/8/12).

Let's have a look at the melodic structure. The motivic development is straightforward. The A sections are clearly subdivided into two-bar phrases (motive – motive – motive – end of phrase), while the B section follows a subdivision into two four-bar phrases. What about the melodic contour as a whole? Things are not that clear, here. Remember that with an AABA format the climax is usually located in the second half of the B section (generally, the high point is found in the last third of a piece). Of course, the B section provides contrast (new motivic material, different chord progression). In addition, the energy level is quite high because of the reversal of the harmonic rhythm (2 bars "weak", 2 bars "strong") and the modulation to E Major (we'll get back to this further down). From a melodic point of view, however, the B section doesn't strike the listener as being particularly exciting. The note D in bar 17, though the highest note of the melody so far, appears at the beginning of the B section. After that, the melody actually loses energy because the important notes of the phrases spell out a descending guide tone line. Remember the discussion of "Just Like That" (p. 303 ff.). If a composition reaches its high point too early, it is difficult to keep the energy level up all the way to the end.

No tune would ever have achieved this degree of popularity without a compelling melodic contour. And for a melody to be captivating, it needs a powerful and well-positioned climax. So where is the primary climax of "All The Things You Are"? Since the B section didn't quite live up to our expectations, the piece has to reach its high point in the last A section. Although this is highly unusual for an AABA tune, it does explain why the last A section of "All The Things You Are" needs a four-bar extension. On the one hand, A3 should repeat what we already heard in A1 (so the first 5 bars are a must). On the other hand, we are still missing a convincing climax. There simply wouldn't be enough time to reach a high point and conclude the piece within the remaining 3 bars of the usual eight-bar format. The extension provides the necessary time and space to accomplish the mission. In bar 30, the melody reaches the high Eb as an initial burst of energy (exceeding the D in bar 17!), only to move on to the F in bar 34 – the primary climax of the tune. Now that the melody has provided the listener with all the necessary ingredients of a satisfying formal design, the piece can come to a close.

As already shown in the chapter "Guide Tone Lines", the melody of "All The Things You Are" consists mainly of thirds and sevenths with a few embellishments. This is, to a certain extent, part of the problem with the high point of this tune. Since voice leading 3rds and 7ths in cycle-of-five chord progressions invariably creates descending guide tone lines, the melody of each section has a strong downward pull. And that, again, doesn't help when trying to create a melodic high point towards the end of any section.

Harmony

As the following analysis will show, the tune is deceptively simple. The piece is in the main key of A♭ Major (4 flats), even though the chord progression starts on F–7. The final cadence at the end of the tune lands on the tonic A♭maj7 (the II-V progression Gø7 - C7 in the last bar merely takes us back to F–7). The key signature is retained throughout the tune, even though it moves through various keys, some of which deviate considerably from A♭ Major.

The first 5 bars simply follow the cycle of fifths diatonically: VI–7 (Aeolian) - II–7 (Dorian) - V7 (Mixolydian) - Imaj7 (Ionian) - IVmaj7 (Lydian). The basic root movement of the diatonic cadence in A♭ Major is continued, but, in place of Gø7 (the diatonic VIIth degree), the secondary dominant G7 (V7/III) appears. We would normally expect C–7 (III–7), but G7 resolves to Cmaj7 instead. Cmaj7 carries more weight than all previous chords since it appears at the end of the phrase and lasts for two bars. For this reason, it establishes itself as a point of focus and must be interpreted as a new tonic (Imaj7). So, working back, we see that G7 is a dual-function pivot chord that can be analysed either as V7/III in A♭ Major or V7/I in C Major. Consequently, the changes move through a pivot modulation from A♭ Major to C Major.

Let's have a closer look at the pivot chord G7. How is it played in terms of its chord-scale relationship? We can keep up the feeling of A♭ Major by playing G7 as HM5/Altered (remember that, for VII7, Altered is the more diatonic and HM5 is the more common scale). This will make Cmaj7 appear as a surprise and emphasise the key change in bar 7. If, however, we use G7 Mixolydian instead, the switch of key happens one bar earlier. Now the G7 will sound surprising and Cmaj7 will be no more than a logical follow-up of the preceding dominant. In this case, the key change will feel more like a direct modulation, since G7 Mixolydian clashes considerably with A♭ Major (4 notes are different). Both options are perfectly valid. It is up to you to decide which alternative you prefer and where you want to switch to the new key. Just make sure to talk to the pianist or guitarist beforehand to verify their view on this. It doesn't sound too great if the soloist and the accompanying musicians don't mesh (however, considering the tempo at which the tune is usually played, it wouldn't really matter anyhow).

In many lead sheets, the G7 is preceded either by Dø7 or D–7 (played as a half-bar II-V). Dø7 - G7 ties the pivot area to A♭ Major because Dø7 (♯IVø7 Locrian) is strongly rooted in the key and clearly implies HM5/Altered for G7. We are still talking about a pivot modulation, since Dø7 - G7 can also be analysed as a modal interchange II-V in C Major. We could also use Locrian(9) for Dø7 and HTWT for G7 in order to establish a closer connection with the target chord Cmaj7. D–7 (Dorian), on the other hand, clearly indicates a break with A♭ Major and introduces the new key one bar earlier. This feels more like a direct modulation.

Bars 9–16 are a repetition of the first 8 bars (sequential approach). The different pitch level (the complete section is transposed down a fourth) and the slight variation in the melody don't alter the fact that this section must clearly be labelled as A2. Since the F–7 in bar 1 was VI–7, the C–7 in bar 9 must be interpreted in the same way. This means, however, that the piece has changed key a second time. After reaching Cmaj7 (Imaj7) in bar 7, the tune immediately modulates to E♭ Major (direct modulation). It will be one of the challenges when improvising over this piece to make it through the rapidly modulating transition from A1 to A2.

For A2, we can apply the same analysis as in the first A section. | C–7 | F–7 | B♭7 | E♭maj7 | A♭maj7 | with its diatonic root movement in fifths is VI-II-V-I-IV in E♭ Major with a pivot modulation via D7 to G Major at the end of the section. D7 is V7/III in E♭ Major and V7 in G Major. As in A1, D7 is sometimes preceded either by A∅7 or A–7, and the same scale choices apply.

At the beginning of the B section, A–7 - D7 - Gmaj7 (II-V-I) confirms the key change to G Major. The piece then modulates to E Major via a pivot modulation. F♯∅7 - B7 is the pivot area, since it can be interpreted either as II-V/VI in G Major (with E–7 as the expected target chord) or as a modal interchange II-V in E Major. If we want the pivot area to sound more diatonic in G Major, we choose F♯∅7 Locrian and B7 HM5/Altered. In this case, the chord progression stays in G Major until the Emaj7 chord appears and the new tonic comes as a bit of a surprise. We can achieve a closer connection to Emaj7 and introduce the switch to E Major earlier by using Locrian(9) and HTWT instead. Sometimes, the progression F♯–7 - B7 (Dorian/Mixolydian) is played instead of F♯∅7 - B7. This prepares the Emaj7 chord and the new key even more clearly and causes a distinct break with G Major (direct modulation).

From bar 25, we return to the thematic material of A1. The tune modulates back to the primary key, with C7 acting as the pivot: SubV/V in E Major and V7/VI in A♭ Major. In E Major, C7 Altered is the most appropriate choice of scale. In A♭ Major, C7 Altered works well, too (even though HM5 would be more diatonic). At first sight, this looks like an easy-to-handle modulation, since C7 can take the same scale in both keys. Nonetheless, in practice, it proves to be rather tricky. After all, we're talking about switching from 4 sharps to 4 flats (with a lot of enharmonic spellings obscuring the transition), and we only have one bar to make the key change. It is interesting that this sometimes poses a problem even for good soloists. The tune itself offers a rather clever solution. The common note G♯/A♭ in the melody bridges the danger zone and acts like a melodic pivot that ties together Emaj7, C7(♭13) and F–7. Without the common note, it is obviously difficult for the ear to find a cohesive link between these relatively remote keys. Some lead sheets indicate C+7 instead of C7(♭13). This would suggest another possible approach to mastering the transition and mitigating the risk of getting stuck when soloing. Starting on an E major triad (Emaj7), you can switch to E+ (= C+) on the C7 and then move on to an F– triad (you're just changing one note from one triad to the next).

Now that we're back on safe ground, the rest shouldn't be very difficult. Up to D♭maj7 (bar 29), everything is as it was in A1. From D♭–7 (IV–7 Dorian), the composition moves via C–7 (III–7 Phrygian), B°7 (♭III°7 WTHT), B♭–7 (II–7 Dorian) and E♭7 (V7 Mixolydian) in a long arch back to A♭maj7 (Imaj7 Ionian).

In "All The Things You Are", the modulations are blatantly obvious and easy to identify, though not that easy to play because the piece modulates frequently and the keys are far apart in terms of their diatonic material. In the following chapters, we will look at tunes that modulate in a much subtler way and where the modulations are sometimes quite difficult to locate.

"Stella By Starlight"

Written by Victor Young in 1944 and first featured as the title tune in the movie "The Uninvited", "Stella By Starlight" has made it to the top ten list of the most frequently played Jazz standards worldwide. For this reason, countless renditions and recordings now exist, some of which have harmonically extended Victor Young's original version considerably. Because the compositions published in the Real Book have, to a certain extent, become the set standard, I think it would make good sense to choose this version for discussion. Whether or not the changes are entirely consistent with the original composition is unimportant. The lead sheet taken from the Real Book is what most Jazz musicians refer to, and that's good enough for me. In any case, I think it would be better to base our analysis on this well-known version, rather than attempt to go back to the lesser-known original for the sake of exaggerated purism. Here's the piece:

As already mentioned, this lead sheet does not entirely conform to the original composition. The melody, of course has stayed the same. The harmony, however, has been subject to a number of transformations. To give you a rough impression of the differences, here are the original changes taken from the soundtrack (bars 1–16): Bb°7 | ∕ | C–7 | F7(sus4) F7 | F–7 | Bb7 | Ebmaj7 | Ab7 | Bbmaj7 | G–7 | D–7 | Bb–6/Db | Fmaj7/C | Bb°7 | Aø7 | D7 | etc. Fascinating, isn't it? In essence, though, it's still the same chord progression.

Bill Evans himself, to whom the Real Book version is generally ascribed, didn't stick to the same changes but used a number of alternative reharmonisations at his discretion. For example, he would play bars 11 + 12 (half-bar harmonic pulse) as | D–7 C–7 | Bø7 Bb–7 |, or in bars 23 + 24, instead of playing 2 bars of Bbmaj7, he'd substitute the first bar with Bb°7 (A/Bb). One of the most inspired and inspiring recordings of "Stella By Starlight" – on Miles Davis' album "My Funny Valentine" (1965) – shows how far you can take the concept of spontaneous reharmonisation. Starting out in a ballad tempo, the band switches to a "double time feel" 1'50" into the recording (at the beginning of the A' section of the theme). Remember that this implies doubling the tempo but keeping the form (e.g. in the C section, the chords would be 4 bars each in the faster tempo). This provides for lots of space to insert additional chords or little harmonic detours and change the chord types or the scale material. The band exploits this space liberally, at times obscuring the original chord progression altogether.

For the sake of the following analysis, we'll stick to the lead sheet supplied by the old Real Book. Once we're done, however, go back to the original changes mentioned above and compare. Find the movie sound track (on *youtube.com*) and see if you can figure out the harmonic similarities or differences in the second half of the tune (in comparison to the Real Book version). We will have another look at "Stella By Starlight" in the chapter "Harmonisation and Reharmonisation" (pdf-F).

Form

As usual, let's start with the formal structure. The piece has 32 bars, subdivided into four eight-bar sections. However, the form is not as clear as the compositions we have already looked at. The first three eight-bar sections differ considerably from each other when comparing the harmonic and melodic content. Not until the last eight-bar section does the piece return to the initial idea. This is the formal structure:

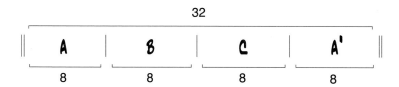

I have chosen the label A' for the last section, since the first and last 8 bars are only partially the same. Let's now look at the individual sections.

A section

The key signature implies B♭ Major or G Minor. It is remarkable, however, that the tonic (B♭maj7 or G–7) does not appear even once throughout the A section. So, how can we be sure that we are truly in B♭ Major? How can we orientate ourselves? The decisive factor is – once again – the melody. I already stated in the chapter "Modulation" that a diatonic melody will always emanate a distinct sense of tonality, no matter how complex or out-of-key the chord progression may be. If we focus on the melody of the A section, the main notes B♭ (first/last note) and F (5) obviously point to B♭ as the tonal centre:

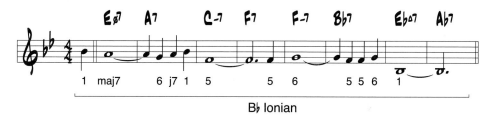

You can't establish the tonality of a melody any more clearly than this. If we add bar 9, there can be no doubt – we are in B♭ Major (sing the melody of bars 1–9 and then a B♭ Major scale for confirmation). So, the changes are a complex harmonisation of a simple, diatonic melody. Here's the analysis:

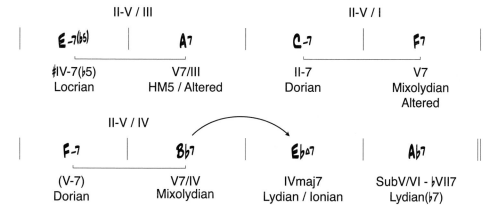

First of all, I'd like you to realise that E–7(♭5) is not only part of II-V/III but also ♯IVø7. We have talked about this sound extensively on p. 207 ff. (in the chapter "Modal Interchange"). Beginning on this function is highly unusual and gives "Stella By Starlight" its unique flavour. I have heard groups play the tune where the musicians would start on Eø7 and then venture out into the wild blue yonder for the following 31 bars (and I mean, really out), only to return to Eø7 at the beginning of the next chorus. So, for "Stella By Starlight", starting on ♯IVø7 is something like a dog tag – it distinguishes this tune from all other tunes. The most basic choice of scales is Locrian for E–7(♭5) and HM5 for A7. We could, however, also use Locrian(9)/HTWT to spice up the sound.

Neither Eø7 - A7 nor C–7 - F7 resolve to the expected target functions D–7 (III–7) and B♭maj7 (Imaj7). For this reason, it is not that easy to improvise over these changes. If we play rote-learned II-V-I patterns, we'll run into harmonic dead-ends because the expected target sounds just aren't there. What we have to do is anticipate the C–7, even though this sound does not correspond with the usual resolution of the II-V. The transition from F7 to F–7 is equally tricky. F7 (V7) could likewise be Mixolydian or HM5/Altered (the melody doesn't help us here). The colour we choose depends on how the progression F7 - F–7 should come across. If we want to have flowing, unobtrusive lines, we should go for Mixolydian (F7 Mixo and F–7 Dorian differ in only one note: A or A♭). In contrast, F7 Altered would create much more tension and disrupt the diatonic flow (which is not necessarily a bad thing).

The E♭maj7 chord (IVmaj7) is normally Lydian (with the A = ♯11). As important as the key of B♭ Major may be, the immediate tonal environment exerts considerable influence. Since the note A♭ plays a decisive role in the preceding cadence (F–7 - B♭7) as well as in the ensuing A♭7 chord (bar 8), E♭ Ionian (with the A♭ = 4) would make a better choice; the A in E♭ Lydian would stick out like a sore thumb (though good voice leading would make it work; try!).

A♭7 in B♭ Major normally leads to G–7. Instead, a deceptive resolution to B♭maj7 (at last!) occurs in bar 9 via the backdoor cadence.

B section

B♭maj7 (Imaj7 Ionian) is followed by Eø7 - A7 (II-V/III), which, unlike bars 1 + 2 of the A section, now resolves to D–7 (III–7) as expected. However, don't be fooled; things are not what they seem to be. We now come to the important bit. Have a good look at the following excerpt (bars 10/11):

These two bars need to be heard as one coherent melodic phrase (sing the melody starting in bar 9, then you'll feel it). The E should therefore not be interpreted as an insignificant passing note, but rather as an important leading tone moving towards the F in bar 11. This has an impact on D–7. Now, if D–7 were III–7 in B♭ Major as expected, the correct choice of scale would be Phrygian. D Phrygian, however, contains an E♭ (♭2). The note E is the major second and therefore out-of-scale. The logical conclusion: This "anomaly" implies a change of function and, possibly, a new key.

If we assume that a modulation has actually taken place, then the D–7 must be consistent with a scale that contains the E. If we restrict ourselves to diatonic functions, only two alternatives present themselves: II–7 Dorian or VI–7 Aeolian (both contain the E). The first implies the key of C Major and the second F Major. At the beginning of the next four-bar segment (bar 13 is a harmonic focal point) we indeed come across Fmaj7 – the notion of a modulation is confirmed. Eø7 - A7 is the pivot area (II-V/III in B♭ Major and II-V/VI in F Major). The following segment (D–7 - B♭–7 - E♭7) must therefore be analysed in the key of F Major.

The attentive listener/reader will have discovered one more – formal – clue to the key change. If we compare bars 8/9 with 12/13, we'll recognise a harmonic-melodic sequence:

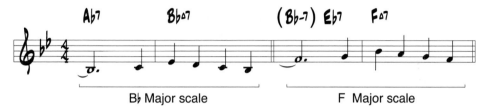

Not only the melodic phrase repeats, the chord progression does, too. A♭7 (♭VII7 in B♭ Major) has the same functional connotation as E♭7 (♭VII7 in F Major). As far as I am concerned, this formal correlation underpins the notion of a key change even more convincingly than the tonal components in bars 10 + 11.

The difficulty, when improvising, lies in the fact that you consciously have to make the switch to F Major *before* you have actually reached Fmaj7. D–7 must already feel like VI–7 (or a minor tonic), otherwise you will not hear B♭–7 - E♭7 as IV–7 - ♭VII7. Once you have reached Fmaj7, everything else falls into place: Eø7 - A7 is II-V/VI and Aø7 - D7 is II-V/II, irrespective of the fact that both II-Vs don't resolve quite as expected.

Moving on to the C section, G7 would be V7/V in the key of F Major, usually played Mixolydian or Lydian(♭7). But, watch out! Always have an eye on the melody. The one note we hear in bar 17 is a prominent E♭ (♭13), not contained in either one of the scales. Conclusion: We are no longer in the key of F Major. Just as the note E initiated the modulation to F Major in bar 10, the reappearance of the note E♭ in bars 17 + 18, where it is hammered home by the melody, launches the modulation back to B♭ Major. If we take the harmony into consideration, the E♭ already starts to make its presence felt subliminally in bars 15 + 16 as part of A–7(♭5) and D7(♭9). Personally, this is where I can already feel the chord progression turning back to the original key. That's why I have marked Aø7 - D7 as a pivot area in the following analysis and ascribed dual functions to both chords. Here's the summary of the B section:

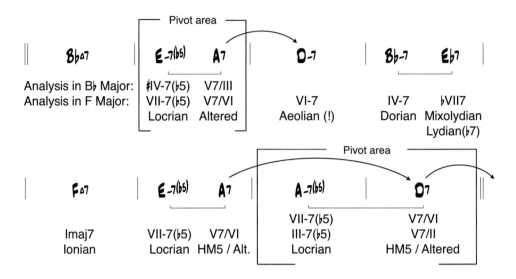

One thing we haven't looked at yet is the strong-weak distribution of the melody and the harmony. Concerning the harmonic and melodic rhythm, this tune is rather ambiguous, particularly when looking at sections A and B. Eø7 - A7 (non-diatonic) and C–7 - F7 (diatonic) set up a two-bar W-S pattern in the A section, which is repeated in bars 5–7 (F–7 - Bb7 is weak and Ebmaj7 is strong). This, too, is one of the many unusual features that characterise this tune. Starting out a chord progression on "weak" is quite uncommon. Bar 8 (Ab7) is weak and reverses the harmonic rhythm, thereby setting up the one-bar S-W pattern found in the B section. While the melodic rhythm follows a one-bar S-W pattern in the A section, it switches to a one-bar W-S pattern in the B section, clearly in contrast to the flow of the chord progression.

As you can see, harmony and melody are at odds both in the A and the B section. The important thing: This is not done arbitrarily. Even though the harmonic and the melodic rhythm are not congruent, both, seen individually, follow a distinct pattern – and that's why the composition works. This, however, is one of the reasons why it's not that easy to improvise on this tune. The soloist has to grapple with conflicting information: two-bar W-S harmonic rhythm and one-bar S-W melodic rhythm in the A section, one-bar S-W harmonic rhythm and one-bar W-S melodic rhythm in the B section. You'll have to base your improvisations either on the structure of the melody or the harmony if you want your lines to make sense. If you try to mix both, you're sure to run into trouble.

C section

In bar 17, we are definitely back in Bb Major. G7 is therefore V7/II. The melody notes Eb (b13) and D (5) imply HM5 as the corresponding scale. In some lead sheets, you will come across the chord symbol G+7 instead of G7 or G7(b13), the reason being that there are soloists who like to play lines based on the Whole-tone scale (though WT doesn't go quite that well with the melody). As expected, G7 resolves to C–7 Dorian. The progression C–7 - Ab7 may look strange on paper (unusual root movement), but it works just fine. If we remember that II–7 and IVmaj7 are both subdominant functions, we'll realise that C–7 (II–7) is simply a replacement for Ebmaj7 (IVmaj7). C–7 - Ab7 - Bbmaj7 is a variation of the backdoor cadence we already encountered in the transition from the A to the B section (bars 7–9): Ebmaj7 - Ab7 - Bbmaj7. Here's the analysis:

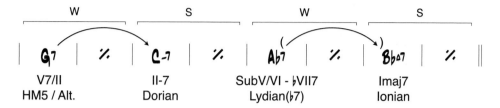

The harmonic rhythm is also worth commenting on. The sudden switch from a one-bar or even half-bar harmonic pulse in the B section to two-bar changes and the reversal of the strong-weak distribution (W-S-W-S instead of S-W-S-W) are ingenious compositional devices that amplify the melodic climax in bar 19. The long, soaring melody notes and their sustained tension (b13 on G7 and 11 on C–7) are like holding one's breath, suspensions in time that intensify the resolution of G7 and boost C–7 as the high point.

A' section

The final section brings us back to the beginning of the composition. This time, however, the chord progression circles back to Bbmaj7, following the cycle of fifths and a sequence of consecutive minor II-Vs. The scale material for improvisation is generally Locrian/HM5. For Cø7/F7, we could also use Locrian(9)/HTWT in order to strengthen the link to Bb Major:

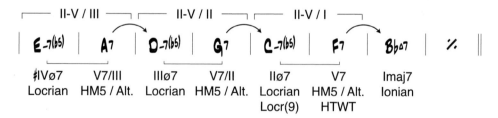

Since this is a sequence, we could also use Locrian(9)/HTWT with each of the minor II-Vs (remember this was also an option for Eø7 - A7 at the beginning of the tune, and it is something you'll come across quite often).

Improvisation

This analysis shows why "Stella By Starlight" is both a difficult and appealing composition. It has surprising harmonic turns and deceptive resolutions from start to finish. Expectations are established only to have them thwarted. A7 sets up D–7, but what you get is C–7. F7 wants to resolve to B♭maj7, F–7 pops up instead. F–7 - B♭7 - E♭maj7 is a II-V-I pattern, however, E♭maj7 is not Imaj7 but IVmaj7. A♭7 doesn't resolve chromatically down to G–7 but deceptively up to B♭maj7. Eø7 - A7 seemingly leads to D–7 (III–7) as expected, but D–7 turns out to be VI–7 in the new key, and so on, and so on. When you practise this piece, concentrate on the unusual harmonic transitions. Ask yourself, for instance, "How do I get from A7 to C–7 (bars 2 + 3), from F7 to F–7 (bars 4 + 5), etc. without breaking the melodic flow?" In the chapter "Improvisation", you will find exercises that will help you with this.

Of course, there are musicians who can play in a very relaxed way over this piece. One of them is the trumpeter Chet Baker. Let's have a look at an excerpt from his solo on the album "Live in Europe" (it's actually two choruses put together in one). The brackets indicate the motivic phrases:

This is how deceptively simple improvisation can (and should) be! This musical gem doesn't sound spectacular, but eminently illustrates the playful ease with which Chet Baker moves through these relatively complex changes.

The first thing you'll probably notice is Chet Baker's sense of form. The basic structure of the composition and its subdivision into eight-bar segments is reflected clearly in the solo. What really strikes the eye and the ear is the amazing consistency with which he develops his motivic ideas. Every formal section tells its own motivic story, enhanced beautifully by the rhythm of the phrases. I have marked the individual motives with brackets in the transcription. Notice how the motivic flow is interrupted by a closing turn at the end of the section in most cases, opening the way for new ideas.

The build-up in the chorus is particularly impressive. If we reduce the improvisation to its essential notes and transitions (Mr. Schenker again), we end up with the following rhythmically simplified guide tone line:

Now you can see the vast melodic arch, tying together the eight-bar segments and progressing from an initially low energy level to a climax and back. Notice that the positioning of the climax in the theme and the solo is identical. Chet Baker is living proof of the ability to keep one's eye on the details as well as the whole.

Let's have a look at the scale material. In principle, the content of the solo is covered by the chord-scale relationships determined in our analysis above. It is worth mentioning, however, that the Eø7 chords in bars 1, 10 and 25 are Locrian(9) and not Locrian (F♯ = 9 in the line). Cø7 - F7 at the end is also Locrian(9)/HTWT and reinforces the key. All in all, the solo rarely departs from the original key despite the frequent changes. Nevertheless, Chet Baker faithfully plays the modulation in the B section – in keeping with the melody (note the E). Otherwise, the lines are mostly diatonic to the key of B♭ Major (the occasional deviations are chromatic passing notes or approach patterns).

Chet Baker is surely one of the tragic heroes in Jazz. There must be only few who have lived through such highs and lows, and, despite the many setbacks in his life, remained faithful to music. If you ever have the chance, watch the documentary movie "Let's Get Lost" about the turbulent career of Chet Baker – in my opinion one of the most touching and beautiful musical portraits ever. Miles Davis is said to have commented drily: "Had it, blew it!" I thoroughly disagree! Chet Baker may not have had an easy life, but he was always in complete control of the music.

"Mornin'"

Compositions on the borderline between Pop and Jazz often deserve a closer look when trying to come to grips with analysis. Since this kind of music is intended for a broader audience, it is likely to be more transparent, comprehensible and easier on the ear than many hardcore Jazz tunes. However, don't be fooled! Don't let yourselves be prejudiced in your judgement of Pop music by writing it off wholesale as banal or unimaginative. There are quite a few recordings that succeed in balancing out commercial packaging with top-class content – tunes that not only appeal to the intuitive listener but also measure up to the expectations of more discerning audiences.

A great example of such a piece is "Mornin'" by Al Jarreau, David Foster and Jay Graydon (on the album "Jarreau", 1983). On first hearing this recording, Jazz musicians may judge it to be a shallow mishmash of catchy melodic lines, mellow Hip-hop, rhapsodic string parts, saccharine synthesiser sounds and kitschy lyrics (and, please, don't watch the video – it will confirm your worst fears). On closer scrutiny, the composition emerges as an ingeniously designed work of art. Even if the melody comes across as a compilation of highly predictable if not simplistic phrases, the apparently trivial and superficial façade of the piece conceals an abundance of harmonic subtleties and surprises. Compared even to demanding Jazz themes, "Mornin'" stands its own ground, which goes to show that some Pop compositions have more to offer than what meets the eye and ear.

Assignment 1

Before we have a look at the lead sheet, I want you to get hold of the original recording. Try to transcribe the general form of the piece (different sections, number of bars per section, climax, points of interest, etc.) and sketch it out on a piece of paper. It would most probably make sense to go for a bar layout (e.g. 4 bars per line) with double bar lines to mark the end of a section. Use A, B, C, etc. to label each section.

Assignment 2

Now, listen to the recording with your layout at hand (see assignment 1). Don't stop the recording until you reach the keyboard solo (2'41"). While you're listening, try to pinpoint the modulations. Make a tick in your layout whenever you have the feeling that a change of key has occurred. This is a purely intuitive exercise because you won't have time to reflect on what you're hearing. So, even if you're not sure, make a tick anyhow. Once we're done with the analysis, go back to this assignment and compare your results.

Assignment 3

I'm not yet going to tell you the purpose of this assignment. Indulge me, just do it. We'll get back to it later in the chapter. What I want you to do is listen to the recording. Start at 1'28" or thereabouts and keep going until you hear the lyrics "Then higher <u>still</u> ..." (round about

2'10"). Now for the actual assignment: Turn off the recording at 2'12" (no later than beat 4 of the bar with the word "still"). Make sure that you don't listen any further! Perhaps you have to do this several times to get it right (if you have to repeat the exercise, always go back to 1'28" and listen to the complete section). As soon as you stop the recording, ask yourself: "What harmonic function am I hearing right now?" To make things a bit easier: You're hearing a minor seventh chord. So, if we consider the most common minor functions (diatonic or modal interchange), it could be I–7, II–7, III–7, IV–7, V–7 or VI–7. Don't think about this exercise too much. Just rely on your intuition and jot down the function that first comes to mind.

Have you finished all three assignments? Then, here's the lead sheet:

D.C. al Coda

Form

Let's move on to our analysis and start with the form. Compared to the structure of a typical Jazz standard, the roadmap of "Mornin'" is more elaborate, even though most of the formal sections are 8 bars long. The following plan shows an overview of the complete recording (the lead sheet above ends just before the keyboard solo for reasons of space).

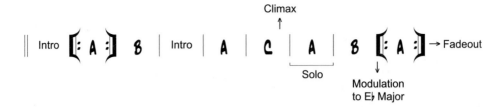

Whereas the intro (4 bars), the A section and the B section (8 bars each) are straightforward, the C section (20 bars) could be broken down into smaller segments: An underlying 8/8/4 subdivision would be plausible, with the last four bars being identical to the introduction. However, because the whole section is based on the same melodic (motivic) idea and clearly follows a progressive build-up towards the high point of the recording, I'd rather interpret C as a 20-bar unit. I'll leave the final verdict to you.

I have mentioned before that simple formal plans such as AABA, ABAC, AAB, etc. are favoured in Jazz because they are easier to "digest" by the subconscious. The more convoluted the formal structure, the more we have to think and the more difficult it becomes to rely on our intuition while improvising. In "Mornin'", the solo section takes up only a small amount of space proportionately, allowing for more compositional leeway and a more complex order of events.

Introduction / A section

The intro firmly establishes D Ionian as the tonality/modality. Dmaj7 is Imaj7. A–7 is therefore V–7 Dorian – a modal interchange function replacing V7. G/A also comes from A Dorian. It is a variation of A–11 (no ♭3) and sounds like A7(sus4). Since A–7 can also be written as C/A, the appeal of this passage lies in the cadential effect created by the two see-sawing triads C and G (I-V-I-V) with A in the bass:

At the end of the introduction (or before the repeat of the A section), we come across the progression A–7 - G–7 - A–7. In addition to V–7, we hear IV–7 Dorian, which is also an MI-function (although, considering the tempo of the harmonic movement, the scale choices are not really an issue; we simply hear a chord shift).

B section

The A section has set up a strong feeling of D Major. Consequently, B♭maj7 must be ♭VImaj7 Lydian – an MI-function. If you listen to the recording, some of you may be under the impression that the tune modulates at this point. Since we've heard two highly uniform A sections with very little variation, we feel a strong need for contrast. Modulation is a commonly used concept to create contrast. Since B♭maj7 deviates substantially from D Major, our first reaction to this sound may be "Ah, change of key!" The chord progression, however, immediately returns to Dmaj7. So, there is no modulation, and our initial assumption (♭VImaj7) is correct.

Like B♭maj7, C7(sus4) Mixolydian has to be analysed as an MI-function from Aeolian (♭VII7). If we choose the symbols G–9/C or B♭maj7/C instead of C13(sus4) – another way of spelling out sus4 chords (see p. 425 ff.) – we'll recognise the connection with two earlier sounds: G–7 and B♭maj7. C13(sus4) corresponds to IV–7 or ♭VImaj7 with a different bass note. Please don't confuse C7(sus4) with the tritone substitute C7 (SubV/VI in D Major), which is usually played Lydian(♭7). Whereas the F♯ (= ♯11) in C Lydian(♭7) ensures the link to D Major, C Mixolydian, on the other hand, contains the note F, which goes against the feeling of D Major and draws us more strongly away from the key (implying D Minor). A7(sus4) is V7 Mixolydian.

As already mentioned, the B section provides contrast. One element of contrast that should catch your eye is the reversal of the harmonic rhythm, arrived at by combining non-diatonic sounds (weak) and diatonic functions (strong): W-S-W-S (2 bars each). It is also worth noting that, with the exception of Dmaj7 and A7(sus4), the intro and both the A section and the B section consist only of MI-functions. The basic mode is D Ionian, and sounds are borrowed from D Mixolydian (V–7) and D Aeolian (IV–7, ♭VImaj7, ♭VII7). Here, the play on various modalities within the same tonality is carried quite a distance. Many of the more contemporary Pop songs thrive on this principle. Because most listeners have a strong need to hear tonality, songwriters are constantly looking for opportunities to extend traditional harmony without leaving the key. MI-functions fulfil this requirement nicely – they add colour without modulating. "Mornin'" is an excellent example of a tune that clearly points out the differences between modal interchange and modulation.

C section

In the first bar of the C section, quite a few of my students tend to hear a modulation (go back to assignment 2 at the beginning of this chapter and see what you came up with). A quick look at the lead sheet, however, reveals that the chord progression, at this point, could hardly be more deeply rooted in the key of D Major. The harmonic pick-up leading into the C section (Dmaj7 - E–7 - F♯–7 - Gmaj7) is nothing but stepwise movement of diatonic functions leading from Imaj7 to IVmaj7. So, why would we hear a modulation? The answer is, compositionally speaking, quite intriguing because it shows how the listener's ear can be tricked into hearing something familiar and simple as something unusual and complex instead. Since we have heard MI-functions almost exclusively up until now, the diatonic material in D Major comes across as fresh and pristine (we haven't heard it yet). As already mentioned several times in this book, the idea of creating a context that relies strongly on MI-functions is a great way of upgrading diatonic sounds, which may have turned stale through overuse. In conclusion, there is definitely no modulation to be found at the beginning of the C section.

The first five bars of the C section are nothing more than a variation of the diatonic cadence in D Major with a few interpolated secondary dominants. Here's the comparison:

	Imaj7		IVmaj7	VIIø7	III-7	VI-7	II-7
Diatonic cadence	D△7		G△7	C#ø7	F#-7	B-7	E-7
Mornin'	D△7 (E-7 F#-7)		G△7	C#7	F#-7	B7	E-7
	Imaj7 (II-7 III-7)		IVmaj7	V7/III	III-7	V7/II	II-7
	Ion Dor Phryg		Lydian	HM5 / Alt	Phrygian	HM5 / Alt	Dorian

I'm sure you agree with this straightforward analysis. "Mornin'", however, shows us once again that the impact of a passage is often influenced by seemingly insignificant details in the arrangement. For this reason, I'd like to draw your attention to some interesting deviations from the expected chord-scale relationships, which pop up in the synthesiser line in the background and are perceived by the ear as little pinpricks of tension:

With Gmaj7, the D# in the secondary voice should catch our eye and ear. We could easily dismiss this note simply as a chromatic approach. But, since it appears in a relatively exposed location, it deserves closer attention. Here, for the first time, we come across a scale variant, which is enjoying increasing popularity in Jazz these days – Lydian(#5):

Lydian(#5) is a member of the group of Melodic minor transpositions (MM3). These modes introduce an abundance of contemporary colours over and above the scales we have already discussed. I'll get back to this topic in the chapter "Voicings" (pdf-E).

On the C♯7 chord, we clearly hear a G (♯11) in the secondary voice. The function is therefore Altered and not HM5. Take note of how smoothly this potentially aggressive sound fits into the tonal framework. Since the keyboard also plays an E (♯9) in the voicing, C♯7 can hardly be distinguished from the diatonic VIIᵗʰ degree C♯ø7 (♯9 = ♭3; ♯11 = ♭5). The only deviation is the relatively unobtrusive major third (E♯) of the secondary dominant (C♯7) concealed in the lower voices of the chord. This again proves that an altered function will not necessarily sound conspicuous or create much tension if it corresponds to tonal expectations (see p. 486 ff.).

Next, look at the G♯ (9) played on the F♯–7 (III–7) – a rather untypical sound for a Phrygian function. This brief departure from the diatonic material in D Major only marginally irritates the ear because of the preceding guide tone line, which distinctly targets the G♯.

We now come to the best part of this passage: bar 4 of the C section. The movement of E♯ to F♯ (♯11 to 5) in the secondary voice, the C (= ♭9) in the melody and the G♯ we heard in the previous bar, which still lingers in the mind, all imply HTWT as the preferred choice of scale for B7. If we listen closely to the rather unusual harmonisation of the quarter note triplet in the second half of the bar, it is quite obvious that HTWT complies with the composer's intentions. We hear a sequence of major triads (upper structures), which are shifted over the basic chord (B7) along with the melody:

Let's start with the A♭ major triad, which can be respelled as G♯ (A♭ was chosen because of the melody note C). The G♯ major triad contains the notes G♯ (13), B♯ (enharmonically seen as C = ♭9) and D♯ (3). This confirms our choice of HTWT. The G major triad, in contrast, with its G (♭13), B (1) and D (♭3 = ♯9), is derived from Altered. The closing F major triad with F (♯11), A (♭7) and C (♭9) can be derived from HTWT as well as Altered:

What initially seems to be a simple parallel sequence of major triads is, in fact, an elegant play on different dominant scales and the upper structures derived from them. This, too, is a subtle form of modal interchange – a blend of various scale forms at close quarters. Again, we will take a closer look at this topic in the chapter "Voicings" (pdf-E).

After reaching E–7 (II–7), the diatonic cadence in D Major with its root movement in fifths is interrupted. The chord progression moves via E–7/D (passing bass note) to C#ø7 - F#7 (II-V/VI). We would therefore expect the relative minor B–7 (VI–7). However, this expectation is not fulfilled. Bmaj7 appears instead. This chord cannot be interpreted as an MI-function because it occurs at the end of an eight-bar section and, unlike the preceding changes, is held for 2 bars (contrary to the one-bar or half-bar harmonic pulse of the preceding chord progression). Besides, there is no such thing as a VImaj7 MI-function. Without a doubt, Bmaj7 must be analysed as a new tonic. So, what we have here is a pivot modulation with C#ø7 - F#7 acting as the pivot area, which can be analysed either as a II-V/VI in D Major or a modal interchange II-V in B Major.

Again, go back to the results of assignment 2 at the beginning of this chapter. How did you do? Did you hear a modulation at this point of the tune? Chances are that you missed it because the harmonic and melodic flow feels so logical. The modulation simply doesn't stick out. That it comes across as unobtrusive is also due to the melody note F#, which belongs to both keys (3 in D Major, 5 in B Major) and has the effect of a tonal bracket (something like a melodic pivot). Furthermore, the high string line and its compelling resolution to the major seventh of the Bmaj7 chord adds to the virtually seamless connection of the two keys:

The sounds that follow can now easily be analysed in B Major: C#–7 = II–7 (Dorian), G#–7 = VI–7 (Aeolian).

We now get to a very interesting point – at least from a psychological point of view. Go back to assignment 3 at the beginning of the chapter. What did you come up with? Ever since I first heard the tune, I have had problems hearing G#–7 as the relative minor (VI–7) in B Major. Many of my colleagues and students have said the same. Of course, many do provide VI–7 as the answer because that's what it is once you've switched to the key of B Major. Quite a few, however, say that G#–7 doesn't really feel like a VI–7 tonic function. Why is this? After all, at least at first glance, there is no other explanation for this chord. Surprisingly, the most frequently quoted alternative is II–7.

So, how do we explain this reaction? We will see that the ear subliminally registers considerably more than the eye recognises at the surface. The C section is not an uninterrupted 20-bar phrase. We clearly sense a division into two subsections: an eight-bar and a 12-bar segment. The end of the first passage is marked by the modulation and the ensuing pause on Bmaj7. Now look at the melody. Can you see that both the pick-up in bar 8 and the subsequent melodic line are identical to the opening of the C section? Of course, we are no longer in D Major because the phrase is transposed up a major third.

And now something astonishing happens: The ear not only remembers the melodic and motivic structure, but also the functional feeling of the changes. Keep in mind that the Gmaj7 (bar 1 of the C section) was IVmaj7 – a subdominant function in D Major. As a consequence, that's what the ear expects in bar 9, too: a subdominant or at least a chord with a similar functional quality. Remember, there are two subdominant functions in the diatonic context of a major key: IVmaj7 and II–7 (see p. 91). G♯–7, if it were a subdominant function, would therefore rather be II–7 and not VI–7 in B Major. If we assume that G♯–7 is II–7, then, logically, a change of key to F♯ Major must have occurred. And, lo and behold, that's exactly what happens. Two bars later, F♯maj7 is targeted as a new tonal centre.

This line of reasoning becomes even more convincing once we compare the interval relationships in the melody:

C section (bars 1–4)

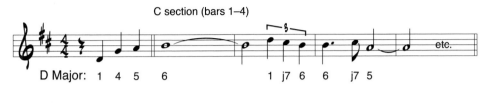

D Major: 1   4   5   6   1   j7 6   6   j7 5

C section (bars 9–12)

F♯ Major: 1   4   5   6   1   j7 6   6   j7 5

Both phrases – based on their respective keys – are identical. What amazes me is the fact that this formal cross-reference is obviously sufficient to create the impression of a modulation on the G♯–7 chord, even though nothing in the melody or in the chord progression points to a new tonal centre just then.

Of course, you could now argue that, once we know how the piece continues, our perception will be tainted by expectation and our ears will anticipate the chord progression modulating to F♯ Major as soon as we reach G♯–7. It is interesting, though, that you can stop the recording at the G♯–7 chord and, starting on G♯, automatically sing Dorian (give it a try!). This wouldn't exactly be the most obvious choice after having heard two bars of Bmaj7 (Ionian). Besides, having arrived at G♯–7, we sense a feeling of movement (which implies a cadence chord) rather than one of rest (which would be the case with VI–7).

What may seem like analytical hair-splitting actually boils down to three decisive points. Firstly, this example proves that composers design their compositions according to an overall formal concept. It is the objective of any analysis to identify this underlying "game plan". It makes no difference whether the composer crafts a piece intuitively or intentionally (or as a combination of both) – a compositional principle is always at play, whether the composer realises this or not. Secondly, it shows that the ear works far more precisely than we would imagine. It is obviously capable of detecting interrelationships and connecting elements, even if they occur far apart from each other. And, thirdly, I would like to repeat for the umpteenth time that it is not the intellect but rather the ear that makes the final decision when it comes to analysis. We only have to learn to trust our aural perception and to interpret it astutely.

Back to the piece! Again, the tune changes key via a pivot modulation with G♯–7 acting as the dual-function pivot (VI–7 in B Major and II–7 in F♯ Major). The second part of the C section can be analysed entirely in F♯ Major: | G♯–7 | C♯7 | F♯maj7 | D♯–7 | is a diatonic turn-around (II-V-I-VI), and | G♯–7 | A♯–7 | Bmaj7 | C♯7(sus4) | is a simple diatonic sequence

(II-III-IV-V). I'm sure I don't have to go into the scale choices; I assume that you can do this on your own by now.

What follows seems to be at first glance a rather brutal reinstatement of D Major (direct modulation). However, this transition actually sounds quite smooth and not at all awkward. Firstly, Dmaj7 can be seen as ♭VImaj7 in F♯ Major. It is therefore a logical follow-up of the preceding chord progression (II-III-IV-V-♭VI). Conclusion: This is a pivot modulation with a dual-function Dmaj7: ♭VImaj7 in F♯ Major and Imaj7 in D Major. More importantly, the melody mirrors the powerful surge of the chord progression. Melody, harmony and bass line all resolve chromatically to Dmaj7, cushioning this rather radical key change.

Note how the melody takes a short breath on the Bmaj7 before making its final dash for the climax of the tune. In the bar preceding Dmaj7, the chord progression alternates between B/C♯ and C♯7, following the quarter-note pulse of the melody. Here, the general chord symbol would normally be C♯7(sus4). The E♯ in the melody (3 of C♯7), however, interferes with the sus4 sound (remember that 3 is an avoid note on sus4 chords). That's why every quarter note of the melody is harmonised differently. If you listen closely to the recording, you'll realise that this is actually a condensed version of the previous three bars with C♯ in the bass: G♯–7/C♯ - A♯–7/C♯ - Bmaj7/C♯ - C♯7 (so the lead sheet is not entirely accurate). Both the melody's and the harmony's stepwise movement accelerate the last bar and propel it into the target sound Dmaj7:

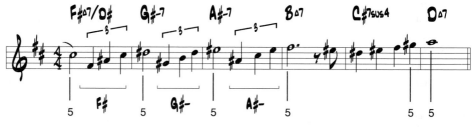

The composition reaches its primary climax with the highest note of the theme, followed by a four-bar fade-out on Dmaj7. This makes good sense because the ear needs time to allow the feeling of F♯ Major to subside and to re-establish D Major. The four bars of Dmaj7 are a repetition of what we already heard in the introduction, which also adds to the feeling of "coming home".

What follows is a short improvisation over the A section. This is one of the classics among keyboard solos. It is a great example of melodic control simply because it says in 8 bars what other improvisations take numerous choruses to say:

The remainder of the recording repeats the material we've already talked about. We hear another B section, followed by a direct modulation to E♭ Major (a popular, though rather mechanical and heavy-handed way to increase the intensity of the piece one last time) and two more A sections with a fade-out.

You may be asking yourselves, for good reason, why we need to think about chord-scale relationships in a mostly through-composed piece like "Mornin'". After all, it is one of the main objectives of a harmonic analysis to define improvisational material. The answer is simple. Firstly, stylistic boundaries are gradually disappearing. As a result, many Jazz musicians are adopting – as a matter of course – the Pop repertoire as a basis for improvisation (I've heard "Mornin'" played as an instrumental version with solos over an AABAC chorus format). Miles Davis, as ever so often, was one of the first Jazz musicians to adapt Pop songs without any reservations or prejudice. Secondly, the intricate harmony, the use of tensions and interesting voicings, the many little secondary lines, the well-designed modulations, etc. demonstrate an in-depth understanding of the way chords and scales interact. Most importantly: You can only write a tune as complex as "Mornin'" if you have truly internalised the harmonic and melodic language of Jazz.

Locating modulations

At this point, let's go back to assignment No. 2 one last time. Did you catch every modulation? After all, the tune modulates four times (which is quite a lot for a Pop song). Surprising, isn't it? Some of you are probably thinking that it is not always a good idea to rely on gut feeling. I often use this example in class to show that it's not that easy to pinpoint a change of key. The modulations in the C section (to B Major and F♯ Major) are fairly subtle and perhaps didn't catch your attention. On the other hand, I can imagine that quite a few of you reacted strongly to the modal interchange functions in sections A and B. It goes to show that MI-functions often have a more disruptive quality than a well-designed pivot modulation.

Be aware of this distinction. Not every sound that sticks out can automatically be equated with a change of key.

Let's quickly run through the various sections. You will have heard strong points of tension in both the A section (maybe) and the B section (definitely). Here we come across sounds that clearly break away from the tonality of D Major: A–7, B♭maj7, C7(sus4). We now know that we're dealing with modal interchange functions, deliberately used by the composer as a means of creating contrast without actually leaving the tonality. They are conspicuous flashes of colour in an otherwise rather bland harmonic environment, inserted to distract us from the persistent major-key texture created by Dmaj7 and A7(sus4). Now for the surprising part. While we clearly feel the MI-functions as a breach of tonality, the modulations are far less noticeable. The chord progression resolves elegantly to the keys of B Major and F♯ Major without the ear detecting anything unusual. The new tonal centres are prepared logically (pivot modulations), fitting in seamlessly with the harmonic flow. The only exception is the modulation back to D Major, which is easily felt by any listener. I'm sure, all of you spotted that one. If you listen to this section of the recording again, see if you can hear the four bars of Dmaj7 at the end as a gradual cross-fade from F♯ Major to D Major (e.g. as 2 bars of ♭VImaj7 and 2 bars of Imaj7).

"Mornin'" should illustrate that modulations do not always create dramatic harmonic change or elicit strong reactions in the listener. As a rule, a new tonic will be more than just a passing chord. It is usually positioned at an important point within the form. In most cases, it is preceded by a cadence, which helps the ear to comfortably settle into the new key.

Lyrics

When analysing Pop songs, it is always a good idea to have a closer look at the way the music underscores the lyrics. Here they are:

A1:   *Mornin' Mister Radio, Mornin' little Cherios,*
       Mornin' Sister Oriole, did I tell you ev'rything is fine,
       In my mind.
A2:   *Mornin' Mr. Shoe Shine Man, shine 'em bright in white and tan,*
       My baby said she loves me and need I tell you ev'rything here is just fine, in my mind.

B: *'Scuse me if I sing, my heart has found its wings,*
       Searchin' high and low, and now at last I know.

A3:   *Mornin' Mr. Golden Gate, I should walk but I can't wait,*
       I can't wait to set it straight, I was shakin' but now I am making it fine, here in my mind.

C: *My heart will soar, with love that's rare and real, my smiling face will feel, ev'ry cloud.*
       And higher still, beyond the blue, until I know I can, like any man, reach out my hand and touch the face of God.

The first two A sections with their happy-go-lucky melody and harmony in D Major set up a light-hearted, carefree mood that supports the feel-good-everything's-just-fine lyrics perfectly. All's well – or so it seems (of course, there's the A–7, which intrudes as a pinprick of anxiety and foreboding). In the B section, we sense a change of inflection. The breezy, day-to-day routine gives way to introspective imagery. The protagonist introduces us to the fact that "he was searching high and low" and his quest for spirituality has finally come to an end because "now at last he knows". The music depicts the dichotomy of the physical and the spiritual by vacillating between diatonic and modal interchange sounds. The third A section marks the transition into the spiritual world. Though still rooted in the down-to-earth, easy-going air of the first two A sections, the words now take on a figurative, if not meta-physical, meaning. The Golden Gate Bridge as a metaphor for the gates of heaven, added to by the underlying urgency of the lyrics, leave no room for doubt – here's a man who has found his true vocation and "can't wait to set it straight".

In the C section, both the music and the lyrics are on the move. The melody arches up, up and away, the chord progression (cycle-of-fifths movement), the harmonic rhythm (one-bar harmonic pulse) and the modulations add to the excitement. The melody soars higher "and higher still" to the words "I know I can, like any man, reach out my hand and touch the face of …" until it finally reaches its climax on the key word "God", strongly emphasised by the unexpected modulation back to D Major. The song has gone full circle. Our protagonist has returned to the point of origin on his road to enlightenment as a changed man and now resumes his everyday life on a higher plane of awareness.

It doesn't get much kitschier than this – but, from a compositional point of view, the tune is sublime. Music and words are in perfect symbiosis. Personally, the sugar-coated lyrics make me cringe. However, speaking as a composer, I have to concede the fact that this is great stuff. Analysis is mainly about how and why things are done, and you have to acknowledge quality, even if you don't like the tune or can't empathise with its message. Personal likes or dislikes aside, "Mornin'" is an ingeniously crafted piece of music. After all, there must be a reason why this tune made the top ten of the US R&B charts in '83 for several weeks.

"Maiden Voyage"

This composition by Herbie Hancock is the title track of the album "Maiden Voyage" (1965), one of the key recordings from the 1960s. Joachim Ernst Berendt, a renowned German Jazz journalist and producer, has praised this album as one of the all-time masterpieces not only of Jazz but of music history as a whole, comparable to works such as *La Mer* by Claude Debussy. However, "Maiden Voyage" is not only a monument to musical creativity and compositional as well as improvisational prowess, it is also a concept album that paints alluring pictures, evoking the mysteries of the ocean and portraying the ebb and flow of the sea. As Herbie Hancock puts it poetically in the original liner notes: "This music attempts to capture its vastness and majesty, the splendor of a sea-going vessel on its maiden voyage, the graceful beauty of the playful dolphins, the constant struggle for survival of even the tiniest sea creatures, and the awesome destructive power of the hurricane, nemesis of seamen." To me, the composition "Maiden Voyage", with its sparse melody and wistful long notes, has always conveyed a mesmerising feeling of endless space and yearning. It's one of those tunes that never seem to lose their appeal.

So, let's break the poetic spell and get down to business. Here's the lead sheet:

D.C. al Fine

The formal structure is straightforward – a 32-bar AABA format subdivided into four eight-bar phrases. From a harmonic point of view, though, this composition is unusual for its time. It consists mainly of shifted 7(sus4) chords and Mixolydian soundscapes. The only exception is the Db–6 chord (Dorian) at the end of the B section. The change of colour from a more complacent and bright Mixolydian environment to the darker and more agitated sound of Db Dorian marks the climax of the piece. There are no functional relationships between the individual chords. So we can say the tune modulates every four bars (direct modulations):

"Maiden Voyage" is a typical example of the early modal era in Jazz. Utilising the terminology that was introduced in the chapter "Modal Interchange", the A section is clearly polytonal/unimodal (D Mixolydian / F Mixolydian) and the B section is polytonal/polymodal (Eb Mixolydian / Db Dorian). However, the use of overblown terms doesn't make a tune special, even if, for the more theoretically minded, these are labels you might want to use. What makes this piece truly remarkable and innovative is its harmony. The chord progression does not follow functional considerations. It lacks a clear tonal centre, although we could interpret D as the main point of reference, since the root movement (D-F-Eb-Db-D) can be analysed – in the broadest sense of the word – as an elongated chromatic approach pattern, which defines the overall structure of the composition. "Maiden Voyage" is a prime example of thinking outside of the box. By circumventing traditional functional expectations and substituting them with a modal and structural approach, Herbie Hancock has come up with a tune that transcends tonal conventions and introduces a new take on harmonic thinking.

The accompanying ostinato (repeated pattern) in the rhythm section that pervades the entire recording is particularly appealing. It is proof that Herbie Hancock spent time studying the music of Olivier Messiaen, in particular his usage of non-retrogradable rhythms – patterns that read the same forwards and backwards (palindromes). Quite clearly a trademark of this composition, the ostinato gives the recording its relaxed mood and serene character. Partly, this is due to the incredibly loose way the band interprets "time" (notably

Tony Williams on drums and Ron Carter on bass). Although the piece is played with an even eighth-note pulse, Tony Williams almost imperceptibly speeds up and slows down the tempo and, at times, even intimates a slight swing feel. There is an elastic ebb and flow to the pulse that aptly ties in with the swell and surge of the waves the tune aims to emulate. It is the rhythmic momentum combined with the transient nature of the Mixolydian scale and the floating quality of the 7(sus4) chord that give "Maiden Voyage" its sense of wide-open space and the impression of gliding on water. The composition effectively portrays what the title refers to: the description of a maiden voyage on open seas.

"Was that it?" you may ask. Well – sometimes things are not that mysterious after all. There is no need to make things more complicated than they actually are. Here we have a deceptively simple tune that is easy to understand (though perhaps not that easy to play), which has its merits more for reasons of its importance in the overall historical scheme of things. "Maiden Voyage" is what the title says – an early and persuasive venture into the uncharted waters of modal Jazz and therefore a must for any budding Jazz musician.

But, hold on, there is a very different way of looking at this composition. Once you feel comfortable playing around with parallel and relative modes, you're likely to stumble across new insights simply by changing the perspective. That said, here's a thought. Have a look at the B section. If you re-interpret D♭–6 Dorian as G♭7(sus4) Mixolydian, you'll realise that both scales contain the same notes. In a next step, look at the harmonic pattern E♭7(sus4) and G♭7(sus4). Obviously, the B section is simply a chromatic transposition of the A section: D7(sus4) - F7(sus4) to E♭7(sus4) - G♭7(sus4). Also consider the fact that a sus4 chord usually implies Mixolydian. However, it could also be interpreted as Dorian, since the third is not defined by the chord symbol (the sound could contain either 3 or ♭3). A 32-bar AABA tune where the A section is based on D and the B section on E♭ – does that remind you of anything? It should! See if you can make the connection before reading on.

The Jazz scene has always been a tight-knit community with musicians feeding off one another's ideas. You will find many compositions sharing similar, if not identical, character traits. It's not so much about blatantly copying material, but rather using certain aspects as inspirational influence. "Maiden Voyage" is a case in point (though, one of the less obvious ones). Same basic idea, different design – in essence, "Maiden Voyage" is a cleverly camouflaged take-off on "So What" by Miles Davis (see p. 175 ff.). A coincidence? I think not! I didn't give Herbie Hancock a call and ask for corroboration, so this train of thought is merely conjecture (and I don't think it's ever been mentioned in any other book on Jazz harmony and analysis). It may well be that Herbie Hancock initially wasn't aware of the correlation when composing "Maiden Voyage". However, this doesn't mean the connection isn't there. It could even be that he eventually realised the similarities and decided to substitute D♭–6 for G♭7(sus4) to throw people off. But, regardless of whether it was a subconscious or a deliberate choice of sounds, there is no denying the fact that "Maiden Voyage" and "So What" share an uncanny resemblance on a structural level.

This demonstrates two things. For one, even great minds copy, wittingly or unwittingly. However, unlike less creative people, they will adopt an idea and almost invariably transform it into something truly original. Secondly, analysis is about assumptions, interpreting clues, getting into the mind of the composer. Every analysis should be an exercise in creative thinking. Analysis is research, and research often leads to unexpected and surprising results. Sometimes, analysis unearths things about a composition even the composer isn't aware of. So, be sure to keep an open mind and learn to read between the lines.

The 7(sus4) chord

Because this composition was quick and easy to analyse, I would like to take the opportunity to talk about a basic chord type that I have neglected until now – *the 7(sus4) chord*. What I did mention at the beginning of this book is that, in Jazz, 7(sus4) chords are regarded and treated as independent sounds. In the majority of cases, the suspension of the fourth is not resolved to the third, as would be the case in Classical harmony. The suspension gives the 7sus(4) chord a floating, ambiguous quality. The scale choice would be Mixolydian, where the avoid note, in contrast to conventional dominant chords, is not the 4 but the 3 (the 4, after all, is a chord tone).

By taking the example of the 7(sus4) chord, I would like to show how a slight change in harmonic thinking can result in new variants in chord symbol notation and the discovery of interesting improvisational concepts. Traditional chord symbol notation is based on chords stacked in thirds (1-3-5-7-9-11-13). The basic structure of a chord (chord tones) is extended into the upper regions (tensions). Of course, we can include individual tensions in any chord symbol, e.g. D13 or D7(♯9/♯11), etc. However, it is quite popular in contemporary Jazz to go one step further by regrouping tensions and chord tones to form self-contained 3-note, 4-note or even 5-note chords commonly referred to as *upper structures* (see pdf-E, p. 18 ff.). These upper structures appear in chord symbol notation as new chords with the original root in the bass.

Let's take D7(sus4) as an example. Whereas the first three sounds in the table below correspond to the usual notation of a 7(sus4) chord with its typical Mixolydian extensions, the voicings that follow show different upper structure variants:

The symbol A–/D would also be an available upper structure. However, this voicing does not truly represent the sound of a 7(sus4) chord because the note G – precisely the 4 – is missing. However, it is actually quite common when working with upper structure triads or four-note chords that the resulting voicing need not necessarily contain every important note of the basic chord. By the way, it should now be clear why a 7(sus4) chord is often perceived as a subdominant function in a diatonic major context (see p. 91). If we consider D7(sus4) as V7(sus4) in G Major, then the upper structures Cmaj7 (IVmaj7) and A–7 (II–7) would both belong to the same functional group (subdominant).

Jazz musicians love to play around with 7(sus4) chords and their upper structures by combining them with other chord types, e.g. diminished voicings in order to create cadences with interesting chromatic resolutions. The following examples show how a D7(sus4) can be used as a starting point for the perfect cadence V-I in G Major:

By choosing a Lydian tonic sound in the last example, it is possible to represent Gmaj7(♯11) as A/G. You'll find a more detailed description of upper structure concepts in the chapters "Licks and Tricks" (p. 587 ff.) and "Voicings" (pdf-E).

How does all of this apply to "Maiden Voyage"? If you listen to Herbie Hancock's accompaniment closely, you will hear many voicings based on upper structures of D7(sus4) (e.g. Cmaj7/D or A–7/D in various inversions) and their transpositions to F Mixolydian and E♭ Mixolydian. The soloists make use of this technique, too. Let's have a look at George Coleman's improvisation. The following transcription is notated *8va* for the sake of legibility:

As you can see in this improvisation, the soloist now has two options: either to think in terms of the basic chord symbol and the corresponding scale or to focus on the available upper structures. The latter approach gives George Coleman the opportunity to use an upper structure in arpeggiated form as part of his lines. For example, Cmaj7/D and Dbmaj7/Eb arpeggios crop up time and again throughout the improvisation. It is also possible to use the upper structure as the point of reference for the corresponding choice of scales. For example, when thinking in terms of A–7/D or Cmaj7/D instead of D7(sus4), you could base your lines on A Dorian or C Lydian instead of D Mixolydian. Although all three scales contain the same notes, the change of perspective will result in different lines. In a second step, you could extract other groups of notes. If you have a close look at George Coleman's solo, you will discover that many of his lines in all three A sections are based on the A minor Pentatonic scale (A-C-D-E-G) – introducing yet another level of chord-scale substitution.

Most of the lines in George Coleman's solo are self-explanatory. In the first two A sections (and most of the last), I have not added any comments since he works with the Mixolydian scale exclusively. It is worth noting, though, that he often organises the scale material in leaps of fourths or fifths, intervals that lend themselves well to the sound and structure of a 7(sus4) chord. Observe the inspired transition to the B section (the last bar of A2) where the phrase in E Mixolydian chromatically links the preceding F7(sus4) to the ensuing E♭7(sus4). In the B section, the soloing concept switches to a more linear and chromatic concept (more of a Bebop approach). Chromatic passing notes and approach patterns are marked with an asterisk (*).

It's a beautiful and powerful solo: rhythmically open in the A sections, with a high energy level and a clear climax in the B section. George Coleman's control and the coherence and fluidity of his lines are superb. Even in the flurry of action (e.g. flying sixteenth notes in the B section), his lines feel laid-back and relaxed. With his smoky tenor sound, he exquisitely captures the mood of the theme and paraphrases the title of the tune. Just look at the transcription graphically – you can actually see the gentle wash of the waves in the rise and fall of the phrases.

Assignment

For further reading and consolidation of the material covered in the theory section of this book up to this point, I would ask you to turn to the following pdf-files:

pdf-A: Tuning Systems

pdf-B: Overview of Functions

pdf-C: The Girl From Ipanema (Analysis)

pdf-D: Blue In Green (Analysis)

pdf-E: Voicings

pdf-F: Harmonisation and Reharmonisation

pdf-G: Arranging 101

Listen

"Es hört doch jeder nur, was er versteht."
"People merely hear the things they comprehend."

Johann Wolfgang von Goethe

Ear Training – a Musician's Nightmare

Ear Training! There is nothing more important to a musician than a pair of good ears. At the same time, there is no greater source of frustration, annoyance, insecurity and, yes, even fear. Ask my students – and, mind you, I am not a teacher who thrives on the discomfort of his protégées. Why is ear training so intimidating? The answer is quite simple. Every Jazz musician, no matter at what level, knows deep down inside that without a highly developed ear he or she will never stand a chance of surviving even the simplest of musical challenges as an improviser. No other idiom demands as acute and sophisticated an ear as Jazz. To be able to interact with the other musicians in an ensemble or to produce more than just haphazard improvisations requires the clearest possible perception of sound in the mind's ear – and the objective of ear training is to develop and establish this imaginative power. The more vivid the vocabulary musicians can draw on for their music, the more articulate their ideas and the more comprehensible their solos will be – a limited supply of mental images results in limited performance. Most of you will probably admit, albeit reluctantly, that your ears have a formidable amount of catching-up to do (it's the exception that proves the rule).

The ear is our gateway to music, the interface between our innermost, imaginative world and the reality of sound. Hearing is the most important of the five senses for musicians. Ears are their antennae, the connection between ideas and the fingers. It is the purpose of ear training to nurture and cultivate this bond and, in doing so, to interlink sounds, feelings, concepts, symbols and the instrument, to train the musical memory and to turn the ear into an organ with the ability to experience, comprehend, evaluate and control:

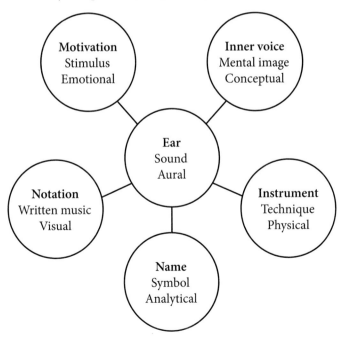

Ideally, every sound should…

- …have a personal and emotional meaning.

- …evoke an image in your mind.

- …trigger a motor reflex on your instrument.

- …be linked to a visual representation of the music (e.g. notation or symbol).

- …be understood theoretically (structure and function).

And this is exactly where the problem lies. Only rarely are sounds truly and securely anchored in all these ways, and ear training exposes our shortcomings mercilessly. Accordingly, the potential for frustration is enormous and a feeling of unease accompanying this issue all too common. It is not pleasant to be reminded of one's own deficiencies over and over again. Before we turn to the actual exercises, I'd like to outline some of the psychological pitfalls that have contributed to the tarnished image of ear training, give some advice on how to avoid them and present a few ideas that will help you approach the matter with more confidence.

Ear training is no fun because …
… we have to switch from hearing to listening

The English language provides us with a distinction that is paramount to the following discussion: the difference between "hearing" and "listening". "Hearing" implies the intuitive, receptive, assimilating, passive perception of music. In contrast, the term "listening" describes taking an active part in a conscious, questioning, searching process by "reaching" into the music with an inquisitive ear. The fundamental objective of ear training is to turn "hearing" musicians into "listening" ones.

For this to happen, you need not only to be able to "feel" music but also to "think" it. This is not a contradiction. It is possible to "switch on" the mind voluntarily and likewise, as a matter of course, to slip back into the unencumbered role of the "hearer". Naturally, I wouldn't want you to lose the ability to appreciate music free of theoretical deliberation (both as players and listeners). But I would like you all to approach music analytically with just as much enjoyment. It can be highly gratifying to consciously delve into a sound, to immerse yourselves in music with a probing mind, to penetrate a sound and to decipher it layer by layer – without experiencing this intellectual process as an obstacle that stands in the way of your emotional perception or aesthetic inclinations. Theory is not a straightjacket. Analysis won't stifle your sensitivity or creativity. If anything, theoretical knowledge will make you aware of things you didn't even know existed. Understanding how music works and why you react to it the way you do will make your listening ears so much more astute. Eventually, you will realise that it is quite possible to alternate between these two mindsets – hearing and listening – at command, that they are not adversaries but two sides of the same coin, which indeed enhance each other.

It is exactly this basic necessity of being able to switch the mind on and off, which many musicians regard with apprehension. Not entirely without reason, they are afraid that the enjoyment of music spoils when you dwell on it theoretically. Students often ask me if I am still able to experience music unimpeded by analytical thought. Now, that's a stupid question, with all due respect. Of course I am! I don't go to concerts or listen to CDs and immediately analyse what I am hearing. Needless to say, I can lose myself in the music, absorb its beauty and energy and set myself adrift emotionally. But when I hear something that intrigues me, something I don't understand, my curiosity compels me to figure out how it works. And then, not necessarily at that very moment, I will try to find out what it was that impressed me.

I am fully aware that conscious listening can take away the magic and the mystery in music. To comprehend something means making it accessible and manageable and that may result in the loss of its appeal. For those of you who don't share the pragmatism of professional musicians, it may be difficult to defer the pleasure of uncritical "hearing" for the purpose of an analytical investigation of music. However, experience shows that only once you understand what excites you, and you use this newly gained understanding to expand on and improve what you already know, will your repertory of sounds evolve and mature. And, the more you know, the easier it will be to overcome any musical hang-ups you may have.

At some point you will realise that understanding a sound can even augment the enjoyment of it, that by figuring out its structure and meaning it has become a close friend. There is such a thing as the "eroticism of awareness", a feeling that is deeply rooted in the pleasure you derive from "being part of the game". Knowledge is sexy! It is a very satisfying feeling to be able to say "Yeah! – I know what that is, *I've got it!*" And it is even more satisfying when you can eventually say "Yeah! – I've got it, and now *I know how to use it!*"

Ear training is no fun because ...
... our ear needs more attention than our instrument

Another pitfall is the widespread discrepancy between listening skills and instrumental proficiency. It is a fact that most music students spend more time on their instrument than on ear training. As a result, their technique improves while the ear progressively lags behind. At the risk of being unfair, I'll assume that you're no different, although you may be reluctant to admit it. Don't get me wrong. I'm not trying to pour on the blame because, on the whole, it's not your fault. The problem lies in the way an instrument is traditionally taught. Understandably, in music lessons, the instrument is the centre of attention. It has to be because, in the end, we need good technique, especially if we are aiming to be an improviser. Without the necessary instrumental expertise, we will not be able to express our musical ideas. However, what good is the finest technique if we only have little to say?

Ideally, teaching music should concern itself not only with turning out good instrumentalists. Seen holistically, the main objective should be to train *musicians*. Do you remember your first lessons on your instrument? Chances are high that you started out by working through the usual etudes, the traditional Classical repertoire, technical exercises, etc. Even if you were lucky enough to find a teacher with a broad stylistic background, I'm convinced that you did not spend much time, if any, on the content of the music, the way it works, theory, ear training, composition, improvisation, music appreciation, etc. Many teachers are out of their depth when it comes to providing more than just the essential instrumental training. It may be that they just don't know any better because they did not have the opportunity to experience a comprehensive musical education themselves. I suspect, though, that the reason is far more mundane. It requires an enormous amount of effort on behalf of the teacher to go beyond the beaten track of the average instrumental program. I'm not suggesting that all teachers are lazy. I do know, however, that many don't teach for the love of it but rather for lack of better choice or simply for the money. Very few go out of their way when it comes to spending time and energy on a stimulating, multi-faceted and personalised teaching program. Unfortunately, there are not that many dedicated teachers and textbooks that encourage creative teaching with the goal of providing a comprehensive perspective. Ultimately, our musical awareness should not be aligned only to the possibilities and limitations of our instrument. Wouldn't it be so much more rewarding to get to know music in the broadest possible sense – from nursery rhymes to Free Jazz, from Bebop solos to Indian *ragas*, etc.? Wouldn't it be great to incorporate all of this into a personal ear-training program and eventually transfer whatever strikes our fancy to our instruments? There's a world of music out there to discover and choose from!

I have met musicians who have mastered their instruments to perfection. Sadly, I have also discovered those among them who have cultivated lightning-like technique as an end in itself, who use this technique as a substitute for musical substance – quite a successful strategy, as can often be observed at concerts. You can get away with murder if you have outstanding technique. Most audiences are easily impressed and bedazzled by technical fireworks. However, I'm sure you agree that it should always be an improviser's intention to control the instrument with his or her musical imagination, rather than allowing the instrument and its particular technical aspects to determine musical content. The instrument should never be a means to an end. It is a tool that comes to life only if you've got something to say.

Many musicians don't notice until very late that their fingers have developed while their ears have stagnated. The moment of truth comes with ear training, and that's often quite a sobering experience. I am convinced that each and every one of you know perfectly well whether you can truly visualise what you want to play in advance or whether you're faking your way through things with the help of rote-learned fingerings and patterns or grandstand razzle-dazzle. It might be possible to hide behind an instrument for a while. The ear will eventually catch you with your pants down. So, don't let your ear and your instrument drift apart too far. The more your ears fall behind your instrumental technique, the harder it will be to bridge the gap. It's psychologically challenging having to work on baby stuff when it comes to ear training, while having breakneck chops to successfully cover up your inadequacies. Consequently, ear training should be right up there at the top of the list of your practice routine from day one.

Ear training is no fun because ...
... our brain works much faster than our ear

Over the course of the past hundred years, Jazz has evolved from an unpretentious form of Folk music into a carefully considered art form steeped in abstraction and sophistication. It is taught in schools and universities, hacked to pieces theoretically, digested in books, minced and puréed – in the true sense of the word, it has been "denatured" academically. Jazz, if you will, has lost its innocence. In compressed form, the personal development of a

Jazz musician happens in a similar way. We all start out as naïve, emotion-driven kids. Fun, groove and energy, playing with other musicians, staying up late and hanging with the guys, etc. is what it's all about. At that stage, theoretical knowledge is not a high priority. At some point, however, we start working more intensively on our music, buy books and get increasingly involved with learning theory. And, as we stuff our heads with new terms and concepts, we gradually lose our natural approach without our noticing it.

Today, Jazz musicians are well versed and immersed in theory. What they tend to forget is that the ear, too, starts out as a naïve, unrefined organ that has to be trained like a muscle. The ear needs a lot of time to store sounds and to make sense of them. In contrast, the mind grasps difficult concepts far more quickly. Consequently, the danger of becoming bogged down in a theoretical quagmire without giving the ear the necessary time to catch up with what the mind has already digested is all too likely. It's so easy to wrap your brain around a theoretical fact in a few minutes, but it takes our ears weeks, if not months or years, to grasp and assimilate the same thing as a mental image of the corresponding sound. Time and time again, I meet participants at my workshops who can hardly put three notes together on their instruments, who can't tell the difference between major and minor or even semitones and whole tones by ear, but who are able to juggle the most complicated theoretical concepts. They may understand a theoretical fact on an intellectual level, but not in terms of its aural equivalent. Speaking as a music and theory teacher, I am fully aware of this problem and try to counteract it daily by trying to balance theoretical input and practical application every step of the way.

Ideally, the ear and our theoretical knowledge should develop in sync. Fact is, however, that our ears usually lag miles behind. Ear training makes us painfully aware of this discrepancy. In the end, it's hard to accept that the ear is still scuffling with basics, while our brain has moved on to more exciting things. I know that it is not pleasant having to backpedal and curb our ambitions in order to enable our ears to catch up with the intellect. Who wants to work on things such as, say, "Baa, Baa Black Sheep" while grappling with "Giant Steps"? Please don't take this as a reprimand, but rather as a warning. Since a large proportion of the current Jazz repertoire requires a certain amount of theoretical background, you can no longer rely on the intuitive ear alone. If you want to make progress, you have to ensure that the ear has a chance of keeping up.

Ear training is no fun because ...
... we often want to play music our ear is not yet ready for

Another reason for the dysfunctional relationship many musicians have with ear training is the gap between expectation and reality. We hear a musician and say: "Wow! I'd like to play like that!" What we overlook is the fact that we are listening to musicians who have developed incrementally over years and years of painstaking hard work. It would be foolish to believe that anyone could simply skip these intermediate steps. It would be like wanting to do your driver's licence in a Formula One car. Our role models often entice us to get on board at much too high a level. Let's be realistic: In most cases, what we would like to do and what we are capable of is simply not the same thing. I'm not suggesting that we should work our way through the entire traditional repertoire or become a Bebop player before we can be

permitted to expose ourselves to contemporary Jazz. I do believe, however, in the importance of a solid base – no building can stand if not built on firm ground. Quotes by musicians
such as David Liebman emphasise that concentrating first on the basics is imperative: "One
has to walk before running. Without a firm knowledge of scales and chords, new concepts
lack foundation".

In this book, I would have loved to introduce you to the music of Vijay Iyer, Kurt Rosen-
winkel, Chris Potter, Brad Mehldau, etc. or the millennials who are shaking up the Jazz
world as I write. It wouldn't have gotten me (and you, for that matter) very far. We have to
take a step back, to the likes of Michael Brecker, Richie Beirach, Bob Berg, Herbie Hancock,
John Abercrombie or Kenny Garrett (to name just a few) – the intermediate generation that
shaped the transition from traditional to contemporary Jazz, which, in turn, was preceded
by several generations of genre-defining Jazz greats: Charlie Parker, John Coltrane, Miles
Davis, Thelonious Monk, Bill Evans, Charles Mingus, Duke Ellington, Louis Armstrong, etc.
In some way or the other, every aspiring Jazz musician is rooted in history. Contemporary
trends don't pop up out of nowhere. They are the result of an ongoing process. We are talking
about evolution rather than revolution – that's what counts in music. Even those musicians
who rebel against tradition need something to rebel against and, ultimately, define themselves in terms of music history in that they reject customs and conventions established over
long periods of time.

Those who involve themselves seriously in Jazz will quickly notice that their idols themselves have their own heroes. When we study music (and I'm not talking only about studying
music at college), we have to accept the fact that in order to understand today's music we
have to go back in history. It is not necessary to go as far as trumpeter Wynton Marsalis and
his "Lincoln Centre Jazz Orchestra". Marsalis, who advocates the "doctrine of true Jazz", has
committed himself to the rigorous and, sadly, rather dogmatic research into his musical
provenance and the history of Jazz. To my mind, he's missing the point by overshooting the
target. Nevertheless, his approach is essentially correct.

For this reason, I would advocate starting off by taking small bites. Give your ears the
chance to grow. Try to retrace the evolutionary steps that led to where you are now without
losing sight of your musical goals and desires. Learn by "looking back". Study the masters
and don't allow yourself to be irritated if you end up in places that seem old-fashioned from
a present-day perspective. I know from experience that it takes a lot of effort to work on
repertoire that doesn't quite match what you'd really like to do. But, believe me, it's good for
your ears!

Ear training is no fun because ...
... we'd rather "do" than "think"

I often come across students who don't even try to hide their disdain for ear training, a topic
they consider to be no more than a petty annoyance, a temporary distraction from the really
important matter of working on their instrument. Particularly among Classical musicians, I
know many great players who make little more than a cursory effort to understand what
they're playing. One explanation for this might be the separation of the roles of the composer
and the performing musician – a development that took place in the late 19th century. While

composers concern themselves with the "what", the musical substance and the underlying concepts, performers focus on the "how", the interpretation and execution of the written music. Sadly, this segregation perseveres as I type these words, perpetuated by music colleges and conservatories with their specialised performance programs.

The pianist Friedrich Gulda spoke out provocatively but refreshingly on this topic in an interview with the German magazine *ZEIT* on 2 June 1989: "… I do not regard pianists who don't compose themselves to be musicians in the true sense of the word. Time and time again, they simply play brilliantly constructed music by other people, most of them long-gone. I regard the separation of performer and composer to be a sign of degeneration originating in the 19th century. Fortunately, with the appearance of Jazz, this evolutionary mishap has come to an end …"

Friedrich Gulda was one of the most brilliant piano players of the 20th century, a colourful, highly controversial, eccentric personality and an *enfant terrible* not only of the Classical circuit. Most famous for his Beethoven and Mozart interpretations, landmarks of Classical music, he was also a composer who moved on into Jazz at an early age. He went through a phase where he focussed on free improvisation, eventually teaming up with Chick Corea and appearing at New York's Birdland as well as at the Newport Jazz Festival. In Jazz, he found "the rhythmic drive, the risk, the absolute contrast to the pale, academic approach I had been taught".

I agree wholeheartedly with Friedrich Gulda's assessment. Until well into the 20th century, most composers were highly proficient instrumentalists and performers. More importantly, many of the great performers were also brilliant improvisers. The clearest indication of this lies in what is referred to as the **concerto cadenza**, in which the soloist is called to play at the end of a movement in order to demonstrate both virtuosity and creativity in terms of the thematic material of the composition. Originally, concerto cadenzas were improvised. Later on, many musicians began composing their cadenzas, avoiding the potential hazards of improvisation. This tradition has all but disappeared. Today, composers write cadenzas for performers! There are only few Classical musicians who write their own cadenzas or dare venture onto the thin ice of improvisation. It is generally accepted in Classical music that composers don't play and performers don't compose or improvise.

As a result, the player has become an accessory to the composer and is concerned only perfunctorily with an understanding of the music. Perfection of performance is paramount – and that is hard work enough in itself. So why burden the ear or the mind with seemingly dispensable insights into the structural make-up of compositions? It is this attitude that relegates the subjects of ear training and music theory to the status of third-rate areas of study. I have found that many Classical students regard ear training as a tedious curricular duty, to be ticked off the list as soon as possible. It is often treated like the proverbial stepmother by members of the faculty, as a dead-turkey subject and a nuisance that infringes on the vitally important work of the instrumental teachers (as always, the exception proves the rule).

In Jazz, this is less of a problem. As an improviser, you are performer and composer in one. Improvisation can only be successful with a lucid concept of sound and an understanding of the formal, rhythmic, harmonic and melodic content of a piece. Sooner or later, every Jazz musician will inevitably have to grapple with theory and ear training. However, even in Jazz, we find a certain reticence. Why is this? Jazz musicians define themselves primarily through their playing! Theoretical considerations are seen as a necessity. However, it's just so much more fun to *do* something than to think about it. This is why many Jazz musicians are reluctant to invest time in things that are theoretical, analytical and systematic. Make sure you always allot a substantial part of your practice program to ear training, transcription and analysis. Last, but not least, write your own music!!! There is hardly a more effective way to train the ear.

Ear training is no fun because ...
... we don't know how to do it

Even educators rarely seem to know what the subject of ear training really encompasses and how it should be taught. What do we actually have to practice in order to improve noticeably? At music colleges and conservatories, ear training has a long-standing tradition. One would like to think that the experience gained over many decades or even centuries would have brought forth an effective and up-to-date methodology. Regrettably, there are still many teachers out there who have a terribly old-fashioned notion of this intrinsically exciting subject.

The big question is: Should we learn by induction or rather by deduction? Traditional ear training works through the process of *induction* (the inference of general rule from particular instances = from the small to the large). This is based on the assumption that you must first master smaller building blocks before you can grasp the greater picture. Unfortunately, even today, there is a widely spread methodological approach focussing on training abstract musical elements and smallest units (the single interval, the individual chord, the isolated cadence, etc.). Nothing much happens beyond the elementary training of intervals, rote learning of cadence formulae on the piano and melodic and rhythmic dictation. Sadly, such lessons are terribly uninspiring and ineffective.

I, too, suffered through this kind of "teaching" during my school years and, with hindsight, must say that I missed out on many things because of it. This approach is utter nonsense because it bypasses the essence of music. Musical perception is holistic. It doesn't start with details. Breaking down music and extracting individual constituent parts from a musical context thwarts our understanding of the bigger picture. Attempting to reduce music to single measurable bits fails to recognise that a listening experience is more than the sum of its quantifiable components. An isolated interval could hardly express a musical idea. Only within a melodic and harmonic context will it have any meaning. For this reason, ear training should rather focus on real music and occur through a process of *deduction* (the inference of the particular by reference to a general rule or principle = from the large to the small)! This is why I always ask you to consider the form as your first step of an analysis. Conscious examination of details only makes sense at a later stage.

Abstract exercises on the piano – another relic of the past – are an even greater abomination. I'm sure you've experienced teachers pounding away at the piano saying "This is a perfect fifth, this is a perfect fifth, this is a perfect fifth …!", hoping that mantra-like repetition will instill enlightenment. This approach won't get you very far. What does determining isolated intervals or chords have to do with real music? These types of exercises can supplement the learning process but never develop an awareness of musical context. Musical reality is far too multi-dimensional and multi-faceted to be reduced to the sound of a single interval or the abstraction of a triad torn from its natural environment. Besides, an individual sound identified on the piano is usually miles away from the many situations in which the same sound could appear in practice (imagine, for example, trying to identify a voicing you initially worked out on the piano now played by a horn section with a rhythm section banging away!).

It should now be clear that many traditional methods used in ear training are outdated. Let's go back to our initial question: What do we need to do to improve our listening skills? My experience shows that *ear training can neither be taught nor learned!* This is no joke and certainly more than just a provocative statement. Since every musician has a unique background as well as different tastes and preferences, attempting to find a single, generally applicable approach to teaching ear training is doomed to failure. Of course, there are objectives and criteria that are equally valid and important to all musicians. However, the route each individual takes will have to be highly personalised. Nobody experiences sound the same way. For this reason, teaching and learning ear training has to be different for each and every one of us.

Conclusion: You have to develop your own ear training program and listening strategies. Always work with the materials you feel closest to. Go to your CD collection, start with the recordings you are most familiar with, spend time with the ones you like best. Many of these are already firmly implanted in your memory. Consciously examine them (melody, harmony, rhythm, form, phrasing, etc.) and learn to understand the principles that govern your favourite compositions and improvisations. Use books, tutorials, ear training software, etc., but use them only as a supplement. It's your personal world of music that should define and direct your practice routine. The following chapters will help you along the way.

Ear training is no fun because ...
... it's easier to rely on written music than to trust our ear

Human beings are predominantly visual creatures. We rely on our eyes for almost everything we do. Scientific studies prove that the eye is the "default" sense our brain falls back on as the "sense of last resort" in critical situations. Even our language says this: "keep an eye on this", "develop an eye for that", "something meets the eye", etc. The written word is often easier to remember than the spoken word. This surely explains why so many musicians panic as soon as you take away their lead sheets or parts. They have little faith in their ears and cling to written music for visual support. However, the more we rely on written music, the more we lose the ability to learn pieces off by heart, to memorise sounds and access them in our mind, and the more our musical imagination withers through lack of use.

Working on ear training makes it painfully evident just how much we rely on the visual stimulus of written music and how little we can trust our musical memory – not an altogether pleasant experience. One of the main objectives of ear training is to wean us from relying on our eyes and to immerse us in the insecure world of listening. So, get rid of your visual crutches, throw away your sheet music, close your eyes and start trusting your ears. There's none so blind as those who will not listen (Neil Gaiman)!

Ear training is no fun because ...
... it's hard work

Ear training (ear straining?) is an extremely tough business. It is hard to measure progress and success. The development of the ear happens incrementally and unpredictably. Only comparisons made over many months or even years show that we have improved. Without really knowing how and when it happened, we suddenly realise: "Hey, this is easy! Why couldn't I do this before?" Besides, the ear's proficiency depends strongly on our daily ups and downs. What we can do well today seems to have evaporated tomorrow. Hearing is a fragile sense on which we can't always fully rely. We might feel comfortable with a particular sound, but if we come across the same thing in a different context, we don't recognise it all. This means we'll often have to reassess things we thought were perfectly clear.

Simply said, we need to work on our listening skills with relish. The ear and the brain need to be challenged persistently in order for them to prosper. Now, please don't get the impression that you have to do ear training exercises every single day. It's hard enough to get through the many other things we need to work on without having to add something as tedious as this. Of course there are – as we will see a little later – exercises that you should do regularly. However, I'm sure it will come as a relief to know that things are actually quite simple: No matter what you do, it will contribute to cultivating your listening skills – ***provided you do it consciously and deliberately!*** It's not about following a specific routine. The objective is simply to soak up sound with an alert and questioning mind. Whatever you do, whether you sing a song, practise your instrument, learn a new piece, go to a concert, listen to a recording or play a rehearsal – as long as you turn on your brain and try to figure out how the music works while doing it, it will help you on your way to a pair of great ears. And then you will realise that ***ear training is fun!***

The Inner Voice

The idea, the musical intention, comes first. Then, in a second step, we attempt to realise this musical objective on our instrument. We should never forget that **our brain is the actual instrument**. The instrument we play is merely a means to an end, the intermediary and extension of our personality – it is the mouthpiece of our thoughts and our soul. We will only develop an authentic and expressive musical language if we have established this flow from the "inner" to the "outer" world. This means that a vital part of ear training is to work on your imaginative powers – your *"inner voice"*. Ideally, this inner voice should drive everything you intend to express on your saxophone, piano or drum set. Your imagination must control your instrument – not the other way around! Comprehensive ear training will help you experience, research, develop, expand and consolidate your musical awareness on both the emotional and intuitive side as well as on an intellectual level, ultimately giving you the ability to realise your very personal sound on your own instrument.

> *"You really have to practise the coordination between the mind and the fingers, the ideas and the body. You have to practise finding the ideas on your horn, getting there at the same time the idea comes into your head. It's a matter of developing instant touch."*

> ## Art Farmer

> *"As a musician I can actually hear the note I create because I imagine it first."*

> ## Percussionist Evelyn Glennie
> (who is almost completely deaf!)

Back to the roots

The first thing I'd like to do is draw your attention to the sounds you have been carrying around inside ever since you were a child. It is a fact that we learn best by merging the new with the old, that we can more easily integrate something new if we establish a connection with what we already know. So, once you understand what you're familiar with, you will be able to grasp new concepts and sounds more easily. This means coming to terms with your "roots". You can't ignore them, even if your tastes have changed over the years. Whether you like it or not, they are firmly anchored in your subconscious. They comprise your musical point of reference, your starting point.

Assignment

Write down the following from memory without the help of your instrument:

- the opening interval of the signature tune of your favourite TV series (starting on C);
- the melody of "Happy Birthday" (in F);
- the rhythmical pattern from Maurice Ravel's "Bolero";
- the chord progression of "Silent Night" in chord symbols (in G);
- the formal structure of "Yesterday" by the Beatles (only the basic subdivision into different sections and the number of bars in each section).

If you happen to be unfamiliar with any one of these examples (something I find hard to believe considering the worldwide popularity of these themes), choose something with which you feel more comfortable. It's not that these particular examples are important. It's more about accessing sounds you've known by heart for years without ever having consciously thought about them, sounds you can conjure up in your mind without having to refer to a recording or your instrument. How many times have you droned along to the tune of "Happy Birthday" at parties? And even if you've only heard the "Bolero" once, its two-bar rhythmic pattern was literally drummed into your head 169 times (!) in a row. Surely, this should be enough to learn it off by heart if you had only listened with a probing mind. "Yesterday" is the most frequently played piece by the Beatles – so I'm assuming that most people will know it. Nevertheless, these sounds don't appear to be quite so familiar when we try to write them down (you'll find the answers in the solutions folder). Make sure that this exercise becomes a permanent part of your practice routine. There are many good old friends stashed away in your memory just waiting to be rediscovered.

Sing, sing, sing

I believe that singing is the most personal form of musical expression. It is the direct link to your inner world of sound. Whatever you can sing is indelibly imprinted on your memory and a permanent part of your inner voice. Singing is the ultimate proof that you are in full control of your musical imagination. And every sound you evoke inside, will, in time, find its way out onto your instrument. It is my experience that all (!) musicians who love to sing and are consciously aware of what they sing not only have a quick and adroit ear – they are also the more creative and tasteful musicians (the trumpet player and singer Chet Baker is a prime example).

Your voice is the instrument you're born with. You always have it at your disposal, and you will carry it around with you until you die. By using your voice, you can practise anywhere, anytime. If you're looking for good ears, then you have to sing, sing, sing… I know that some of you firmly believe they can't sing – and you're not alone. Most adults find singing quite daunting. Some think they have a bad voice. Others simply lack confidence. Some are happy to sing in private but are terrified of having to sing in front of an audience. Others claim they can't sing in tune, and so on, and so on… There is no limit to the excuses people will make just to avoid singing – something that came so naturally and spontaneously to us as children.

So, the first thing to do is come to terms with your voice. Don't feel intimidated. You don't need a great voice – just a can-do attitude, a positive mindset and determination. The main thing is to sing with enthusiasm. Sing whenever and wherever you can – at home, in the car, in the shower. Sing out loud, and don't worry about other people giving you the evil eye. With time, you will overcome your reluctance to sing and get over any reservations you may have about your voice.

I'm convinced that what we sing is often closer to our inner voice than what we play. All too often, our ideas are inhibited by the nature of our instrument and its technical demands. The instrument tends to define what is musically feasible. It often infringes on our imagination and interferes with the flow of our inner voice. I have met students who could sing beautiful lines, none of which could be found in their playing – their inspirations and aspirations strangled by technical inadequacies and compromised by mechanically rote-learned fingerings. For example, there are many guitarists out there who resort to pentatonic scale patterns exclusively in their solos – not because that is what their inner voice tells them to do, but simply because those licks are easy to play. Conclusion: You have to find ways to practise away from your instrument. And that means singing!

While singing, you can assess whether a melodic line is as clearly established and tangible as you would like it to be. Any slip of the voice or missed note, any problem with intonation immediately tells you: "I only have a vague idea of what this phrase should sound like". The more we sing, the clearer our musical ideas will become. What we can sing is firmly anchored in our musical memory. If we learn to play like we sing, our music will always come from within and sound authentic.

Of course, you can't do without an instrument. Especially in the early stages, when ear training still holds more threats than thrills, you need a safe way of checking up on what you're doing while practising. It makes good sense to use a piano or keyboard at first because you won't have to struggle with intonation problems. As you get more confident and your hearing becomes more acute, you can begin to rely on an instrument that doesn't have fixed tuning.

Vocal range

The first thing to do is establish your personal vocal range. Start with what is referred to as the *modal register* or *chest voice* (colloquial) – the register used in normal speech and most singing, also called the *tessitura* (the most comfortable range for a singer). Ascend and descend chromatically without straining and make a note of your lower and upper limits. These will naturally change with practice. Don't forget to check out your high vocal range, known as the *falsetto register* or *head voice* (colloquial), and the transition from modal voice to *falsetto* (you will feel your voice switching from a "chesty" to an "airy" quality). Additionally, factors such as the time of day or how we feel will influence our voice. For this reason, it's not that easy to establish an exact vocal range. The high range can vary considerably, while the bottom cut-off is usually less open to change. Most people have a range of about one and a half octaves (trained singers, of course, have wider ranges):

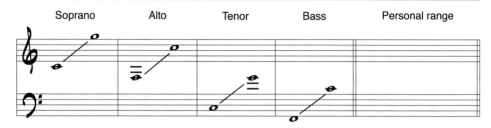

Untrained singers often tell me that they can't sing something because it is too high. Of course, there are limits, and we don't want to ruin our voices. My experience shows, though, that this problem has less to do with the voice itself and more with the lack of a clear musical imagination. Even melodies with a wide range and many leaps are no problem if you can truly visualise the notes you're reaching for in your mind. It's quite simple: If you can hear a line inside, you can sing it. Of course, you may have to stretch to hit a high note. But, if you have a clear picture of it in your mind's ear, you can almost always reach it by using the *falsetto* range. If necessary, transpose it down one octave to a more comfortable register.

My work with music students over the years has led me to the conclusion that a good ear is – amongst other things – influenced by two important factors: our personal vocal range and the range of our instrument. We hear best within the frequency range we're most familiar with. I have observed that most people hear well in the middle register (where most of our voices are located). The same is true for ranges we experience every day on our instruments (e.g. bassists hear well in the lower register, flute players feel more comfortable in the upper register, and so on). Conversely, the frequency ranges we are not consciously aware of can sometimes be like uncharted territory. We must be able to hear equally well in all frequency ranges.

Assignment

Select several recordings from your CD collection (different styles and instrumentations). However, instead of listening to the sound as a whole, try focussing on different layers and registers (including the extreme high and low parts of the sound). Concentrate on each instrument separately and try following it exclusively for some time without letting yourself become distracted by the other parts.

Silent singing

Singing in your head is a great way to train the ear. Here are a few preliminary exercises to become acquainted with the concept:

- Choose any note in the lower part of your vocal range and sing a Major scale upwards. Gradually change to *falsetto*. Try to get as high as you can without straining (sing softly). When you reach the point where you feel you can't go any higher, stop singing aloud but continue in your head (for at least another two octaves). Concentrate on the notes you hear in your mind and try not to let them slip away. If this exercise is too abstract because you can't visualize the sound of your voice beyond its actual range, then substitute it with an instrument you might have heard in the high register (e.g. a flute or violin). The goal is to extend the range of your perception and to have a vivid, tangible notion of every note in your head. Now do the opposite, using a descending Major scale (choose a trombone or a bass in your imaginary low register).

- Next, start the exercise really low or high (way beyond your vocal range) and silent-sing the notes of the Major scale, moving through your vocal range, without actually singing. This exercise can encompass 5 octaves or more. Then, repeat the exercise and silent-sing a maj7 arpeggio. Apply this exercise to other scales or arpeggios.

- Finally, choose melodies you know by heart and run them through your head. Silent-sing in time. Don't be sloppy. Make sure you can hear every note clearly and check your intonation on the piano every now and then. Even though you are not singing aloud, pitch control is important.

Internalising notes

Let's start with a few preparatory exercises:

- Play any note on the piano *within* your vocal range (short attack, no sustain). Give your ear some time to "lock in" and internalise the note. Then sing the note on "ooh" or "aah". Make an effort to sing in tune – don't let your voice wobble or slip. Concentrate on holding the note. Gradually speed up this exercise until singing back the note you have just played becomes an automatic response.

- Alternating with the above exercise, select a note outside of your vocal range (significantly higher or lower). Trying to sing the actual pitch obviously makes no sense (don't strain!). You have to rethink the note – transpose it internally – before you can sing it. If you have some difficulty with this, approach it step by step: Name the note you've just played, play the same note within your vocal range, sing it, hold it and play the original note once again. Do you hear the similarity?

Take particular care not to sing back low notes at the bottom of your range, which is what most people instinctively do. Sing the notes an octave higher. The higher you sing, the more in tune you will be. If you drone away in the lower range of your voice where the frequencies of two adjacent pitches are closer together, it will be more difficult to hit and hold the note. So, for example, always sing bass lines in your upper range.

Now apply the above exercises to real music. Play a recording and stop it randomly. Pick any component of the last sound you heard: e.g. the melody note, bass note or lead note of the piano voicing. Lock into it and memorise it. Don't make the mistake of wanting to sing it back immediately. Give your ear some time for the note to sink in. Wait until you can clearly visualise it in your mind. Only sing the note when you are absolutely sure you've got it. With a little practice, this will help you filter out individual notes from any sound, no matter how dense or busy the context might be. Expand this exercise to include not only single notes but also short sequences of notes and, eventually, longer melodic phrases.

Work regularly on these exercises, even if they appear to be simplistic and easy to do. It is important to speed up your reaction time. This will enable you to grasp a note quickly, isolate it – independent of its register, instrumentation and colour – and sing it back straight away. Singing helps guarantee that you have a clear impression of the note or phrase, an image you can fall back on anytime. Once a sound has been stored in your mind, you can access it on demand, work with it, look at it through a magnifying glass and think about it without having to listen to the recording over and over again.

Root and tonality

Go back to the exercise on p. 36 ff. (recognising the tonal centre of a sound). Your ability to identify the root of a melody or chord progression should now be so reliable that you can depend on it at any time (if not: keep practising!).

Assignment

Listen to **tracks 20–25** and locate the root of each example. If you're not sure, then sing the note which you think is the root (in the upper register of your vocal range). Turn off the recording. Now sing *downwards* in stepwise motion, following your memory of the recording. Take your time with every note and ask yourself: Does it feel like "home base"? If you initially located the actual root, you will be able to sing a complete scale before you once again get the feeling of coming to rest and locking into the note with the least tension. Remember that it is not uncommon to mistake the fifth for the root. Check!

Assignment

One of the most important things is the ability to keep the root in your head, no matter how much time has passed since you last consciously heard it, independently of what has happened musically in the meantime. Here is an exercise that requires a lot of concentration but will help develop your ability to retain sounds. Play a note on your instrument before you leave the house in the morning. Carry this note around with you all day, consciously sing or hum it every now and then and as soon as you come home, check if you've still got the same note.

The Chromatic scale

Without having mastered the chromatic subdivisions of the octave, it is impossible to develop a good ear. After all, the half step is the basic unit of our melodic and harmonic world. We constantly need to refer to the Chromatic scale for orientation. For this reason, it has to be an integral part of our musical memory.

Assignment

Sing any note in the lower range of your voice. Starting on this note, sing an ascending Chromatic scale (or what you believe to be the Chromatic scale ☺). Sing slowly, holding each note. Take your time to clearly imagine the next note before singing it. Try to sense when you've reached the octave (count the notes if you have to). Reverse and repeat this process by starting on a note in the upper range of your voice and try to sing a descending Chromatic scale.

Repeat this exercise with the help of the piano. Locate the note you started with in the previous assignment. Sing the Chromatic scale (without the instrument) up to the octave and back again. Check if you've stopped on the right note by playing it on the piano. If both are not the same, try this:

1. Play the Chromatic scale a number of times on the piano in order to get an impression of the sound.

2. Try the exercise again, but this time by singing and playing simultaneously (slowly).

3. Sing the exercise without the support of the instrument.

4. Check what you've just sung on the instrument.

Be aware of the fact that you are not only singing a series of uniform half steps, but also a sequence of specific intervals. After all, you started on a note that will now act as a point of reference (root). Use the Chromatic scale as a "ladder" (in the true sense of the word) to work your way from one interval to the next step by step. Sing the following exercise:

Sing the exercise at a very slow tempo (BPM = 60) – you should have enough time to imagine each note clearly *before* you sing it. Check what you are singing: First imagine the note, then sing it, then play it on the piano and, finally, compare the two. Do this exercise a number of times and think aloud by saying: "Now I'm singing a minor third, now I'm singing a perfect fifth, and so on". Once you've reached the octave, think/say: "This is the root!" Sing the upper and lower root alternately a number of times in order to establish the span of the octave.

While singing the descending exercise, keep in mind that you may, for example, be singing down a minor second but that you are still hearing a major seventh. The point of reference is C, no matter whether it is in the upper or in the lower range, and a B is the maj7, regardless of where it is sung or played. What we're talking about, here, is the concept of *complementary intervals*. It is important to understand that any two notes will form a specific interval, but that any one note can relate to a predetermined root as an intervallic function. For example, the notes e′ and c″ relate to each other as a minor 6th. If, however, we define C as the root, the E will always be a 3, no matter in which octave it appears.

I'd like to share a few thoughts on this topic. Most people have the habit of thinking intervals from the lower to the upper note. Even though this is the customary way of learning and constructing intervals, it has its drawbacks. In practice, we are often confronted with situations where the root is **not** at the very bottom of a sound (e.g. in the bass). This means you should be able to recognise interval relationships independently of where the point of reference is located. Once a root (of a scale, a melody, a single chord or chord progression) has been established, all notes relate to this root – e.g. a ♭3 is a ♭3, regardless of whether it is part of the bass line, the top note of a piano voicing or a melody note played by a trumpet. Because we are so used to thinking intervals "bottom up", many people have a hard time hearing the intervallic function of a note when it appears in the lower register and the root happens to be above the note they are trying to identify. When trying to define an interval, they first have to sing the root below the note in question and then the note itself in order to figure out what it is. We have to rid ourselves of this habit and should strive for the ability to pinpoint any note immediately as a specific intervallic function, no matter in which octave it is played or by which instrument.

Before we move on, here are the four golden rules of ear training:

- Practise slowly – your ear needs time to get used to a new sound and to store it permanently.

- Practise daily – you will only see progress if you do it regularly.

- Practise patiently – it may take some time before you notice progress, but it will happen eventually if you stick to your routine.

- Don't give up – *keep practising!*

Whole-tone, WTHT, HTWT

Most likely, you have learned to think of scales as complete entities – and you probably store scales in your memory in the same way. The result is that most of us sing and hear stepwise movement in melodies without consciously realising where the half steps or whole steps are. We fall back on our deeply ingrained reflexes based on major and minor melodies without thinking. This is hazardous. We have to learn to recognise melodic steps (♭2 and 2) independently of the context.

Assignment

Sing a Whole-tone scale (from root to root and back). This will show you to what extent your ears are programmed through habit. When you sing upwards from the root, you may notice how your ear and, accordingly, your voice – profoundly influenced by the Major scale – struggle when moving from 3 to ♯4 (you have to fight the inclination to sing the 4) and, even more so, from ♯4 to ♯5/♭6 (singing the 5 feels more natural). On the way down, the beginning is easy (1/8-♭7-♭6) because it reminds us of Aeolian. However, the step from ♭6 to ♭5 is more difficult because the ear calls for the fifth. The next step (from ♭5 to 3) will create problems, too, because the ear expects the 4. Consistent movement in whole steps goes against the familiar structure of Major and Minor scales and forces us to hear whole-tones independently of our intuitively acquired diatonic habits in major and minor. Be sure to check your intonation on the piano every now and then. Practise WTHT and HTWT scales using the same method. Their symmetrical structures will initially generate similar problems as with the Whole-tone scale.

Intervals

As self-evident as it may seem, singing one note and, at the same time, thinking about a particular interval implies the awareness of *two* notes simultaneously: the note you're singing and the reference note you're visualising. If you say: "I'm singing a major seventh", then you should hear the note you are singing in relation to the root resonating in your mind. The fact that you are thinking of a specific interval will give the sung note a unique quality. Every interval has its characteristic flavour – a ♭3 has a different feel to it than a 5. This ability to hear more than what is actually there – e.g. a specific note and its imaginary point of reference – is an important feature of a well-developed inner voice.

Assignment

Sing any note. Now, let's say that you're singing the top note of a major third. Can you visualise the root? Can you hear it materialising in your mind? Resist the temptation to actually sing the root. You should sense how the thought of the major third alone colours the note you sing, how the imagined root turns your sung note into a major third. Now redefine the same note as 5, ♭2, 6 and so on. Take your time to allow your inner ear to switch to the new root. Do you hear it? Do you sense the difference in quality of the note you're singing now that you've changed the point of reference? Can you visualise your note as part of a major or minor triad? Can you sing a 5 and fill in the missing notes in your imagination (1 and ♭3/3)? Can you conjure up the full triad – if not as distinct pitches then at least as a vague smudge with a major or minor character? If you do hear things clearly, are you able to imagine the triad in root position, first or second inversion? Can you hear your note as part of the Phrygian scale (e.g. as ♭2 or ♭7)? Can you picture your note as the opening of "All The Things You Are" and hear the complete melody as a result?

What's this exercise for? Firstly, it is meant to help you develop an imagination for sound. A third or a fifth should not remain an abstract phenomenon; it must be transformed into a tangible colour, a recognisable aural entity. The second reason is even more important. In my experience, all musicians who have good ears perceive more than they are actually hearing. They can visualise a single note as a constituent part of a more comprehensive sound. They not only perceive the isolated note, they can also identify its colour and therefore grasp its meaning as part of a chord, a voicing, a scale, a theme, etc. Good ears can figure out a musical principle or context from a single sound.

Scales

Let's start with the linear stepwise motion of a scale. For this purpose, let's go to the various modal play-alongs **tracks 1–9**.

Assignment

First repeat the exercise from the chapter "Modality" (p. 64 ff.) and locate the root of the play-alongs (listen to the bass). Then, starting on the root, sing to each recording (very slowly!!!), moving stepwise to the octave and back. Take your time with every note, decide whether it fits in with the recording and is actually part of the scale. Think while you sing and analyse the intervals (for example: "Now I'm on the 2, this is what a 9 sounds like; and now I'm on the ♯4, this is the characteristic Lydian note, etc."). Be aware of the fact that every note you sing will have a unique quality: some notes are consonant (chord tones), some will create a certain amount of dissonance (tensions) and some will feel terribly wrong (avoid notes or chromatic notes). Be careful: not every note that sounds dissonant is out-of-scale!

Assignment

Sing the following exercise and concentrate on keeping the root stable and in tune (check regularly on an instrument):

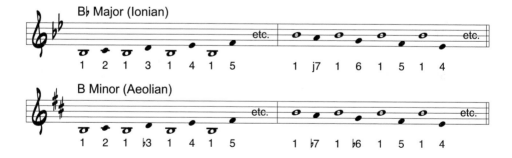

Repeat this exercise with all (!) the scale types you know and sing them along with the corresponding play-alongs.

Assignment

The next exercise is a combination of some of the previous assignments and helps to develop the ability to switch from one key area to another. Begin on any note and define it as e.g. the fifth of a Major scale. Now sing the scale upwards or downwards until you reach the root. Stay on this note and redefine it as a new scale degree. Think actual notes and intervals while you sing (e.g. "This is the note F, which is the 3 in the key of Db Major.")! Sing aloud either the degrees of the scale (e.g. 4-b3-2-1) or the actual names of the notes (e.g. Bb-Ab-G-F in F Minor). You will have to use enharmonic equivalents when switching from flat to sharp tonalities. The next thing you could do is to mix scale types and even work only with scale segments without singing back to the root. This is what the exercise could look like:

When following the example shown above, play the first note on the piano. Then continue on your own without the help of the instrument. Finally, check if you have again reached the correct starting note.

Of course, it is very important to have good control over the stepwise movement of a scale. In reality, however, melodies can leap around quite a bit (though not arbitrarily). For this reason, we have to be able to recognise interval relationships without having to rely on the linear scale structure.

Assignment

The following table is a true instrument of torture! Sing any note in the lower part of your vocal range – this will be your root. Now, sing the numbered degrees *above* this root, using all heptatonic scale types. Start with the Major and the Natural minor scales (as well as MM and HM). In a second step, extend this exercise to the church modes and their variants. *Have fun!*

2	4	5	3	6	7	5	1	8	2	6	4	3	8	7	1
6	5	2	7	8	3	4	6	1	4	8	5	7	3	1	2
4	1	5	8	2	1	3	5	4	2	6	3	7	6	8	7
5	3	6	1	4	8	6	2	8	1	7	2	4	5	7	3
1	6	4	7	8	5	1	2	3	8	7	5	2	6	3	4
8	2	7	1	4	5	7	4	6	2	8	3	6	5	3	1
2	4	8	1	7	3	5	2	6	8	5	4	7	6	1	3
8	6	4	2	1	5	6	7	2	5	1	4	3	7	8	3
6	5	8	4	5	3	2	8	7	1	2	7	4	6	3	1
7	5	2	3	4	1	8	2	6	1	3	5	7	6	4	8
3	6	2	4	7	3	8	6	7	8	1	5	4	2	5	1
4	5	6	8	5	2	1	6	3	7	4	3	2	7	1	8

Repeat this exercise by choosing a note in your high register, define it as the root and sing the interval series *below* it. Develop your own random sequences of intervals.

Telephone books are a good source of numbers, too. Sing the numbers of the New York telephone book (or the Mumbai phone book, for all I care): 1 = root, 2 = second, etc., 9 = ninth, 0 = tenth (this will take you out of the range of an octave!). You will have enough practice material to keep you busy until the end of your days.

Assignment

Deliberate and conscious singing of melodies is probably the most effective way of developing a sense of the intervals and their relation to a root. Take any song you know well and sing it a number of times, making sure that the melody is clearly established in your mind and you're singing in tune. Locate the root and determine the intervallic relationship for each melody note.

The common practice of learning intervals by using the opening notes of well-known tunes as a point of reference is not such a good thing, as far as I'm concerned. On the one hand, this focusses only on the intervallic relationship between the first two melody notes and disregards their connection to the overall key. For example, stating that "The Days Of Wine And Roses" begins with a major sixth (c'-a') ignores the more important fact that we're dealing with the 5 and the 3 in the key of F Major. Secondly, it restricts the ear to only one of countless situations in which an interval could appear. This method hampers the ear's flexibility and its ability to react to different situations.

In *solfège* or *solfeggio* – a system of vocal exercises – teachers and books usually work with *solmisation techniques*, in which every note is assigned a special syllable as a mnemonic aid to support pitch recognition when sight-singing. Many different systems exist worldwide.

The earliest can be found in Indian traditional music and employs the syllables "Sa (the tonic), Re, Ga, Ma, Pa, Dha, Ni", representing the pitches of a 7-note scale. The prevailing system in Western music is the "Do-Re-Mi-Fa-Sol-La-Ti" method, dating from the early 11th century and ascribed to the Italian monk Guido d'Arezzo. I'm sure many of you know the song "Do-Re-Mi" from the Rodgers and Hammerstein musical "The Sound of Music" (used by Maria to teach the children the notes of a Major scale).

Nowadays, two fundamentally different approaches are in use: "*fixed Do*" (pronounced "dough/doe" and not "doo"), where "Do" is always C, no matter what key we are in and "*movable Do*", where "Do" is always the tonic independent of the key, "Re" is the second degree, etc. Whereas I feel that "fixed Do" is a public hazard when dealing with tonal music because you're only learning names of notes and not their functional significance, the system has its merits when dealing with atonal melodies and music that modulates often. The "movable Do" principle, on the other hand, is quite useful when working on intervals in tonal music because the syllables correspond not to specific pitches, but to scale degrees and therefore represent the same intervallic relationships in every key (e.g. "Mi" is always the third).

The basic problem with both methods is that they concentrate only on the seven diatonic degrees of a Major scale (the naturals). This means that accidentals do not affect the syllables used: "Re" equally applies to D/Db/D♯ (in "fixed Do") or 2/b2/♯2 (in "movable Do"). So, what do you do with the chromatic notes in between? There are ways of expanding on the basic system by adding endings such as "i" for raised notes and "a/e" for lowered notes. The result is a highly confusing business. Starting on C, we would sing a Chromatic scale as Do (C) - Di (C♯) - Ra (Db) - Re (D) - Ri (D♯) - Ma (Eb) - Mi (E) - Fa (F) - Fi (F♯) - Se (Gb) - Sol (G) - Si (G♯) - Le (Ab) - La (A) - Li (A♯) - Te (Bb) - Ti (B). Accordingly, in "movable Do", a Natural minor scale would be sung as "Do-Re-Me-Fa-Sol-Le-Te". As you can see, a lot of time and energy has to be spent and – in my opinion – wasted on learning these syllables. This is why I prefer working with numbers.

Assignment

Play **tracks 1–9** again. Pick a play-along, locate the root and sing the scale from the root to the octave and back again along with the recording, using the appropriate numbers (for Dorian sing: one – two – flat three – four – five – six – flat seven – one). If the root is too low for your voice, then sing from 5 to 5 rather than from 1 to 8. It's not important for you to sing in time. Stay on each note until you've internalised it aurally and intellectually. Feel how it fits into the overall sound of the track. Sense, for example, what the 2 in Dorian sounds like, what colour it has and what tension it creates. As soon as you can sing all notes of the scale with confidence and follow the series of intervals in your mind, speed up the exercise, and continue doing so until you have absorbed each scale without having to think about it. Frequently check that you haven't slipped into some other mode by accident (maintain a speed that allows you to sing each individual note in tune). Keep note of the scales that need more work.

Assignment

Repeat the previous exercise, but now improvise to the play-alongs. Don't try to think about what you are doing. Just sing intuitively, immerse yourself in the sound of the recording and try to be as musical as possible. Sing little motivic ideas, sequential phrases, arpeggios – whatever comes to mind. Whenever you reach the final note of a phrase, however, stop for a moment, turn on your brain and analyse the note you have landed on. If necessary, check the note on the piano to make sure that you have analysed it correctly.

Sound and written music

The connection of what we hear and what we see on the written page is equally important to the development of our inner musical imagination. When looking at a page of sheet music, the aim is not only to understand it intellectually but also – at least to a certain extent – to be able to hear it in your mind. Ideally, the sound should jump off the page when you look at a lead sheet, a transcription or a score. Conversely, your musical imagination should be so clear-cut, that, when hearing music within, you can immediately visualise what it should look like in notation.

I know from my own experience that these abilities require an unbelievable amount of practice. I work as a composer and arranger and I've learned to accept – despite the many years of training and involvement in a multitude of musical projects – that I can't always immediately hear everything I see on paper nor immediately write down everything I hear in my head. Studies have shown that composers – measured according to today's life expectancy – only reach their zenith at the age of about 50. That's how long it takes to acquire the necessary knowledge and technical skills when it comes to handling the instruments of varying ensembles confidently and to hone your creative and imaginative powers. It takes a lot of time and patience to develop a highly refined, reliable inner voice and to perfect the ability to translate imagined sound into written music.

Assignment

Sing the following lines. First, play each root on the piano and check this root regularly during the exercise. For each key signature, alternately choose the root of the Major scale or the corresponding relative minor (e.g. E♭ Major or C Natural minor for the first line). Sing each row of notes very slowly and think about the intervallic functions ("now I'm on the 3, the 4, and now on the 6"). Don't sing from one note to the next. For example, in the first line, don't think "I'm singing a minor third from F to D" but rather "I'm singing from the 2 to the maj7 in the key of E♭ Major"! Think about and anticipate the sound of every interval relative to the root, no matter how much the notes jump around. Consciously experience how a 2, 3, 4, etc. actually feels, how the sound of each note appears in your mind *before* you sing it. Check the notes you sing on the piano. Even if the lines approach the limits of your vocal range, try hard to hit them and sing them in tune (don't push, rather sing soft *falsetto*). The point is to stretch for each note, to really want it. Transpose the notes beyond your vocal range into a more comfortable register:

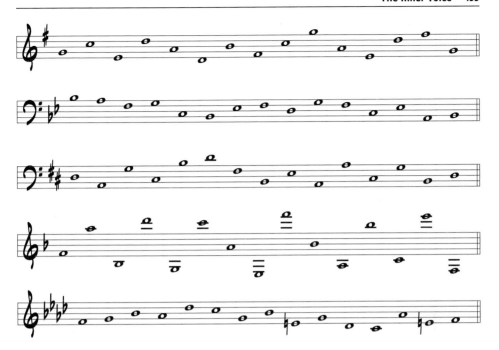

Write similar random note exercises for all major and minor keys in treble and bass clef (include Aeolian, HM and MM for the minor keys). The exercises should contain a healthy mixture of stepwise movement, leaps and notes on the ledger lines. Don't forget to use key signatures. Take these sheets out of your drawer at regular intervals to see how your tonal reflexes have improved.

Assignment

Apply the exercise above to real pieces. Use nursery rhymes (why not!) and Folk tunes because of their simple structure. Here's how to do it:

- Sing the melody a number of times and locate both the root and the starting note (the two might not be the same).

- Write down the tune in different keys. Don't be frustrated if you have difficulties initially. The more often you try this, the easier it gets. Be sure not to restrict yourself to the "simple" keys (i.e. 2 flats to 2 sharps). Get used to the more difficult key signatures, too (3 flats/sharps or more). Our goal is to develop a conscious connection in all keys between the written page and its representation in our mind.

- Analyse the melody (write down the intervallic functions as numbers under each of the notes).

- Sing the tune in slow motion so that you can think along and sing the scale degrees or, alternately, the names of the notes.

Switching modes

Here's a fantastic exercise to help you come to grips with the nuances of the various types of scales and to improve interval and root recognition: the transformation of a melody into a *parallel* mode. What we do is transpose melodies into other modes *without changing the root.*

Let's take "Happy Birthday" as an example. ***Don't look at the following piece of music yet!*** Go back to the assignment on p. 442. You were asked to notate the melody based on the root F. If you didn't do it then, do it now! Once you've written down the melody, add the scale degrees by numbering each individual note according to its interval relationship with the root.

So, what did you come up with? Here's what your result should look like:

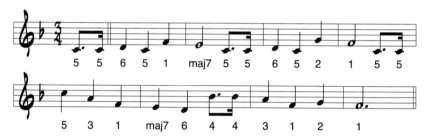

Now let's try to sing this melody in a different mode *while retaining the root* (F). For example, let's switch from F Ionian (the mode "Happy Birthday" was originally in) to F Aeolian. You will have to change certain notes of the melody to adjust it to the intervallic relationships inherent to Aeolian. In the following example, I have still used the key signature of F Major so that you can see the necessary changes more easily:

Sing the Aeolian version. Make sure you sing in tune. It may be a good idea, at first, to play the root on the piano every now and then so that you don't lose your bearings. Later on, however, try to do this exercise without the help of the piano. After all, you are trying to train your inner voice. Work slowly, so that you have enough time to think about the scale degrees while singing and the opportunity to consciously experience the quality of each individual interval. Gradually speed up the exercise so that you internalise the melodic flow and the colour of the scale as a whole.

While doing this exercise you will discover that every mode has its own mood: Whereas the Ionian version of "Happy Birthday" sounds lively and spirited (as well it should, considering its purpose), the Aeolian variant has a rather melancholic and reticent quality (reserved for your odd friends!). So, the atmosphere of a melody is clearly dictated by the character of the tonal material used (by comparison, the intervals ♭3, ♭6 and ♭7 give the melody a more sombre feel).

Assignment

Practise "Happy Birthday" this way in F Lydian, F Mixolydian, F Dorian, F Phrygian, F Harmonic minor, F Melodic minor, F HM5, F Lydian(♭7), F Mixo(♭9) and F Mixo(♭13) or in any other 7-note scale you can come up with (for those of you more daring, try F Locrian, which starts on the ♭5!). Find Folk tunes, nursery rhymes or Christmas carols – they should contain all 7 scale degrees – and work on them in the same way as with "Happy Birthday" in the modes I have listed.

Don't underestimate this exercise! It is – even if it doesn't look it – one of the most important exercises in this entire book. Don't see it as a one-off assignment, but rather as an ongoing one that will keep you busy for years to come. Use new songs and different scales as you move along (how about your national anthem in Double Harmonic major or minor?). Make it part of your regular practice routine. Gradually – without noticing it – this exercise will improve your ability to recognise roots, interval relationships, scales and their individual colours and characteristics.

Fact and fiction

At this point, I'd like to issue a warning. I often come across students (even very capable ones) who try to sing back a melodic line and fail to reproduce the phrase, but who, nonetheless, stubbornly insist they have sung accurately. Why might that be? The reason lies in the fact that the ear, or rather the cortex of the brain, adjusts and distorts difficult or unusual sounds to make them fit something we're familiar with. The voice and the ear act as a unit. And because both tend to be rather lazy, they are reluctant to accommodate what is challenging, new or strange. This even applies to sounds that are only marginally unfamiliar (to you personally). In the end, the important thing is to understand that this is how your ear works. Accept that it is able to create its own reality. It wants to hear what it knows. This is why every "natural" response to a sound must be evaluated and tested to prevent the ear falling victim to its own habits, hearing what it wants to hear rather than what is really there.

So, please be very careful when working on an exercise. It is quite possible that you intend to do one thing, and the ear starts playing tricks on you. You could be 100% convinced that you've carried out the task correctly, but if you look at the result objectively (e.g. record yourself or have someone else check), you may find that you have just sung what is easiest. And because the natural response – though wrong – feels good, you think you got it right.

Here are several examples. Earlier on, I mentioned that it is difficult to sing an ascending Whole-tone scale, especially when moving from 3 to ♯4 and from ♯4 to ♯5/♭6. After the 3 we expect to hear the 4 and not the ♯4 because of the strong influence of the Major scale (this is why Ionian is easier to sing than Lydian). Once you come to terms with Lydian, the ♯4 shouldn't be a problem, but we still get stuck on the ♯5 because the ear expects 5 (Lydian is easier than the Whole-tone scale). Conversely, it is difficult to sing a descending Dorian scale starting on the octave. The hard thing is singing from ♭7 to 6. The ear expects the ♭6 because we're more used to Aeolian than Dorian on the way down. Quite possibly, you'll slip into the more comfortable mode inadvertently.

Assignment

Take the minor modes Aeolian, Dorian, HM and MM. Sing any note in the upper register of your voice. This is the root (octave). Now sing downwards to the fifth and back up to the octave a number of times while alternating between the various minor scales. The exercise could look something like this: 1/8-♭7-♭6-5(Aeolian) – 6-maj7-1/8(MM) – maj7-♭6-5(HM) – 6-♭7-1/8(Dorian) – maj7-6-5(MM) – ♭6-♭7-1/8(Aeolian) – ♭7-6-5(Dorian) – ♭6-maj7-1/8(HM).

Have you noticed how difficult it is to go against the natural melodic tendency of 5-6-maj7-1/8 (Ionian/MM ascending) and 1/8-♭7-♭6-5 (Aeolian descending)? The interesting thing about these exercises, even though they are comparatively easy, is that they show how readily the ear takes the path of least resistance and tries to circumvent the less familiar. So, while you're singing, always ask yourself: "Am I really doing what I think I'm doing?" Take your time, work slowly and check every note. As soon as you speed up beyond what your conscious brain can process, you'll be riding on your automatic systems without the ability to monitor or modify. You will start relying on reflexes – and these could be wrong without your noticing it.

Develop similar exercises – not necessarily with the aim of practising scales (this will happen anyhow) but rather to find out how your ear is programmed and which habits stand in your way.

Arpeggios

Sing a C. This is your note of reference, which we will interpret as the root, third or fifth of a major or minor triad. Sing the following exercise (if it is too high or too low, transpose it):

Here are a few tips:

- If you start on the third or the fifth, **_do not sing downwards to the root_** for orientation! Instead, try to imagine the root in your mind. Think: "I'm on the third, and it sounds like a third because it produces a particular colour in combination with the imagined root. I don't need to actually sing the root first because I can feel it resonating in my head automatically when I visualise a third."

- Always sing from the starting note upwards to its octave and back. You must *complete the full octave*. With inversions, this will carry you past the root and further develop your ability to deal with octave transpositions.

- Don't think in intervals from one note to the next. For example, don't say: "I'm singing a minor triad from the third to the fifth, so that means I have to sing a major third." Rather say: "Now I'm on the third, and now I'm on the fifth of the chord, etc."

- Since we're working on triads, be careful not to slip into four-note chords accidentally. When singing from 5 to 8 (or 8 to 5 on the way down), make sure you don't add notes to fill the gap.

- Check yourself on the piano at regular intervals. We all have a tendency, by force of habit, to return to the root position of a chord because it is what we know best. Take your time. Allow every note to appear in your mind before you sing it. Sing slowly and deliberately. When you reach the root (irrespective of the triad and inversion you're singing), stay there a little longer to allow the sound of the triad as a whole to settle in.

Choose a note in the upper register of your vocal range and sing the same exercise in the opposite direction (downwards from the upper octave and back). Once you feel comfortable with major and minor triads, start working on augmented and diminished triads, too.

Do the same exercise for four-note chords (maj7, minor7, dominant, sus4, diminished, half-diminished, augmented) and their most important variants in all inversions:

The objective of these exercises is not only to sing the arpeggios in tune (which is a given) but, more importantly, to be able to imagine harmonic structures *without actually singing them*! So, the next thing to do is to repeat each exercise mentally (silent singing). Run through the various chord types and their inversions in the same way as you did when singing them aloud. Think about them note for note (successively), and remember to take your time. Don't be satisfied until you have an absolutely crystal clear inner image of every note. If this exercise seems a little too abstract, do it while imagining the sound of an instrument (guitar, trombone, flute, etc.).

Assignment

Now for the difficult part: Try to imagine the overall sound of an entire harmonic structure – not as a single-note arpeggio but as a full triad or four-note chord. Choose any chord tone. Position it as the lowest voice (bass) or the top note (lead voice) of the chord. Sing the chosen note aloud or imagine it (silent singing) and add the tonal material of each corresponding triad or four-note chord above or below this note (simultaneously) in your mind. Be aware that it will not be possible to distinguish individual notes. You will perceive the harmonic structure as a blurred smudge or blob of sound with a specific colour and a characteristic feel. Again, imagining instruments makes this exercise a little easier (visualise a piano or guitar voicing, a brass section, a choir, etc.).

It can take a long time for us to establish a tangible harmonic impression of every chord type in our imagination. For this reason, come back to these exercises at regular intervals. At some point, you'll suddenly realise that you've developed the ability to recognise not only single notes and their functional meaning, but also harmonic structures according to their specific colours. One day, you will be able to identify sounds immediately as maj7, –7(b5) or sus4 chords without knowing how and why. This ability is crucial, for example, when it comes to transcribing chord progressions. It is often impossible to filter out individual notes or specific voicings from a recording, either because the sound quality is bad or the piano gets drowned out by the other instruments and is barely audible. In such cases, only intuition, a general feeling for the harmony and intelligent guesswork will help you.

Chord or scale?

Remember: Chords are vertical scales and scales are horizontal chords. Make sure you're constantly aware of this while listening, singing and playing. The link between chord and scale should be so well established internally that the chord symbol is not only interpreted as a vertical stack of intervals, but also melodically as a horizontal succession of notes. Vice versa, you should be able to recognise the harmonic substance behind a melodic phrase. Have another good look at all the scales we talked about and the way they relate to specific chord types. If, for example, you hear a melodic line consisting of Dorian scale material, you should immediately know that you are dealing with a minor seventh chord. Conversely, the chord symbol F7 should automatically trigger Mixolydian (or any other dominant scale) as the corresponding sound in your mind.

Assignment

Listen to **track 39**. You will hear a succession of four-bar phrases – each phrase is based exclusively on a single chord and a related scale. The progression is random, so you won't recognise familiar harmonic patterns or functional relationships. Here's the problem: The keyboard player not only plays voicings (chords), he also adds little fills and melodic phrases. Your assignment is to determine the chord type behind each four-bar phrase. At first, play the whole recording (there are 18 different four-bar sections) and write down each of the chord types while listening, using general four-note symbols without tensions (e.g. –7, °7, 7sus4, etc.). The purpose of this first run-through is to find out which sounds you can already identify intuitively. If you're not sure, make an educated guess. You know that there are only 7 basic chord types, so try to exclude the less probable ones. You're invited to repeat the exercise as often as you like, but resist the temptation to stop the recording. This first part of the assignment is not meant to be easy, so it's OK if you miss out on quite a few of the sounds.

Once you've done this exercise as a whole, listen to each of the four-bar phrases individually by looping it with the A/B-function on your remote. First, try to find the root (listen to the bass). Now, while the recording is playing, sing the scale corresponding to each four-bar loop starting on the root. Sing slowly, feel how each note locks into the sound and analyse what you're singing. Think, for example, "Now I'm on the 1, the 2, the b3, 4, 5, 6, b7, 8 – OK, I got it, this is Dorian. This must mean that I'm hearing a minor seventh chord." Then sing the chord tones (in root position) up to the octave and back. Think, for example, "I am now singing the 1, the b3, 5, b7, 8/1 – this is what a minor seventh chord sounds like, and here it is Dorian." Compare the result with what you discovered and notated in the first part of the exercise.

Repeat this exercise at regular intervals over a longer period of time – not only with **track 39**, but also with the other play-alongs. An even better idea would be to use the many recordings in your own CD collection. The day will come when you will be able to identify a sound as soon as you hear it (scale and/or chord type). At this point, it is not important to know why your immediate response tells you, for instance, "this is an altered dominant". You'll just know it. It is no longer necessary to dissect every sound into its component parts in order to understand it. When I listen to something consciously, I very rarely think about individual notes. I listen to the sound as a whole and react to its basic concept first. Only in a second step, do I go into detail and ask myself which specific notes I am dealing with.

Chord progressions and functions

You will find a whole series of exercises in the coming chapters on improvisation dealing with chord progressions and important functional relationships (which you should not only play but also sing!). For this reason, I will only address basic diatonic functions in major and minor keys at present.

Assignment

Remember that every note of a scale automatically implies harmony (see pdf-F). Sing the root F. Sing the F Major scale from f' to f'' and back (male voices sing an octave lower). I know it's high, but you can get it with *falsetto* voice. In the following exercise, each scale note is the *top note* of the corresponding triad or four-note chord. Sing down the notes of each chord. For example, think: "I am now on the G, the 2nd scale degree in F Major, and this note implies the dominant (the C major triad or C7):

Take your time with this exercise. Try to imagine the notes of the triads or four-note chords simultaneously (vertically) as well as successively (horizontally). Repeat this exercise in F Minor. Write out the F Harmonic minor scale and harmonise each scale note with F–, Bb– or C/C7. Then sing the resulting chord sequence.

Assignment

Sing the following lines making sure that you are aware of how each individual note connects to the tonal environment – as part of the overall scale/key or as part of the immediate chord. While singing, think about the harmonic functions: "I'm on the tonic, the V, the IV, etc.":

Look for melodies that contain leaps and arpeggios and sing them, conscious of the important melody notes (long notes or notes on strong beats) and the chord functions they outline. Folk music, nursery rhymes and Christmas carols are, as usual, particularly good for this purpose (have a closer look at the melody of "Silent Night", for example, and the harmony it implies).

Assignment

Now, we'll turn things around a little bit and check your functional perception. Go to **track 20**. You will hear a 16-bar loop in Bb Major containing only diatonic functions (one-bar harmonic rhythm). Draw up a 16-bar grid on a piece of manuscript paper and try to write down the chord progression using functional notation as the recording is playing. How did you do? The goal of this exercise is to be able to identify each sound immediately as III, VI, IV, etc. Repeat this exercise as often as you need to (if necessary 100 times) until you are able to identify each function as soon it appears (say them out loud to the recording). If you have difficulties, it would make sense to first mark the bars where you think you're hearing the tonic (I) and work your way backwards by figuring out how the chord progression resolves to these cornerstones.

The next thing we'll do, is convert our chord progression into a melodic line made up exclusively of triads and four-note arpeggios. Learn the following exercise off by heart and sing it to the recording:

Apply the two previous exercises to **tracks 12** and **21–38**. From now on, these tracks constitute your program of functional recognition exercises. Have a look at the chord progressions for these tracks in the appendix. Analyse them and listen to the corresponding recordings over and over again, consciously thinking about each function. Think "Now I am hearing II-7 Dorian, a minor subdominant, a Blues tonic, a Locrian VIIᵗʰ degree, ♯II°7", and so on. Try to imagine these functional progressions without the help of the recordings. You should at least have a vague impression in your mind when you try to recall a specific track. Write several melodic exercises similar to the one shown above for every one of the tracks (consisting mostly of arpeggios) and sing them to the recordings.

See the symbol, hear the chord

Exercises only make sense when put into a practical context as soon as possible. In order to come to grips with the chord progression of a composition, we have to concentrate on its vertical aspect for a while. Let's try doing this by applying the previous exercises to one of the most widely known Jazz standards: "All Of Me".

Assignment

First, have a look at the chord progression (you'll find the lead sheet on p. 339 ff.):

- Sing the roots of the chords (in time).

- Sing the chords in root position over this bass line (firstly as triads and then as four-note chords) so that you get a general feeling for the tonal material (sing out of time).

Remember to check your intonation with the help of the piano. At first, you should do this quite often (after every chord) to make sure that you don't lose your bearings without noticing. Later on, you can try to sing a complete chorus before going back to the instrument for confirmation.

Let's turn the progression of triads and four-note chords into a melodic exercise consisting mainly of chord tones. "All Of Me" is particularly well suited to this. Because the changes occur every two bars, we can spend a lot of time with each sound. In addition, the melody begins with a sequence of arpeggiated chords, which serves as the perfect starting point for our exercise:

Concentrate at first on the notes, ignoring the rhythm. Sing slowly, in tune, and name every interval. Think while you sing: "Now I'm on the 1 of C, on the 5 of E7, on the 1 of A7, etc." Once you have done this, set your metronome to about 100–120 beats per minute and sing the exercise in time – until you can do it perfectly without tripping up. This exercise could take some time. It's important to realise that we're trying to practise two things at once – the vertical aspect of each chord as well as the horizontal flow from one chord to the next (voice leading). We must learn to be consciously aware of both perspectives and to be able to switch from one to the other in our minds with ease.

Once you can sing these lines without conscious effort, you'll be able to imagine the chord progression without having to rely on an accompaniment. It will be like a movie playing in your head, guiding you safely through the piece from beginning to end. Moreover, you will be able to anticipate any unusual part of the chord progression that doesn't follow expected patterns. You shouldn't have any problems with the first 8 bars of the piece. But how do we get from D–7 to E7? Here, the progression neither follows the cycle of fifths nor can it be explained diatonically – it is simply a shift from one sound to the next without any cadential connection. This makes the transition hard to grasp. With the help of this exercise, we now have at least one way to get through the danger zone without tripping up. I don't mean to say that this exercise is the cure for all ills. But it is a good starting point, and we have to start somewhere, after all. Naturally, I would expect you to look for other solutions.

Assignment

Work through the piece "There Will Never Be Another You" in the same way (see p. 78). Work on your entire repertoire using the previous and the following exercises!

The main objective of the previous exercises is to assemble an image of a piece in your mind, a mental map that you can draw on at any time, an inner representation of the chord progression that encompasses every harmonic twist and turn, every stumbling block and every peculiarity. If you can visualise all of this, you've got it made. Ideally, you should now be able to sit down, close your eyes and let the piece unfold from start to finish in your imagination. This is quite similar to Formula One drivers or downhill ski racers, who are able to project the entire race in their heads because they know their circuits and slopes inside out. In fact, they could probably get around them blindfolded. During their pre-race routine, world-class skiers often enter a trance-like state of mental preparation where they try to emulate the actual race (almost to the second). They can anticipate every obstacle and experience every bump or turn in their minds in real-time. During the race, they no longer consciously need to think about what they're doing because their trained reflexes kick in, almost like on autopilot. They have acquired a "physical memory", very much like the one we develop on our instruments and with most everything we do in life. This is exactly what we should try to aim for, too, as improvisers: creating a realistic and tangible image of a tune in our minds.

Some musicians take this even one step further. Having reached a high level of proficiency on their instrument, they can practise mentally. They are able to develop melodic, harmonic or rhythmical ideas in their minds (by the way, this is how Charles Mingus practised the bass while working for the U.S. Postal Service). Once our musical ideas are crystal clear – assuming that we've worked hard on our technique – the fingers only have to follow our imagination. Ideally, as soon as we pick up our instrument, we should know and feel exactly what to do in order to turn our ideas into sound – as if we've been playing them forever.

Instant touch

We now get to a crucial point. Everything we've worked on should serve to create a direct link between our "inner voice" and our instrument. Whereas, up until now, we've been attempting to translate written music into imagined sound, we are now talking about translating our musical imagination into the corresponding fingerings on our instrument (both abilities, by the way, are essential prerequisites for good sight readers). So, how do we develop this elusive thing that Art Farmer so aptly called *instant touch*? Let's do an experiment! Again, we will go back to our roots rather than beginning with the Jazz repertoire. Read on only once you have your instrument in your hands.

Assignment

So – are you ready? Choose any note in the lower register of your instrument. Now, starting on this note and without further premeditation or preparation, play "Happy Birthday". On your mark, get set, go!

Well? How did it turn out? Not good? Then try again. Don't cheat! You're not supposed to play "stop and go", to start off tentatively, make a mistake and start again, speed up when things are easy and slow down when you're not sure of what you're doing, get stuck, repeat a phrase, become impatient, skip over a difficult part, muddling your way through to the final note. Simply try to play in time, steadily and evenly, as slowly as the melody needs to be played in order to get from the beginning to the end without tripping up.

If you did well, move on. If you still can't manage it, then choose a note in the lower register of your vocal range and *sing* the melody. How did you do this time? My experience tells me that anyone, and I mean *anyone*, can sing "Happy Birthday" (and with its big leaps, it's not the easiest of melodies). Why is it that you're having difficulties playing a tune that you've heard and sung hundreds of times? How do you expect to cope with new sounds and complex Jazz themes far less familiar to the ear if you have such a hard time handling even a basic tune on your instrument? It's obvious that your ears and fingers are not in sync. On the one hand, you have the ability to visualise the sound of a melody (the "inner voice") but, on the other hand, your instrument is not following what's in your head. Only when both aspects are inextricably connected will your fingers be able to complement your musical imagination.

Assignment

Work out a comfortable fingering on your instrument so that you can easily play a Major scale over two octaves (almost all well-known tunes lie within this range). Now try to play melodies that are based on the Major scale, staying with this fingering. Apply this exercise to all the many melodies you know by heart. Switch your fingering to other keys and repeat this exercise until you can play any nursery rhyme, Christmas carol or Folk tune faultlessly, starting on any note. Remember that this merging of the ear and the instrument is a process that can take many years. You'll probably have to continue working on this exercise for a long time.

Assignment

Sing short and simple phrases (no more than 3 or 4 notes at first) and play them back on your instrument. With time, you can move on to longer and more complex lines. Nevertheless, you should always be aware of the limitations of your imaginative powers, the point at which your musical ideas begin to fall apart because the sound in your head is too vague. Have you noticed just how tangible your phrases have to be before you manage to sing them, let alone play them? This exercise not only develops "instant touch" but also enhances the clarity of your ideas. You will learn to accept that your solos only radiate confidence if you have a clear conception of what you want to play *before* you play it. Singing is a great way of making sure that you are in control of your ideas. If your instrument allows you to do so, *sing and play simultaneously*. Musicians such as George Benson, Tania Maria or Keith Jarrett can sing along to any line they play on their instrument (even though Keith Jarrett "moans" rather than sings, you can always sense the strong connection to what he is playing).

Assignment

Go back to "All Of Me". Take your instrument and try to play the exercise you have learned to sing. Make sure that your inner voice controls what you are doing and that you hear every note internally *before* you play it. Feel how your inner voice guides your fingers. At first, stick to the exercise and play it exactly as it is, without changing or adding a single note. See if you can do this several times without making a mistake. Eventually, you can try to be more musical. Start improvising, varying the lines rhythmically and embellishing them. Don't try to play anything too complicated or you'll get stuck. If you lose control, go back to the basic exercise. Keep practising until the lines become part of your very being. Don't let the exercise become boring. Only when your fingers have completely absorbed every note can you afford to branch out and be more creative.

It is, of course, possible that you still make mistakes long after this exercise has become routine. This, however, is most probably no longer due to your not being able to imagine the lines. It is more likely that you are still grappling with technical problems on your instrument. If the problem is "merely" technical and not musical, you have won the battle. It would be far more troubling if your problems were musical in nature and attributed to a lack of imagination. Difficulties on your instrument, however, can be solved because you can always recall what you wanted to play, and, accordingly, you will always know what to practise.

If You Wanna Hear It, You Gotta Feel It!

A good ear is one that has the ability to identify, classify, name, compare and distinguish sounds. A good ear would tell us: "Oh yeah, I've heard this sound before", or "It sounds a bit like this or that – but not quite. What's the difference?", or it might tell us "It's definitely not sound X, Y or Z – what else could it be?" What we need to develop is a perpetually growing archive of sounds – a library that organises the countless different chords, voicings, scales, rhythms, cadences, modulations, etc. in all their manifestations and configurations, and makes them available to us at the flick of a switch. The more storage compartments our internal file system has, the easier it will be for us to access a new sound and lodge it permanently in our mind. I'd like to give you a few tips on how to build your very own directory of sound.

The magic triangle

This book deals a lot with musical terminology. We have become accustomed to describing and measuring sounds by using labels such as major or minor thirds, half or whole steps, maj7 or –7 chords, etc. However, the more we fiddle with words and definitions, the greater the danger of losing track of what the terms are actually supposed to represent and which emotions the corresponding sounds stimulate. Sounds have meanings that often defy definition. Talking about Dorian simply isn't sexy – the sound itself certainly can be. Therefore, every theoretical discussion raises a fundamental dilemma. On the one hand, we use abstract terminology to categorise musical structures and content, but, on the other hand, we should never forget that music acts on an emotional level. So, a vital concern of ear training must be to establish a connection not only between a theoretical concept and the sound it symbolises, but also between the sound and the feeling it elicits:

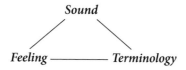

It is my aim to link these three areas. It's not enough to simply understand the terminology. Only when there is a close, mutual relationship between a theoretical term, the corresponding sound and its emotional impact, does theory become more than just lifeless knowledge and inanimate thought. Without this connection, you run the risk of developing primarily on an intellectual level while gradually losing your emotional rapport with the music.

From sound to feelings

Most musicians would agree with me that we only play convincingly and expressively if what we play has emotional meaning. The same applies to hearing/listening. In all my years of teaching, one thing has become apparent – the more theoretical knowledge you accumulate, the more you dissociate yourself from what a musically uneducated but nevertheless sensitive audience quite naturally possesses: the ability to experience a sound in a naïve and childlike way.

For most people, music is an essential part of life. Music has accompanied us from day one. Without our realising it, our brain has accumulated and stored an amazing amount of information that is closely tied to literally thousands, if not millions, of musical bits and bytes. More than any other means of recollection (e.g. smell or taste), music provides us with memory markers. Music acts as a trigger. Ever so often, it's a recording or a melody, a sound associated with some place or moment in your life, that catches you by surprise and transports you back through space and time, evoking with startling resonance and clarity a memory you had all but forgotten. Now, all you have to do is exploit this link. Once you activate a specific memory, sentiment or emotion and consciously connect it to a related musical event, you will always recognise this particular sound for what it is, simply because it has acquired meaning beyond its connotation as merely a theoretical and therefore rather dispassionate concept.

When I ask students, for example, what they associate with a 7(♯9)-chord and what this sound means to them, they invariably come up with the following answers: seventh chord, altered dominant, 3 and ♭3 in the same voicing, dissonant sound, etc. – connotations predominantly concerned with technical terms and abstract musical terminology. When I ask them if the symbol "7(♯9)" evokes some sort of inner counterpart, an emotional equivalent, I often get puzzled looks or a simple "no" for an answer. At best, they have no more than a blurred, vaguely tangible memory of the sound. Only in rare cases do they make a connection, for example, to the Blues, to the introduction of "Spinning Wheel" by Blood, Sweat and Tears or a chord fingering on the guitar, etc. – a connection that relates to real music or something familiar on their instrument. When I play those same students a 7(♯9) chord in various situations, I have to acknowledge that only a small fraction of them can identify it. More often than not, there's absolutely no correlation between the term and the sound. And, after all, we're talking about students who have spent many years of their lives immersed in music.

But, what baffles me the most is that many musicians have a hard time describing how a sound feels, what kind of emotional impact it has. Sadly, the term "7(♯9) chord" doesn't seem to trigger any emotional response whatsoever. It isn't perceived as a unique sound that can be put into expressive words beyond the use of musical terminology. I have never heard anyone describe a 7(♯9) chord as being sensual, smoky, grimy, red, abrasive, vulgar, obscene, aggressive, as something that makes you itch and tingle all over, etc. Those are some of the attributes that cross my mind when I think of the term "7(♯9)". The important thing: They help me remember and recognise this particular sound. Whenever a chord sets off these emotional reactions, I know I am hearing a 7(♯9) chord – not because I'm counting intervals, but because I'm aware of how the sound feels.

Of course, I know these descriptions to be highly subjective and therefore not necessarily universally shared. Quite on the contrary – it would be a pity if we all reacted the same way. Everyone should be free to tap into his/her very personal emotional world. However, I can't emphasise enough the importance of experiencing sounds and musical terms in this way. Try to remember how you perceived music as a child. I would like you to activate all your emotions, pictures and memories that you've been carrying around with you for years, some of which – at first glance – have nothing to do with music. On the other hand, why shouldn't you also use your other senses (sight, touch, taste, smell) to experience your own world of sound more vividly? To me, music has the scent of spices and perfume.

Try to get to the core of a sound by describing it in as many ways as possible – not only with conventional musical terminology, but also with every figurative and emotional reaction the sound spontaneously elicits in you. Here is a random and, of course, incomplete compilation of words that come to mind when I hear something. Many of these criteria are generally used (e.g. by music critics) and would probably be endorsed by most musicians. Some of them, however, are very personal and reflect my own feelings and the way I relate to music. A few are technical terms, but most of them are common expressions – after all, it's important to include everyday life in your music. I've tried to pair up opposites (antonyms), which I don't want to be seen as antipodes – as either-or – but rather as tendencies with gradations and many intermediate shades and hues (e.g. a sound can be *vaguely* familiar, *rather* smooth, *relatively* diatonic, *quite* bright, *very* stable, etc.). Also, this list should not imply that all words in the left-hand column belong together or all words in the right-hand column have a similar connotation – every set of two words stands on its own:

inside	outside
natural	artificial
dull	shiny
clichéd	unique
hip	square
meaningless	significant
simple	complex
boring	exciting
appropriate	inappropriate
right	wrong
conventional	unconventional
white	black
open	congested
salty	sweet
small	large
yes!	no!
cheerful	sad
meek	brazen
smooth	rough
cool	flustered
vacillating	resolute
often	seldom
consonant	dissonant
abnormal	ordinary

winter	summer
light	dark
brave	timid
elegant	vulgar
blunt	sharp
neat	messy
beautiful	ugly
native	alien
colourful	drab
calming	upsetting
airy	earthy
stable	volatile
relaxed	agitated
mundane	original
transparent	dense
thin	fat
land	sea
juicy	dry
expected	surprising
moving	stationary
graceful	clumsy
shrill	mellow
diatonic	chromatic
soft	hard
uplifting	depressing
conspicuous	unobtrusive
warm	cold
tonic sound	cadence sound
heavy	light
red	blue
jazz club	concert hall
bland	biting
yin	yang
familiar	unfamiliar
normal	strange
tonal	atonal
orderly	chaotic
bland	spicy
majestic	humble
luscious	sparse
aggressive	restrained
round	angular
fluid	solid
opaque	clear
extroverted	introspective
mysterious	straightforward

```
elated  -------------------------------- subdued
empty  --------------------------------- full
```

and many thousands more …

I have deliberately jumbled up these pairs of words to emphasise that there is no hierarchy or degree of importance implied. I simply wrote out what first came to mind. Expand on this list by adding your own criteria, experiences and descriptions.

Make sure you know what these terms mean. Sit down, think about every word or pair of words and see what sort of sounds they imply to you. Here are two examples from my own stock of sounds:

```
  bright  -----------------------x-------- dark
  stable  ------------------------x---- unstable
familiar  ----x------------------------ unfamiliar
diatonic  ----x------------------------ chromatic
    soft  ----------x--------------- hard
   small  ----x------------------------ big
  pretty  -----------------------x------- ugly
```

This sums up my impression of a D–7(♭5) chord in the key of E♭ Major (the VIIᵗʰ degree). The fact that this sound feels rather "dark", "small" and "ugly" to me must not be understood as a value judgement – I enjoy improvising on half-diminished chords. This is simply how I first experienced the sound, and that's how I have stored it in my mind. I have to stand by this description because it is exactly what sets this sound apart from others.

Here's another example. What do you think I mean by this description?

```
  natural  ------------------------x------ artificial
consonant  ------------------------x------ dissonant
   simple  ------------------------x------ complex
     calm  ------------------------x------ hectic
  angular  ----x------------------------ round
```

In my catalogue of sounds, this is how I would describe a chord or phrase consisting of material taken from the HTWT scale.

Basically, we can describe any musical event in this way – be it a single note or a whole piece. This may not be all that easy at first. Don't be embarrassed to delve into your world of sound in this rather naïve and unpretentious way. As already mentioned above – if we only think about music theoretically and in technical terms, we may run the risk of losing touch with its sensual aspects.

The important thing, here, is that these descriptions and sentiments are not incontrovertible fact – they are constantly in flux. Let's take, for example, the word "familiar". Familiar sounds are …

- … those you grew up with;

- … part of your personal repertoire;

- ... the ones you are currently practising at home or rehearsing with a band;

- ... on your favourite CDs;

- ... ones you associate experiences and impressions with (pleasant or unpleasant).

Because our understanding of music is constantly progressing and expanding, the content of the box marked "familiar" will change, too. We should therefore consciously test and re-evaluate the way we feel about certain sounds at regular intervals.

It is even possible to assign emotional meaning to something as artificial and abstract as a scale. Let's take Lydian as an example:

1 = I'm at home.
2 = I'm walking briskly uphill.
3 = A warm summer breeze.
♯4 = The sun beats down mercilessly and sweat stings my eyes.
5 = Let's take a break and catch our breath.
6 = Time to move on, it's a steep climb; what an amazing view.
j7 = My legs and joints are aching, I'm almost there.
8 = I've reached the mountain cabin and it's been a great but strenuous day.

Join me on my little outing. Sing a Lydian scale, stop on every note and key into the interval-lic relationships with the root. I live in Switzerland and the association with the aspiring and bright characteristics of Lydian reflects a lot of what I feel close to and experience in every-day life. Lydian, even in its most rudimentary form – the scale itself – is not an abstract collection of notes, but rather a sound with a unique quality.

Conversely, I can translate a mood into a mode. Here is an example: I feel depressed and would like to express my state of mind using an appropriate scale. I choose the following series of intervals:

1 = I'm feeling low today.
♭2 = I lack motivation, everything is dragging me down.
♭3 = The sky is grey.
4 = I need to get my act together and do something.
5 = Fatigue and exhaustion require time for recovery.
♭6 = I have to overcome my weaker self and carry on.
♭7 = I'm not doing terribly well, but I have to keep at it.
8 = I tried, to no avail – I'm going back to bed.

Can you empathise? The outcome is Phrygian – a melancholic and gloomy sound that matches my depressed mood. Smile if you will. Now you should understand why, for exam-ple, there are *ragas* in Indian music for different days, seasons, events, states of mind, etc. A mode is nothing more than a "way of life".

So, in the same way that a scale is not simply a uniform succession of notes but rather an assembly of different tension and energy levels, it stands to reason that even a single note may acquire emotional significance. Depending on the context, it can be a chord tone (little tension), a tension (more dissonance), an avoid note (grating tension) or a note foreign to the scale (very unpleasant tension = wrong?) and assume its very own individual colour and potential.

To me, it makes a huge difference whether I imagine a minor third within the context of a minor chord or an augmented ninth in a seventh chord. Even though it is, enharmonically spelled, the same note, the ♭3 feels dark, full-bodied and mellow, whereas the ♯9 elicits a sharp pain in the back of my head when it clashes with the major third of the seventh chord.

Assignment

Play a minor triad (for example C–) on the piano. Play it repeatedly (with the sustain pedal) and sing a Chromatic scale to the chord. Move up the scale step by step and hold each note. Determine whether a note "locks in", elicits extreme tension, creates a pleasant rub or makes your hair stand on end. Sit on each note, even if it hurts. This will intensify the feeling of rest when singing chord or scale tones. Try to find a figurative description for each note and the way it feels. Here's my immediate reaction when relating the notes to a minor triad:

1	=	a complacent Buddha-smile
♭2	=	pain
2/9	=	unfulfilled yearning
♭3	=	a warm blanket
3	=	a kick in the shins
11	=	floating in mid-air
♯11	=	ouch!
5	=	what a relief
♭6	=	ties my stomach in knots
6	=	ready for adventure
♭7	=	neither fish nor fowl
maj7	=	up, up and away
8	=	home at last

Work through all main chord types in this way. Based on your emotional response, decide which notes to avoid in a particular situation, which notes serve the chord or which intervals are particularly good ones to land on because they create interesting and exciting colours (tensions). Since you're doing this exercise with isolated chords, it may be that some of the notes termed avoid notes in a functional environment may actually sound quite thrilling when added to the basic triad or four-note chord. Be aware of this distinction.

Assignment

Play your favourite CDs or the play-alongs accompanying this book, go to concerts, jam sessions, etc. and describe what you hear in your own words – try to find a story, your story, behind the music. Play and sing (improvise) in one mode for a long time (repeatedly play the root on the piano and let it ring) and experience the various scales and their respective sounds as moods, pictures, poems … Play various chord types (with or without tensions) and try to find descriptions that go beyond just the tonal material. How does a sus4 sound feel, what effect does a 7(♯11) voicing have, etc.? Whether you are thinking about your holiday in Bali, fear, the Moscow underground, your first kiss, Albus Dumbledore or a rainbow – these are your own unique experiences and associations, your personal link to the music you're listening to.

Assignment

Imagine something and choose sounds that express what you want to say. Try to tell a story on your instrument. Improvise melodies or compose pieces – but always with the intention to communicate something specific, to arouse feelings or create moods.

Make sure these assignments become a regular part of your practice program. I'll return to this topic in the section "Playing".

Those of you who would like to delve more into this way of thinking should go to the movies more often. Film music is a fantastic medium. This is where you will find the closest and most direct connection between pictures, stories and the emotional content the music tries to depict (by the way, this would be a convenient way to justify the many hours you spend in front of the television).

Programmatic music (or program music) belongs here, too. In many works of instrumental Classical music, we find the portrayal of a story, an event or a theme (e.g. nature). Good examples of this are the compositions "The Moldau" by Friedrich Smetana, "The Four Seasons" by Antonio Vivaldi, "The Planets" by Gustav Holst or "Till Eugenspiegel" by Richard Strauss. Equally important is the principle of the **Leitmotiv** (from German) – the motivic illustration of people, concepts or events in music, by tying a short, striking, and easily recognisable musical phrase to a particular character, place or incident in the story. The German composer Richard Wagner used this technique extensively in his music-dramas, though it needs to be said that he went a great deal further in his desire to create a **Gesamtkunstwerk** (literally: "complete work of art") that united all art forms – music, poetry, dance, painting, drama – in one great masterpiece. On a less ambitious note, the well-known composition "Peter and the Wolf" by Sergei Prokofiev is a beautiful example of how the illustration of individual characters can go beyond the motive. Each figure in the narrative not only has its own melodic theme but is also represented by a specific instrument (Peter = strings, the bird = flute, the duck = oboe, the cat = clarinet and the wolf = French horn, etc.). Check out the music to "Lord of the Rings" by Howard Shore or movies such as "ET" or "Jaws": You will find an abundance of motivic ideas linked to individual characters and venues.

In Jazz, the most noteworthy composer of programmatic music is Duke Ellington. His suites "Black, Brown and Beige" ("a tone-parallel to the history of the American Negro" as Duke described it himself), "Such Sweet Thunder" (also called the "Shakespearean Suite" because the compositions are based on Shakespeare's plays, themes and characters) or the "Far East Suite" (inspired by a tour of the Middle East and a visit to Japan) are clearly programmatic in content and sound.

The lyrics of songs are also often expressed musically. Good songwriters always try to complement the meaning of the words with matching sounds. Have another look at the A section of "Over The Rainbow" (see p. 298). This is a beautiful example of how the melody underscores the essence of the text. The octave leap on the word "some-where" evokes a feeling of longing for a wonderland far away yonder. The major sixth and the long notes on the words "way up high" also support the lyrics and paint a picture of space and upward movement. The melody then gradually relaxes (descending line, more step-wise movement), ending on the word "lullaby" – as if the melody is literally singing itself to sleep. The entire phrase, introduced by the sweep of the opening octave, arches back to where it started and communicates the impression of vastness and openness – rather like a rainbow. Lyrics and music are in perfect symbiosis.

I would like to tell you an anecdote illustrating how instrumentalists can be inspired by lyrics. Ben Webster, one of the great tenor saxophonists in Jazz, was known for first learning the lyrics of a new composition before he practised it on his instrument. The words helped him tell stories with his playing, often determining the mood of his improvisations. One evening, during a concert, he suddenly stopped playing in the middle of a solo. After finishing the piece, he apologised to the audience and – to the questioning looks of the other members of the band – said sheepishly: "I'm sorry – I forgot the lyrics."

> *"The old timers always used to tell horn players to learn the lyrics just as a singer does, so that they know the meaning of the piece."*
>
> **Dizzy Gillespie**

From feelings to terminology

Ear training is more than just an analytical process. It should also kindle your awareness of how you experience music. So far, in this chapter, we've talked about music and the way it can stimulate reactions in terms of images and emotions. Now, in a second step, we will try to translate emotional impact into musical terminology and theoretical fact. A good ear is capable of inferring the objective content of a musical event from a subjective reaction to the sound by establishing a link between a visceral response and the corresponding musical principles. There are three things I'd like to achieve by means of the following discussion:

- Trust your feelings.
- Learn how to describe what you feel.
- Try to interpret your feelings in musical terms.

Conscious, effective listening depends on the intuitive perception of superordinate formal structures and functional relationships as well as the energy levels, the increase and decrease in tension, the overall direction and flow of the music, etc. within these structures, which is then translated intellectually into concrete terminology. In brief, think about the character, the atmosphere and the mood of an individual sound or a longer passage and ask yourself which musical resources are necessary to evoke these feelings.

Assignment

A simple example should show how astutely your ears work and how – in a few easy steps – you can elicit detailed information from a sound and deduce musical facts just by analysing your reactions. Listen to **track 27**. Allow yourselves to be drawn into the recording and describe what occurs to you spontaneously on an emotional level. Look for figurative and graphic descriptions, no matter how silly they might appear to be at first. Try to be as openminded as possible when you play this game, even if you find it difficult to describe music in this way. When contemplating the recording, try to avoid anything to do with abstract musical terminology. Don't think about scales, tensions, functions, and so on. Just write down what occurs to you on an intuitive level while listening. Don't read on until you've put down your reactions on paper.

Are you done? Then let's move on. I've tried this exercise with my students many times. Here are some of their observations and the conclusions that we can draw from them:

"I hear six different loops, each with a repeat. Each loop consists of two colours alternating every two bars. One sound has little tension, feels homely, bright and lush, while the other is restless and wants to resolve. Harmonically, I hear the chord progression oscillating back and forth between relaxation and activity. The first sound is always the same, whereas the second sound changes its character every other loop. The chord progression seems very familiar and is nothing special."

What can we conclude from this rather vague description? The fact that the recording in general appears to be fairly commonplace leads to the assumption that we're dealing with an elementary chord progression. The reason for the second sound of each loop wanting to resolve and the fact that it keeps changing must have something to do with a function that can be varied while maintaining the basic principle. The question is: "What kind of chord with a high level of tension has many faces?" The answer is obvious: a dominant seventh chord because this chord type needs to resolve and goes with a number of different types of scales. Since the first sound is relatively stable, it's probably a tonic chord. The fact that it sounds bright would indicate a maj7 chord. In conclusion, we could venture a guess and say that the chord progression consists of the two alternating functions: Imaj7 and V7. And this is absolutely correct! If you listen carefully to the bass and determine the tonal centre, it will confirm this assumption. We are hearing Fmaj7 and C7 in the key of F Major.

It could be that you recognised this immediately. Well – good for you and a big pat on the back! It could also be that the way we arrived at the above conclusion may seem a bit trite. However, the thought process I have just described with the help of a very simple musical situation is something that can be applied to far more complex chord progressions.

Let's go into more detail and have a closer look at C7. Since we're talking about a dominant seventh chord, the change in colour every second loop must be the result of different scales and tensions being used. This, again, should immediately trigger a chain of thought. We need to delve into our scale library and think about the various commonly used dominant scales in terms of their tonal material and their effect. Let's examine the individual loops. The vocabulary used to describe each loop is taken from answers given by my students to just this exercise. Your reactions and therefore your reasoning may not be quite the same. Don't worry! My intention is to show how to deduce a technical term from an emotional quality, and you will most probably come up with similar, if not identical, results using your own descriptions:

- *Loop 1*: Here, we hear nothing unusual. The dominant sound is familiar, warm, bright, unobtrusive, plain and simple. The tonic and the dominant produce a similar feeling and match in colour. Even if they differ in tension, we don't really notice the transition. Conclusion: Both chords are based on the same tonal material. Therefore, if Fmaj7 is Ionian, then C7 must be *Mixolydian* and the tensions are 9 and/or 13.

- *Loop 2*: Here the dominant feels edgy, biting, raw and darker. It still seems familiar (a colour we often hear), but it has a lot more tension and sounds more aggressive, with more push and pull. The accompaniment, too, feels less smooth and is more percussive. The tonic and dominant are now very different in quality. Conclusion: We are hearing an altered dominant, in which the tensions ♭9, ♯9, ♯11 and/or ♭13 could be expected (in reality we only hear ♭9, ♯9 and ♭13), so the scale is *HM5* or *Altered*.

- *Loop 3*: Trouble is on the way. The sound seems acerbic, noxious, artificial, unfamiliar, symmetrical, harsh, dense, is downright nasty with a lot of sharp edges and spikes – a rather unusual sound. Conclusion: There can be only one interpretation – *HTWT*. This is the only dominant scale that stimulates such a reaction. The HTWT scale contains many half steps (points of dissonance) and has a symmetrical structure (artificial). The tensions are therefore ♭9, ♯9, ♯11 and 13 (it is especially the combination of ♭9/♯9 and 13 that produces this effect – whereas we also find the combination of ♭9, ♯9 and/or ♯11 in Altered).

- *Loop 4*: Here, we are confronted with something very different. The sound suddenly ends up on "cloud nine", floating in mid-air, has hardly any tension at all, seems spacious, peaceful, mellifluous, bright, kitschy, elegant, but at the same time familiar and unspectacular, similar to the C7 in the first loop. Note how the special colouring of the dominant motivates the pianist to change the feel of his accompaniment. He now plays less percussively, with more pedal, sustained voicings, etc. In this case, too, there is only one conclusion: It must be a sus4 chord, which has no tritone (almost no tension), has a floating quality as a result of the suspension of the 4th, and therefore sounds smoother than a normal dominant. The scale is – as was with the first loop – *Mixolydian* (with 9 and/or 13 as tensions).

- *Loop 5*: Something fundamental has changed here. The sound is now boiling away darkly. It seems more cramped, blurred and obscure, has a lot of tension and a stronger tendency to want to resolve than, for instance, the C7 in loop 2. Assumption: Now that we have dealt with most of the important variations of a dominant chord in the previous loops, we are talking about a sound that acts like a dominant, but must be something else. Conclusion: We're no longer hearing C7 but rather the tritone substitution G♭7 (listen to the bass). Because this sound has a relatively high level of tension and because ♭II7 and Imaj7 feel rather different, the scale for G♭7 must be *Lydian(♭7)*. This scale corresponds to C7 Altered and therefore contains a number of chromatic deviations from the key of F Major.

- *Loop 6*: The basic principle has not changed from the last loop. We are still hearing the tritone substitution G♭7. The colour is even darker, though. At the same time, the tension has decreased a bit. Particularly at the transition from ♭II7 to Imaj7, we don't hear a clean break (this means that the scale material of these two chords must be quite similar). All of this allows for only one possible conclusion: Gb7 must be *Altered* – the tonal material seems darker than with Lydian(b7), but it creates less tension because it does not deviate as much from F Ionian.

Our conclusions could be summed up like this:

It is clear that we were able to compare the colours very nicely because we only had an isolated V-I cadence to deal with, and it was easy to focus on the dominant. Nonetheless, this example does show how a close interrelation of emotional response and analytical thinking can help us to hear more accurately.

With this discussion, and especially with the next chapter "Transcription" in mind, I'd like to encourage you to approach a sound firstly from an emotional perspective. I have learned from experience that we should not look to abstract terminology too soon when trying to describe sounds. Jumping to conclusions and prematurely coming up with labels can prevent the ear from taking in a sound without bias and prejudice. Once you have settled on a specific term, it is hard to get rid of it. It may stand in the way of the ear and it can even happen that you start hearing what the wrongly chosen term implies (something like a self-fulfilling prophecy).

Terminology is treacherous. It can obscure the view of the actual musical event and – if you don't watch out – even supersede it. Although theoretical terms are symbols that help us describe things in words, they are no more than a stylised and schematic rendering of an actual musical event, a sterile substitute for the real thing. Music is far too multi-faceted to be forced into a corset of words. Music speaks for itself and can, as I've said before, live happily without verbal description and explanation. For this reason, I'd like you to approach a sound the way you experience it head-on – not intellectually, but sensually. Seduced by dry rationality, the mind can construe a reality of its own. Feelings, however, recognise what is really there.

Normality and surprise

Human beings react strongly to the unexpected and the unusual. Trivial as this may seem, it shows us the route to a sophisticated way of perceiving sound because, if there is such thing as "the special", there must be such thing as "the ordinary". Translated into a specific listening experience, this means that as long as we have a feeling of normality, the music will follow standard procedure and conform to the cliché. Harmonic and melodic rules and stereotypes as well as our personal expectations and habits will be confirmed. The expected and the familiar will be unobtrusive ("inside"). However, as soon as we perceive a moment of tension or surprise, we immediately know that something unusual has happened. Every unexpected note or sound will imply a deviation from the norm. The higher the level of tension, the further away we find ourselves from the cliché, the less ordinary or traditional a sound (increasingly "outside"). We might not yet know what is actually going on. But, what we do know, without any doubt whatsoever, is what is *not* happening – namely the habitual, familiar, customary and expected in this particular situation. And at least we now know what *not* to look for.

So, it is vitally important to be acquainted with the rules that govern a musical situation and the context within which a chord or melodic phrase appears. If we understand how a progression works and which sounds it normally consists of, if we know what determines our habits and expectations in a specific situation, then we will be able to interpret any feeling of surprise (or the lack thereof) correctly. When listening to a piece of music analytically, your train of thought should run down the following lines:

- "The usual" = little or no tension = expected sound = familiar = following the rules = cliché/norm (e.g. diatonic sounds)

- "The unusual" = lot of tension = surprise = unfamiliar = breaking the rules = special case (e.g. chromatic sounds)

Assignment

Two examples will show you what I mean. Play **track 4**. In the meantime, you know that this is in Bb Dorian (see p. 65). Listen to the recording up to 1'50" a number of times (always skip back to the beginning at this point!). So far, the recording is exclusively diatonic. The more often you listen to it, the more firmly the Dorian scale material will become anchored in your ear as the tonal framework of this piece, and the more this framework will determine your perception. Can you feel how your ear gradually locks into the "normality" of this piece and how the Dorian sound becomes more and more familiar? Now listen to the whole track. Towards the end of the recording, you will hear a number of short sections that go against what you have become acquainted with – nothing particularly unusual or spectacular, but brief periods of tension, which you should be able to spot. Here are the time codes for the deviations: 1'57", 2'05", 2'14" and 2'20". It's not (yet) important to know what happens at these very moments. But, what we do know for sure is that the pianist is using sounds that don't agree with Bb Dorian. This is why we feel little pinpricks of dissonance disrupting an otherwise homogenous scale environment.

The analysis of the unusual bits should present no serious challenge. You know at least what it *isn't* – namely Bb Dorian. This means you don't have to look very far. It could be a different scale, a chromatic embellishment or chord displacement, a strange voicing or a phrase structured in an unusual way, etc. See, if you can figure out what it actually is.

Assignment

I'd like to try a little experiment. Let's listen to Larry William's keyboard solo on "Spain" (on "This Time" by Al Jarreau). Get hold of the recording and do the following. Prepare a 24-bar grid on a separate sheet of paper and fill in the changes (see p. 336). OK, here we go. Start the recording. Once you reach the solo (3'05") – while listening – mark every bar where the lines convey a feeling of strangeness. I am not talking about dramatic dissonances. After all, there is not one wrong note in the entire solo. Every single phrase can be explained in terms of the theoretical concepts presented in this book. Nevertheless, it is still possible to play within the bounds of convention and create more or less tension, depending on which im-provisational concept you are working with. These tendencies can be clearly felt. Don't read on until you've completed the assignment.

If you need more time to think about a certain section of the solo, stop the recording before reaching the next chord. You might have to practise getting this right! Tap along with the solo in half notes on 1 and 3 (*alla breve*) and see if you can stop just before the bar line. You should not listen to the next chord change because it would interfere with your immedi-ate reaction:

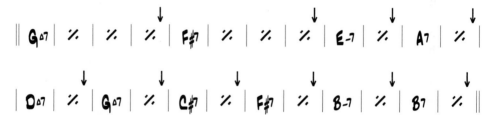

So, let's do it again! Each time you stop the recording, ask yourself what you feel. Did the passage before the stopping point sound familiar (inside) or strange (slightly outside)? The results of your "stop-and-go" exercise could look like this:

Familiar				Strange				Familiar		Strange	
G△7	∕.	∕.	∕.	**F#**7	∕.	∕.	∕.	**E**-7	∕.	**A**7	∕.

Familiar		Familiar		Strange		A bit strange		Familiar		Strange	
D△7	∕.	**G**△7	∕.	**C#**7	∕.	**F#**7	∕.	**B**-7	∕.	**B**7	∕.

Can you feel both choruses progressing in a similar way? If you do, it means you are reacting perfectly in accordance with Larry Williams' lines. It is easy to make out where he stays within the constraints imposed by the tonality and where he has deliberately worked with scale material that disregards the diatonic expectations of the overall key

Now the question arises as to why some parts sound "strange" and others not. It is obvious that the diatonic functions don't attract attention. Conclusion: Larry Williams improvises over all diatonic chords within the bounds of the tonal cliché – and this means we hear lines that confirm our expectations. However, on the dominant chords (all dominants!), we feel something that goes against the grain. Second conclusion: He no longer sticks to the chord-scale relationships we would expect to hear. You may be a bit unsure about the F♯7 in bars 19 and 20 – to some, this may sound normal, while others experience considerable tension.

Analyse the dominant chords (even though the tune is clearly in B Minor, think in terms of D Major for simplicity's sake). You should come up with the following functional analysis and the corresponding chord-scale relationships: F♯7 (V7/VI) = HM5, A7 (V7) = Mixolydian, C♯7 (V7/III) = Altered, B7 (V7/II) = HM5. Obviously, this is *not* what Larry Williams plays.

So what does he do? There are two possible explanations. Remember the scale cliché for dominants: they are either Mixolydian (when resolving to a major target chord) or HM5/Altered (when resolving to a minor chord). So, one possible solution is the reversal of this principle, which would account for the fact that all dominants create considerable tension. But – to cut things short – this is not what happens (though the possibility should cross your mind). There is, however, a second explanation if you consider concepts that can be applied to any dominant chord. It stands to reason that Larry Williams uses material that generates tension with both types of dominants. Question: Which scale creates tension with every dominant function? Answer: Half-tone-whole-tone. With an otherwise Mixolydian dominant, the ♭9, ♯9 and ♯11 cause considerable unrest, with a dominant usually played HM5 it is the 13 that sticks out like a sore thumb.

And this is exactly what Larry Williams does. As the transcription of the first chorus on p. 133 ff. shows, F♯7, A7, C♯7 and B7 are all played HTWT. Since this scale sounds like a mixture of Mixolydian and Altered, it clashes with our expectations every time. You can also see this clearly in the written music once you compare the transcription with the results of our little experiment. Whenever the deviations from the basic diatonic environment are more pronounced, more accidentals appear (resulting in a higher level of tension).

The question remains: Why does the F♯7 in bars 19 and 20 sound unusual, even though the function is played HM5/Altered, as would be expected? If it's not the scale material, then it must be the structure of the phrase that tickles our ear. If you look closely, you'll see that the line can also be interpreted as A minor Pentatonic. We are hearing the usual scale material arranged in an unusual way – and this causes the tension some of us experience.

I have carried out this experiment with many musicians. What never ceases to amaze me is that all (!) of my guinea pigs have reacted in more or less the same way. This goes to show that the feeling for what is normal or unusual is *independent of how experienced or knowledgeable* the listener is! Beginners sense this in the same ways as pros do. It makes absolutely no difference how far we have probed into unusual sounds in our musical development. Even musicians for whom dissonance is an everyday occurrence, those who can play "outside" and therefore have a highly developed sense of tolerance for the unusual, are still able to distinguish between "inside" and "outside" when listening to tonal music.

This shows that our perception has less to do with a sound as such, but rather more with the context in which it is used. The context determines the rules (the norm) as well as the exceptions (the unusual). As an example, let's look at the tritone. Within a purely diatonic, major framework with its consonant triadic layers of thirds and relationships based on the cycle of fifths, the tritone is a seriously disrupting factor, and this is how we perceive it – as a nasty dissonance (the "devil in music"). However, when it appears in the Blues, it is nothing special at all. It just slips by the ear without making much of an impression. Here, it is a fundamental element because all basic functions are seventh chords (I7, IV7, V7) and the ♭5 in the melody is one of the main stylistic features of the Blues (a blue note). In this context, the tritone is an essential ingredient – the standard sound – and therefore consonant.

I hope it is now clear to you how important it is to be aware of the context in which a sound appears – the context determines its effect and the way our ear reacts to it. This means that the same sound may stimulate a completely different response when appearing in another setting. And now to the decisive point: Anyone can feel the effect of a sound, but we can only interpret it if we know which rules and principles govern the framework within which the sound occurs. These principles give a sound meaning, and we need to understand them in order to assess the reason for our reaction to the sound correctly. So, a good ear has a lot to do with what you know. The more you know, the better you will understand a sound and the way it works.

From terminology to sound

I quoted Goethe at the beginning of this section ("Listening"): "People merely hear the things they comprehend". Some of you may want to contradict this. However, after 30 years of teaching ear training, I can categorically state that this quote hits the nail right on the head – we have to know and understand something before we can actually hear it. Of course, I'm not talking about hearing in a clinical sense – what I mean is recognising something we hear for what it is. Here's a fact: We will not notice something we know nothing about. The narrower our thinking, the more rudimentary and unrefined our musical perception is. To lay listeners, a musical event probably appears as nothing more than a vague cloud of sound that affects them in a general, holistic way, which they can enjoy on an emotional level but not understand intellectually. The trained musician, however, will discover a multitude of minute details beneath the surface, which forever remain hidden to the untrained ear. The more limited and superficial our musical knowledge, the more restricted we are in our ability to delve into the structure of music. Here's an example. If you don't know anything about the concept of "upper structures", you will not be in a position to recognise them as such when they appear in a solo or an accompaniment. Even worse, what you don't know about you won't practise, and what you don't practise you will probably never play. So, you first have to know that upper structures exist before you can appreciate them or think about using them.

Much of what is going on in Jazz these days is impossible to understand without a well-grounded knowledge of theory and a fabulously well-developed ear. The more complex the music is, the harder it gets to access melodic, harmonic, rhythmic or formal aspects of a composition solely on an emotional and intuitive level. It is increasingly necessary to "think" music first before dealing with it "hands on". This is where terminology comes into play. Terms, labels and theoretical descriptions make us aware of new concepts and help us include yet unfamiliar colours in our musical vocabulary by sorting and storing them and putting them in juxtaposition with familiar sounds. Terminology is not simply there to describe musical concepts we already know about. It is also a way of introducing us to things that are not yet part of our musical repertoire. This means, however, that, more often than not, we will learn concepts *before* being introduced to the corresponding sounds. It is quite normal for us to juggle theoretical terms that are not yet tied to actual music. Of course, you may have come across the sound in question at some point, but it most probably will have slipped by because the link between the theoretical term and its aural equivalent has not yet been established.

Why is this of importance? It is an old truth that terminology influences our perception of things. The choice of a particular term is often quite relevant to how we identify and memorise the corresponding sound. Because we tend to hear things the way we think about them, we must take care *how* we learn and use new terminology. I have already touched on this problem in the chapter on secondary dominants (p. 118). Remember, for instance, that I introduced the symbols V7/V as well as II7 for the secondary dominant G7 in the key of F Major. The first term (V7/V) is linked to the dominant's need to resolve and points us towards the expected target chord (C7). The second (II7) puts G7 in relation to the diatonic scale degrees and defines it as a replacement for II–7 (G–7). Depending on which symbol we use, we can interpret G7 either as an active sound (V7/V) or as a stationary diatonic substitution (II7). Both approaches are justified, and it would be limiting to focus only on one of the two. It was my intention to confront you with two different theoretical angles for one and the same sound, in the hope of enhancing your ability to commit this specific sound to memory as well as improving the flexibility of the ear.

Let's take another example. I assume that you – like most people – are used to placing the root at the bottom of a chord or scale with the rest of the notes added *above* it. This means you have acquired the habit of thinking *from the bottom up* – and all theory books support this approach without realising its implications. My experience has shown that most people don't even consider looking for the root anywhere else. When I ask my students to sing the root of a recording, they start droning away somewhere in the lower register of their vocal range (where you can't properly intonate, even if you were paid for it). I have never (!) heard anyone respond to this exercise by singing the root somewhere in his or her upper range. The same goes for the octave – it is always assumed that the upper octave is meant. Many musicians have remarkable difficulty equating the upper octave with the lower root, in other words, saying 1 rather than 8 when dealing with the upper octave. The intellect knows that we are talking about the same note, but the reflex "the root is at the bottom" predominates.

So, what's so mind-shattering about this revelation? Let's have a look at intervals. I regularly find in my teaching that larger intervals (sixths/sevenths) are harder to hear and sing than smaller ones (seconds/thirds). Why – for heaven's sake – would that be? In the end, sixths and sevenths are only "large" if, by force of habit, we think of an interval as a pair of notes with the root at the bottom and the second note propped up on top of it. If we were to transpose the root up an octave and think about the interval *from the top down*, the sixth would turn into a third and the seventh would turn into a second, resulting in smaller, easier intervals. As soon as we have defined a root, it should be of no consequence whatsoever where we hear a note – a maj7 is always a maj7, whether it is played on the bass or the piccolo.

Give it a try! Sing a note in the lower range of your voice, define it as the root and sing the maj7 above it. Not so easy, is it? Now sing the root an octave higher and the maj7 below it. You only have to sing a half step down – and this is so much easier. Even if this exercise seems trivial, it clearly shows us something fundamental: If we don't think about viewing the upper octave as the root we would never think of using the principle of complementary intervals and sing the maj7 below the root. And if we don't use this idea, a major seventh will always be a hard interval to sing and hear.

The same discussion applies to chord inversions. Again, it is my experience that triads or four-note chords are much easier to sing in root position than in inverted form. Go ahead and try! Pick a note in the lower range and define it as the 5 of a major triad. Now sing the triad upwards. Be honest! How many times did you have to try before you were sure that you are singing the right thing? How often did you instinctively slip into a root position? How much mental gymnastics did you have to perform to avoid following the urge to automatically sing the basic chord structure with the root at the bottom? As a result, many of my students have a hard time identifying chord sounds that are *not* played in root position (and if you refer to the chapter "Voicings", pdf-E, you will realise that there are many sounds where the root is not the bottom voice).

What can we conclude from this? The way we learn terminology and the way we use terms influences our ear. The way we think determines to a large extent how we approach new sounds. For this reason, it is important to examine and understand your own thought processes. The more flexible your thinking is, the easier it will be to assimilate a new sound. It stands to reason that those of us, who feel the need for narrow, strict definitions and who understand theory in a one-dimensional way, will hear poorly as a result.

Assignment

One example should show you how dangerous it is to assign immutable sound characteristics and properties to a specific musical term. Let's do another experiment. On a separate sheet of paper, write down everything you associate with the term "Altered". Only read on once you are satisfied you have an exhaustive list of descriptive attributes.

My students almost invariably come up with the following reactions to this assignment: "highly dissonant", "out of character", "aggressive", "notes foreign to the key", "it's nice to be back again after having used this sound" – only to mention a few. I assume that your responses are fairly similar. After all, the Altered scale is presented as an aggressive colour in all textbooks and "altered tensions" are described as being far more dissonant than "natural tensions" (diatonic extensions).

This goes to show how decisive it is how we are first exposed to a new term or concept. I guess that most of you have learned "Altered" as an alternative to a Mixolydian dominant within a major key context (V7 Altered → Imaj7 Ionian). And in this specific case, it is true that V7 Altered is a special and highly aggressive scale option – it goes against the tonality and creates an inordinate amount of tension. However, both of the following dominants in the key of G Major clearly show that the actual effect of a scale and the degree of dissonance are primarily influenced by the harmonic environment and the overall tonality:

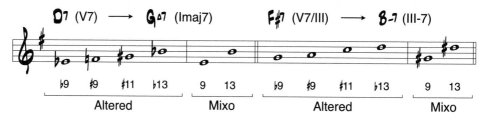

Remember – the context determines the effect of a sound. Whereas all tensions of an altered D7 chord (V7) go against the feeling of tonality (high level of dissonance), the alterations of F#7 (V7/III) are an integral part of G Major (less dissonance). Inversely, Mixolydian would be a far more dissonant choice of scale for F♯7 because 9 (G♯) and 13 (D♯) clearly deviate from the key. So, it is easy to see that alterations do not automatically imply higher levels of dissonance. In some cases, altered tensions are the ordinary sound, the cliché and the more neutral, inconspicuous colour (and, vice versa, natural tensions are not always as easygoing and bland as you might expect).

Here's the essential point. Depending on the context, an altered sound – as I have just shown – *may or may not* trigger a feeling of tension! So, if you associate the term "Altered" with the phenomenon "high level of dissonance", you could well misinterpret or completely overlook an altered sound that *does not* sound dissonant. If we view musical terms too narrowly, we will have difficulty coming to grips with the multi-faceted nature of music. However, if we are aware of the different implications of the terms we use to describe sounds, we will be able to analyse musical situations far more quickly and reliably. We would not need to start from scratch each time, having to filter out countless possibilities in order to come up with the correct solution. Your awareness of the context will immediately whittle down the multitude of options to a relatively limited number of probabilities. If you hear, for instance, an F♯7 chord in G Major that seems to zip past in a rather normal and unobtrusive way, then you just *know* that you're dealing with the cliché, and that the tensions you hear must include ♭9, ♯9, ♯11 or ♭13. You might not immediately know precisely which alteration(s) are actually used, but you will certainly stop looking for 9 and 13.

The previous assignment shows that we can only label a sound correctly if we can interpret our reaction to the sound and understand in which context it is likely to create what kind of effect. With this, our magic triangle is now complete. Sound, feelings and terminology belong inextricably to one another. The better you are able to link what you feel with what you know, the more acutely you will be able to hear. And one day you will be able to say without hesitation: That's a ♯9. You won't know why; you'll just know that that's what it is. A ♯9 has its own flavour – and you can taste it on your tongue that very moment. A ♯9 is a ♯9 is a ♯9 is a ♯9 … and you don't have to waste a single moment thinking about it. Your intuitive reaction tells you that it can't be anything else. But, be careful! Once you think you have completely absorbed the ♯9, you suddenly stumble upon a maj7 chord that is not played Ionian but rather Lydian(♯9) – quite an unusual sound that doesn't "fit in", that baffles the ear because you have never run across anything like it or didn't even know it existed. And suddenly, the ♯9 is once again a stranger and the game begins anew. No matter how certain you feel you may be, there will always be something unusual and unfamiliar waiting for you around the corner to be discovered. And this is the delightful and thrilling thing about music!

Transcription

"When you're very young, you don't have the harmonic knowledge to create solos yourself, so you begin by copying things that sound good in other people's solos."

Benny Bailey

The well-known trumpeter Clark Terry responded to the question as to how he learned to improvise by saying:

"Imitate, assimilate, create, innovate"

It is not possible to put this in any better way. The fascinating thing is that all Jazz musicians say the same thing – sometimes even using the same words.

For example, the pianist Walter Bishop Jr.: *"You move from the imitation stage to the as-similation stage when you take little bits of things from different people and weld them into an identifiable style – creating your own style. Once you've created your sound and you have a good sense of the history of the music, then you think of where the music hasn't gone and where it can go – and that's innovation."*

Or the trumpet player Lonnie Hillyer: *"All the great Jazz musicians have also been great teachers. Their lessons are preserved for students on every recording they made."*

Let's start with imitation. **It is not a criminal offense to copy what inspires you!** Every musician will have looked to role models for orientation at some point or other in his or her development. There are no better teachers! Even though the number of available workbooks, online courses and instructional materials for the aspiring Jazz musician has increased ex-ponentially over the past years, books can never substitute the real thing. After all, Jazz is improvised music and can't be learned by reading books (dear reader, I am fully aware of the inconsistency). If we want to get to the heart of the matter, we are compelled to fall back on the only source that gives us permanent access to all the wonderful improvisations that have enticed us to become a Jazz musician – our CD collections. This is our personal library of sound, which we can draw on when putting together a practice program that reflects our musical taste. Whereas Classical musicians rely primarily on sheet music or printed scores and parts when practising, Jazz musicians have to create their own study tools. One of the most important elements of the everyday practice routine of a Jazz musician – and some-thing quite alien to a Classical musician – is to transcribe recordings.

Transcription (from the Latin *scribere* = to write) means: **listening** to improvisations, chord progressions, bass lines, voicings, rhythmic patterns, etc., **memorising** them, **analys-ing** them, **writing** them down, **playing** them on your instrument over and over again until they are completely internalised and then **translating them into your own ideas** so that they become an inherent part of your personal musical language. Transcriptions were, are and always will be the single most important means of consciously and deliberately studying, comparing and integrating the musical vocabulary of our favourite Jazz artists. Transcription is the most comprehensive and effective way of acquiring a good ear. It disciplines, organises and trains our musical memory, forces us to think analytically and creates a link between sound, the written page and the instrument. This will also help composers/arrangers formulate their ideas more precisely as well as help studio musicians with their sight-reading. As committed Jazz musicians, we should have the desire to immerse ourselves deeply in the recordings that touch and impress us. These recordings are the starting points of our personal development and transcribing them should become an integral part of our daily routine.

Before we get down to the nitty-gritty, I'd like to dispose of a common misconception. Music is like any other language. You learn your mother tongue aurally at first. You speak before you can read or write. Why should Jazz be any different? Ultimately, the goal of any transcription is to capture a sound, internalise it and, eventually, weave it into something personal. Acquiring a mental image of a sound and translating it to your own instrument is what it's all about. The word "transcription" is therefore misleading, because it insinuates that we are aiming for a written result. You couldn't be more wrong! Writing down a solo is nothing but an intermediate stepping stone. As a matter of fact, there are many (highly successful) Jazz musicians who sidestep the writing aspect of transcription and go straight for the instrument. Personally, however, I believe that writing things down has its merits because it forces you to take decisions. As you will see, there are many things to be considered, figured out and scrutinised analytically before you can put a sound down on paper. A written representation will also help you with visualising and memorising the music. In addition, you will always be able to go back to a transcription if you should ever forget a particular detail. I therefore endorse the written product, but only if it is preceded by absorbing a sound aurally and is followed up by diligent work on your instrument and the creative process of turning the transcribed material into something original. For the sake of this book, we'll stick to the following procedure: *listen – memorise – analyse – notate – play – transform*.

I am fully aware of the transcription software available on the market. There are programs that work with spectrum analysis and offer a number of features (e.g. slowing down the recording without change of pitch, "note and chord guessing", change of playback pitch, fine tuning, looping, etc., to name just a few), which can facilitate transcription considerably. Sounds great, doesn't it? ***Don't use them!!!*** You would only be cheating yourself out of an important part of ear training (so I'm not going to endorse any transcription program). I know that transcribing can be a tedious business! But, I encourage you to take the difficult route. It will pay off eventually.

Of course, there are also countless transcriptions available commercially. I can't emphasise strongly enough how important it is to avoid these at all costs. Firstly, they often contain annoying errors, which we adopt inadvertently. Secondly, the easy way out has never been the key to success. The ear has to be challenged in order to develop! *Strain to train* – only the transcriptions we have worked on ourselves will really stick and become part of our subconscious inner voice.

Transcribing is an art that needs to be practised! It is time-consuming work, at least at first – work that requires a lot of tenacity and self-discipline. Approaching it systematically is essential. The following pages will serve as a guide.

"Really, the best way to learn is to take tunes off records, because you're utilizing your ear. It takes a lot of knowledge and experience to do this, but it becomes so easy to hear pieces in their component parts if you actually do the work yourself. Then you start trying to write the changes out by ear. In the beginning, you're going to write things out wrong. You're not going to know what's wrong for the first few years that you do this. But in the end, you see your mistakes and you really learn it."

Howard Levy

Choice of material

Why do we transcribe? Because we hear something we like and want to get to know better. I'm sure you've often thought: "Great solo! I want to play just like that!" However, don't forget that the players on the recordings probably have decades of experience on you. Most of the frustrations we experience with transcriptions are due to the fact that we recklessly overestimate our abilities. We venture too quickly into uncharted territory and become overwhelmed and discouraged with the mammoth task at hand. As a result, we shy away from future attempts. You have to accept that you can't catch up 20 years' worth of work in 20 minutes. You must start at your own level and work your way up gradually.

So, lower the demands you impose on yourselves and first try to transcribe recordings that correspond to where your ears are at. Choose a familiar piece, one you might have played already (e.g. a Blues or a well-known standard). The tempo should not be too fast (about 100–140 BPM). Don't begin with a ballad – the time feel of ballads is often floating, indistinct and hard to lock into. Stay away from complex chord progressions. Pick something relatively tonal without modulations and in a key with a simple key signature (up to 2 sharps or flats) – in other words, something that is easy to handle. The theme or solo should be relatively easy-going and relaxed (simple rhythms, a fair amount of rests, not too many leaps or fast-moving lines, etc.). I'd recommend recordings by Chet Baker (tp), Paul Desmond (as), Stan Getz (ts), J.J. Johnson (tb), Kenny Burrell (g) or Ray Brown (b). Think about whether you would like to transcribe the entire recording or just a short section.

When transcribing solos, you should start off with improvisations played on your instrument. Being familiar with its sound as well as its technical peculiarities (fingerings, typical phrases, etc.) will make it easier for you to key into the music. Every instrument has its characteristics due to the way it is constructed. For instance, something that is easy to perform on a saxophone is sometimes virtually impossible to do on a guitar (although there are guitar players who try and succeed). Be aware of these differences. Later on, in order to broaden your musical horizons, be sure to transcribe solos played on other instruments, too. Remember that every instrument has its own unmistakable sound, which we should get to know. In addition, looking to other instruments will supply you with ideas you most likely would not come up with if you exclusively rely on material played on your own instrument.

Don't focus on solos only. Transcribe themes and arrangements. This will give you the opportunity to become acquainted with different instruments and their roles within an ensemble. Additionally, arrangements are useful because they are usually based on written material and are therefore played quite accurately. Solos can be ambiguous at times (especially in terms of rhythm).

I would like to avoid letting this become too dry and academic by working on three recordings, which demonstrate very different aspects of transcription:

- *"Moving Out"* by Isla Eckinger on the album "Magic Box"
- *"Waltz For Ever"* by Joe Haider on "Joe Haider – Bert Joris Anniversary Big Band"
- *"Walking Tiptoe"* by Bert Joris on "Joe Haider – Bert Joris Anniversary Big Band"

Listen to these pieces (**tracks 42–44**). I hope you like my choice of tunes – after all, transcription should be fun. I recommend you keep pdf-H ("Transcription Workshop") at hand while reading this chapter. It would make sense to refer to an actual recording while working on every one of the following points.

Goals of transcription

The next thing to decide is why we are doing the transcription. If we are transcribing a theme, are we aiming for an exact copy of what was played, including all instruments and musical components right down to the last minute detail? Or do we want to end up with a lead sheet, in other words, a more general, abridged version. If so, we need to deliberately transcribe less accurately (chord symbols instead of exact voicings, rhythmic and melodic simplifications, etc.). After all, a lead sheet is the condensed portrayal of a piece that can be used by many different instruments (remember: The more specific the notation, the less improvisational freedom for the players).

Whereas a theme can be notated more sketchily, transcriptions of solos should be as accurate as possible. Here, you have to consider and notate every little ingredient: dynamics, articulations, phrase marks, ghost notes, slurs, trills, slides, etc. Ultimately, the objective of a solo transcription is not only to capture the correct notes as such but also to be mindful of the way the lines are shaped. Once you transfer them to your instrument, you should practise them *exactly* the way they were originally played. Consequently, the notation should reflect the sound of the recording as closely as possible.

Transcribing arrangements (from small band to big band) is also a great ear training exercise, even though this may be quite a challenge at first. Since arrangements are usually carefully constructed and designed down to the last dot, they give us the chance to focus not only on writing down the more prominent and easily discernible elements of a composition but also those aspects that are less obvious and harder to grasp: secondary parts, horn sections, bass lines, piano voicings, detailed drum grooves, etc. So, with arrangements, we will have to decide how far we want to take them.

Getting to know the recording

I have observed many students working on transcriptions in my time. The less experienced ones tend to work along the following lines (with a bit of exaggeration on my behalf): The recording is played and immediately switched off as soon as the very first note has sounded; then it's off to the piano, hectically trying to find the note. The first attempt is usually wrong, by which time the memory of the right note has faded away into oblivion. So, it's back to the recording, off to the piano, play another note, miss the right one, try again, miss, try, miss, try... until, at last, the note is found and written down – eureka! Then, of course, it's off to the second note, and the whole cycle starts afresh. Same story! And so, we move through the recording in itsy-bitsy, teeny-weeny steps.

Few students first take the time to listen to the complete recording from beginning to end. In their hurry to get something down on paper quickly, they chop it up into small, seemingly more palatable bits and pieces. *This makes absolutely no sense at all and couldn't be less effective!* No one listens to music in this way, and it is definitely not how we commit music to memory. After a concert we're usually left with nothing more tangible than a ticket stub to remind us of the music we just heard. How many of you have ever commented on a performance by saying something like: "The F7(♯9) chord on the third beat of bar 92 in the fourth tune of the first set really blew me away!"? Who listens to CDs and stops every two seconds to think about a particular note? When we listen to music we listen to the whole piece, and if we like it we say "Yeah!" or "Wow!" or, if we're not that impressed, "Oh well, I dunno ..." – nothing more and nothing less. This is exactly how we should approach our transcriptions – *as a whole*. Just sit back and allow the recording to work its magic on you. At first, try not to think too much about anything. Don't try to name or analyse details, and, especially, don't write things down. Simply delve into the music and absorb the sound.

Then press "stop" and try to recap the recording in your head. Here, too, you should not think too analytically. At this stage, we are not yet concerned with figuring out specific notes, chords, progressions, rhythmic patterns, etc. Simply allow the sounds to pass by your inner ear and give your memory the chance to store a vivid image of the piece. Take your time with this. Listen to the recording as often as you need to. Try to recall it "in tempo" – your memory should be as close to the original as possible. It is not important to concern yourself with individual instruments or minor details for the moment – at this point, it is much more important to develop a reliable overall impression of the tune, which you can draw on at any time without having to listen to the recording again.

Now switch on the brain and start thinking about what you have just heard. Try – as best you can with whichever words come to mind – to describe what you have noticed and identified in terms of general aspects as well as detailed elements. Recapitulate your impressions from memory and make a list of the things you remember and the thoughts that occured to you while listening – no matter how straightforward or complex, trivial or significant they may appear to be.

First, focus on the basic structure of the piece (e.g. think: "I hear a section and then something different, then the first section is repeated, followed by a closing passage – so, we're most probably dealing with an ABAC tune format."). Try to remember how the theme or the solo breathes, where the breaks and formal subdivisions are, where melodic ideas begin or end. We aren't talking about scales, chords or rhythms yet. We're just trying to get the gist of things – the general sequence of events. Only with a good overview will you be able to hear at different *zoom levels*, to "zoom in" on details without losing touch with the overall picture and to listen to passages at different "magnifications" – from one single note or chord to a complete formal section. You will not only be able to work deductively (from the large to the small, i.e. drawing detailed conclusions from general assumptions) but also inductively (from the small to the large, i.e. making generalisations based on individual aspects).

Instrumentation

Successful transcription, however, does not only depend on the ability to take in the sound of a recording as a whole. It is equally important to be able to filter out and identify individual instruments or parts. Listen to the recording a number of times and try to determine what instruments are playing. Be as exact as you can. You are not just hearing a saxophone, for instance, but rather a sopranino, soprano, alto, tenor, baritone or bass sax, each with its very own unique sound. Do you hear a trumpet or a flugelhorn? What mute is being used (cup, harmon, straight, plunger, etc.)? Are you hearing an electric bass guitar or a double bass? Is the double bass being plucked (*pizzicato*) or bowed (*arco*)? Are we talking about an acoustic or electric guitar (a Classical guitar with nylon strings, a steel-string acoustic, acoustic or semi-acoustic Jazz guitar, solid body, etc.)? What effects does the guitarist use (reverb, chorus, wah-wah pedal, etc.)? What parts of the drum set can you identify (hi-hat, snare, bass drum, floor tom, etc.)? Is the drummer playing with sticks, brushes, Hot Rods, mallets? Is there a percussionist (congas, bongos, timbales, claves, maracas, tambourine, etc.)? How many trombones can you hear? Is the line played by one instrument only or by several instruments in unison? And so on, and so on …

To cut a long story short – these questions should show that there is much more to a transcription than notating chords, melodies and rhythms. Consider the character, the overall effect and the peculiarities of each instrument. The better you get to know the sound of an instrument and the more you understand its technical properties, the easier it will be for you to transcribe what is being played. Sometimes, an understanding of the mechanics of a particular instrument will give you decisive clues as to whether you're on the right track or whether a line you think you've transcribed correctly must be wrong simply because it's technically not feasible. In time, your ear will be sensitive to such a fine degree that you will even start recognising specific musicians based on their sound and the way they articulate and phrase their lines.

I am aware of the fact that it takes a long time to develop these recognition patterns. Make a point of familiarising yourselves with a wide range of instruments. I have already suggested (under "Choice of Material") that you should initially choose pieces or improvisations played on your own instrument. Later on, you must transcribe other instruments, too. That is why I have chosen "Waltz For Ever" and "Walking Tiptoe" for you to transcribe (pdf-H). Since both pieces are written for big band, the recordings will help you get to know the most commonly used instruments in Jazz.

As soon as we have determined the instrumentation of a piece, we get to a seemingly trivial, but nonetheless vitally important part of any transcription (this exercise was already given in the previous chapter). Play the recording a number of times and focus on *one* instrument or group of instruments each time without letting the other parts divert your attention. Allow yourselves to be drawn deep into every layer of the sound. Don't just focus on the obvious parts of the recording such as the melody or the soloist. Try to follow the less conspicuous instruments, too (the bass line, elements of the drums such as the bass drum, snare or hi-hat, the piano accompaniment, etc.). Being able to concentrate on individual instruments is important because seemingly insignificant details in the background often provide us with vital clues about melodic, harmonic, rhythmic and formal aspects (chord types, scales, functional relationships, etc.). It will become easier for you to discern the specific ingredients of a composition once you are able to isolate individual instruments. Don't yet think about what you hear, just be aware of each instrument as a distinctive voice.

Pulse, tempo, time signature and style

Thus far, we haven't written down or played a single note of what we've been listening to – and that's the way it should be! Transcription should always move from the general to the specific. So, instead of getting bogged down in detail, we should focus on the basic aspects that constitute the framework of the transcription. What is the first thing we should listen for: the root, the key, the melody, the chord progression, etc.? No! We should first concern ourselves with something more elementary, apparently self-evident, without which you wouldn't be able to notate anything at all: We have to determine the basic pulse and the tempo of the recording. Without pulse, there's no tempo, no time signature, no form.

So, the question is: What is the basic pulse? In most cases, this is quite easy to figure out. Tap along with the recording. What you are reacting to is probably the quarter-note pulse. But watch out – pieces in a faster tempo sometimes come across as having a slower pulse because you are feeling groups of beats rather than each individual beat. There are styles (e.g. fast Latin in 4/4) that are felt and played *alla breve* (in half notes), also referred to as *cut time* (indicated by the symbol C with a vertical stroke). This means we feel a half-note pulse, while the tempo is actually double the speed and counted in quarter notes. In 3/4, faster pieces often have a dotted-half-note feel (the downbeat of each bar is felt as the basic pulse). In 6/8, the dotted eighth note is quite a common subdivision of the bar. In 12/8 Afro-Cuban, you'd be counting in 8th notes, but you would rather feel a slow 4/4 with a triplet feel (three 8th notes to the beat), and so on. If you are not sure about the pulse, ask yourself: "How would I dance to this piece?" Your sense of how you would move to the music will tell you if it is a slower or a faster piece. Here are the most common styles and grooves and the way they are "counted":

- *Swing*: in quarter notes (swing 8ths)
- *Bossa Nova*: in quarter notes (straight 8ths)
- *Samba*: in half notes (the actual pulse = fast quarter notes)
- *Funk*: in quarter notes (with a subdivision in sixteenth notes)
- *Shuffle*: in quarter notes (with a triplet subdivision)

Once you have established the pulse, take a metronome and check the exact tempo. This is a very important step. After all, the reason you are transcribing is to absorb and "save" a sound to memory in the hope of implanting it firmly in your musical vocabulary. Because you will probably spend quite some time on a transcription and listen to the recording repeatedly, knowing the exact tempo will help you subconsciously develop a good feel for the corresponding metronome marking. The recording itself becomes a point of reference in your mind for this particular tempo. Ideally, you should have a reference tune for almost every metronome marking from 60 to 240 BPM. Eventually, you will be able to associate each metronome marking with a specific tempo by keying into a specific piece. For example, "Fantasy" by Earth, Wind and Fire is my link to 90 BPM. "The Groove Merchant" by Jerome Richardson (as played by the Thad Jones / Mel Lewis Jazz Orchestra) conjures up "medium shuffle" (as the style) and also triggers 130 BPM. "The Kid From Red Bank" by Count Basie / Neal Hefti (on "The Atomic Mr. Basie") is inextricably tied to 280 BPM, and so on. I have a whole list of recordings covering almost every metronome marking from 50–300 BPM. So, get used to determining the exact tempo of a piece and writing it down at the top of your transcription as one of the first things you do.

The next step would be to figure out the time signature (also referred to as "metre"). Don't forget what I said earlier about melodic rhythm in terms of "strong" and "weak". The feeling of "strong" (= point of emphasis) usually coincides with the first beat (the downbeat) of the bar. Just to be sure, you should count your way through the whole piece and conduct along to the recording. Here are the most common conducting patterns the way they would be executed by a right-handed person (from your perspective). The patterns for left-handed people are the mirror images of these:

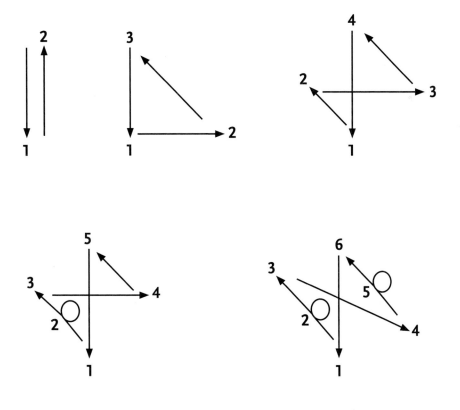

Practise these patterns with various recordings. Most pieces have a fixed time signature, as do all tracks accompanying this book. If, however, you lose your place while conducting, if you find that your "one" is no longer in sync with the points of emphasis in the melody, it may mean that there is a change of metre somewhere along the way.

Assignment

Sing "Happy Birthday". Can you feel the pulse? What time signature is it in? Try to conduct while singing. Start with a 4/4 conducting pattern (beginning on "Happy"). You should feel how the points of emphasis in the melody time and again fail to coincide with the downbeats of the conducting pattern. Now try to conduct in 4/4 starting on <u>Birth</u>day ("Happy" being a pick-up). That doesn't work either. Repeat the procedure using a 3/4 conducting pattern. And, lo and behold, you will come up with the correct solution. Amazingly, I have come across quite a few music students who are not immediately able to spot the fact that "Happy Birthday" starts with a pick-up and is in 3/4.

Assignment

Listen to the piece "I'll Be Here For You" by Al Jarreau (on the album "Jarreau") and try to figure out the time signature of the theme. Feel the (slow) basic pulse, conduct along to the recording and write down your solution. Don't read on or look at the result further down before you've tried this a few times.

During the introduction and the chorus, you will have no problem conducting a 4/4 pattern. In the verse, however, you will notice that it is not possible to keep up the 4/4-pattern. You will trip up on the way because the stressed (= accented) beats are not where you would expect them to be. Conclusion: There must be a change of metre somewhere. If you closely follow the points of emphasis and consider the melodic and harmonic rhythm while conducting, you will end up with the following metric distribution:

It might be possible to use 6/4 instead of switching from 4/4 to 2/4 (you would still have to include a 2/4-bar at some point in the first half of the verse). I think, however, that the strong-weak distribution verifies what I have suggested (conduct to the recording and decide for yourself which version feels the most plausible). It is interesting that many musicians who know this piece have never noticed that there is something odd about the verses. It goes to show once again that, even in Pop music, it is possible to incorporate time signature changes and odd-bar sections as long as the basic pulse keeps going.

Form

Now that you've determined both tempo and time signature(s), listen to the general structure of the piece (AABA, ABAC, etc.) and figure out the number of bars contained in each individual section. With contemporary pieces, which often display somewhat irregular formal characteristics, this is not always easy. If you are uncertain, focus on the theme. The melody will often provide you with the necessary clues as it usually takes a breath at formal junctions. This will help you recognise points of transition from one section to the next and point you towards important downbeats. You can also depend on the drummer, who usually provides the clearest indication of form, e.g. by marking phrase beginnings and setting up each new section with a fill. In terms of what we have just discussed, the composition "I'll Be Here For You" follows an AAB format (B being the eight-bar chorus subdivided into two four-bar phrases).

Assignment

Let's transcribe the form of a tune I believe all of you know: "What's Love Got To Do With It" by Tina Turner (1984, on the album "Private Dancer"). You've most probably heard it a number of times, however, without focussing on any particular aspect of the piece, so I'm sure you won't have more than a vague recollection. Get hold of the recording. Listen to the introduction, check the basic pulse as well as the time signature and determine the tempo. Don't forget to conduct while you're listening! Now play the complete piece twice (without interruption) and focus on a different topic each time. During the first run, just concentrate on the general form. Ask yourself: "Which are the important subdivisions? Are there repeated sections? Where do I hear something new or different?" Write down the road map. Label each individual section as A, B, C, and so on (same or similar sections are labelled with the same letter). During the second run, try to count how many bars there are to each section. Don't read on until you have completed the assignment. Go...

  So, here's the solution. The pulse should be quite obvious (if not, tap your foot to the recording). The tempo is approximately 99 BPM. Here's the formal structure of the recording and the subdivision of each section:

A = 8 bars (2 x 4, introduction, in 4/4)
B = 13 bars (7 + 6, 1st verse)
C = 8 bars (2 x 4, chorus)
B = 13 bars (7 + 6, 2nd verse)
C = 8 bars (2 x 4, chorus)
D = 7 bars of 4/4 and 1 bar of 2/4 (interlude, the solo is based on the changes of C)
E = 8 bars (bridge, entirely new material)
C = 7 bars of 4/4 and 1 bar of 2/4 (chorus, repeated 3 times including fade-out)

Quite elaborate, isn't it? I'm sure you didn't anticipate some of this. For a No. 1 chart hit, the form looks rather ambitious. For starters, we have quite a few sections (A–E), each containing different material. Compared to the average Jazz standard, that's a lot. Of course, it may look a bit strange to label the introduction as A. However, when transcribing a recording, we're not necessarily referring to the basic song formats found in Jazz (AABA, ABAC, etc.) but rather outlining the actual sequence of events. We could take this even one step further. When notating extended arrangements, it is quite common to ignore the fact that some sections are repeated. The lettering of each section simply follows the alphabet, regardless of whether we've heard it before or not. So, another way of labelling the form of "What's Love…" could have been: A (intro), B (1. verse), C (chorus), D (2. verse), E (chorus), F (interlude/ solo), G (bridge), H (chorus)…

Let's take a closer look at the form of "What's Love…". Here, too, we run into several unexpected twists. For one, we have a 13-bar verse. As suggested, the B section could be subdivided into 7 bars of verse and 6 bars of pre-chorus or broken down into even shorter phrases (4/3/2/2/2). However, I'd prefer to interpret this as a complete 13-bar section (mainly because of the lyrics). When thinking about form, don't overdo things, by chopping up everything into small pieces. At this stage of a transcription, we're looking at the general form, not the individual motivic phrases.

The second surprising element is the bar of 2/4, cleverly introduced the first time at the end the D section (solo) and then repeated in the last sections (chorus) of the recording. It is slipped in as a formal contraction in order to increase the energy level. The cross-fade into the next section works smoothly – I could imagine some of you didn't even notice it until you actually started counting bars. It's a nice little quirk that doesn't bother the ear at all because the pulse is not interrupted. However, subliminally, it adds an element of excitement.

Assignment

Transcribe the general form of "Moving Out", "Waltz For Ever" and "Walking Tiptoe" (**tracks 42-44**). We will need the information when working on these recordings in the chapter "Transcription Workshop" (pdf-H).

Root and key

The next step is to establish the key(s) of the piece. Concentrate on the beginning and the end of each chorus or the section you want to transcribe – this is where the feeling of tonality is most noticeable. Harmonically, you can focus on the first chord (mostly Imaj7 or I-7) or the final resolution where you will almost always hear a basic cadential formula such as V-I or II-V-I.

Ask yourself if you have the feeling of a pervading tonality, or whether you can sense a change of key. Tunes containing modulations usually begin and end in the same key. Tunes can modulate more than once. But, be careful not to interpret every unusual colour as a modulation. For instance, modal interchange functions can create the false impression of a key change because they deviate strongly from the tonality. However, in most of these cases, the chord progression quickly returns to the diatonic material of the initial key. Only if the ear loses its bearings for more than just a bar or two and struggles to maintain a feeling of "tonal continuity", chances are that a real modulation has taken place.

When it comes to figuring out the basic key, the theme is a reliable source of information. It is an elementary feature of traditional melodies to strongly imply either a Major or Minor scale, no matter how complex the chord progression may be. Sing the theme a number of times (break it down into phrases or shorter sections) and ask yourself whether you hear an underlying scale or get the feeling of a tonal centre. Trust your intuitive ability to hear a root, which, whether you know it or not, has always been with you ever since you were a child. Your musical heritage and education has prepared your ear to lock into certain sounds automatically. Because you have all grown up with tonal music, you will definitely hear a tonal centre as such without necessarily knowing why.

Concentrate on important notes and try to determine their intervallic function in the overall key (e.g. "… this melody note sounds like a major third …", "… this one implies a perfect fifth …", etc.). Here, too, it is important to focus on the beginning and especially the ending of themes, since most traditional tunes end on the root. Listen to the melody a number of times and then sing the note that "sticks out", i.e. the one that is most prominent in your memory and seems to "settle in" the most when scanning the recording. In most cases, your tonally conditioned ear will hit the right note. Once you have decided on a root, *for the first and only time* check this note on your instrument.

Assignment

Listen to the **play-alongs** that came with this book and try to determine the root of each recording (with the exception of **tracks 11** and **37–40**).

Ask yourself, even if it is immediately apparent, if the recordings are in a major or minor key (get used to asking certain questions as a matter of routine). Which colour predominates, minor or major? Check your answer by singing a scale to the recording – instinctively (!), without thinking – from the note you think is the root. Take your time and don't sing too fast. Pause on every note, listen and try to feel if the note "locks into" the overall sound or not. Play the recording again if you are not sure. The very second you sing a wrong note it will override and "destroy" your inner image of the sound. Once you are sure of your intonation, turn off the recording and sing up and down the assumed scale (from the root to the upper octave and back) – still without thinking about what you're singing. Only when you have the scale firmly anchored in your mind's ear, switch on the brain. Ask yourself: "Are we dealing with a major or minor third here, a major or minor seventh, etc.?" Sing the scale (aloud) while verbalising the names of the scale degrees: 1-2-♭3-4-5-6-♭7-8 and back. Conclusion: I got it! The basic character of this piece is Dorian.

Assignment

Go back to "What's Love Got To Do With It" and apply the previous exercise to the recording. Listen to sections A and B. Try to determine the root, the basic character of the piece (major or minor) and the underlying scale of both sections. Check the root on your instrument.

All of this should also be applied to compositions that modulate. Most of these have a main key, which the tune then departs from at some point (mostly at an important formal "intersection") and returns to at a later stage somewhere near the end of the piece. Remember the analysis of "Mornin'" (see p. 409 ff.). This example should illustrate that we all need a certain amount of experience in recognising modulations. They are not always sufficiently obvious to create a dramatic harmonic change. As a rule, a new tonic will be more than just a passing chord. It has to be positioned at an important point within the form and, in most cases, is "confirmed" by a preceding cadence for the ear to comfortably settle into the new key.

Assignment

Let's try locating modulations. Again, I'd like to use "What's Love Got To Do With It" as an example. Return to the general formal layout you prepared a few pages ago. Start the recording and make check marks as you go along whenever you have the feeling that a modulation has occurred. For the moment, just try to pinpoint the sections where you are no longer able to hear the key of origin. In a second run, try to determine the exact points of transition. As an additional challenge, you could try to transcribe the changes using basic chord symbols. Only read on once you have repeated this exercise several times and finalised your assumptions.

Have you decided on the places where the modulations might be? If you've completed the previous assignment, you already know that the piece starts out in G♯ Minor (Aeolian). You couldn't possibly miss G♯ as the root, since the bass is pounding it out mercilessly. In both the introduction and the first half of the B section, the main chord is G♯–11. The only change of colour (every two bars) is a switch to F♯/G♯, which sounds like a G♯7(sus4). In the second half of the verse, we hear the triads E (♭VI) and F♯ (♭VII) alternating. Both are diatonic in G♯ Aeolian. So, what about the C section (chorus)? To some of you, this may feel like a change of key. The trouble is, all we have is a switch to B Major (the relative major of G♯ Minor). As I said before (in the chapter "Modulation"), a change from a minor key to its relative major key (or vice versa) is not really a modulation in my book. The chorus (C) is not sufficiently different to substantiate a change of key. After all, we're still dealing with the same tonal material (melody and chords), albeit with a change of perspective. The chord progression is a simple two-bar loop with half-bar changes: B - F♯ - E - F♯ (all triads). Even though the two triads E and F♯ were ♭VI and ♭VII in G♯ Minor, I'm quite sure you now hear them as IV and V in B Major. That's OK. We're still talking about the same thing.

Let's move on to the interlude (solo). Here, you should definitely hear a direct modulation. The complete D section simply shifts up a whole step to C♯ Major. Since the solo is based on the same changes as the chorus, we're hearing the chords C♯ (I), F♯ (IV) and G♯ (V). So far, so good. In the E section (the bridge), however, things get convoluted. From a harmonic point of view, this is definitely the most dramatic part of the song. It starts out with 4 bars of C♯7(sus4) alternating with a C♯ triad, which could be interpreted as V7/IV in C♯ Major (without the expected resolution to IV), followed by one bar each of A (triad), B/A (Lydian slash chord), G♯–7 and C♯ (triad). Since the section begins and ends with C♯, this can't be a modulation. So, why do we hear such a distinct change of mood and harmonic colour? Again, we should remember what we learned when analysing "Mornin'": MI-functions often have more impact than modulations. And that's exactly what happens here. C♯7(sus4) Mixolydian (I7) is a first distraction that pulls the ear away from C♯ Ionian without changing the tonality. The A major triad (♭VI), B/A (a variation of ♭VI) as well as the G♯–7 (V–7) are clearly MI-functions, which more than tickle the ear before circling back to the C♯ major triad.

It is worth noting that the tune does not return to the initial key of B Major towards the end. The last few sections (chorus) are all in the key of C♯ Major. If I were to notate this recording, I would most probably start out with the key signature of B Major (5 sharps) and switch to C♯ Major (7 sharps) as of the D section (and no, I don't think you should be in awe of 7 sharps).

The layout of the music

Let's return to our general topic: developing a game plan that will help us transcribe more efficiently. Now that we've determined the time signature(s), the root, the overall key signature and the basic form of the tune, it is time to draw a grid of bar lines on the page. In order to do this, we need to be clear as to the purpose of the transcription and how simple or complex it should be. So, the first thing to decide is exactly what you want to transcribe and how many staves you need for notating the various parts. One stave is enough for a theme or a single-note solo including the changes (the chord symbols are written above the stave). If you are opting for a more accurate transcription that contains additional information (bass lines, piano voicings, horn parts, etc.), you will need two or even three staves (multiple staves are called a system). Don't try to squeeze too much into one stave – give the music space to breathe! Draw an appropriate clef and the key signature at the beginning of *every* stave. The time signature only appears at the beginning of the transcription (unless, of course, a change of metre occurs).

The next thing to do is to draw bar lines corresponding to the formal structure of the chorus or section you are transcribing. Most traditional pieces are divided into 4-bar, 8-bar and 16-bar sections, so a good approach is to work with 4 bars per single stave or system. If the formal structure is irregular, this makes less sense. Since the layout should reflect the phrase subdivision, we would have to vary the number of bars per stave accordingly so that the end of each formal section coincides with the end of a stave/system (e.g. a five-bar phrase would call for 5 bars to the stave). The same goes for repeats with first and second (or more) endings. Don't forget to incorporate sufficient space for a pick-up at the beginning, if there is one. Mark the end of each of the formal sections with a double bar line. Here's a simple example of a layout (including a pick-up and a repeat):

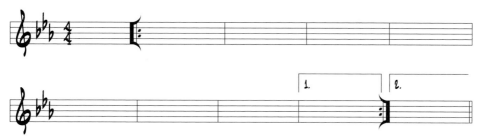

If a solo is very busy (lots of 8th or 16th notes), you should go for three or even two bars per stave/system. Make sure the bars are equally long, even if there isn't much happening in one bar and a lot in the next. After all, the pulse is usually steady, and notation should always reflect the flow of the music. One line could look like this:

Starting with a page of blank bars is an important psychological step. On the one hand, the structural framework of the piece is defined and the whole exercise becomes less daunting and more quantifiable. On the other hand, a neatly laid out page gives us a good overview. Sketchy, untidy work often dooms the transcription to failure right from the start. Make an effort to write neatly. You may want to return to what you've written, so you need to be able to decipher it even after a number of years.

Preparing a neat layout is not only psychologically helpful. It also gives us the opportunity to dive into the transcription at any point and start with the parts we personally find easiest to do. We don't have to begin with the first note and work our way from A to B to C, and so on. A transcription is a bit like a big jigsaw puzzle. Some parts will come to us immediately while others may require more consideration. Once we have figured out the cornerstones and important target notes or chords, the more difficult sections become easier to transcribe. In many cases, the missing bits simply fall into place because they follow the logic of the music.

So, you can start wherever you like, jump around, initially avoid the harder bits, concentrate on easier sections first. The approach may vary from person to person. Every one of us will develop his or her own techniques or shortcuts and set different priorities according to our musical backgrounds, preferences and abilities. It stands to reason that pianists will (and should) transcribe very differently from sax players or drummers.

Melody and improvisation

Let's turn our attention to melodies and/or improvisations. Right from the start, it should be our goal to transcribe everything – even complicated and fast passages – in context rather than note for note so that the ear is trained to memorise phrases as a whole. Longer melodic lines can be chopped up into shorter segments of one or two bars, if necessary.

Approach this step by step:

- Choose a phrase, listen to it *closely* a few times and focus on the ending. As soon as you have a clear inner image of the phrase, press pause immediately after reaching the final note to avoid being distracted by the next phrase. Sometimes this might mean reacting within a fraction of a second, especially if you have to break down a longer melodic section into smaller chunks. In this case, it may be necessary to aim for a rhythmically important or melodically prominent point in the line (e.g. the note on the first beat of the bar, an accent, the highest or lowest note, etc.) where it is easy to stop the recording. In any case, you have to be quick. You might even need to practise punching in and out of a line on your computer or CD player. If you have the technical means, loop the section in question.

- Listen to the phrase. First, give it some time to settle. Run it through your mind a number of times without the recording. Don't make the mistake of trying to sing the phrase or to play it on your instrument immediately. Our initial responses are often wrong and every wrong note will obscure or maybe even wipe out what we have just heard. Trust your memory – it is better than you think.

- Once you have established a clear image of the phrase in your mind, try to *sing* it (along with the recording as well as without it) without thinking about intervallic functions or names of notes. Do this until you are as close to the original as possible.

- Next, try to recapitulate the phrase in your mind and – *by scanning it in slow motion* – begin taking it apart. *Only now* should you break down the line into its components and think about the tonal and rhythmic content. Start with general questions about the structure of the phrase. Does it mostly move horizontally (step-wise motion), vertically (leaps and arpeggios) or symmetrically (intervallic patterns)? Does it move up and down (wave-like) or is there a distinct direction? Is there a scale feeling, a tonal quality? Does it seem diatonic, chromatic, inside, outside? Do you hear a uniform flow of eighth notes or are there syncopations, triplets, pattern displacements, etc.? Every line has characteristic elements and qualities we can isolate. Every one of these seemingly simple questions brings us closer to a result.

- Trying to focus on too many things at once can bog you down. When transcribing a melodic phrase, it therefore makes sense to separate the notes from the rhythms. Start out with the rhythmic structure. More often than not, this intermediate step greatly simplifies things. Sing the phrase in time and think about the note values (don't forget to conduct to make sure that you're on the right track). Jot down the rhythms on a separate piece of paper.

- Now's the time to start thinking about actual notes. Since you've already settled on a specific key, sing the notes you're trying to pinpoint and analyse their intervallic quality in relation to the tonic of the piece. For example, the note on the downbeat of the first bar in "What's Love Got To Do With It" (on the word "must") feels like the 5; since we're in the key of G♯ Minor, it must be a D♯. The highest note of the first four bars is a ♭7, so it must be an F♯, and so on. Take the phrase apart note by note. Do this in your head (after all, you know the phrase by heart). Don't listen to the recording anymore, otherwise you may run into conflicting aural information because your ear can either relate a note or phrase to the general tonality and its corresponding scale (horizontal context) or to the root of the underlying harmony (vertical context) and get confused by the different points of reference. Make sure that you think relative to 1 (of the key) regardless of what the chord of the moment is. Ignore the harmony for now.

- Try to write down the phrase and check it on your instrument.

- Finally, practise the phrase by first repeatedly singing and then playing it on your instrument. Begin very slowly, speeding up gradually until you can do it at the original tempo. Your mental image will lead you, even if your voice is not capable of executing the phrase because, perhaps, it is too fast or intricate (after all, most of you are not professional singers). You might be singing out of tune or missing notes, but your inner ear will be visualising it accurately (of course, on the instrument, you should be able to play the phrase without any mistakes and as close to the original as possible, including phrasing and articulation). Once you've worked on every note and every twist and turn of the phrase, return to the recording and you will make an interesting discovery. As if you're hearing everything in slow motion, the phrase will be completely transparent, almost as if you've become one with the sound. Even at faster tempos, every note will be tangible, and you will be able to hear and correct any mistakes or inaccuracies right away.

You should repeat these steps a number of times. Here are a few tips:

- As already mentioned at the beginning of this chapter, there are computer programs that give you the possibility to slow down difficult passages without affecting pitch. Don't be tempted! You must work on transcriptions at the *original tempo*. Ultimately, transcribing has less to do with the notation of the music, but rather with becoming acquainted with, memorising and absorbing the actual sound. Slowing down the recording profoundly influences the effect of the music. Even if you can reduce the speed without changing the pitch level, more often than not the quality of the recording suffers considerably. The most important thing, though, is that the integrity of a phrase gets lost when you slow it down. You will no longer hear it as a unit but rather as a loosely connected, fragmented succession of individual notes, which your memory will not retain as an entity. This applies especially to rhythms – the slower the tempo, the more disjointed the line will feel, resulting in an unclear pulse, diffuse note values, seemingly sloppy timing and phrasing, etc. Slowing down the recording is something we should only turn to at the very end of a transcription, as a last resort in order to figure out particularly obscure and elusive details.

- I recommend you first focus on the most obvious and conspicuous parts of a phrase (first, last, highest or lowest note, accents, etc.). Divide longer lines into shorter segments and figure out the notes that occur on the beat, especially on the strong beats of the bar. The rest of the phrase should fall into place quite easily once you've isolated the most important notes. Place them in your layout where they occur rhythmically and fill in the missing parts of the line later. Transcribe by jumping back and forth in the recording. Every piece of the mosaic that is correctly allocated will contribute to the final product.

- Very fast phrases or lines consisting mainly of 16th or even 32nd notes (lines many of us would baulk at and rather prefer to ignore) are not that difficult to transcribe as long as you don't make the mistake of wanting to isolate every single note. Soloists will play such lines without premeditation. They don't think about individual notes but rather draw automatically on what they have practised and internalised. Since nobody practises without strategy, every fast line will instinctively follow some kind of principle or concept. Accordingly, we should approach high-speed solos structurally rather than as a succession of individual notes. With this in mind, try to get a feeling for the overall design of a phrase. Think about whether you can recognise a particular scale, an intervallic structure, a motivic or sequential idea, etc. Ask yourself whether the phrase is diatonic or whether it contains chromatic passing notes, whether it follows stepwise motion, or whether you can hear leaps. Once you've answered these questions and established the rhythmic structure (which is usually easy when it comes to faster lines because they rarely include complex rhythms) as well as the first and last note, the rest of the phrase is often a piece of cake.

- Sometimes, it is a lot more efficient to transcribe *backwards* than forwards. You will discover that the structure of a phrase is easier to grasp once you know what the ending is. Ultimately, every melodic line follows a logical development, which we will only understand once the phrase is completed. Once we know what the target note is, we will also have quite a clear idea of how the phrase got there. Inversely, it is by far more difficult to start on the first note and grope your way through the line. Consider the psychology. Based on your personal experience and playing habits, your ear has the propensity to anticipate the way a line will evolve. This means that the ear works on assumptions. It tries to extrapolate and predict the line's direction and structure (we're talking milliseconds, here). Theoretically, however, anything can happen at any point in the line. You can never be sure of how the phrase will actually unfold. So, whenever something unexpected happens, the ear is thrown off balance. As a result, you'll be forced to listen to the recording again and again each time you run into anything unforeseen. The smart thing to do is start with the final note of a phrase and work your way backwards bit by bit. Ask yourself: "Did the line resolve from above or below, stepwise or by leap, diatonically or chromatically, and so on?" Once you know how the whole phrase is structured, there are no surprises and these questions will be easy to answer.

- It is a common mistake to want to listen for too many things all at once. It's easy to get caught up in detail and lose sight of the bigger picture. At the risk of repeating myself, consider writing down the rhythm of an entire solo first and only filling in the pitches later (or the other way around). In this way, the ear can concentrate on one thing at a time and is able to cope.

- Don't ask yourself *what you are hearing*, but rather *what you're not hearing*. Asking "what" is often akin to looking for a needle in a haystack. Approach the problem through the back door – apply your knowledge by excluding what is unlikely, gradually working towards what is more likely. In this way, you not only solve the problem at hand, but also – as a side effect – touch on almost your entire musical vocabulary.

- Never be immediately satisfied with what you have found. Check every assumption with the help of a simple exercise. Don't make the mistake of writing down the first thing that comes to mind. Once something is written down, it has probably wormed its way into your memory and may possibly interfere with the actual sound. You start hearing what you want to hear because it's on paper, and, if it's on paper, it has to be correct. I call this "the phenomenon of parallel realities". Our ear, in the belief that it has found the right solution, starts creating a sort of "alternate universe", which may override what we are actually hearing. Once established, it's often hard to fend off and revoke preconceived notions. For this reason, it is important to find the simplest possible way to verify everything you've written down. In the chapter "Transcription Workshop", you will find many little exercises and clues on how to check your findings.

- Even though it is sometimes necessary to use an instrument to verify your results, I would ask you not to run off to the piano to check every little note. In my opinion (and I'm not alone on this), we should complete transcriptions to the largest possible extent without the help of an instrument. The more you force your ear and your brain to bear the brunt of the work, the sooner the music will become an integral part of your vocabulary.

- Sinking your teeth into a problem with persistence is a worthy and desirable character trait. However, getting stuck on a brainteaser for too long is not going to help. The capacity of the ear to absorb a phrase will not necessarily improve by stubbornly listening to the recording over and over again. Quite the opposite – our lack of success often has a counter-productive effect. If you get bogged down, move on to a new bit and return to the original problem with "fresh" ears at a later point in time.

- Sometimes, you try and try again, yet you still fail to figure out a particular chord, line or rhythmic phrase. This might not be your fault. Quite often, it's the lousy quality of the recording that prevents you from being successful. You will run into situations, where the music sounds muffled or badly balanced. And, never forget: musicians, after all, are human beings. They play a little out of tune, may be rhythmically off, rush a phrase or play behind the beat, "ghost" some of the notes, make mistakes, etc. So, don't be frustrated if you're not able to grasp every little detail.

- If you don't succeed despite all efforts, it is entirely acceptable to abandon the transcription for a while. Sometimes you simply have to accept that your ears are not yet up to the job. Work on other things until your listening skills have improved sufficiently before returning to the task at hand. Oftentimes, you will be surprised that when you go back to your initial problem a few days or weeks later, everything magically falls into place and you wonder why you ever had any difficulties.

Mistakes

One of the most contentious issues when it comes to transcribing is the question whether mistakes or slip-ups – if they can be recognised as such – should be corrected. I have come to the conclusion that, as we progress in our ability to transcribe, we improve our ability to discriminate between "right" and "wrong" or, more precisely, to differentiate between the soloist's intention and what he or she actually played. Over time, we will develop quite an astute ear for whether a soloist has slipped up or whether a phrase was meant to sound the way it does. All musicians work on particular patterns, which appear in their improvisations. They don't just start playing haphazardly but rather move within the framework of what they have practised and internalised. Most phrases therefore follow a certain structure: a scale, sequence, arpeggio, etc. – principles that are not only appreciated in retrospect but, in many cases, can be anticipated by the proficient listener after having heard no more than just a few notes. If something happens in a solo that deviates strongly from what we expect (not to speak of "losing it altogether"), it could conceivably be a mistake. The more experienced you become as an improviser in your own right, the more quickly you will see through the habits of other soloists and develop the ability to evaluate if what you hear is intentional or accidental.

So, the question is: Should we ignore the mistakes we hear (and accept them as a natural part of any faithful reproduction) or should we correct them and follow the musical intention of the soloist? There are purists who think that every note the Master plays is nothing less than the Word of God, and there are more pragmatic, down-to-earth listeners, who know, as a matter of course, that musicians are not machines or gods and that they are fallible. I'm sure you can tell by my choice of words which side I am on. Just because an improvisation is credited to Miles Davis doesn't mean that we have to treat it with uncritical veneration. How often have you missed a fingering or messed up a line? To a lesser degree, the same goes for any professional musician. The professional, however, is smart enough to accept that there is no such thing as the perfect solo – discounting wishful thinking. Quite to the contrary, perfection is considered to be a rather questionable quality by most Jazz musicians. It is sometimes even regarded as something undesirable because it does not agree with the "spirit" of Jazz and improvisation. Those who risk venturing into uncharted territory and those who are prepared to take chances are the ones who are sometimes going to miss the mark. Nobody is perfect – and that is something a Jazz musician puts up with, not only on stage but also in the recording studio.

For this reason, I think it's permissible to correct the most obvious mistakes. Why should we copy them if we know they are slip-ups? When correcting mistakes, I usually select a series of notes or a rhythmic pattern in keeping with the phrase as well as with the musical and stylistic logic of the piece. Try to choose something that coherently connects the material leading up to the mistake with the next part of the phrase. This will probably come closest to the soloist's intentions. For the sake of accuracy, I would put the corrected passages in brackets, though, to indicate where the transcription deviates from the recording.

Rhythm

Rhythmic notation is a special issue that is often the topic of discussion and even contention among Jazz musicians. I would briefly like to explain why, when speaking of rhythmic perception, what we see notated in a transcription may – and sometimes must – differ from what we hear in the recording. The following remarks are by no means intended as a comprehensive investigation of the intricacies of rhythm in Jazz. They should serve as an introduction and make you aware of some of the problems.

When you listen to Jazz recordings, the first thing you sense is the constant pulse, the *beat*. This is the "timekeeper", the energy source and steady heartbeat of the music. If you key into the driving force of the beat, you will experience what is commonly referred to as the *groove* – a flow of energy that sweeps away both musicians and listeners.

The beat, however, is no more than a foundation on which Jazz musicians base their rhythmic ideas. It is the unique way Jazz musicians play with the time flow that makes rhythm in Jazz so special and appealing. Jazz is characterised by the mastery of time. In no other music is the sovereignty over time so important as in Jazz. Although the steady beat is always present, accomplished Jazz musicians stretch and compress it, circle around it, anticipate or delay it, ***but never lose it***. This rather schizophrenic tension – a symbiosis of absolute precision (objective time) and endless variety (subjective time) – is probably what largely contributes to that elusive thing known as *swing*. The ability to follow the beat while moving freely within the metrical framework means working on two seemingly conflicting levels simultaneously. All good Jazz musicians combine these two worlds, which is what makes them swing. No matter whether a Jazz musician is playing on his own or with a rhythm section, he or she will always make the listener feel the pulse. The way in which Jazz musicians toy with the beat and how they move within its confines is known as *timing*.

Anticipations are a typical example of how Jazz musicians deal with tempo and pulse. Let us look at the following rhythmic pattern:

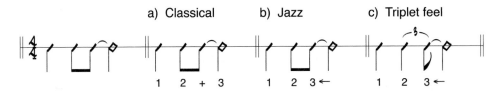

The traditional interpretation of this pattern would be to count and to play the tied eighth note as part of the second beat of the bar – on the subdivision "two and" (a). Jazz musicians, however, interpret the same note as an anticipation of beat three (b). Anticipations imply a shift of emphasis, creating the impression of the beat speeding up a bit, displacing and thereby accenting it, generating a sense of "acceleration" by pushing the beat forward without actually changing the tempo.

The interesting thing is that every Jazz musician anticipates differently. When anticipating a beat (as in our little example shown above), the degree of anticipation can vary from hardly noticeable to a version that comes close to the traditional interpretation of the tied-over eighth note. When Jazz musicians have to play in unison (e.g. in a big band), these differences can result in quite a bit of confusion. In an attempt to avoid this predicament, a standard way of dealing with anticipations has established itself, bringing the huge variety of interpretations to a common denominator: The beat is divided into triplets and the anticipation is played as a tied-over eighth-note triplet (c).

The division of the beat into triplets does not only apply to anticipations, though. In Jazz, consecutive eighth notes are not played uniformly. A beat is not subdivided evenly (two eighth notes to the beat) but rather "long-short". *On-the-beat* eighth notes are played long and correspond to the value of two eighth-note triplets. *Offbeat* eighth notes are short, equaling one eighth-note triplet. Depending on the style, the interpretation (phrasing) of consecutive eighth notes can be defined either as *even 8ths* (two equal eighth notes per beat = traditional) or *swing 8ths* (two notes per beat with a long-short subdivision based on a triplet feel = Jazz). Unfortunately, both of these variants are notated identically. The only clue we have as to how to phrase a line is the performance indication "straight eighths" or "even eighths" (traditional phrasing) and "swing" or "swing eighths" (Jazz phrasing), usually displayed at the beginning of the piece. Please, please, please don't notate "swing eighths" as a dotted 8th note (long) and a 16th note (short). This is often found in older publications. Melodies phrased in this way sound terribly square:

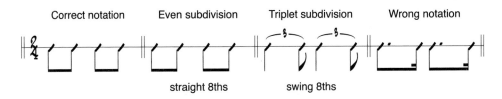

Please keep in mind that the concept of using the triplet feel as a means to mastering swing phrasing is no more than an approximation and an abstract model. It helps, but it's definitely not the road to ultimate success. The two rhythmic phrases in the following example illustrate the point. Depending on whether an offbeat 8th note appears as part of a line containing consecutive 8th notes or as an anticipation of the beat, its interpretation is fundamentally different:

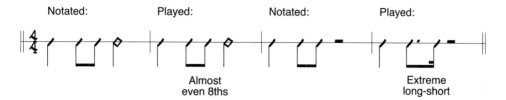

Whereas the consecutive 8th notes in the first example are played close to "straight eighths" (almost on "two and") because of the note on beat 3, the second example is commonly played as an extreme "long-short" subdivision of beat 2 (the "three" is anticipated by a 16th or even less). Again, both situations are notated identically!

Most popular styles are based on a quarter note pulse subdivided either into 8th or 16th notes. As a rule, if the subdivision is in 8th notes, the quarter notes are even and the 8th notes are played either even or swing, depending on style. If the subdivision is in 16th notes, the 8th notes are even and the 16th notes are played either even or swing. For example, Latin-American music (Bossa Nova, Samba, Salsa, etc.) is played straight (even 8ths/16ths). Jazz and Jazz-related styles (e.g. Shuffle) usually follow an 8th note subdivision using swing 8ths. In Funk, the quarter note beat is subdivided into 16th notes. This means that the 8th note is always played even. The 16th notes, however, can be either phrased even (the most commonly used phrasing) or with a swing feel (e.g. in Funk Shuffle or Second Line). Jazz musicians are expected to interpret the written music accordingly. They should also be able to switch from one feel to another off-the-cuff.

Jazz musicians often change their phrasing during a solo. On the one hand, the tempo influences the phrasing considerably. With slower tempi, soloists may switch from "hard swing" with a pronounced long-short feel to an interpretation of consecutive 8th notes that is almost "straight" within one and the same line (sometimes from bar to bar or even beat to beat). The faster the tempo, the "straighter" the eighth notes become and the less conspicuous the long-short feel is. On the other hand, phrasing often depends on the melodic flow. Every melodic line demands its own rhythmic phrasing – depending on whether it is ascending or descending, whether it is horizontal (step-wise movement) or vertical (leaps and arpeggios), on the beat or with a lot of syncopation.

Even when it comes to tiny details, Jazz musicians have their own way of phrasing, their personal *micro-timing*. Some play **on top of the beat** (slightly ahead of the beat) and create the impression of excitement and breathlessness without actually speeding up (e.g. Charlie Parker). Some play uncompromisingly **on the beat** with mind-blowing effect (e.g. Michael Brecker). Others play **behind the beat**, or **laid back**, as it's known, seemingly dragging the tempo in a relaxed but nonetheless intense way (e.g. Dexter Gordon). This is why some groups sound better than others: Musicians will only work well together if they have a deep appreciation for the phrasing "philosophy" of the other band members and are able to find common ground (especially bass and drums).

This is where Jazz differs radically from Classical music. Traditional music is played as written. Rhythmic patterns consist of pre-defined and precisely "countable" note values. What happens musically is inextricably linked to the exact subdivisions of the beat. Of course, traditional music is *agogic* – denoting an effect produced by lengthening or contracting the time value of notes and, accordingly, speeding up or slowing down the tempo. This is essential to expressive interpretation of the music and includes performance indications such as *accelerando* (gradual acceleration), *ritardando* (gradual deceleration), *rubato* (freedom of rhythmic interpretation, floating time), etc. The point, however, is that in all these cases *every change of tempo affects the beat or the pulse* – and this is *never* the case in Jazz (at least not in mainstream Jazz).

In Jazz, the constant beat and the actually played rhythms are merely two loosely connected layers, which occasionally coincide and "lock in" to one another (e.g. on the first beat of a bar, at the beginning or end of a phrase, on an accent, etc.). They can, however, also shift relative to each other and exist independently for a limited period of time. It is important to remember that these subtle shifts in tempo and phrasing – other than in Classical music – do not affect the steady beat.

So, what does all of this have to do with transcription? It is virtually impossible to capture these nuances using traditional notation. It would be pointless to attempt notating them, as they vary from player to player and often depend on the other members of the band. For this reason, it makes much more sense to notate approximately. Trying to work with exact subdivisions of the beat can sometimes obscure what is actually happening. Many transcriptions go awry in pursuit of pinpoint accuracy. I have seen improvisations transcribed right down to the very last rhythmic detail, resulting in hopelessly cluttered pages full of practically unplayable precision (including 32nd or even 64th notes). Unfortunately, this sort of transcription rarely has much to do with reality.

To cut a long story short: You can't relate everything to the beat. It would be a ridiculously foolhardy venture to meticulously notate every anticipated 32nd note, which was most probably not meant to be a precise 32nd in the first place, but rather an anticipation in general. Just as a septuplet with seven notes to a bar of 4/4 will more likely be a sequence of 8th notes played very laid-back. We have to learn to understand the player's rhythmic intentions. This – and nothing else – should be what we end up notating. Try rather to figure out the basic rhythmic ideas behind a seemingly complex line. Think horizontally (line) rather than vertically (beat). Soloists rarely think in terms of highly complicated rhythmic structures (though, in contemporary Jazz, you will come across some rather sophisticated rhythmic concepts). Usually, the rhythmic intention is quite simple, but, because a pattern is slightly shifted against the beat, it would look outrageously complicated on paper when trying to tie everything to the beat level. Try to sense whether the soloist intended to play an eighth-note line, eighth-note or quarter-note triplets, a syncopated phrase, on the beat or an anticipation, etc. – no matter whether this scrupulously corresponds to the beat or not. Your rhythmic notation should always be an approximation of what is actually played – otherwise you're not doing the music justice.

Phrasing and dynamics

How something is played is just as important as *what* is played. It is not enough only to play the correct notes. It is often much more important how a phrase is interpreted. With this in mind, transcriptions should include vital information on articulation, phrasing and dynamics. Here are the most commonly used notational symbols and performance indications:

Staccato

Notes played "staccato" (indicated by a dot above or below the note heads) are played shorter than their actual note values. In Jazz, a staccato is usually not as short as in Classical music. Although a Jazz staccato still clearly separates one note from the next, it is phrased relatively "fat" or "with body":

Staccato is not only used to indicate notes played short. Sometimes it is used to simplify notation. The above example should more accurately be written as follows (this is what the line actually sounds like):

So, we do away with the rests and write staccato quarter notes instead, making the line much easier to read.

Tenuto

Notes played tenuto (indicated by a dash above or below the note heads) are held for their full value but are not connected with the next note (the notes have to be attacked separately):

In Jazz, quarter notes are a law unto themselves. They are generally phrased long when on the beat and short when syncopated. Unfortunately, this is no more than an unwritten agreement among Jazz players, making misunderstandings inevitable. For this reason, accomplished arrangers have developed the habit of marking *all* quarter notes as either staccato or tenuto.

In Funk music, where the pulse is divided into equal 16th notes, the quarter notes are always long, whereas the eighth notes have to be defined clearly as long or short:

Legato

Playing legato means that the notes of a line are smoothly connected. A tie (or slur) above the phrase indicates that the notes should not be played separately but "on one breath" (e.g. wind or brass instruments) or "on one bow" (strings):

Accents

Notes to be emphasised are marked with an accent (>) or a *marcato* (^). Generally, the accent can appear on any note (long or short), whereas the marcato is reserved for accented notes played short (essentially a combination of accent and staccato). Quarter notes can be marked with either depending on the tempo:

Glissando

This is when two notes are connected by a "run" or a "slide". There is a difference between an *articulated glissando* (the connecting notes can be heard as discrete pitches, e.g. on a saxophone or piano) and an *unarticulated glissando* (sliding like a trombone or a violin), the latter also referred to as *portamento*:

Unarticulated   Articulated

Slide

A note is approached by a glissando from below (less commonly from above):

Drop/Fall

This is when a note is concluded with a downward glissando. The duration and the range of the drop is usually indicated by the length of the line:

Grace notes

In contrast to the slide, the grace note is a clearly defined single note directly preceding the target note (also called the "principal"). Grace notes are usually written as small eighth notes with a slash through the note stem to indicate that they have no actual durational value (they are played as short as possible). Grace notes are usually located a half step or whole step below the target note (less often above):

Ghost notes

These are notes that are deliberately "swallowed" or muted, almost to the point of near silence. They contribute to the rhythmic flow of the line but are not articulated clearly. The listener therefore hears them subconsciously, as a hint of a note. As a result, the notes around the ghost notes stand out more and the line has a more dynamic contour. Ghost notes are notated as "x" note heads (older publications sometimes bracket the note heads):

Dynamics

Dynamic indications relate to the volume of a sound or a note: *piano* (soft = *p*) or *forte* (loud = *f*) and their gradations *ppp, pp, p, mp, mf, f, ff, fff* (the "m" stands for *mezzo* = "moderately soft/loud"). The terms "crescendo" and "decrescendo" (indicated by "hairpins") are used to denote a gradual increase or decrease in volume:

So, always be sure to include articulations and dynamic indications in your transcriptions. In time, you will be able to recognise individual musicians by the way they phrase and articulate.

Harmony

> *"Probably the most frustrating thing was trying to figure out the hipper voicings from records. It was no problem for me to get the basic character of the chord, to figure out what chords were major or minor, but you can drive yourself crazy trying to figure out the notes in between the bass notes and the treble notes."*

> ## Kenny Barron

Let's talk about the changes – one of the major stumbling blocks to any transcription. Even if you have a lead sheet at hand, you cannot blindly rely on the given chord symbols; they serve, at best, as a guide. In many cases, your lead sheet is based on a different recording than the one you are trying to transcribe. Also, your recording may differ considerably from any original changes you may be familiar with. Firstly, reharmonisations are common – all Jazz musicians arrange pieces according to their personal tastes and styles, looking for their own version. Secondly, not only do the soloists improvise, but the rest of the band does so, too. So, the original chord progression could easily have been changed spontaneously. Thirdly, reckon with the possibility that each player in a group may have a different harmonic notion of the piece. It could even happen that the soloist, the pianist and the bassist – at least in places – all work with a different set of changes simultaneously (e.g. as in Rhythm Changes). Have a look at the turnarounds on p. 236 ff. It is conceivable that the players in a group are playing a turnaround, but each follows a different version. This would work musically, but the question remains as to which version should be notated in the transcription.

Even more problematic is the fact that we usually do not know who created the lead sheet. Someone, somewhere, at some point in time listened to a piece, interpreted it and put it down on paper according to their personal experience, awareness of sound, listening skills, understanding of theory, knowledge of terminology and notational habits. How can we be sure the author of a lead sheet is up to the task and knows what he or she is doing? Of course, every lead sheet is made with the best of intentions. Alas, experience tells me that faith is a lousy advisor and that the quality of lead sheets is often more than questionable. Musicians transcribe as best they can. But, it is a matter of choice as to what symbols to use, what to include and what to leave out. These decisions are based on personal judgement. Much of what is out on the market is generally OK, but a lot of it is not. I maintain that if 100 musicians were to notate the same piece based on the same recording, we would probably end up with 100 more or less differing outcomes, depending on how well each musician hears and which priorities he or she sets. That's why there is no such thing as a flawless transcription. However, despite the fact that it is virtually impossible to come up with a perfect result, doing the job yourself will definitely increase your awareness and improve your ability to evaluate the quality of other transcriptions and lead sheets. You, too, will not always be sure how to name or notate something. But you will eventually learn to make decisions – even if you are still in doubt.

I'd like to illustrate a typical problem with the example of "Naima" by John Coltrane (on the album "Giant Steps"). Here is the A section:

Whereas the theme (line 1) is reasonably self-explanatory, there is as good as no agreement on the harmonic notation. Line 2 is the version from the old Real Book, line 3 is from the New Real Book (Vol. 2), line 4 is what the pianist Wynton Kelly actually plays on the original recording and line 5 is organised according to melodic-horizontal rather than harmonic-vertical considerations (a commonly used notational practice these days). Amazingly, *all four versions describe the same sound!* So, how do we resolve the resulting chaos?

Line 3 actually comes closest to the real thing when considering an adequate symbolic notation. But even in this relatively successful rendition, a minor error has managed to creep in: bar 3 should be G+maj7/E♭ and not Gmaj7/E♭. Line 2, however, is catastrophic. For a long time, this was the only available version. Whereas the first 2 bars are basically correct, the chords in bar 3 are utter nonsense. What has B7(♭5) got to do with Amaj7/E♭ (check this yourselves)? Line 5 is somewhat questionable. The scale nomenclature gives us the correct improvisational material but not the specific structure of the piano voicings. If we showed lines 2 and 5 to a pianist who doesn't know "Naima", it would be highly unlikely that he or she would play anything remotely like what is on the recording. Just as the vague indication "E♭ pedal" taken from the old Real Book (line 6) can hardly represent the carefully constructed bass line with its repetitive rhythmic pattern and octave transpositions as played by Paul Chambers (line 7).

Of course, it is not always your goal to transcribe the recording right down to the very last detail or to play the original version exactly as it is on the recording. Depending on your intentions – the precise reproduction of the original or a portrayal that leaves room for interpretation and improvisation (e.g. a lead sheet) – the final product could look very different. If we compare various transcriptions of one and the same piece, the most common disagreements are about the interpretation of individual harmonic sounds. This is to be expected and nothing to make a fuss about. Sketch summaries – and that's what lead sheets are – will naturally differ from one another simply because our ears react differently.

Marked differences are often found when it comes to interpreting chord progressions. Chord symbols are, after all, approximations of real sounds. Just as there may be a large number of different voicings (chord structures) implied by any one chord symbol, any one voicing could be represented by a variety of chord symbols. Have a look at the following voicing and a small selection of conceivable interpretations:

As in the example shown above, it is often hard to choose an appropriate chord symbol in practice. Even if the harmonic context provides obvious clues, a lot of experience is needed to find the right interpretation. To cut a long story short – having faith in other people's listening skills is fine, but checking the results is always better. You can't avoid having to question every lead sheet and check every transcription. ***Don't put your trust in other people's ears!*** Undue modesty is totally out of place. There are enough posers out there in the music business who, despite second-rate ears, are presumptuous enough to flood the market with substandard sheet music. Even the most professional transcription is not free of the occasional stupid little mistake (including the ones in this book!). With practice, you will eventually be in a position to interpret sounds with the necessary confidence. Learn to live with the fact that you may end up with transcriptions looking different from those of your friends or colleagues. This does not mean that your results are wrong.

Where are the changes?

Let's get back to the main topic. Work on the changes layer by layer. Listen to the recording a number of times and ask yourself a first question: Where can you actually sense a true change of chord? Even this initial, seemingly simple question is not always easy to answer. What might appear at first to be a new chord may turn out to be nothing more than a variation of the current sound. A pianist, for example, may play a number of voicings based on one and the same chord symbol, all differing in register, number of notes, structure, choice of tensions, etc. In this case, however, we get a sense of motion but no real change of colour because the various voicings usually relate to the same scale material. It could also be that the pianist lays out for a bar or two, so all you can hear is the bass line, which, as we will see in a moment, is not always all that clear-cut either. Last, but not least, chord progressions are reharmonised and expanded on spontaneously during performance. Although we may hear an actual change of chord in this case, these harmonic add-ons are of subordinate importance because they are merely embellishments of the basic chord progression. So, you're up against quite a few obstacles when transcribing the harmony.

Harmonic rhythm

As I've said before, don't make the mistake of wanting to transcribe bar by bar. When trying to locate the changes, it is important not to focus on each individual chord too soon. Start out by thinking in terms of larger sections. I would much rather you initially get an overview of the harmony than getting lost in attempting to figure out single sounds. In a first step, concentrate on one of the most important topics when it comes to successful transcription: harmonic rhythm. Ask yourself:

- Where do I hear movement, tension, chords that want to resolve, etc. – in other words: cadences?

- Where do I hear points of rest or a feeling of resolution – in other words: target chords?

There is no need to immediately define the actual harmonies. It is more important to understand the ups and downs of the chord progression and to get a feeling for areas of activity and moments of rest. Look for target chords first. Cadential patterns are easier to determine once you have worked out the points of resolution. Don't forget that the chord changes in most Jazz compositions occur at regular intervals and predominantly follow a half-bar, one-bar or two-bar harmonic pulse. Once you have established the harmonic rhythm, mark the location of each chord as well as the cadential areas (weak) and target points (strong) in your transcription layout.

If you listen to the various recordings of "There Will Never Be Another You" (**tracks 13–19**), the first half of the chord progression could look something like this (each arrow denotes a change of chord):

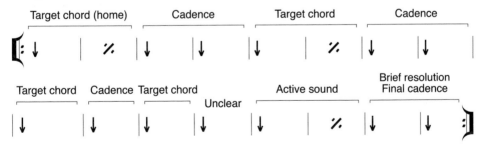

Assignment

Take any recording from your CD collection and try to follow the changes as suggested above. Locate each individual chord as you listen and determine its individual quality either as a cadence or target sound.

Harmonic patterns

The next thing to do is to listen for familiar progressions. This still has nothing to do with determining specific bass notes or chord symbols. Ask yourself: Are the sounds diatonic to the key (you have already established the tonal centre), or is there a strong push and pull that goes against the feeling of tonality? Can you hear familiar harmonic formulae and patterns (e.g. root movement in fifths, II-Vs, turnarounds, extended dominants, etc.)? Listen to the bass line. Does it move stepwise, in leaps, in scale, chromatically, etc.? Does the recording remind you – at least partially – of other tunes, which you could use as a comparison? Are there any unusual or elusive passages that might suggest the use of modal interchange functions or intimate a modulation? The answers to any one of these questions will bring you closer to figuring out the chord progression.

Bass lines

Let's try to determine the root of each chord. Concentrate on the bass first, the harmonic foundation of the band. The bass outlines the root movement of the chord progression. At the same time, it is also the "time keeper" along with the drummer. While bass lines consist mainly of roots and chord tones in most popular styles, things are a bit more complicated when it comes to bass lines in Jazz. In mainstream Jazz, a typical bass line follows a steady quarter note pulse, commonly referred to as a *walking bass* – the throbbing heart, the backbone, the driving force behind the band. Walking bass lines not only support the vertical structure of the harmony, they also have a strong melodic quality and generate a powerful forward drive. In addition to the mandatory roots and chord tones, a good walking bass line will consequently contain an abundance of diatonic or chromatic passing notes, which add to the melodic flow but can also obscure the actual root of a chord. For this reason, and so that your ear knows what to listen for, I will briefly introduce you to the various ways in which a walking bass line can be constructed.

Here's the basic principle in 4/4 time: Chord tones (1/3/5) occur on the strong beats (1+3) of the bar, and passing notes (in-scale or chromatic) occur on the weaker beats (2+4). You will find exceptions to this rule, but only if they contribute to the flow of the line. It is particularly important for the bassist to create fluid transitions from one bar to the next and from chord to chord. In order to produce a smooth line, the strong beats of the bar (1+3) are approached stepwise (either diatonically or chromatically). Bass lines can also contain larger leaps (mostly fifths and octaves) to enhance the impact of the line. Let's, for example, take a look at the first five bars of a Blues in F (the bass sounds an octave lower than it is notated):

- Only chord tones and diatonic passing notes:

- Chord tones and chromatic passing notes:

- Linear (focussing on stepwise movement using diatonic and chromatic notes):

- With leaps:

The bass lines are graded according to complexity. Whereas the first example is very basic (here the ear should have no difficulty in identifying the chords), the other versions become increasingly intricate and elaborate although they clearly imply the same changes. Analyse each line. Make a distinction between notes that are important because they define the basic chord and notes that can be ignored because they merely contribute to the line as passing tones. Even though this may be straightforward in most cases, be careful. Example No. 3, for instance, shows that a chromatic passing tone may occur on a strong beat if the line calls for it. In the first bar, the G♯ appears on beat 3. For the line to resolve smoothly to the B♭ in bar 2, this is the only choice, since the first bar starts out with a diatonic step (F-G). However, if you were to transcribe the bass line and rely on the strong beats to define chord types, you might misinterpret the G♯ (= A♭) as a minor third and wrongly assume the corresponding chord to be an F–7 (in that case, the A would be a chromatic approach). Example No. 4 shows nicely why you shouldn't jump to conclusions when analysing a bass line. In bar 4, the E on beat 2 could be misleading. The leap makes it sound important and in combination with the C on beat 1, you would probably arrive at C7 instead of C–7, which would require an E♭ if we think in terms of the chord. Here, however, the note E works just as well (as a chromatic approach to the F on beat 3). And so on…

Assignment

Complete the four bass lines above, continuing the respective style of the first few bars. Choose a different extended Blues format for each of the lines. Make sure that your lines do not only comply with the changes, but also have melodic quality. They should have a clear sense of direction, rise and fall, contain climaxes, etc. The range can cover two octaves or more – a double bass ranges from E1-g ("Contra E" to "small g"; check the instrumentation table at the end of pdf-G). Of course, the bass can play higher than that (good bass players often use the extreme upper range when soloing). This is, however, rarely done as part of a bass line because it would no longer supply the necessary harmonic support.

Now that we have discussed the basic constructional principle, let's try to interpret a bass line harmonically. Here are the first 16 bars of a well-known Jazz standard. Try to analyse the bass line before you read on:

Bar 1 clearly outlines Gmaj7 (the avoid note C on beat 3 is no more than a passing note and clearly part of a chromatic line beginning on B and landing on D in bar 2). Bar 2, at a first glance, could imply D7, assuming that the chord changes occur every bar. However, the G (4 = avoid note of D7) appearing on a strong beat (on 3) makes D7 unlikely. It is more plausible to consider two bars of Gmaj7, with the 5 (D) on beat 1. This is confirmed by the leap to B (on beat 4). Even if we interpret the B as an "in-scale" preparation of the next bar, it doesn't alter the fact that bar 2 basically delineates a G major triad.

In bars 3 and 4 we encounter a Bb on beat 1 and an Eb on beat 3. The first problem: How can a Bb be interpreted in the key of G Major? Here are the various possibilities: Bb7 (SubV/ II), Bbmaj7 (bIIImaj7), Bb–7 as part of a Sub(II-V) progression and bIII°7 (expected resolution = A–7). Bb7 would normally be Lydian(b7) – but the Eb (4) would contradict the feeling of this scale. Bbmaj7 would be an MI-function and, as a consequence, Lydian – but, once again, the Eb makes little sense. Bb°7 is also unlikely – on the one hand, the bassist would have played an E and not an F on beat 2 of bar 3, and on the other hand, there is a G on beat 1 of bar 5, contradicting the idea of A–7 as the target chord of Bb°7. If we consider the Eb on beat 3 (fifth root movement) and the leap to the Db in bar 4 (on beat 2), we are left with only one possible solution: a half-bar II-V progression (Bb–7 - Eb7), which is repeated (with the A on beat 4 of bar 3 acting as a chromatic approach note).

In bars 5 and 6, we encounter almost the same bass line as in bars 1 and 2. Conclusion: The bassist plays the same thing twice because the changes are the same (two bars of Gmaj7).

In bar 7, we see a B on beat 1 and an E on beat 3. At this point, we should make the connection between the immediate bar and the overall design of the piece. Every composition is conceived with a certain degree of structural coherence. For reasons of continuity, the possibility that bars 5–8 are a close copy of bars 1–4 is not at all far-fetched, suggesting a half-bar II-V pattern: B–7 - E7. Moving on to bar 8, we see our hypothesis confirmed: B on beat 1 and G♯ (= 3 of E7) on beat 3 validate our assumption. Further evidence is provided by bar 9: The A on beat 1 and the C on beat 3 clearly imply the target chord A–7 (II–7). Instead of B–7, Bø7 is conceivable as part of the minor cadence II-V/II. Here, we will have to listen a little more closely to the piano accompaniment because the F on beat 2 of bar 7 could be either a chord tone or a chromatic approach note.

Bars 9–12 are tricky. Following the A–7 in bar 9, the chord progression seems to backtrack to Bø7 - E7. How else should we interpret the B on beat 1 and the E on beat 3 of bar 10? Here, the F on beat 2 is most probably a chord tone. In bar 11, we obviously return to A–7. But, what about the B on beat 1 in bar 12? It is highly unlikely that we should, once again, arrive at B–7 or Bø7 (chord progressions rarely sit on the same chords for too long). The solution to this puzzle is quite simple: The key to bar 12 is the A on beat 3. B and B♭ are no more than chromatic approach notes (bass players often use this technique of delaying important notes to make the bass line less obvious and to create more flow). Bars 11 and 12 therefore are both A–7.

As you will notice, bars 13 and 14 resemble bars 1 and 2. Conclusion: Again, we are confronted with a two-bar chord. Two possible interpretations present themselves: E♭maj7 (a modal interchange ♭VImaj7) or E♭7 (a SubV/V). Neither the minor seventh (♭7 = D♭) nor the major seventh (maj7 = D) appear in the bass line. E♭7 is more likely because it creates a strong cadential feeling in the direction of bars 15 and 16, which must be A–7 - D7. A high level of tension makes formal sense as we find ourselves at the end of a 16-bar section where we would usually expect a climax (E♭maj7 would not create as much tension in G Major as E♭7 does). Note the F on beat 3 of bar 16: This has no harmonic importance (so don't make the mistake of thinking D–7). When dealing with extended chromatic movement (e.g. E-F-F♯-G), you will automatically find chromatic notes on the strong beats, too.

Well – that took us some time! Quite often, you will need a super-sleuth's mind to decipher the harmonic implications of a bass line. So, get used to this kind of thinking. According to our discussion, the most likely chord progression would be the following:

| Gᴬ⁷ | % | B♭–7 E♭7 | B♭–7 E♭7 | Gᴬ⁷ | % | B–7 E7 | B–7 E7 |

| A–7 | Bø7 E7 A–7 | % | E♭7 | % | A–7 | D7 | Gᴬ⁷ |

Though characteristic of this piece, the harmonic rhythm is rather irregular and therefore quite unusual (two-bar and half-bar changes alternating all the way through). Those of you who have some knowledge of the standard repertoire may already have a good idea as to what piece this is: the first half of "Out Of Nowhere" by Johnny Green. The bass line (played by Todd Coolman) can be heard on Jamey Aebersold's play-along Volume 22 (1st chorus). Despite the erratic changes, the bass line is remarkably executed and clearly reflects the chord progression. Listen to the recording to see if your ear confirms our analysis (it should!).

Assignment

It is essential to develop the ability to read a bass line harmonically. Here are the first two choruses of a recording from Jamey Aebersold's Volume 25, "17 All-Time Standards" (as played by Steve Gilmore). Try to figure out the changes without listening to the CD. The first chorus will make life a little easier because the bass line moves mostly in half notes and therefore must be quite fundamental (fewer notes imply that the bass line contains more harmonically important notes and less approach and passing notes). This sort of bass line is known as *half-time bass* or *two-beat bass* for obvious reasons. On the other hand, it is quite hard to figure out the chord types because the bass line consists mainly of roots and fifths (we need the second chorus for this):

Now go to the Aebersold-CD mentioned above. See if you find the corresponding tune just by listening to the recording. Once you have found it, compare the changes shown in the accompanying booklet with your bass line analysis.

Assignment

Go to the play-alongs accompanying this book once again, listen to the various versions of "TWINBAY" (tracks 13–19) as well as the harmonic loops (tracks 20–39) and transcribe the bass lines. I know this will keep you busy for a long time. Nevertheless, give each example a try. You can look up the chord progressions for each play-along if you get really stuck.

Where is the root?

Back to our transcription. Now that we have a notion of how bass lines are constructed, we could try to transcribe the bass and figure out the roots of the chord progression. It won't be necessary to write out the complete bass line. Just focus on the downbeat of each bar or the first bass note of a chord, since you already know where to expect a change of chord. This is easier said than done. Most people have a hard time locking into a root quickly enough before the note disappears from memory because it has been superimposed by the sounds that follow. Bass notes are difficult to isolate. Frequently, the first thing we react to is not the bass but rather the melody. The ear has the inclination to go for the most obvious part of the sound, which is usually some high or loud note. However, what may initially seem like a handicap can actually be turned into something advantageous.

Most people instinctively try to transcribe chords "bottom up", starting with the bass note and gradually working their way into the upper extensions (that's how people generally think when dealing with harmony). However, if the bass is hard to hear (e.g. on older recordings) you will have to change that routine and apply a different strategy. Instead of dejectedly groping around in the lower regions of the recording where the sound is muddy and individual notes are hard to identify, let's try to approach the problem from a completely different angle.

Be aware of the fact that every melody note has its own particular intervallic quality *because* the bass line resonates along with the upper parts and gives them colour and tension. This means that *any note* can be used to deduce the bass notes. By switching to a higher and more transparent register, you can focus on important notes or parts of the melody that are easier to grasp and use them to figure out the bass. What I am suggesting is that you reverse the process and – instead of working "bottom up" – transcribe "top down". This might take some getting used to because we are so accustomed to thinking of chords by starting from the bottom, and that is hard to shake off.

So, how does this work? Listen to the recording first, pick any conspicuous note (e.g. a melody note or the top note of a piano voicing, etc.), memorise the time code, stop the recording immediately after reaching that note and ask yourself what scale degree you are on, e.g. a ♭3, a ♭9 or a 5, etc. It is not essential to know why you have the impression of a particular interval. Trust your instincts and rely on your intuitive abilities to recognise intervallic relationships (you've worked on this for some time, after all). As soon as you think you have figured out the scale degree, decide what note it is (or look at the transcription, since you have already written out the melody) and deduce the bass note from this note. For example:

You listen to the melody/solo and pick a prominent note; you hear this note as a ♭3; you know that it is a C, so the bass note must subsequently be an A. Repeat this process with every new chord as marked in your transcription.

However, when doing this exercise, always keep in mind that the ear instinctively reacts to one of two different points of reference. It will either hear "globally" or "locally". "Global" perception relates to the root of the overall key, whereas "local" interval cognition is based on the root of the immediate chord. If, for example, we are in the key of E♭ Major, the chord is F–7 and the melody note is G, the ear will either hear a 3 (in E♭ Major) or the 9 (of F–7). Be aware of this distinction and make sure you check which perspective your ear is reacting to. In this exercise, we should try to focus on "local" perception.

The next step would be to sing the notes you think to be the roots to the recording. First, write down the roots of the chord progression on a separate piece of paper (as whole or half notes) and practise singing this "bass line" in time independently of the recording until you can do it without getting stuck (use a keyboard or piano to check). Don't make the mistake of wanting to sing the bass line in its actual register (you won't be able to sing that low anyhow). More importantly, intonation is harder to control in the lower register (try droning away at the bottom of your voice and see how difficult it is to sing in tune). Sing the line in the middle or even high range of your voice, where it is easier to distinguish the notes from one another. The fact that you are singing several octaves higher than the bass is of no consequence. To the contrary – if you sing along with the recording in a more comfortable register, your voice will not get lost in the thicket of sound. After all, there are enough other problems to solve as it is: You're trying to sing a line to a recording, to hit every note despite the other instruments and sounds going on at the same time, to listen to what you are doing while you're doing it and to decide whether each note "locks in" and creates the expected "root feeling" or not. That's a tall order. I'm sure you realise that you will have to do this exercise over and over again before you develop the necessary calm and detachment to listen to yourself sing and successfully evaluate the result while the music is playing.

One of the difficulties when determining the root of a chord is due to the fact that chords can appear in root position as well as in various inversions. If the main notes of a bass line move stepwise or chromatically, this is one of the first things you should consider. The example on p. 19 of pdf-F – "Harmonisation and Reharmonisation" – shows how a chord progression predominantly following the cycle of fifths can be completely obscured by the use of inversions.

If there are certain parts where things are still unclear, try using common sense and logic. Your knowledge of harmonic rules and clichés should give you at least a hint of what you are looking for. As always, trust your intuitive musical perception. A feeling of "normality" usually means that the progression is following a common pattern. In many cases, we can predict how a chord progression will unfold (II-V progressions, extended dominants, turnarounds, etc.). Conversely, the sudden appearance of tension would indicate something unusual. Think about the way the progression moves. Is it proceeding downwards or upwards, is it moving stepwise or in leaps, diatonically or chromatically? What can we deduce from the answers to these questions? What seems most likely? Hazard an *educated guess* if all else fails. Any assumption can be tested and will help us narrow down the possibilities.

Don't forget that, in traditional Jazz, we are dealing with chord progressions that repeat every chorus. The changes we are trying to figure out will reappear several times over the course of the recording. Jump to the same passage in another chorus – you might find things easier to figure out in a subtly different context (the bass line may be more obvious, the piano voicings easier to identify, etc.).

Assignment

Once again, go to **tracks 13–19** and **20–39** or to the bass lines from the tracks you have hopefully transcribed and analysed by now. Write down the main bass notes (only the roots) of each chord on a separate page – one note per chord. The result will look something like this for "TWINBAY" (octave transpositions must naturally be chosen according to your vocal range):

Learn each line by heart and make sure you can sing it in time without missing a note. Then sing the line along with the recording. You will probably have to do this a number of times to get through it without being distracted by the music (it's not easy to stay in tune with so many other things happening at the same time). Eventually, you should be so sure of what you're singing that you can listen actively to both the recording and yourself. Then you will sense how the notes you are singing fundamentally lock into the music and how the bass line moves in and out of the roots of the chord progression.

Chord types

Now try to determine the chord types. Work, once again, from the general to the specific. Remind yourselves that there are only seven essential chord types on which almost all other sounds are based: major (triad or maj7), minor (triad or –7), diminished, (° or °7), augmented (+), dominant seventh (7), suspended dominant seventh (7sus4) and half-diminished (ø7). Actually, considering the fact that augmented and 7sus4 chords are commonly used as substitutes for dominant seventh chords, there are only five basic types (maj7, –7, 7, ø7, °7) to reckon with. Don't worry about the extensions at this point. It makes little sense to concern ourselves with details without yet having assigned a sound to one of these basic chord categories.

I must add that the use of **slash chords** has become quite common over the past 30 years. These sounds have a unique and special quality, even though some of them also relate to the basic chord types. I don't want to make things overly complicated by introducing them at this stage. They will, however, play a key role when dealing with the contemporary Jazz repertoire. Similarly, the use of special intervallic structures (e.g. voicings in fourths, clusters, etc.) may confuse the ear considerably. Though often based on one of the fundamental triads or four-note chords and their corresponding scales, they tend to obscure the underlying chord type. Again, I would like to ignore this particular problem for the moment. For those of you interested in these topics, please refer to pdf-E "Voicings" for further information.

So, to which basic chord category does the sound we are listening to belong? In many cases, this question alone will lead to a quick answer. Most of you have the intuitive experience and the necessary reflexes that can immediately distinguish between major and minor. The other sounds are not that hard to narrow down either: Diminished and augmented chords produce quite a bit of tension with a need to resolve and have this distinct symmetry that sets them apart from all other chord types; sus4 chords have a floating, open quality; −7(♭5) chords sound subdued and dark. Sit down at the piano, play the various chord types (without extensions) and try to characterise each of them in your own words. Any description will help you classify and memorise the sounds.

As soon as you have transcribed and analysed a bass line, you at least have the root of the chord you're looking for – and this root can be interpreted functionally as part of the tonal environment and the key of the moment. If we consider the various chord functions we have talked about for major keys (diatonic, secondary and substitute dominants, modal interchange, etc.), it is possible to predict which chord types we can expect on each chromatic step. In the following table, I have listed all functional degrees and arranged the corresponding sounds according to their probability (in major keys). Chord types at the top of the table are most likely to occur. As you go down the list, the probability decreases:

I	♯I/♭II	II	♯II/♭III	III	IV	♯IV/♭V	V	♯V/♭VI	VI	♭VII	VII
maj7	7	−7	7	−7	maj7	°7	7	7	−7	7	ø7
7	°7	7	°7	I/3	−7	ø7	7(sus4)	maj7	7	maj7	7
−7	maj7	ø7	maj7	7	7	7	I/5	°7			V/3
°7				ø7			−7				°7
											−7

Influenced by the standard repertoire and following the logic of harmonic patterns, certain sounds are more likely to occur than others. Conversely, there are certain chord types that we never, or hardly ever, find in a particular situation. You will notice that for every functional degree there is at least one basic chord type missing. For instance, half-diminished chords simply do not occur on the Ist degree (I); the same applies to −7 chords on the ♭II degree, and so on (even though you may find exceptions if you dig deep enough).

Assignment

Try to come up with a similar table for minor keys.

How does this help us with our transcription? If a chord sounds straightforward, it most probably is. Don't waste your time looking for something that is highly improbable. If a chord feels unusual, think of one of the more unexpected options. So, knowing which chord types are likely to occur on which degrees will help us come up with an assumption for any specific root.

Assignment

How do we check our assumptions? Let's go back to the **play-alongs**. Play one of the examples of which you have transcribed the bass line, sing the roots along with the recording and stop the recording at the end of the bar in question (don't stop at the beginning of the bar because the ear needs all the information it can get). Now, from this root, spontaneously sing the arpeggio (four-note chord going up in thirds to the octave and back) following the automatic response of your ear. Don't think about anything. Just sing whatever first occurs to you. Try not to be sloppy and make sure you sing in tune (don't sing too fast). Let your inner voice lead you. Don't try singing to the recording (as I have already mentioned, it is quite difficult to concentrate on your own voice while the music is playing; in addition, you wouldn't have much time before the next sound appears and blanks out whatever you may have had in mind). Repeat the arpeggio several times to stabilise the sound in your head. Gradually change to slow motion so that you can isolate every note. Only then, start thinking about what you are singing, analyse it and write it down. What basic chord type did you sing? Compare the result with your assumption to check if your analysis corresponds.

Repeat the exercise by first singing the chord type you assume it to be (practise until you can sing the arpeggio accurately). Then play the recording, stop it as soon as the chord in question has sounded for a few beats (before it reaches the next chord!), sing the arpeggio and ask yourself if what you are singing agrees with what you hear in the recording. If technically possible, you may want to consider looping a small section of the play-along to help you focus on the immediate problem.

This is another exercise you might have to keep doing for a long time – maybe even months or years. I promise, it will eventually pay off! One day, your reflexes will have improved to a point where you ear is able to lock into a sound instinctively, recognise it and label it on the spur of the moment.

Hearing more than there is

One of the biggest problems for the untrained listener is to develop an "eye" for what is essential. The inexperienced ear tends to get easily distracted by irrelevant things like an embellishment, a chromatic passing note, an unusual voicing, an unexpected little reharmonisation, a surprising rhythmic idea or other insignificant details, which obscure the more important aspects of a sound: the general principles, concepts and rules governing it. Before we can develop the ability to recognise a specific sound, we must first understand its basic idea:

- the basic chord type, often concealed by inversions and extensions or transformed by the structure of the voicing, etc.;

- the functional concept of a chord progression as well as the function of each individual sound relative to its harmonic and melodic environment;

- the scale material or sequence of scales on which a melody is based;

- the construction principle of a melodic phrase.

Instead of getting lost in detail, take a step back and focus on the more general elements and concepts of the music first. This will help you look in the right direction and speed up the process of finding a solution.

How does this way of thinking help us when transcribing? Let's apply this approach to the recognition of basic chord types. I hope you agree that chords are vertical scales and scales are horizontal chords. Use this knowledge. The ear is able to cross-reference and make use of seemingly disparate information. It sometimes recognises chords not because a particular harmonic structure is apparent but rather because the melody, bass line or any other ingredient triggers the feeling of a scale, which, in turn, can be interpreted as a chord. Here's an example of what I mean: We recognise – maybe because it is a very typical and unique sound – HTWT as the basic idea behind a melodic phrase. Without having to look any further, we can conclude that the corresponding chord must be a dominant sound with the tensions ♭9, ♯9, ♯11 and/or 13.

As you can see, we don't necessarily need to concentrate on the changes in order to determine chords. Instead, we can direct our attention to the melodic (!) components and assemble them into a more general picture (= scale), which then leads us to the corresponding chord type. Sometimes it is sufficient to hear only a few melody notes from which we can derive the harmony. Let's say, for example, we hear 1, 5 and ♭6 in a traditional setting. This should immediately precipitate the following questions:

- Which scales contain 1, 5 and ♭6?

- Which scales can we eliminate because they do not include these scale degrees?

- Which other notes must we focus on in order to isolate the actual scale?

- What chord type can we deduce from the resulting scale?

Connecting melodic material to a scale will lead us to the basic chord type as well as its expected tensions. All we have to do, is listen for other key notes that will help us narrow down our choices. We know that 1, 5 and ♭6 (especially the ♭6) appear primarily in minor modes. So, if we hear a ♭3 somewhere along the line, the first thing we should turn to is a –7 chord. However, watch out! A commonly used scale containing a major third and a ♭6 is HM5. We would therefore also be on the lookout for a 3 in the melody or the accompaniment. If it appears, we know that the scale must be HM5 and the corresponding chord a dominant seventh. Even if we should come across a ♭3, HM5 would still be an option. Why? Because HM5 may contain a ♯9. Then, however, we would need to hear both 3 and ♭3 (which in this case would be more correctly labelled as a ♯9). We might, in passing, think of Altered and HTWT because they, too, relate to a dominant seventh chord and contain 3 and ♯9. However, both scales have to be excluded because Altered does not contain a 5 and HTWT has no ♭6. Ultimately, it doesn't make much of a difference because all three are dominant scales and relate to seventh chords. In minor, the combination 1, 5 and ♭6 appears in quite a few modes with the exclusion of Dorian, Melodic minor (both contain 6 instead of ♭6) and Locrian (♭5 instead of 5). So, we're left with Aeolian, Phrygian and Harmonic minor. If we hear a maj7, we know that our choice must be HM and the corresponding chord a –maj7. If we hear a ♭7, we know that only Aeolian and Phrygian remain in the frame. The difference, here, is between 2 and ♭2. No matter which of the two notes actually appears, we already know we're dealing with a minor 7th chord because the same basic chord type applies to both scales. In the end, we have found our way to the chord type by considering three notes (actually two, because the root doesn't really count) and applying a bit of educated guesswork, conjecture, knowledge and quick reasoning.

Could you follow this train of thought? It is this kind of thinking that makes for good ears. You might argue that it took us half a page to run through this sequence of questions, assumptions and conclusions. In real life, however, this process will be almost instantaneous and take up no more than a fraction of a second – if you know your theory! In a flash, your ear will key into little bits and pieces, which start making sense in a more general way when combined with a theoretical understanding of how music works. I'm sure you have met (or will meet) musicians with amazing ears. Don't feel overawed. In most cases, they just have a lot of experience linking the little things they hear to an abundance of things they know. Drawing conclusions from minor details is something that can be learned, even though it requires years of practice. To sum things up: The more you know, the easier it will be to come up with a quick solution with almost no information at hand.

Tensions

Now we get to the extensions. Here, too, begin with the general and work gradually towards finding specific notes. Don't make the mistake of jumping to conclusions and accepting the first thing that crosses your mind. Don't go looking for a ♭9, 13 or ♯11 straight away. You will most probably end up by poking around in a haystack. Be sure to consider the possibility of hearing no tensions at all. Especially, when transcribing a simple Pop tune or something comparable, you have to acknowledge that tensions are used rather sparsely. In fact, you may be hearing nothing but triads instead of four-note basic chord types. Don't transcribe what's not there!

So, let's assume we're listening to a Jazz recording. Remember the discussion in the previous chapter. What do we react to most strongly? To surprising and unexpected events. This, again, implies that there has to be "the ordinary" (otherwise you wouldn't be surprised). As a result, if you're listening to something and everything feels straight ahead and sits comfortably with the ear, then you can almost be sure that you are dealing with chords, scales and tensions that follow the harmonic rules and conventions, determined by the tonality or by traditional performance styles. On the other hand, if you sense dissonance, then there is probably something unusual happening that goes against the grain. Here are two examples:

- We have an F♯7 chord in the key of D Major and we hear nothing out of the ordinary. Conclusion: Business as usual. The expected scale is HM5 and its related tensions (if present in the melody or the voicing) must be ♭9 (G), ♯9 (A) and/or ♭13 (D), all of which are diatonic to the key. If we hear moderate tension in an otherwise familiar sound, then we should think of Altered: The added ♯11 (C) would apply a certain amount of pressure.

- We are again on an F♯7 chord in the key of D Major and we hear something strange. Conclusion: *Houston, we have a problem.* HM5 is eliminated immediately. If you hear a lot of dissonance, you should think about Mixolydian or one of the symmetrical scales (HTWT or WT). Mixolydian with its tensions 9 (G♯) and 13 (D♯) would sound particularly out of place in D Major. An unusual mix of tensions (e.g. ♯9/13 or 9/♭13) would also create quite a bit of unrest.

Again, we use our theoretical knowledge to interpret the feeling we get when listening to a sound. The function of a chord, its tonal environment and the expectation it creates in our ear provide us with the clues necessary to figure out the scale and the related tensions. This certainly does not mean that all available tensions of the scale are actually present. All we are trying to do is narrow down the possibilities to prevent us from heading in the wrong direction. Only when you have decided on the general scale do you go off looking for specific tensions.

Assignment

Go to **track 13** ("There Will Never Be Another You"), and listen to the piano. Ignore the intro and move on to the first chorus. Listen to it several times, concentrating only on the question of "usual versus unusual". The impression you should get is a feeling of familiarity pervading throughout. This means that the accompaniment follows the chord progression as expected, generally using the most "inside" scales and commonplace tensions. The only sounds that stick out clearly can be found in bars 16 (B♭7), 20 (G7) and 29–31 (A♭7 - G7 - C7 - F7 - B♭7). Let's try to pinpoint the special events – you first (don't read on until you've tried to figure out what's happening on your own).

In bar 16, the B♭7 sounds rather dissonant – nothing dramatic, but it definitely has more tension than you would expect if the dominant were played Mixolydian (the "inside" choice). Conclusion: Most probably, we're hearing an altered dominant with HM5(+♯9) or Altered as the scale material. Because the tension level is not very high, I'd rather lean towards HM5(+♯9) – and that's what it is.

In bar 20, the G7 sticks out like a sore thumb (in a good way). You can hear three piano voicings, which all have pretty much the same quality. If you follow the top notes of the voicings, you will realise that the pianist is just shifting the same structure down in minor thirds. Considering the high level of dissonance and the fact that the identical voicing can be symmetrically sequenced in minor thirds, only one conclusion makes sense: The G7 is played HTWT (the structure of which repeats in minor thirds). The tensions A♭ (♭9), A♯ (♯9), C♯ (♯11) and E (13) give this sequence its special colour.

Now listen closely to bars 29–32. Note how the tension level increases from chord to chord. While A♭7 still sounds as expected, the dissonance gets stronger and stronger, starting with G7 at a fairly low level and culminating with F7. By comparison, the B♭7 is almost back to normal again. You should also notice the sequential character of this passage. The pianist obviously uses the same principle with every chord. Of course, the rhythmic activity adds to the intensity of the voicings. What can we deduce from these preliminary statements? This section is not that easy to decipher. The A♭7 (SubV/III), though, should be straightforward. Since the sound doesn't jar and the most inside solution in the key of E♭ Major would be Lydian(♭7), that's what we should go for. With G7 (V7/VI), we should remember that it is generally played as HM5(+♯9) in E♭ Major. Considering the slight increase in tension, we should come up with Altered as a possible solution, with the ♯11 adding some spice (and that is correct). Next, contemplate the sequential character of the accompaniment. If our assumption holds true, we can speculate that whatever is used over G7 is continued over the following chords. This means that C7 (V7/II), which is normally played HM5(+♯9) or Mixolydian(♭13) with a natural 9, and F7 (V7/V), which usually takes Mixolydian or Lydian(♭7), are both played as Altered, too (this would account for the high level of tension on the F7). To cut a long story short – this is exactly what happens. With Bb7, the choice of scale more or less returns to the expected (you should, however, feel a slight pinprick when listening to the voicing). We will go into more detail further down in this chapter.

Voicings

Sometimes we may want to transcribe the exact structure of a sound or even a longer succession of voicings. How do we approach this? Here are a few tips that should facilitate the first steps in transcribing piano or guitar voicings, vocal groups, brass or saxophone sections, etc. Consider the following aspects and try to answer the corresponding questions while listening to the recording (of course, you'll have to listen repeatedly and focus on a different topic each time):

- *bottom note* or *lead note* (the outer parts provide us with the framework of a voicing);
- *root* (Be careful! Who says that the bottom note is always the root? It could be an inversion. Check! Quite often, the root is only provided by the bass and is not included in the voicing);
- *scale* (Does the voicing trigger a sense of scale material?);
- *harmonic expectation* (What chord type is likely to appear in this particular situation?);
- *degree of tension* (How consonant/dissonant, simple/complex or usual/unusual is the sound?);
- *functional notes* (Where are the thirds and/or sevenths?);
- *tensions* (How many and which extensions are there in the voicing?);
- *voicing technique / intervallic structure* (layers of thirds, voicings in fourths, clusters, upper structures, slash chords, etc.); go to the chapter "Voicings" (pdf-E) for further information;
- *density of the voicing / number of parts* (How many notes/parts are there?);
- *distribution of parts* (Which elements of the voicing are e.g. in the left hand or right hand of the piano, which parts are played by the trombone, sax or trumpet section in a big band arrangement, etc.?);
- *voice leading* (A voicing is not an isolated event; follow the progress of individual parts into and out of the sound; this especially helps with the middle parts, which are always hard to hear)
- *instrumental "reflex"* (How do the voicings "feel"? Thinking as a pianist or guitarist – can we recognise voicings according to familiar fingerings?).

It makes absolutely no difference which of these points you figure out first – the important thing is to get a foot in the door and to go on from there.

Let's go back to the recording of "TWINBAY" (**track 13**) and the last 4 bars of the first chorus (the section we talked about further up when considering choice of scales). Listen to the accompaniment again several times (loop it on your computer or CD player if you can). Remember that I mentioned the sequential character of this passage. So, let's assume that the pianist not only follows a scale concept but also a voicing strategy. If you listen closely to the right hand of the piano, you should hear that, structurally speaking, it sounds very coherent. This, again, should lead you to the assumption that the pianist uses the same voicing concept throughout (he does). In addition, we should take into account that a piano player generally tends to play 4-note or 5-note two-hand voicings when comping. For those of you who are already familiar with the concept of "upper structures" (see pdf-E for further information) it will be obvious that the piano player is using triads in the right hand and important chord tones (3/♭7) in the left hand.

First, transcribe the top notes of the piano accompaniment. Then, referring back to the scales we decided on further up, try to figure out the exact triads in the right hand. Finally, add 3 and ♭7 in the left hand and consider how a pianist would probably position them. Don't look at the following example before you've tried to work out a possible solution.

This is what you should come up with:

Analysis

> *"It may be helpful just to see what someone like Miles Davis played, but books don't really teach you anything about why Miles did what he did, what his thinking was. That's what's needed."*
>
> ## Benny Bailey

Now it's time to analyse our transcription. By this, I don't just mean describing the actual musical content. Trying to understand the principles and the person behind the notes is of even greater importance. Analysis should always transcend the purely descriptive stage. Stating that a note is a ♭9, a melodic phrase is Dorian or a dominant chord is a V7/V is stating the obvious and merely scratching the surface. Trying to find out *why* a soloist plays a particular phrase is far more exciting and rewarding than to analyse *what* is played. You have to learn to ask questions that look beyond the immediately apparent facts – questions that help reveal the intention, the approach, the "philosophy" of a player. All musicians work on concepts – whether they are aware of it or not. You need to look for these concepts. You should try to understand how other musicians actually think and how they might have practised, so that they would have immediate access to the musical vocabulary expressed through their lines. Analysis should never be a matter of external perspective alone. Being merely a casual observer is not enough. Trying to get to the core of things by putting yourself into the position of the soloist or composer is what it's all about.

Let's take Larry Williams' solo on "Spain" (see p. 133 ff.) as an example. When analysing the actual notes, we see that he plays almost every dominant as HTWT. This is obviously his strategy – at least for this improvisation. Now we get to the decisive point. Larry Williams was not thinking about any of this while soloing. At this tempo, no one has time to think. It's all about automatic responses and reacting to musical situations on the spur of the moment. However, to make these lines happen, he must have worked exhaustively on HTWT dominants and all possible resolutions in major and minor keys again and again over a long period of time in order to establish this direct link between the sound and the fingers, to make this tricky material immediately available. Especially when it comes to sounds such as the HTWT scale, which are not automatically part of our playing habits, meticulous practice is imperative. Our ear initially rejects sounds that sidestep tonality and diatonicism, and it takes time before they become part of our musical vocabulary. It is all the more impressive when someone has managed to master sounds like these with such ease and dexterity.

Transcriptions not only show us what notes to choose and how to apply them in a specific harmonic situation. They also reveal underlying concepts and strategies that will tell us how great musicians think. Here's another phrase taken from the same solo (2nd chorus, bars 9–11):

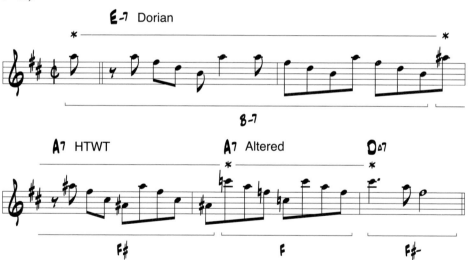

Here are a couple of things Larry Williams must have worked on for him to be able to play this particular line at this tempo in such a relaxed way:

- dominants that are played HTWT or Altered and resolve to major chords;

- upper structures (triads and four-note chords) derived from these scales and superimposed on the basic changes (e.g. B–7 over E–7, an F♯ or F triad over A7);

- constructing ascending guide tone lines over a II-V-I progression (A - A♯/B♭ - C - C♯) instead of the usual descending GTLs;

- voice leading the arpeggios upwards instead of following the natural reflex of moving downwards chromatically (F♯ to F);

- incorporating all the preceding concepts into a flowing line, starting "inside" on II–7 (E–7), getting increasingly dissonant over V7 (A7) and landing "inside" again on Imaj7 (Dmaj7);

- using rhythmic displacement.

These things don't "just happen". Lines such as the one shown above are the result of pains-taking work with concepts and sounds that don't follow well-trodden paths and common-place patterns. They require premeditation before we can practise them, let alone use them. The phrase reveals far too much structural control and is too smoothly executed for it to be coincidental. You have to burn gallons of midnight oil to develop "instant touch" for such a complex sequence of events. It may even be one of Larry Williams' "stock phrases" over a II-V-I, something he would use time and again with minor variations.

In conclusion: Keep working hard on the "behind-the-scenes" aspects of your transcrip-tions. Never be satisfied with a superficial analysis limited only to scale choices or harmonic functions. It's not only about the *what* but rather the *how*, *when* and, particularly, the *why*.

Fast thinking = good ears

One of the goals when transcribing is to get the maximum result from a minimum amount of information. Successful transcription has a lot to do with deduction, cross-referencing, guesswork and quick thinking. Listening to a recording over and over again while hoping that divine inspiration will strike and answers will drop like manna from heaven is a waste of time. As a rule of thumb, those who think fast hear well, and those who think faster hear even better. We have to learn to filter out the right answers from an abundance of possibili-ties, to draw intelligent and pertinent conclusions from seemingly insignificant or incongru-ent details, to collate the experiences and memories we carry around, to weigh up what seems likely and unlikely and to extract precise information from general musical observa-tions. The faster this associative process takes place, the more accurately and acutely we hear. The ear tells us e.g. "It's neither this nor that, but it does remind me a little of something I've heard in another tune, so, maybe that's what it is.", or "This sounds unusual, it feels strange, I've never heard anything like it before", etc. The mind evaluates the information our ear gives us and says: "That seems likely in this context.", or "That is highly unlikely, here.", or "If this holds true and I consider that, then it could only be this.", etc. You will be surprised how quickly your listening skills will develop when the ear and the mind collaborate.

Students often ask me how it is that I manage to come up with the correct (or at least a likely) solution right away when listening to something for the first time. The answer is simple. It's not that I can hear better than other people. It makes no difference whether you are a teacher or a student, amateur or pro – we all hear the same sounds. It's the interpretation of what we hear that poses the problem. As a battle-scarred musician, I simply have a zillion subliminally stored sounds, more listening strategies, more know-how and more theoretical background to rely on than the less experienced musician. Countless deliberately memorised musical facts and ready-to-use images in my mind are constantly at my disposal as points of reference. I can immediately apply this arsenal of knowledge and experience to evaluate and compare anything new that comes my way. I have developed the ability to access a recording with little or no prior information and to get to the point more quickly than the untrained listener, who usually has no idea where to start, gets bogged down thinking about irrelevant details and ends up asking the wrong questions. I have learned to clearly distinguish between "important" and "unimportant" and, as a result, manage to latch onto a sound quickly, even if it is initially unfamiliar. Let me tell you, it didn't happen overnight.

All musicians with a good ear rely on the same associative process. They hear a sound and can name it on the spur of the moment, seemingly without having to think about it. This may appear to be magic to some, but it is nothing more than incredibly fast information processing based on a lifetime of facts leading immediately to the right answer. Sound and concept are so inextricably linked that an immediate reflex is triggered and recognition is instantaneous. And now for the good news – anyone can do this, albeit at different levels.

The more you know and play, the more you will recognise. Sometimes, it takes just a small step to make a big difference. Here's a little anecdote to prove my point:

A colleague had a student, who could play basic piano and knew almost nothing about music theory. One day, they talked about II-V-Is. My colleague played him a few examples and gave him several piano exercises to work on. A few days later, the student was back and said: "I'm hearing II-V-Is all over the place. Before, I couldn't, because I didn't know what to listen for, even though they were out there all along."

Having a reliable listening strategy means asking the right questions at the right moment, and for that to happen, you need knowledge – the more, the better. So, work on your theory and learn to apply it. It is not that important to be able to come up with the right answers immediately. It is much more important to ask pertinent questions. Try to find questions that are easy to answer. Start simple!!! Your questions should correspond to your personal level of knowledge and listening capabilities. Each answer should lead to further logical questions and an increasing understanding of what it is you're hearing. The answers may initially be conjecture and must be verified. For this reason, you need to practise coming up with exercises that will either confirm or refute your assumptions. And that's what we'll do in the "Transcription Workshop" (pdf-H). There, I have laid out examples and exercises as a question-and-answer game, following a set line of reasoning:

- What do I know about the context, the harmonic, melodic, rhythmic or formal environment?

- Regarding the context and seen from a theoretical point of view, what would I expect? What would be commonplace, familiar or rather unusual?

- Which explanations would make sense considering the effect of the sound in question?

- Which one of these explanations is the most likely?

- How can I check my assumptions?

- What conclusions can I draw once I've checked these assumptions?

I will use the pieces "Moving Out", "Waltz For Ever" and "Walking Tiptoe" (tracks 42–44) to show you how you can practise doing transcriptions.

From transcription to instrument

"If you hear something intriguing in somebody else's solo, the main thing is to find out how it works, to find out what's intriguing about it, and then to apply it differently in your own way."

Benny Bailey

We now come to my last point. Ultimately, transcriptions are there to help you expand your repertoire and instrumental vocabulary. For this reason, your transcriptions must be transferred to your instrument and practised down to the tiniest detail. Once you've transcribed a solo, work on every little embellishment, every accent, every glissando and every dynamic subtlety. Play the lines in real time along with the recording and play them unaccompanied, just with a metronome. In any case, practise a solo until you can play it note-perfect. I have colleagues whose record collections merely crackle and pop – worn down after years of being listened to and used as a play-along literally thousands of times (with CDs, iPods and so on, this, of course, is no longer an issue). It is worth going to the absolute limit and then some. As a final step, the most important elements of your transcriptions, the concepts of the soloists and your favourite phrases should be incorporated into your daily practice routine. You will find detailed exercises in the chapters "Improvisation" and "How To Practise" (pdf-K).

However, playing any idea (line, solo, voicing, etc.) exactly as transcribed is only a first step. Eventually, you will have to leave the comfort zone of imitation and transform the material into something personal. Be sure to focus on the creative use of what you've practised. Extract those parts of a transcription that you are particularly fond of and try to include them in your improvisations. Embellish, vary, reshape, develop and change them, thereby creating your own interpretation. Sooner or later, you will realise that certain phrases are indelibly imprinted on your musical memory and have become second nature to your playing – not as set "building blocks" but rather as malleable and flexible ideas that have merged with other parts of your musical vocabulary.

Assignment

Go to pdf-H and delve into the "Transcription Workshop" as soon as possible.

Play

"I can show you the basic theory you need to play Jazz in a few hours, but you will spend the next five to seven years studying it before you can make much use of it in your playing."

Wynton Marsalis

Improvisation

"There are still a few die-hards who believe ... there is such a thing as unadulterated improvisation without any preparation or anticipation. It is my firm belief that there has never been anybody who has blown even two bars worth listening to who didn't have some idea about what he was going to play, before he started ... there has to be some thought preceding each phrase, otherwise it is meaningless."

Duke Ellington

Cultural and music theorist Bert Noglik once wrote in an article: "… the problems of improvisation … cannot be solved with the help of premeditation and behaviour-oriented planning, only by means of situational adroitness and process-related responses." Put more simply – you can't prepare for improvisation. Essentially, Noglik is right, of course. Free improvisation calls for the ability to create meaningful and coherent results from coincidental events. How could we possibly practise this in advance? Improvisation can only be experienced through the improvisational process itself, by doing it. If we also understand improvisation as something that mainly occurs within a group of musicians, where we react to the stimulus of others or, likewise, provide impulse and impetus to the band, it becomes patently obvious that we're talking about an ability that cannot be developed in the seclusion of our private practice room.

I don't intend to philosophise on the essence of improvisation – others have done so quite eloquently. One thing, however, should be absolutely clear: We are not going to talk about "free improvisation" in this book. We will primarily focus on what the guitarist Derek Bailey (one of the most influential personalities in Free Jazz) calls *idiomatic improvisation* in his treatise "Improvisation – Its Nature and Practice in Music". In his sense, the word "idiomatic" means being part of and in accordance with the rules and conventions of a particular style. In contrast, the term *non-idiomatic improvisation* is used to describe an expressive form free of stylistic constraints.

It is in the very nature of mainstream Jazz (and that is what this book is about) that we improvise over changes, that solos are driven by the melodic, harmonic, rhythmical and formal criteria of the underlying musical compositions. So, Noglik's statement must be false if improvisation occurs within a framework determined by specific vocabulary, a stylistic language following certain rules and displaying typical attributes. If musicians – as in traditional Jazz – rely on a standard repertoire, if specific chord progressions are agreed upon as the basis for improvisation, then – to follow up on the introductory quote by Duke Ellington – it is inherently necessary to be well prepared.

The context determines what is appropriate and what is not. And I am fully aware that the rules we have to follow and the habits we have to develop as Jazz musicians are fraught with the danger of becoming rigid in our thinking and mechanical in our playing. In this respect,

Free Jazz can be seen as a logical development, an attempt to liberate improvisation from the shackles of traditional dos and don'ts. However, when we improvise, for example, over a II-V-I progression in F Major, we can't avoid having to accept certain facts that are critical to the musical flow in this particular situation. Sure, we could just dive in, play anything we like and hope that everything will turn out just dandy. More likely, the outcome will be a terrible mess. Then again, we could simply doodle around in the key of F Major. This would not be entirely wrong, but the result would not sound very coherent or reflect the changes adequately. On the other hand, if we work with chord tones, tensions, guide tone lines and motivic phrases in keeping with G–7, C7 and Fmaj7, we would most probably come pretty close to a meaningful melody.

According to the Viennese flugelhorn player Franz Kogelmann, improvisation is "… a demonstration of acquired skills on the one hand and spontaneous invention on the other". I subscribe wholeheartedly to this sentiment even though, later on in Kogelmann's essay, he clearly implies that, to him, a true improviser is one who aims to avoid the use of prefabricated material and is solely committed to the necessities of the moment. Kogelmann says publicly what many Jazz musicians think – that improvisation can never be the result of premeditation and practice, otherwise the spontaneity of creation will be lost. To some it is sacrilege to plan an improvisation. They glorify improvisation as a mystical process, suggesting to beginners that "some simply have it and some simply don't".

Actually, the daily grind of a Jazz musician is far more sobering. The ability to find suitable answers to the questions posed by other musicians during an improvisation is based on a musical and instrumental vocabulary that is the result of very hard work and has absolutely nothing to do with esoteric hogwash. One of my favourite sayings is:

"Chance favours the prepared mind."

If we want to mitigate the risk of failure, we have to be prepared. Of course, it is our objective to switch off our thoughts while improvising, to depend entirely on the ear, intuition and instinct. After all, reflexes are faster than thoughts. However, reflexes can be developed, and only with a well-trained and firmly ingrained vocabulary can we *play* in the true sense of the word.

Of course, we often come across the allegation that improvisations in the mainstream Jazz idiom are no more than the regurgitation of pre-packed formulae. However, the history of Jazz has shown that it is possible to follow rules and still be creative. Quite to the contrary, the narrower the framework, the bigger the challenge it is for musicians to tell interesting stories despite these limitations. True creativity emerges independently of style and its standards. Never blame a lack of creativity on the constraints of the idiom.

Granted – not everyone has the talent and the perseverance to become a John Coltrane or Miles Davis. But, as much as we may try to attribute the achievements of such musicians to a higher level of awareness or even divine inspiration, the bottom line is this simple fact: They could unquestionably speak the "language of music" better than most of their contemporaries. And, just like learning a language, we have to come to grips with vocabulary and grammar in order to be able to express our thoughts coherently. People who really knew and admired John Coltrane have boiled it down quite profanely – he was not a genius, but simply the most obsessive workaholic ever to walk down Jazz Street (as we all know: Genius is 1% inspiration and 99% perspiration).

What I am really trying to say is that improvisation can be learned! And I am wildly determined to lift the veil of mystery from a phenomenon, which is all too often considered to be something inexplicable and even unattainable. I would like to pursue the question as to what distinguishes a good improvisation. Regrettably, I will have to do this without being able to touch on the most important point: the communication and interaction between musicians. Improvisation doesn't mean "standing in front of the band doing your thing, while a couple of slaves in the background provide a rhythmic and harmonic carpet". Of course, in a traditional setting, it does mean that, for a while, one of the musicians takes on responsibility by stepping into the limelight as a soloist, inspiring the others in the group. However, the excitement of improvisation depends largely on the degree to which fellow musicians react, how they support and contribute to the ideas of the soloist. This interplay can simply not be dealt with in a book. It can only be learned through practical experience. For this reason, I will have to limit myself to exercises we can tackle on our own.

The six pillars

Six basic elements determine the flow of an improvisation:

- Motivation

- Sound

- Form

- Rhythm

- Melody

- Harmony

Whereas motivation describes the inner world of feelings, thoughts and the personal intentions of a player (cause), the other five aspects embody the actual music (effect). These aspects naturally overlap and should not be seen as separate. Quite to the contrary – they influence and complement each other profoundly. They will, however, take on differing degrees of importance and emphasis depending on the musician, his or her tastes, individual strengths and weaknesses, the character of the composition, style, etc.

The order in which the six elements are listed above is not random. I have aligned them in such a way that they follow a hierarchy that moves from …

- … conceptual to concrete;

- … subjective to objective;

- … personal to general;

- … vague to precise;

- … subliminal to perceptible;

- … emotional to cerebral.

Motivation comes first because it is the essential catalyst for any artistic activity. It is the fundamental reason why people pick up an instrument or write a piece of music. What motivates you is both highly personal and inherently elusive because it could be anything you deem important enough to act as a starting point. Motivation is the all-embracing term for whatever inspires you and spurs you on – be it a trip to Moscow, the moon, peace, flowers, fame, a lover, the word "harumpff", money, chop sticks, etc. It is hard to talk about and narrow down motivation because it is up to you and you alone to decide what it is that motivates you. Motivation defines the "why" in music.

Sound comes next. Again, like motivation, sound is hard to pinpoint or describe. Sound includes many things – the inflection of a single note, the way you articulate a phrase, the timbre of an instrument, the orchestration of a piece, the "signature sound" of a musician or band, the mix of a recording, the characteristics of a style, etc. Sound encompasses anything that gives music its distinctive flavour (e.g. the romantic quality of an *"oboe d'amore"*, the guitar playing of Pat Metheny, the Motown Sound, etc.). Sound is what translates motivation into actual music. Sound is the superordinate term that unites all other aspects, **the** primary parameter that makes (your) music recognisable. Sound defines the "how" in music.

Form is the general term for the way music moves through time, the way rhythm, melody and harmony interact to create a flow perceived as a whole. It is the way a story is told. When we hear a piece of music, we react strongly to how it unfolds, to its contour, the ups and downs, the swell and surge. Of course, there are standardised forms that govern the way sectional units are combined to create a piece (e.g. AABA, ABAC, 12-bar Blues, etc. in Jazz, the "verse-chorus" format in Pop music, minuet, rondo or sonata forms in Classical music, etc.). There are, however, a multitude of other concepts that are used to determine the structure, architecture or design of a piece (many of which we've talked about in detail). Form defines the "when" in music.

We now move on into the more specific and quantifiable areas, the "what" in music. *Rhythm* is the most primal of musical elements. It is the one aspect our body experiences most strongly. We dance to rhythm. Some cultures rely almost entirely on rhythm as their principal means of expression. This does not imply that their music is less complex than most of Western music, which focusses more strongly on melody and harmony. African music is highly polyrhythmic, Indian *talas* take years to learn and even Techno does rather well with almost no melody or harmony to speak of. Rhythm encompasses all aspects of movement: pulse, beat, measure, tempo, metric structure, groove, timing, *accelerando*, *ritardando*, floating time, etc.

Melody is next in line. Melody is what we experience first as kids (by singing ourselves or listening to our parents sing). Discounting rhythm, it is our most direct access to music. Melody is what we remember best when conjuring up a piece in our mind. We have talked extensively about the structural elements of melodies in previous chapters, so I'll move on.

Harmony comes last because it the most sophisticated and conceptual topic. Harmony, seen historically, is an outcrop of melody. It evolved from melodic polyphony, which, in the course of time, introduced the vertical aspect into music. Harmony is the most scholarly of topics with the clearest set of rules. It can be viewed academically and analytically – more so than any of the other elements. And that is why there are zillions of books on harmony (☺) and almost none on motivation or sound. It's much easier to talk about harmony, melody and rhythm, to define a "right" or "wrong", to set up exercises and follow a verifiable learning curve. It is almost impossible to say the same for motivation and sound.

So, our list of 6 elements moves from the most subjective, emotionally driven aspect (motivation) to the most quantifiable, objective element (harmony). This book is mainly about harmony and melody. However, the effect, vitality and vigour of Western music in general (including Jazz) with its refined, filigree harmonic and melodic language depends largely on the feeling of motion (rhythm), the sense of being part of a whole (form), how the music is played and presented (sound) and what induces us to express ourselves through music in the first place (motivation).

What does all of this have to do with improvisation? Only if we move away from spending our time almost exclusively with harmony, melody and rhythm and shift our focus to the more impalpable topics (form, sound and motivation) will our improvisations have personality and depth. Since motivation and sound are topics that are seldom written about, I would like to make a few comments on them, here.

Motivation

What motivates you to pick up your instrument and start making music? Why do we get on stage? Why do people write music? What is it you want to say? What's your "message"?

Exercise – part one

Think of something – a picture, story, mood, scene, person or feeling. It doesn't have to be anything special. You could choose something quite ordinary – the main thing is that it has touched you and moved you in some way. Allow this idea to take shape in your imagination and work its effect on you. Then go to your instrument, close your eyes and improvise. Think only about what you are trying to convey. Don't think about scales, changes, exercises you're working on, technical studies and, especially, not about anything you have read in this book. Just play! Allow yourself to be drawn into your inner world and try to express your emotions with the notes you play. Imagine you are playing for an audience. When you are done, think back and ask yourself if you told your story truthfully and convincingly.

Exercise – part two

Do the same as in the first exercise, with one exception – now you have exactly one minute to tell your story. So, what any painter has to content himself with when starting on a 50 × 70 cm canvas should not be unusual for musicians when having to play within the confines of a limited timeframe. While you are playing, look at a clock and think:

00 seconds – Beginning
15 seconds – Now I should gradually get going
30 seconds – Half time
45 seconds – Now I should gradually come to the end
60 seconds – End

Now, think back. Have you said what you wanted to say? How do you feel about your sense of time? Did you feel stressed, under pressure? Did you manage to tell the whole story or did the clock interrupt you? Are you happy with the outcome of the exercise? Be aware of how the imposed time limit affected you, how it forced you to think in proportions and work with a time line. Did this influence your ideas? Did you have to stretch, compress, accelerate or slow down your phrases in order to end on time? A minute can be endless or go by in a flash.

Exercise – part three

Play **track 13**. You now have three choruses in which to tell the same story you tried to tell in the previous exercises. Go ahead and try it a few times if you don't manage at first.

So, did you run into problems? How much did the fact that you were trying to follow an inner scenario get in the way of your musical ideas? Was it difficult to keep your story in mind, and, at the same time, to consider all other factors the composition forces you to observe and execute while you are improvising? For the improviser, this is the greatest challenge of all: to create emotional impact and simultaneously respect the technicalities of the tune.

Never forget that, even when you are working on exercises concerning scales, chords, motives, rhythms, etc., the incentive should always be to tell a good story. Fill every note with meaning! The instrument is your mouthpiece, the mirror of your soul. What is it you want to say? What message does the tune convey (title, lyrics)? Which pictures, colours, emotions or experiences do you want to express? Improvisation is not "the special moment on the stage". Try to see improvisation as part of your day-to-day life, a reflection of all the many memories, events and impressions you carry around with you. Do you want your improvisations to be colourful, articulate, passionate, touching, energetic? I'm sure, you do. If it is your desire to play a spirited improvisation, the decisive question should always be: Which musical resources do I want to (or have to) use to tell my story convincingly? Don't play a note just because it's there, play it because it serves your cause!

At this point, I'd like to recommend a book that has become iconic and widely recognised in the world of contemporary Jazz: "Effortless Mastery – Liberating the Master Musician Within" by Kenny Werner. It is the only book I know of that provides comprehensive and empathic insight into the manifold psychological aspects of improvisation. I know a number of Jazz musicians for whom this book was a turning point in their careers. It will help you develop your creative skills and enhance your ability to tell the many stories that fuel your motivation with greater conviction.

Sound

We talked about the origin of sound at the beginning of this book. Of course, it is possible to break down the sound of an instrument into mathematically and physically intelligible components. And yet, it is the personality of the player that brings the instrument to life. We could speak about the trumpet in the abstract, but it takes the sound of a Miles Davis or a Chet Baker to give it emotional meaning and its typical colouring. The sound is what distinguishes one musician from another. It is a trademark, a personal signature. All great soloists have their own distinctive and unmistakable sound. It is what makes them stand out from the crowd. There is hardly an issue that occupies musicians more and to which they react more sensitively, if not touchy. If our sound isn't right, we don't feel right. Most musicians spend their entire lives searching for *"their very own sound"*.

At the same time, nobody knows what the term "sound" really means. Sound is the most individual and therefore least tangible aspect of a musician's attributes. There is no "right" or "wrong" – it is a very ambiguous criterion. You can't really teach sound. You can make a student aware of the topic. But, in the end, you can only chaperone the quest for an individual voice. To have a signature sound is a never-ending story that encompasses a lot more than just a specific technical approach to the instrument. It also includes articulation, the way the notes are formed, dynamics, timing, individual physical attributes (e.g. embouchure), the ear, role models we emulate, intonation, style, melodic and rhythmical ideas, typical phrases, etc. – in a word, it is a combination of many, many factors.

Why do I attach so much importance to this subject? Without a very personal sound, nothing we play emanates meaning. Only once we add features such as vibrato, glissandi, slides, drops, accents, ghost notes, embellishments, etc. to a melody, does it come alive, convey moods and tell stories. It makes no difference *what* you play – it is *how* you present it that counts. The notes themselves are merely amorphous matter. It is the way they are articulated, phrased and formed that brings them to life. This doesn't mean that the packaging is more important than the content. However, you can play as many "right" notes as you like, and they will sound like nothing at all until you imbue them with colour. It is the sound that gives an improvisation personality and vitality. Because this book is on harmony, my focus lies on your playing the right notes. However, don't fall into the trap of thinking that you've got it made once you've mastered a chord progression and are capable of playing nice lines. That's only part of the story. Concentrate on the way you perform a phrase. Be aware of its feel and impact. The first note you play sets a mood and invites the listener to follow your musical narrative. If you spend more time on this topic, then chances are high that you will, eventually, not sound like a dime a dozen.

Composition vs improvisation

Many musicians equate improvisation to "composing on the spur of the moment" or "*instant composing*" – and they are right. *Improvisation is spontaneous composition!* Of course, there are differences. Improvisation thrives on the "here and now", it exploits the excitement and emotional disposition of the players and depends on their immediate interaction. Therefore, it sometimes lacks structure and concept. Composition, on the other hand, is the working of a plan, a matter of design and proportions and focusses on the way individual parts are put together to construct a whole. As a result, it often lacks the vigour and spontaneity of improvisation. Whereas composers develop their ideas with contemplation and leisure at a desk (well, perhaps not, if you have a deadline looming ahead), improvisers work with an immediacy that denies ever going back on what has been played. However, when evaluating the outcome of an improvisation or a composition, both are judged on the same criteria: coherence, flow, originality, creativity, form, concept, emotional impact, etc. So, in the end, it is only the time factor that sets the two apart.

Improvisers can learn a lot from composers. An understanding of compositional principles will help give your improvisations a higher degree of integrity. In essence, composition is an idealised form of improvisation, a model case. Inversely, a convincing solo will stand up on its own as a theme. There are, in fact, improvisations that have become compositions in their own right because they are so beautifully structured. The best-known example of this is "Donna Lee" by Charlie Parker, a piece that emerged from a solo on "Back Home in Indiana" by J. F. Hanley. "Donna Lee" is a good example of a *"perfect solo"* that has firmly established itself as part of the standard repertoire (much to the frustration of many Jazz musicians who have tried to make head or tail of its hellishly difficult lines!).

A sure sense of structural balance (repetition, variation, contrast), dynamics, tension and release, continuity, etc. is indispensable both to composers and improvisers. The ability to conceive coherent musical ideas, to develop motives, phrases, sections and to generate a compelling formal contour, to imagine the whole as well as the many details that constitute the final result – all these skills, likewise, contribute to the creation of an inspiring improvisation as well as a powerful composition. The confidence of the composer to take unequivocal decisions with the necessary clarity of thought – the ability to make a strong statement – is by the same token of central importance to the improviser. This is why, to the budding Jazz musician, analysis is a vital step on the way to playing a successful solo. Composition can often bring the various musical aspects together more consistently than improvisation, which by its very nature depends on a higher degree of chance and is therefore likely to contain more incongruities.

We have already looked at the excerpt from the Sonata in C Major for violin solo by J. S. Bach (see p. 120), in which he manages to unite all constituent parts of a good composition *in one single line*. The phrases are so intelligently conceived and linked that the harmony is implied quite clearly without the need for accompaniment. Even more importantly – Bach's phrases are part of an overall, compelling and coherent formal arch. This, of course, is incredibly difficult to achieve in a solo. Nevertheless, there are examples of improvisations in Jazz that come very close to this compositional ideal.

One of these gems is the 16-bar solo (yes, you don't need more space to create a work of art!) by the trumpet player Chet Baker on "It Could Happen To You" (on the album "Chet Baker Sings"):

These 16 bars alone show that Chet Baker is one of the greatest soloists ever. Remember the six elements? We could only speculate about his motivation (other than his lifelong quest for beautiful music) – but his sound is unmistakable. His rather melancholic timbre has become a trademark that every Jazz musician immediately recognises. His feeling for form is impressive. His clearly structured phrases, the motives, the overall contour of the solo, the undulating surge and swell of energy, the carefully prepared climax in bar 9, the identical starting and finishing note (at the same time the lowest note = the point of minimum tension) – all of this is witness to absolute intuitive control. His rhythmic ideas are truly full of life. We don't hear – as we so often do – a torrent of eighth notes, but rather a colourful mixture of different note values. The melody has a tremendous forward drive (try to find the guide tone lines concealed in this improvisation!). Every phrase leads perfectly to the next. The harmony is also clearly reflected in the line. The phrases consist mainly of arpeggios and resolve to chord tones at decisive moments. Despite the relatively complex changes, this improvisation is predominantly diatonic. It is worth noting, however, that almost all harmonic deviations from the tonality are also incorporated into the solo. All characteristic notes occur at the beginning or on the main beats of the bar. These are clearly points Chet Baker was aiming for, not chance hits. And now for the most remarkable fact of all: We are listening to a *sung* improvisation. We are not listening to an instrument and preconceived fingerings. We are listening to internalised sound, pure music, to a voice – the unadulterated and most direct link between the soul, the personality and the outside world.

The objective of the following chapters will be to give you an understanding of how Jazz musicians think and to touch on some of the psychological aspects of improvisation. I would like to get to the bottom of what it is that gives a solo such as the one by Chet Baker the qualities we appreciate so much. And I'd like to help you make the distinction between a poor solo and a good one.

Assignment

While working on the next few chapters, don't forget to consult the pdf-files mentioned below. They will provide many practical tips on how to effectively work on your instrument, how to put together a successful practice program and how to efficiently learn pieces off by heart:

pdf-I: Technique and Scales

pdf-J: Same Old Changes

pdf-K: How To Practise

Play-Alongs

What is the ultimate reason for practising? Because we want to get out there and play! And what do we play? Tunes! This might seem obvious, but it means that everything you practise must relate to real music! As a matter of principle!! Always!!! Abstract exercises are only of limited value. Practising scales, arpeggios, sequences, patterns, etc. is good for your technique, but it only has meaning if it serves the repertoire you want to play. Of course, it is necessary to isolate technical or musical problems and practise them separately – but in the end, every sound must be applied in a practical context.

The first and most important step: *Find yourself a band!* Make sure you track down fellow musicians at your level (or preferably better) who are willing to practise regularly (once a week or more). Don't be shy about your playing. Whatever you've practised, you have to apply it in a live situation. This will help consolidate your repertoire. Hands-on experience is what counts! Only "locking horns" (pun intended) will give you the necessary confidence as a soloist and an understanding of what it means to interact with other musicians. If you can't find the right people to play with in your immediate area, attend as many Jazz workshops as possible. This is where you'll meet like-minded souls who share the same goals and who are only too happy to get together every now and then.

Sadly, not everybody has the opportunity to hook up with a band. Fortunately, there is an alternative: *play-alongs* – recordings featuring professional rhythm sections (mostly piano, bass and drums), which provide the accompaniment to a vast number of Jazz standards. Play-alongs constitute the only way to work on your repertoire at home in a simulated musical environment that comes close to a real playing situation. The best-known collection of play-alongs is the *Jamey Aebersold* series, consisting of more than 130 CDs covering a wide range of tunes and styles.

However, be warned that play-alongs are a controversial issue. I often hear colleagues belittle them because they represent an artificial setting in which it is not possible to experience and develop the main thing Jazz is all about – interplay. This point of view is not entirely unjustified. With a recording, there can be no interaction with other musicians. You always practise to the same track, subsequently running the risk of getting used to one, and only one, accompaniment. You react to specific bass lines, drum fills, piano voicings, rhythmical accents, and so on, *which never change*. And that's what you file away in your head. Next time you play the same piece at a jam session or a concert, you may find yourself confronted with a completely new situation. Different musicians, a different version of the tune, different changes, a different key, tempo or style – all of this calls for different reactions and a different approach. Whatever you've practised at home with the play-along might not be musically relevant or appropriate any more.

For this reason, it is quite understandable why many Jazz musicians cheerfully badmouth the Aebersold series. However, most of them are pros and in the enviable position of rehearsing and playing concerts regularly with a variety of musicians. The average amateur has a more fundamental problem to solve: How do you practise soloing? How many of you have access to a band that is prepared to slave away while you're trying to get your act together? From this perspective, play-alongs are the most patient rhythm sections you could possibly find. Besides, how many of us will ever have the chance to be accompanied by great musicians such as Ron Carter, Billy Higgins or Hal Galper? Just remember that play-alongs cannot replace a real band. They're only the second best choice! From an educational point of view, however, I have grown to be a big fan of Mr. Aebersold and his steadily increasing collection of CDs.

I would recommend using a play-along for every tune you're working on. If you can't find one, make your own (Band-in-a-Box, sequencer or, even better, a recording of your own band without soloist or theme).

"TWINBAY"

It was not my intention to copy the Aebersold series with this book. So – what's the reason for the 7 play-alongs of "TWINBAY" (**tracks 13–19**)? What can't be found in most play-along collections I know of are recordings of one and the same piece in different versions. In the Aebersold series, almost all tunes are presented only in the original key and in one tempo and style (with few exceptions such as Blues, Rhythm Changes and a small selection of all-time favourite standards). However, learning tunes in all keys is a must, especially when dealing with compositions that contain frequently used chord progressions, which pop up in many other situations. This will help you generalise basic harmonic patterns and make them applicable to other pieces. Learning new tunes will be so much easier if you can rely on material you're already comfortable with.

I have chosen "There Will Never Be Another You" as the principal standard used throughout this book as a sort of "boot camp". This piece is just manageable for beginners and still interesting enough for more advanced players. Additionally, it contains many typical functional progressions (secondary dominants, secondary II-V progressions, etc.). It is therefore what we could call a "mandatory standard". The most important point is that many of you – whether consciously or not – will probably know this tune. Apart from the fact that it is an exemplary training ground for all levels of players, the title of this piece should always remind you that everybody has something very personal and special to say.

Along with this book, you will find seven play-along tracks of "TWINBAY" in different keys, tempos, time signatures, grooves, styles and formats (e.g. long-metre and short-metre changes). For reasons of space, I have not notated the chord progression in the keys used in the recordings. I believe it's a good exercise to transpose the changes yourself (see p. 78 for the lead sheet in E♭ Major).

Here is a summary of the recordings and their "road maps":

Track 13: E♭ Major   Medium Swing   (150 BPM, regular form)

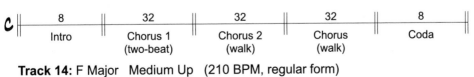

Track 14: F Major   Medium Up   (210 BPM, regular form)

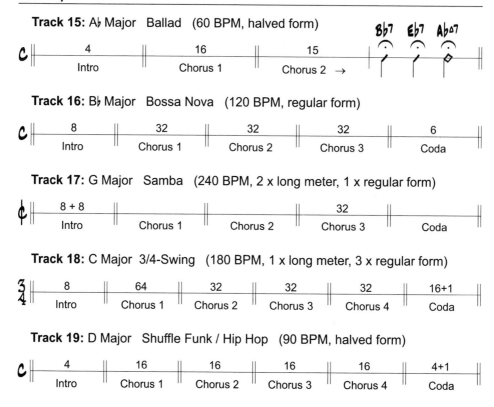

Track 15: Ab Major   Ballad   (60 BPM, halved form)

4	16	15	Bb7 Eb7 Abᐃ7
Intro	Chorus 1	Chorus 2 →	

Track 16: Bb Major   Bossa Nova   (120 BPM, regular form)

8	32	32	32	6
Intro	Chorus 1	Chorus 2	Chorus 3	Coda

Track 17: G Major   Samba   (240 BPM, 2 x long meter, 1 x regular form)

8 + 8			32	
Intro	Chorus 1	Chorus 2	Chorus 3	Coda

Track 18: C Major   3/4-Swing   (180 BPM, 1 x long meter, 3 x regular form)

8	64	32	32	32	16+1
Intro	Chorus 1	Chorus 2	Chorus 3	Chorus 4	Coda

Track 19: D Major   Shuffle Funk / Hip Hop   (90 BPM, halved form)

4	16	16	16	16	4+1
Intro	Chorus 1	Chorus 2	Chorus 3	Chorus 4	Coda

Before we continue, I'd like to issue a warning. Even though play-alongs are rather artificial simulations of a live performance, the musicians, at least in principle, try to play as they would in their own bands. The Aebersold series is actually recorded with a soloist to ensure an authentic result (if you listen very closely, you may catch a hint of the suppressed alto sax solo of Mr. Aebersold himself). Some of the accompaniments you hear on these play-alongs are therefore pretty close to the real thing. This, however, means that the rhythm sections take considerable liberties with the lead sheets that go with the recordings. What you're hearing may not necessarily reflect the theoretically "correct version". The changes may differ marginally from one chorus to the next because they are reharmonised or expanded on spontaneously. Tensions are chosen freely (for example, where a dominant actually should be Mixolydian, you might find it played HTWT). You have to learn to accept this as part of the game. Therefore, always assume that you might not be dealing with the version you know.

Assignment

Listen, for example, to the recordings of "All Of Me" on Vol. 95 of the Aebersold series, "Stella By Starlight" by Stan Getz on the album "Anniversary" as well as the various versions of "TWINBAY" (**tracks 13–19**) and compare them with the lead sheets presented in this book. What differences do you hear? Are the same changes used in every chorus? Which tensions does the pianist play? Can you hear reharmonisations? Do the bass lines correspond to the piano voicings? And so on…

Guide Tone Lines Again

We have seen earlier on that we can derive a scale for any chord depending on its function. But, how do we apply this material? How do we avoid solos that simply run up and down the scales? How do we generate meaningful and coherent melodic phrases when moving from one chord to the next? How do we make sure that we produce more than just a mechanical succession of isolated scale fragments?

The reason for the powerful forward drive of a good line usually lies in its melodic focal points and their relationships to one another. If the most important melody notes (the first, last, highest, lowest notes, accents, points of emphasis, target notes, etc.) follow a consistent pattern of development, a coherent phrase with a clear contour will emerge. In most cases, you will find that these melodic cornerstones add up to a guide tone line (GTL), which threads its way through a phrase giving it direction as well as harmonic integrity. In order to be able to play compelling and articulate melodies, we need a basic repertoire of GTLs for every chord progression.

Voice leading and chord tones

From a traditional point of view, it is the mark of a good solo that it outlines the harmony in the melody. "Playing the changes" is something that all great soloists have mastered. When analysing their solos, it is evident that most lines incorporate important chord tones at decisive points along the way, for example, at a point of chord change or at the beginning of a bar. This ensures that the vertical aspect of the changes, the chord sound, is always apparent. All the same, we never get the feeling that the melodic continuity is compromised. So, it is possible to acknowledge the harmony and, at the same time, create flowing melodies.

If we want to spell out the changes as part of an expressive melody, we have to emphasise the characteristic chord tones – primarily the third and the seventh. We have already talked about voice leading thirds and sevenths and the resulting elementary guide tone lines when dealing with chord progressions following the cycle of fifths (see p. 240 ff.). Since chord progressions in Jazz are suffused with root movement in fifths, I would like to use the diatonic cadence to show you how to turn a chord progression into a line – working only with chord tones and arpeggios at first.

Let's take, for example, the beginning of the diatonic cadence in E♭ Major (E♭maj7 - A♭maj7). The following four basic patterns demonstrate how to advance through cycle-of-fifths chord progressions by voice leading thirds and sevenths (one chord per bar):

The 7/3-resolutions always occur at the transition from one chord to the next. The roots and fifths are placed in between as a link, creating a variety of patterns, which move the line into the upper or lower register with regard to the starting note.

Next, let's have a look at the entire diatonic cadence in E♭ Major and two of its variations. The first eight bars are purely diatonic. The second eight-bar cycle includes all secondary dominants and helps us to get a feel for the notes that deviate from the diatonic framework (functional chromaticism, see p. 118 ff.). The third eight-bar example contains a mixture of diatonic functions and secondary dominants (Dø7 has been replaced by D7 and C−7 by C7):

As you can see, the maj7 or ♭7 of a chord always resolves to the 3 or the ♭3 of the next chord.

Of course, it is possible to combine the various patterns randomly. In the examples shown above, I have limited the range of the lines by always combining two patterns moving in opposite directions (wavelike motion) to ensure that you can sing them (consider the assignment given!). By consistently using the same pattern for several bars, it is, however, possible to cover a much larger range and augment the dynamic impact of the line:

Assignment

Please go to **tracks 21–24**. Remind yourselves of the corresponding chord progressions (in the appendix), transpose the previous exercises and apply them to each of the variations of the diatonic cadence. Practise these lines until you can do them faultlessly. Then play them along with the recordings. As soon as you have them firmly implanted in your ear, start improvising on this "basic material". Try embellishing it, play around with it, change the rhythms, but always try to retain the original line as a common thread. Try soloing without the play-alongs (in time). After a while, you should be able to improvise without the accompaniment and still hear the chord progression in your lines.

It stands to reason that you should transfer these exercises to real pieces. The following exercise on "All The Things You Are" consists almost exclusively of chord tones that have been connected in the way suggested above (added passing notes have been marked with an asterisk):

Naturally, this is not much more than a soulless etude, but if you liven up the mechanical succession of quarter notes by inserting a few diatonic or chromatic passing 8th notes, substituting some of the chord tones, adding syncopations, embellishments and approach patterns, this simple exercise will develop a life of its own and come close to a good improvisation. Here's a fairly complex example. The important notes correspond to those in the previous exercise, but the lines take considerable liberties in terms of the tonal material. Analyse the chorus and see if you can still locate the GTLs (3/7 voice leading):

Assignment

Sing both choruses shown above and learn them off by heart. I know this will take a considerable amount of time, but, I assure you, it's worth the effort. Depending on your vocal range, you may have to transpose some of the lines up or down an octave (try to keep at least a full section within the same octave). Once you can sing both choruses in time (the second, in particular) at ca. 120 BPM, you'll make several discoveries. Firstly, you will have acquired a feel for important target notes and you'll be able to anticipate the final resolution of a line well ahead of time. Secondly, there are many motivic ideas to key into, e.g. sequences based on a variety of guide tone lines. Thirdly, the more active chorus provides insight into the micro-timing of phrases and the exact placement of individual notes. Since the lines contain a fair amount of chromatic passing notes and approach patterns, you will come to understand how each phrase has to unfold for it to resolve correctly, either by using chromatics to slow it down or resorting to diatonic material to speed it up. In bar 9, for example, the chromatic line resolves smoothly to the ♭3 of F–7. In bar 11 (B♭7), however, I had to use an approach pattern instead, otherwise the line would have resolved too early. The same applies to bar 18 (D7). In bar 20 (Gmaj7), by contrast, the chromatic line must be resolved by a diatonic whole step (!) at the end of the bar, otherwise it would land on an A# and not the A (♭3 of F#ø7). The most important result, however, is the ability to imagine the changes while singing. Since you are aware of the essential notes and their meaning in relation to each individual chord (not intellectually but aurally), you will actually hear the entire chord progression internally while you sing – not as specific voicings but rather as fuzzy colours. Finally, speed this exercise up to ca. 200 BPM. You will no longer be able to sing everything in tune (after all, most of you are not singers). But – surprise! – the line will still be crystal clear in your mind. So, you may sing a wrong note, but you won't lose your bearings

Assignment

Transfer the same exercise to "TWINBAY". Use the patterns presented at the beginning of this chapter wherever the chord progression follows the cycle of fifths. If a chord carries on for more than one bar, fill the line as smoothly as possible by using chord tones and notes taken from the appropriate scale. Here is what the first eight bars might look like:

Complete the chorus and write a second one. This time, however, make the lines more active and melodious by using 8th notes, approach patterns, chromatic passing notes, etc.

The world of guide tone lines

All previous exercises focussed primarily on the lower parts of the chord symbols (1/3/5/7). We have already seen in the first chapter on guide tone lines (see p. 244 ff.) that *any* note of the scale can be part of a GTL (with the exclusion of avoid notes). I'd like to demonstrate how to work on GTLs systematically by taking the example of a simple turnaround in F Major: Fmaj7 - D7 - G–7 - C7.

First, analyse the changes and write down the corresponding scale material on a separate piece of paper. Make sure that you always write down the scales "in key" by using the appropriate key signature. This is a useful visual aid, which will help you pinpoint out-of-key notes not part of the diatonic framework. It will also ensure that you don't overlook any one of the available GTLs (later on, this step can be done in your head). Here are the scales for the turnaround in F Major (avoid notes are in brackets):

I have chosen Altered for both D7 and C7 in this example in order to confront you with a more dissonant dominant colour and chromatic voice leading (of course, you could do this exercise using dominant scales that are more diatonic). You would, however, run into problems when improvising to the play-along (**track 36**).

Voice-lead the scales (initially only one note per chord) by starting on *each* note of Fmaj7 in turn (exclude the avoid note – it would be far too exposed in this context). The basic idea of this exercise is to get a feel for the most logical way a note wants to resolve when changing scales. Starting from any given note there are three basic possibilities:

- *Hold the starting note* when moving from one chord to the next (following the principle of common tones). Only change the note by moving it up or down a step if absolutely necessary (e.g. because it is not part of the following scale or to bypass an avoid note) and return to the starting note as soon as possible.

- *Move downwards* consistently in stepwise motion (descending GTL) by switching to the closest available note of the next scale.

- *Move upwards* consistently in stepwise motion (ascending GTL) to the next available scale note above.

It is self-evident that the resulting GTLs will contain chord tones as well as tensions (the more tensions appear, the more colourful the GTLs will be).

Before we take a closer look at these GTLs, I want to raise an important point. A GTL is always the backbone of a more elaborate melodic phrase. For any phrase to present itself as a self-contained whole, it needs to resolve (remember the quote by John Coltrane: "… always play the cadence!"). Consider the harmonic rhythm of our four-bar turnaround. For a GTL to be complete, it should not end on C7 (weak) in bar 4 but rather on Fmaj7 (strong) in bar 1 of the following loop. For this reason, it is important to bring every GTL to a close by extending it into the next four-bar section and resolving it to the expected target chord Fmaj7. This said, here are the GTLs:

Not all of these GTLs work equally well. Some of them feel awkward because they break the rules of traditional voice leading, fail to follow the expected harmonic cliché, counteract the usual strong-weak stress pattern of the turnaround or simply because they don't satisfy our personal preferences. The following commentary relates to the numbering in the list of GTLs shown above and explains the reservations I have about some of the lines:

1) The root of the key, to me, is a rather drab sound, lacking in tension, with a low energy level and little colour. I'm not alone on this. The tenor sax player Jerry Bergonzi states quite categorically: *"Never start on 1, never end on 1!"* This applies predominantly to the tonic Imaj7 because of the undesirable clash with the maj7 of the chord. With other chord types (–7, ø7, 7, etc.) and secondary functions the problem is not that pronounced. Using the F on D7 (as a #9) and G–7 (as a ♭7) actually sounds quite nice. So, be cautious when using the root.

2) Here, too, it would be better to hold the E (= maj7), even if it does not follow the traditional resolution of the leading tone.

3) The 5 only occurs in HM5. I have added this GTL because it is quite commonly used. You would have to move either to F# (#11) or A♭ (♭13) with Altered on the C7. Give these options a try, too.

4) The #11 does not occur in Ionian. Nevertheless, it is a popular target note because it extends the chromatic line into the tonic (and because it sounds so good!).

5) The 6 is not an effective target note (weak close); rather keep the E.

6) Same as point number 5. In this case, because of the preceding D♭ (♭9) on the C7, the resolution to C would be the more logical and satisfactory choice.

7) This line sounds a little awkward because a high level of tension (#11) is followed by an almost total lack of colour (1) when moving from one chord to the next.

8) Here, we have to keep the D because the expected E = 6 in G–7 Dorian is an avoid note (at least in this functional context).

9) The #9 of C7 (E♭ = D#) tends to resolve upwards to the E (= maj7) rather than back to the D (6 = weak close, again).

10) Here, we would rather expect the D (= 5) and not the F because of the preceding ♭9's strong downward pull; resolving the E♭ upwards by a whole step is poor voice leading.

11) This line sounds most unusual because, with the exception of the final resolution, it consists only of whole steps (the Whole-tone scale is a "special sound" for the ear).

The last three GTLs should serve as a reminder that guide tone lines don't always have to progress by common tones or small steps only. Basically, any line – whether it consists of chord tones and/or tensions – will serve as a GTL as long as it follows a conceptual pattern and has a clear sense of direction. The first example is very dynamic because of the powerful ascending movement. It also has a high level of integrity because the notes add up to an Fmaj7 chord, contributing to the feeling of tonality. The second example, despite its seemingly haphazard leaps, sounds perfectly coherent because it has a strong motivic quality. If you start the line on middle C instead, you will notice that it consists of ascending leaps in perfect fourths (C-F-Bb-Eb). Because the first two notes are transposed up an octave and the first and last notes are identical, we get a GTL with a cyclical quality. The last GTL is a combination of ascending and descending movement (wave-like).

As you can see, there is an amazing abundance of available GTLs for just one simple turnaround. By using a wider variety of scale choices for D7 (HM5, HTWT, WT) and C7 (HM5, Mixo, HTWT, WT) we expand our possibilities. If we use more than one note per chord or bar (more active GTLs with half notes or even quarter notes) the possibilities become almost infinite.

It's always worth looking for more than just the straightforward GTLs. You won't play anything outside the box (from your point of view) if you don't come up with variants beyond the obvious solutions. Pieces like "All The Things You Are" are a case in point. The melody itself is a combination of the two basic GTLs following traditional 3/7-movement of the diatonic cadence (go to p. 241 as a reminder). So, when practising this tune, you will automatically absorb the voice leading of the melody, and that's what you will just as automatically use when improvising. If you want to arrive at more than just an emulation of the melody, if you want to expand your solo vocabulary, you have to start digging for options that give you a different slant on the piece. Have a look at the following GTL for the A section:

This example focusses exclusively on the upper functions of each individual chord (mostly the tensions). In addition, the line moves in contrary motion to the fundamental 3/7-GTLs supplied by the melody and counteracts their strong downward pull. With its special qualities, this is exactly the kind of line that doesn't come naturally. These sounds don't just *happen*. They must be premeditated and worked on, and it may take years to establish them as a permanent part of your vocabulary. You will only use them in your playing if you hear them inside.

I'd like to make a brief comment in this regard: Many of us "think about things", which implies that we think about them *after* the fact – we *reflect* on them. However, if you reflect on things while improvising, it's too late. You have to work on the ability to *think ahead*. No matter where you are in your solo, you need to be able to sense exactly where you are going at any given moment in order to get there with the necessary confidence. Working with GTLs will help you with this.

Assignment

Go back to the turnaround we worked on earlier in this chapter and accompany yourself at the piano with basic voicings (1/3/7) while singing the GTLs. Take your time with each individual sound. Let your ear lock into each note so that an image of the sound and the tension it produces develops in your mind. Try to anticipate every note before you sing it, and don't sing it until you are absolutely sure how it is going to sound. You must physically feel the next sound approaching. Always be acutely aware of exactly what it is you are practising. Think aloud – e.g.: "I am starting on the 5 of Fmaj7, going down via the ♭13 of D7 to the 9 of G–7 and the ♭13 of C7, finally landing on the 9 of Fmaj7, etc." Speed up the exercise so that you get a feel for the way the individual sounds connect.

Assignment

Go to **track 36**. Sing and then play the GTLs along with the recording. Now everything happens in time, and that means you have to move from note to note at the right moment and fit the GTLs into the turnaround correctly. First, concentrate on the same GTL for the full duration of the play-along. You'll have to skip every other four-bar loop so that you can resolve the GTL to Fmaj7 and its target note. Repeat this exercise for each of the GTLs a number of times. It is not enough to have done it well just once. It takes a long time for these lines to settle into the ear so that they can be called upon while you are improvising.

Later on, you can link two or even more GTLs. Here's an example that combines two lines – one ascending, the other descending – thereby creating an eight-bar cycle:

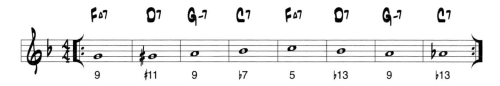

You could also cover a larger range by moving on in the same direction when switching from one GTL to the next: e.g. "E-F-G-A♭-A-B♭-C-D♭-C" going up or "E-E♭-D-D♭-C-B♭-A-A♭-G" going down, etc.

Now pick a few of the GTLs you like best and start improvising by playing around with the rhythm, adding embellishments, motivic sequences, approach patterns, arpeggios, etc. Make sure you don't get lost. Stick to the GTLs despite the additional material!

Assignment

Apply this principle to the changes of "TWINBAY". You have already analysed the chord progression and decided on a choice of scales. Now write down *all* GTLs starting on *every* possible note (you have written out some on p. 249). It would be impossible to manage the entire 32-bar structure with one line (you would run into problems in terms of the range of your instruments if you consistently try to move in one direction). So, break down the chord progression into smaller sections (4, 8 or 16 bars) and combine the resulting GTLs indiscriminately. At any rate, it is not common to stick to one single GTL for a longer period of time. Most Jazz musicians jump to a new one every few bars.

Even if you manage to compile all GTLs contained in a chord progression, it would be impossible to find the time to practise them all to the same extent. Choose the ones you like best and focus on these. You can always return to the others at a later stage.

And now for the most important part of the exercise: Once you have a certain repertoire of GTLs, randomly start on any note and see where the line will carry you. While you're singing/playing to the recording, always ask yourself if you can truly anticipate how the line should progress and if it will land on a note that works with the next chord. Here's an example that will show you the various problems you may run into when constructing GTLs. Start the exercise on D and move consistently upwards (initially 1 note per chord):

Watch out for the following:

- Line 1: If you sustain the D for the first two bars, you will land on E♭ – the avoid note of Dø7 – in bar 3 (♭2 in VIIø7 Locrian). It would be better to switch to E♭ in bar 2 (and move to the F in bar 3) or to keep the D for three bars and switch to the E♭ on G7.

- Line 2: If you choose the F for Dø7 and move to the G on G7, you would subsequently land on an A♭ on the C–7 chord, which is also an avoid note (♭6 of VI–7 Aeolian). You could resolve the line to the A (= 6/13) because VI– can also be played MM. However, this would take us out of the key at a point of resolution where the GTL should rather "lock in" (bar 5 = strong). The alternative of holding the G when moving to C–7 wouldn't work that well either because the cadence G7 - C–7 calls for a melodic resolution, too. It is not musical to consistently move a line and then interrupt the flow by sitting on a note while the chord progression resolves. The best solution would be to keep the F on G7 and move to the G on the C–7.

- Line 3: The movement from C–7 to B♭–7 is easy (G to A♭). However, you can't keep the A♭ on E♭7 because it is an avoid note (A♭ = 4). It would only be possible to hold on to the A♭ if the chord were an E♭7(sus4). The nicest option would be to switch to the A (= ♯11) with E♭7 and move on to B♭ (= 9) with A♭maj7. This, again, is a sound that needs getting used to because the A clashes with the tonality of E♭ Major. In addition, the A♭ (♭7 of B♭–7) would want to resolve down to the G (= 3 of E♭7) and not upwards!

Timing is the crucial factor when mapping out a GTL. If the line develops awkwardly in terms of the harmonic flow and, as a consequence, hits a chord on the wrong note, it's too late. Sometimes it is necessary to anticipate more than just the next chord. You may have to sense the direction in which the line wants to move a number of bars or even a whole section in advance. In many cases, you will have to delay or speed up the line, or you'll find yourselves running into roadblocks sooner or later. That is why it is important to work on longer lines and not just short phrases. Here is a suggestion for the first 17 bars of "TWINBAY" (starting on the D as discussed earlier):

It is important to stockpile several GTLs for every part of a chord progression. Once you start improvising, you'd better be ready. There is just no time to do any thinking once you're under way. You need to trust the lines you have internalised implicitly. Only once you have developed the ability to predict intuitively where a line wants to go will your improvisations exhibit the amazing consistency and coherence we admire so much in the great soloists.

This would be a good time to get back to the "problem" of "TWINBAY". Do you remember the last four bars and the likelihood of crash-landing an otherwise great solo at the very end because of the half-bar changes and the tricky ending (see pdf-K, p. 21 ff.)? Well – GTLs are a great way of making it through the danger zone. Here are three possible GTLs (G7 could naturally be replaced by G–7 and F–7 could be replaced by F7, although different GTLs would result):

If you base your improvisation on one of these three options and add a few embellishments, you might not end up with a spectacular solo, but you would get through the difficult passage unscathed.

Assignment

Figure out several GTLs for the various sections of "TWINBAY" and play them to **tracks 13–19** (transpose the GTLs to the corresponding keys).

From guide tone line to melody

Although GTLs are the basic substance of a melody, they constitute only the first step in the creation of dynamic lines. So far, we have only talked about and practised how to connect the changes in a logical way. We have set up a "model case", stripped a melody down to the bare bones and reduced it to its most essential component – the transition from one chord to the next. Now we have to transform a rather inanimate and mechanical GTL into a persuasive melody. Here are the three most important creative tools:

- *rhythm* (repeating notes, syncopations, accents, anticipations, etc.);

- *embellishment* (playing "around" the notes of the GTL);

- *motivic sequencing*, in which the GTL comprises the focal points of the sequence.

Again, let's go back to the turnaround and apply these techniques. In the first of the following examples, only the rhythmic design has been changed and the GTL remains highly conspicuous. The second example shows the use of diatonic and scale embellishments. In both cases, the GTL is clearly discernible. You should, however, detect a two-bar sequence that gives the line a motivic quality. The third example follows up on the concept of the motivic sequence. Whereas the first line is straightforward and simple, the second line is very active and obscures the GTL to a certain extent:

Note the octave transposition of the GTL in bars 3 and 4 of the last example. This is quite a common device used to create continuity without being too obvious. Despite the change of register and the high level of melodic activity, the ear still picks up the GTL subliminally.

In the following example – the A section of "Rhythm Changes" – I have created a motivic sequence. In the first half of the phrase, the notes of the GTL (marked with an asterisk) relate to both chords in each bar (the note reappears on beat 4 as part of the pick-up phrase):

The GTL for "TWINBAY" suggested further up could be translated into a melody looking something like this:

This example shows the GTL quite clearly. The important notes are located at the beginning of the bar. In practice, though, GTLs are rarely positioned so conspicuously. More often than not, they are camouflaged by other parts of the melody. It can happen that the notes of a GTL only pop up intermittently – as cornerstones of the line (e.g. as the highest or lowest notes of a phrase). But even so, we perceive them as a thread running through the fabric of the whole section. The ear senses the steady development subliminally and makes the connections.

This chapter is about the ability to predict the future. Good improvisers are "psychic" in the sense that they can extrapolate where a line wants to go long before they actually play it. Improvisation doesn't mean that we react to the immediate moment (then it's too late). We have to anticipate the development, to feel the route into the next sound and the ones beyond before they arrive. Only then will our lines have vitality and direction. Speaking for myself, I no longer hear a chord progression as a series of vertical events. Once I know a tune well, I can conjure it in my imagination as what I can only describe as a cloud of sound suffused with a multitude of GTLs. I can visualise the chord progression and hear it in time just by following one or more of these lines. I can't get lost because I always find a GTL that carries me on. Guide tone lines are like escalators. They take us somewhere. And while we are on the move, we look around and ahead and can feel where the journey is going.

Licks and Tricks

"The old guys used to call those things crips. That's from crippled. In other words, when you're playing a solo and your mind is crippled and you cannot think of anything different to play, you go back into one of your old bags and play one of your crips. You better have something to play when you can't think of anything new …!"

Tommy Turrentine

We now come to a rather delicate matter that raises a lot of questions and to which many Jazz musicians turn up their noses – playing *licks*, also referred to as *crips* or *patterns*. Licks are short clichés or set phrases that crop up regularly – more or less as fixed units – and are combined with other melodic fragments. To some people, this falling back on ready-made material may smack of betrayal, considering the spontaneity attributed to improvisation. In practice, however, no Jazz musician manages without licks. Indeed, I have colleagues who claim they never play licks because they never practise them and even make a point of actively avoiding them. However, on hearing their own recordings, they have to admit that the same lines tend to pop up time and again.

Let's be honest – it may be that every musician is determined to deliver improvisations containing nothing but fresh, new, original and unique material. The reality is different, though. At home, we practise specific skills and techniques – arpeggios, scales, sequences, rhythmic patterns, etc. Should none of this count when soloing? It stands to reason that the things we have worked on exhaustively and can play intuitively will automatically keep turning up in our improvisations. We simply don't have time to think during a solo. We have to rely on our instincts and reflexes (especially when dealing with fast tempos). Without having phrases deeply anchored in our subconscious, we would surely run the risk of stumbling or getting stuck. Every phrase we have absorbed will reappear every now and then in our solos and can be termed a lick – and there is nothing wrong with that.

John Coltrane's solo over "Giant Steps" proves that even the Jazz giants – despite their seemingly inexhaustible reservoir of ideas – are mere mortals who have obviously done their homework and who, at crucial moments, call on pre-fabricated phrases. Here is the first chorus (ghost notes are indicated by an "x"). Analyse the lines in relation to the chords. Because this piece modulates frequently, the segments in different keys are bracketed below:

This solo radiates tremendous energy, but it is incredibly redundant as well. I wouldn't want to make light of Coltrane's performance – composition and improvisation are undoubtedly landmarks in the history of Jazz (as the title suggests and – unwittingly at the time – predicted). There is no denying the sublime way in which Coltrane moves through the rapidly spiralling, remote tonalities. Equally impressive are the power and consistency of his lines and the ease with which he plays this seemingly simple but extremely demanding piece. Nevertheless, the fast tempo and the unconventional modulations force the improvisation into a straightjacket from which not even a soloist of John Coltrane's caliber can extricate himself. The extent to which he uses standardised and premeditated melodic phrases becomes apparent when comparing the first chorus with the rest of the solo. A few examples should illustrate that John Coltrane, too, was a creature of habit (a hardworking one notwithstanding):

Bars 5 - 7 (2nd chorus)

Bars 1 - 4 (3rd chorus)

The similarities are even more obvious in the next example:

Bars 1 - 11 (4th chorus)

Parallels such as these can be found throughout the solo. If we also look for similar passages and not just identical ones, we realise that the entire improvisation consists of a limited number of basic patterns that are rehashed over and over again, marginally varied and reassembled in different combinations.

This example demonstrates that even one of the most influential Jazz musicians of the 20th century couldn't manage without ready-made material. It also dispels the myth that good improvisations perpetually feed on some inexhaustible source of fresh inspiration. For this reason, we should stop treating our idols with awestruck reverence. Basically, the difference between an average Jazz player and the brilliant soloist is that the latter has a vastly larger vocabulary he or she can draw on at any moment. The more phrases you assimilate, the more variable, surprising and less redundant your improvisations will sound. You will also be able to react more spontaneously to your band members.

Licks

There are licks that are part of the universal Jazz vocabulary and therefore recur time and time again in the improvisations of many players. Other licks are highly individualised trademark phrases ascribed to specific players. And then there are the licks we create ourselves, which will, hopefully, help define our personal style. It is beyond the scope of this book to provide a comprehensive list of typical licks for all possible harmonic situations. Nevertheless, I would like to show you how to build your own collection of patterns.

Let's take, for example, the II-V-I progression. Especially when dealing with such a basic and omnipresent harmonic formula, it is worthwhile stockpiling an extensive repertoire of phrases. Here are some typical licks in B♭ Major. All these examples are taken from actual improvisations and have been transposed, whenever necessary, to facilitate a comparison of the tonal material. Analyse each of these phrases and make sure you understand its structure (scale material, principal notes, driving factors, target notes, points of resolution, etc.) as well as its formal logic. You will notice that the dominant, in particular, is important in terms of how each line unfolds. I have chosen these specific examples so as to encourage you to practise a variety of melodic concepts:

- diatonic II-V-I patterns with Mixolydian dominants;

- use of chromaticism;

- split dominants (V7 switching from Mixolydian to Altered);

- delayed dominants (by extending the II–7 chord);

- patterns using Altered or HTWT for V7;

- sequences.

You should have a commensurate collection of phrases for II-V-I progression in minor keys. Here are a few patterns in C Minor:

Up until now, all patterns were based on chord changes occurring once every bar. It is equally important to have a stockpile of phrases for half-bar changes. Here are a few examples in F Major and D Minor:

I could go on and on and give you hundreds of phrases just like these – and there are many books that do just that. However, it is more important that you find your own licks by re-searching improvisations, transcribing the lines you like as well as designing and composing your own.

Most of the II-V-I phrases shown above were randomly chosen, although I have ensured that they start and end on different scale degrees for the sake of variety. When developing your own lines, it is worth adopting a more systematic approach. In the following examples, the beginning of each phrase is always the same. With beat 3 of the first bar (C–7), however, the lines branch off in different directions. For the downbeat of the second bar (F7), I have used almost every possible target note within a range of two octaves that can be derived from the various dominant scales relating to F7. Depending on which target note you are heading for, the design of the first bar has to be adjusted so that the phrase has a good flow and re-solves logically and smoothly. It is intentional that these examples consist exclusively of eighth notes. This will force you to practise three scenarios:

- The starting note (C–7) and the target note (F7) are at approximately the same pitch level. This means you have to limit the overall range of the first bar by using approach patterns or circling back to the starting point for the line to stay in the same register despite the consistent eighth-note movement.

- The target note is a little higher (or lower) than the starting note. This means that the line gradually has to progress up or down in a wave-like movement (e.g. by using sequences).

- The target note is much higher (or lower) than the starting note. Because the line now has to change register quickly, you have to work with a mix of scale fragments, arpeggios and leaps in order to give the line enough momentum for it to span the large gap between the starting point and the target note in a logical way.

With these options in mind, practise the following licks:

Assignment

Take the three scenarios mentioned above and write your own II-V-I lines in major and minor keys (one chord per bar as well as half-bar changes). Here are a few starting phrases to work with:

Assignment

- Practise the licks in this chapter *in all keys!*
- Write lines for a variety of four-bar turnarounds (see also p. 236 ff.).
- Develop lines for II-V progressions (major and minor) in different time signatures (e.g. 3/4, 6/8, etc.).

The last point is especially important. Different time signatures require different lines. If you only practise in 4/4, you will run into problems when trying to use the same lines in 3/4 or 6/8 (or any other time signature, for that matter). You will have to adjust the timing of your phrases (by adding or subtracting notes), otherwise they will resolve too early or too late. This means you should have an extensive repertoire of licks in other commonly used time signatures, notably in 3/4.

Assignment

Play all your phrases (the ones in this book and the ones you have composed yourself) and decide on a couple you really like. Then practise these until your fingers and ears have soaked up every note. While doing this, don't just concentrate on the notes you're playing. Focus your attention on your timing, your phrasing and the dynamic flow of the line – play with *spirit*! Practise with a metronome. Start very slowly (60 BPM). Give the ear a chance to absorb every detail. Gradually increase the tempo – with time, you should be able to play the lines at least at 240 BPM without tripping up. Don't underestimate the technical aspect. Because many of these phrases are partly chromatic and since most of us have predominantly worked on diatonic scale exercises, some of the lines will present quite a challenge.

Let's go back to "TWINBAY". Choose one of these phrases for each of the II-V progressions in the piece and try to connect them in the simplest and musically most logical way. The result could look something like this (the licks are taken from the list on p. 571 ff.):

Lick 21

Lick 15

Lick 35

Lick 3

Lick 30

Lick 7

Lick 9 (1st half)

Lick 37

Lick 36

Assignment

Learn this chorus by heart. Then, compose a number of choruses following the same principle (in E♭ Major) and practise them until you can play them in time. Transpose the various
choruses to F Major and B♭ Major and play them along with **tracks 13, 14 and 16**. This will
force you to manage this basic vocabulary in various keys, styles and tempos.

It may well be that the last assignment appears artificial. And some of you may even be a
little disappointed. Naturally, it is not the objective of improvisation to simply combine
pre-fabricated phrases mechanically. But as Tommy Turrentine said: "You better have something to play when you can't think of anything new." Although, from a musical point of view,
it might be better to play nothing at all if you can't come up with anything worthwhile listening to. After a while, these licks will become a natural part of your playing and your repertoire. Eventually, you will start creating your own favourite phrases, and one day you will
discover that you have developed what you could call your own personal style.

It is quite OK to put together a solo and to play it over and over again until you can do it
in your sleep. I once asked Pat Metheny whether I had only imagined hearing him play the
same or at least a similar solo over one of his pieces two concerts in a row. He answered: "I
like what I play. It feels good – so why should I change it?" So, you see, even a "favourite solo"
can be some sort of "lick".

Assignment

Compose two improvisations over "TWINBAY": one over *one* chorus and the other over *two*. Get used to the differing formal lengths of the solos. Approach this assignment as you would a composition. Try to tell a good story by moving through secondary and primary climaxes as well as using motivic development.

The play-alongs

Let's transfer what we have worked on in terms of II-V-I progressions (developing phrases, practising them and applying them to actual music) to other harmonic formulae. The time for **tracks 20–35** has arrived (the chord progressions are in the appendix):

Track 20:	Diatonic functions in Bb Major
Track 21:	Diatonic cadence in Eb Major
Tracks 22–24:	Variations on the diatonic cadence in G, F and Ab Major (with secondary dominants)
Track 25:	Diatonic cadence in Bb Major with secondary II-Vs
Track 26:	Diatonic cadence in C Minor
Track 27:	V-I and SubV-I in F Major (with different colours for C7 and Gb7)
Track 28:	II-V-I in C Major (with different colours for II and V)
Track 29:	Turnaround in G Minor (with different colours for II and V)
Track 30:	All SubV functions and their expected resolutions in D Major
Tracks 31/32:	Diminished functions in F Major and G Major
Track 33:	I-IV in C Dorian
Track 34:	Phrygian cadence (bIImaj7) in F with resolution to F–7 and Fmaj7
Track 35:	The most important MI-functions in C Major

Assignment

I'd like to use **track 35** to show you how to work with play-alongs. This track contains the most important modal interchange functions in C Major (always alternating with Cmaj7 every two bars; every four-bar section is repeated). Fast forward to the second and third patterns (0'20" and 0'37"). You will hear Cmaj7 - F–7 - Bb7(sus4) and Cmaj7 - F–maj7 - Bb7. First, figure out the scale material. F–7 Dorian and Bb7(sus4) Mixolydian can be seen as a unit – both scales contain the same notes. F–maj7 MM and Bb7 Lydian(b7) can also be seen as a pair. Make sure you clearly understand the characteristic difference between both versions (it is only one note). While F–7 - B♭7(sus4) clearly breaks with the key of C Major (because of the E♭), F–maj7 and B♭7(♯11) establish a much closer connection with the key because of the characteristic note E (the major 3rd in C Major).

Loop these sixteen bars (both eight-bar sections) using your CD player's A/B function. Now improvise – for hours on end, if necessary – to these changes. Start off simply and concentrate initially on the important notes and the way they move: G (over Cmaj7) and A♭ (over F–7 and F–maj7) as well as E (over Cmaj7) and E♭ (over F–7). Be sure to understand that, when playing over the second four-bar section, you must hold on to the E and may not change to E♭. As you progress, start playing more elaborate lines, but make sure they still incorporate the guide tones mentioned above. At first, think about what you are doing and control the tonal material you are using. Once you have developed a certain amount of confidence and a feel for the sounds, you can start playing more intuitively. Switch back to "thinking mode" from time to time to check if your intuitive playing has allowed mistakes to creep in unnoticed.

Develop your own licks and loop them many, many times. Here is a line for each of the four-bar sections and two examples for half-bar changes:

The last step involves the practical application of the material you have worked on. For every function presented in this book, I have quoted at least one composition that includes each specific sound in a typical way. I recommend you make all these tunes part of your repertoire and practice routine. Start using the licks you have developed with the play-alongs and transform them into longer phrases. I would suggest – among others – the pieces "Joy Spring" (IV–7) and "The Days Of Wine And Roses" (IV–maj7) for the functions we have just practised. Both of these pieces are in F Major. Transpose the phrases shown above and integrate them into longer melodic phrases. Be sure to prepare and resolve the licks smoothly and in a musically logical way. Here is an example for the A section of "Joy Spring" in which I have used one of the half-bar phrases shown above:

Assignments

Write a solo for the first 8 bars of "The Days Of Wine And Roses" incorporating bars 3 and 4 of the second four-bar phrase shown on p. 581.

Write a number of phrases for each of the play-alongs I mentioned on p. 580 and work on them until you know them like the back of your hand. Transpose them to different keys. Look for pieces containing each of these sounds and include your phrases into longer melodic lines.

Jazz vocabulary

When talking about licks, we mean to include the notion of "phrases typical to a particular style". All styles have their own specific vocabulary. Without mastering the idiomatic terminology of Jazz (at least pertaining to mainstream), our improvisations will not be taken seriously. There are certain standard phrases that show the seasoned player or listener that you have done your homework – "figures of speech" belonging to the stock phraseology of Jazz, which are anchored in melodic tradition and are still played by many Jazz musicians today.

Quite a few years back, I experienced just how deeply some licks are ingrained in our collective memory. I was doing a sound check with my quintet, and while we were warming up, we played a standard. During the improvisations we suddenly realised that every single one of us (discounting the drummer, of course) was playing exactly the same line at a particular place in the piece – so obviously and conspicuously that we decided to black-list the phrase for the concert (by the way, I am talking about the Altered lick on p. 145). To raise the stakes, we agreed that every time someone played this lick (or any of its variants) he would have to pay ten dollars (the pianist kept score!). Although we all tried our hardest to avoid the phrase, we ended up with more than five hundred dollars in the kitty by the end of the evening! We went out and had a feast.

This anecdote illustrates just how deep-rooted certain lines are. It is quite impossible to steer clear of them. And why should we? When we speak, we use the same vocabulary, follow the same grammar and talk about the same things time and again. Why should we suddenly, just because we're dealing with music, be so much more creative and innovative? Why should we force ourselves to avoid certain sounds just because they come to mind readily?

Art and artificiality are sometimes a hair's breadth apart. I personally know several Jazz musicians who simply cannot play relaxed for fear of repeating themselves.

I believe that we must learn the idiomatic language of a specific style if we want to play it convincingly – although I am fully aware that some of my colleagues would not agree when it comes to Jazz. They perceive clichés as crutches, designed to relieve people from the burden of having to engage in original thought. And I agree – clichés are dangerous! They quickly become stereotyped platitudes, accessible at the flick of a switch, tempting us to evade the responsibility of being creative. The commonly heard allegation that all mainstream Jazz musicians sound the same cannot be disregarded entirely. Nevertheless, it is precisely these clichés by which we can tell if someone has truly grasped and absorbed the particularities of a style.

On the other hand, we could choose to see this in a more positive light. Is it not a good thing if musicians speak the same language and use the same vocabulary? The more common ground you and your colleagues share, the easier it is to communicate successfully. It is definitely a lot of fun to be able to figure out in advance where the ideas of the other band members are heading. Someone passes you the ball, you juggle it a bit and pass it on to somebody else – always in the knowledge that you can fully rely on the other players' support. When musicians are so comfortable together, they start finishing each other's sentences. Once you can feel this intimacy and closeness of ideas, you will risk more – and this will help you be more spontaneous in your improvisations. In an ensemble that has developed the art of conversation, players are on a journey together, where each of them can go on their own excursions and outings without ever losing touch with the others. You see – a common vocabulary is not such a bad thing after all. Of course, ideally, every band should eventually develop an individual style and unique sound with its own "speech patterns". To start things off, though, it does make sense to have a mutual understanding of the Jazz language.

Over the next 30 or so pages, I want to introduce you to a few sounds that are typical to the general Jazz vocabulary. This selection is by no means exhaustive, but the examples do show quite well, what the term "vocabulary" can imply. The choice ranges from an isolated note to a generic concept. Most of these techniques are hard to grasp on an intuitive level because they do not follow our deeply ingrained and long-standing tonal habits. We have to access them intellectually at first and work on them consciously before we can actually practise, let alone apply, them.

II7 and the ♯11

Let's begin with a single note that has become a trademark of every accomplished Jazz soloist: the use of ♯11 over V7/V (II7). Yes, even an isolated intervallic function within a very specific harmonic situation can have a personality of its own! Though nothing extraordinary, it is nonetheless a conspicuous sound that can be heard in almost every solo over changes containing II7 – a typical example of a melodic cliché that doesn't come naturally to the ear but should be matter-of-course for any proficient "straight ahead" Jazz player.

The theory states that we can play Lydian(♭7) over II7 (V7/V). Good to know. But what use is this bit of knowledge if you can't hear the corresponding sound in your head and therefore can't utilise it? Remember that we normally would play II7 as Mixolydian, this being the scale most consistent with the overall key (go back to p. 122 if you can't recall the reasoning). Consequently, the ♯11 clashes with our tonal expectations. Many years of teaching have shown me that this sound does not simply appear out of nowhere. Without having been exposed to it extensively (either by hearing it used over and over again by our colleagues or having worked on it as part of our daily practice routine), we won't make it happen. Only once we have actually experienced the ♯11 and internalised it within the framework of a specific chord progression will it become more than an abstract phenomenon or theoretical fact (also see p. 127).

How do we make the ♯11 a part of our personal playing habits? As always, we have to devise an exercise that leads nicely up to this unfamiliar sound and resolves it just as smoothly, making it an integral part of a longer melodic line. The best way to do this would be – as you probably guessed – to use a guide tone line that moves into and out of the ♯11 with as little change as possible. Look at the following exercise and play/sing it along with **track 13**. At first, run through the GTL exactly as it is. Give your ear a chance to get used to the sound:

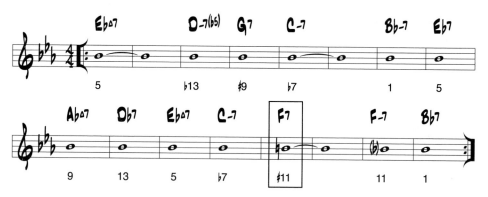

This exercise develops the ability to anticipate the ♯11 well in advance. We need to sit on the B♭ (as the 5 of the key) for quite some time to prepare the ear for the move to the B. Hear the sound approaching, work towards it, control your timing and make yourselves land on the B exactly on beat one of bar 13. If you don't manage at first, don't give up and don't get bored! It needs a lot of discipline to stick to such a simple exercise without losing focus. Once you do succeed, don't stop! Repeat the exercise. You need to experience the same sequence of events many times in a row for this sound to become a good friend.

Be sure to understand how the ♯11 should be resolved when moving on from the F7 chord through the II-V pattern to E♭maj7. The ♯11 normally has a strong upward pull. Consequently, there are two popular ways of resolving this melodic function:

Assignment

Transpose these exercises and play them to all play-alongs of "TWINBAY" (**tracks 13–19**). Be aware of the accompaniment when reaching the II7 chord. If you listen closely, you will hear the ♯11 in the piano in almost every chorus at this spot. I made a point of *not* asking Hubert Nuss to do this (I wanted to find out if he would use the sound without my suggesting it prior to the recording). The result is conclusive: He used it anyhow – *because it feels good, sounds interesting and is idiomatic.* You can be hell-bent on avoiding such a melodic or harmonic standard under the misguided assumption that it will stifle your creativity. But, the incontrovertible fact of the matter is that it is an inextricable part of traditional Jazz vocabulary. So, don't try to fight it – embrace it and move on!

Here is a final comment on this topic: The ♯11 is essentially an important note over other chord types, too – notably maj7 chords because of their potential Lydian quality (♯11 is not used over –7 or sus4 chords; with °7 and ø7 chords the ♯4/♭5 is a chord tone anyhow and will not create additional colour). Practise the ♯11 in every conceivable situation, even if it doesn't belong to the fundamental scale material (make it part of a guide tone line so it can be approached and resolved smoothly). The ♯11 is a typical "spice" that should always be at your fingertips:

Assignment

Come up with several choruses over "TWINBAY" and expand the various GTL examples into more elaborate melodic lines by adding motivic material, more active movement, passing notes, embellishments, approach patterns, etc.

Altered dominants in major keys

My second example is also an integral part of every Jazz musician's repertoire. Altering a dominant 7th chord that would normally be played Mixolydian is something you would not consider if it were left to tonal intuition. Altered dominants are a first step in creating increasingly chromatic colours.

Assignment

Go to the GTL exercise on p. 558 (turnaround in F Major: Fmaj7 - D7 - G-7 - C7) and familiarise yourself with the most important ways of approaching and resolving the altered tensions of C7 (all possible alterations are contained within the GTLs). Play these GTLs with the play-along **track 36**. At first, practise every line as it is (no embellishments) so that your ear can really lock into the sound of each note. In a second step, play more actively. But, don't forget, the important thing is to always land decisively on the intended alterations and – even more importantly – to imagine well in advance what each altered tension will sound like, otherwise your ear will not overcome its fixation with diatonic material.

Let's now have a look at the first half of "TWINBAY". We already know that G7 (bar 4) is Altered or HM5 in the key of E♭ Major. D♭7 (bar 10) and F7 (bars 13 & 14) are both Lydian(♭7) – we won't worry about these two sounds. What remains are the dominants E♭7 (bar 8) and B♭7 (bar 16). These are the ones we want to play Altered. Here, too, we should approach the altered target notes by means of good voice leading. Starting with the C–7 chord in bar 5, write GTLs (ascending and descending) that deliberately land on the ♭9, ♯9, ♯11 or ♭13 of E♭7, and then resolve them to the A♭maj7 chord in bar 9. Here are some examples:

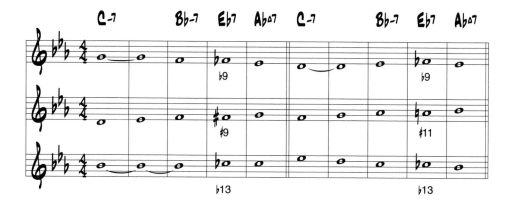

Transpose the GTLs to F–7 - B♭7 - E♭maj7 (bars 15 to 17) and play them to **track 13**. Then go to the II-V-I licks (C–7 - F7 - B♭maj7) on p. 571 ff. and filter out the patterns containing altered dominants (there are quite a few). Transpose them to B♭–7 - E♭7 - A♭maj7 and F–7 - B♭7 - E♭maj7 and develop more phrases along the same lines. You don't have to slavishly follow the voice leading I have suggested above. Just make sure that your phrases land firmly on the ♭9, ♯9, ♯11 or ♭13 of E♭7 and B♭7, carry on in Altered and resolve smoothly to A♭maj7 and E♭maj7 respectively. Finally, transpose the GTLs and the II-V-I patterns to the corresponding keys of the other play-alongs of "TWINBAY" (**tracks 14–19**). Play them with the recordings and incorporate them into longer melodic lines.

OK! In the meantime, a few years have gone by ☺. Your repertoire of altered phrases should be well developed by now. So, it's time to move on to the next level. The use of altered material is the starting point for an array of playing concepts, which, layer upon layer, result in increasingly complex and exciting sounds.

Chord/Scale superimposition

At this point, I'd like to introduce a way of thinking that has established itself as one of the most important tools of the contemporary Jazz soloist. The concept is straightforward and easy to understand but not that simply put into practice. The general idea is to choose a structure – be it a chord (triad or four-note voicing), a chord progression or a scale – and superimpose it on the basic changes provided by the accompaniment. The clash of these two layers – the original changes and the superimposed structures – makes for a lot of excitement and tension.

Upper structure triads

Let's begin with the superimposition of major or minor triads. This is a technique, which is used by just about every Jazz soloist today. To understand the theory, please go to the file pdf-E and turn to the section "Upper Structure Triads". There you will find a brief introduction to the topic and a chart showing a variety of scales and the triads that can be derived from each one. Also indicated are the upper structures that sound the most colourful.

How are upper structures put to use? Go back to the excerpt of Larry Williams' solo on "Spain" on p. 533 ff. That's a really nice example of this approach. Let's see how we can apply this concept to a simple turnaround in F Major (Fmaj7 - D7 - G–7 - C7). The first step is to choose appropriate scales for each chord. The second step is to select an upper structure triad derived from each of these scales. Most effective, of course, are USTs that contain at least one tension (preferably more) and therefore exert a certain amount of pressure. Here's an example:

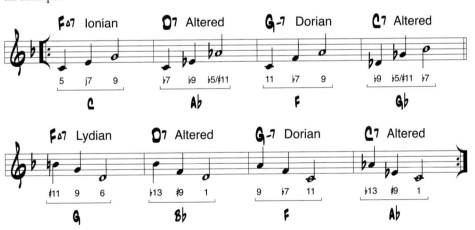

Make sure you understand why the various triads were chosen and how they relate to the underlying scales. Note the Lydian tonic in bar 5 and the G major triad used as an upper structure. It's a nice sound that often appears in improvisations to spice up the Imaj7 chord, which would otherwise sound relatively boring.

Now go to **track 36** and improvise while using the USTs suggested above. Start out by simply playing the triads to the recording. Your ear will first have to get used to the sound of the USTs. Gradually add more notes, embellish the triads and try to include them in longer phrases. It will take some time to create a pleasing melodic flow. USTs tend to sound artificial if they simply pop up as isolated elements. Make a point of moving into and out of the USTs as smoothly as possible. It is not necessary to play a UST in every bar. The technique loses value if you overdo things. It is far more effective to introduce these special colours intermittently as an element of surprise. I would therefore suggest you play phrases that touch on a UST every other bar or introduce a UST at a different point of the four-bar phrase each time 'round.

Let's have a look at the first 17 bars of "TWINBAY". Some of the USTs I've chosen relate to the turnaround exercise we looked at before. There are, of course, many other possibilities depending on your choice of scales (especially when it comes to dominants). Note that the triads follow the guide tone line shown on p. 563 (GTLs are a commonly used voice-leading principle when connecting consecutive USTs):

Assignment

- Analyse the intervallic functions of the notes in relation to the corresponding chord symbols and determine the triads they constitute (I've done the first few bars to give you an example). Write down the scales from which the triads are derived.

- Try to come up with USTs for the second half of the tune (bars 17–32).

- Go to **track 13** and play the triads to the recording. Stick to the basic triadic structure at first and give your ear the chance to lock into each individual sound. Use different inversions in order to cover the full range of your instrument. Gradually embellish the triads.

- Improvise several choruses and develop phrases that include USTs every now and then as brief highlights (as mentioned before, don't play USTs on every chord – with overuse, the effect wears off).

- For piano players, I would also suggest working on voicings that include the use of USTs in the right hand and basic changes in the left hand. Go to the example shown on p. 532 (the last few bars of "TWINBAY") to see how this concept works.

Eventually, you will begin to recognise USTs when they appear in the solos or accompaniments of other players. I strongly advise you to spend quite a bit of time on this topic since it is the basis for many exciting sounds to be found in modern playing and composing.

Secondary Sub(II-V)s

If you go one step further, you can superimpose lines drawn not only from single chords but also chord progressions while the rhythm section sticks to the original changes. I'd like to show you how this approach works using the example of secondary Sub(II-V)s (if you need a reminder, go back to p. 160 ff.). Remember that all SubV functions can be played Lydian(♭7). If we replace Lydian(♭7) with Mixolydian, the SubV can be preceded by a Dorian IInd degree, thereby expanding it to a secondary Sub(II-V) progression (both chords now use the same scale material).

From an improvisational point of view, we can apply a Sub(II-V) to any II-V situation. If we do this in "TWINBAY", we could, for instance, replace Dø7 - G7 with A♭−7 - D♭7. The result won't yet sound very spectacular because, in E♭ Major, G7 is generally played Altered/HM5, and the expected scale for D♭7 would, accordingly, be Lydian(♭7) – so the choice of Dorian for A♭−7 and Mixolydian for D♭7 would therefore agree with the tonal scale cliché quite closely. Things are quite different, though, with the II-V progression B♭−7 - E♭7, instead of which we could use E−7 - A7, the corresponding Sub(II-V). This chord substitution results in a very unusual sound that clashes considerably with the tonality. Its out-of-key quality will also be clearly reflected in the number of accidentals necessary when notating a line containing this sound (this progression can also be found in bars 4 and 5 of "West Coast Blues" by Wes Montgomery).

The most important aspect of this improvisational concept is a smooth incorporation of the "foreign body" in an otherwise tonal environment. The point is to create flowing melodic transitions. Here is an example:

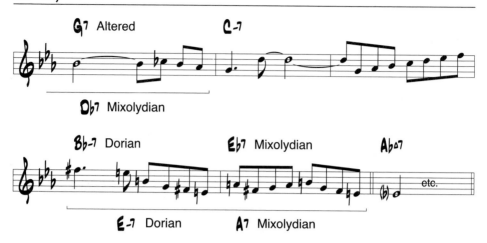

Practise the line and play it to **track 13**. While Db7 (bar 4) still corresponds closely to the Altered sound of the substituted dominant G7, the A7 (bar 8) is very distant and clashes considerably with Eb7 Mixolydian. The real difference, however, lies in the preceding II–7 chords Ab–7 and E–7. When applying this technique, it would actually make sense to focus mainly on the Dorian II chord of the Sub(II-V). Don't get too preoccupied with the V7. It is the Dorian flavour of the II that creates the most distinct clash with the underlying chord progression. In the above example, I have deliberately chosen target notes that work aggressively against the original changes. On paper, the phrases look wrong, but they work musically because the II-Vs are coherent units in themselves and fit smoothly into the overall line. What we get is a second harmonic level superimposed onto the original harmony. Here's one last bit of advice. Make sure you don't use any chromatic passing notes or chromatic approach patterns. The Sub(II-V)s should be played Dorian and Mixolydian exclusively. Think in terms of "undiluted" II-Vs. Any additional chromaticism will automatically cancel out the effect of the Sub(II-V) in relation to the overall tonality.

Assignment

Look for II-V passages in your own repertoire, substitute them in this way, develop phrases that include the alternate changes and practise them to a play-along.

In a next step, it is possible to precede *any* chord with a Sub(II-V). For example, go to bars 5 and 6 of "TWINBAY". Instead of playing two bars of C–7, we could, for example, substitute the second bar of C–7 with the Sub(II-V) Gb–7 - Cb7, thereby setting up the ensuing Bb–7. The same goes for the two bars of F7 in bars 13/14. This being the high point of the first half of the tune may suggest an additional boost of energy, arrived at by inserting the Sub(II-V) pattern Db–7 - Gb7 in bar 14 (half-bar changes), which resolves to the F–7 in bar 15. You could, of course, continue to B–7 - E7, as a Sub(II-V) replacing F–7 - Bb7 in bars 15 and 16, thereby creating a sequence of cycle-of-fifths Sub(II-V)s that create considerable dissonance: F7 | Db–7 | Gb7 | B–7 | E7 | Ebmaj7 (watch out for enharmonic spelling). Don't concern yourself with the fact that you are using material that deviates considerably from the underlying harmony – that's exactly what this technique is all about.

Assignment

Go to "TWINBAY" and map out a strategy for a complete chorus by inserting various Sub-(II-V)s as suggested above. Now play to the recording (**track 13**) and see if you can work out lines that incorporate the superimposed cadences.

Pentatonic scales

In the same way as upper structures and superimposed Sub(II-V)s help us create interesting sounds (chord on chord), we can also derive superordinate melodic structures from the scale material (scale on scale). The most common technique is the use of *Pentatonic scales*. This is one of the first scales most musicians learn. It therefore makes a lot of sense to apply this comparatively simple structure within a more complex setting. We will find pentatonic groupings in almost all other scale types.

Assignment

Screen all scales for pentatonic groupings (including avoid notes for the moment, even though we will focus on the groupings which exclude avoid notes for practical reasons). You will find a number of possibilities in most scales. Draw up a table with every basic chord type, the corresponding scale options and the Pentatonic scale groupings contained within each. It makes no difference whether you use the major Pentatonic scale or its relative minor as a point of reference. Both approaches lead to the same result – at least, when looking at the notes (I prefer to think in terms of the major Pentatonic scale).

You will realise that some scales do not contain pentatonic groupings – notably the symmetric scales (Whole-tone, HTWT, WTHT).

Now write out the Pentatonic options for each basic chord type and its corresponding scale(s). Here are two examples:

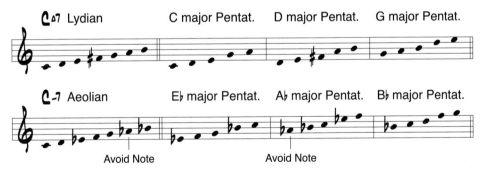

Lydian has no avoid notes. This is why all three Pentatonic scales are available. Aeolian contains one avoid note (♭6). In a functional context, the A♭ major Pentatonic would therefore not be a good choice for C–7 (VI–7).

Let's look at a turnaround in F Major (G–7 - C7 - Fmaj7 - D7). I'd like to concentrate primarily on Altered as the choice of scales for C7 and D7. The appeal, here, is the very simple and clear sound of the Pentatonic scale. This simplicity stands in effective contrast to the dissonant quality of the Altered scale:

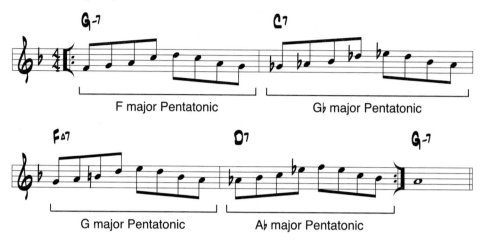

Since I have chosen Lydian as the basic scale for Fmaj7 (Imaj7), a series of chromatically ascending Pentatonic scales results.

Assignment

Go to **track 36**. First, play this exercise to the play-along. Of course, you will have to shift the phrase, since the four-bar turnaround in the recording starts on Fmaj7 (I-VI-II-V), while the line shown above begins with G–7 (II-V-I-VI). In a second step, use the material in a more musical way (different rhythms, motivic ideas, a more extended range of the phrases, etc.).

If you consult your table – hopefully complete by now – you will notice that Dorian contains a major Pentatonic scale starting on the ♭7, Altered on the ♭5/♯4, Lydian on the 2, Locrian on the ♭6, etc. We can therefore assign the following Pentatonic scales to the changes of "TWIN-BAY". Again, I have chosen Lydian for the maj7 chords independent of their functions – for the simple reason that it sounds interesting and gives us more pentatonic options than Ionian:

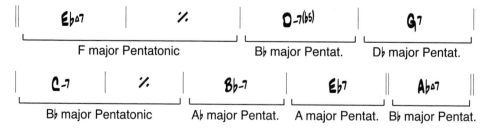

The material presented rather mechanically in the turnaround above (in order to explain the principle) has been applied a lot more musically in the following example over the changes of "TWINBAY". Notice the different ways the pentatonic material has been structured:

Assignment

Again, practise the line, play it to **track 13** and see if your ears are willing to adjust to the unusual character of the phrases. Using pentatonic groupings will result in a rather different melodic quality compared to a more traditional approach.

Try to see this little example as a starting point for an improvisational concept in which the complete scale material of a chord progression can be replaced with various Pentatonic scale superimpositions. If you go back to the chart shown on p. 76 in the chapter "Modality", you will realise that there are other Pentatonic scale types worth considering when applying this technique. I don't want to open a can of worms at this stage. The topic is just too vast to cover in detail and goes beyond the scope of this book. I just wanted to introduce you to the general idea. File it away for now and check it out whenever you feel ready. However, I do want you to remember that there are other 5-note groupings beyond the basic major/minor Pentatonic scale.

Chromaticism

Chromatic passing notes and chromatic approach patterns are a fundamental feature of Jazz improvisations. They are seen as a trademark especially of Bebop and Hard Bop. Extensive chromaticism, though not usually found in the melodies of the average Jazz standard, is an indispensable part of the Jazz soloist's vocabulary even today. There is hardly a musician in modern Jazz who doesn't use it. It is an idiomatic element by which any expert can dependably judge whether or not players have done their homework and have studied and analysed the great improvisers in depth. Tiny things such as a badly positioned approach pattern, an incorrectly timed resolution, etc. immediately betray whether chromatisicm is just being used to fill gaps haphazardly or whether the soloist has internalised the concept and knows how to apply it in terms of the idiom. Let's outline a couple of scenarios in which you can practise a more chromatic approach.

Assignment

Have a look at the following exercise in F Mixolydian – an 8th note scale pattern sequenced up one octave and back again. The diatonic version is at the top, the chromatic version below. It should be your aim to be able to play both variants equally well. Whereas the diatonic version most probably presents no problem whatsoever, I can imagine that the chromatic approach patterns will make you trip up time and time again. Apart from the unfamiliar fingerings, the difficulties lie in the unusual structure of the lines. Observe carefully how the pattern changes, depending on whether the shift from one diatonic target note to the next occurs by a whole step or a semitone (over the F7 chord, we are talking about the melodic movement A to B♭ and D to E♭). In some places, you can choose from two different approach patterns (indicated by two note heads):

Try to connect the diatonic and the chromatic versions – e.g. by playing the first half of the bar diatonically and the second half chromatically, or by switching every bar.

It is the main objective of our line to ensure that its underlying scale (in our example this is F7 Mixolydian) is still recognisable despite the chromatic embellishments. If we can no longer hear the changes, then the timing of our phrases is off. If we just go ahead and play chromatically at random, blindly relying on luck, the chromatic material may obscure and overpower the fundamental sound completely. For this reason, we have to develop a feel for what is "important" and "unimportant". Target notes are important – they occur mostly on the beat. Chromatic notes are "unimportant" – they are passing events that fill in the gaps and usually occur on the offbeat 8th notes. This guarantees that, even in the midst of extreme chromaticism, the changes and the corresponding scales can still be heard clearly. The chromatic material may even emphasise the basic colour of the underlying chord progression because it helps the ear focus on the important notes (chord tones, diatonic target notes).

Assignment

Practise the following exercise with a metronome (start with 60 BPM and, eventually, move up to ca. 240 BPM). It may take some time to get accustomed to the strangeness of these meandering phrases. In addition, you will find some of them technically quite challenging. Generally, aim for faster tempos (150 BPM and beyond). When played at a slow tempo, these lines tend to sound rather awkward and artificial because of their mechanical structure and the many chromatic notes. In up-tempo situations, however, the chromatic material is effectively used as a means of building and maintaining momentum by creating eighth-note lines that span several bars within a limited range (with purely diatonic phrases, it is actually quite difficult to keep going for more than a bar or two without coming up against the range restrictions of the instrument). Practise the exercise as a whole or in sections (after all, if you're a horn player, you have to breathe every now and then). Analyse each note either as a diatonic or a chromatic component of the line in relation to the chord (F7) and the underlying scale (Mixolydian):

Now transpose the above exercise to D7, practise it and play it to **track 3**. You will hear the progression D7(sus4) - D7. When using chromatic embellishments, 7(sus4) chords are treated like regular dominants without regard to the suspension. Note that the ♯11 can appear on 7(sus4) sounds without causing any problems if it is positioned as part of a chromatic approach pattern. This works because the ♯11 does not act as a tension, but as a passing tone that resolves to the 5. It is therefore perceived horizontally (as part of the line) and not vertically (as part of the chord).

Assignment

Right – in the meantime a few weeks will have passed! Can you now play these lines by heart? In your sleep? At any tempo? Without making any mistakes? In F, D, B♭, G, etc.? If so, we can move on. Go to **track 33** and play the F7 lines along with the recording. Take note that the pulse you are hearing (BPM = 105) will force you to play the lines in double time (in other words, you will have to use 16th notes). Playing 8th notes may be a good idea at first to familiarise yourself with the sound. However, the true effect of these lines will only become apparent if you play them at a fast tempo.

Did you notice anything unusual while doing this exercise? We hear the progression C–7 - F7 in the recording (with an emphasis on C–7). This implies that all chromatic F7 lines can also be played over C–7. We have discovered an important principle: What works over seventh chords can also be applied to other chord types. It should be easy to understand, though, why chromaticism is particularly well suited to seventh chords. The purpose of a dominant is, after all, to create tension, and that is exactly what chromatic material adds to. In contrast, –7 and maj7 chords are comparatively stable sounds and, as a result, trickier to handle when it comes to chromaticism. However, we can play chromatically over these chords, too, as long as we accept that they tolerate less tension and, in general, have to be treated more diatonically.

So, how do we approach minor chords? We interpret them as part of a II-V pattern and use the same chromatic material over II–7 as for the V7 chord, which we have already practised. The actual scale for the –7 chord (Dorian, Aeolian, Phrygian) is of no great significance because chromatic passing notes and approach patterns resolve predominantly to chord tones, and these are the same for all scales mentioned above. For half-diminished chords, the thinking is a little different: They are treated as upper structures of a V9 chord starting from the third (e.g. Aø7 is the upper structure of F9, so you can use the chromatic lines based on F7 for Aø7).

Assignment

Transpose the chromatic lines you can play well to E♭7. Go to **track 4**, which by now you know is in B♭ Dorian. Play the E♭7 lines to the recording. Does this work? Of course – even though playing lines with a high level of cromaticism to this almost exclusively diatonic play-along may take some getting used to. But, with time, I am sure you will realise that you now have musical vocabulary at your disposal that will enable you to break away from the smooth, easy-going, clean Dorian sound and start playing more aggressively by introducing dissonance as a means of contrast. And that's exactly what the chromatic concept is all about – creating disturbances without destroying the general framework.

If you transpose your chromatic lines to A7, you can play them along with **track 7**, which is entirely in C♯–7(♭5) Locrian.

Assignment

Ask yourselves what you would have to do to use chromatic material with maj7 chords. The following solo examples will give you a hint.

Before we apply chromaticism to any particular chord progression, I'd like to raise a warning sign. Chromaticism is not an end in itself. It is something extra, an ornamentation and extension of an already coherent diatonic phrase. That's why we have to begin with a distinct melodic intention before we can start adding chromatic elements. Just diving into a chromatic line while hoping to produce something logical and musically satisfying is wishful thinking. We at least have to have a rough melodic outline in mind. If we don't hear specific diatonic target notes, we cannot approach them chromatically. So, as a starting point, let's look at the first 17 bars of "TWINBAY" and a simple, almost entirely diatonic melody that clearly delineates the chord progression:

If we want to safeguard the harmonic and melodic essence of the previous line, we have to group our chromatic patterns around the chord tones and the central melodic notes in such a way, as to allow the essential target notes to occur on the strong beats of the bar:

Practise this excerpt, learn it off by heart and play it along with **track 13**. You will notice that it is sometimes necessary to play a "wrong" (= chromatic) note at important points (on the beat, and even on the downbeat of a bar). These "wrong" notes become "right" once they have been resolved to a target note. For instance, we have to begin on a chromatic note in bars 2 and 11 if we want to time the line and its resolution correctly.

Assignment

Finish writing this chorus. Write a number of your own choruses following the same principle. Use the phrases I introduced you to in the chapter "Chromaticism" on p. 253 ff.

A comparison of the two examples presented above – the chromatic and the underlying diatonic version – shows us that chromaticism is a great way of creating excitement and additional tension. The increase in melodic activity might well give us the impression that the chromatic version moves at a faster tempo. If we used only diatonic melodic material in extended eighth-note lines, we would quickly come up against the range restrictions of our instruments. By introducing chromaticism, we can reduce the range of a line without losing momentum. Besides, we can also "stretch" or "stall" a phrase before reaching an important target note so that the line resolves smoothly. However, as with anything used in excess, chromatic material loses its value and charm if you overdo things. Chromaticism is a spice, a means of creating little surprises. So, use it sparingly, and don't ruin the dish.

    By incorporating chromaticism, you have taken the first step towards playing "outside". The more chromatic your lines are, the more you will depart from the tonal framework of your music. This will eventually increase your familiarity with tension and tolerance for dissonance. And the more dissonance you can handle, the easier it will become for you to play "outside". And so, on to our next topic.

From inside to outside

Let's go back to what we have already discussed briefly at the end of the chapter "Chromaticism": *inside-outside* playing. I'm sure you all can recall situations where you are listening to a soloist and you suddenly hear something that makes you instinctively prick up your ears and say: "Wow! What was that?" That is exactly the feeling you will have when experiencing what is known as "playing outside of the changes". All modern Jazz players are familiar with the concept of playing outside – i.e. deviating from the changes while the rhythm section sticks to the original chord progression.

Remember the discussion on "the ordinary" and "the special" when talking about the choice of scale material: ordinary = tonality = cliché = little tension; special = departure from the tonality = unusual = a lot of tension. In essence, we are applying the specific concept of V-I in a more general way – as the interplay of tension (V7 = outside) and release (I = inside). When looking at a chromatic approach pattern, for example, the chromatic notes (outside) resolve to chord or scale tones (inside). Here, the principle works on the level of a single beat or bar, with individual chromatic passing notes and approach patterns embellishing an otherwise diatonic tonal framework. When talking about the concept of "playing outside", the same principle is translated into longer, multi-bar units. Now we are talking about complete phrases or longer melodic segments clashing with the tonality. Outside passages sound unusual because they break away from the ordinary (= diatonic) environment, fundamentally toying with the tonal expectations of the listener.

Jazz musicians who play "outside" define what they play in relation to an "inside" environment. Remember the quote by Ramon Ricker on p. 263: "You can't play hip outside, if you can't play hip inside!" Just as *yin* and *yang* complement each other despite their dissimilarity, there is no "outside" without an "inside". The important thing is a certain degree of balance between the two extremes. Even the most aggressive player needs moments of rest and alternates between the two opposites. Like any other effect, the concept becomes self-destructive if overused. Playing outside exclusively is boring because everything sounds equally strange. If "way-out" becomes the norm, we're missing the essence of the concept. However, if "way-out" pops up every now and then in an otherwise traditional = conventional context, then the ear says "Wow!"

Passages played "outside" must make sense, have structure and follow a conceptual pattern – otherwise they simply sound "wrong". When analysing "outside" lines, we quickly discover that they are actually transposed "inside" phrases. So, when playing outside, we are playing something familiar and consonant, turning it into something strange and dissonant by shifting it away from the home key. Actually, we end up playing inside all the time – just not quite how the ear expects to hear things. This means we do not have to learn new lines to be able to play outside. We can use what we already know and can do. But because we apply it in an unconventional way, it acquires a completely different meaning. Let's have a look at a few approaches that result in "outside" sounds.

- *Bitonality*: The rhythm section sticks to the original changes while the soloist is thinking and playing in a different key. The further apart the key signatures, the more "outside" the outcome and the stronger the feeling of strangeness. Conversely, the more notes common to both keys, the weaker the resulting tension. In practice, the key the soloist plays in would have to differ by at least three sharps or flats to have much impact. Go to p. 260 and have a look at Miles Davis' solo on "Tune Up" by way of example.

- *Chromatic displacement*: This technique is also known as **sidestepping**. You take a phrase and, instead of playing it in scale, you shift it up or down by a semitone. The result will sound highly dissonant because of the big difference in the number of sharps or flats relative to the overall key. However, because you are using a coherent phrase, which in itself sounds inside, the resulting line will still make sense. Sidestepping is very popular because it creates the most dramatic effect of all inside-outside approaches. Quite often, it is not the soloist but a member of the rhythm section who uses this technique. For example, the soloist stays in key and the piano player shifts a voicing up or down a half step every now and then, creating pinpricks of dissonance on the way. A well-rehearsed group of musicians can take this even further by shifting collectively, the whole band simultaneously weaving in and out of the chord progression. This, however, calls for great ears and outrageously fast reaction times.

- *Modulating sequences:* Remember the distinction between exact (real) and diatonic (tonal) sequences as a means of motivic variation (p. 272 ff.). Diatonic sequences follow the expected scale material and fit into the overall key. Exact sequences, on the other hand, shift the entire motivic idea regardless of tonal considerations. They are a great way of creating outside lines, because they automatically modulate and break with the tonality. The result is nevertheless coherent because the motivic idea is developed consistently. You can control the amount of tension by either gradually shifting a phrase out of key (e.g. sequencing up/down in intervals of major seconds, fourths or fifths) or by using intervallic transpositions, which push the phrase out of key more radically (minor seconds, minor/major thirds, tritone).

All three techniques mentioned above result in similar "outside" effects. Let's have a look at a few examples that put these concepts to work:

Bitonality:

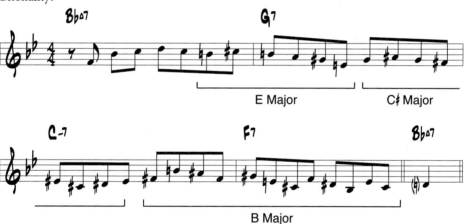

In this example, it is no coincidence that the line touches on key areas, which relate to the roots of the underlying chord progression by the interval of a tritone (B♭maj7 / E Major, G7 / C♯ Major, F7 / B Major). Transpose the example up a perfect fifth to F Major (or down a perfect fourth, depending on the range of your instrument), learn it by heart, play it to the turnaround (**track 36**) and enjoy.

Real (exact) sequences:

Chromatically displaced and real (exact) sequences:

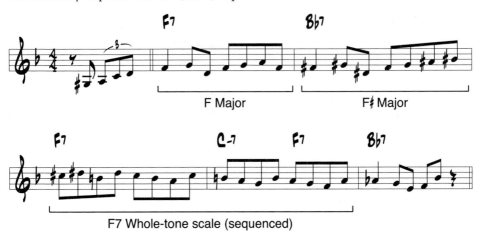

Playing outside is primarily a matter of will and guts. You have to approach every outside phrase with confidence – only then will it sound good and not "wrong". You have to be able to handle the tension that results from the conflicting tonal layers. This may be difficult at first. Sounds that turn against our diatonic needs and musical habits, inherited over years, if not decades, will initially feel strange. Playing outside may even cause physical discomfort. All the same, give it a try. Evaluate your acceptance of dissonance from time to time. The more at ease you are with discord, the further "outside" you'll be able to venture. Let's create a few exercises to help you cross this threshold.

Assignment

Go to **track 4** (B♭ Dorian). Improvise "in scale" for a while. Once you feel comfortable, switch to B Dorian or A Dorian every now and then. Practise various combinations – e.g. 6 bars of B♭ Dorian, 2 bars of B Dorian (or 4/4, 8/8, 12/4, etc.). Alternately, you could try other key shifts (e.g. in minor thirds):

Every outside phrase has to be incorporated smoothly into the basic tonal framework. The hardest thing with playing outside is the seamless link between the inside and outside passages (e.g. 4 bars of B♭–7 alternating with 4 bars of A–7):

In the following assignments, concentrate on the entry and departure points with the goal of getting the change from one tonality to the next to sound logical. Map out the transitions first. If necessary, figure out specific lines and write them down.

Assignment

Play along to **track 13** and start out by improvising over the basic changes for a while. Then take the cadential elements (the II-V progressions) and replace them with sounds that, for example, are a semitone above the target sound. Reverse this principle and replace only the target sounds with outside material:

		C#-7				A△7			
Eb△7	⁒	D∅7	G7	C-7	⁒	Bb-7	Eb7	Ab△7	etc.

		E△7				C#-7		A△7		
Eb△7	⁒	D∅7	G7	C-7	⁒	Bb-7	Eb7	Ab△7	etc.

Assignment

Choose an easy Blues play-along (e.g. Aebersold). The changes should only consist of basic functions (no secondary dominants, etc.). Improvise over the entire Blues form in various keys other than the original tonality, using only the functions I7, IV7 and V7 (either in the basic Blues scale or in the Mixolydian scales corresponding to the individual seventh chords). Choose keys that differ greatly from the original to increase the feeling of tonal conflict. Try to avoid the use of chromatic passing notes or approach patterns. If you use chromaticism, you will cancel out the effect!!! Learn to tolerate the tension:

E7	A7	E7		A7		E7		B7	A7	E7	B7
Bb7	Eb7	Bb7	⁒	Eb7	⁒	Bb7	⁒	F7	Eb7	Bb7	F7

Summary

I would like to show you a long excerpt that should illustrate how these concepts (♯11 over II7, Altered dominants, chromaticism and playing outside) are applied in the real world. This is a recording with solos by Woody Shaw (trumpet), Kenny Garrett (alto sax) and Kenny Barron (piano) over "TWINBAY" taken from the album "Solid" by Woody Shaw. I have included brief comments in the score so that you can easily spot the different techniques (chromatic passing notes are marked with an asterisk, approach patterns are marked with "AP" and passages without comment follow the scale cliché). Nonetheless, listen to the recording, work carefully through all six choruses in detail and analyse every note and phrase in relation to the changes:

Essentially, all three improvisations are quite traditional. What is noticeable, though, is the effortless ease with which each soloist injects occasional moments of dissonance into his lines, only to return just as nonchalantly to the more consonant and conventional concept of "playing the changes". A word on the outside passages: They are clearly visible in the score because they display a high number of accidentals, highlighting the material foreign to the key.

Assignment

Learn the six choruses off by heart and play them to **track 13**. Play them over and over again until your ears and fingers have completely absorbed them. Then transfer them to the other "TWINBAY" play-alongs (**tracks 14–19**). Of course, you'll not be able to use the material without changing some of the phrases considerably. Apart from the transpositions, you will need to compress or extend some of the lines, change the rhythms and use different phrasing on account of the varying stylistic approaches, tempos and time signatures. The goal is not to transcribe something only to keep it exactly as it was originally played. When you are working with other people's improvisations, they should be no more than a starting point. Of course, transcriptions supply new phrases, which you are supposed to copy diligently at first. Ultimately, however, they should add to the musical vocabulary already at hand, merge with the many lines you are already familiar with and inspire you to create new ideas.

How to handle mistakes

It has taken us hundreds of pages to learn to do the right thing – to choose the right scale material, to use the right tensions, to play the right voicings, to practise efficiently, to avoid tripping up. At some point or another, the question must arise: What do I do if things go wrong during an improvisation (and they will)? How do I deal with mistakes? Let's end this chapter with a topic that is one of Jazz's great taboos.

"Do not fear mistakes. There are none."

Miles Davis

There are many musicians who, like Miles Davis, endorse the notion that **there is no such thing as a wrong note**. Be aware, however, that this sentiment is founded in the psychology of the Jazz musician. Jazz is the Great Unifier, Jazz is open to any style, Jazz is the music of individualists, Jazz is freedom of choice, Jazz knows no boundaries, and so on and so forth. Everyone has the right to his or her very own and unique voice in Jazz. Who would dare attempt to decree what is "right" or "wrong" in the very music to which tolerance and open-mindedness is paramount. This would contradict everything that Jazz has ever stood for. Talking about mistakes clashes with the very "spirit" of Jazz. Anything is possible in Jazz. And, if anything is possible, then nothing can be "wrong" and, as a consequence, there can be no mistakes – end of story.

   Yeah, right, you wish! To me, this is taking the easy way out and nothing more than a convenient and self-serving assertion. It means dodging the responsibility of having to decide what works best, what is appropriate or not. Of course, there are mistakes – and even the very best of soloists concede the fact. The guitarist John Abercrombie once said to me after a (great!) concert:

"You know, all I'm trying to do while improvising is make my mistakes work."

I don't believe he was fishing for compliments. But, even if there is a certain degree of coquetry behind this statement, it goes to show that all musicians, at whatever level, have to deal with the same difficulties. Even Miles Davis made mistakes, but what set him (and other greats) apart from the less proficient musician was the fact that he could effectively turn any potential mistake into something that worked and, in the end, made the wrong note sound right. Good soloists have an uncanny and almost infallible sixth sense for what is appropriate, for the demands of the moment. They feel intuitively where a line wants to go – not as a conscious effort, but rather as a sort of premonition that is founded on decades of experience and a highly responsive ear. And when they hit a "wrong" note (which happens more often than you might think), these reflexes kick in and help them to keep going, to maintain the momentum of the line and to bring it to a satisfying close. This is what this section on mistakes is all about. Desperately trying to avoid mistakes is not a good approach (ultimately, if that were to be our main objective, it would be better not to play at all). The important thing is not to get stuck or lose control *despite* the mistakes – to move on and turn a mistake into something "right".

What is a mistake, actually? Basically, there are only two types:

- We hit a wrong note and don't notice it. Remember: The context determines the rules, and the rules determine what is "right" or "wrong". If we don't know the rules, i.e. the vocabulary, the grammar, the right "pronunciation", etc. of a style or a specific composition, we will inevitably make mistakes without knowing it. When this happens, there is nothing we can do about it (at least for the time being). If we are not aware of our mistakes, we obviously can't correct them. The problem will only be solved with more experience, growing theoretical knowledge, better instrumental technique, an increasingly sophisticated inner voice and a more developed ear. A dedicated teacher, who monitors your practice sessions and makes you aware of the things that go wrong, would be helpful, too.

- We hit a wrong note and realise it. This means we had a specific idea in mind but couldn't carry it off. We had the intention to play something in particular (e.g. a motivic idea) and our intention comes across as: "Listen up! This is what I'd like to say!" This triggers expectations, which we set up for ourselves as well as for our band members and the audience. If we mess up what we set out to do, it will be heard as a mistake (this could be a single note or an entire phrase). The clearer our intentions up to this point, the more noticeable the mistake will be. The good thing, though, is that this is something that can be solved because we know what we wanted to play – so we can remember the mistake we made, go back to it in our practice room and work on it.

Naturally, we are going to focus our attention only on the latter category and discuss the remedies that may help us survive if we run into trouble. For a start, we need to recognise a wrong note or phrase as such. The distinction is, however, not that clear-cut. Whether we perceive something as a mistake or not depends, firstly, on our individual tolerance for tension and, secondly, on the musical context. Some sounds can put up with wrong notes better than others. An "out of scale" (= wrong) note will be less conspicuous when used over a dominant chord with its strong tendency to resolve and an inherently high degree of dissonance than in the context of a consonant maj7 chord. Minor chords, with their various scale options, are also comparatively "tolerant" and flexible when it comes to mistakes. It is likewise not easy to draw the line between "right" and "wrong", here. Let's have a look at the main chord types (maj7, –7 and 7) and compare their potential for accommodating "mistakes":

- maj7 chords (usually played Ionian or Lydian) – wrong notes are ♭2, ♭3, ♭6 and ♭7;

- minor chords (played Aeolian, Dorian, Phrygian, MM or HM) – the only wrong note is 3; all other notes are contained in either one of the minor scales mentioned afore;

- seventh chords – the only wrong note is the maj7 if we take into account all possible dominant scales.

A major 7th chord is clearly the most unambiguous sound of the lot, with little scope for variation. Mistakes are therefore more likely to happen, and they will carry more weight simply because they will be more noticeable in this context. It is easier to wriggle your way out of situations involving minor chords and dominants.

Assignment

Pick any note on your instrument and play it along with **track 39** (random chords). Keep this note and repeat it at least once per bar throughout the entire exercise. Whenever a new sound appears (every four bars), decide …

1. … whether your note feels right or wrong and,
2. … if it feels right, what degree of the chord and the corresponding scale it is (try to be exact: e.g. 3, ♭7, ♯9, 11, ♭13, etc.).

Repeat the exercise, randomly choosing a different note each time.

Rely on the feeling of tension each note triggers in you. Decide whether the note creates a lot, little or no tension at all. If it has little tension, we can assume that it is a chord tone. The root itself is likely not to produce any dissonance. The root will give us a strong feeling of being "at home". If our note irritates the ear and the feeling of tension is unpleasant, it is likely to be an avoid note or out-of-scale. If the note, on the other hand, creates considerable dissonance in a good way, it will invariably be an available tension. We will be able to sit on these notes comfortably despite their dissonance because they are actually part of the sound (the scale belonging to the chord). Although they might want to resolve, we sense the tension as satisfying and even exciting.

Help is on its way

What do we do when we make a mistake? Since we have always practised with the intention of playing "right", most mistakes catch us by surprise (otherwise they wouldn't happen!). So, what we need is a survival strategy when things go wrong. Have you learned enough licks or patterns to get you out of the predicament? How quick is your reaction time? Is there something you can automatically rely on to bail you out? If not, then what should you do? You can't rectify your mistake after the event. You can never correct a phrase you are unhappy with because *the music never stops*. It just keeps on going and you have to go along with the flow. Of course, you could always resort to taking a break, make a dramatic pause, not play for a while, gather your wits and sort things out before you continue. This would not be the worst of choices, and it would definitely be better than to go on stumbling about in the dark. Interrupting your solo, however, will draw the attention of the listener to the mistake and make it stick out like a sore thumb. It would therefore be better to go on playing.

I would like to show you a musical, an instrumental and a psychological strategy, each of which you can use to manoeuvre yourself out of a sticky situation. The goal: *learning to live with mistakes*. So, let's contrive a couple of settings in which you can practise making mistakes, learn to accept them as inevitable and find a way to move on without tripping up too badly. Don't think this is going to be easy. As I have already mentioned under the heading of "playing outside" – the fact that we have spent our entire lives trying to play correctly makes it hard to go against the grain and suddenly feel comfortable with something we have always tried to avoid.

Tonality

Most mistakes happen while trying to capture every minute detail of the chord progression, while scrupulously "playing the changes". When we think vertically, we relate our melodic phrases to each individual chord. This again means that every melody note is viewed in terms of the underlying chord, either as a chord tone, tension or passing note. Because we are so focussed on the function of a note, we are automatically very sensitive to whether a note is "right" or "wrong" and it sometimes takes just one wrong note to throw us off track. When we think horizontally, however, by focussing more on the flow of the phrases, the occasional mistake will not be that noticeable. The melodic contour is of greater significance and the occasional mistake doesn't carry that much weight. Based on this observation, we can derive a simple rescue formula: *Play tonally!*

Instead of trying to address each and every chord, switch to thinking in terms of the larger picture and rely on the one basic aspect that governs every traditional chord progression: the tonality. All the many sounds we have discussed in this book relate in some way or another to a key. This is particularly apparent with dominant functions. Remember the principle of scale construction: chord tones + tensions that establish a close connection to the key.

So, the first rescue remedy is: *back to the basics*. If you feel disoriented or get stuck, fall back on the diatonic material of the overall key, instead of trying to deal with each individual chord. You will still make mistakes because the phrases – seen vertically – won't always strictly correspond to the changes. However, the result will sound acceptable because – seen horizontally – the line consistently follows a particular scale colour. If, in addition, your phrases have a strong rhythmic and motivic quality, the ear of the listener will automatically focus on this aspect and not pay attention to the odd mistake.

Let's take the first 9 bars of "TWINBAY" as an example and compare the different approaches. The first line is based on the principle of "every chord its own scale", the second subdivides the chord progression into harmonic phrases consisting of important target chords and their preceding cadences and the third line follows the idea of the changes being part of an overall key area:

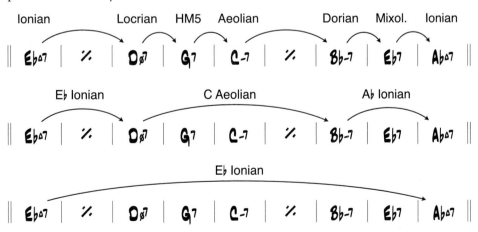

If we resort to the principles shown in lines 2 and 3, we're pretty much on the safe side and our improvisation will sound quite coherent. Remember, though, the less sophisticated or refined the approach, the higher the number of potential sources of error. If we improvise only in E♭ Ionian (as in line 3), we would not play the essential note D♭ over B♭–7 and E♭7. Neither would we play a C♭ over the D♭7, which is the next chord (not shown in the example). The result, however, would still sound acceptable because the line is held together by its diatonic quality and its motivic development.

Let's have a look at Chet Baker's improvisation on "Stella By Starlight" (see p. 406 ff.). Bars 21 and 22 show that horizontal melodic thinking is more effective than compulsive adherence to vertical harmonic requirements. The expected scale over A♭7 (♭VII7) would be Lydian(♭7). Seen from this perspective, the notes G (= maj7) and A (= ♭9) are wrong. Most Jazz musicians would have tried to adjust the flow of the melody to the harmony by playing G♭ and A♭ instead. Since the four bars leading up to A♭7 are clearly diatonic in B♭ Major, the notes G♭ and A♭ would feel strange (sing the phrase with the A♭ and G♭). The line containing G and A, as played by Chet Baker, sounds much smoother:

Theoretically correct

Musically preferable

What may appear to some of you like nit-picking, shows that every line demands consistency, and that an actual "wrong" note could very well be the "right" choice if it serves the logical flow of the phrase – and the logic of Chet Baker's line is: tonality and motivic sequence. *Playing wrong notes can therefore sometimes sound right.*

Assignment

Play along with **tracks 22–25** (diatonic cadences containing secondary dominants and secondary II-Vs). Play exclusively in the actual key of each track without thinking about the changes (use only notes from G Major for track 22 and F Major for track 23, etc.). This doesn't mean you should doodle around aimlessly. Play musically, in time, use motivic ideas and strive for clear melodic phrases. You will notice that – despite minor incongruities – it doesn't sound at all bad. Do the same with the various "TWINBAY" play-alongs. Play, for instance, only in E♭ Major on **track 13** and stick to F Major on **track 14**, A♭ Major for **track 15**, etc. Next, go back to the same play-alongs and "play the changes". Make sure you're doing justice to every chord and its corresponding scale. As a final step, combine these two techniques (e.g. play 8 bars thinking only in terms of the tonality and 8 bars with consideration to every chord, etc.). You should feel equally at home with both approaches. Being able to switch from one to the other arbitrarily will give you the necessary confidence to circumvent any problem you may come up against while soloing. So, if you run into a mistake while "playing the changes", immediately switch to the diatonic approach and continue as if nothing had happened.

Chromaticism

With our 12 chromatic notes and our customary 7-note scales (or rather six, if we don't include the almost inevitable avoid note), the probability of hitting a correct note is 50:50 or better. Isn't it good to know that you are more likely to play "right" than "wrong"? The fact is – if we hit a wrong note, there is always a right note a half step above or below. Therefore, when dealing with mistakes, chromaticism is an indispensable means of recovery (there are scandalmongers out there who suggest that the inside-outside concept arose only as a result of musicians making mistakes and resolving them chromatically). So, the second rescue remedy is: *The wrong note will show you the way to the right one!* Whenever you land on a wrong note, just shift it chromatically up or down a half step and you will automatically find yourself on firm ground once again. As soon as you're back on track, the familiar sound will set you off on a new string of melodic ideas and fingerings. None of this can be planned, though. We have to live with what first occurs to us. It *is*, however, possible to practise how to survive when ambushed by the unforeseen wrong note.

Assignment

Choose any "TWINBAY" play-along and set up a 1- or 2-chorus loop with your A/B function. Play the recording and choose a random note on your instrument. If it turns out to be wrong, shift chromatically and then continue playing the changes for a few bars. Then interrupt your improvisation and start again on a different random note. The main incentive of the exercise is to start off on a wrong note as often as possible in order to practise your chromatic rescue reflex. Get used to playing wrong notes. This will help you avoid panicking when it actually happens and train you to keep your cool while manoeuvring your way out of the predicament. At the same time, this exercise will help sharpen your ear in terms of how individual notes relate to the changes.

When wrong, play strong

A beautifully executed and formally consistent improvisation will always sound "right" no matter how many "wrong" notes it contains. Remember the discussion on the topic of "playing outside"? The step from "outside" to "wrong" is minimal. Here's the difference – when we play "outside" we sense a clear intention, whereas "wrong" signifies: "Whoops, that's not what I was trying to do!" Taking this to its logical conclusion, we come up with a third escape route, which often proves itself to be highly effective: *When wrong, play strong!*

As soon as you turn something "wrong" into a principle, it will start sounding "right/outside". Repetition is what it's all about. A wrong note or phrase becomes right once it is repeated often enough and played with assurance and commitment. Repetition implies intent. The listener will say: "Although this sounds pretty weird, it's clearly deliberate, otherwise the player would not be so obstinately repetitive." Ideally, the reaction would be: "Wow!

That sounds hip. Where does this guy get his ideas from?" Persistence is the magic word, here. Dealing with mistakes confidently will always result in a persuasive solution. I'd like to give you a few examples of how to use this concept and extricate yourselves from an uncomfortable spot.

Have a look at the following excerpt from Kenny Barron's solo on "TWINBAY" (bars 9–16 of his second chorus; see p. 608 ff.):

Although the line only makes occasional sense in terms of the expected chord-scale relationships, the passage sounds premeditated and highly convincing. Why? Kenny Barron plays so "strong" that there can be no doubt as to his intentions. This is what he wanted to play and nothing else. When someone plays with this clarity and confidence, the listener's ear mercifully "turns a blind eye" to any incongruity. Because both the solo and the accompaniment are so coherent in themselves, these two levels temporarily can move independently of one another without this being perceived as a problem.

Let's look at a second, subtler, example. Go to Phil Woods' improvisation on "Just The Way You Are" (see p. 247 ff.). Have a look at the last four bars (E7 - A7). E7 (V7/V) takes Lydian(♭7) as its corresponding scale, and we hear the expected A♯ (♯11) as an important part of the line. For motivic reasons, Phil Woods plays the same phrase over the ensuing A7 (V7). Again, the ♯11 (D♯) is the main note. If you have the recording and listen to it very carefully, though, you will notice that the keyboard plays E7(sus4) and A7(sus4)! Surprisingly, what amounts to a serious tonal collision on paper doesn't disturb the ear at all. On the one hand, this is because of the compelling motivic sequence. It carries the solo through the melodic-harmonic mismatch – the horizontal (i.e. the line) takes precedence over the vertical (i.e. the harmony). On the other hand, the sax and the keyboard sound sufficiently different to prevent the melodic and harmonic layers from blending too much. Because both the solo and the accompaniment work so well, seen individually, this sort of "mistake" is hardly noticeable.

Another example shows that compositions may also contain "mistakes". Here is "Cantaloupe Island" by Herbie Hancock (the first 8 bars):

The four-bar phrase is played twice, harmonised first with F–7 and then with D♭7. Note that the C in the melody reappears on the repeat (= maj7), despite the fact that it is now used in conjunction with a dominant seventh chord. Because the melody is motivically consistent, the ear accepts the collision of maj7 in the melody and ♭7 in the chord. No Jazz musician would consider this to be a problem. What I find intriguing, however, is that "Cantaloupe Island" appeared in a Schweppes tonic water TV commercial several years ago. In the ad, the theme was changed at the decisive spot (C♭ instead of C) to fit the D♭7 chord. It could be that the producer of the new version felt that he should correct the "mistake" in view of a less open-minded audience. The melody works well in the new version, of course. Personally, however, I think it is a pity that the interesting glitch, intentionally included in the composition and perhaps the one original thing that sets "Cantaloupe Island" apart from similar tunes, was smoothed over. The fact remains that I have often used this piece in workshops and never met anyone who considered the C unpleasant. This goes to show once again that the repetitive horizontal (motivic) concept of the line takes precedence over the vertical discrepancy.

Here's one last, more complex compositional example. Check out one of the most beautiful and unusual ballads you'll ever come across: "The Peacocks" by Jimmy Rowles (you'll find the lead sheet in "World's Greatest Fake Book"). Go to the B section, bars 3–5, and you'll discover something rather strange: Cø7 - F7 with a prominent E and E♭ø7 - A♭7 with an equally conspicuous G in the melody. Using major 3rds over ø7 chords and major 7ths over dominant chords would seem to be quite a daring concept. Surprisingly, it works. Considering the general chromatic quality of the B section, I am sure that Jimmy Rowles was looking for a special sound that would hold up as the climax of a tune already teeming with dissonant tidbits. His choice serves the cause admirably. And now for the main point: Since the melodic continuity is so strong (the motive appears 3 times), the ear accepts the extreme clash of melody and harmony.

Assignment

Let's do a little experiment. Go to any one of the "TWINBAY" play-alongs and think up a simple motivic idea that fits the first chord (Imaj7). Now play it to the recording. Start with your phrase and develop it sequentially following a specific principle of your choice (e.g. ascending chromatically, descending in whole steps, etc.). Don't worry about the changes. This exercise is not about hitting the right notes. Just stick to your motivic idea (melodically and rhythmically), move it according to the concept you've chosen and put up with whatever strange sounds you may run into. The result could look something like this when played to **track 13** (the opening motive is shifted up chromatically):

Well? How did it feel? It might be that there were moments when your hair stood up on end. But, be honest – somehow it worked, didn't it? Here is the reason: You were consistent; you developed the idea convincingly and resolved it well at the end (to A♭maj7). Try the same thing with different single-bar or two-bar motives, varying the direction as well as the intervallic concept of the sequence. Don't forget the option of repeating your motivic idea for a longer period of time without moving it at all. Also, consider beginning on a phrase that is not in key (start "outside" and repeat your idea or move it up or down). No matter how bizarre the result may be, it will give the listener the impression that you know exactly what you're doing.

Conclusion

We have now reached a point where we should take another look at the way we perceive mistakes. In many cases, the term "outside" may be closer to the truth than "wrong". The ear must learn to accept that way-out, unusual, weird, dissonant, etc. does not automatically imply "wrong". If we manage to turn the unexpected strange note into something intelligible, a clear statement radiating intention and conviction, then it will sound "right". This does not mean we can get away with bullshit just by claiming something was intentional. And, of course, we will still run into wrong notes while improvising. Our inclination to tonality will continue to lead us for the most part to play inside notes. That's what we feel comfortable with. However, if we learn to feel equally comfortable with an unexpected outside note or phrase we will lose our fear of wrong notes.

And one day, you will realise that Miles Davis' quotation is more than just rhetorical. There are no wrong notes. At worst, there is a wrong time for the right note. All things considered, a note itself cannot be wrong. It can only feel wrong if it fails to comply with your intentions. Once you learn to weave your inaccuracies into something acceptable, you will feel at ease despite your mistakes. As Jazz musicians say, not in resignation but in acquiescence: *Shit happens!* The best soloists in the world know that the perfect improvisation doesn't exist. Improvisation and perfection are mutually exclusive. Even though all Jazz musicians dream of that singular moment where everything comes together and falls into place, we all know this to be a rare occurrence. No improvisation is without risk – otherwise it wouldn't be an improvisation. Things may (and will) go wrong. That, however, shouldn't keep you from going out on a limb time and again. How does the saying go? *No risk – no fun!*

To cut a long story short – embrace mistakes, don't feel bad about them. Appreciate them as lessons learned the hard way. And welcome the fact that, ever so often, a mistake will be the starting point for something new. Mistakes can safeguard you from falling into the rut of playing the same things over and over again. As James Joyce, the great writer, once put it: "Mistakes are the portals of discovery."

Playing the Form

"Soloists elaborate upon what the structure of the piece has to say, what it tells them to do."

Tommy Flanagan

Form is the very breath of music, the driving force that controls the hills and valleys, the shape of a composition or improvisation. It is the governing principle, the framework within which rhythmical, melodic and harmonic events acquire their significance. The effectiveness of a phrase depends to a large extent on how it is embedded in the formal structure of the piece. Once again, it is of greater importance *when* and *where* something is played, rather than *what* is played. Remind yourselves of everything we've discussed in the chapters "Form", "The Motive" and "Melodic Contour and Climax". Choosing the right notes alone cannot guarantee good music. Only when transformed into a formally convincing melodic flow will they have meaning and exude vitality.

Beginning and ending

"Start strong, end strong and in between it's nobody's business!"

Stephane Grapelli

What do listeners remember best? Naturally, the beginning and the ending of a solo. So, let's set up the framework of a convincing improvisation. One of the most important truisms attributed to the world of advertising and job interviews is:

"You never have a second chance to make a first impression!"

When listening to good soloists, you will notice that their improvisations always start with loads of self-confidence. You don't hear any reluctance, hesitation, insecurity or "tinkering around" – every note means something. You recognise from the start that these musicians know what they want, that they are "ready to go". Listen to the solo pick-ups of tenor saxophonist Roman Schwaller's solo on "Moving Out" (**track 42**) and Hank Mobley on "The More I See You" (**track 41**). There is no room for discussion, not the shadow of a doubt – these guys take a stand.

The beginning of any convincing solo relies on a strong appearance, a powerful "declaration of intent". The first step is:

"Make a clear statement!"

Don't edge your way into a solo – say something from the first note!!! Begin with a vigorous, bold and clear-cut idea.

Your solos should end just as decidedly as they begin. If you want to tell a good story with what you're playing, then you have to finish your solo conclusively, too. Make sure you let your band members (and your audience for that matter) know that your solo is coming to an end by gradually lifting your foot off the pedal. Give the rhythm section a chance to follow and to "cool down" with you. And when you hit the last note of your solo, make sure that everybody feels that "this was it". No meandering or rambling on incoherently, no fumbling around – just a clear full stop!

What next?

So, let's imagine you've played your first note or phrase. Now comes a much harder, but nonetheless decisive, step. Every musical statement, be it a single note, a motive, a rhythmical pattern, etc., sets a mood, has its own momentum and triggers expectations as to how it should continue – in the listeners, the band members and yourselves alike. So, instead of relentlessly overloading a solo with new ideas or playing rote-learned platitudes, sensitive musicians follow up on their first idea, allowing it to unfold by letting it take the lead in terms of direction, structure, shape, dynamics and energy. A highly memorable quote by Art Farmer hits the nail on the head. Replying to the question how he always manages to play remarkably coherent solos, he told me:

"I let the music play me."

What a beautiful concept. Every idea has enormous potential and the power to guide us through the next part of our solo – if we let it happen. The music knows perfectly well where it wants to go, without our interfering. If we give our initial idea sufficient time and room for development, it will evolve and weave musical fabric as if it possesses a life of its own. We simply have to follow the natural flow of the line. A good solo bows to what the music needs without seeing this as a straitjacket. If we are prepared to serve the music, to allow ourselves to be drawn into its surge and swell, just about any starting point will grow into longer melodic phrases and maybe even into an entire solo. The biggest mistake we can make is to go against the inherent forward drive of our first statement. A few quotations show that Art Farmer is not alone in his approach:

"The phrases you play are your message while you're playing. They should relate to one another and they should be logical."

Tommy Flanagan

"The vital part is thinking while you're moving. Once the momentum has been started, I don't like to break it. I'm concerned with the continuity in motion. If you're not affected and influenced by your own notes when you improvise, then you're missing the whole essential point."

Lee Konitz

Improvisation is not an ego trip despite the responsibility we have to take for every note we play. Good soloing requires a healthy portion of humility and the ability to resist the temptation of wanting to control everything. Not until the opening statement has been clearly established and developed does the musician take initiative again by introducing the next idea. It is the balance between two seemingly contradictory virtues that distinguishes the great Jazz soloists – being able to exercise control and, likewise, to let go and give in to the demands of the music.

The first note you play sets the music in motion. After this, the music dictates – at least for a few bars – how things should continue. As every action is followed by a reaction, so it is in music. Be aware of the impact of that first note. By playing your first phrase, you are making a promise – and if you don't follow up on this promise, your solo will not sound coherent. If you, however, allow yourself to be led by the requirements of the music, it seems unlikely that anything but a meaningful and musically convincing solo will result. The big question is: How do we acquire this ability? How do we practise the art of making the right choices?

Motive and sequence

Do not fear repetition! It is a widespread misconception that every improvisation has to be new, fresh and exceptional, and everything you play must always be unique and should never be redundant. What nonsense! To the contrary, many Jazz musicians cultivate what I call "the art of joyful repetition". What we come across in every good solo is motivic thinking and the persistent development of ideas. We *have to* repeat ourselves in order to be consistent. There are soloists who build entire improvisations from a single idea. Some even like to toy with their audiences by repeating a phrase remorselessly, modifying it, milking it to the max, turning and twisting it inside out. This creates an enormous amount of excitement and suspense. The listener's need for change, for contrast, becomes overpowering. And when something new does – at last – occur, the effect is breathtaking. You must learn to enjoy repetition.

One of the biggest problems while improvising is that it's hard to remember – under stress – what we've just played. Benny Bailey once told me: "Try to learn your solo while playing, and continue what you started with, then your lines will always make sense." But how should we be able to repeat or even consistently develop something if we've lost track of our opening phrase? That's why it is so important to begin every solo with a meaningful and convincing idea. The clearer and simpler it is, the easier it will be to remember. Then follow up on your first statement. Don't try to say something new every second bar. If you do, you'll most probably go off on a wild goose chase. The result will be no more than patchwork, a hodgepodge of incoherent lines. Instead, learn to listen carefully to yourself while you're playing, try to keep your opening idea in mind and allow it to unfold in the subsequent phrases, thereby giving your solo overall meaning and integrity.

Again, I would like to quote Art Farmer, with whom I had the pleasure and honour of playing and who was definitely one of the greats when it comes to creating extraordinary solos. What impressed me time and again was the fact that he could begin his improvisations with a phrase and come to a close with the same idea ten choruses later. Commenting on this, his laconic statement makes things sound so simple: "It's easy, it's like coming home at the end of your solo. You just have to remember where home is."

Obviously, one of the most important principles when it comes to playing convincing solos is the use of *motive, sequence* and *motivic development* – in short, the repetition and variation of a motivic idea. Just as most compositions start with a phrase that grows, develops, keeps reappearing and ultimately determines the entire piece, good solos thrive on a continuity of ideas. If you want your lines to sound coherent, you will have to stay with one idea for a while. Don't keep jumping from one thought to another. On the other hand, try to develop a feeling for how long you can hang onto an idea before it becomes stale and the ear calls for new material.

So, say something meaningful! Say it again, so that your fellow musicians understand what you are trying to do. Say it a third time, so that the other band members can begin to interact with your idea and the audience has a chance of "jumping on the bandwagon", too. Say it a fourth time, so that the band as a whole can develop something based on the original idea. Say it a fifth time in a slightly different way, to make sure that the idea doesn't lose its vitality. Say it a sixth time so that you and the band can start building momentum. Say it a seventh time so that everybody can enjoy the energy created by collective effort and mutual understanding. Now it's time for change and something new …

Assignment

Take a simple motive (no more than three or four notes, no big leaps at first) and stick to it exclusively during the entire (!) solo by…

- …repeating it consistently and changing it as little as possible (only if necessary, e.g. for a change of scale material);

- …playing it in every or every other bar (depending on the harmonic rhythm);

- …creating variety (e.g. by using inversions, embellishments, etc.);

- …deliberately shifting it around a lot, covering a large range on your instrument;

- …changing it rhythmically (using triplets, syncopations, displacements, etc.);

- …connecting it to guide tone lines (sequence);

- …incorporating it into longer and more active phrases.

The last two points are particularly important when trying to control the development of a motive because they help you anticipate the direction in which the solo progresses. In "TWINBAY", as with all chord progressions that follow the cycle of fifths, the main guide tone lines (based on thirds and sevenths) lead downwards. Controlling thematic ideas moving upwards is more difficult because you're not following the natural flow of the harmony. Without GTLs helping you voice-lead a sequence, you'll have a hard time handling upward movement. For the moment, stick to the GTLs you know best. However, don't forget to go back to pages 562 ff. for some more GTLs to work with.

Let's start with the simplest method of motivic development: blatant repetition! At first, force yourself to hold on to the identical motive as long as you can. Learn to listen ahead and to anticipate whether or not the motive will fit the following changes. In some cases, you'll have to change certain notes to adjust the motive to the scale material of the next chord(s) or to achieve good voice leading. Try to retain as much of the motive as possible. Here's an example (practise it and play it to **track 13**):

As you can see: The motive only needs to be moved on the Bb–7 chord to be consistent with the voice leading of a II-V progression (remember that the G = 6 is an avoid note over Bb–7 because it would prematurely introduce the 3 of Eb7). This example follows the "principle of common tones" (analyse and observe how the G changes its colour in relation to the chords). Of course, this is no more than a simple étude. But it is important to temporarily exaggerate or even over-do certain things for the principle to really sink in. If you can't anticipate (at least for a few bars) how a line should or could continue, your solos will not emanate the necessary confidence.

With a little rhythmical variation and a bit of ornamentation, this rather mechanical exercise can be turned into quite an acceptable melodic line:

Now, try moving your opening motive consistently in one direction (upwards or downwards) with minor variations. For example:

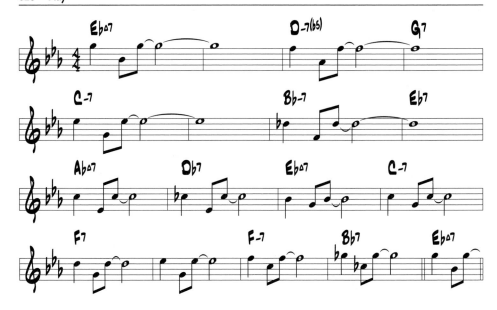

Develop a number of exercises according to the same principle using the chord progression of "TWINBAY". Work with various motives and starting notes. Be as consistent as you can (hang on to the motive or move it persistently in one direction). Transpose these exercises and use them with the various play-alongs of "TWINBAY" – keep doing this until you can visualise every note in your head well before it appears. Eventually, you should be able to not only hear the development of a melodic line in advance but also the harmonic environment within which the melodic phrases will appear. A melody note should automatically generate harmonic awareness and not just be perceived horizontally. Look at the last 5 bars in the example above. While you are still dealing with F7, you should already hear the guide tone line F-Gb-G coming your way as a logical continuation of what you have played so far. In addition to this horizontal perception, you should also hear the GTL as part of the cadence F–7 - Bb7 - Ebmaj7. Accordingly, the Gb, for example, should not only be heard as part of the GTL but should also trigger the sound of an altered Bb7 in your mind – **well before you get there**.

As soon as you have mastered a specific pattern, you can gradually start toying around with it: embellish it, use chromatics, change the rhythms, develop it into more extended phrases (two or four bars long), etc. Try to be less mechanical and more musical in your approach, think of the flow of the melody and not in terms of an exercise. Here is an example that is based on the motivic sequences shown above:

As a next step, take the exercises and work them into complete choruses. It is not necessary to stick to your opening idea too closely. You can depart from the initial statement after a while and combine it with different material, but make sure you return to your motive from time to time. Only if you are able to repeat your opening idea will you have the chance to develop it. If you stay away for too long, you'll run the risk of losing control and playing non-related material. While you are playing, try to get a feel for your ability to remember your first idea. You should play so clearly and simply that it is easy to think back to the beginning of your chorus at any time. Here is an example:

Practise this chorus until you can play it by heart and analyse it. Play it to **track 13** and listen to how the phrases relate to each other motivically. This chorus is nothing special, but it is very consistent in terms of motivic development and melodic contour. Notice how the first 8 bars are repeated as of bar 17 (with a slight variation of the opening statement). Returning to something you have played before is an important part of successful soloing. Of course, if you can't remember what you played, you can't repeat it. This is exactly what the next assignment is all about: memory training.

Assignment

Choose one of the play-alongs of "TWINBAY" (preferably **tracks 13** or **14**). Decide on a simple motivic idea (later on, you can do this exercise without premeditation). Your initial motive should be fairly short – no more than one or two bars. A longer phrase would probably be too unwieldy and overtax your memory. However, with a little practice, you will eventually be able to manage complex ideas, too. Begin with the motive you've chosen and then continue improvising. Don't reflect on what you're doing or consciously think about developing the motive – just play and follow the flow. Now for the actual assignment: Once you get to bar 17, repeat your opening motive – identically, if possible, or at least similarly. Here's the tricky part: As soon as you reach bars 15 and 16, try to visualise your thematic idea so that you can anticipate the repeat in bar 17 and approach it in a musically logical way. You are not just simply trying to repeat the same phrase after a longer period of time (so, don't just jump into it abruptly), you are also trying to get ready for the repeat in a way that will give you a "soft landing" on the opening phrase. Try to limit the risks you take with this exercise by restricting the range of your improvisation, avoiding leaps and working with simple rhythms at first.

Ideally, despite the many things that happen at any time during an improvisation, the ear should always be connected with the past as well as with what's to come. Try to remember where your lines originate and learn to anticipate where they want to go. Equally important is the ability to pay attention to detail as well as the larger picture simultaneously. However, zooming in on each individual phrase and zooming out to see how it relates to the overall solo at the same time (while playing, make no mistake) is only possible if your ideas are absolutely clear and tangible in your mind. This is the actual goal of this exercise – to develop the clarity of your ideas. Clean up your phrases so that there are no unnecessary notes – reduce to the max! The more notes you play the more likely it is that you come up with superfluous, awkward or even wrong-sounding ideas (wrong in terms of scale material and placement of the notes). Busy lines are hard to control. Only very good soloists can handle many notes without tripping up. Perhaps I am being too much of a purist. I would, nonetheless, want you to be aware of whether you are moving your fingers just because that's what is expected of them, or whether you're moving them because you have given them a job to do – namely to play a clear-cut idea.

Rhythm

"I hear rhythms, mostly, and then I put notes to them."

Dizzy Gillespie

What would a melodic phrase be without rhythmical structure? Form – in essence – is structured time. Accordingly, form is primarily a rhythmical phenomenon. I know I've said this ad nauseam: Improvising isn't just about playing the right notes at the right time. The far more important thing is how they fit into the rhythmical flow, how they contribute to the groove, and how they are phrased. It is common knowledge that our capacity to remember rhythmical structures is greater than our ability to recall series of notes. The rhythmical contour of a line is generally the most memorable aspect for the listener. For this reason, we must also conceive our motives from a rhythmical point of view. Always try to play a rich variety of rhythms. Persistent eighth-note passages (often heard in uninspired Bebop solos) are tiring in the long run. Good solos need contrast – rhythmical contrast.

Assignment

- Play lines consisting only of the same note values (only half notes, quarters, eighths, quarter-note and eighth-note triplets, sixteenths) to develop a feel for a steady flow in different tempos.

- Play lines that are a colourful mix of different note values.

- Play only on the beat or offbeats (syncopations) exclusively; play phrases alternating between "on the beat" and "off the beat".

- Play in "stop and go" mode, alternating between longer and shorter note values, accelerating and slowing down your lines; play a lot, then again nothing at all.

- Deliberately play less. Use only long notes and rests. This will help you feel the meaning of each individual note and give you more time to concentrate on its colour and impact.

The last point – developing a feeling for long notes and rests – is particularly important. We often play out of habit – or for fear the listeners might think that we've run out of ideas if we don't play. Try to eliminate everything superfluous from your solos. Never play simply to fill space; only play if you really feel the urge to say something. The more you work with rests, the easier it will be to keep control over your solos. By playing more economically, you will have more time to listen to your lines, to develop your ideas more effectively and to anticipate the direction in which your phrases should go. And – last, but not least – if you play incessantly, there is no room for interaction with your band members.

Let's get back to rhythms. Practise rhythmic displacements! I get itchy fingers when I hear a line moving against the basic feel of the time signature. I like it when soloists work with simple means and few notes and still manage to achieve impressive results and great impact. I love the excitement resulting from the clash between the basic pulse, the metre and the line. The following example works with *metric modulations* – a concept where the phrases are based on beat groupings that create the impression of a different time signature. In our example, the motivic cells are grouped in units of three quarter notes, simulating 3/4 time. This effect gradually disguises the 4/4 feel, blurring the bar line and creating increasing tension as the line proceeds:

Play this exercise using **track 13**. Learn it by heart so that you can consciously listen to and enjoy the tension created by the rhythmic displacements working against the underlying form while you are playing. Then transpose the line to F Major and play it to **track 14**. Metric modulations are particularly effective when working with faster tempos.

A good example of a metric modulation (3/4 over 4/4) can be found in the chapter "Licks and Tricks". Take a look at bars 10–16 of the transcription of the second solo chorus by Kenny Barron on "TWINBAY" (on p. 610).

Assignment

Write similar exercises following the same principle and play them to **track 13**. Start with shorter phrases at first (four-bar or eight-bar periods). The longer you keep up the pattern displacements, the more likely it is that you will lose your bearings. The difficult thing with metric modulations is following the changes (which, of course, still relate to the original harmonic rhythm in 4/4 time). The phrases should reflect the chord-scale relationships of the underlying harmony (this may necessitate changing scale in the middle of a pattern). Choose differing points of entry. Don't begin the displacement on the first beat of the bar only, start on the other beats, too. Make sure that the line resolves convincingly at the end (usually when reaching an important point within the form). Think mathematically when designing these exercises. Calculate how many repetitions you need to reach a specific point of resolution (e.g. try to hit the downbeat of the next A or B section). If necessary, add to or subtract from the line to ensure a clear ending. By doing this you will develop different ways of initiating and – even more importantly – resolving a metric modulation without getting lost.

One last word before we move on. Whenever you are dealing with rhythms and whatever exercises you may be working on, there is one topic that cannot be stressed strongly enough and which should always be lurking in the back of your mind, something more important than any wonderful note, line or voicing you might come up with:

Timing, timing, timing, timing, timing…

This is the bottom line of good Jazz playing. You have to be acutely aware of time in everything you play. No matter whether you are practising or playing a gig, soloing or accompanying, always, always, always play so that everyone can clearly feel the time (and I'll refrain from using the world-famous Duke Ellington quote…). We won't have time (pun intended) to go into this in detail. After all, this is a harmony book, although there is a section on Jazz phrasing in the chapter "Transcription" (pages 507 ff.). Just always keep in mind: Sloppy, inaccurate, shaky timing in Jazz is disastrous. If your solos lack rhythmic definition and don't emanate a strong sense of time, you won't connect to the players around you. You can't lean on the other band members for support. Self do, self have! True mastery of time comes from within.

Harmonic and melodic rhythm

Most books on Jazz harmony focus on which notes to use in a specific harmonic situation. This is psychologically dangerous. If we only concentrate on what we should play, we easily forget that the bits where we don't play are just as important to the overall effect of a solo. Busy solos come across as cluttered and hectic (horn players, at least, need to breathe from time to time!). Those of us who play incessantly run the risk of getting lost in meaningless musical babble. So, be aware of how your improvisations move within the formal framework of a piece. Always monitor the way your lines breathe and control the activity of your phrases, even if you are just working on an exercise. Try to consciously pace yourselves when you practise. Use rests deliberately, or just simply play less than you feel you need to every now and then. In this way, the things you do play will have more meaning, your lines will seem better structured, your ideas will become more discernible and listeners will be able to follow your solo more easily. Above all, you will have more time to listen (to yourself and the others), and it will be easier for your fellow musicians to react to what you are doing. Leaving space will do wonders for communication in the band.

Assignment

While improvising, there is so much to watch out for (sound, scale material, timing, phrasing, etc.) that the formal aspects often fall short (or we are simply not aware of a deficiency or a lack of perception in this area). So, let's try to isolate this issue by concentrating only on the formal structure of your lines, aiming to strike a balance between motion and rest.

Begin with the scale play-alongs (**tracks 1–9**). Since each recording is completely diatonic in a single mode, you won't have to deal with a specific chord progression. Prepare a fingering on your instrument for each of the modes so that you don't have to worry about the tonal material. Now practise: play – don't play – play – don't play, etc. To begin with, don't think so much about the length of the phrases. Simply practise putting in rests. Exaggerate "not playing". Learn to feel comfortable when you're not playing. Delay your next phrase deliberately. Wait for the right moment and then play with conviction. Alternate between equally long segments of play and rest. Do this asymmetrically as well: long phrase – short rest, short phrase – long rest. Be aware of the fact that some of the play-alongs have a certain subdivision. In some cases, the piano switches from comping to soloing every 16 bars. Even though you are not hearing a chord progression, since each play-along is in a single mode throughout, you should still be observant of a certain periodical quality in your playing (try to think in 2-bar, 4-bar or 8-bar phrases).

The fundamental challenge of any improvisation is to control the formal flow provided by the composition and to translate it into lines that reflect the rise and fall in energy determined by the chord progression and the melodic contour. Of course, there are many examples of soloists playing around with the formal structure of a piece, e.g. by deliberately shifting the harmonic rhythm against the melodic rhythm (see, for example, "Line Up" by Lennie Tristano on p. 347 ff.). In most cases, though, the shape of a successful solo goes in hand with the ups and downs of the changes. So, let's move on to chord progressions.

Assignment

Let's begin with a simple turnaround (e.g. **track 36**). Follow the harmonic rhythm of this chord progression (strong = rest; weak = motion) by consciously alternating between rests and activity. Try to get your lines to breathe:

First, alternate strictly between rests and motion one bar at a time. Don't forget that "rest" also implies holding a long note or playing very little by comparison! Exaggerate this for a while (strong = don't play; weak = play a lot without thinking about the tonal material) so that you can clearly feel the effect of what you are doing. Then gradually begin your active phrases a little earlier (with a pick-up) and finish them a little later, allowing the phrase to cross the bar line. This will make your lines sound less symmetrical. The bar line will become less obtrusive, the phrases will flow better and feel more natural and less "disjointed".

Assignment

Now transfer the previous exercises to the chord progression of "TWINBAY". First, carefully look at the changes in terms of their harmonic rhythm. Go back to p. 284 where we already discussed the harmonic rhythm of "TWINBAY" in detail.

Be sure to realise that the melody – at least in the A section – moves inversely to the harmony. This is not – as you may think – coincidental. Because it happens twice (bars 1–4 and 5–8), it has a motivic quality and is obviously an intentionally used compositional device. In the diagram below you will find the melodic rhythm above and the harmonic rhythm below the changes:

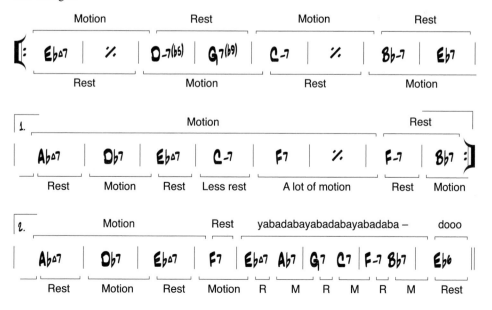

So, when working on this tune, there are two options you can pursue. Use the various play-alongs of "TWINBAY" and alternate between concentrating either on the movement of the harmony or the movement of the melody. Be sure to end every phrase convincingly. This is why the brackets in the diagram above, which indicate the phases of motion, always reach across the bar line and extend into the next bar. This should remind you that *lines do not stop at the end of a bar – they end at the beginning of the next bar with the resolution of the phrase.* Don't forget that the closure of a phrase (a long note or rest) is still part of the phrase. Landing on a final note does not mean that the line is finished – it's completed when the next line begins!

Melodic contour

Have another look at Chet Baker's chorus over "Stella By Starlight" on p. 406 ff. Carefully study how determinedly he develops his motivic ideas. Notice, how faithfully he sticks to the form in his lines? Every eight-bar segment follows a self-contained train of thought. Chet Baker develops his ideas only as long as necessary – it's the form that tells him where to conclude an idea and where to begin with a new one.

Resolve your phrases with as much conviction as you can. When an idea comes to an end, that's it, you're done, end of story! Don't go on playing. Learn to make clear closing statements. Every melodic line needs room to breathe and should be bracketed by points of rest to make it more tangible. Every player, too, needs time for reflection every now and then to prepare new thoughts and ideas. So, when practising, concentrate not only on the phrases themselves but also on the end of each formal section. Enjoy the wait before you move on to the next melodic idea. Spotlight these pauses – appreciate them as important parts of your solo.

The melody of "TWINBAY" is very well suited to illustrating this principle. In the A section, we clearly hear two four-bar phrases with 2 bars of movement and 2 bars of rest (remember that you can reverse this alignment if you follow the harmonic rhythm instead). In the B section, which has to have more energy for formal reasons, we hear a more active eight-bar segment coming to a standstill in bar 15 (on "strong").

Assignment

Try to follow this play-stop structure in your improvisations:

Exaggerate this at first by clearly stopping on the downbeat of bars 3, 7 and 15. If possible, hold the last note for two bars. Depending on which note you land on, you will probably have to adjust the line to fit the changes (so it's not so much about not playing at all but rather about playing less). For this to work more naturally, you could play a little further into the bar and stop on beat 2 or 3 (this will sound less mechanical). Do the same for the phrase beginnings. At first, start on the downbeat of bars 1, 5, and 9, making the entry of each phrase clearly noticeable. Then gradually move the beginning of your phrases back to include part of the preceding bar by playing a pick-up.

Again, remember that we had the option of focussing either on the melody or the harmony when working with "TWINBAY". I hope you realise that we've been emulating the melody with our play-stop strategy. Repeat the exercise and go with the harmonic rhythm instead (stop on target chords and play on cadence chords).

The structure of a solo and the climax

Make a conscious effort of controlling the flow of energy in your improvisations. Most soloists start their improvisations at a low energy level (economical phrases, less rhythmical activity, a lot of rests, softer dynamics, lower register, etc.). The solo then gradually picks up speed and increases in intensity, tempo and density. Supported and encouraged by the rhythm section, the soloist gradually moves into a higher and more dynamic range of the instrument – until the climax is reached. Subsequently, the energy level drops off and the solo calms down before coming to a close.

If we want to maintain a high energy level for a longer period of time, we have to have excellent control over our instruments and the necessary stamina to manage the physical exertion that comes with faster, louder and more complex lines in the upper register (this is definitely something to work on when exercising your instrument). Naturally, we need to be able to rely on support from the rhythm section whatever we do. After all, the first and foremost duty of the rhythm section is to ...:

"Make the soloist sound good!"

Alert accompanists will try to follow the flow of the solo and to maintain a high energy level once the climax is reached until the soloist wants to ease off a bit. Of course, we shouldn't be entirely dependent on the rhythm section. It is our obligation as the soloist to show the band where our improvisation is headed. We need to take command, to "turn up the heat" or "cool things down" if we want the rhythm section to make sense of our intentions. It is therefore vital to practise playing at different energy levels and to control the ups and downs of our lines, even if we're on our own.

At this point, it is necessary to move on to the larger picture – the overall contour of an improvisation. I have already shown, while discussing Mike Mainieri's solo on "Pools" (see p. 325 ff.), that great soloists are capable of controlling both the smaller and larger subdivisions of the formal structure of a composition at the same time. The points I made earlier about the harmonic and melodic rhythm at the level of the bar or the multi-measure period are equally valid to the larger structural units: the longer melodic phrase, the formal sections, a single chorus, up to an entire solo consisting of several choruses. This rise and fall in tension, the principle of "tension and release" – in other words the alternation between "strong" and "weak" – is noticeable on every one of these levels (remember the illustration of this issue on p. 291).

If we layer the various formal subdivisions (bar, period, section, 1ˢᵗ and 2ⁿᵈ half of a chorus) of "TWINBAY" one on top of the other, we end up with the following chorus outline (in a very general way):

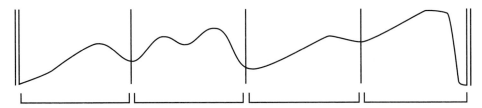

Assignment

Choose a "TWINBAY" play-along and improvise two choruses following the solo contour shown above. Your second chorus should generally be on a higher energy level than the first. Initially, exaggerate the formal ups and downs by deliberately playing much less (or not at all) on the "strong" parts (rests, long and low notes, etc.) and increasing the musical activity in the "weak" parts (eighth-note movement, syncopated lines, high notes, etc.). Try to time your lines so that the 8-bar, 16-bar and 32-bar segments relate to one another, too (A = strong, B/C = weak, 1ˢᵗ half of a chorus = strong, 2ⁿᵈ half = weak, 1ˢᵗ chorus = strong, 2ⁿᵈ chorus = weak). Begin relaxed (e.g. in the lower register of the instrument) and play economically at first – this will provide room for development.

The formal contour shown above is the "general case" found in many solos, but there are alternatives. How would you develop your solo, for instance, if the previous soloist ended on a very high energy level? Would you wait for the rhythm section to first cool down before you begin? Or would you take over at the same level of intensity? How would you continue from there? Would you have to turn up the heat even more or choose a completely different approach? The important thing, therefore, is to have a number of strategies "up your sleeve" in order to handle a variety of situations.

In addition, the overall duration and thus the formal timing of an improvisation are of vital importance. We need different strategies depending on whether we are playing a long or a short solo. In a short improvisation, we need to get to the point more quickly; otherwise, things will be over before we really get going. Especially in Pop music – where improvisation plays a subordinate role – very short solos are predominant. In this situation, we cannot afford to experiment. Every note has to fit and every idea has to be flawless from the start. This is the ultimate test as to whether a soloist has what it takes to say everything that needs to be said within just a few bars – with a clear opening idea, an equally clear ending and a convincing musical statement, which is neither hectic nor cluttered. The tenor sax player Michael Brecker, for instance, was a master of the perfect miniature solo – as proven on literally thousands (!) of recordings as a sideman. In longer improvisations, we need to hold back and develop things in a more deliberate way. If we reach a high energy level too soon, we face the danger of running out of steam prematurely. This is often a matter of physical staying power. We need stamina to gradually pour on the pressure and keep the energy going over a longer period of time.

Assignment

Make sure you practise different solo shapes. The following diagrams should serve as models for your improvisations. They only suggest the energy levels and contours of a solo without implying the time aspect (they can be applied to short and long solos likewise). Improvise over the various "TWINBAY" play-alongs and vary the length of your improvisations. Play 8 or 16 bars only, or stretch out for one, two or even three choruses in order to improve your flexibility:

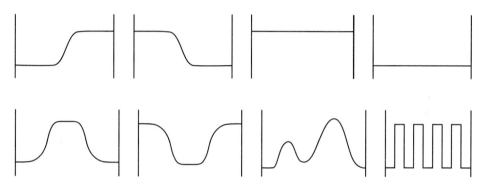

Monologue and dialogue

Now there is only one more topic I would like address in this book – *interplay*. The most important element of an improvisation is the interaction with the other band members. Ultimately, the sound of any band is defined by a mutual understanding of form, energy, groove and time. These are the things that need to be practised as a group. You have already seen in previous chapters how differently the form of a composition can be interpreted. So, when you are rehearsing with your band, make sure you don't only practise themes and arrangements. More than anything else, you have to find common ground when it comes to improvising. You actually have to work on a collaborative concept of improvisation – as strange as this may seem when talking about an art that essentially lays claim to spontaneity and creation on the spur of the moment. You have to develop a collective awareness of the formal components of a composition, a shared perception of how the piece breathes and flows, a shared appreciation of the liberties each individual musician can take and the criteria that have to be fulfilled in order to do justice to the piece as one voice. I have noticed that very few ensembles practise like this. It is, however, interesting that, for example, Miles Davis and his colleagues met several times a week for nearly two years before they got together to record the album "The Birth of the Cool" – primarily to explore various concepts and ideas, not only working up the repertoire, but also finding common ground in terms of interplay.

However, before you are able to put together a collective concept with other musicians, you must have something to say in your own right. In the United States, there is a popular, but rather malicious, practical joke that is played on new musicians to check them out – *strolling*. Right in the middle of an improvisation, the rhythm section suddenly drops out without prior warning (an extremely unpleasant and nerve-wracking experience that I myself have been through a number of times). The soloists are then expected to play several choruses entirely on their own without losing form, tempo or changes – and to top things off, everything must make musical sense, too. Even if this is quite a nasty form of social Darwinism (in Europe musicians tend to treat each other a little bit more civilly), I fully agree with the fact that any good Jazz soloist should be able to improvise over a composition without the support of the other band members. A persuasive improvisation can stand alone – without having to depend on other musicians rolling out the red carpet.

Assignment

Take "TWINBAY" (or any other piece you know well) and play a solo over a number of choruses …

- … only accompanied by a metronome;

- … without any accompaniment at all.

The exercise without accompaniment is probably the most difficult because you have to be able to put together the various components of a composition without relying on a time-keeper. Playing a "monologue" like this will show you exactly which parts of a piece and which musical aspects you have securely at your fingertips and where you are still struggling. Try, despite the problems you may experience with form, changes and timing, to play as melodically as you can. Don't try to "show the changes" by running up and down the corresponding arpeggios or scales – that will not give you musical results. The idea is to play good motivic phrases and to time your lines in such a way that you land on important chord tones at harmonically strategic places (e.g. on a target chord of a cadence).

Improvisation also means being involved in a dialogue with oneself. Learn to ask a melodic question and to provide an appropriate answer by playing a subsequent phrase following the principle of "call and response". Play relatively short, expressive phrases – the simpler your questions are, the easier it will be to find an appropriate answer. What is the difference between a question and an answer? It is primarily the direction of the melodic movement. While the major part of both phrases will be similar or even identical, the phrase endings differ: Questions tend to end with an upward movement whereas answers usually have a descending closure (remember "Here's That Rainy Day" and the discussion on pages 295 ff.). The element of repetition therefore plays an important role. Try to repeat two-bar or four-bar lines and vary the ending of each phrase: "questions up, answers down".

Once you can argue your way through an entire solo all on your own, you can be sure that you have something meaningful to say. Then you will be in a position to lead the members of your band as a soloist. Here, too, there has to be continuous "call and response". Your melodic and rhythmical ideas, the structure of your solo – all of this must be presented in such a way that the members of your band are not only able to follow but can actually predict what you are about to do. Ask questions and give your colleagues time and space to answer back. Speak, scream, whisper – but always say something the other band members can understand and relate to.

Conversely, you will be required to listen to and let yourself be drawn into what is going on in the rhythm section. The name of the game is "to lead and be led", a game in which the roles and responsibilities alternate and the focus can shift from one musician to the next at any moment. All musicians are continually engaged in dialogue. But only an ensemble that speaks the same language and agrees on a mutual "topic of conversation" will experience the intuitive understanding necessary to create the moments of musical magic we so admire when listening to the greats. In short – great bands tell great stories!

Assignment

Go to pdf-L and have a look at the transcription. You will find an introduction, the theme and seven choruses on "TWINBAY" – played by Stan Getz on "The Steamer" (1956). Don't spend too much time analysing the tonal material and the chord-scale relationships (however, check those out, too, eventually). More importantly, concentrate on the formal aspects of the improvisation, the motivic ideas contained within the lines, the structure of the individual melodic phrases, the development of the various choruses and, ultimately, of the entire solo. This improvisation shows the ease and mastery of a soloist who is completely in tune not only with the changes but also with every formal nook and cranny of the composition. Last, but not least – try to find the recording and listen to how the quartet interacts.

Great – isn't it? It's one of the most relaxed and laid-back renditions of the tune I have ever heard, despite the bright tempo of close to 230 BPM. Every chorus tells a story. Stan Getz's sound is unmistakable – warm, lush and mellow – and his lines have a lyrical quality unsurpassed by most of his contemporaries. Practise this solo. Copy every detail on your instrument – not just the notes as such but also the way they are played (phrasing, articulation, timing, dynamics, etc.). Play the solo (at least partly) to the play-alongs of "TWINBAY". Do this until you can play every phrase in your sleep. Gradually, you will absorb the lines and they will become part of your musical vocabulary. The most important thing is that you will subliminally develop a feel for the ebb and flow of a good solo on the way.

Postlude

So, we come to the end of this book. Again, have a look at the following chord progression:

$$\| : E\flat^{\triangle 7} \quad | \quad \% \quad | \quad D^{-7(\flat 5)} \quad G^{7(\flat 9)} \quad | \quad C^{-7} \quad | \quad \% \quad | \quad B\flat^{-9} \quad E\flat^{13(\flat 9)} \quad |$$

$$| \quad A\flat^{\triangle 9} \quad | \quad D\flat^{7(\sharp 11)} \quad | \quad E\flat^{\triangle 7} \quad | \quad C^{-11} \quad | \quad F^{13(\sharp 11)} \quad | \quad \% \quad | \quad F^{-9} \quad | \quad B\flat^{13} \quad : \|$$

What do you associate with these changes? What music do you hear in your mind? Can you conjure up specific sounds simply by looking at the chord symbols? Are they more than just an abstract collection of notes? Do you recognise a particular piece? Does the progression relate to anything you've already played or practised? What seems familiar at this point, what feels obscure? Could you write down the notes of each chord? Can you feel how the tensions add to the underlying four-note structures and how they influence the basic sound of the harmonies? What scale material does each chord imply? Could you notate it? Can you hear melodic phrases, guide tone lines or voicings that go with this chord progression? Are you aware of the formal ups and downs of the changes? Does the progression give you a feeling of development? Do you understand how the chords relate to each other functionally? Could you analyse them? Do you sense the push and pull of the chord progression, the harmonic energy, the feeling of tension and release? Can you sense harmonic phrases, sections, cadences, resolutions, points of rest, a climax…? Are your fingers itching to improvise over this chord progression on your instrument? Can you hear a bass line, a drum groove or possibly even a full band? Anything else…?? Anything at all…???

If you are now able to answer these questions, at least in part, this book will have been of some help. Now it's up to you. As with anything worth doing, Jazz takes work, application, lots of listening, oodles of playing, dedication and an unassailable love of the music. So, open your heart and mind, limber up your ears and fingers and aim for that pot of gold at the end of the rainbow – with curiosity, energy, motivation and, above all, fun. Share your music and don't ever forget:

THERE WILL NEVER BE ANOTHER YOU!

Appendix

Acknowledgements

This book would not have been finished without the help of a bunch of clever people who didn't mind me picking their brains and using them as a sounding board. I would like to offer my grateful thanks to those who gave so generously of their time and expertise: in particular Amit Sen (my consulting editor) who cast a microscopic eye over every word and musical example, Francis Montocchio (co-translator) and Max Zentawer (for cleaning up my music files). Of course, anything I've got right is down to them and anything I've got wrong is down to me. Thanks go to the wonderful musicians for the recordings: Hubert Nuss, Ingmar Heller, Sebastian Netta, Philip Henzi, Stefan Reinthaler, Martin Stadelmann, Peter Gromer and to recording engineer Benoît Piccand. A big thank-you is due to my publisher Schott Music, in particular Elke Dörr, Julia Baldauf and Nico Schellhammer who showed remarkable forbearance in the face of an author who ignored every deadline. I hope I haven't abused your patience beyond repair. Not least, I'm indebted to my many students for serving as guinea pigs over the past 30 years. They have – not always knowingly or wilfully – contributed greatly to this book and helped me make it happen. My family deserves special mention for years of unfailing support. My wife Regula, in particular, had to put up with a lot, enduring my mood swings. I dearly hope the revenue from this book will help prop up her annuities in the long run. Finally, I wish to thank my readers for embarking on a journey that, while hopefully enjoyable for the most part, will be an uphill ride time and again. I am gladdened by the knowledge that this book is bought and read. I hope it makes a difference.

Chord progressions to the play-along tracks

Track

20 Diatonic functions in B♭ Major

4x

Bb∆7	F7	G-7	D-7	Eb∆7	Bb∆7	C-7	F7
Bb∆7	Eb∆7	D-7	G-7	C-7	F7	Bb∆7	%

21 Diatonic cadence in E♭ Major

Eb∆7	Ab∆7	D-7(b5)	G-7	C-7	F-7	Bb7	Eb∆7 Bb7sus4

22 Diatonic cadence with secondary dominants in G Major

G∆7	G7	C∆7	F#7	B7	E7	A7	D7
	Mixo		Altered	HM5	HM5	Lyd(♭7)	Mixo

23 Diatonic cadence with secondary dominants in F Major

F∆7	F7	Bb∆7	E7	A-7	D7	G-7	C7
	Mixo		Altered	Phrygian	HM5	Dorian	Mixo

24 Diatonic cadence with secondary dominants in A♭ Major

Ab∆7	Db∆7	G-7(b5)	C7	F-7	Bb7	Bb-7	Eb7
			HM5		Lyd(♭7)		Altered

25 Diatonic cadence with secondary II-Vs in B♭ Major

Bb∆7	F-7 Bb7	Eb∆7	Eø7 A7	D-7	Dø7 G7	C-7	F7
	Dor HM5		Locr HM5		Locr HM5		HM5

26   Diatonic cadence in C Minor

‖: C-7 | F-7 | Bb7 | Eb△7 | Ab△7 | D-7(b5) | G7 | C-7 G7 :‖

Aeolian Dorian Mixo Ionian Lydian Locrian HM5 Aeol HM5

27   V-I in F Major (with different scale choices for C7)

‖: F△7 | ✗. | C7 | ✗. :‖: F△7 | ✗. | C7 | ✗. :‖: F△7 | ✗. | C7 | ✗. :‖

Mixo   HM5   HTWT

‖: F△7 | ✗. | C7sus4 | ✗. :‖: F△7 | ✗. | Gb7 | ✗. :‖: F△7 | ✗. | Gb7 | ✗. :‖

Mixo   Lyd(b7)   Altered

28   II-V-I in C Major (with different colours for II and V)

‖: C△7 | ✗. | D-7 | G7 :‖: C△7 | ✗. | D-7 | G7 :‖

Dorian Mixo   Dorian Altered

‖: C△7 | ✗. | D-7(b5) | G7(b9) :‖: C△7 | ✗. | D-9(b5) | G13(b9) :‖ C△7 ‖

Locrian HM5   Locr(♮9) HTWT

29   Turnaround in G Minor (with different colours for II and V)

4x   4x

‖: G-7 | E-7(b5) | A-7(b5) | D7(b9) :‖: G-7 | E-9(b5) | A-9(b5) | D13(b9) :‖ G-7 ‖

Locrian Locrian HM5   Locr(♮9) Locr(♮9) HTWT

30   Substitute dominants in D Major

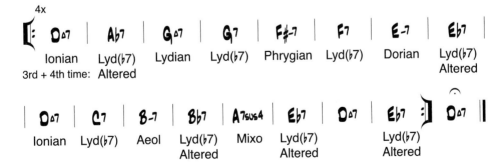

4x

‖: D△7 | Ab7 | G△7 | G7 | F#-7 | F7 | E-7 | Eb7 |

Ionian Lyd(b7) Lydian Lyd(b7) Phrygian Lyd(b7) Dorian Lyd(b7)
3rd + 4th time: Altered   Altered

| D△7 | C7 | B-7 | Bb7 | A7sus4 | Eb7 | D△7 | Eb7 :‖ D△7 ‖

Ionian Lyd(b7) Aeol Lyd(b7) Mixo Lyd(b7)   Lyd(b7)
                    Altered   Altered   Altered

31   Diminished chord functions in F Major (1)

4x

| F∆7 | F#°7 | G-7 | G#°7 | A-7 | A♭°7 | G-7 | G♭7 |

32   Diminished chord functions in G Major (2)

6x

| G∆7 | G7/8 | C∆7 | C#°7 | G∆7/D | D#°7 | E-7 | D7sus4 |

33   Dorian cadence I–7 - IV7 in C Dorian

| C-7 | F7 |

Dorian   Mixolydian

34   ♭IImaj7 in F Phrygian and F Major (MI)

4x   4x   4x   4x

| F-7 | G♭∆7 | F∆7 | G♭∆7 | F-7 | G♭∆7 | F∆7 | G♭∆7 | F∆7 ‖

Phryg Lydian   Ionian Lydian

35   Important MI-functions in C Major

| C∆7 | ∕. | C-7 | ∕. | C∆7 | ∕. | F-7 | B♭7sus4 | C∆7 | ∕. | F-(∆7) | B♭7 |

Ionian   Dorian   Dor   Mixo   MM   Lyd(♭7)

| C∆7 | ∕. | G-7 | ∕. | C∆7 | ∕. | D♭∆7 | ∕. | C∆7 | ∕. | E♭∆7 | ∕. |

Dorian   Lydian   Lydian

| C∆7 | ∕. | A♭∆7 | ∕. | C∆7 | ∕. | B♭∆7 | ∕. | C∆7 | E♭∆7 | A♭∆7 | D♭∆7 |

Lydian   Lydian

36   Turnaround in F Major (assignment "Guide Tone Lines")

8x

| F∆7 | D7 | G-7 | C7 | F∆7 ‖

Ionian   Altered   Dorian   Altered

37   Diatonic functions in E♭ Major

|| E♭∆7 | ⁒ | ⁒ | ⁒ | F-7 | ⁒ | ⁒ | ⁒ | G-7 | ⁒ | ⁒ | ⁒ | A♭∆7 | ⁒ | ⁒ | ⁒ |

| B♭7 | ⁒ | ⁒ | ⁒ | C-7 | ⁒ | ⁒ | ⁒ | D-7(♭5) | ⁒ | ⁒ | ⁒ | E♭∆7 ||

38   Diatonic functions in G Melodic minor

|| G-(∆7) | ⁒ | ⁒ | ⁒ | F#7 | ⁒ | ⁒ | ⁒ | B♭∆7(#5) | ⁒ | ⁒ | ⁒ |
MM   Altered   Lyd(#5)

| E-7(♭5) | ⁒ | ⁒ | ⁒ | C7 | ⁒ | ⁒ | ⁒ | D7 | ⁒ | ⁒ | ⁒ | G-(∆7) ||
Locr(♮9)   Lyd(♭7)   Mixo(♭13)   MM

39   Random chords (without functional relationships)

Ionian	Mixolydian	Aeolian	Altered	Locrian	MM
A♭∆7	E7	C-7	A7	B-7(♭5)	E♭-(∆7)

Lydian	Mixolydian	WTHT	Lyd(♭7)	Mixolydian	Aeolian
B∆7	G7sus4	E♭∆7	D♭7	B♭7	F#-7

HM5	WTHT	Ionian	Lydian	Mixolydian	Dorian
F7	G∘7	D∆7	F∆7	D♭7sus4	A-7

Tune quotes

The following list shows the copyright owners of the works mentioned in this book. At the same time, it may provide an overview of tunes you should know.

A Child Is Born (Thad Jones)
D'Accord Music (Co.) Inc.

All Of Me (Gerald Marks)
Bourne Co.

All Of You (Cole Porter)
Chappell Co. Inc.

All The Things You Are (Jerome Kern)
Universal Polygram International Publishing

Autumn Leaves (Joseph Kosma)
Enoch and Cie
Morley-Music Co. Inc.

Bag's Groove (Milt Jackson)
Reecie Music

Beatrice (Sam Rivers)
Rivbea Music Co.

Black Orpheus (Luiz Bonfa)
Meridian Editions
Euterpe Edicoes LTDA
Soc Meridian

Blue Bossa (Kenny Dorham)
Orpheum Music

Bluesette (Toots Thielemans)
Universal/Reuter-Reuter Forlags AB

Blues For Alice (Charlie Parker)
Criterion-Music Corp.

Blue In Green (Miles Davis)
Jazz Horn Music Corp.

Bye Bye Blackbird (Ray Henderson)
Redwood Music LTD

Chameleon (Herbie Hancock)
Funkdivity Music
Hancock Music
Cigum Music Company

Darn That Dream (Jimmy van Heusen)
Bregman-Vocco-Conn Inc.

Desafinado (Antonio Carlos Jobim)
Editora e Imp. Musial Fermata do Brasil

Dolphin Dance (Herbie Hancock)
Hancock Music

Donna Lee (Charlie Parker)
Screen Gems-emi Music Inc.

Falling Grace (Steve Swallow)
Wonderbuns Inc.

Far Away (Freddie Hubbard)
Emi Unart Catalog Inc.

Freedom Jazz Dance (Eddie Harris)
Seventh House LTD

Giant Steps (John Coltrane)
Jowcol Music

Goodbye Pork Pie Hat (Charles Mingus)
Crazy Crow Music

Have You Met Miss Jones (Richard Rodgers)
Chappell Co. Inc.

Here's That Rainy Day (Jimmy van Heusen)
Bourne Co.

I Love You (Cole Porter)
Chappell Co. Inc.

I Mean You (Thelonious Monk/Coleman Hawkins)
Embassy Music Corp.

In A Sentimental Mood (Duke Ellington)
Emi Mills Music Inc.

I Remember Clifford (Benny Golson)
Time Step Music

In The Wee Small Hours Of The Morning
(David Mann/Bob Hilliard)
Bourne Co.
Rytvoc Inc.

Israel (John Carisi)
Beechwood Music Corp.

Joy Spring (Clifford Brown)
Cherio Corp.

Juju (Wayne Shorter)
Miyako Music

Just Like That (Peter Herbolzheimer)
Self-published

Line Up (Lennie Tristano)
Hill and Range Southwind Mus S A

Little Sunflower (Freddie Hubbard)
Hub Tones Music Co.

Lucky Southern (Keith Jarrett)
Kunhdalini Music

Minority (Gigi Gryce)
Totem-Music Co. Inc.

Misty (Erroll Garner)
Octave-Music Publ. Corp.
My DAD's Songs Inc.
Reganesque Music Company
Pocketful of Dreams Music Pub.
Marke-Music Publ. Co. Inc.

Mornin' (Al Jarreau/Al Foster/Jay Graydon)
Garden Rake Music Inc.
Aljaareau Music
Peermusic III LTD

Mr Sandman (Ballard/Morris)
Morris Edwin H Co. Inc.

My Funny Valentine (Richard Rodgers)
Chappell Co. Inc.

Naima (John Coltrane)
Jowcol Music

Nardis (Miles Davis)
Jazz Horn Music Corp.

Night And Day (Cole Porter)
Warner Bros Inc.

On A Clear Day (Burton Lane)
Chappell-Co. Inc.

On Green Dolphin Street (Bronislaw Kaper)
Feist Leo Inc.

Once I Loved (Antonio Carlos Jobim)
Corcovado Music Corp.
Universal Music Pub. S L

Peace (Horace Silver)
Ecaroh Music Inc.

Pools (Don Grolnick)
INTUITION Music Pub. GmbH

'Round Midnight (Thelonious Monk)
Thelonious Music Corp.
W B Music Corp.

Sack O'Woe (Nat Adderley)
SM Pub. (POLAND) SP. Z O.O.

Satin Doll (Duke Ellington)
Campbell Connelly and Co. LTD

Saving All My Love (Michael Masser/Gerald Goffin)
Inkwrite Music, Ddubau Music Pub.,
MG Gold Songs, Thaaristocrats, SONY
ATV Tunes, Emi Blackwood, UNIVERSAL
Music Corp., Copyright Control Shares

Someday My Prince Will Come (Frank Churchill)
Bourne Co.

So What (Miles Davis)
Jazz Horn Music Corp.

Somewhere Over The Rainbow (Harold Arlen)
Feist Leo Inc.

Spring Is Here (Richard Rodgers)
Emi Robbins Catalog Inc.

Stella By Starlight (Victor Young)
SONY ATV Harmony

Stolen Moments (Oliver Nelson)
NOSLEN Music Company LLC

Sonnymoon For Two (Sonny Rollins)
Son Rol Music Company

Sweet Georgia Brown (Ben Bernie/Maceo Pinkard)
WARNER BROS Inc.

Take Five (Paul Desmond)
DERRY Music Company

Take The 'A' Train (Billy Strayhorn)
TEMPO Music Inc.

The Blues Walk (Clifford Brown)
HENDON Music Inc

The Days Of Wine And Roses (Henry Mancini)
WARNER BROS Inc.

The Girl From Ipanema (Antonio Carlos Jobim)
NEW THUNDER Music Co.
UNIVERSAL Duchess Music Corp.

The More I See You (Harry Warren/Mack Gordon)
Bregman-Vocco-Conn Inc.

There Is No Greater Love (Isham Jones)
JONES-ISHAM-Music Corp.

There Will Never Be Another You (Harry Warren)
Morris Edwin H Co. Inc.

Three Flowers (McCoy Tyner)
Emi Music Pub. LTD

Tune Up (Miles Davis)
PRESTIGE Music Co.

Twelve Tone Tune (TTT) (Bill Evans)
ORPHEUM Music

Walking Tiptoe (Bert Joris)
self-published

Waltz For Ever (Joe Haider)
JHM Publishing

Wave (Antonio Carlos Jobim)
Corcovado Music Corp.

Yearnin' (Oliver Nelson)
NOSLEN Music Company LLC

Yes Or No (Wayne Shorter)
MIYAKO Music

You Are The Sunshine Of My Life (Stevie Wonder)
Black Bull Music Inc., Jobete Music Co. Inc.

About the author

Frank Sikora (*1956) was born in London and grew up in Hong Kong and Paris. Due to his father's work as a diplomat, he travelled the world from day one, something he has been doing ever since. Coming from an art-loving environment, he was drawn into music at an early age, singing in choirs, playing piano and guitar and fronting his own rock bands. He drifted into Jazz when he was 15, playing in numerous swing, bebop and gypsy groups while still in school.

Frank initially studied biochemistry (sciences being his other major area of interest), but then succumbed to his first love, venturing into a career as a musician. After completing his studies at Berklee College of Music and New England Conservatory in Boston/USA, majoring in composition, arranging and guitar, Frank spent more than 15 years on the road, performing amongst others with Art Farmer, Dieter Ilg, Victor Bailey, Joe Haider, Slide Hampton and Pony Pointdexter. He then focussed on composing and arranging for a wide variety of professional ensembles (big band, vocal groups, orchestra, radio bands, etc.), acting as musical director for a number of projects (e.g. the Zurich Jazz Orchestra 2003–06).

Frank eventually launched into teaching as his primary calling, running more than 400 workshops worldwide over the past 30 years (improvisation, theory, ensembles). He taught ear training and arranging at the State University of Music and the Performing Arts Stuttgart/Germany (1987–2007). Since 1988 he is in charge of the theory department and the master program in Jazz Composition & Arrangement at the University of the Arts Bern/Switzerland, teaching harmony, counterpoint, composition, arranging, ensembles, etc. with a distinct "hands-on" approach, helping students recognise their creative potential. This book attempts to emulate what he has been trying to achieve throughout his teaching career. Frank currently lives in Switzerland with his wife Regula and his son Loris.

MP3 track list

The audio files are an essential part of this book. Please visit **www.schott-music.com/ online-material** to download the MP3 files for free using the following voucher code: **JHSi4or8**

Track

01	Abmaj7 Lydian	2:04
02	Fmaj7 Ionian	1:57
03	D7 Mixolydian	2:38
04	Bb–7 Dorian	2:45
05	G–7 Aeolian	2:31
06	E–7 Phrygian	2:08
07	C#–7(b5) Locrian	2:04
08	C–6 Melodic minor	2:03
09	A–maj7 Harmonic minor	2:01
10	C Half-tone-whole-tone	1:50
11	Messiaen Mode III (in C)	2:56
12	Turnaround in F Major	7:57
13	"TWINBAY" in Eb Major (Medium Swing)	3:31
14	"TWINBAY" in F Major (Medium Up Swing)	2:57
15	"TWINBAY" in Ab Major (Ballad)	3:07
16	"TWINBAY" in Bb Major (Bossa Nova)	3:35
17	"TWINBAY" in G Major (Samba)	3:24
18	"TWINBAY" in C Major (3/4 Swing)	3:05
19	"TWINBAY" in D Major (Shuffle Funk)	3:16
20	Diatonic functions in Bb Major	2:22
21	Diatonic cadence in Eb Major	1:42
22	Diatonic cadence with secondary dominants in G Major	1:25
23	Diatonic cadence with secondary dominants in F Major	1:25
24	Diatonic cadence with secondary dominants in Ab Major	2:04
25	Diatonic cadence with secondary II-Vs in Bb Major	2:14
26	Diatonic cadence in C Minor	2:02
27	V-I in F Major (with different scale choices for C7)	2:05
28	II-V-I in C Major (with different colours for II and V)	1:26
29	Turnaround in G Minor (with different colours for II and V)	1:27
30	Substitute dominants in D Major	2:23
31	Diminished chord functions in F Major (1)	1:24
32	Diminished chord functions in G Major (2)	1:45
33	Dorian cadence I–7 - IV7 in C Dorian	1:45
34	bIImaj7 in F Phrygian and F Major (MI)	1:35
35	Important MI-functions in C Major	2:43

Solutions

Please visit **www.schott-music.com/shop/32750** to download the solutions to the assignments in this book. Note that beginning with the section "Listen", only select solutions may be provided due to the nature of the assignments.